200 YEARS IN IMAGES

The cover presents a pictorial history of John Wiley & Sons, Inc., including Wiley family and leaders, authors, and inventors; these images portray highlights of the technological and cultural innovations of the past two centuries. From New York to Bangalore to the World Wide Web, Wiley is knowledge for generations.

1. A 1754 engraving of the first printing press, invented by Johannes Gutenberg in the fifteenth century. (© *Hulton Archive/Getty Images*)
2. Archival map of New York, NY. (© *Corbis-Bettman*)
3. John Wiley (1808–1891) *(Wiley Archives)*
4. Lithograph of Wall Street as seen from Trinity Church. Charles Wiley's shop was located at 3 Wall Street. (© *P. Maverick. 29.100.2286 — The J. Clarence Davies Collection. Courtesy of the Museum of the City of New York)*
5. James Fenimore Cooper (1789–1851). American author. Colored, stipple engraving, 1831. (© *The Granger Collection)*
6. John "Jack" Wiley (1748–1829) and family. He is standing by the wall of Trinity Church at the foot of Wall Street with his mother, Mary Tillinghast, and his two sisters, Mary and Patty. *(Wiley Archives)*
7. Portrait of feminist and American author Margaret Fuller (1810–1850). From a daguerreotype. (© *Bettmann/Corbis Images)*
8. William H. (The Major) Wiley (1842–1925). *(Wiley Archives)*
9. Nathaniel Hawthorne, American author (1804–1864). Stipple engraving 1851. (© *Humanities and Social Sciences Library/Henry W. and Albert A. Berg Collection of English and American Literature/New York Public Library)*
10. The Brooklyn Bridge. (© *Silvia Otte/Photonica/Getty Images)*
11. Thomas Edison (1847–1931), American inventor, in his chemistry laboratory (1917). (© *Roger Violett/Getty Images)*
12. Galápagos tortoise at the edge of Vulcan Alcedo, Galápagos Islands. (© *Frans Lanting/Minden Pictures, Inc.)*
13. Marie Curie (1867–1934) French physicist and winner of the 1903 Nobel Prize for Physics, which she shared with her husband, Pierre Curie, and Henri Becquerel. She was the first woman to win a Nobel Prize. (© *Hulton Archive/Getty Images)*
14. Engineering students, Ohio State University (1907). *(Courtesy of Ohio State University)*
15. A woman carrying a banner with the suffragette slogan, "Votes for Women," during a demonstration at Westminster (1912). (© *Hulton Archive/Getty Images)*
16. Assembly line workers inside the Ford Motor Company factory at Dearborn, Michigan (1928). (© *Hulton Archive/Getty Images)*
17. William Bradford Wiley (1910–1998). *(Wiley Archives, photo by Andy Washnik)*
18. A family watching television, 1950. (© *Harold M. Lambert/Getty Images, Inc.)*
19. Aerial view of New York City, New York. (© *VCL/Taxi/Getty Images)*
20. A sample of Wiley's publications. *(Wiley Archives)*
21. DNA. (© *PASIEKA/Photo Researchers, Inc.)*
22. Wiley InterScience online. *(Wiley Archives)*
23. Wiley's Hoboken office. *(Wiley Archives)*
24. Bangalore, India. (© *David R. Frazier/Danita Delimont)*
25. Wiley colleague, Toni Chow, executive assistant to the president and CEO *(Wiley Archives)*

Back Cover Photo: © *iStockphoto*

KNOWLEDGE

BICENTENNIAL
BICENTENNIAL
1807
WILEY
2007
BICENTENNIAL
BICENTENNIAL

for

GENERATIONS

KNOWLEDGE

for

GENERATIONS

Wiley and the Global Publishing Industry

1807–2007

TIMOTHY CURTIS JACOBSON

GEORGE DAVID SMITH

ROBERT E. WRIGHT

PETER BOOTH WILEY

SUSAN BROPHY SPILKA

BARBARA L. HEANEY

EDITORS-IN-CHIEF	Peter Wiley, Susan Spilka, and Barbara Heaney
PRODUCTION EDITORS	Barbara Russiello/Kelly Tavares
CREATIVE DIRECTOR & DESIGNER	Harry Nolan
PAGE DESIGN & LAYOUT	Lee Goldstein
COMPOSITOR/PAGE LAYOUT	Elizabeth Brooks
SENIOR PHOTO EDITOR	Jennifer MacMillan
PHOTO RESEARCHER	Elyse Rieder
PHOTOGRAPHERS	Lattelle Solomon and Andy Washnik
SENIOR ILLUSTRATION EDITOR	Anna Melhorn
ILLUSTRATION STUDIO	Hadel Studio
COVER DESIGN	Harry Nolan
COVER PHOTO CREDITS	See front endpaper

This book was set in 11/16 Times New Roman PS by Wiley Composition Services, Indianapolis, and by Lee Goldstein. It was printed and bound by RR Donnelley & Sons Company, Jefferson City. The case cover was printed by Brady Palmer Printing Company and the dust jacket was printed by Phoenix Color.

This book is printed on acid-free paper. ∞

To order books or for customer service, please call 1-800-CALL WILEY (225-5945).

Library of Congress Cataloging in Publication Data:

Jacobson, Timothy C., 1948-
  Knowledge for generations : Wiley and the global publishing industry,
1807–2007 / Timothy Curtis Jacobson, George David Smith, Robert E. Wright.
    p. cm.
  ISBN 978-0-471-75721-4 (cloth)
  1. John Wiley & Sons—History. 2. Publishers and publishing—United
States—History. I. Smith, George David. II. Wright, Robert E. (Robert
Eric), 1969– III. John Wiley & Sons. IV. Title.
  Z473.J67J33 2007
  070.50973—dc22
                        2007042803

Printed in the United States of America

10 9 8 7 6 5 4 3 2 1

Foreword

John Wiley & Sons has published three books describing aspects of its history. *Wiley: One Hundred and Seventy-Five Years of Publishing,* the third of these, was published in 1982 to mark our 175th anniversary; it was the first effort at a comprehensive history of Wiley.

We are honored to publish this fourth volume on such a memorable occasion—our 200th anniversary. Charles Wiley opened a print shop in lower Manhattan when Thomas Jefferson was president of the United States. Charles's printing press bore a remarkable resemblance to the one that Johann Gutenberg invented in the middle of the fifteenth century. Publishing and Wiley have traveled a long road since then, moving in the last two decades at what from Gutenberg and Charles's perspective would have seemed like the speed of light.

Today we still publish print products and will continue to do so for as long as our customers want them. As a result of significant investments in enabling technology, we are actively engaged in the rapid delivery of quality content from our authors to our readers. In addition, our content is accompanied by digital tools that facilitate search, discoverability, and customization.

Wiley's history is unique in the annals of publishing. Accordingly, we decided to tell our story in a way that we believe is distinctive in comparison to other corporate histories by providing a candid account of "the good and the bad" in Wiley's history. We believe that our readers will learn more about our Company and its singular culture in this way. Further, we included, wherever possible, descriptions of the work life of our colleagues during the course of Wiley's history. Hence, this is a book about the evolution of publishing as a business and as a craft, as well as a history of Wiley— all in the context of the external environment within which the Company at times barely survived and at other times thrived. We hope *Knowledge for Generations* will inform and entertain our readers, and perhaps even inspire them.

With members of the sixth and seventh generations of the Wiley family and a team of dedicated colleagues who are collaborating around the world, we look forward to writing the next chapter in the ongoing story of John Wiley & Sons, Inc. We are proud of our rich heritage; humbled by the challenges ahead; and inspired to sustain a Company culture in which the next generation of authors, partners, customers, shareholders, and colleagues will thrive. We sincerely appreciate your interest and support.

PETER BOOTH WILEY
Chairman of the Board

WILLIAM J. PESCE
President and
Chief Executive Officer

Preface

$\mathcal{K}$nowledge *for Generations* documents a remarkable feat in the histories of publishing and business: the growth and survival of a family firm over two centuries. Once a humble printing shop in lower Manhattan, John Wiley & Sons, as the company came to be known, has evolved from a hand-to-mouth start-up into a far-flung, $1.2 billion, multinational corporation, publishing and distributing knowledge from more than 20 offices around the world. Since its early days, its mission has been to publish things people need to know. Today Wiley nurtures the creation of content and delivers it in a variety of media to students and academics, professionals and professional and learned societies, researchers, practitioners, and general readers.

Two hundred years of survival is no small accomplishment. Publishing was a durable enclave of family-owned and -operated businesses well into the twentieth century, but today one can count the number of substantial family-controlled publishing houses on the fingers of one hand, while the number of family-controlled businesses worldwide generating over $1 billion in revenues is probably less than three hundred. Traditional publishing firms have largely disappeared, as the drive toward scale in a hotly competitive, increasingly global industry has compelled most family publishers to cede control to the "logic" of modern corporate finance. In the process, many once-great publishing houses have failed or merged themselves out of memory into larger corporate entities or exist only as imprints within larger publishing companies. Not Wiley.

This rendering of its history will show that Wiley's progress over two centuries was far from linear; the company has gone through many twists and turns, ups and downs. Each and every year the company has been in business, it has had an opportunity to fail. Episodes in the company's history in which it seemed on the brink of extinction form an important part of our story. Wiley has survived and flourished because it is the cumulative product of generations of mostly good management, some measure of good fortune, and a family sensitive enough to understand the difference between the two.

Into the 1980s, succeeding generations of Wiley family leaders kept the business afloat, in a gradual, if not always steady, upward trajectory of growth. Starting in the late 1960s, the modern patriarch of the Wiley family, William Bradford Wiley, began to turn the day-to-day control of the company's operations over to non-family, professional managers. The transition was far from easy, reaching crisis proportions in the late 1980s, but since that time, a new generation of professional managers has steered Wiley through the most expansive, technologically dynamic, and consistently profitable phase of its history.

In the meantime, the Wiley family has firmly—some might say stubbornly—resisted lucrative opportunities to sell its controlling interest. In an industry where mass consolidation has been the rule, rather than *be* acquired, Wiley has actively acquired assets and people, transforming them into knowledge producers, in accordance with what has become highly efficient and creative Wiley business methods. For its part, the Wiley family continues to be what it has always seemed to be: nothing more than a publishing family. The family provides patient capital and oversight, which, when combined with good management, have proven supportive of a business that relies above all on the cooperation of highly creative people who control all the processes by which important knowledge is selected, made ready for publication, and sold. Managers manage, the family watches over, and the result is a company that, insulated from the short-term pressures of the public stock market, is able to plan for the long term while making money in the short term.

This book was undertaken for the occasion of John Wiley & Sons' bicentennial in 2007, at the behest of the company and current family members who also play key roles in its operation: Peter Booth Wiley, the company's non-executive chairman, Brad Wiley II, his predecessor, and Deborah Wiley, the one remaining family member in a high management position. *Knowledge for Generations* is a commissioned work, contracted through The Winthrop Group, Inc., an association of business, economic, and technology historians. It is a work researched and written to scholarly standards. The first six chapters were written by the named authors,

outsiders privileged to have an inside view of the company along with complete access to corporate records and personnel, in the hope that it would yield an independent interpretation of the history. They accept sole responsibility for the story told in those chapters. The last three chapters, which cover a time period within living memory of most of the participants, are based on a more collaborative effort in which a number of Wiley colleagues conducted interviews, did research, and wrote text in addition to what the Winthrop historians developed on their own. Responsibility for the content of those chapters lies with John Wiley & Sons.

Peter Booth Wiley, author and historian in his own right, championed the project and judiciously counseled the authors whenever he thought important information might be overlooked. His contributions make him an author in all but name, and the authors of record thank him in particular for a level of intellectual engagement that made their job consistently stimulating.

TIMOTHY CURTIS JACOBSON,
GEORGE DAVID SMITH,
ROBERT E. WRIGHT
The Winthrop Group, Inc.
Spring 2007

Acknowledgments

A book of this size and with all its graphic elegance is a complex production; many heads and hands shaped it along the way. We thank all those Wiley colleagues, past and present, as well as Wiley friends, who have contributed so much of their assistance, expertise, and time to this project. We see the future of Wiley within their strengths.

PETER BOOTH WILEY
SUSAN SPILKA
BARBARA HEANEY

Editors

ANN GROGG, *line editing*
JOHN LEHMANN-HAUPT, *writing and interviewing*
CHARITY ROBEY, *art editing and accuracy checking*

Researchers

NICOLE LUCE-RIZZO, MARY MCFADDEN and
VERITY WAITE, *researchers*
ED MELANDO, JIM READ, ED SPERLING, and
KRISTEN WEILER, *financial data*

Creative Services

HARRY NOLAN, *creative director, cover and
interior design*
LEE GOLDSTEIN, *page and layout design*
JENNIFER MACMILLAN, *photo editing and research*
HILARY NEWMAN and ELYSE RIEDER, *photo research*
LATTELLE SOLOMON and ANDY WASHNIK, *photography*
CECELIA DISKIN, *photo montages/borders*
ANNA MELHORN, *illustration management*
FRED HAYNES, *illustrator*
RICHARD J. PACIFICO, *design of bicentennial logo*

Production and Manufacturing

ANN BERLIN, BARBARA RUSSIELLO, and KELLY TAVARES,
production management
BETTY PESSAGNO, *copyediting*
GLORIA HAMILTON, *copyediting, proofreading,
and fact checking*
JANICE BORZENDOWSKI, *proofreading*
LAURA ALBERT, *senior proofreading and quality control*
RASHELL SMITH, *senior graphics illustrator*
ELIZABETH BROOKS, *senior page layout*
ERIN ZELTNER, *senior page layout*
KATHIE RICKARD, *manager, page layout*
CLINT LAHNEN, *supervisor, graphics processing and
imaging*
DEBBIE STAILEY, *director, composition services*
KATHY COLLINS, *director, corporate manufacturing*
RON TESORO, *director, paper planning and purchasing*
MARK VANDEVEN, *manager, transportation logistics*
COURTNEY LESHKO, *production assistant*
WANDA HENDERSON, *senior assistant, product information*
KELLY RICCI, *Aptara senior production editor*
STEVE RATH, *Aptara indexer*

ACKNOWLEDGMENTS

x

Advertising and Promotion

AMITA CHEN
DIANE IMUS
JULIA LAMPAM
LORI SAYDE-MEHRTENS
MARGIE SCHUSTACK
ALIDA SETFORD
MARSHALL WILEN

Attorneys

PEGGY GARRY   GARY RINCK
DEIRDRE SILVER NANCY E. WOLFF

Executive Assistance

TAMARA KELLY   YOLANDA PAGAN   MARY MCFADDEN

Corporate Communications

ALEXANDRA BROWN
SARAH FEWSTER
LATTELLE SOLOMON

Previous Wiley Historians

RICHARD BLODGETT, *interviews and research for this 200-year history*
JOHN HAMMOND MOORE, *Wiley: One Hundred and Seventy-Five Years of Publishing,* 1982
[KENDALL B. TAFT, ED.]: *The First One Hundred and Fifty Years: A History of John Wiley and Sons, Incorporated* 1807–1957 [20+ contributors]

Photo Acknowledgments

JO BACCHI
KATHY BENDO
ANN BERLIN
MARK F. BERRAFATO
MARK BERTILS
JOSEPH BLUM
ALEXANDRA BROWN
BETHANY CARLAND
CAMILLE CARTER
JULIAN CLAYTON
ELIZABETH DOBLE
CATHERINE EELES
SUSAN ELBE
DON EMBLER
RYAN FLAHIVE
TODD FRIES
LISA GEE
LEE GOLDSTEIN
SHEENA GOLDSTEIN
MARSHA GORDON
LISA HART

TED HOFFMAN
JOAN KALKUT
RABEA KAPSCHAK
JOYCE KRIEGER
TOM KULESA
CELIA KUPFERBERG
JOHN LEHMANN-HAUPT
FRANK LYMAN
MATHEW MCHUGH
CAROL MCNELIS
JESSICA MARKS
BARBARA MELE
AMANDA MILLER
MARIO MULLER
HILARY NEWMAN
HARRY NOLAN
YOLANDA PAGAN
INEZ PETTIS
ALINE PHILLIPS
ERICA RENZO
CHARITY ROBEY

HELEN RUSSO
GREGORY ST. JOHN
TARA SANFORD
BEATRICE SHUBE
STEVE SCHULTZ
ALIDA SETFORD
JOY SIKORSKI
GEORGINA SMITH
LATTELLE SOLOMON
GEORGE STANLEY
KAREN STAUDINGER
RON TESORO
ELLINOR WAGNER
VERITY WAITE
CHRIS WALLACE
AUDRY WEE-CHIANG
CARL WEIR
DEBORAH, PETER, AND BRAD WILEY
AMY ZARKOS
WILLIAM ZERTER

Vendors

APTARA

BIND RITE ROBBINSVILLE

BRADY PALMER PRINTING COMPANY

COSMOS COMMUNICATIONS

COURIER CORPORATION

RR DONNELLEY & SONS

HADEL STUDIO

HORIZON PAPER

LYNCH EXHIBITS

PHOENIX COLOR

UNIMAC GRAPHICS

UNITED PARCEL SERVICE

VERSO PAPER

Interviewees, Reviewers, and Advisers

PEGGY ALEXANDER

MARK ALLIN

WAYNE ANDERSON

WILLIAM ARLINGTON

MARTHA AVERY

JANET BAILEY

WARREN BAKER

RUTH BARUTH

JAY BECK

ARUN BHARTI

DOUG BLACK

JEFF BROWN

PHILIP CARPENTER

NATALIE CHAPMAN

DOMINIC COPPOLA

ELLIS COUSENS

MARY CURTIS

DEBBIE DAVIS

JACK DAY

GEOFFREY DEAN

JIM DICKS

ELIZABETH DOBLE

PETER DONOUGHUE

SUSAN ELBE

CHARLES ELLIS

ALLEN FERNALD

KHEE HOW FOO

WARREN FRISTENSKY

BERNADINE GALWAY

HARTMUT GANTE

IAN GARRARD

ROBERT GARBER

PETER GÖLITZ

ANN-MARIE HALLIGAN

TADASHI HASE

HEE-JEONG IHN

ED IMMERGUT

RITA IRONS

JOHN JARVIS

GWENYTH JONES

SUSAN KANTROWITZ

JOHN KILCULLEN

NILS KINDWALL

TIMOTHY KING

STEPHEN KIPPUR

ERNEST KIRKWOOD

KRISTIN KLIEMANN

STEVEN KRAHAM

HANA LANE

ALAN LESURE

MADELYN LESURE

THERESA LIU

RICK LEYH

BONNIE LIEBERMAN

ROBERT LONG

RICHARD LYNCH

JOHN MARION

RUTH MCMULLIN

MARC MIKULICH

CLIFF MILLS

KAREN MILNER

STEVEN MIRON

JEAN MORLEY

GEOFF NAYLOR

ANDREW H. NEILLY JR.

CARLOS NORIEGA ARIAS

LARRY OLSON

MEHDI OMRANLOO

WILLIAM J. PESCE

CHARITY ROBEY

BONNIE ROESCH

RICHARD RUDICK

EDWARD RUSSELL

BRUCE SPATZ

GREGORY ST. JOHN

MARGIE SCHUSTACK

MICHAEL SILVERSTEIN

STEPHEN SMITH

LIZANNE STOLL

WILLIAM R. (BERT) SUTHERLAND

ERIC SWANSON

GEORGE TELECKI

CRAIG VAN DYCK

ROBERT WILDER

BRAD WILEY

DEBORAH WILEY

EVA ELISABETH WILLE

GILBERT WINDHEIM

NANCY WOLFBERG

DIANE WOOD

WILLIAM ZERTER

Brief Contents

CHAPTER 1   1

Family Craft and Business:
Evolution
1807–2007

CHAPTER 2   17

Charles Wiley:
Bookman of the "Literary Republic"
1807–1826

CHAPTER 3   55

John Wiley:
Foundations
1826–1865

CHAPTER 4   101

And Sons:
Transition to Modern Publishing
1865–1925

CHAPTER 5   143

The Cousins:
Conservative Change During
the Fourth Generation
1925–1956

CHAPTER 6   197

William Bradford Wiley:
The Transition to Professional Management
1957–1979

CHAPTER 7   267

A Turbulent Decade:
Experimentation and Survival
1979–1989

CHAPTER 8   333

Renaissance:
Rebirth as a Global Company
1989 and Beyond

CHAPTER 9   431

Ushering In
Wiley's Third Century

Contents

CHAPTER 1   1

Family Craft and Business: Evolution
1807 — 2007

Change and Continuity

Themes, 8   The Long Horizon, 12

CHAPTER 2   19

Charles Wiley: Bookman of the "Literary Republic"
1807 — 1826

The New York of Charles Wiley

The Road to Publishing, 20
  PROFILE: JOHN (JACK) WILEY, 21

The Demand for Books, 24

The Book Trade, 26

THE PRINTING CRAFT: GLYPHS, FRAMES, AND HAND PRESSES, 28

Print Shop Beginnings, 29

The Van Winkle Partnership, 31

INSIDE THE BOOKS: THE TRIANGLE, 32

Charles Wiley & Co. and Wiley & Halsted, 35
  PROFILE: WASHINGTON IRVING, 39

Wiley and the Book Business in America, 41
  Cooperation in the Book Trade, 42

The Emergence of American Literature, 44

Wiley and James Fenimore Cooper, 47
  PROFILE: JAMES FENIMORE COOPER, 48

Troubled Times and Decline, 50

CHAPTER 3 55

John Wiley:
Foundations
1826 — 1865

Charles Dickens and the Copyright Law

John Wiley's Beginnings as Book Agent and Publisher, 59

  Portrait of a Bookstore, 61

Publishing in Antebellum America, 65

  INSIDE THE BOOKS: GIFT BOOKS, 68

  THE PRINTING CRAFT: NINETEENTH-CENTURY ADVANCES IN TECHNOLOGY, 71

Wiley & Putnam's Early Years, 73

PROFILE: GEORGE PALMER PUTNAM, 76

PROFILE: EVERT A. DUYCKINCK, 79

The Glory Years, 80

  PROFILE: MARGARET FULLER, 85

  PROFILE: EDGAR ALLAN POE, 86

The Fight for International Copyright, 89

Shift and Split, 94

CHAPTER 4 101

And Sons:
Transition to Modern Publishing
1865 — 1925

Wiley and Edison at Menlo Park

  PROFILE: JOHN RUSKIN, 106

An Industrialized Economy, 108

Scientific Wiley: Its Market and Competitors, 110

  PROFILE: DAVID VAN NOSTRAND, 112

Practical Knowledge and Engineering, 116

  PROFILE: JOHN CRESSON TRAUTWINE, 119

  PROFILE: MAJOR WILLIAM HALSTED WILEY, 120

  THE PRINTING CRAFT: THE LINOTYPE AND SMYTH SEWING, 122

Working at Wiley, 124

The Art of the Textbook Trade, 126

Editors and Authors, 128

Marketing Books, 129

  INSIDE THE BOOKS: THE WILEY COLOPHON, 132

Connections Abroad, 133

Wiley Series Books: A Case Study, 134

  PROFILE: JAY BROWNLEE DAVIDSON, 136

Between Family and Firm, 139

CHAPTER 5   143

The Cousins:
Conservative Change During the Fourth Generation
1925 — 1956

The Cousins and Their Times

The Cousins Come into Their Own, 146
  PROFILE: WILLIAM O. WILEY, 146
  PROFILE: EDWARD P. HAMILTON, 147

New People, Ideas, and Practices, 152
  PROFILE: MARTIN MATHESON, 153

Books and Reading Between the Wars, 155

THE PRINTING CRAFT: INNOVATION AND THE DRIVE TO EFFICIENCY, 158

Wiley Weathers the Great Depression, 160

Celebration, Cooperation, and Competition, 164

INSIDE THE BOOKS: ARCHITECTURAL GRAPHIC STANDARDS, 166

Family Matters, 169
  College Travelers, 170

The Big War, 172
  Scientific and Technical Evergreens, 174

Postwar Bonanza, 175
  PROFILE: NORBERT WIENER'S CYBERNETICS, 178

Postwar Changes and Challenges, 179

INSIDE THE BOOKS: MERIAM'S MECHANICS, 186

The Search for Overseas Markets, 189

Old to New, 192

CHAPTER 6   197

William Bradford Wiley:
The Transition to Professional Management
1957 — 1979

Sputnik Launches a New Era

The Right Wiley, 200
  PROFILE: WILLIAM BRADFORD WILEY SR., 201
  PROFILE: WARREN "SULLY" SULLIVAN, 202

Babies, *Sputniks,* and Publishing, 203

The Textbook Revolution, 214

INSIDE THE BOOKS: SCHIFFERES' HEALTHIER LIVING, 215

The Urge to Merge, 216

Reorganization, 222
  PROFILE: GORDON S. IERARDI, 223
  PROFILE: CHARLES STOLL, 224
  PROFILE: MICHAEL HARRIS, 225

Expansion Through Acquisitions, 226

Exploring Opportunities in Professional and Trade Publishing, 229

Andrew Neilly and Nonfamily Professional Management, 233

Wiley Goes Global, 235
  PROFILE: OVE STEENTOFT, 238

Exploring Behind the Iron Curtain, 243
  The Wileys as Ambassadors, 244

The International Corporation, 245

Moving Books, Managing Information, 247
  Computers and Wiley, 248
  Halliday and Resnick Define Physics, 250
  Wiley and Geography, 252

Make, Buy, or Ally?, 257
  PROFILE: JOHN BALBALIS, 258

THE PRINTING CRAFT: THE COLD TYPE REVOLUTION, 260

Transition, 264

CHAPTER 7   267

A Turbulent Decade:
Experimentation and Survival
1979 — 1989

The Challenges Ahead

Facing Uncertainty, 271

Neilly's Imprint, 275
  PROFILE: ANDREW H. NEILLY JR., 276

The Higher Education Market, 279
  INSIDE THE BOOKS: KIESO AND WEYGANDT
  AND WILEY ACCOUNTING, 282

Professional Publishing, 287

Journals Publishing, 289
  The Knowledge Explosion, 290

Medical Publishing, 292

International Expansion and Contraction, 293
  New Challenge to Copyright, 304

Wiley Learning Technologies and
  the Promise of Wilson Learning, 305

New Technology from Existing Product Lines, 308

1985: A Pivotal Year, 309

Searching for New Leadership, 313

Attempted Turnaround, 316

The Turnaround Sours, 317

Worklife at Wiley in the 1980s, 321
  THE PUBLISHING CRAFT:
  FROM HANDWORK TO COMPUTERS, 322

Wiley Remains Independent, 325
  PROFILE: BEATRICE SHUBE AND TED HOFFMAN, 328
  PROFILE: STELLA KUPFERBERG, 329

CHAPTER 8   333

Renaissance:
Rebirth as a Global Company
1989 — 2002

A New World

New Leadership, New Energy, 336

Charles Ellis: Focus and Renewal, 336
  PROFILE: CHARLES ELLIS, 337

Planning for a Renewal, 338

Will Pesce: Vision and Execution, 344

PROFILE: WILLIAM J. PESCE, 345

Higher Education, 347

Embedded in the Curriculum Reform Movement, 351
  CALCULUS REFORM, 352

Leveraging Technology, 353

Evolving Technology in Higher Education, 354

Higher Education Acquisitions and Partnerships, 359

Inside the Books: Tortora's Anatomy and Physiology Titles, 360

Science, Technology, and Medical, 366

Inside the Journals: InterScience, 369

Library Consortia and Digital Content, 371

CrossRef, 372

STM Acquisitions, 373

Profile: VCH, 374

The Societies Initiative, 380

The Cochrane Collaboration, 381

STM Books, 383

Professional/Trade, 385

Expansion of the Trade List, 387

P/T Acquisitions, 390

Profile: Jossey-Bass, 392

Profile: For Dummies, 394

Culinary Publishing, 396

Toward Global Publishing, 398

Information Technology: Going Global, 400

United Kingdom, 402

Australia, 405

Canada, 409

Asia, 412

India, 415

China, 416

Japan, 417

Latin America, the Middle East, and Africa, 418

The Move to Hoboken, 419

Computers and Worklife at Wiley, 420

Protective Engagement, 421

The Publishing Craft: Digital Production Comes of Age, 422

CHAPTER 9   431

Ushering in Wiley's Third Century

❋

Publishing Without Boundaries

危機轉機機會 Embracing Risk, 432

A Long Courtship, 433

Profile: Blackwell Publishing, 434

"In Dreams Begins Responsibility," 440

轉機 *Zhuan Ji*: Transition, 441

轉機機會 Adding Value, 442

Pirates of the Printed Page and More, 444

The Price and Value Proposition, 446

轉機機會 Print *and* Electronic Delivery, 449

機會 The Global Marketplace, 450

Sustaining Value and Ramping Up Investor Relations, 452

All Wiley, All the Time, 456

Persevering in the Middle, 456

Notes, 463

Photo Credits, 507

Name Index, 511

Subject Index, 519

Family Craft and Business: Evolution 1807–2007

Chapter One

✳

Change and Continuity

By American standards, John Wiley & Sons, Inc.[1] is a very old firm. No other American publishing company can match it in age. For two centuries it has produced books and, against long odds, it has remained an independent, family-controlled business. This Wiley publication, Knowledge for Generations, *is written for the firm's bicentennial in 2007. It is the story of how Wiley has endured and prospered, and it suggests how its long history shines light on the path ahead.*

Founder Charles Wiley, who opened a print shop in New York in 1807, would scarcely recognize either the book business or its environment today. New York at that time covered the southern tip of Manhattan Island, and Greenwich Village was just that, a village. Country estates and farmland spread off to the north. Today the only green places left in Manhattan are parks, and the city itself has covered Manhattan and expanded to Staten Island, the western end of Long Island, and a goodly chunk of land north of the Harlem River. Across the Hudson River to the west, the New Jersey shore—once dotted by small towns separated by forests and farms—is now an extension of the city, with high-rise apartment buildings, office towers, and the new world headquarters of John Wiley & Sons in Hoboken defining the skyline.

View of Manhattan looking south with the Hoboken waterfront to the right, by John Bachmann, 1866.

View of New York in a lithograph by Currier and Ives, 1876, showing the Brooklyn Bridge still under construction. At top left is the Hoboken shoreline, future home of John Wiley and Sons.

Location of Wiley's world headquarters, 2007.

Location of Charles Wiley bookstore, 1814–1826.

Some of Wiley's offices worldwide:

Boston

Tokyo

Melbourne

Edinburgh

Oxford

Singapore I

Copenhagen

Chichester

Indianapolis   Singapore II   Toronto   San Francisco   Weinheim   Brisbane   Somerset   Hoboken

*P*ublishing companies like Wiley have also grown apace from small shops run by a proprietor and a helper or two to complex multinational corporations. In the early years, Charles Wiley published a mixture of American originals, English reprints, and an occasional translation of a European title. Today, the largest publishers manage clusters of offices spread around the world—from New York to Tokyo, from London to Delhi, from Moscow to Beijing—recruiting authors on an equally international basis and delivering the results from one end of the earth to another.[2]

Books themselves have changed physically as what was once a book's content has escaped from the confines of its covers into the digital world. At first glance, a recently published book and a well-preserved one from the early nineteenth century may seem alike. Both are printed on paper enclosed between two covers. They contain similar parts, too: a title page, a table of contents, some prefatory remarks, and a body of text. But while Charles and his helpers edited a handwritten manuscript, set it in type, printed each sheet on a hand-operated press, and then had the sheets cut, sewn, and bound between covers, books today are edited and designed online, sent to the printer via the World Wide Web, printed, and then assembled by machine.

Some say that the old artistic qualities have been lost, yet modern machines put out books of uniform quality for a fraction of the cost—and readers no longer have to cut pages—while acid-free paper has extended their usable shelf life. No one in Charles's day could begin to imagine the lush colors and elaborate illustrations that one finds in a modern text or coffee-table book. While books—and printed journals in Wiley's case—remain essential to almost every publisher's offering, Wiley describes itself as a company that "serves the needs of students, lifelong learners, professors, researchers, medical practitioners, professionals, and consumers for educational, professional, and personal development" by working with authors to create, market, sell, and distribute "must-have content and services in the global marketplace."[3]

What used to appear between the covers of a book is now available in a dazzling variety of formats via tape, compact disk, the Internet, even MP3 and the iPod®. Wiley has gone beyond the mere distribution of content to the creation of tools with which customers can search, shape, and use content in new ways. For example, a student using *WileyPLUS*, the company's online educational platform, can take tests based on a particular text, assess the outcome, and be referred to parts of the text for further study. And in its 200th year, Wiley introduced a new type of textbook: one where instructors can search Wiley's content to create a text designed for a specific course.

The way books are sold has also changed. In the nineteenth century,

*W*iley began as an American literary pioneer and evolved into a global provider of must-have content and services.

peddlers pushed titles door to door and field to field. Prepublication subscriptions were sought, and editors and reviewers, when not the authors themselves, were often paid for favorable notices. Today, formal distribution systems are precise, efficient, and highly specialized, with dedicated sales teams servicing everyone and everything from big franchise stores to online retail outlets to library consortia that license numerous journals and major reference works in a single transaction. Through a little work at a personal computer, a publisher can gather detailed information from Amazon and BookScan about how each title is doing in the marketplace. Although the occasional author may surreptitiously tout his own book in an anonymous online review, for the most part today's review system is honest and informative.

Publishing has its constants and traditions, too. Whatever the form of the final products, the publishing functions that lead to them—acquiring, editing, producing, marketing, and selling—have remained largely unchanged through the years. So has publishing's intermediary character remained constant—in between a business and a craft. Editors bring their individual creativity to their work in shaping and refining manuscripts. Designers, even with sophisticated computers, still must combine artfulness with practicality as they develop the right look for every title. And marketers apply both intelligence and intuition in their

> **What used to appear between the covers of a book is now available in a dazzling variety of formats.**

5

$\mathcal{W}$iley met the literary and practical needs of a young nation with its early publications, many preserved in its corporate library. Its history is intertwined with the advance of publishing, the growth of a nation, the evolution of modern science and technology, and the emergence of a global economy, as its titles continue to meet the needs of its customers.

understanding of the marketplace. At the end of the day, commercial publishers must sell the fruits of their labor profitably in the marketplace or fail as businesses. They must also exercise respect for time-honored ways when dealing with the world of words and ideas, where authors, editors, and designers together create works of usefulness, insight, and sometimes even beauty. Behind locked glass doors along the softly lit corridor that leads to Wiley's executive offices in Hoboken, today's visitor can see masterpieces of the craft of bookmaking—the physical artifacts of a family's patrimony and a firm's history. That same visitor, from the comfort of home, can also go to the company's website for information about current titles and for samples of Wiley's technology offerings.

Publishing about important topics is intrinsically satisfying, even exciting. Ideas in print can and do change the world. Every now and then a book spawns profound social change or shifts the way we view the world: John Locke's *Second Treatise [of Civil Government]*, Karl Marx's *Communist Manifesto*, Harriet Beecher Stowe's *Uncle Tom's Cabin*, Charles

Darwin's *Origin of Species*, Rachel Carson's *Silent Spring*, none of them published by Wiley. But Wiley has published a great many works that have been part of gentler evolutions as they serve the practical requirements of readers with a need to know. *Dairy Engineering* (1925), *Poultry Breeding* (1932), *Sampling Inspection Tables* (1944, 1945, 1959, 1970, 1998), *Television: The Electronics of Image Transmission* (1940), or *Simplified Drafting Practice* (1953), *Physics* (1960), *[You-name-it] For Dummies*, all Wiley publications, convey important knowledge and help make lives better. Large and small knowledge gains add up, together contributing to humanity's material and cultural well-being. Books are important and can be profitable. They are a business themselves, and they, along with journals, are the business of John Wiley & Sons.[4]

The Wiley Family

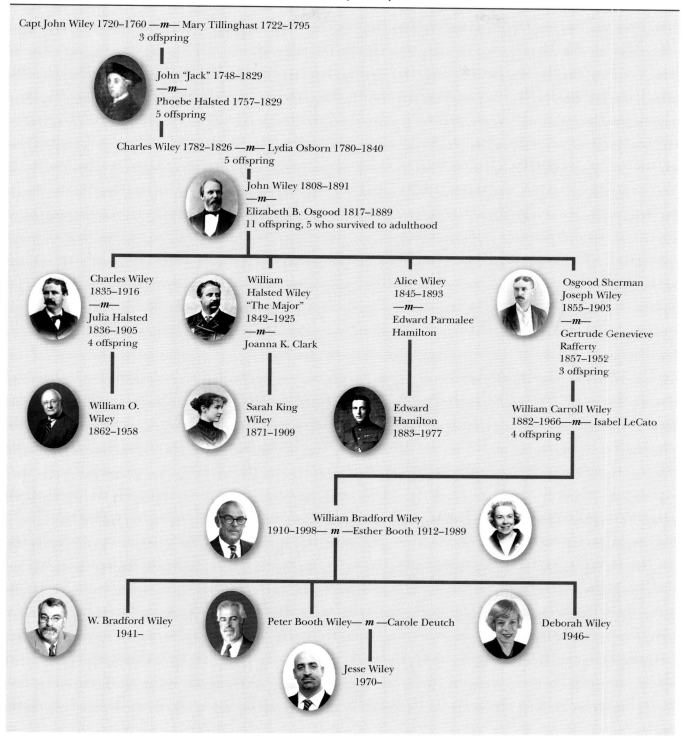

Capt John Wiley 1720–1760 —*m*— Mary Tillinghast 1722–1795
3 offspring

John "Jack" 1748–1829
—*m*—
Phoebe Halsted 1757–1829
5 offspring

Charles Wiley 1782–1826 —*m*— Lydia Osborn 1780–1840
5 offspring

John Wiley 1808–1891
—*m*—
Elizabeth B. Osgood 1817–1889
11 offspring, 5 who survived to adulthood

Charles Wiley
1835–1916
—*m*—
Julia Halsted
1836–1905
4 offspring

William
Halsted Wiley
"The Major"
1842–1925
—*m*—
Joanna K. Clark

Alice Wiley
1845–1893
—*m*—
Edward Parmalee
Hamilton

Osgood Sherman
Joseph Wiley
1855–1903
—*m*—
Gertrude Genevieve
Rafferty
1857–1952
3 offspring

William O.
Wiley
1862–1958

Sarah King
Wiley
1871–1909

Edward
Hamilton
1883–1977

William Carroll Wiley
1882–1966—*m*— Isabel LeCato
4 offspring

William Bradford Wiley
1910–1998— *m* —Esther Booth 1912–1989

W. Bradford Wiley
1941–

Peter Booth Wiley— *m* —Carole Deutch

Deborah Wiley
1946–

Jesse Wiley
1970–

Themes

The story of John Wiley & Sons moves along a number of lines. The first is the character of knowledge publishing: how knowledge gets created and crafted, bought and sold by publishers. As used here, the term "knowledge" is distinct from mere data, the simple agglomeration of numbers and discrete facts. Knowledge need not necessarily be "true" in an eternal sense, nor is it necessarily "fact," though it has a factual basis. It is at bottom a social construct: what intelligent people believe, because of research or study, to be the best understanding of a topic or question at a given time. A nineteenth-century understanding of physics certainly differs from today's understanding, after the discovery of quantum mechanics. But for knowledge to advance, it must be spread and tested, verified and built upon. Of all forms of media, books and journals have long been the most

Wiley's customers have included libraries, such as The New York Public Library, whose Rose Reading Room is as large as a football field. The South Reading Room (left, restored in 1998) gives patrons the setting of the grand European libraries. The North Reading Room has accommodations for patrons' computers as well as offering the use of free computers.

Wiley's *Introduction to Inclusive Education* by Anne Jordan (Wiley Canada Series in Education) is one of many higher education titles that offer *WileyPLUS* as a tool for learning beyond the boundaries of the physical book.

The need for knowledge is constant, from these civil engineers in the field, circa 1900, to students at the Culinary Institute of America studying from the Institute's *The Professional Chef*, 8th edition, © 2006.

authoritative mediators of knowledge, and the more respectable the publisher, the more authoritative the work. Much has been written, over the last 30 years or so as telecommunications and computer revolutions spread, about the end of publishing. Much if not all of it has turned out to be wrong. Books, journals, magazines, and newspapers,

> While delivery formats may change, the need for the transmission of knowledge through writing remains.

as well as some of the firms that produce them, have proven to be hardy stock. We have learned, and learned with a certainty, that while delivery formats may change, the need for the transmission of knowledge through writing remains. Even if ink-on-paper publications had given way utterly to ether—which they haven't—society would still

*C*olleagues from 20 nations work at Wiley-VCH in Weinheim, Germany. Members of the Wiley-VCH football team were excited about the World Cup in June, 2006.

*W*iley's third Asian sales meeting, 1995, Hua Tin, Thailand. Operations, sales, and marketing staff met to develop strategies for the coming year.

need someone to create, mediate, and disseminate knowledge.

The Wileys over their first three generations moved from publishing a broadly based list of both fiction and nonfiction titles to focus on scientific and technical works. From there Wiley the company, through various permutations of its basic publishing program, moved on to "need-to-know" content for specific targeted audiences. Today Wiley is organized into three businesses—Higher Education; Professional/Reference; and Scientific, Technical, and Medical (now Wiley-Blackwell). Later chapters will describe how each of these businesses emerged and blended to become the company's essential publishing portfolio.

Today Wiley operates in a global context.

Publishers arose and remain with us for good economic reasons. Wiley as an organization of entrepreneurs and intermediaries fulfills important economic functions that authors and readers cannot efficiently provide for themselves. Publishers carry most of publishing's substantial risks, managing their lists of publications not unlike portfolios of equities. Moreover, as raw information proliferates, they function as intermediaries in another sense, negotiating a seemingly infinite amount of knowledge to meet the necessarily limited needs of readers. For Wiley, publishing is a business, a way to make a living. When it is well-run, as it usually but not always has been, the business earns profits,

Wiley's legal group at the new corporate headquarters in Hoboken, N.J.

International Foreign Language Association conference held in Bangkok, Thailand, in August 1998 with Jaslyn Tan (far left), Marketing Manager of Wiley Singapore, meeting a professor who was brought to the booth by Mrs. Pranom Anuwatkunnatham (far right), Manager of PB ForBooks Company.

Chichester (U.K.) colleagues at the opening of The Atrium in 2002.

sustains itself, and grows. It pays taxes, wages, royalties, and dividends. It directly creates economic wealth and indirectly promotes economic growth.

Closely related is the story of how the Wileys—*corporate* Wiley beginning with the family's third generation—managed to develop new and successful publishing programs in response to changing demand. How and why Wiley, for example, developed its engineering list over 16 decades or expanded on its Dummies technology list over a shorter period of time is part of the same story of opportunism, occasional luck, and increasing attention to planning. Over much of its history, Wiley reviewed, renewed, discarded, and on occasion revisited publishing programs once discarded. After World War II, the search for opportunity was more formally codified through strategic planning. As elements of the publishing craft, such as editing, design,

and financial analysis, were refined and differentiated, Wiley moved from a largely intuitive approach to publishing—based, albeit, on constant contact with the market—to a more orderly and disciplined approach. The new approach does not preclude, however, the instincts of a fine editor, designer, salesperson, or marketer. We will see that it took a generation and more for Wiley to effectively link the formulation of plans with their successful implementation.

Today Wiley operates in a global context. Charles and John Wiley's world was the Atlantic Basin. They interacted and competed with British publishers while publishing translations of French and German titles at a time when the national and international copyright laws were weak and piracy was common. In 1838, Charles's son John sent his new partner, George Palmer Putnam, to London to open an office through which Wiley &

Putnam increased their import business, arranged to publish popular British writers, such as Charles Dickens, published an occasional title in the United Kingdom, and pushed for a copyright regime that would protect their growing list from piracy. Later, as a scientific and technical publisher, Wiley participated in the flow of knowledge in fields such as chemistry and engineering, which at first ran from Europe to the United States but would soon flow equally in the opposite direction. In the years after World War II, Wiley set up numerous overseas companies and a smaller number of joint ventures. Most of these companies became publishers in their own right, making Wiley in 2007 a truly global operation with publishing offices in nine countries.

> Publishing . . . is a business of long horizons.

The Long Horizon

For two centuries, Wiley has not only survived, grown, and flourished, but it has done so as a family-controlled business in a competitive environment that has become more so since the era of globalization began in the 1980s. With a staff of 4,700 and $1.2 billion in sales at the end of fiscal year 2007 (April 30, 2007), Wiley is a substantial organization, but in its chosen areas of publishing, it is smaller than some of its peers, such as Reed Elsevier. Three of its major competitors (Bertelsmann, McGraw-Hill, and Von Holtzbrinck) remain under family control. Through at least two waves of consolidation starting in the 1950s, however, most family publishing firms were sold, becoming, if they survived at all, imprints within larger houses. Even the large and strong sometimes succumb, but Wiley has not. Why not? The answer lies first with good fortune in navigating the often dangerous shoals of generational transitions.

Wiley was, is, and for the foreseeable future will remain a family-controlled company. The relationship between family and firm has evolved from a time at the start when Wiley was a sole proprietorship and the family and the firm were essentially identical, to the current day when professional managers operate the firm while the family, working with independent board members, oversees it.[5]

Family control may be perceived as a pronounced disadvantage in many industries, especially when families manage their properties to their personal advantage at the expense of other stakeholders. Not so with firms like Wiley, argue the authors of a recent study. Extensive research demonstrates that publicly traded firms "with founding family presence outperform those with more dispersed ownership structures." The salient factor that limits family opportunism and leads to better performance, the authors continue, "is the relative influence of independent and family directors."[6]

Today, Wiley shares are traded on the New York Stock Exchange. The Wiley family elects 70 percent of the board of directors but has learned through good and bad experiences that a board with strong, independent members responsible for guidance and oversight is one of the keys to success. Additionally, the Wileys have always been patient investors, providing the stability creative people need to do their work. With their responsibilities for managing an important part of the company's capital structure, the family has had an interest in the continuation of the enterprise from one generation to the next. Their patience continues to complement the business well: Publishing, especially knowledge publishing, is a business of long horizons where economic return, though often substantial, is seldom quick.

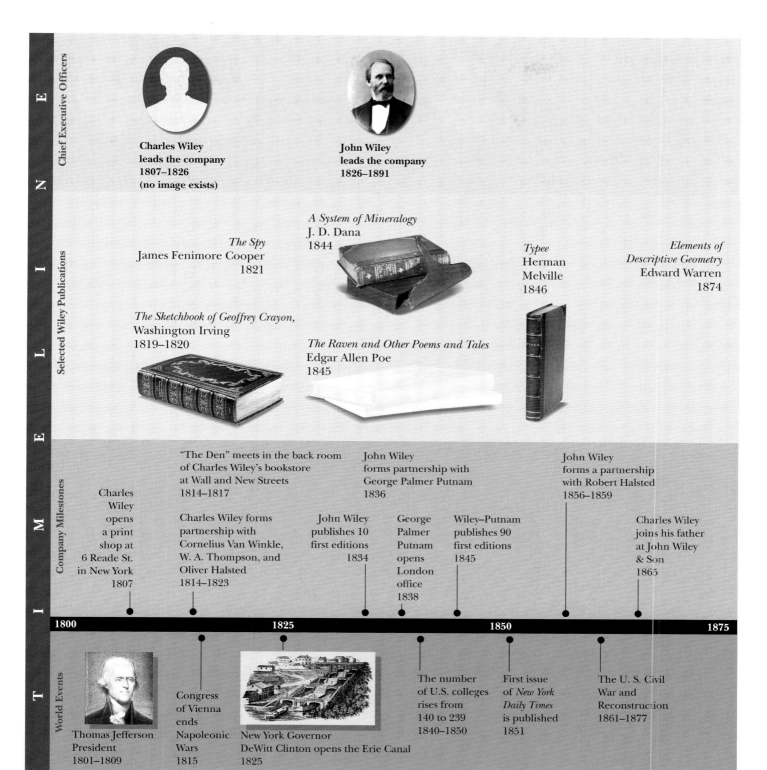

Chief Executive Officers

Charles Wiley
leads the company
1807–1826
(no image exists)

John Wiley
leads the company
1826–1891

Selected Wiley Publications

A System of Mineralogy
J. D. Dana
1844

The Spy
James Fenimore Cooper
1821

Typee
Herman
Melville
1846

*Elements of
Descriptive Geometry*
Edward Warren
1874

The Sketchbook of Geoffrey Crayon,
Washington Irving
1819–1820

The Raven and Other Poems and Tales
Edgar Allen Poe
1845

Company Milestones

"The Den" meets in the back room
of Charles Wiley's bookstore
at Wall and New Streets
1814–1817

John Wiley
forms partnership with
George Palmer Putnam
1836

John Wiley
forms a partnership
with Robert Halsted
1856–1859

Charles
Wiley
opens
a print
shop at
6 Reade St.
in New York
1807

Charles Wiley forms
partnership with
Cornelius Van Winkle,
W. A. Thompson, and
Oliver Halsted
1814–1823

John Wiley
publishes 10
first editions
1834

George
Palmer
Putnam
opens
London
office
1838

Wiley–Putnam
publishes 90
first editions
1845

Charles Wiley
joins his father
at John Wiley
& Son
1865

| 1800 | 1825 | 1850 | 1875 |

World Events

Thomas Jefferson
President
1801–1809

Congress
of Vienna
ends
Napoleonic
Wars
1815

New York Governor
DeWitt Clinton opens the Erie Canal
1825

The number
of U.S. colleges
rises from
140 to 239
1840–1850

First issue
of *New York
Daily Times*
is published
1851

The U. S. Civil
War and
Reconstruction
1861–1877

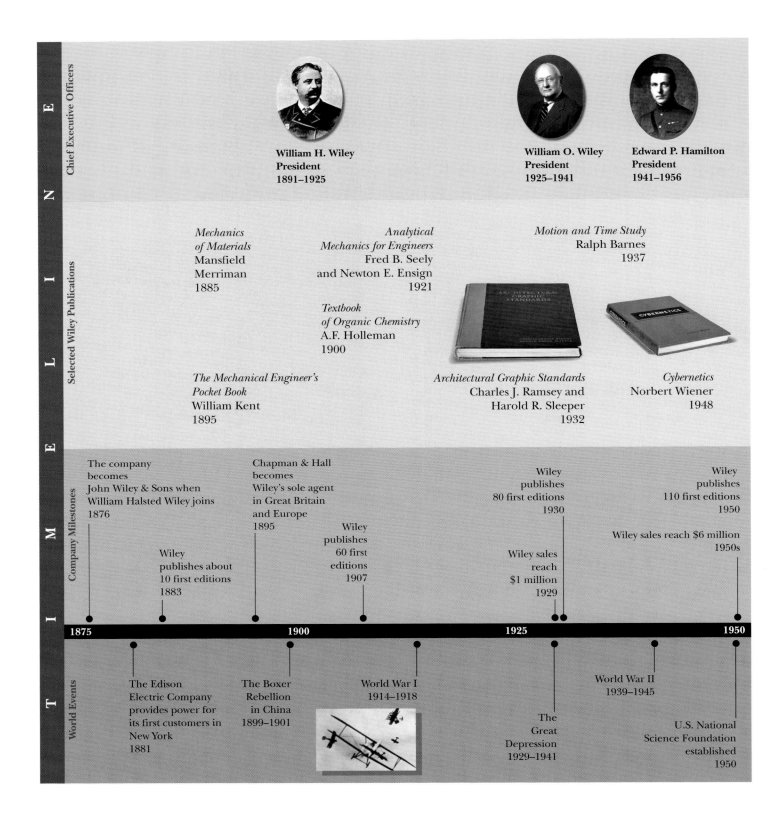

Chief Executive Officers

William H. Wiley
President
1891–1925

William O. Wiley
President
1925–1941

Edward P. Hamilton
President
1941–1956

Selected Wiley Publications

*Mechanics
of Materials*
Mansfield
Merriman
1885

*Analytical
Mechanics for Engineers*
Fred B. Seely
and Newton E. Ensign
1921

Motion and Time Study
Ralph Barnes
1937

*Textbook
of Organic Chemistry*
A.F. Holleman
1900

*The Mechanical Engineer's
Pocket Book*
William Kent
1895

Architectural Graphic Standards
Charles J. Ramsey and
Harold R. Sleeper
1932

Cybernetics
Norbert Wiener
1948

Company Milestones

The company
becomes
John Wiley & Sons when
William Halsted Wiley joins
1876

Wiley
publishes about
10 first editions
1883

Chapman & Hall
becomes
Wiley's sole agent
in Great Britain
and Europe
1895

Wiley
publishes
60 first
editions
1907

Wiley
publishes
80 first editions
1930

Wiley sales
reach
$1 million
1929

Wiley
publishes
110 first editions
1950

Wiley sales reach $6 million
1950s

1875 · **1900** · **1925** · **1950**

World Events

The Edison
Electric Company
provides power for
its first customers in
New York
1881

The Boxer
Rebellion
in China
1899–1901

World War I
1914–1918

The
Great
Depression
1929–1941

World War II
1939–1945

U.S. National
Science Foundation
established
1950

W. Bradford Wiley
CEO
1956–1979

Andrew Neilly
CEO
1979–1989

Ruth McMullin
CEO
1989–1990

Charles Ellis
CEO
1990–1998

William J. Pesce
CEO
1998–

Virology
S.E. Luria
1953

Physics of Semiconductor Devices
Simon Sze
1981

*Encyclopedia of Polymer
Science and Technology*
Herman Mark,
Norman Gaylord,
and Norbert
Bikales
1964

Biochemistry
Donald and
Judith Voet
1990

Intermediate Accounting
Donald E. Kieso and
Jerry J. Weygandt
1974

*The Journal
of
Image-Guided Surgery*
1995

Windows XP for Dummies
2002

15

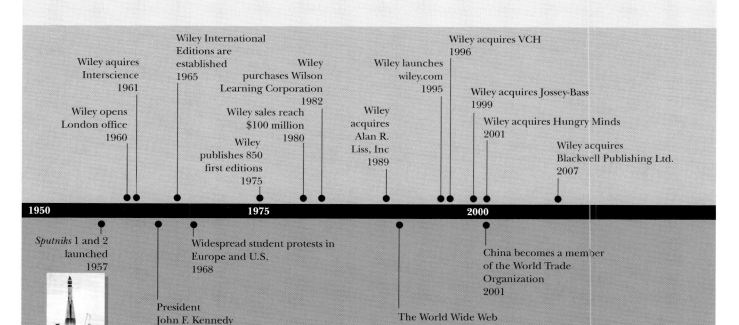

Wiley aquires
Interscience
1961

Wiley International
Editions are
established
1965

Wiley
purchases Wilson
Learning Corporation
1982

Wiley launches
wiley.com
1995

Wiley acquires VCH
1996

Wiley opens
London office
1960

Wiley sales reach
$100 million
1980

Wiley acquires Jossey-Bass
1999

Wiley
publishes 850
first editions
1975

Wiley
acquires
Alan R.
Liss, Inc
1989

Wiley acquires Hungry Minds
2001

Wiley acquires
Blackwell Publishing Ltd.
2007

1950

1975

2000

Sputniks 1 and 2
launched
1957

Widespread student protests in
Europe and U.S.
1968

China becomes a member
of the World Trade
Organization
2001

President
John F. Kennedy
assassinated
1963

The World Wide Web
launched
1991

Broadway near Bowling Green

Charles Wiley: Bookman of the "Literary Republic"

1807–1826

Chapter Two

❋

The New York of Charles Wiley

In fact and imagination, great cities remain forever associated with the industries that made them great. For Pittsburgh, it was steel; for Chicago, railroads; for Detroit, automobiles; and for New York, finance, commerce, and publishing. By the late eighteenth century, New York was a booming urban center, proudly polyglot and facing outward across its great harbor toward the world. At the start of the nineteenth century, which was when Charles Wiley set up his book business, New York was the place to be—infused with freedom, disorder, boundless possibility, and the risk that came with being young in the young republic.

Lower Manhattan beckoned the fashionable and the ambitious. An English visitor at the time, used to the splendors of Georgian London, was not unimpressed. Broadway and Bowery Road, he reported, were the city's "two finest avenues," with houses "lofty and well-built" and universally made of red brick. Just to the north up and around Broadway spread the city's principal tradesmen and merchants with "commodious shops of every description well-stocked with European and Indian goods, and exhibiting as splendid and varied a show in their windows as can be met with in London." At his earliest locations, Charles Wiley's shops—and probably his home, too, for it was usual then to live over the store—were in more modest neighborhoods, where

The corner of Greenwich and Warren streets in 1809. Typical of the neighborhoods where Charles Wiley worked and lived before moving to 3 Wall Street in 1814.

The Tontine Coffeehouse (left), where the city's merchants gathered to haggle and deal, was at the corner of Wall and Water streets, four blocks east of Charles's shop and home between 1814 and his death.

two-story buildings accommodated both work and living quarters. In any case, nothing was very far from anything else in Manhattan. To get there, one walked.[1]

Manhattan's shops, including its several extensive bookstores, were windows onto this world of trade. Trade is, of course, indifferent to social justice, and Charles Wiley's New York displayed all the disparities of wealth and poverty, hope and despair, happiness and squalor, that the market could create. It was filled with old and newly rich joined with new poor. Native-born Americans jostled with newcomers, sometimes angrily, for place and advantage. Charles was a witness. When he finally settled down permanently at 3 Wall Street in 1814, his bookstore and his home were in a prime location on a street that ran between the busy wharves of South Street on the East River through the business district to Broadway at Trinity Church. Nearby was the Tontine Coffeehouse, a favorite gathering place for the city's merchants, and a little farther still was the notorious Five Points district.

To the north, the city was bounded just beyond the new City Hall, which opened in 1811, by a fetid swamp known as The Collect into which raw sewage drained. Throughout the city, two- and four-legged creatures of all sorts ran in the crooked streets. The place was a bedlam of carriages and wagons in summer, sleds in winter and year-round horses, cattle, dogs, and hogs, let to wander freely in exchange for their services as primitive agents of waste management.

From such a stew might have boiled up social unrest, even violence and revolution. It had been known to happen in European cities, where those lured by the metropolis overwhelmed its opportunities or failed to create them fast enough. There were few safety valves in slums like Five Points. In Charles's New York, however, revolution did not happen. Instead, economic growth enabled a social mobility that produced a large and lively middle class, ever ambitious to improve itself materially and in other ways. Their New York was both business powerhouse and cultural center. Books equaled culture for every man and woman who was literate, and most Americans were literate—excepting, of course, most slaves. New York booksellers held the first ever literary fair in the United States in 1802, where dealers snatched up half a million volumes in less than a week. Libraries opened, and schools expanded to serve more and more of the young. Clubs and societies abounded—the Uranian, Horanian, Calliopean, the Law and Philological—where New Yorkers gathered to discuss literature, politics, and science. The professions gradually became more professional. In 1797, two New York physicians launched the Medical Repository, the country's first professional journal. Painting, music, and theater put down roots.

The notorious Five Points district, a neighborhood once populated by artisans, would go down in history as America's first "slum," rife with crime, pestilence, and overcrowding. Immigration, then largely unregulated, brought thousands to New York each year, some strong and ready for enterprise, soon to make a place for themselves or move on, others weak and inviting exploitation. To both strong and weak and everything in between, Five Points was home.

The corporate history of old family companies is personal, rooted in fascinating foundings, in unlikely paths to success, in sad tales of decline and happy ones of renewal. The course of the company is entwined in the lives and dreams of its founders: the people who thought it up, made the first moves and mistakes, took the first risks, most often witnessed the collapse of their endeavors, and may not have lived long enough to enjoy the benefits.

John Wiley & Sons is no exception.* Charles Wiley's print shop at 6 Reade Street, Manhattan, evolved in the two decades after 1807 into something akin to a modern publisher. But when Charles died in 1826, the company almost died with him. Why did Charles enter the book trade at that particular time and place? Why did he persist in a business whose stresses must have shortened his life? How did he manage to keep the company going through embargo, war, financial panic, and changing technological and business environments? With the scant documentation available, we attempt to answer those questions.

The Road to Publishing

The Wiley family settled in New Brunswick, New Jersey, where John Wiley (1720–1760), a sea captain from Scotland, became a partner in a distillery in 1744. John Wiley married Mary Tillinghast and then moved to New York City where he leased land from Trinity Church and built two still houses between the west wall of the church yard and the Hudson River. When John died a prosperous merchant in 1760, he left his still houses to his wife and children, one of whom was also named John (1748–1829) but often called "Jack," or "Captain Jack." Jack continued in his father's business, owning, according to his grandson, "several small brigs and schooners which

brought sugar and molasses to his distillery and took back to the West Indies 'Old Jamaica' freshly made." A member of the Sons of Liberty, he joined the First New York Infantry as a first lieutenant at the start of the American Revolution, abandoning the city along with General George Washington as British forces closed in. Jack was promoted to captain within a year, and the next year to brigade-major. A mysterious fire swept the west side of New York in September 1776, and Jack lost everything. In 1777, he wrote that he feared for the Continental Army, then retreating before the British troops, because privateers were siphoning off recruits while merchants and quarter-masters cheated on supplies. Jack saw action in numerous engagements until 1780, when he married Phoebe Halsted and became Commissary of Purchases for the New York line. That proved an opportune position for a merchant-

Captain Jack Wiley's brother William was one of the leaders of the Stamp Act riots of 1765, after which he and his fellow Sons of Liberty wanted to assure the authorities that they were still loyal subjects of the king. William therefore helped raise funds for this statue of George III, which Jack helped pull down in 1776. George's head *sans* nose was raised on a pike in front of a tavern.

*For the sake of clarity, we generally refer to individual Wiley family members by their first names or nicknames and, when necessary, middle initials or numbers. Also, we use an ampersand [&] to distinguish business partnerships from multiple individuals.

PROFILE

JOHN ("JACK") WILEY

When Jack and his family returned to New York after the war, he planned to rebuild, but Trinity Church insisted on better terms for Jack's lease. He became so outraged, according to his grandson, that "he tore up the lease, threw the fragments into the faces of the committee appointed to confer with him, and left them with a benediction which would probably burn holes in the paper if literally translated." Instead, he built his new distillery in Newark, New Jersey, in 1787. The business survived at least through 1790, when John and several partners announced the erection of a cider mill in neighboring Elizabeth Town. They likely sold cider as well as rum to mercantile firms like Gelston & Saltonstall of New York for distribution in Pennsylvania, New Jersey, New York, and New England. John also engaged in real estate, selling lots along the Passaic River.[2]

Major John Wiley and Family. Major John Wiley is standing by the wall of Trinity Church at the foot of Wall Street with his mother, Mary Tillinghast, and his two sisters, Mary and Patty.

turned-soldier who once claimed that he thought himself "duty bound to even spare the coat off my back to supply the necessities of the brave soldier who at the risque of life and health nobly steps forth to defend our *Glorious Cause.*" He and Phoebe had five children, the eldest of whom, Charles (1782–1826), founded Wiley.[3]

According to an early biographer, Charles was educated with the intent of his entering a learned profession, but reverses in the family business induced him to become a printer, an occupation he supposed would accord with his literary tastes. Other sources concur that Jack found himself in financial difficulty; we know for certain that he had financial claims against the federal government that went unpaid during his lifetime. Yet other sources suggest that Jack drank to excess. Both Jack and Phoebe died in 1829.[4]

The specter of drunken fathers destroying the lives of their sons loomed large in the nation's early years, an all too believable set-piece of subsequent cheap fiction. Many males of the Revolutionary generation and sons born into Charles's birth cohort (1776–1800) avowed temperance. We cannot be certain of Charles's views on drinking, but the use of hard liquor was increasingly frowned upon, and Charles may have had profoundly personal reasons for shunning the family liquor business.[5]

He also had sound business reasons. Distilling was risky. Liquor imports were enormous, competition intense, and U.S. distillers had no clear comparative advantage. In fact, they suffered several disadvantages. By shattering century-old

THE SUBSCRIBERS having nearly compleated their Distillery at Newark, beg leave to inform the public that they are daily receiving Cyder for distillation, and that such Persons who send any for that purpose may depend on being paid the full amount of what may be due to them by the 15th instant, after which time immediate payment will be made, on the delivery of the Cyder at said Distillery, in proof Spirits, of an excellent flavour, and in the proportion usually given.   JOHN WILEY, & Co.

Newark, September 4, 1787.

N.B. In order to prevent a detention of the teams and casks at said Distillery, a number of cisterns are conveniently placed below the ground to receive any quantity of Cyder that may be sent for distillation.

ELIZABETH-TOWN: PRINTED BY SHEPARD KOLLOCK.

Announcement that the John Wiley distillery in Newark, N.J., was nearly completed: 1787.

trading relationships, the American and French revolutions fundamentally altered the trans-Atlantic economy. Some American industries wilted, while others prospered. The price of domestically produced rum fluctuated wildly as it absorbed the shocks of war and diplomacy as well as frequent changes in duties and excise taxes on sugar and molasses. At the same time, the use of slaves and indentured servants in distilling declined, their labor replaced by wage workers whose contracts were short-term and volatile. Finally, many consumers—then as now—judged imported spirits superior to domestic.[6]

By contrast, the mercantile trade steadily thrived in the 1790s, particularly in New York. The same forces that made liquor production risky provided America's merchants with opportunities undreamed of in the colonial period. Freed from British regulation, American merchants ventured to China, Latin America, Africa—wherever trade promised profit. Neutral during the wars between France and England, American merchantmen prospered in the trans-Atlantic trade.[7]

After 1797, just as Charles was coming of age, Britain and Napoleonic France sought to deny one another access to American shipping. In retaliation for the impressment of American seamen by the British, the administration of Thomas Jefferson imposed a controversial trade embargo in 1807 that hit the new nation hard. Uneven enforcement only increased uncertainty. With U.S. exports forbidden, ports were closed, fleets grew idle, and businesses everywhere were shuttered. In New York, the coffeehouses and quaysides along South Street fell silent; "not a box, bale, cask, barrel or package . . . the few solitary merchants to be seen walked about with their hands in their pockets." Exports shrank

by 80 percent, imports by 60 percent. The embargo lasted two years, and soon after it was lifted New York bustled once again.[8]

Distilling, with its dependence on international trade, must have seemed a very unappealing business choice for a young man of slim capital. The book trade, in contrast, must have looked good. Like distilling, it entailed some manufacturing processes, but it was neither dependent on foreign raw materials like molasses nor subject to fitful taxes and duties. Unlike American distillers, American printers had several advantages over foreign rivals. Right after the Revolution most books could still be gotten more cheaply from Britain than they could be printed in America. This soon changed. Domestic paper manufacturing had flourished during the war, and type and ink were produced in increasing quantities after the first American type foundry opened in Philadelphia in 1796. By the mid-1790s American publishers could manufacture and sell even large series of law books as cheaply as those sent from Britain. Of course, American publishers often pirated British books, paying only for the relatively cheap incremental copies and not the very expensive first copy.[9]

In addition, printing and publishing could be conducted profitably on a small scale, in contrast to distilling, which required a larger labor force. And while the book trade was connected to the trans-Atlantic economy, it was not dependent on it. Rather, the book trade gave bookmen, as Charles was to become, the option to import and export, but it required no more than domestic demand to sustain itself and grow. And except for intermittent economic downturns, that demand was rising. America's population grew

> American publishers often pirated British books, paying only for the relatively cheap incremental copies and not the very expensive first copy.

View of New York harbor from Battery Park, Castle Clinton Battery on the right. With the greatest of harbors on the eastern seaboard, New York belonged as much to the Atlantic as to the American world. On a map New York may have looked, from London, to be on the periphery of things. After all, its population in 1810 was 120,000 compared to London's 1.3 million. But from New York's perspective, the city was at the center. New York was connected to London in a web of commerce, trading in everything from sugar to rum to cotton to slaves to financial services, even to books.

In 1807, the year Charles entered the book trade, Robert Fulton confounded skeptics by making a successful maiden voyage up the Hudson in his paddlewheel steamboat, later named the *Clermont*. A large crowd gathered the morning of August 17 at the Christopher Street pier, some no doubt expecting—even hoping—for smoke, fire, and a big bang. Instead, the little vessel chugged against the current all the way up to Albany at a stately four-and-a-half miles per hour, opening a new era in the history of technology. Ironically, Fulton had to travel to England for his technical education and to France in search of support. Within another generation, American technologists could get all the education they needed right here at home, and the scientific and technical subjects that commanded their mastery were a lucrative market for publishers.

rapidly, from 3.9 million in 1790 to 5.3 million in 1800 to almost 10 million by 1820. New York's population also soared, from 33,000 in 1790 to 123,000 by 1820. Just as important, per capita annual income surged upward from $1,150 in 1790 to $1,350 in 1800 to over $1,500 by 1820 (all figures historically adjusted). Demand for books, which were what economists call "luxury goods," increased even more quickly.[10]

> In the early nineteenth century, most Americans could read . . . America was a land of libraries.

Demand drove supply, and the publishing business, which one way or another dealt with printing and selling words on paper, flourished. The country was at the dawn of a new era of technological change that would open up demand even further.

The Demand for Books

In the early nineteenth century, most Americans could read. About 75 to 90 percent of them, depending on time and place, were literate enough to read the Bible, and so were also able to read books and newspapers. But they did not have much time to do so. Eight in every ten Americans were farmers, working sunup to sundown. Even merchants and artisans worked long hours, six days a week. But the coldest part of the winter and the hottest part of the summer brought some spare time, when reading could bring both enjoyment and self-improvement.[11]

The Scoville Memorial Library, in Salisbury, Connecticut, founded in 1827, was typical of the libraries founded in the early nineteenth century. Membership at that time cost $3.34.

Many Americans owned books outright. The wealthiest among them owned impressive libraries. Most famous was Thomas Jefferson's collection of 6,487 volumes, which would become the nucleus for the Library of Congress; but less exalted citizens, too, bought books and presumably read them. By December 1820, Henry W. Pearce's collection numbered 3,850 titles. Six years earlier, Charles Riche of Burlington, New Jersey, boasted a fine library of 142 titles, many of them classic volumes by Plutarch, Shakespeare, Alexander Pope, David Hume, and Jonathan Swift. Probate records reveal that book ownership was widespread—almost ubiquitous—among Americans who owned any property at all at the time of their death. Of a random sample of 37 people (35 men, 2 women) who died in Maryland and Virginia between 1800 and 1810, 28 (or 75 percent) owned at least one book. Even the poor could buy books produced by printers like Samuel Woods and John Low of New York, who brought out cheap editions specifically for "country pedlars, house maids and mariners."[12]

Those too poor or disinclined to purchase books could still read them because America was a land of libraries. College and municipal libraries had been established by the end of the seventeenth century, but in the late eighteenth and early nineteenth centuries "social libraries," like the Library Company of Philadelphia, founded

Number of U.S. Libraries, 1790–1825

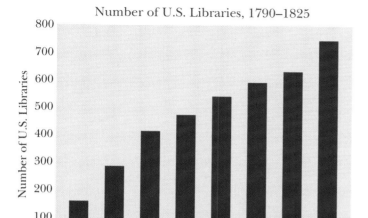

Source: Haynes McMullen, *American Libraries Before 1876* (Conn.: Greenwood Press, 2000), 48.

U.S. Libraries Per Capita, 1790–1830

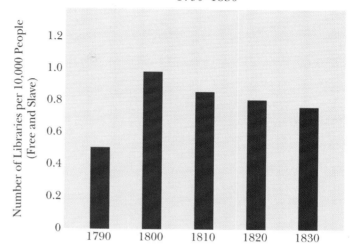

Source: Haynes McMullen, *American Libraries Before 1876* (Conn.: Greenwood Press, 2000), 51.

by Benjamin Franklin and others in 1731, grew in number and importance. By 1802, there were at least 100 social libraries in Massachusetts alone. Funded by membership dues, social libraries allowed patrons to borrow books for a nominal fee. Others, modeled after elite British institutions called "atheneums," were essentially joint-stock corporations that offered member-stockholders access to a wide range of books and periodicals. There were also numerous "circulating libraries"—essentially bookstores that rented books. For a nominal fee, customers of circulating libraries could enjoy a few days with Adam Smith's *The Wealth of Nations* or Daniel Defoe's *Robinson Crusoe*. Churches, colleges, all kinds of societies (agricultural, artistic, historical, literary, musical), and other organizations (fraternal orders, fire companies) also established libraries for the use of their members. The number of libraries almost doubled in per capita terms in the nation's first decades. Books also attracted charity. In 1812, Philadelphia bookman William Bradford donated 367 books to the local prison for the Sabbath use of its inmates. In 1821, Charles Wiley and his partner Oliver Halsted collected books for donation to the "Sailor's Floating Library," which distributed them to the sailors of 21 different vessels.[13]

Of course, not everyone who was literate chose to read, and undoubtedly some books collected dust. Yet most Americans found books too dear not to use them. Evidence abounds that people did not just buy books; they craved them. In 1805, some disgruntled Philadelphians threatened to form a "Literary Society for the Importation of Books" if the directors of the Library Company of Philadelphia persisted in keeping all the new books to themselves. Twenty years later, some New Yorkers established a "book club" designed to allow members to read, in random order, important new books, including Wiley titles like James Fenimore Cooper's *Lionel Lincoln*, soon after publication. Dues, fines, and sale of used books at auction paid for additional new titles. About that same time, Wiley author Richard Henry Dana wrote to Cooper that "reading is now a sort of fashion & the great object is, to be first in the fashion, & in order to do that, to be the first in getting a new publication, the first in getting thro it, the first to talk about it, & the first in talking about it." Books were the medium of the early republic, as Americans gathered in their shops, stalls, and over the fence in the field to discuss the latest things between covers.[14]

Publishing appealed to budding literary nationalists, like Mathew Carey and Charles Wiley, who thrilled at the prospect of an authentic American literature.

$\mathcal{M}$athew Carey was a newspaper publisher, an Irish rebel, a political prisoner, and the first great American publisher. Called "The Father of American Trade" because he crusaded on behalf of America's publishing industry, he had dealings with Charles and employed John Wiley after Charles, John's father, died.

The Book Trade

Charles Wiley likely learned the attractions of the book trade because of the exertions of Philadelphia printer Mathew Carey, who crusaded so vigorously on behalf of America's nascent publishing industry that he was called "The Father of the American Trade." In 1801, Carey called for "*A Literary Fair*, as nearly on the plan of those of Frankfort and Leipzic [*sic*], as possible" in order to create a national market for books. He confidently predicted a great increase in the number of books printed in

the United States. Bookmen from around the country responded to his call, convening five fairs between 1802 and 1805, three of which met in New York, one in Newark, and one in Philadelphia.[15]

Charles may well have attended one or all of those fairs. If so, he would have learned that both the economic and the legal climate favored the growth of American publishing. As Carey explained at the 1802 fair in New York: "THE LAW OF COPY-RIGHTs, by securing a reward to the labours of genius, gilt the laurel that enwreathed [the industry's] brow." He was saluting the copyright laws of 1790 and 1802, which provided authors, cartographers, and engravers residing in the United States with a nationwide copyright good for at least 14 years. These laws assured the growth of the publishing industry, but publishing was more than good business. Publishing had a special appeal to moralists, like Carey, who saw themselves as guardians of the press and the virtue of the people. And it appealed to budding literary nationalists, like Carey and Charles, who thrilled at the prospect of nurturing an authentically American literature.[16]

Despite early competition from Philadelphia and Boston, New York became the center of the publishing

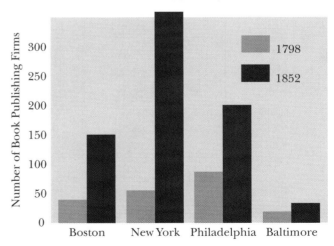

Growth of the Book Trade in Major U.S. Cities 1798–1852

trade. In 1795, it already had 29 print shops and 24 booksellers, and by 1807, 40 print shops and 37 booksellers. (No distinction was made between a printer and a publisher at the time.) New York's deep-water harbor and connection to the Erie Canal, partially open in 1819, ensured its preeminence as America's commercial center. By the mid-1830s, Manhattan would also be the undisputed financial heart of the country. These were all distinct advantages for New York publishers.[17]

Charles was able to attract manuscripts from New England because, in the words of Bostonian Richard Dana, "it is far better to send to New York for general distribution than to attempt sending from such an out of the way place as Boston to different parts of the United States." Relatively easy and fast access to short-term business loans also helped New York publishers attract authors and compete against publishers elsewhere, especially in the south and west. As a result, the number of persons and firms in the book trade in New York grew much more rapidly than in Boston, Philadelphia, and Baltimore. By the middle of the nineteenth century, New York would far outstrip all its rivals.[18]

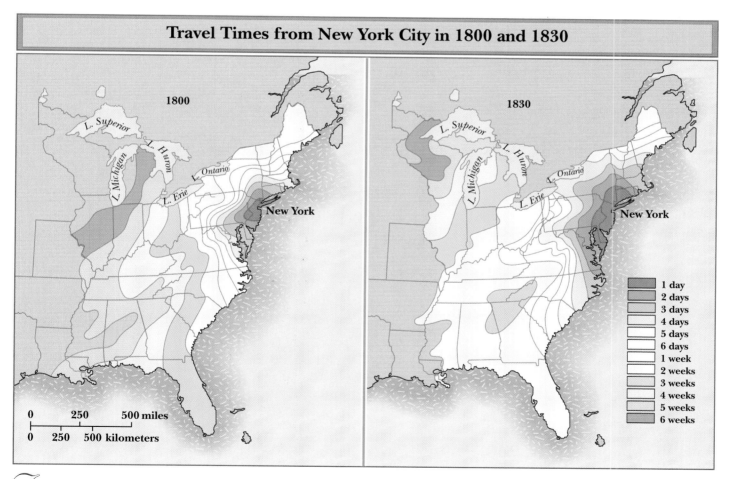

Travel Times from New York City in 1800 and 1830

1800

1830

L. Superior
L. Michigan
L. Huron
L. Ontario
L. Erie
New York

1 day
2 days
3 days
4 days
5 days
6 days
1 week
2 weeks
3 weeks
4 weeks
5 weeks
6 weeks

0   250   500 miles
0   250   500 kilometers

*T*he transportation revolution of the early nineteenth century, which contributed to a growing market for books, made possible much more rapid travel within the United States.

THE *Printing craft*

GLYPHS, FRAMES, AND HAND PRESSES

In the early nineteenth century, the craft of printing was highly regulated by printers themselves. The New York Typographical Society set the rules for apprenticeships. An apprentice had to work for two or three years before achieving journeyman status. Many journeymen chose to work for other printers rather than go into business for themselves because the costs of starting a shop were significant. Not only was the equipment expensive, but the skills required to run a shop were varied and complex. Printing was definitely a labor-intensive craft.

Within print shops, work was subdivided by skill. Compositors set type, placing glyphs one at a time in a composing stick until a line of type was complete. Then they transferred it to a metal or wooden frame. The process was repeated, line by line, until a page was completely typeset. The frame was then locked and placed on the printing press. After the

page was printed, the glyphs were removed from the frame and cleaned. They were then redistributed to the type case for the next job, likely later pages of the same book. If a book were ever required to be reprinted, composition had to begin all over again.

The printing press itself was hand-operated. Most eighteenth-century presses were made of wood, though iron presses were replacing them. Either way, operating a press required considerable brawn. The type had to be inked, a dirty job if there ever was one, and then the page placed upon it. The press was then screwed down on top so the paper would be imprinted with the type. Next the tension was released and the damp page removed and hung to dry for later printing on the other side. Then the finished pages were collated, folded, and cut. Perhaps some of the run would be bound, a task sometimes completed in-house and sometimes by an outside binder, with the residue remaining unbound to facilitate storage, long-distance shipping, and orders for special, usually extravagant, bindings.

In 1812, stereographic technology was first introduced in the United States. It represented a major advance because it obviated the need to compose type anew for each reprinting. Instead of imprinting on paper, glyphs made indelible impressions on metal plates, from which the printed pages were produced. The plates were durable and could be stored and transported with relative ease—a new, permanent, physical embodiment of the work of the author and publisher.[19]

This wood engraving (American, circa 1800) shows a typical printing office of the time.

Print Shop Beginnings

To start in the book trade as he did, first as a printer, Charles would have needed experience and capital, and the record is dim as to how he acquired either. The New York Typographical Society required all printers to serve apprenticeships of two, three, or more years, so it is almost certain that Charles served as a printer's apprentice at some point. Fragmentary evidence suggests he may have apprenticed under printer and bookseller Isaac Riley (1770–1824), who was extensively engaged in the law book trade. Similarly, we can only speculate as to how Charles raised the funds—as much as several thousand dollars—needed to rent a shop, buy one or more printing presses and type fonts, and otherwise supply his business with ink, paper, furniture, and sundries. His father and members of his mother's family may have supplied the funds, but there are other possibilities. Given the stop-and-go nature of the firm's early years, it seems clear that Charles's backers, whoever they were, never lavished him with cash.[20]

Wiley under Charles traversed six distinct business phases, during each of which the company operated under a different name and maintained a distinct emphasis. Like many early businessmen, Charles changed partners frequently. The focus of the following discussion is on the publishing side of his business, but Wiley under Charles is better described as a proto-publisher. Sometimes he published books in the modern sense; that is, he assumed the financial risks of acquiring, printing, and distributing. Much more of his effort, however, went into areas no longer considered part of the publishing business proper. He ran a bookstore and a print shop. He also functioned as what today would be called a vanity press, charging authors for the production cost of their books and assuming none of the risks of production or sale himself. The few agreements that survive indicate only two things: that there were no standard arrangements between early Wiley and its authors and that the line between real and vanity publishing was blurred.

)) all Street in 1814.
Charles Wiley's shop
was located at 3 Wall Street.

Moreover, Wiley's publishing program looks diffuse and opportunistic, especially in the beginning. Like all early publishers, Charles was a jack-of-all-trades, acquiring manuscripts, editing them, and even overseeing the typesetting and sales. As the firm participated in the growth of its industry, a division of labor began to develop, with Charles leaving the difficult, dirty job of printing to his partner or, eventually, entirely to other firms. Throughout his career, however, his early background in printing held Charles in good stead when it came to quoting prices to prospective authors and critiquing the work of other printers.[21]

During Wiley's first phase, from 1807 through 1811, Charles started out with a print shop on Reade Street, perhaps continued in later years, though that seems unlikely. (Charles and his family moved to Flatbush, Long Island, in 1808, remaining there until at least 1810. Commuting from Long Island by ferry would have been time-consuming and expensive, and most businessmen lived in the same building as their shops.) So one can speculate that he was working for another printer. In 1811, Charles, working in a shop at 28 Provost (now Franklin) Street, printed one of the Franklin Company's first books, William Ballantine's legal treatise on the statute of limitations. For reasons unknown, the Franklin Company folded later that year and sold its stock at auction. If Charles printed or published any other books between 1807 and 1812, no record has survived.[22]

In Wiley's second phase, Charles printed a handful of titles out of his print shop, located at 61 Hudson Street in 1812 and at 26 Provost (now Franklin) Street in 1813. Some for the legal profession he financed and distributed. These included a reprint of Joseph Chitty's *A Practical Treatise on Pleading* and the second edition of William Cranch's nine-volume *Reports of Cases Argued . . . in the Supreme Court.* Other books associated with Wiley in this period, such as *The Young Traveller, or, Adventures of Etienne in Search of His Father; The Mirror of the Graces,* and *Travels in Various Countries in Europe, Asia, and Africa,* appear to have been just printing jobs for Cornelius Van Winkle (soon to become

Charles's partner), William B. Gilley, Isaac Riley, or other established publishers.

Printing was a relatively low-status occupation, but Charles used it to make contacts and build a network. In 1813, for example, Bradford & Inskeep of Philadelphia used Charles to print James Kirke Paulding's *The Diverting History of John Bull and Brother Jonathan*, a comedic satire inspired by the War of 1812 about the settlement of the colonies and the Revolution. Similarly, Charles printed *The Analectic Magazine*, which was edited and published by Moses Thomas of Philadelphia. For the *Analectic*, Washington Irving collected essays from British periodicals but also published his own biographical sketches of American naval heroes.[23]

Whether Charles turned a monetary profit on *John Bull* or the *Analectic* is unknown, but the jobs undoubtedly increased his reputation within a circle of aspiring New York literati, of which Irving and Paulding were leading members. Paulding was no lover of publishers. He changed them frequently because he thought them all "Philistines" and "rogues." Nevertheless, he was careful to protect the interests of Charles and his partner Cornelius S. Van Winkle, telling Mathew Carey that he considered himself "bound to take care they are not injured."[24]

Nevertheless, life for Charles in this second phase of his career could not have been easy. The War of 1812 dampened business, and two-thirds of the city's printers shut down. In 1815, after the war had ended and trade with Britain reopened, the New York Typographical Society tried to forestall price competition by setting a minimum fee schedule for typesetting, but Charles's business was already expanding.[25]

The Van Winkle Partnership

The third phase of Charles's career began in 1814, even before the War of 1812 ended, and lasted until September 1817. With a retail bookstore at 3 Wall Street, a great deal of printing at a plant run by Van Winkle at 101 Greenwich Street, and a flurry of true publishing activity under the imprint of Van Winkle & Wiley, Charles and the company prospered. Tax assessors assessed the building at 3 Wall Street, a prime location on an important thoroughfare, at $7,000 and Charles's personal estate at $2,000. The printing plant on Greenwich Street was assessed at $4,000 and Van Winkle's personal estate at $2,500.[26]

Opening a bookstore was a savvy business strategy. While retail premises increased the overhead, they were also a place to sell books, Wiley's own as well as others, and to take subscriptions for books yet to be published. The store also allowed the company to sell other products, such as tickets to live performances, and even to run an art contest associated with the Wiley book *The Triangle: A Series of Numbers upon Three Theological Points*, an attack on New England theology written by Baptist minister Samuel Whelpley. The store was a convenient place for proprietors to meet with authors and

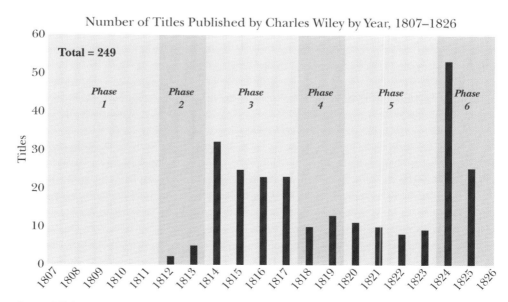

Number of Titles Published by Charles Wiley by Year, 1807–1826

Total = 249

Phase 1 · Phase 2 · Phase 3 · Phase 4 · Phase 5 · Phase 6

Titles

Source: OCLC.

INSIDE THE BOOKS

The Triangle

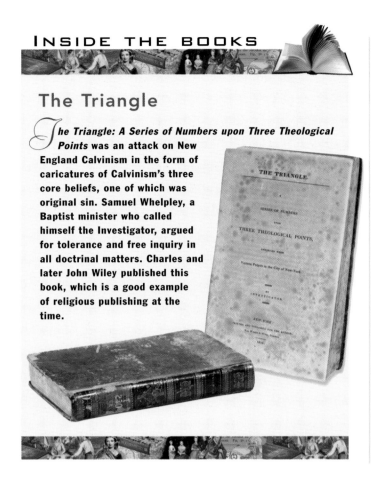

The Triangle: A Series of Numbers upon Three Theological Points was an attack on New England Calvinism in the form of caricatures of Calvinism's three core beliefs, one of which was original sin. Samuel Whelpley, a Baptist minister who called himself the Investigator, argued for tolerance and free inquiry in all doctrinal matters. Charles and later John Wiley published this book, which is a good example of religious publishing at the time.

newspaper editors. Indeed, the store's back room became well-known as The Den, a gathering place for writers and artists, including William Cullen Bryant, James Kirke Paulding, Gulian Verplanck, Asher Durand, Samuel F. B. Morse, and Mordecai Manuel Noah.[27]

Combining printing, bookselling, and publishing under one management is an example of what economists call "vertical integration." Clearly, it served to reduce the transaction costs of book manufacture and distribution, still high in Charles's era. Booksellers and printers were frequently at odds over remuneration, both seeking a larger share of the revenues generated by each book. Van Winkle & Wiley avoided such conflicts by taking on all the risks for the books they printed, published, and sold themselves—and corralling all the profits for themselves.

Wiley's move into retail may also have reflected a change in the way that Americans bought books. From the very invention of books, the best way to sell them was by no means clear. Should they be sold passively, like blankets? Or should they be pushed aggressively, like life insurance? Should they be sold and then printed,

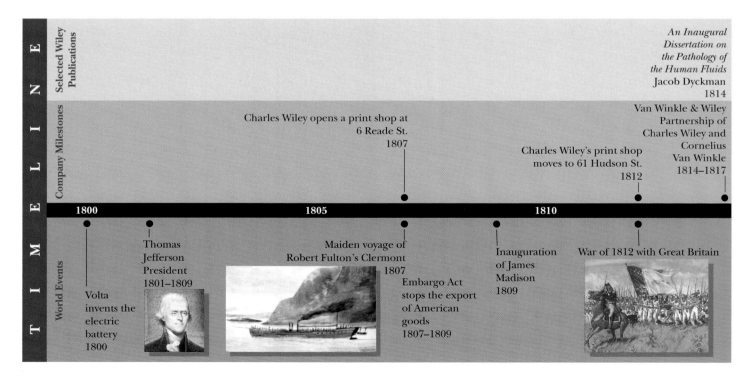

TIMELINE

Selected Wiley Publications

An Inaugural Dissertation on the Pathology of the Human Fluids Jacob Dyckman 1814

Company Milestones

Charles Wiley opens a print shop at 6 Reade St. 1807

Charles Wiley's print shop moves to 61 Hudson St. 1812

Van Winkle & Wiley Partnership of Charles Wiley and Cornelius Van Winkle 1814–1817

1800   1805   1810

World Events

Volta invents the electric battery 1800

Thomas Jefferson President 1801–1809

Maiden voyage of Robert Fulton's Clermont 1807

Embargo Act stops the export of American goods 1807–1809

Inauguration of James Madison 1809

War of 1812 with Great Britain

or printed and then sold? Early in Charles's career, most books were offered first by subscription—sold, after a manner, then printed. In 1795, for example, Thomas Bradford of Philadelphia sought subscribers for *Summary of the Law of Nations*. Some fifty lawyers and law students from the Carolinas to New England signed up to buy the book upon its publication. Sometimes publishers asked for cash up front. When that failed, they sought a simple promise to buy, or a note that fell due upon delivery of the book.[28]

Wiley continued to sell books by subscription, but the bookstore afforded two additional means of reaching customers, retail and wholesale. The retail trade was a tough business because it entailed selling a book or two at a time, often on credit. Its real if nonquantifiable value lay in the market information it provided, as customers and even mere browsers conversed with the staff, describing what they were looking for and discussing books they had already read. The wholesale side of the business had the prospect of larger and easier sales. In the first decades of the nineteenth century, country merchants and roaming

book peddlers purchased books in bulk, especially books that were, explained Mathew Carey's traveling agent (and early biographer of George Washington) Mason Weems, "from 25 to 50 or 75 cents—*interesting subjects*—popular titles—fascinating frontispieces & showy binding." These book peddlers and sales agents crisscrossed the countryside, hawking books. Their efforts greatly expanded the market for books, and their orders of a dozen or even a hundred copies at a time made matters much easier for bookstore owners like Charles.[29]

In 1814, the newly formed partnership between Van Winkle and Charles published Wiley's first medical title, Jacob Dyckman's *An Inaugural Dissertation on the Pathology of the Human Fluids*, and its first "textbooks," syllabi for medical and science courses at Columbia College and the College of Physicians and Surgeons. That same year, it teamed up with Isaac Riley to publish Wiley's first cookbook, *The Universal Receipt [Recipe] Book*, likely the production of Richard Alsop under the pseudonym "Society of Gentlemen in New York." Its first biographies appeared, too, reprints

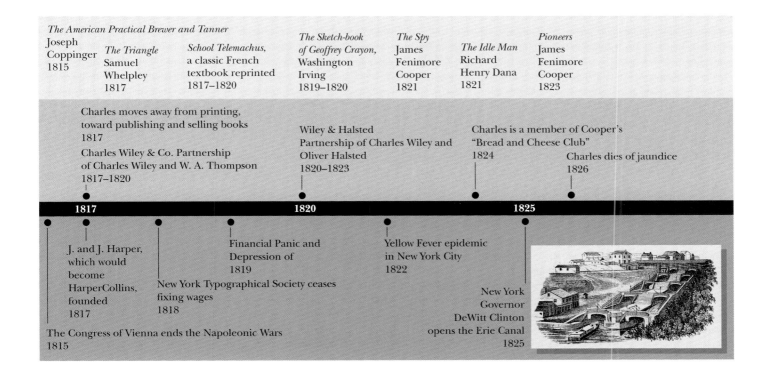

The American Practical Brewer and Tanner
Joseph Coppinger 1815

The Triangle Samuel Whelpley 1817

School Telemachus, a classic French textbook reprinted 1817–1820

The Sketch-book of Geoffrey Crayon, Washington Irving 1819–1820

The Spy James Fenimore Cooper 1821

The Idle Man Richard Henry Dana 1821

Pioneers James Fenimore Cooper 1823

Charles moves away from printing, toward publishing and selling books 1817

Charles Wiley & Co. Partnership of Charles Wiley and W. A. Thompson 1817–1820

Wiley & Halsted Partnership of Charles Wiley and Oliver Halsted 1820–1823

Charles is a member of Cooper's "Bread and Cheese Club" 1824

Charles dies of jaundice 1826

1817   **1820**   **1825**

J. and J. Harper, which would become HarperCollins, founded 1817

New York Typographical Society ceases fixing wages 1818

Financial Panic and Depression of 1819

Yellow Fever epidemic in New York City 1822

New York Governor DeWitt Clinton opens the Erie Canal 1825

The Congress of Vienna ends the Napoleonic Wars 1815

of studies of famed philanthropist John Howard, playwright and journalist Henry Fielding, and Arthur Wellesley, the Duke of Wellington, which a reviewer called "an interesting work." The partners broke into history as well, with the publication of *An Extract of a Translation of the History of New Sweed Land*. The company and other partners, publishers like Isaac Riley, David Huntington, T. C. Fay, W. B. Gilley, A. H. Inskeep, and Griffin & Rudd, also ventured into literature, in 1814 bringing out a four-volume edition of Miguel Cervantes's *Don Quixote*, William Cowper's *The Task and Other Poems*, and other classics. A Wiley travelogue appeared in 1814, a reprint of Vicomte Chateaubriand's *Travels in Greece, Palestine, Egypt, and Barbary During the Years 1806 and 1807*. That year the partners also began printing with alacrity various addresses, discourses, orations, and speeches for religious, historical, and philosophical societies and by famous people of the day, such as the politician and diplomat Gouverneur Morris. Sometimes on his own account and sometimes with Riley, Charles continued printing/publishing legal titles, too, including the *Reports* of New York's highest courts and John Rodman's treatise on the commercial code of France.[30]

Van Winkle & Wiley tried to turn the War of 1812 with Great Britain to its advantage, rather than be victimized by the commercial disruptions it inevitably caused. So in 1814, they printed up blank military forms, including inspection returns for cavalry and infantry units, muster rolls, pay rolls, and sundry military account books. They also began churning out war-related titles—the proceedings of a trial held on the *USS Constellation* and reprints of an account of a European battle and of a geographical and historical description of St. Helena, the island to which Napoleon Bonaparte was exiled in 1815. The partners published William Cobbett's *Letters on the Late War Between the United*

> In a common arrangement, Coppinger paid . . . to print the book . . . retained the copyright and took all the financial risk.

States and Great Britain, Mrs. Hofland's heart-tugging *History of an Officer's Widow and Her Young Family*, and, in conjunction with W. B. Gilley, *The Poet's Pilgrimage to Waterloo*, by Robert Southey, and Sir Walter Scott's *The Field of Waterloo: A Poem* (and also pirated Scott's classic novel, *Waverley*).[31]

In 1815, Van Winkle & Wiley published its first juvenile titles, *The Happy Sequel* and *Ellen, the Teacher*, and its first religious titles, *Strictures on a Pastoral Letter* and *Devotional Somnium, or, A Collection of Prayers*, allegedly written by a young woman in a coma. That year they also expanded their printing of proceedings of the Medico-Chirurgical Society of New York and the American Academy of the Arts. The partners' travelogue list grew, too, to include Edward Clarke's *Travels in Various Countries in Europe, Asia, and Africa*. Adding to their growing list of medical titles were John W. Francis's *Cases of Morbid Anatomy*, Elias Marks's *Conjectural Inquiry into the Relative Influence of the Mind and Stomach*, John Scudder's *Diseases of Old Age*, and a pair of short books by David Hosack, *Observations on the Laws Governing the Communication of Contagious Diseases* and *Remarks on the Treatment of the Typhoid State of Fever*. Law titles continued to come out, now solely under the imprint of Van Winkle & Wiley. They also extended their relationship with Paulding by printing his *The United States and England* for A. H. Inskeep of Philadelphia. In 1815, the partners also published their first technical works, William MacNeven's *Chemical Examination of the Mineral Water of Schooley's Mountain* and Joseph Coppinger's *The American Practical Brewer and Tanner*.

Like many other Americans then and now, Coppinger believed that beer was a healthy beverage essential to a good life. He also hoped to wean Americans from imported brew and therefore described a method for malting Indian corn. In a common arrangement,

Coppinger paid Van Winkle & Wiley to print the book while Coppinger retained the copyright and took all the financial risk. He also presold the book to subscribers, another common practice. After publication, Coppinger ran newspaper advertisements and placed copies with bookstores. He even wrote to former president Thomas Jefferson, who replied: "I had noted the advertisement of your book in which the process of malting corn was promised and had engaged a bookseller to send it to me as soon as it should come out. We tried it here the last fall with perfect success, and I shall use it principally hereafter."[32]

In 1816, Wiley branched into another new field, political economy, with the publication of an anonymous tract called *Brief Remarks on the Proposed New Tariff*. It also published its first scientific treatise, *An Essay on the Botanical, Chemical, and Medical Properties of the Fucus Edulis of Linnaeus* by Augustus Griffen. Law reports, war stories, religious tracts, medical dissertations, histories, novels, and poems continued to pour from Van Winkle and Wiley, some as mere print jobs, others as reprints of foreign works, others as joint productions with other publishers, and still others under the company's own imprimatur. Aside from the tract on the tariff—a hot political issue as Congress placed high tariffs on imported manufactured goods to protect new American industries—the most timely title may have been a short pamphlet, *Hints to Emigrants from Europe*, printed and published for the Shamrock Society of New York.

With the reprinting of the *Memoirs of Napoleon Bonaparte* in 1817, Van Winkle & Wiley began another strong year. Speculation about the authenticity of the memoirs prompted Charles to circulate proof sheets to newspaper editors so that they could stir up even more interest before the book hit the market. In 1817, the partnership also continued to grow all its lists—biography (*Dr. Poedagogus*), literature (Samuel Taylor Coleridge's

> **Charles soon came to specialize in publishing and selling, leaving printing to others.**

Biographia Literaria and Thomas Moore's *Lalla Rookh*), medicine (*Action of Poisons*), military matters (*Handbook for the Drill . . . of the Companies Attached to Field Pieces*), poetry (Lord Byron's *Manfred*), political economy (*Encouragement of Domestic Manufacturers*), religion (*Minutes of the New-York Baptist Association*), science (*Science of Physiognomy*), and travel (*Voyage Round the World*)—and continued its usual eclectic mix of print jobs, reprints, and joint publishing ventures.[33]

Charles was by this time a success as a bookman. Like most of his peers he was active in printing, retailing, wholesaling, and publishing. Like those of many of his peers, his publishing program was broader than it was deep. That would not change, but Charles soon came to specialize in publishing and selling, leaving printing to others.

Charles Wiley & Co. and Wiley & Halsted

It is not clear why Van Winkle & Wiley dissolved, but the first sign of trouble appeared in early August 1817, when the company advertised to rent the bookstore at 3 Wall Street, calling it an excellent "stand" for a jeweler or confectioner. Apparently, there were no takers. On September 16, the partnership dissolved "by mutual consent," with Van Winkle keeping the print shop on Greenwich Street and Charles taking the bookstore at 3 Wall Street. Charles immediately formed a partnership with W. A. Thompson, styled "Charles Wiley & Co." Thompson was a New York attorney who probably provided the partnership with more cash than expertise. Along with its publishing activities, the new company imported an assortment of books from London and also claimed to have "constantly on hand all the new works." To support the bookstore part of the business, Wiley ran frequent advertisements in the local newspapers.[34]

31

SONG.

I.

There's a barrel of porter at Tammany Hall,
  And the bucktails are swigging it all the night long.
In the time of my boyhood 'twas pleasant to call
  For a seat and segar, 'mid the jovial throng.
That beer and those bucktails I'll never forget;
  But oft, when alone, and unnoticed by all,
I think, is the porter cask foaming there yet?
  Are the bucktails still swigging at Tammany Hall?

II.

No! the porter was out long before it was stale,
  But some blossoms on many a nose brightly shone;
And the speeches inspir'd by the fumes of the ale,
  Had the fragrance of porter when porter was gone.
How much Cozzens will draw of such beer ere he dies,
  Is a question of moment to me and to all;
For still dear to my soul, as 'twas then to mine eyes,
  Is that barrel of porter at Tammany Hall.

This first edition of *Fanny*, by Fitz-Greene Halleck, was published in 1819. This satirical poem was perhaps the most successful of Charles Wiley & Co.'s publications, even garnering praise in Britain. A social commentary about a poor merchant and his daughter who unexpectedly rose into high society, the poem was similar to other works that helped Americans to grapple with the fundamental changes transforming the nation's economy and society. In early America, the poor could gain riches and, as the Panic of 1819 made clear, the rich could reap bankruptcy and imprisonment. Perhaps Charles read in the lines of *Fanny* something of his own family's up-and-down fortune?

During this fourth phase of Charles's career, which ran from the breakup of Van Winkle & Wiley in September 1817 through the dissolution of Charles Wiley & Co. on March 1, 1820, the firm's printing and publishing program slackened. During its brief existence, Charles Wiley & Co. reprinted and published titles in biography (*Recollections of Curran*), history (*Roman Antiquities*), literature (William Godwin's *Mandeville*), poetry (Fitz-Greene Halleck's *Fanny*), political economy (*Disquisition on Imprisonment for Debt* and *Prohibiting Slavery in . . . Missouri*), religion (*Religion of the Indian Tribes*), science (*A View of the Lead Mines of Missouri*), technology (*A Treatise on Agriculture*), travel (*A Tour from . . . New York to Detroit*), and a reprint of a French classic used at Columbia College (*School Telemachus*).[35]

The company no longer printed for other publishers, and the title pages of many of its own books began to list other companies, including Charles's erstwhile partner C. S. Van Winkle, as printers. The fact that Wiley no longer served only as a printer on others' publishing projects partly explains the slowdown in the number of titles in 1818, 1819, and 1820. Another cause was the slump following the Panic of 1819. Yet in February 1819, Charles claimed to be doing well financially. He was offered $2,500 for the lease of his house and store, a figure that accords well with the surviving tax records. Moreover, he owed less than $5,000, and his accounts receivable and inventory he valued at $10,000 each. That was by no means an unusually high sum. When bookseller A. H. Inskeep auctioned off his inventory in 1815, for example, his "splendid collection" included some 50,000 volumes. At a dollar per book on average, Inskeep's store was five times the size of Charles's. Despite his strong balance sheet position, however, liquidity problems dogged Charles, forcing him to borrow $700 from a friend, wealthy capitalist Henry Brevoort.[36]

The company's early account books are lost, and little detailed information about the business remains. If Charles's bookstore was anything like that of Thomas Clark of Philadelphia, it was a sleepy place that generated a fitful and generally small stream of cash. (When he died on April 2, 1819, Clark had less than $5 on hand, not even enough to bury him.) But by 1819, Charles's bookstore probably more closely resembled that of Hugh Maxwell, whose wholesale and publishing operations dwarfed his relatively tiny retail trade. On October 8, 1804, for example, Maxwell sold only a single item, a lead pencil for twelve and a half cents. But on January 2, 1805, $97.30 of books and other genteel merchandise (dice, playing cards, a backgammon table)

*A*n engraving from *A View of the Lead Mines of Missouri, Including Some Observations of the Mineralogy, Geology, Antiquities, Soil, Climate, Population and Productions of Missouri and Arkansaw* by Henry R. Schoolcraft, published by Charles Wiley & Co., 1819.

went out the door to bookseller Christopher Morris of Staunton, Virginia.[37]

One thing is certain: The fact that Charles borrowed money in 1819 should not be taken as a sign of trouble. Then as now, most businesses borrowed short-term to smooth out cash flows, particularly during business slumps. The Panic of 1819 and the subsequent depression were hard on all businessmen, not just those in the book trade and not just on Wiley. New York was particularly hard hit. As luxury items, books suffered from sharply decreased demand. In February 1820, Schaeffer & Mound told Carey that business was so slow that not even Bibles, a perennial bestseller, were selling. If anything, the fact that Charles was able to borrow was a good sign—he was creditworthy, even at a time when, according to publishing legend Samuel Griswold Goodrich, "it was positively injurious to the commercial credit of a bookseller to undertake American works."[38]

Perhaps to protect his loan, Brevoort entrusted to Charles a valuable asset in the form of one of the few books certain to sell even in the aftermath of a panic: Washington Irving's *The Sketch-Book of Geoffrey Crayon*. Irving, of a wealthy New York merchant family, practiced law while he wrote and edited in his spare time. After the end of the War of 1812, he moved to England to help in the family business. There he wrote *The Sketch-Book*, a collection of tales, including the soon to be famous "Rip Van Winkle" and "The Legend of Sleepy Hollow," which he submitted to John Murray, a leading British publisher. When Murray turned it down, Irving sent the manuscript to his friend Brevoort in New York, to find a publisher there. Brevoort, in turn, gave the manuscript to Charles, who selected his former partner Cornelius Van Winkle to print it. *The Sketch-Book* appeared in seven paperbound installments between June 1819 and September 1820, and was available simultaneously in bookstores in New York, Boston, Philadelphia, and Baltimore. (Books were often sold in paperbound installments to be bound together, not in the paperback format as we understand it today.) Readers loved it, purchasing an estimated 5,000 copies in its first two years of publication. Within a decade, over one percent of Americans purchased a copy of the book, the equivalent of a book today selling three million copies. *The Sketch-Book* confirmed Irving's status as the premier American author, and the sketches would go on to be printed in primers for students as models of American prose. Charles must have made money on this publication. According to one account, Irving earned 40 percent of the revenues of the installments, and the printer, Van Winkle, 35 percent. Of the remaining 25 percent, 20 percent went to retailers in the form of a discount off the list price, and 5 percent was allowed to the wholesaler, the role played by Charles. Irving's take has been estimated at $10,000 in the first two years, suggesting that the book's total revenues were $25,000 and that Charles made about $1,250 for his role in bringing it out.[39]

Irving's book also won critical acclaim and financial success in Britain. The *Literary Gazette* praised *The Sketch-Book* and published extracts. Rumors swirled that a pirated edition was in the works, so Irving, who was still residing in England, arranged for an authorized British edition replete with additional stories. Murray was now eager to bring it out, and in 1821, he purchased the copyright from Irving outright, keeping the title in print into the 1830s.[40]

The title page of the U.S. edition of *The Sketch-Book* lists C. S. Van Winkle as printer but does not mention Wiley. New York's most important literary figures surely knew, however, of Charles's involvement, as did those who saw his advertisements for the book in the *New York Commercial Advertiser* or the *Evening Post*, which explicitly stated that Wiley had "this day published" the title. Though Irving would never again publish with Wiley, *The Sketch-Book* helped to establish Charles's reputation as a publisher of American authors who knew how to successfully sell and distribute a large number of copies. He advertised the installments more than 100 times in 1819 and 1820 in the New York papers alone.[41]

Despite, or perhaps because of, the success of *The Sketch-Book*, Charles Wiley & Co. dissolved on March 1, 1820. Charles and his cousin, Oliver Halsted, formed Wiley & Halsted. The new company sold a "general assortment of Law Books" as well as the laws of the United States. In this fifth phase, Wiley published a modest number of books but of a different sort than in

> Within a decade, over one percent of Americans purchased a copy of [The Sketch-Book], the equivalent of a book today selling three million copies.

PROFILE

WASHINGTON IRVING

With his brother William and a friend, James Kirke Paulding, Washington Irving edited *Salmagundi* (1807–1808), a witty periodical published by Wiley. His affectionately humorous *A History of New-York*, written in 1809 under the pen name Diedrich Knickerbocker, describes the lives of the Dutch settlers of Manhattan. Irving moved to Liverpool in 1815 to help the family business, exporting American goods to Britain. The business failed in 1818, but Irving stayed in England to try his hand at writing full time.[42]

Irving's *The Sketch-Book*, published in 1819 and 1820 under another pen name, "Geoffrey Crayon, Gent.," was a popular and critical success in America and Britain. Its tales, including "Rip Van Winkle" and "The Legend of Sleepy Hollow," have been loved by generations of children and adults ever since. Although *The Sketch-Book* was the only book Irving published with Charles Wiley, it helped to establish Charles's reputation as a successful publisher and distributor of American authors.

A great traveler, Irving was the first American author with an international reputation. He wrote travel literature, including a book about Spain's Alhambra, a biography of Christopher Columbus, and two books about the fur trade and exploration of the Pacific Northwest, *Astoria* (1836) and *The Adventures of Captain Bonneville* (1837), having been provided access by John Jacob Astor to Astor's business records. Irving returned to the states in 1832, establishing his home, Sunnyside, on the Hudson River in what is now Irvington, New York. President Tyler appointed him minister to Spain in 1842, and he traveled throughout Europe as an American diplomat. Never married, Irving died in 1859.

Born in New York City to a wealthy merchant family in 1783, Washington Irving began practicing law in 1807 but wrote in his spare time. A great traveler, he was the first American author with an international reputation and probably the first to make his living from writing alone. Never married, he died in 1859.

CHAPTER TWO

39

the past. Many were high-quality originals, not mere reprints of British classics.[43]

By this time Charles had completely abandoned printing. The reasons are not hard to guess. Between 1809 and 1818, the New York Typographical Society had fixed the wages that Charles and his workers received for typesetting. After the state legislature forced the Society to stop interfering with wage scales, wages became more volatile. Some printers continued to pay the old wages but others hired "runaway

or dismissed apprentices for a small compensation." Those so-called "two-thirds men" allowed printers to slash prices so much that rival printers were forced to cut wages or workers or both. The decrease in wages and their instability, combined with the change in technology to new presses and printing techniques, probably pushed Charles away from printing. At the same time, an affinity for books themselves was pulling him toward the more intellectual side of the trade—book selling and publishing.[44]

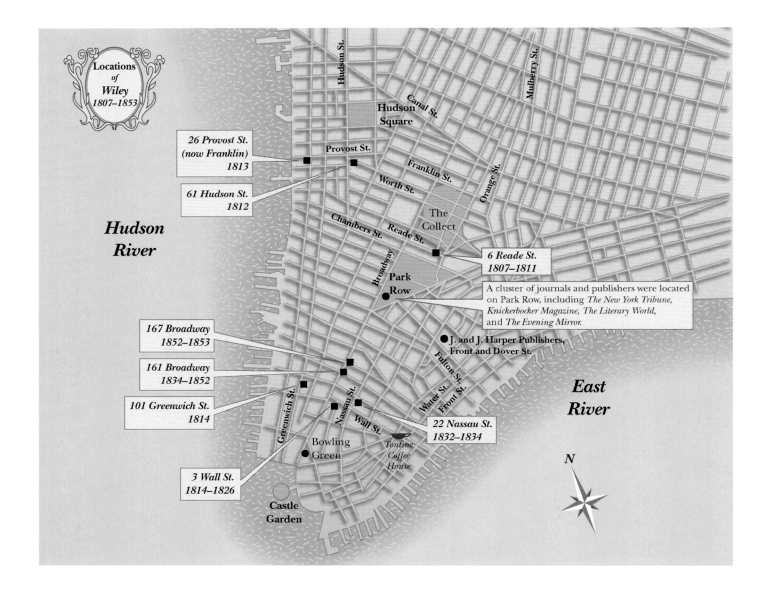

Locations of Wiley 1807–1853

Hudson St.

Canal St.

Mulberry St.

Hudson Square

26 Provost St. (now Franklin) 1813

Provost St.

Franklin St.

Worth St.

Orange St.

61 Hudson St. 1812

Hudson River

The Collect

Chambers St.

Reade St.

6 Reade St. 1807–1811

Broadway

Park Row

A cluster of journals and publishers were located on Park Row, including *The New York Tribune*, *Knickerbocker Magazine*, *The Literary World*, and *The Evening Mirror*.

167 Broadway 1852–1853

J. and J. Harper Publishers, Front and Dover St.

161 Broadway 1834–1852

Fulton St.

East River

101 Greenwich St. 1814

Greenwich St.

Nassau St.

Water St.

Front St.

Wall St.

22 Nassau St. 1832–1834

Bowling Green

Tontine Coffee House

N

3 Wall St. 1814–1826

Castle Garden

Wiley and the Book Business in America

The sixth phase of Wiley's development lasted from the dissolution of Wiley & Halsted in 1823 to Charles's death in January 1826. Throughout both phases, Wiley continued to publish a wide variety of books, including scientific titles small in number but that foreshadowed things to come, and literary works large in significance but ultimately abandoned. Some of these books did better than others, and there is no denying the appearance that it was a fitful business. To fully appreciate how it worked, we must first understand the business and cultural environments in which the company operated.

The members of America's early book trade seldom worked alone, but rather relied on networks of friends and advisors to help cull, acquire, edit, print, and sell books, and even, using pseudonyms, to write favorable reviews of them. Authors helped other authors and publishers; publishers came to the aid of authors and even other publishers. It was not unusual for Charles to receive correspondence from perfect strangers designed to aid Wiley authors. In 1823, for example, Alexander Wylly (no relation), a fan of James Fenimore Cooper's *The Spy*, offered Charles and Cooper his services on Cooper's Revolutionary War novel *Lionel Lincoln*. Wylly had served in the army during the entire Revolution and had numerous anecdotes he was happy to share.[45]

Cooperation in the book trade extended into finance. Like other early bookmen, Charles was caught up in a web of credit relationships. To ease the necessity of raising cash, bookmen sometimes bartered books with each other.

> Cooperation in the book trade extended into finance. Like other early bookmen, Charles was caught up in a web of credit relationships.

Before book exchanges became commonplace, publishing in America was somewhat regional in character. Great books published in out-of-the-way places, like *The Algerine Captive* by New England attorney Royall Tyler published by a press in Walpole, New Hampshire, languished for want of a market. Charles certainly exchanged books with others in the trade, including Carey himself. By 1825, the book exchange system appeared to wane, and Charles and eight other bookmen combined to hold a more structured wholesale book auction. They sold items from their catalog, which contained about 400 entries, to the highest bidder. Purchasers of less than $100 worth of books had to pay cash, but larger purchasers could take books on credit of up to six months. The institution caught on. For at least thirty years, at least one auction sale was held each year in both New York and Philadelphia, which helped to create a more national market for books.[46]

Books also secured debts. In 1820, for example, William Robinson wrote Mathew Carey that "the books sent out of this city for sale on delivery to subscribers are to be transferred as a security for the payment of the debt due Mr. Bailey, Mr. De Silver and yourself and likewise for the same purpose the proceeds of the books which have been sold in Philada [*sic*] or delivered by De Silver to various booksellers." Charles also had occasion to secure his debts with his books.[47]

Book publishers cooperated with newspaper and magazine editors, too. The latter needed content, the former, coverage for their titles. One of the more marketing-oriented of the proto-publishers of his day, Charles claimed that "no work, however meritorious,

COOPERATION IN THE BOOK TRADE

Especially when allied through credit and book exchange networks, bookmen often cooperated, if only to protect their own interests. In 1795, for example, New York printer James Rivington told Philadelphia bookman Thomas Bradford that a particular book was not selling because its title was "inexplicit." It would sell "vastly brisker," Rivington argued, if Bradford could induce his friend "Peter Porcupine" (*nom de plume* of famed British expatriate William Cobbett, 1763–1835), "to read it through, and give . . . a title expressive of its contents, which should be inserted in the Title page of each Volume." Bookmen also bartered books with each other to ease the necessity of

paying cash. In 1794, for example, Thomas Allen of New York told bookseller Thomas Bradford that he had "just published a very neat Edition of Miss Williams' Letters on the French Revolution 4 vols bound in Two. Also Peter Pindar's Works Complete in 2 Vols." "If you should want any of these," he informed Bradford, he would "take some more of St. Quentin's Grammar" in exchange. According to Mathew Carey, the "*general* interchange of publications" commenced in earnest in the last years of the eighteenth century. The practice allowed publishers to increase profit margins by making possible the "striking off of *large editions.*"[48]

$\mathcal{W}$illiam Cobbett, British expatriate author; James Rivington, New York printer; Thomas Bradford, Philadelphia bookman.

will sell without the assistance of the newspapers." At a minimum, he hoped for benign mentions. Better were full-blown reviews, the more glowing the better. Charles carefully cultivated newspaper editors and even controlled a journal, *The Literary and Scientific Repository*, to promote Wiley's growing list of authors.[49]

Cooperative at one level, the book trade was at the same time extremely competitive. Like businessmen in other industries where entry was easy and players numerous, publishers tried to limit competition as best they could. Sometimes their efforts were overt. For example, Philadelphia publishers in the first years of the nineteenth century associated as the "Book Sellers Company." The company itself published a few books, but its major economic function was to protect publishers who pirated and reprinted foreign works from competition. On May 8, 1802, the company "resolved, that in every case of the claim of a new work not already printed by the Company or any individual member, the person who first produces a copy to the Secretary & registers his intentions of printing it in the Secretary's book, shall have the exclusive privilege of printing the same." Just a month later, Carey, the company's president, tried to convince those attending the nation's first book fair that "where a large sum is invested by one man in a particular work, and liberal terms of sale offered to his brethren, it were ungenerous to the last degree to start an opposition." In short, Carey and his company did just about everything they legally could to decrease competition between publishers.[50]

U.S. copyright law in the nineteenth century applied only to American authors (see Chapter 3), so American printers were free to pirate foreign books and magazines. Piracy could be profitable, because printers did not have to pay royalties for content or expend any time or effort culling, developing, and editing manuscripts. Perhaps most important, pirates enjoyed a considerable amount of market information that the original publishers did not. Specifically, they could better gauge what demand would be and then reprint proven commercial successes while avoiding the inevitable and more numerous laggards. Wiley, too, reprinted the most valuable British novels, treatises, and journals.

> **U.S. copyright law in the nineteenth century applied only to American authors, so American printers were free to pirate foreign books and magazines.**

Piracy had its own problems though, because markets easy to enter were easy to saturate. All one needed was a copy of the book, a printing press, and bookmaking materials. Mathew Carey and the publisher J. & J. Harper (later Harper & Brothers), established in New York in 1817, took their commercial rivalry to extremes over the republication of Edward Bulwer Lytton's *Rienzi*. Both received a copy from London on the same day, but Carey & Hart gained the upper hand by paying 12 printers to work on it all day and night. The afternoon after the book arrived, Carey & Hart shipped 500 copies to New York by express stage and beat Harper's in its own neighborhood.[51]

When overt efforts to stymie intense competition failed, publishers, printers, and booksellers tried gentlemanly rules that recognized the rights of first publishers. Similar extralegal rules also evolved in Britain. These worked at times when the stakes were small, though ultimately efforts at friendly collusion failed. The book trade remained cutthroat. Whenever and wherever profits increased, new bookbinders, booksellers, printers, and publishers crowded into the market, drove up supply and, predictably, sent average profits back down to what Adam Smith called their natural rate—or lower if competition became cutthroat.[52]

Cutthroat competition was fine for consumers, the readers who had access to a steady supply of inexpensive books. It was not good news for producers. If they wanted to earn more than the going rate of return, or even stay in business, they had to seek out niches where reasonable profits were possible. For publishers, such niches could be as narrow as a single book or the literary productions of a single author, or as wide as entire areas of knowledge that had received relatively little attention. Though in the beginning Wiley appeared broadly opportunistic in what it published, the company under Charles slowly learned to probe for such profitable niches, and market realities began to drive a strategy. He found two niches, both of them emerging growth areas: the literary productions of American authors, such as Irving, who were seeking to define a new national literature, and scientific or technical titles that would increase the fund of knowledge and know-how in the new American republic. In monetary terms, Charles's success was limited, but it was enough to leave a small but indelible stamp on the development of American *belles lettres* and a bigger one on the later development of American science and technology.[53]

> **Charles slowly learned to probe for profitable niches.**

Scientific publishing in America was still very much in its infancy in Charles's day. According to Philadelphian Joseph Delaplaine, his periodical *The Emporium of Arts & Sciences* was the only work of the kind that had ever been undertaken in the United States. Scientific publishers were active in Europe but America was not quite ready. *The Emporium* appeared only once every two months between 1812 and 1815, then folded. Perhaps encouraged by the success of the New York Literary and Philosophical Society, which promoted "medicine & chemistry . . . Natural History . . . Mathematics, Astronomy . . . Geography . . . Husbandry, Manufactures, & the Useful Arts," in July 1820 Wiley & Halsted published the first number of a new journal, *The Literary and Scientific Repository*. But it fared no better than Delaplaine's *Emporium*, lasting just two years. Perhaps the journal, which was heavily studded with excerpts, reviews, and discussions

> **"In the four quarters of the globe, who reads an American book?"**

of the work of Halleck, Irving, Paulding, and other Wiley authors, had too much of the appearance of a house organ.[54]

Charles also continued to publish in political economy. *The Repository* reprinted extracts of Adam Seybert's *Statistical Annals of the United States*, and articles (and long reviews) on American resources, finance, taxation, trade, and whaling. In 1822, Charles pushed Mathew Carey's *Appeal to Common Sense and Common Justice*, a tract that called for the imposition of a higher tariff to protect American manufacturing interests. Charles sold two copies, lamenting "that the people of this country are so lukewarm to their most important interests." We don't know if Charles was as ardent a protectionist as Carey or if he was simply supporting an important business associate. Given Charles's strong support for American authors, however, it seems probable that, like Carey, he supported protective tariffs too.[55]

The Emergence of American Literature

In 1820, English clergyman Sidney Smith asked in the *Edinburgh Review*: "In the four quarters of the globe, who reads an American book?" Some Americans accepted the criticism and looked for scapegoats. The *North American Review* blamed the dearth of worthy American literature on American booksellers and publishers busy pirating foreign works. In more nationalist quarters, Smith's question was ridiculed. Hezekiah Niles, editor of *Niles' Weekly Register*, simply pointed to the undeniable if selective success of American authors. One year after

ALFRED MOORE

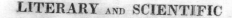

THE

LITERARY AND SCIENTIFIC

REPOSITORY,

AND

CRITICAL REVIEW.

No. I.

PUBLISHED QUARTERLY.

NEW-YORK:

WILEY & HALSTED.

CLAYTON & KINGSLAND, PRINTERS.

JULY, 1820.

The Literary and Scientific Repository, Wiley's first journal, was first published by Wiley & Halsted in July 1820. Edited by Charles K. Gardner, the national quarterly was a mixture of reprinted and original material on agriculture, chemistry, cryptography, demography, economics, geography, and mechanics.

Cooper's *The Spy* was published (by Wiley in 1821), the novel had passed through three editions. Somebody was reading an American book, and not just Americans. Tens of thousands, Niles predicted, would read Cooper's next novel *The Pioneers*—in Britain.[56]

American literature, though young in the 1820s, was healthy and growing. By 1838, British publishers had reprinted some 600 American titles, and the number grew from there. By 1868, American literature had a canon of its own so considerable that one might ask, instead, who does *not* read American books? Wiley would be a leader in the development of this new literature.[57]

As early as 1821, John Mennons, a publisher based in Greenock, Scotland, befriended a young New York–bound Scot, James Lawson, with one view in mind: to help him to reprint the literary production of

American authors. Given the frequency with which American publishers pirated British works, it hardly seemed unfair. In subsequent letters Mennons stressed that his interests would also serve the interests of American authors and beseeched his friend to forward any printed material favorable to American literature. Washington Irving, he supposed, must not be the only American who knew how to write.[58]

With Lawson's help, Mennons identified Charles Wiley as one of the most important publishers of the best American writing. Mennons was particularly taken by Washington Irving's *Sketch-Book* and Fitz-Greene Halleck's poem *Fanny*, which Wiley first published in 1819, followed in 1821 by a second edition with 50 new stanzas. Mennons called that 67-page production "a most acceptable treat." Though he eventually declined to reprint *Fanny* in his journal *The Literary Coronal* on the grounds that it was too long and too local, he urged Lawson to push for more Halleck. Other British publishers were less concerned with *Fanny*'s suitability, and before the year was out G. & W. B. Whittaker of London, W. & C. Tait of Edinburgh, Reid & Henderson of Glasgow, and D. Weir of Greenock all had reprinted the poem to favorable reviews.[59]

Another Wiley publication soon caught Mennons's attention: *The Idle Man*, a little periodical partly authored and partly edited by a reclusive New England scholar-poet named Richard Henry Dana. This should have been happy news for Charles, who thought the periodical had suffered from "inattention in the public prints," despite his efforts. Charles had sent free copies of the first number to four New York newspaper editors and to two businessmen of a literary bent. He also advertised it and pressed William Coleman, editor of the *New York Evening Post*, to take notice. When Coleman finally published a review, it may have been authored by Dana himself, as it was common that such notices were written by the author or the author's

friends, or when a sufficient "contribution" had been made to the paper. This review was mixed; the periodical, said the reviewer, had not created much "buzz." A review in *The Literary Companion* was also mixed, finding some pieces written with warmth and imagination and others in a style that was labored, its sentiments redundant. Despite a few favorable notices, and long excerpts in *The Ladies' Literary Cabinet* and *The Literary Companion*, sales fizzled in New York, though they were good in Boston. Charles had priced the 50-page periodical at 50 cents, a price he thought would yield a good profit for Dana even with a 25 percent allowance to booksellers—except for himself; as "the distributing publisher" he claimed a discount of one-third.[60]

Dana paid his bill of $119.50 for paper and printing at the end of July 1821 and undertook, at Charles's prodding, a second number. The second volume did less well overall, however, until *The American* and the *Baltimore Patriot* gave it notice. In mid-September, a very favorable review appeared, prompting Charles to urge Dana to pay to print 1,000 copies of a third number because each new number sustained interest in previous ones. Events proved Charles correct. After appearance of the third number, Charles noted that "we often sell the work in sets, and few . . . who have purchased the first number have failed to buy the others." Ultimately Dana turned out six, possibly seven numbers, but sales languished. The fourth number arrived in the dead of winter when the yellow fever epidemic that swept New York in the fall of 1822 killed Charles's clerk, made Charles himself gravely ill, and sent the Wiley family scurrying to the New Jersey countryside. Most stores in the city were closed.[61]

Ever hopeful, Charles urged Dana to try a novel, which of course he calculated would drive sales of the remaining copies of *The Idle Man*. Dana never did write a novel, but his son, also Richard Henry, an apparent

COMMUNICATION.

Mr. Coleman:—Will you permit me, through the medium of your paper, to draw the attention of the public to a late publication which attracted my notice by accident: I speak of " The Idle Man," recently published by Messrs. Wiley and Halsted, and for ought I know by the other booksellers of this city. As I have not heard this little work mentioned, I suppose it has not been much read, and I fear that it may not attract the degree of notice which I think it well merits. It is evidently the production of no ordinary writer, for both its beauties and defects are of a marked character. There is a quaintness in the style, which most readers would deem affected, and yet I am inclined to believe that it is the result. or rather expression, of a peculiar cast of mind, nurtured, probably, by early and long-continued habit. The Idle Man certainly possesses very keen sensibilities, and enjoys and suffers much from causes which probably excite little sensation in those of coarser temperament. For myself I am rather inclined to sympathise with most of his feelings and opinions, though I can readily imagine that others, and those sounder judges than myself, may think them overstrained and unnatural. One of the subjects treated in this little book, (Mr. Kean.) ... propos at the present moment, and ... the first effort of a ... ushed by a fortuitous

... tle work is of a very ... will meet with very ... one at all. I think the ... ch way the die turns. ... ows that he is not rich ... nts solely for the gratifi... public, I hope he will ... pense of the publication.

AN IDLER.

The Idle Man, a literary journal, was partly authored and partly edited by a reclusive New England scholar-poet named Richard Henry Dana. Although financially disappointing, *The Idle Man* did win Dana a degree of literary fame.[62]

collaborator on *The Idle Man*, became even more famous with his memoir, *Two Years Before the Mast* in 1840.[63]

Meanwhile, Mennons, the Scottish bookman, found merit in the *Poems* of Dr. James G. Percival, published by Charles in 1823 but first printed in New Haven in 1821. Charles paid Percival an advance of $60 and had 780 copies printed, but Percival and his friends—author James Fenimore Cooper, publisher Samuel Goodrich, and poet James Hillhouse—had to do much of the marketing. They were so successful that Percival's medical practice dried up. "When a person is really ill," Percival later complained, "no one sends for a poet to cure him." Conversely, when his poems were published in London, they failed to catch on.[64]

Mennons went on to publish books composed wholly of American poetry and other reprint projects, but he found it increasingly difficult to compete against the big London publishing houses. In November 1823, he thanked Lawson for forwarding various American novels but explained that London publishers had already brought them out "*as British works* and *original writing*." Indeed, even marginal American novels like *Logan*, *Seventy Six*, *The Wilderness*, and *Justina* (the last a Wiley title; authors all long forgotten) were pouring out of British publishing houses and selling well. At the same time, the novels of another Wiley author were selling in large numbers on both sides of the Atlantic, and in a league entirely of their own.[65]

Wiley and James Fenimore Cooper

Charles Wiley met James Fenimore Cooper in 1819 or 1820, perhaps when Charles was touring upstate New York, trying to sell books. The two must have liked each other because Cooper, in 1820, began to contribute to Wiley's *Literary and Scientific Repository*. Then in 1821, Cooper offered Charles *The Spy*, his second novel,

PROFILE

JAMES FENIMORE COOPER

While reading a novel to his wife one day, Cooper remarked that he could do much better. She challenged him, and he took her up on it.[66]

Charles published Cooper's second novel, *The Spy*, in 1821 to critical acclaim; here, at last, was a truly American historical romance, the genre so closely associated at the time with Sir Walter Scott. Charles also published *The Pioneers*, the first of the Leather-Stocking Tales, in 1823, and *The Pilot*, a sea novel, in 1824. Because of their financial arrangement, in which Cooper assumed most of the risks, he also reaped most of the profits, though Charles benefited as well. Charles then bought the right to print and sell Cooper's *Lionel Lincoln* in 1825 with promissory notes; the novel's failure created financial difficulties for Charles. Charles and Cooper reverted to their old arrangement, with Cooper assuming the risks of publication, for his next novel, *The Last of the Mohicans*.

Unfortunately, Charles died early in 1826 before the novel could be published, and Henry Carey of Carey & Lea published *The Last of the Mohicans* in March 1826. Set in 1757 during the French and Indian War, this romantic novel, one of the Leather-Stocking Tales, is thought by many to be Cooper's masterpiece.

Charles's death clearly shook Cooper, who professed to love "Poor Wiley." Though he had come to think of Charles as "credulous and weak . . . in some respects," he also believed his friend "at bottom an excellent fellow, and of great good sense—nay, even of talent."

Cooper did not shy away from controversy, sometimes defending and sometimes attacking his fellow countrymen. His literary reputation suffered from the uneven quality of his works; Mark Twain later enumerated his "literary offences" but others, including European critics, praised him. Today, Cooper is often viewed as the first true American novelist, preceding and influencing Hawthorne and Melville.

Born in 1789, James Fenimore Cooper grew up in Cooperstown, New York, a frontier town established by William Cooper, his father. One of the youngest in a large family, Cooper had a checkered youth. He entered Yale at age 13, was expelled for pranks, joined the navy only to resign his commission in 1811, two years after his father died leaving him in charge of a large and tangled estate. Cooper was prolific, producing over 30 novels as well as many political and travel writings before his death in 1851.

a romantic tale of espionage set in the American Revolution. Charles agreed to publish the book but would not pay cash for the copyright, leaving much of the financial risk with Cooper. He had reason to hesitate, as Cooper's first book, *Precaution*, had fallen flat. One reviewer called it stupid and inane. Cooper blamed the printer, who was slow and did a shoddy job.[67]

The Spy was no mere print job, however. Charles accepted it and began having it typeset and printed even before Cooper finished writing it. Parts of the novel appear, in Cooper's own words, "crowded and hurried" because in fact they were written at the last minute under tight page requirements. Even so, both Charles and Cooper had high hopes, and the book sold even better than expected. The first printing of 1,000 copies sold in just three weeks of the December 21, 1821, publication date. Within four months, 8,000 copies were gone, a figure that many books today never achieve. By December 1822, Wiley had paid Cooper $2,700 over and above expenses. With few exceptions, early reviews of *The Spy* were strong. Poet and Wiley author Halleck called it "among the best novels that have been written." At least seven other reviewers showered it with praise, and Charles's father John was so impressed that he offered upon Cooper's "arrival in the Mamoroneck stage to take off the horses, and with the assistance of others to drag [his coach] throughout the City" in tribute.[68]

Cooper's and Charles's friendship grew as both moved confidently among New York's several literary cliques, including a small group of poets called the Athenian Society or Literary Confederacy that actually signed a document promising to "preserve a friendly communion" among themselves "in all the vicissitudes of life." The Literary and Philosophical Society of New York was a larger and much more eminent group that sought "to promote the useful arts, to diffuse knowledge, and to enlighten the human mind." Many Wiley authors, like DeWitt Clinton, David Hosack, and Hugh Williamson, were members, and Wiley printed the

society's proceedings throughout 1815. But due to its informality, Charles's own literary den at the back of his store was the ultimate meeting place for writers and artists. The old City Tavern was directly across New Street, at 4 Wall Street, attracting printers and authors, all of whom were renowned for their hard drinking. On at least one occasion, Cooper ordered through Charles a dozen bottles of sherry.[69]

Given the friendship, it was almost a foregone conclusion that Charles would publish Cooper's next novel, *The Pioneers*. This was the first in a series of five novels—eventually called the Leather-Stocking Tales—that featured the frontier hero Natty Bumppo. Though publication was delayed by the yellow fever epidemic that also slowed sales of *The Idle Man*, Cooper's *Pioneers* sold well, wholesaling 3,500 copies when it appeared in February 1823.[70]

As with *The Spy*, and Cooper's sea novel *The Pilot*, published in 1824, Charles provided his imprimatur and coordinated the printing, binding, advertising, and wholesale distribution for *The Pioneers*, but Cooper assumed the big financial risks of publication and reaped most of the profits. Yet Charles showed a shrewd marketing sense. Accurately sensing that *The Pioneers* did not carry the same appeal as *The Spy*, Charles created a buzz for the book that was so effective as to draw reviewers' attention. Newspaper editors were eager to publish excerpts from the forthcoming novel and speculated about the book's progress and Cooper's rumored trip to Europe. Charles likely enjoyed dropping bits of information to the press, and literary nationalists like Hezekiah Niles rejoiced when 3,500 copies of *The Pioneers* sold by noon of the official publication date.[71]

Some critics praised *The Pioneers,* others found fault: it was as good as Sir Walter Scott (a model for both Irving and Cooper and also a rival) but also guilty of murdering the King's English. That judgment is not surprising, given that the book went directly from

Cooper's desk to the printers. Cooper himself had not read it in print, leaving it up to Wiley to edit it, which evidently Charles did not do.[72]

Richard Henry Dana tried to soothe Cooper's feelings by noting that reviewers were often cruel beasts and that he did not doubt that the "voice of praise" would reach Cooper "from the other side of the water, tho it should not come to you down the Connecticut." (Cooper responded by joking that Dana's *Idle Man* was "too Lazy" and ought to appear in public more often.) Other Wiley authors came to the book's defense, with Paulding dedicating an entire chapter to it in his 1823 book, *Koningsmarke: The Long Finne*.[73]

As Dana had expected, British critics were stunned to learn that the American reviewers were not appreciative of *The Pioneers*. The British publisher John Miller offered to split his profits with Cooper, provided that Cooper supply him with page proofs sent by different ships to ensure timely arrival in case a ship should encounter a storm, a shoal, pirates, or unfavorable winds. (Other British publishers, including Murray and Colbern, also shared their profits with Cooper in exchange for early copies of his books.) Cooper was willing to enter such arrangements after losing badly on *The Spy*, which several British publishers, including F. & W. B. Whitaker, had pirated. It was partly Cooper's fault, for he neglected to send an early copy to Colbern, and Murray declined to publish the book after his outside reader, the prolific British author William Gifford, gave a cool report. Washington Irving advised Charles and Cooper to avoid Murray, whom he regarded as insufficiently enthusiastic about things American and slow in service. Irving thought Colbern a better choice and ultimately advised Cooper to market his work through Miller, a solidly pro-American bookseller in Fleet Street.[74]

Cooper agreed and went with Miller. Their arrangement worked well with *The Pilot*, which Miller received in time to print 1,000 copies before other printers had a copy on hand. First mover advantage and extensive advertising enabled Miller to wholesale 800 copies on the day of publication. The book was a smashing success, and though it did less well in America, Charles still found it necessary to employ five printers to keep up with demand. Continuing vigilance was essential though, and Miller warned Cooper of efficient pirates' agents in New York ready to send off to Britain copies of popular works the instant they appeared. If Cooper neglected to send the proofs of his next novel, *Lionel Lincoln*, with dispatch, warned Miller, it could be appropriated by another publishing house in just four days. As it turned out, Miller and Charles may have wished they had never heard of the book.[75]

Troubled Times and Decline

Early Wiley authors considered Charles a good companion and reliable promoter of their work: the ideal bookman. He was the only publisher invited to membership in Cooper's famous Bread and Cheese Club, a direct outgrowth of Wiley's den. In the early 1820s, Charles's reputation looked secure as one of the country's "enterprising" publishers who "ranked high in the trade." Modern scholars generally agree, calling Charles "one of the major personalities of the publishing world." But by January 1826, Charles was dead and his business in shambles.[76]

The first real signs of trouble emerged in 1823, when Cooper essentially gave *Tales for Fifteen*, the rump of another never-completed work, to Charles to "help him along." Unfortunately for Wiley, the book, which Cooper later admitted he wrote on a "rainy day, half asleep and half awake," did poorly and may have actually cost Charles money. That same year, Charles published George Tucker's first major work, *The Valley of Shenandoah*, a tragic novel about the decline of a Virginia plantation family. Better known for his work on political economy, Tucker had initially approached Harper & Brothers with his hastily composed novel, but when offered just $500 for the copyright, he took it to Charles, who agreed to publish it and split all costs and profits. Due to Charles's illness or negligence, however, the book contained numerous printing errors. Before his death, Charles gave Tucker no cash but "some hundreds of copies," which Tucker struggled to distribute. Even before this, however, rumors swirled that Wiley was bankrupt.[77]

Despite Cooper's success as a writer, Charles, as publisher, had not had equal success. Cooper controlled the finances, but he wanted to write, not to manage a small business. Charles, on the other hand, no doubt sought greater profit. He must have realized that if he had purchased *The Spy*'s copyright, he, and not Cooper, would have been getting rich. So the friends devised a new contract for *Lionel Lincoln* whereby Charles and New York merchant Abijah Weston gave Cooper $5,000 of promissory notes in exchange for the exclusive right to print and sell up to 10,000 copies of the two-volume novel within one year. But Charles had chosen the wrong Cooper novel to back. In Cooper's own words, *Lionel Lincoln* "failed, and perhaps justly."[78]

In an attempt to dig himself out of the financial hole created by *Lionel Lincoln*, Charles ventured onto new ground by publishing and reprinting drama. The more than 60 comedies, farces, and tragedies that the company put out in 1824 and 1825, did little, however, to help its short-term prospects. Nor, evidently, did high-quality nonfiction such as William Cardell's *Essay on Language, As Connected with the Faculties of Mind*, which critics hailed as "an ingenious and philosophical essay on Grammar," and Gulian C. Verplanck's highly respected *Essay on the Doctrine of Contracts*.[79]

Meanwhile, Cooper was being courted by Philadelphia publisher Carey & Lea. In early 1825, Henry C. Carey, Mathew's son, let Cooper know that, had Cooper accepted the risks of publication for *Lionel Lincoln*, as he had with his earlier books, he would have realized significantly more even on this failed project. So in July, when Cooper signed a contract with Wiley for *The Last of the Mohicans*, he again assumed the risks of publication, and its rewards. By August, Charles told Miller that he had already "made considerable progress in printing *The Last of the Mohegans* [sic] and the September issue of *The United States Literary Gazette* listed it as "in Press," under Wiley. But by October the book still had not appeared, probably because of Charles's serious financial difficulties and possibly because of illness as well. Cooper helped out by paying Charles's note for $300 to Halleck and endorsing three of Charles's notes totaling $1,280.88. To secure the debt, Charles assigned to Cooper all his remaining copies of and rights in *Lionel Lincoln*, *The Pilot*, *The Spy*, Paulding's *John Bull*, and Verplanck's *Essays on the Nature and Uses of the Various Evidences of Revealed Religion*. Then, on January 9, 1826, Charles died.[80]

Charles's obituary noted that he had had "a lingering illness," described as "jaundice." Jaundice, as then understood, was directly caused by blockage of the "free emission" of bile through the liver into the intestines. An indirect cause of jaundice was heavy long-term consumption of alcohol. Or it could be that Charles never fully recovered from yellow fever, which attacked the liver and kidneys making its victims look jaundiced. In any case, Charles had probably been ill for some time but continued working. Then early in 1826, he suffered an unexpected and acute attack that ended his life. Some scholars of Wiley's literary productions suggest that Charles's business and health deteriorated together. It is strange, then, that he died intestate, especially as others seem to have realized that his death was imminent, and by 1825, his son John was working in the shop with him.[81]

Cooper now turned to Carey & Lea, with whom he had already begun negotiations, for the publication of his next novel. Henry Carey had responded carefully in November 1825: "Not knowing the nature of your arrangement with Wiley, or what kind of one you would wish to make," he answered, "I can hardly make any proposition, but if you will submit your views, we will be able to give you a reply without delay." There matters apparently rested until after Charles's death. Then Cooper switched his publishing activities to Carey & Lea. Carey quickly took over, telling Cooper that he need "never again humble" himself "with printers, paper makers, & bookbinders."[82]

In March 1826, *The New York Review* noted that Carey & Lea published *The Last of the Mohicans* because, while it was in press, "Mr. Charles Wiley, whose name the author has given to enduring remembrance by a former epistle dedicatory, was removed from the cares of this world; and took his journey to another, where there is no writing, publishing, nor reviewing." The notice continued, almost as a memorial to Charles and a tribute to the New York book trade: "We record, with regret, the loss of a publisher who was acquainted with the inside as well as the exterior of books; and are sorry that our metropolis, in which

the literary career of Mr. Cooper was begun, with a popularity which no other American had ever succeeding in approaching, should no longer be the source from whence his works first emanate."[83]

Wiley under Charles was not a commercial success, but he did establish the name Wiley as a major figure in the New York publishing world while publishing in many fields where Wiley would later prosper, starting with the sciences. In addition to publishing as we now understand the term, Charles printed books for a fee and retailed the books of other printer-publishers. By the time of his death, Wiley had abandoned the printing business altogether and focused increasingly on publishing books at its own risk and expense, a practice Charles's son and successor John, in line with other leading publishers, would extend. Moreover, Wiley under Charles was present at the creation of an authentic American literature, a literature featuring American heroes in American settings. In the spring of 1826, just months after Charles's death, New York City bestowed a silver medal upon Cooper for writings that "added to the glory of the Republic." The renown of American letters soon spread abroad as well.[84]

New York itself was only growing in vitality, in part because of the Erie Canal, completed in 1825, the year before Charles died. The Erie Canal represented technical and engineering brilliance in a class all its own. The canal linked the city of New York to the continental hinterland as securely as the Atlantic linked it to the world, and it assured New York's commercial preeminence. The market for books that captured, created, and disseminated that know-how grew with it.

As far as we can tell, Charles's personal life was a happy one. He appears to have remained emotionally and physically close to his aging father even

> "We record, with regret, the loss of a publisher who was acquainted with the inside as well as the exterior of books . . ."

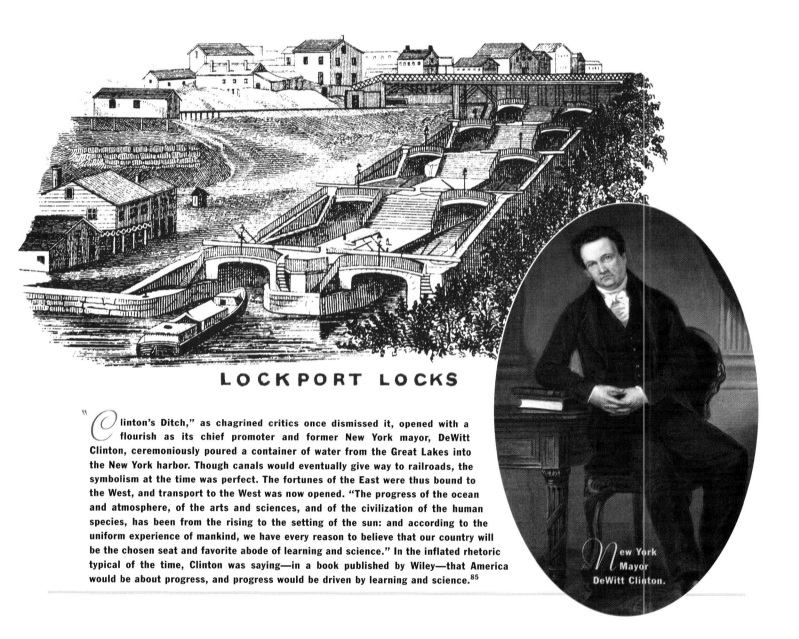

LOCKPORT LOCKS

"Clinton's Ditch," as chagrined critics once dismissed it, opened with a flourish as its chief promoter and former New York mayor, DeWitt Clinton, ceremoniously poured a container of water from the Great Lakes into the New York harbor. Though canals would eventually give way to railroads, the symbolism at the time was perfect. The fortunes of the East were thus bound to the West, and transport to the West was now opened. "The progress of the ocean and atmosphere, of the arts and sciences, and of the civilization of the human species, has been from the rising to the setting of the sun: and according to the uniform experience of mankind, we have every reason to believe that our country will be the chosen seat and favorite abode of learning and science." In the inflated rhetoric typical of the time, Clinton was saying—in a book published by Wiley—that America would be about progress, and progress would be driven by learning and science.[85]

New York Mayor DeWitt Clinton.

while raising a family of his own. In 1805, he had married Lydia Osborn (1780–1840), and they had five children: Mary, John, Charles, Martha, and Augustus. John (1808–1891) would be Charles's successor, the one who placed the family business on a firm foundation and gave it its enduring name. John apprenticed in his father's shop beginning in 1824 but had not learned enough by Charles's death to continue the

family business immediately, and, only 17 years old at the time, he could not enter legally binding contracts. Money was also a problem. Legend has it that Cooper tore up Charles's promissory notes on hearing of his death, but it is unlikely that other creditors were so kind. By the end of January, a stationer moved into 3 Wall Street; the literary den became a storehouse for self-sharpening pencils. The fate of Wiley hung in the balance.[86]

A view of Broadway looking south toward Trinity Church in 1834, the year that John Wiley opened a bookstore just north of here at 161 Broadway.

John Wiley: Foundations

1826–1865

Chapter Three

❀

Charles Dickens and the Copyright Law

Things changed quickly in nineteenth-century New York, but not quite everything. By the 1840s, when John Wiley had been 20 years in the publishing business, regular steamship service was beginning to replace the packets which sailed between the city and Liverpool, gaslight illuminated the better streets and houses—and scavenger pigs still ran free in the city. Charles Dickens, the most widely read writer of the century, remarked on them in his account of his visit in 1842. "Ugly brutes they are," reported Dickens, with "scanty brown backs like the lids of old horsehair trunks." With a novelist's flair Dickens represented the scavenger pig as indicative of the young republic: "He is in every respect a republican pig, going wherever he pleases and mingling with the best society, on an equal, if not superior footing, for every one makes way when he appears": the very model of "self possession and self-reliance."[1]

Dickens was the season's main event, the most renowned visitor to America since the Marquis de Lafayette, hero of the Revolution, had made his farewell tour in 1825. Thousands of New Yorkers had bought Dickens's books, and thousands more would buy his books to come, some of which would be published by John Wiley and his partner. Though Dickens was only thirty at the time of his visit, few authors of his era could match his critical acclaim; none could touch his sales.

When Dickens arrived in New York that January with his wife Catherine, he came with two purposes. One was to gather material for the travel book whose sales he intended would pay for the trip. The other was to voice a grievance over the lack of copyright protection that cheated authors of rightful income. In Britain, Dickens's work would soon be protected by the Copyright Amendment Act that passed Parliament later that year, with his support and that of fellow author and Member of Parliament Thomas Babington Macaulay. But abroad, Dickens was commonly read in pirated editions. The United States was Dickens's single largest foreign market, and American law protected only the domestic copyright of American authors. It was an awkward subject, and American friends warned Dickens not to raise it during his visit. But he did.

Dickens liked to think of himself as something of a radical, at home with American democratic ideals, but when, in Hartford, he launched into a plea for international copyright, the room went chilly. He held up not his own example (for Dickens had good agents and lawyers; over his lifetime he earned approximately £10,000 from U.S. sales even in the absence of copyright protection) but that of the legendary Sir Walter Scott, pirated into ruin and despair at the time of his death in 1832: "My blood so boiled," Dickens wrote later of the evening, "as I thought of the monstrous injustice that I felt as if I were twelve feet high when I thrust [my argument] down their throats." Wiley and his partner George Palmer Putnam heartily agreed, but for this additional reason: as long as American publishers could steal foreign works with impunity and sell them cheap, they would never support American writers adequately enough to establish a truly national literature. It was a battle that would not be won in their lifetimes.[2]

Although Dickens was ready to see "the wonders that await us in your mighty land," he went away deeply conflicted about the young republic. In speeches early in the trip he spoke warmly of being an honorary American. He probably liked Boston, his first stop, but soon wearied in the role of distinguished foreign guest. Traveling by rail, coach, and riverboat, he went to New Haven after Hartford and then to New York, Philadelphia, Washington, Pittsburgh, and west as far as St. Louis. He witnessed slavery in the South, despised it, and said so. A glimpse of the western prairie left him unmoved. He seemed to like ordinary Americans, though he might have preferred to meet them in smaller doses: "They are friendly, earnest, hospitable, kind, frank, very often accomplished, far less prejudiced than you would suppose, warm-hearted, fervent, enthusiastic." His primary biographer, Peter Ackroyd, speculates that this extended exposure to young America made Dickens realize how truly old English he was.[3]

Dickens (on opposite page) and his wife Catherine danced at the "Boz Ball" given in his honor. ("Boz" was an early Dickens pseudonym from the 1830s.) The Park Theatre, converted into a ballroom accommodating 3,000 guests, was festooned with satin drapery, candelabra, and large plaques representing each of his books. At the center, as if an object of worship, was suspended a portrait of the great man himself.

American Notes *suggests Dickens's ambivalence. An oddly large portion of it dwells on prisons, asylums, workhouses, and orphanages, though the reformer in Dickens judged America's—or at least New England's—efforts more enlightened than those he knew at home. He wrote the book, a chapter a week, that summer; it was pirated in America almost immediately. Harper's purloined edition sold for 12.5 cents. Strong sales correlated with the controversy it provoked. Washington Irving, who had corresponded with Dickens before his tour and hosted a festive dinner for him at New York's City Hall, now found Dickens "outrageously vulgar—in dress, manners, and mind."[4]*

Except for the fixation on the pigs, American Notes *treats New York reasonably well. Dickens was an urban creature. Outside of London, a city of 2.2 million and Dickens's literal and literary home, New York was the greatest English-speaking metropolis. (Manhattan and its surrounding boroughs, none yet consolidated, numbered some 400,000 denizens in 1842 and were growing fast.) Strolling up the fashionable stretch of Broadway, Dickens heard echoes of Piccadilly and Regent Street. Squalid Five Points, which he visited under escort by two policemen, offered choice venues for many a local Fagin's den of* youthful pickpockets, and Nancy might have met her sad end along any number of dank alleys down by the river. He eyed "singularly beautiful" New York ladies (with so many parasols), "pimping and pandering" journalists, omnibuses, hackney cabs and sleek phaetons, bowling saloons, and oyster bars. The whole place seethed and smelled of life. Dickens did not mention visiting a bookstore. Had he done so, American Notes *might have recorded how his spirits were at once lifted— "Oh, how much these New Yorkers read!"—and depressed—"Oh, how much these New York publishers steal!"[5]*

When Dickens visited New York, John Wiley was only four years older than Dickens, but John had been working in the publishing business for half his lifetime. Charles Wiley, his father, had died in 1826 just as the effects of a financial panic in Britain were being felt in America. The dramatic slowdown in British publishing that began in 1825 hit New York publishing by early 1826. By April, the situation was so dire that London publisher John Miller refused to honor James Fenimore Cooper's draft on him. Miller wrote of "the frightful state of the money market here & the desolation that is all around" and of unsold books—including most of Cooper's—stacked up in the warehouse. Even Sir Walter Scott's main publisher, Constable & Company, failed.[6]

Charles's eldest son, John, just 17,[7] was working in the family business when Charles died, but the legal documents that must have been generated after Charles's death have not been found and so the company's condition is not fully known. What is known is that the Wiley family quickly moved out of 3 Wall Street, and by the end of January 1826 a new tenant had moved in, setting up a stationery shop. Yet the company appears to have continued in business. On February 15, 1826, about five weeks after Charles died, Philadelphia publishers Carey & Lea wrote to Cooper: "Last Friday

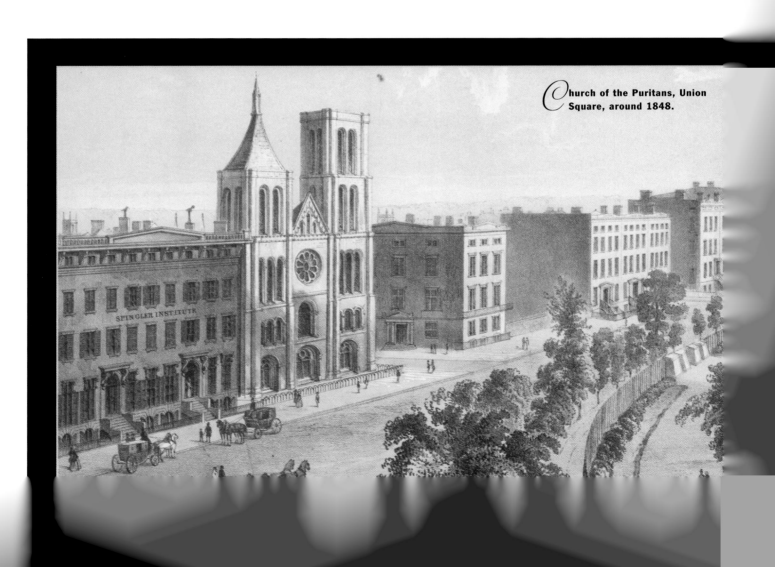

Church of the Puritans, Union Square, around 1848.

Wiley had orders for some copies which he could not supply owing to the delay of the last Hundred copies." The "he" suggests reference to John, who probably did the bulk of the physical work. Charles's widow, Lydia Osborn Wiley (1780–1840), must have technically run the business at least until early October, when John reached majority and could begin to sign contracts. She may have continued leading the company for some years. City directories from 1826 through 1829 list Lydia as Charles's widow, suggesting that she was the head of the household and possibly the head of the firm. It was not unusual in this period for widows to take over the businesses of their deceased husbands until the eldest male was ready, and Lydia had been a shopkeeper before marrying Charles. Lydia, like other wives of poor and middling businessmen, may have helped to run the bookstore during her husband Charles's lifetime, especially when he traveled. Even if she had not, her constant physical proximity to the bookstore—the Wileys lived over the Wall Street shop for years—would have ensured that she knew much about the business.[8]

John Wiley's Beginnings as Book Agent and Publisher

Wiley's future, however, rested with John. In his father's shop he had received "a good practical education and considerable experience of the details of bookmaking and bookselling," a newspaper later reported, and he seems to have quickly made his way in the book trade on his own. In 1828, Thomas Wardle of Philadelphia employed John as an agent in his extensive import business. By

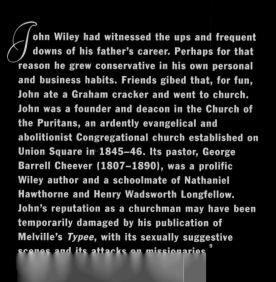

John Wiley had witnessed the ups and frequent downs of his father's career. Perhaps for that reason he grew conservative in his own personal and business habits. Friends gibed that, for fun, John ate a Graham cracker and went to church. John was a founder and deacon in the Church of the Puritans, an ardently evangelical and abolitionist Congregational church established on Union Square in 1845–46. Its pastor, George Barrell Cheever (1807–1890), was a prolific Wiley author and a schoolmate of Nathaniel Hawthorne and Henry Wadsworth Longfellow. John's reputation as a churchman may have been temporarily damaged by his publication of Melville's *Typee,* with its sexually suggestive scenes and its attacks on missionaries.[9]

*T*hought to be Elizabeth Osgood Wiley (1817–1889), the daughter of Reverend Samuel Osgood of Springfield, Massachusetts, with her granddaughter, Sarah King Wiley. Elizabeth married John Wiley in 1833. Together they had 11 children. Only five survived to adulthood. The three surviving sons—Charles, William Halsted, and Osgood—all joined the family business.

1829, John was also a New York agent for Carey & Lea. In 1831, he appears in the New York City directory as a "book agent" at Wall Street near Broad, two blocks from his father's store. His precise duties as agent are unknown, but he probably served as the New York sales representative for the Philadelphia publishers. What other business activities, if any, John undertook in these years remain obscure. But we do know that in 1832 he

opened a bookstore "up stairs" at 22 Nassau Street (again nearby) and published his first book, a reprint of a Van Winkle & Wiley religious title, Samuel Whelpley's *The Triangle: A Series of Numbers upon Three Theological Points*.[10]

The facility with which John moved into the book trade was, of course, owing to his father Charles, from whom came the acquaintance with the authors and bookmen who had frequented Charles's literary den at 3 Wall Street. And the Wiley name would have held John in good stead with the aging but still important literary clique that included James Fenimore Cooper, James Kirke Paulding, and Washington Irving. Charles also bequeathed to John an approach to publishing in two potentially profitable business niches. With American literature John tried hard, until failure of the U.S. international copyright movement caused him to leave fiction behind. With scientific and technical publishing he found a more promising future.[11]

In 1833, John married Elizabeth Osgood. The marriage produced 11 children, 6 of whom died at very young ages. John was a pious Christian whose faith was often reflected in what he published. Before their marriage, he wrote to Elizabeth, "I have frequently said that when settled with you as a companion I should better enjoy religion." Two titles that appeared in the same year as his marriage exemplify the Christian, morality-building genre—an edition of Mrs. Anna Brownell Jameson's *Characteristics of Women: Moral, Poetical, and Historical*, an analysis of Shakespeare's heroines that has

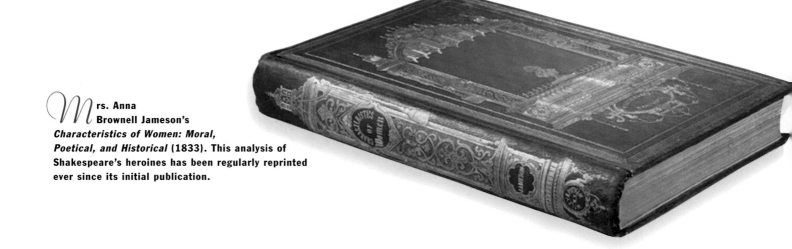

*M*rs. Anna Brownell Jameson's *Characteristics of Women: Moral, Poetical, and Historical* (1833). This analysis of Shakespeare's heroines has been regularly reprinted ever since its initial publication.

PORTRAIT OF A BOOKSTORE

Bookstores could be found in remote areas. Publisher J. C. Derby, who began his career as a bookman in 1834 clerking in a store in Auburn, New York, described bookstores as "the natural resorts for the intelligent class of the community, who usually met there to discuss the topics of the day or to learn what was new in the book world." Auburn boasted a theological school, so theological treatises and textbooks were staples at the store, but the novels of Sir Walter Scott, James Fenimore Cooper, and Washington Irving were also in demand. On annual pilgrimages to New York, Derby acquired the books his patrons needed for school or desired for diversion.

been regularly reprinted ever since, and *Manly Piety in Its Principles* by Robert Philip, a Methodist minister, which also went through multiple printings. John soon published three more of Philip's religious self-help titles, including *Christian Experience, or, A Guide to the Perplexed*. Little of John's correspondence survives, so instead of probing his character to help interpret his business and life decisions, it is necessary to do the reverse. His marriage to a minister's daughter, his publishing interests, and his business decisions suggest that John was a conservative businessman, persistent in his pursuit of the book trade despite unfavorable business cycles. Perhaps he saw publishing as a calling, as a way of promoting morality, though he also, of course, sought profit and was willing to publish some freethinkers. It is likely that he favored the Whig and later the Republican parties, and certain that he opposed slavery.[12]

In the same year as his marriage, John, in company with Peter Hill, M. Bancroft, and G. & C. & H. Carvill, began publishing the *American Monthly Magazine*. Edited by a recent arrival from England, Henry William Herbert, the magazine was devoted to apolitical fiction, biography, travel, and moral essays. Though it garnered positive reviews, it was more of an attempt to follow the market than lead it. Such general miscellanies as well as more specialized periodicals would soon flood the reading market. "Every pursuit in life, and almost every shade of opinion," observed Henry C. Carey, son of Mathew Carey, in 1853, "has its periodical." "A single city in Western New York," he noted, "furnishes no less than four agricultural and horticultural journals, one of them published weekly, with a circulation of 15,000, and the others, monthly, with a joint circulation of 25,000." Merchants, bankers, doctors, and lawyers could choose from multiple publications. Even dental surgery boasted five periodicals, one with a circulation of 5,000. Not all were top quality, and competition from established (and pirated) British periodicals like *Blackwood's* and the *Quarterly Review*, made for a tough business. Even so, *The American Monthly*, which struggled financially in the face of pirates, continued for five years, when it joined the many victims of the Panic of 1837.[13]

John lived elsewhere but kept his Nassau Street store through 1834, where he was known to have sold

maps in partnership with Andrew T. Goodrich. The pair also published three travel titles: *A Visit to Texas*, which the *Southern Literary Messenger* called an "unpretending and agreeable narrative"; Theodore Dwight's *The Northern Traveller*; and *A Sketch of Bolivar in His Camp* by Hiram Paulding, a naval hero during the War of 1812, which recounted a 1,500-mile trek through the Andes with rebel general Simon Bolivar, the "George Washington of Latin America." That same year John also launched the short-lived *Father's Magazine*, a pious version of Abigail and Samuel Whittelsey's

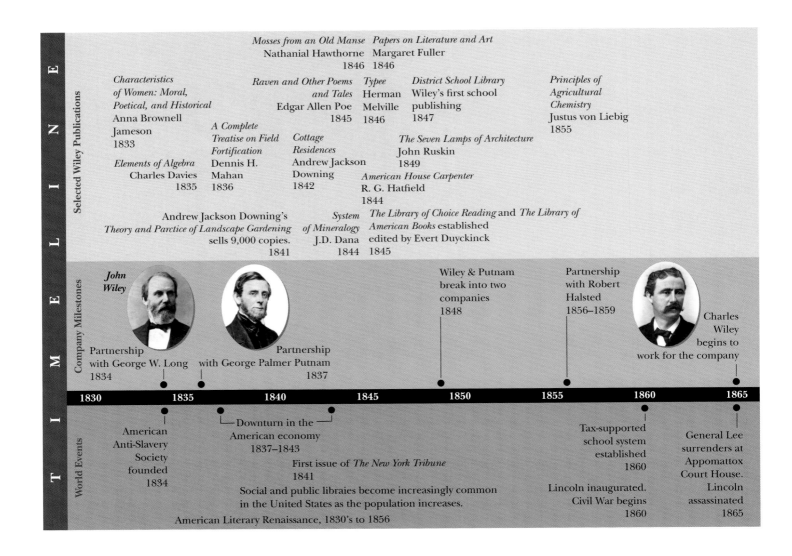

TIMELINE

Selected Wiley Publications

Mosses from an Old Manse — Nathanial Hawthorne — 1846
Papers on Literature and Art — Margaret Fuller — 1846

Characteristics of Women: Moral, Poetical, and Historical — Anna Brownell Jameson — 1833

Raven and Other Poems and Tales — Edgar Allen Poe — 1845

Typee — Herman Melville — 1846

District School Library — Wiley's first school publishing — 1847

Principles of Agricultural Chemistry — Justus von Liebig — 1855

A Complete Treatise on Field Fortification — Dennis H. Mahan — 1836

Elements of Algebra — Charles Davies — 1835

Cottage Residences — Andrew Jackson Downing — 1842

The Seven Lamps of Architecture — John Ruskin — 1849

American House Carpenter — R. G. Hatfield — 1844

Andrew Jackson Downing's Theory and Parctice of Landscape Gardening sells 9,000 copies. 1841

System of Mineralogy — J.D. Dana — 1844

The Library of Choice Reading and *The Library of American Books* established — edited by Evert Duyckinck — 1845

Company Milestones

John Wiley

Partnership with George W. Long — 1834

Partnership with George Palmer Putnam — 1837

Wiley & Putnam break into two companies — 1848

Partnership with Robert Halsted — 1856–1859

Charles Wiley begins to work for the company

| 1830 | 1835 | 1840 | 1845 | 1850 | 1855 | 1860 | 1865 |

World Events

American Anti-Slavery Society founded 1834

Downturn in the American economy 1837–1843

First issue of *The New York Tribune* 1841

Social and public libraies become increasingly common in the United States as the population increases.

American Literary Renaissance, 1830's to 1856

Tax-supported school system established 1860

Lincoln inaugurated. Civil War begins 1860

General Lee surrenders at Appomattox Court House. Lincoln assassinated 1865

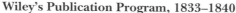

Wiley's Publication Program, 1833–1840

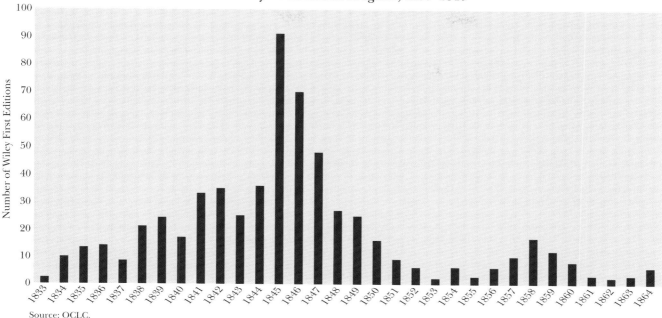

Source: OCLC.

successful *Mother's Magazine* (1833–1849) but for men, and he helped to distribute the New York City directory to booksellers. In retrospect, this was also the year in which Wiley took a strong turn toward serious literature.

James Fenimore Cooper reentered John's life in 1834 when the author encouraged Carey, Lea, & Blanchard to publish *The Monikins* by threatening to "print at my own risk, through John Wiley." The Philadelphia firm relented and the title appeared the next year. Perhaps to assuage John, or perhaps because Carey had initially passed on the book, Cooper turned to Wiley to publish *A Letter to His Countrymen, by J. Fenimore-Cooper*, a sharply critical attack on American cultural provincialism in which Cooper threatened to stop writing. Reviewers were unkind; one went so far as to call Cooper a "spoiled child," and in the words of a Cooper scholar, the book was "a masterpiece of miscalculation."

If with the Cooper name John hoped to bolster his reputation and his profits at the same time, he was disappointed. Thereafter, Cooper used John solely as a bookseller and as an agent to handle some of his publishing transactions.[14]

Late in 1834, John entered a partnership with George W. Long, the son of the Long who had worked with Charles Wiley on various projects. They set up a bookstore at 161 Broadway and published a range of titles, from self-help and Christian moralism to compendiums of useful, practical knowledge. The latter included works on mathematics and surveying by Charles Davies and on engineering by Dennis H. Mahan, who was professor of mathematics and engineering at the U.S. Military Academy at West Point from 1830. West Point was the country's first engineering school, and Davies and Mahan were pioneers, writing some of the first textbooks in English for the country's first engineering students. Before this, with the exception of one

The United States Military Academy at West Point, New York, the nation's first engineering school, around 1828.
West Point Museum Art Collection, United States Military Academy, West Point, N.Y. #6954

Wiley & Long established ties to the United States Military Academy, the country's first engineering school, in the 1830's, publishing four titles by Charles Davies: *Elements of Algebra, A Treatise on Shades and Shadows, Elements of Surveying,* and *Elements of Descriptive Geometry*. Davies was one of the most prolific and popular mathematics authors of the nineteenth century, and Wiley eventually put out 10 of his 25 books, most in numerous editions. Wiley & Long also published Dennis H. Mahan's *A Complete Treatise on Field Fortification* in 1836, which became an enduring classic. Like Davies, Mahan would emerge as a major figure on Wiley's list.[15]

The bookstore at 161 Broadway attracted numerous authors, including Edgar Allan Poe, making it one of the best known literary addresses in New York City. The store housed Wiley & Putnam and then reverted to Wiley when the partnership ended in 1848 and Putnam moved down a few doors to 155 Broadway.

translation of a French text into English, West Point cadets were required to learn French so that they could use French language texts. Dennis H. Mahan's *A Complete Treatise on Field Fortification*, which Wiley published in 1836, became an enduring classic.[16]

This was the start of a long connection between Wiley and the publication of mathematics, surveying, and engineering works that fed on the rise of science and engineering education in America. With two later heads of the company trained as engineers, Wiley would become renowned worldwide for its engineering titles and remains so today.

For the most part, Wiley now was publishing as we think of it, with the publisher assuming the costs and risks of bringing a work to market in exchange for all the profits, minus authors' royalties, and exerting a large degree of editorial control.[17]

The growth and quality of Wiley's list attracted the attention of another young bookman, George Palmer Putnam. By 1832, he was associated with Jonathan Leavitt, then the senior partner of famed publisher Daniel Appleton, and had written a first successful book, *Chronology, or, An Introduction and Index to Universal History, Biography, and Useful Knowledge*, an impressive work for a teenager. And John was impressed. In 1836, Putnam came into the company as a junior partner. He traveled in Europe on behalf of Wiley & Long and invested $150 in the company before Long retired at the end of the year. The new firm, Wiley & Putnam, appeared in the 1837 city directory, located at the former Wiley & Long bookstore at 161 Broadway.[18]

Publishing in Antebellum America

John's persistence in his early years suggests a decision to stay in the book business and not turn to another, as a man under thirty might have done. The record does not speak directly, but something can be pieced together about whether his decision to remain in the book trade was a good one. From a personal view, the answer is probably yes. John remained in the business for over half a century and from what we can tell he loved it in his own quiet way. From a business point of view, the answer is probably also yes, with qualifications.

*A*n American parlor in the Victorian Era. Thomas Bailey Aldrich memorial, Portsmouth, N.H.

Demand was certainly auspicious: Americans were reading. Cooper once remarked that he could not remember ever entering an American house where there were not books, and the growth of the book trade amazed poet and New York newspaper editor William Cullen Bryant, who observed, "The circle of knowledge widens every year" and with it the market for books. Henry C. Carey of the publishing family and a leading political economist, thought the American book market "unparalleled in the world." In 1855, George Palmer Putnam, now publishing on his own, claimed that the "sheet from our book presses alone, in a single year, would reach nearly twice round the globe." The industry's growth outpaced the nation's growing population and increasing wealth. With few exceptions, demand for books rose each year, as the population of Manhattan, the Northeast, and the nation bounded upward, from 12.9 million nationally in 1830 to 31.4 million on the eve of the Civil War. The population of the Northeast, then Wiley's most important market, almost doubled in the same period, from 5.5 million to 10.6 million.[19]

The nation also grew richer, with per capita GDP increasing from about $1,500 per year in 1826 to $2,340 in 1860.[20] More wealth allowed more people to buy more books. Book prices fell somewhat, especially in the early 1840s when a recession induced publishers to put out unbound, abridged, and condensed editions on massive folios of newsprint priced as low as 6 cents. Quality books, however, remained fairly expensive in the antebellum period, about a dollar, or a day's pay for a common laborer, for a hardcover novel. Paperback reprints of British

> Putnam . . . claimed that the "sheet from our book presses alone, in a single year, would reach nearly twice round the globe."

Growth of U.S. Libraries, 1830–1875

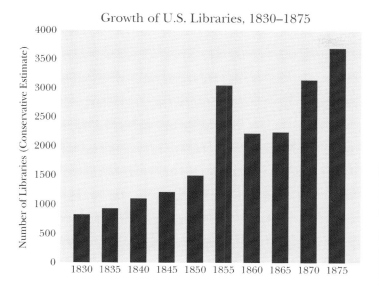

Source: Haynes McMullen, *American Libraries Before 1876*, Westport, Conn.: Greenwood Press, 2000), 48.

York Mercantile Library) of 20,000 volumes for just two dollars per year. Other major libraries included the New York Society Library (40,000 volumes), the Boston Atheneum (around 32,000), the Library Company of Philadelphia (52,000), and the Library of Congress (25,000). Social libraries were not just a northern metropolitan phenomenon. Charleston, South Carolina, had one with 15,000 volumes, and other smaller collections abounded. Most were not circulating libraries, but collections could be freely consulted during regular hours.[22]

By the 1850s, the public or "free" library was beginning to supplant the old social and circulating libraries of Charles Wiley's era. The opening of a tax-supported public library in Boston in 1848 set the standard. In 1850, 1,217 public libraries housed 1,466,015 books, about a quarter of the 4,537,811 library books then in the nation. The Civil War slowed the trend, but

authors could retail for as little as 12.5 cents, but 50 cents was more common. As incomes grew, so did the ability to afford such prices. Rising incomes also made indoor gas lighting and eyeglasses more affordable, and these made reading easier and so also increased demand for books. The best available estimate is that the number of American readers increased from 6.44 million in 1840 to 15.3 million in 1860.[21]

Those who could not buy books could almost always borrow them. Wiley author Lydia Maria Child wrote in 1831 that it was hard to imagine anyone who really wanted a book not obtaining one. And that was before free public libraries were common. A New York reader boasted in 1844 that he had access to a fine library (probably the New

*C*lassroom, circa 1850, in the Emerson School for Girls (Boston, Massachusetts).

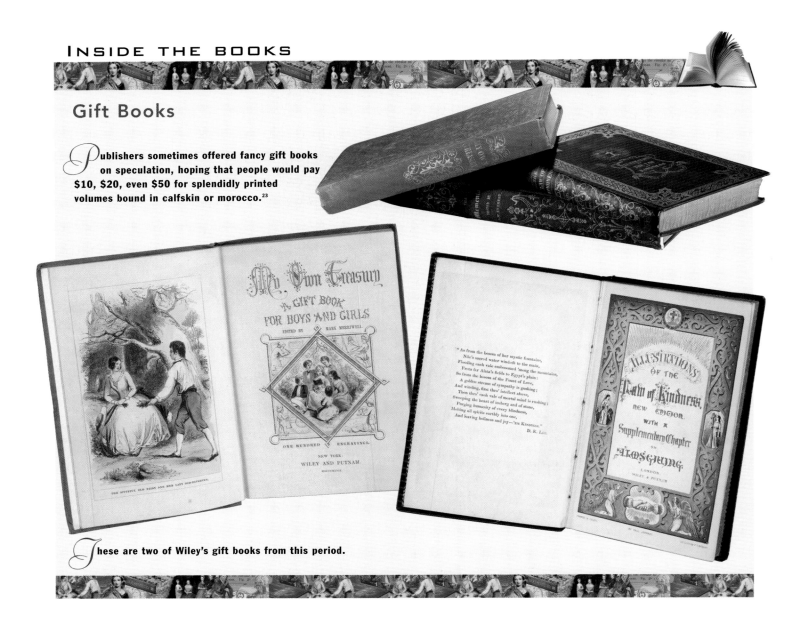

INSIDE THE BOOKS

Gift Books

*P*ublishers sometimes offered fancy gift books on speculation, hoping that people would pay $10, $20, even $50 for splendidly printed volumes bound in calfskin or morocco.[23]

*T*hese are two of Wiley's gift books from this period.

68

by 1875, municipal public libraries numbered over 2,000. Surviving records indicate that the nation's libraries, of all sorts, were well used.[24]

Demand for books was, of course, related to literacy rates, which scholars put at about 90 percent for antebellum America. Rates were higher in the industrializing North than in the agricultural and slave South, but on the whole they were higher than in Britain, where literacy in this period hovered at about 60 percent. In 1850, about 600 million newspaper pages, or 24 per person, were printed in the United States, compared to just 2.5

newspaper pages per person in Britain. While literacy is not the same as schooling, antebellum Americans did get some formal education—some public, some private, some a mixture of the two. In New York State in 1850, for example, there were 778,000 students in public schools and another 75,000 in private ones. Schools, of course, needed books. The Empire State's school libraries alone contained about 1.5 million volumes, and these were available to all. Highly successful schoolbooks could sell a million copies, at the rate of 70,000 or more a year for extended periods.[25]

Colleges also grew in number and enrollment during the antebellum era. By the early 1840s, America had 103 colleges with total enrollments of almost 20,000, 28 medical schools with 3,250 students, and 39 theological schools with 1,300 students all told. The libraries of these institutions housed some three-quarters of a million books. In 1853, the number of American colleges had increased to 120. Academic titles, which in the early part of the century attracted few sales, could by the 1850s sell up to 50,000 copies a year, and scores of college-level books regularly sold 5,000 to 10,000 copies a year.[26]

Americans, then as now, thought books made good gifts. Publishers and organizations sometimes put out special "gift editions" for this purpose, but often people simply purchased regular trade books for giving to others. In the 1840s, for example, Philip Milledoler gave his children more than 150 books on topics including biography, history, logic, mathematics, travel, and, of course, religion. This kind of gift list, together with library circulation records and other sources, indicates that antebellum readers were very much polymaths, consuming titles on everything from military history to logic, the useful arts, agriculture and animal husbandry, to literature and cheap novels.[27]

For publishers, more people, greater wealth, expanding libraries, growing schools, and a constant love of reading added up to sales. By the early 1850s, print runs for the front-list books of major publishers were as high as 100,000, up from the 100s or 1,000s common during Charles Wiley's era and surpassing all but the most popular Cooper titles from the 1820s. Even modest titles were printed in runs of 10,000. Publishing

industry revenue was up as well, increasing from $2.5 million in 1820 to $16 million in 1856. New York publishers accounted for 37.5 percent of the latter figure, Boston and Philadelphia publishers for half of New York's share each. New York remained the country's most important publishing center.[28]

If demand was good, developments on the supply side also proved the wisdom of John's decision to stay in the publishing business. The technological revolution in printing that began during Charles's career accelerated; it is no exaggeration to say that the changes in printing that took place between about 1820 and 1850 were as revolutionary as the changes that took place between 1970 and 2000. Many antebellum publishers attributed their growth and success to stereotyping, improvements in composition and papermaking, and—most importantly—the steam-driven cylinder press.[29]

Improvements in work organization accompanied advances in mechanization. By 1855, Harper & Brothers ran a large, multi-story factory where unskilled workers received raw materials, put them through mighty steam presses, dried, flattened, and folded the printed sheets, then sewed and stitched them in preparation for the fitting of covers and the trimming of edges.[30]

Other technological advances aided the book industry, though less directly. In Charles's day, most goods, including books, moved by horseback, wagon, or small boat. Books were both heavy and fragile—they lost most of their value if they came into contact with water or mud—and transporting them was costly and slow. By the 1840s, in John's era, railroads laced the eastern countryside, moving books efficiently from

> Many antebellum publishers attributed their growth and success to stereotyping, improvements in composition and papermaking, and—most importantly—the steam-driven cylinder press.

69

*H*arper & Brothers counting room provided space for a warehouse and shipping operation, sample cases, bookkeeping, and the Harper brothers' desks. By the end of the 1840s, Harper & Brothers was the largest publisher in America and one of the largest in the world. The Harpers' operation overshadowed Wiley & Putnam's bookstore-office. In 1856 after a fire, the firm built an impressive two-building complex on Franklin Square in lower Manhattan. This virtual publishing factory provided space for hand typesetting and typesetting by electro-typing machines; printing on 28 steam presses; folding, binding, and covering; paper marbling, gilding titles on bindings and covers, and a sprinkling process to give leather-bound volumes a mottled look; and a warehouse, mail room, and front office.[31]

publishing centers to the periphery. Publishing began to centralize, as local publishers were supplanted. Railroads, steamships, and the telegraph also regularized business communications, making them more predictable and dependable as well as faster and cheaper. By 1850, a network of railroads linked the Northeast to Pittsburgh, Cincinnati, St. Louis, and Chicago. These developments, in turn, allowed publishers to run their businesses more evenly throughout the year, less subject to changing weather and money-market conditions. The railroad also modernized book distribution by making returns possible: Booksellers could return unsold copies to

publishers within a reasonable period, usually about a year. While this system threw most of the risk onto publishers, it enabled booksellers to increase their offerings. The old subscription and peddling systems soon withered away.[32]

All these factors encouraged entry into the book business, or at least they made it look tempting. Between 1800 and the end of the Civil War, the number of printing and publishing firms increased, by one estimate from fewer than 300 to more than 4,500, or roughly from one firm for every 18,000 Americans to one firm for every 7,000 Americans. With competition like that,

THE *Printing craft*

NINETEENTH-CENTURY ADVANCES IN TECHNOLOGY

Stereotyping was one of the early nineteenth century's most important printing innovations. In stereotyping, the type was hand set, as before, but was then used to cast a metal printing plate—after which the type was taken apart and the plate retained. Once type was impressed on metal plates, typesetting became permanent. The plates could be stored, transported, and reused; books could be printed from them again and again without ever having to be typeset and proofread. In this way, a publisher could reduce his risk by issuing a small first edition to test the market. If that initial printing sold well, subsequent editions could be published from the plates without having to reset type.

As stereotyping was perfected, a set of plates for a popular book became a valuable asset. Publishers even rented and sold plates to other publishers; sometimes the author received additional money from the second publisher, depending on the terms of the author's agreement with the first publisher. In 1846, Wiley & Putnam published the first edition of Nathaniel Hawthorne's *Mosses from an Old Manse*. When Wiley and his partner, George Palmer Putnam, went their separate ways in 1848, Putnam retained most of the literary properties, including the plates for *Mosses*. Putnam subsequently published editions in 1850 and 1851 and then sold the plates to Boston publisher

*S*team driven presses at the Harper & Brothers printing factory.

$\mathcal{G}$eorge Bruce

Ticknor & Fields, which produced its own first edition in 1854.

Stereotyping was introduced into the United States by George Bruce, a Scot born in Edinburgh in 1781 who had followed his brother David to America. In 1806, they had a print shop in New York, just a few blocks from where Charles set up his shop a year later. Unlike Charles, however, George and David were more artisans than bookmen. It was printing, not publishing, that interested them, and they transformed printing. Although George brought the secret of stereotyping to the United States in 1812 after a trip to England, the type of the time was not suitably cast for it, and stereotyping was not in common use in Charles's day. George

Bruce also pioneered innovations in type design that helped stereotyping to spread.[33]

Typesetting speeds increased, too, after the introduction in 1841 of a steam-driven, typewriter-like contraption that allowed "rapid girlish fingers, touching keys like those of a piano" to set type "about four times as fast as the quickest compositor." David Bruce's son, also David, carried on with new type-founding technology, and his aging uncle George in 1854 invented a way to substitute air for water in the cooling of hot lead type.[34]

Papermaking also improved, with the coming of the Fourdrinier belt-based machine in the 1810s and Thomas Gilpin's cylinder-based machine in the 1830s that allowed, for the first time, the production of continuous rolls of large-width sheets. Traditionally made from cotton and linen rags, paper remained relatively expensive until manufacturers turned to wood pulp in the mid-1850s.[35]

Even bookbinding was mechanized to some extent, with the introduction of the stabbing machine around 1820, the rolling press and the folding machine around 1840, the rounder and backer in 1854, and sundry trimming and cutting machines. Sewing, though, remained a hand process until late in the nineteenth century.

Only when steam began to power both plates and paper would the printing process itself be fully mechanized. Use of an iron frame, a larger screw, and better fulcrums and levers in the early nineteenth century, as in George Clymer's "Columbian Press," had made presswork more efficient, though still a manual task. Horsepower substituted for manpower on some new presses in the 1820s, and in the 1830s Isaac Adams perfected the steam-driven flatbed press, which was ideal for the production of high-quality books. It was Robert Hoe's cylinder press, however, that from the late 1840s ushered in the age of rapid, cheap printing. Savings were enormous: A magazine produced by hand in 1852 consumed 3,170 man hours at a cost of $302.50. That same product, using the latest technology, required only 15 hours and a cost of $4.63.[36]

price-cutting, in the form of discounts allowed to retailers, soared. So did advertising expenses, which could exceed 15 percent of revenue. According to William Cullen Bryant, publishers, especially those specializing in reprinting foreign works (the easiest of all approaches to the business), "have sprung up and died off, two or half-a-dozen a week, in every city in the country." Some simply did not know their business. An 1855 trade publication described a hapless bookseller who had listed Robert Burton's philosophical *Anatomy of Melancholy*, published in 1621, under the category of "Surgery." According to the *New-Yorker* (a periodical published between 1836 and 1841), the bookseller was to the author as the wigmaster was to the schoolmaster: "one is learned on the outside, and the other on the inside of the article he furnishes."[37]

> Despite the downturn, Wiley & Putnam [continued to] publish or copublish.

Wiley & Putnam's Early Years

John was much brighter than the run-of-the-mill bookseller, and he correctly perceived that publishing was a growing business with profits for the quick and the smart. Nevertheless, Wiley & Putnam, the partnership that John entered with the young George Putnam, began in a bad year—1837—as a panic related to international business cycles and the economic policies of the Jackson administration produced a recession that lasted until 1843. While the causes of the downturn are debated, its effects were clear: per capita output in current prices dropped from $119 in 1836 to just $85 in 1843, essentially throwing the economy back to 1830. Business failures were ubiquitous, publishers among them. Many slashed prices below costs in an effort to maintain market share, an untenable long-term strategy. Others, though technically not bankrupt, were insolvent, meaning that they

simply could not raise enough cash to pay their bills. Those who survived did so by retrenching, cutting back on the number of titles published. The growth of Wiley's list was uneven during these years. Soon after the recession began, for example, it dropped at least one major project, an "American anthology" of mammoth proportions.[38]

Despite the downturn, Wiley & Putnam published or co-published in some broad subject areas that reflected current interests and foreshadowed future successes.[39] In 1841, for example, the company published *The Principles and Practice of Book-keeping*, an accounting manual that provided instruction in debits and credits, journals and ledgers, and assets and liabilities. To this day Wiley remains an important publisher of accounting titles. That same year, the company also published the autobiography of early American portrait artist Jonathan Trumbull (1756–1843). An ardent patriot who ironically learned much of his craft in England, Trumbull devoted his life to painting scenes of the Revolution and its leaders. No doubt Wiley & Putnam published the autobiography of this influential painter because it fit both the company's nationalist inclination and its profit projections.

In the years of the recession, Wiley & Putnam also found it expedient and profitable to publish education and economic policy books like *Education Reform* (1837), *An Address on Primary Education* (1840), *The Remedy, in a National Bank of the People* (1838), *Remarks on the Currency of the United States* (1840), *Reasons for the Inexpediency of Chartering a National Bank* (1841), and *Suggestions on the Banks* (1841), the last by Albert Gallatin, who served Thomas Jefferson and James Madison as Secretary of the Treasury. Americans have never been completely satisfied with their banks or their schools, and recession usually spurs both the supply

The Middle Kingdom, by S. Wells Williams and published by Wiley in 1847, was the first serious academic-reportorial study of China.

of and the demand for works calling for reform of both. Banking, in particular, had been a white-hot political topic during the 1830s, during and after Jackson's 1832 veto of the rechartering of the Second Bank of the United States, which would leave the country without a central bank for three-quarters of a century to come.

Wiley & Putnam's interest in the education system was likely piqued by its sales to schools and colleges. Though a clear distinction between textbooks and trade books had yet to arise, the company published a large number of nonfiction titles that must have found their way into classrooms or the eager hands of the country's numerous autodidacts. In its first years, Wiley & Putnam published historical works including *History of the Revolution in Texas* (1838), *Memoir, Historical and Political, of the Northwest Coast of North America* (1840), and *The Official and Other Papers of . . . Alexander Hamilton* (1842); language primers for French, Hebrew, and Greek; mathematics books like *Elements of Trigonometry* (1838) and *Elements of the Differential and Integral Calculus* (1842); medical works including *The Pathology and Treatment of Asiatic Cholera* (1840), *A Practical Treatise on the Diseases of*

Children (1841), and *Hints to Mothers* (1842); military tracts such as *An Elementary Treatise on Optics, Designed for the Use of Cadets of the United States Military Academy* (1839); philosophy texts like *Elements of Moral Philosophy* (1837); and reference works such as *A Comprehensive Atlas* (1838). Suggesting even greater things to come, the company in the late 1830s and early 1840s also built an impressive list of scientific works, including *Elements of Chemistry* (1837), *A Flora of North America* (1838), *An Elementary Treatise on Astronomy* (1839), *Stories Illustrative of the Instinct of Animals* (1841), and *Bees, Pigeons, Rabbits, and the Canary Bird* (1842); and technical titles like *Laboratory Calculations* (1837), *Treatise on Topographical Drawing* (1837), *A Catalogue of the Shells, Arranged According to the Lamarckian System* (1839), *Treatise on Sheep* (1841), and *The Poultry-Yard* (1841).

The early Wiley & Putnam continued to publish fiction by Charles Dickens, Samuel Goodrich, Nathaniel Hawthorne, and Edgar Allan Poe, and poetry by Thomas Campbell (1838), William Cullen Bryant (1842), and others—a harbinger of efforts to come. Its interest in travelogues continued, while it explored hybrid genres with books like *The Poetry and History of Wyoming* (1841) and *The Middle Kingdom* (1847), a survey of the Chinese empire and its people. It also published *War and Peace* (1842), but not the famous one by Leo Tolstoy.[40]

These years also saw the publication of several very good sellers, including the work of the horticulturalist, landscape gardener, and architect Andrew Jackson Downing. His architectural works mark the beginning of Wiley's interest in architecture and construction; Wiley is still a leading publisher in these areas. Downing was an early advocate of the suburbs as a refuge from "the too great bustle and excitement of our commercial cities" and of urban parks as a safety valve against social disorder. His books were more practical than polemical, however, and found large audiences. *The Theory and Practice of Landscape Gardening* (1841), which sold 9,000 copies at a

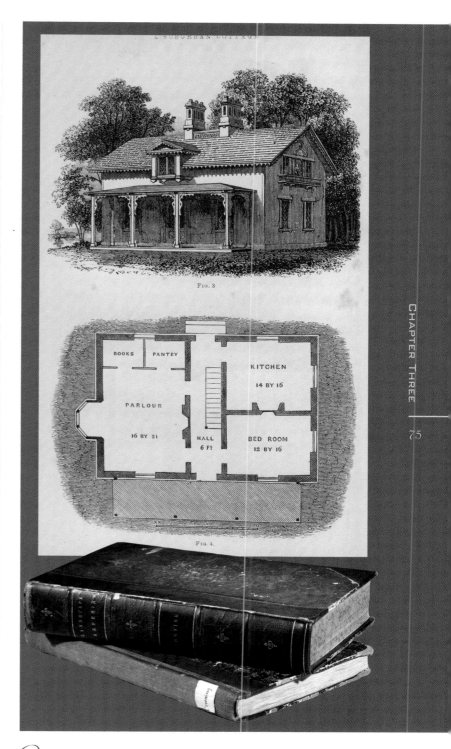

Cottage Residences, by Andrew Jackson Downing, was published by Wiley & Putnam in 1842 and sold handsomely. The book helped define and launch the popularity of the house pattern book and the idea that a house, as a home, was the basis of a moral society.

PROFILE

GEORGE PALMER PUTNAM

A conscientious publisher with high standards and an early campaigner for an international copyright law, George Palmer Putnam, much like John, led a career marked by numerous ups and downs. Unlike John, Putnam left the book business for a time but like John managed in the end to bequeath to his heirs a substantial business.

Putnam went to work for Wiley & Long, and in 1836, as junior partner, was sent to Europe for eight months to arrange for the purchase of foreign books. The following year he became secretary of an association formed to fight for an international copyright law, a cause John also strongly endorsed. About this time Putnam replaced Long as John's partner.

In 1838, Wiley dispatched this affable, alert young man to London. Wiley's prime goal was to import British publications to America. This moderately successful venture lasted about ten years, but the true benefits accrued to Putnam's son, George Haven Putnam, who in succeeding decades was able to capitalize on literary connections his father had forged.

In addition to meeting with Elizabeth Barrett Browning, Robert Browning, and other leading writers of the day, Putnam wrote articles for the *New York World*, the *Commercial Advertiser*, and the *Evening Post* and published several books on America and Europe. His *American Facts*, 1845, stressed his belief that the "promiscuous introduction" into America of English authors, unrestricted by copyright law, tended to impede the development of American literature.

In 1847, Putnam returned to America with publishing ideas of his own, and within a few months amicably dissolved his ties with Wiley. Putnam's son deeply regretted this split, believing that the more conservative Wiley possessed sound critical judgment that often curbed Putnam's more erratic flights of fancy. Five years later Putnam launched *Putnam's Monthly Magazine*, devoted exclusively to American material and containing no reprints from British journals. Soon he was in financial trouble, his problems aggravated by the 1857 panic, but with the assistance of old friends such as Washington Irving he was able to salvage his operation.

Then, distressed by business complexities arising from the Civil War, Putnam abandoned publishing for a

George Palmer Putnam was born in Brunswick, Maine, in 1814, the son of a lawyer and prep school proprietor father and a schoolteacher mother, from whom he acquired a sound education. Putnam at age eleven began a four-year apprenticeship in the rigid household of a Boston uncle who sold carpets. He fled his uncle's stern authority in 1829, taking a job as an errand boy in George Bleeker's Manhattan bookstore. For the next four years he worked hard, educating himself at night by reading assiduously, all while earning only his board and $25 per year.

In 1841 he married Victorine Haven. The couple set up housekeeping in a house christened "Knickerbocker Cottage," in the London suburbs. Their home became a salon of sorts, attracting such diverse figures as Washington Irving, Italian revolutionary Giuseppe Mazzini, and Louis Napoleon Bonaparte, later Emperor Napoleon III. Putnam used his travels and his connections to buy books for the U.S. market, recruit British authors for an important Wiley & Putnam series, and publish some titles in London.

After returning to America in 1847 and leaving both Wiley and then publishing for a while, Putnam eventually established G. P. Putnam & Sons (1866). He collapsed and died in his office in 1872, the end apparently hastened by a severe blow suffered a few years earlier during an accident at a Manhattan construction site.

time, placed his book list with Hurd & Houghton, and accepted a lucrative post as U.S. collector of internal revenue for the Eighth District of New York. In 1866, after being dismissed by President Andrew Johnson for failing to pay the usual campaign assessment, he established G. P. Putnam & Son, which five years later—like Wiley—became "& Sons." Putnam also revived his magazine, which lasted six more volumes before merging with *Scribner's*.[41]

respectable $3.50 a copy, and *Cottage Residences* (1842), which sold over 6,000 and listed at $2.00, must have been profitable for both himself and Wiley.[42]

Reviews of Wiley & Putnam's books in this period indicate that Wiley authors generally knew their subjects and how to write about them, and they are important primary evidence of how Wiley's work was received at the time. The *New-Yorker*, for instance, said of William Channing's *Reformation of Medical Science* (1839) that "its arguments are woven together like chain mail armor and the weapon that would sever them must be weighty enough to crush the whole science which they enclose." One reviewer called the *Mineral Springs of Western Virginia* (1842) by William Burke, "a *vade mecum* which every invalid should take with him, who desires to know what he ought to do when he arrives upon the spot, for the regaining of his health." Some titles, however, received scant praise. *Arcturus*, a periodical edited by future Wiley editor Evert A. Duyckinck and Wiley author Cornelius Mathews, wondered just what could have induced Wiley & Putnam to republish "so stupid a book" as *The Book Without a Name* (1841), a mere "collection of disconnected miscellanies" suffused with "execrable" puns. Opinion must have averaged out to the good, however, as by the 1840s Wiley and Putnam had gained a reputation as "enterprising publishers" and successful importers of European books into America and exporters of American books abroad.[43]

The firm accomplished much with a very small staff, which apparently numbered only the proprietors, John's younger brother Augustus, and a bookkeeper whose services were indispensable, as John discovered whenever he took ill. The partnership's first years were nevertheless tense, focused more on survival than

The London branch of Wiley & Putnam imported American books and exported European titles.

expansion. Perhaps the most interesting move on the company's part was the establishment of a branch office in London in 1838, the first of its kind for an American publisher. It was a risky move, but one made easier by regular transatlantic packet service.[44]

Staffed by Putnam, the London branch of Wiley & Putnam actively imported American books and exported European titles ordered by American customers, including Yale University. One was a Gutenberg Bible, now part of the Lenox collection at the New York Public Library. By 1843, Wiley & Putnam was a familiar presence on gritty Paternoster Row, where London's book trade mingled with butchers, bakers, and tallow makers. From there, in the words of New York politician and editor Thurlow Weed, the company "pushed" America's "literary wealth" "all over Europe."[45]

When it came to publishing in London, Putnam moved cautiously. In 1839, he solicited the advice of Sir Thomas W. Talfourd, a member of Parliament and leading British literary figure, regarding the publication in London of the tragedy, *Velasco; a Tragedy, in Five Acts*, by the American playwright and poet Epes Sargent. After apologizing for his delayed response, Talfourd wrote that he liked the five-act play, noting it was "very elegantly written; ~~sometimes~~ [*sic*] not rarely rising into beauty." Nevertheless, he felt success in London unlikely. "I am afraid a drama, not represented on our English stage, and not sanctioned by a reputation antecedently acquired," he judged, had poor chance of commercial success, however good the art. So Wiley passed, but Harper, a much larger, integrated publishing house with a modern production plant, a backlist of over 1,500 titles, and a handsome cushion of capital, took the book.

John tended to do most of the firm's publishing from the New York office, shipping sheets to Putnam for binding and sale in Britain. But the London office did do some publishing on its own, and so occasionally unbound Wiley sheets were carried by westbound packets.[46]

In New York, the company aimed to become the primary distributor to major libraries, including the New York State Library, the "most important of all the American Libraries of its class," and the venerable Library Company of Philadelphia. Writing for the New York State Library in late June 1840, John Canfield Spencer thanked Wiley for its "full and explicit" letter regarding its business policies. Intimating that the company was being considered for the library's book orders, he suggested a meeting in July, when he was scheduled to visit Manhattan. That October, the company also wrote to John Jay Smith, president of the Library Company of Philadelphia, of its confidence at giving satisfaction if entrusted with the library's business. As its 1841 catalog made clear, the company could purchase European books for U.S. libraries at 10 to 20 percent less "than the current Prices even in London" because it compared prices and, when appropriate, bought in bulk. That catalog showed that the company offered for sale 82 pages worth of titles, 79 in English, 2 in French, and 1 page of Bibles and books in Italian and German, the result of two years' research in the finest bookstores and libraries of Europe. The outcome of these efforts is not clear.

Chastened by the loss of the *American Monthly* in 1837, at least partly at the hands of American pirates, Wiley & Putnam in 1840 negotiated for special rates with British journal publishers. Putnam succeeded in convincing several of them, including John Murray, to supply to Wiley at a discount. In 1841, Wiley sold imported copies of *Blackwood's Magazine* (affectionately known as "*Maga*"), *Quarterly Review, British Critic, Civil Engineer and Architect's Journal, Practical Mechanic and Engineer's Magazine*, and

other leading British journals at prices competitive with those offered by reprint specialists. The pirates responded by cutting corners and costs, winning back the bottom part of the market. In early 1844, Americans could choose from four versions of *Blackwood's*: a very cheap reprint at $2, a cheap reprint at $3, a cheap "colonial" import at $3, or the original, through Wiley & Putnam, at $4. It was apparently too much, and within 6 months only the $3 reprint remained. The publisher of *Maga* considered cutting off the pirates by agreeing to provide an American publisher with advanced sheets or even plates, but it would not consider contracting with Wiley, describing John enigmatically as "too protestant." Wiley & Putnam continued to import other British journals like the *London Quarterly Review* and the *Edinburgh Review*, which were not popular enough to be successfully pirated, but imports of *Maga* slipped away. The company also sold American periodicals in London, including *The American Almanac* and *Repository of Useful Knowledge*.[47]

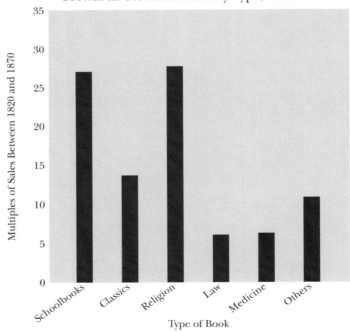

Growth in U.S. Book Sales by Type, 1820–1870

Source: *First Century of National Existence* (Hartford, Conn: L. Stebbins, 1875), 269.

PROFILE

EVERT A. DUYCKINCK

According to the editors of *The Orion, A Monthly Magazine of Literature and Art*, Evert A. Duyckinck (1816–1878) was a "young gentleman of New York of sound judgment, excellent talent, and a proper sense of moral responsibility." *The Orion*, edited from 1842 to 1844 by the artist and travel writer Thomas Addison Richards and his brother William Cary Richards, also thought him one of the "most promising" writers in the city. Duyckinck grew up around books, had a good inheritance, graduated from Columbia in 1835, was admitted to the bar, and traveled widely in Europe before settling into several editorships in New York in the early 1840s. His townhouse on Clinton Place was renowned for its 17,000-volume library and its boisterous dinner parties where Young Americans solved the problems of the world and sorted out the future of American letters. Duyckinck originated and edited Wiley and Putnam's two important series, the Library of Choice Reading and the Library of American Books.[48]

The son of a well-to-do Water Street bookseller and publisher, Duyckinck belonged to the first generation of New Yorkers for whom literature was more vocation than avocation.

Unlike Charles and his grandfather and namesake, John was intensely religious, professing and practicing a strict Protestant piety. Probably owing to John's abolitionist connections, Wiley & Putnam in 1839 published William Ellery Channing's *Remarks on the Slavery Question in a Letter to Jonathan Phillips.* Channing, the acknowledged head of Unitarianism, argued that "slavery is as insane as to seek health and prosperity by rebelling against the laws of nature, by sowing our seed on the ocean, or making poison our common food." In 1841 John published Reverend Ralph Gurley's *Letter to Henry Clay . . . on the Colonization and Civilization of Africa.* Gurley (1797–1872) played a leading role in the establishment of Liberia as an independent African state for the repatriation of freed American slaves. There was also, in 1844, Marmaduke Sampson's *Slavery in the United States.*

Although an abolitionist movement had existed in the United States since the Revolution, most early proponents had favored gradual change. In the 1830s and 1840s, however, abolitionism increasingly came to mean immediate emancipation. The movement had a strong religious base, including Quakers and many northerners affected by the revivalist fervor caused by the Second Great Awakening in the 1830s, and also economic and political components rooted in the growing fear that slavery weakened the nation's economic and political institutions.[49]

John's preference for religious and morally earnest tracts may have been rooted in personal conviction, but his publishing decisions were subject to business judgments. In this instance, they must have been easy enough to make. Religion was a major growth area for publishers between 1820 and 1870, its revenue increasing over 25 times, slightly outpacing the growth in revenue from education titles. Religious titles such as *An Inquiry into the Moral and Religious Character of the American Government* (1838), *History of the Christian Church* (1839), *The Christian Layman* (1840), *Sacred Melodies* (1841), and *Mormonism* (1842) were both popular and profitable. Wiley & Putnam also started a religious magazine, *Bibliotheca Sacra,* which is still in print, but no longer published by Wiley.[50]

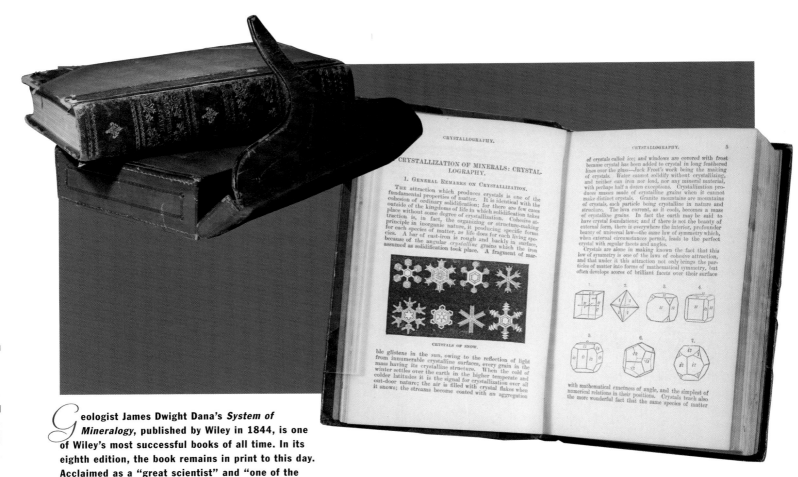

Geologist James Dwight Dana's *System of Mineralogy*, published by Wiley in 1844, is one of Wiley's most successful books of all time. In its eighth edition, the book remains in print to this day. Acclaimed as a "great scientist" and "one of the most learned geologists of the world," Dana wrote books that were "universally read" by the scientific elite. Born in Utica, New York, in 1813, Dana died in New Haven, Connecticut, in 1895 after a long, distinguished but illness-ridden career at Yale.[51]

The Glory Years

As economic conditions improved in 1843 and 1844, Wiley & Putnam took advantage by expanding its eclectic and serious publication program. *Littell's Living Age* called George Fownes's *Chemistry, as Exemplifying the Wisdom and Beneficence of God* (1844) a "very able one" and noted approvingly "it is short." In 1844 Wiley published James Dwight Dana's *System of Mineralogy*, still a classic in the field of geology.[52]

But before Wiley & Putnam would begin to specialize in such important scientific work, it focused for a few more brief but exciting years on the finest of

American *belles lettres*, much of which was exportable. In April 1843, the company promoted its books (its own and those published by others) and its pro-American ideology in its *American Book Circular*. Responding to the claim of a British historian that "European habits and ideas" were prerequisites to the development of American literature, Wiley & Putnam countered that American works sold extremely well, original American titles outnumbered reprints in most categories, and British publishers regularly pirated American titles. Listing 1,172 "original American works," the company's catalog of books offered at retail and wholesale was ample evidence of its nationalist viewpoint.[53]

This interest in *belles lettres* was announced by the launch in 1845 of the *American Review: A Whig Journal of Politics, Literature, Art, and Science*. In these years, New York and American literary culture was split into two factions vying for primacy. The Whig Knickerbockers had a literary monthly, *The Knickerbocker*, that was nationally influential, while the Jacksonian Young Americans were represented first by Evert Duyckinck's *Arcturus* and then by the *Democratic Review*, which endorsed literary nationalism, international copyright (so that American authors might have a better chance of publication in their own country), and Manifest Destiny. Wiley & Putnam's *American Review* aimed to bolster the Whig faction.[54]

In the same year, the company picked up an idea from a series "at once small in price and tasteful in execution" that had already met its demise. The series had begun in 1844, when "certain gentlemen interested in literature" in New York "reflecting on the unhappy condition of publishing matters & hoping to see it amended" recommended a series of publications under the rubric "The Home Library." The prospectus for the series, which was edited by Duyckinck and published by Isaac Platt, promised authors a share of the profits. The first volume in the poetical series, *The Whitefooted Deer and Other Poems* by Wiley author William Cullen Bryant, received rave reviews, as did the first prose title, J. T. Headley's *Letters from Italy*. "It is beautifully printed," observed one critic. Even so, Platt discontinued the series, probably because profit margins were too thin.[55]

Wiley & Putnam picked up the idea of publishing work in a series with this innovation: They developed two series of moderately priced books with a literary theme—The Library of Choice Reading and The Library of American Books. To assist in this endeavor John enlisted the aid of Duyckinck without advice from Putnam, who was nonetheless delighted, as he had met the young man of letters in London years earlier and liked him. The Library of Choice Reading

reprinted works by the most famous European authors, such as Elizabeth Barrett Browning, Thomas Carlyle, Charles Dickens, William Hazlitt, Victor Hugo, William Makepeace Thackeray, and others. Wiley & Putnam more or less pirated some of the foreign classics, but the firm, like Hurd & Houghton (a predecessor of Houghton Mifflin) and a few other

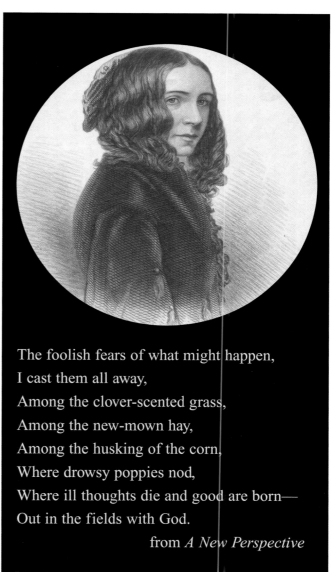

The foolish fears of what might happen,
I cast them all away,
Among the clover-scented grass,
Among the new-mown hay,
Among the husking of the corn,
Where drowsy poppies nod,
Where ill thoughts die and good are born—
Out in the fields with God.

from *A New Perspective*

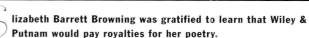

Elizabeth Barrett Browning was gratified to learn that Wiley & Putnam would pay royalties for her poetry.

*B*ritish historian Thomas Carlyle in approximately 1846. Negotiations between Carlyle and Wiley & Putnam produced a rich contract for Carlyle but poor royalties, as piracy by other American publishers reduced potential sales.

American publishers, also went to great lengths to make reasonable arrangements with foreign authors. Elizabeth Barrett Browning was pleased with her arrangements, while relations with Carlyle were strained by a confusing correspondence involving John in New York, Putnam in London, Ralph Waldo Emerson in Boston, and Carlyle himself. Only Putnam's personal visit to Carlyle's home in April 1846, and one of the most favorable contracts yet consummated between a British author and an American publisher, saved the relationship, and then only for a time. Carlyle ended it in 1847 because he thought his royalty check far too paltry, even after the

amount was verified by a bank clerk inspecting Wiley & Putnam's account books in New York. The problem— and it was no small one—was that pirates cut into sales deeply, injuring both the firm and its esteemed author.[56]

The Library of American Books was even more expansive in vision, looking to establish a new national canon by publishing original works by America's leading literary lights, including Margaret Fuller, Nathaniel Hawthorne, Herman Melville, Edgar Allan Poe, and John Greenleaf Whittier. It attracted both the New England authors and the New York-based Young Americans. The literary nationalism movement of which it was an important part inspired Herman Melville to urge Americans to "first praise mediocrity even, in her own children, before she praises . . . the best excellence in the children of any other land. Let her own authors, I say, have the priority of appreciation."[57]

Both series were massive undertakings, and Duyckinck deserves much of the credit for their rapid growth and critical quality. He was an outstanding editor who knew the magic of simultaneously chiding and flattering his authors. He also knew how to bring out the best in them. For example, when Commodore Horatio Bridges's *Journal of an African Cruiser* came in on the dreary side, he suggested Nathaniel Hawthorne might be of help. Hawthorne was willing, and able, and a revised Bridges's *Journal* sold out its first reprinting of 2,000 copies in just a few months. But in the meantime Hawthorne had neglected his own writing, prompting Duyckinck to jest, with an edge: "I hope you will not think me a troublesome fellow if I drop you another line with the vociferous cry, MSS.! MSS.! Mr. Wiley's American series is athirst."[58]

Actually, the American series was not the least bit parched. Without the whole of European literature to borrow from, it did grow more slowly than the Library of Choice Reading, but it was by far the more intellectually bold of the two projects. Duyckinck eventually pried out of Hawthorne *Mosses from an Old Manse*, a series of tales about alchemy and science that was published in 1846 and remained in print for eight years. Unfortunately for Wiley, Ticknor & Fields later captured Hawthorne's bigger work, Fields claiming to have played a crucial role in the final form of *The Scarlet Letter* (1850). Washington Irving helped by introducing Herman Melville's brother to Putnam in London. Putnam and John Murray agreed to simultaneous publication in New York and London of Melville's first book, *Typee: A Peep at Polynesian Life.* The son of an unsuccessful New York merchant, 22-year-old Melville had gone to sea in 1841 for what was supposed to have been a four-year voyage. But with bosom companion Toby Greene, he jumped ship in the Marquesas in the South Pacific, where he encountered the supposedly fierce Taipis or Typees tribe.

*N*athaniel Hawthorne served Wiley & Putnam as editor of Horatio Bridges's *Journal of an African Cruiser*, author of *Mosses from an Old Manse*, and favorable reviewer of Herman Melville's *Typee.*

The Typees turned out to be more cordial than anticipated, allowing Greene to leave their valley fastness to find medical attention for Melville, who had injured his leg. The Typees allowed Melville to sail away, too, a month later, aboard an Australian whaler.[59]

Hawthorne, a good friend of Melville's and Duyckinck's, provided a favorable review of the book once it was published. (The world of writers and publishers was still a small one.) Hawthorne liked the writing style and the content, a vivid reporting, he thought, of "barbarian life." *The Brooklyn Eagle's* Walt Whitman described the book as the sort of book to savor dreamily on a summer day. Other critics, however, thought Melville must have made the story up, and the Protestant press, including John Wiley's church newsletter, was particularly upset by the sexually suggestive nature of some of the content and Melville's attack on missionaries. John apparently did not take time to read the proofs sent from London in his hurry to match Murray's publication date.[60]

Murray had taken the first cut at the manuscript, deleting some explicitly sexual scenes and others that were merely suggestive. Melville cut even more at Murray's request. And then John, chastened by the negative publicity in the Protestant press and likely from the horrified responses of his fellow parishioners, sat down with Melville face to face to make further cuts. Gone from the "Revised Edition" were scenes such as the description of a prominent Marquesan lady who, in order to display her tattoos during a visit aboard a French ship, turned away from her hosts, lifted her skirts, and showed them her backside, and another section in which the islanders visited Melville's ship, leading to a scene of "riot and debauchery" in which "not the feeblest barrier was interposed between the unholy passions of the crew and their unlimited gratification."

The new edition did include, however, fresh material, "The Story of Toby," a sequel about what happened to Greene, which served somewhat to salvage Melville's credibility.[61]

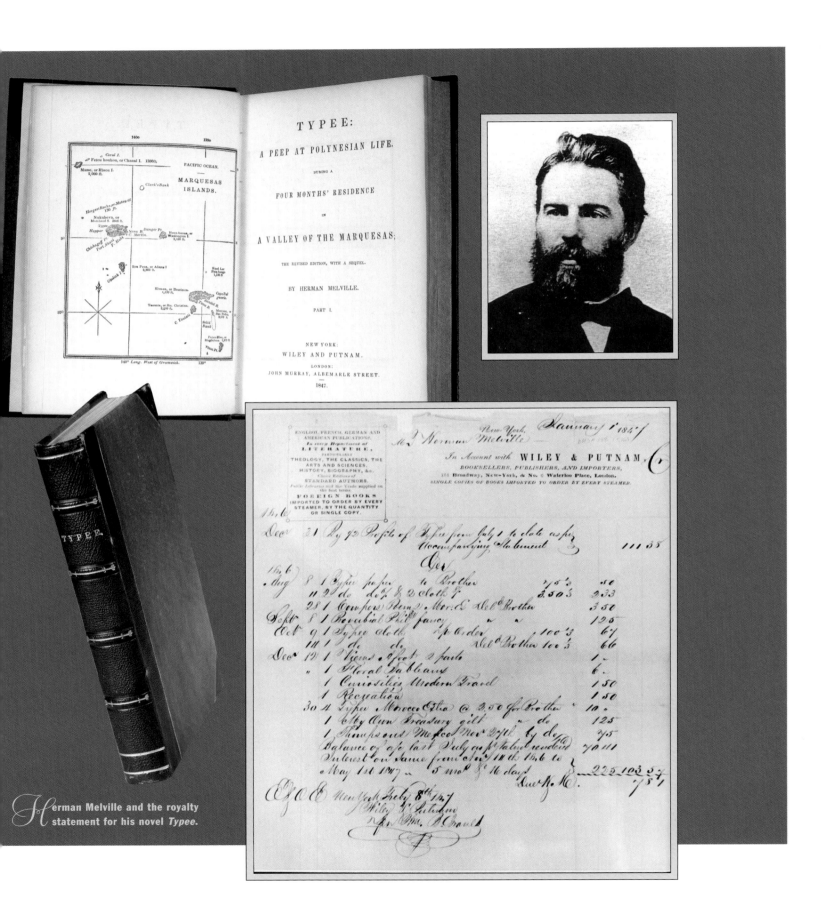

*H*erman Melville and the royalty statement for his novel *Typee.*

𝒫 ROFILE

MARGARET FULLER

M argaret Fuller, Wiley author and early women's rights advocate, resented John's interference with her criticism of religion in *Papers on Literature and Art*. A leading Transcendentalist, she was also well known for her radical views on women's rights. For the *New York Tribune* she covered the city's cultural life while writing about social issues, such as immigration and conditions in mental hospitals. Following Wiley & Putnam's publication of her *Papers on Literature and Art*, she went to Europe, where she continued to write for the *Tribune*, making her the country's first female foreign correspondent. She traveled to Rome, where she fell in love with and apparently married an Italian nobleman who was a follower of Giuseppe Mazzini. With him she participated in and wrote about the Italian revolutionary uprisings of 1848–1849. She, her husband, and their child drowned off the coast of Long Island in 1850, as she was returning home.

𝒲 argaret Fuller was born Sarah Margaret Fuller on May 23, 1810, in Cambridgeport, Massachusetts.

Melville appeared to take the editing (for which John did not charge him) in stride. "*Typee* has come out measurably unscathed from the fiery ordeal of Mr. Wiley's criticisms," he wrote Duyckinck. His sister, years later, reported a different response: Melville "was very cut up that in all later editions—all mention of Missionary's [sic] was omitted. He saw how much evil they were doing and thought it should be shown." Clearly, something soured, and when John turned down his next book, *Omoo: A Narrative of Adventures in the South Seas*, which was harsher yet on missionaries, Melville turned to the Harper brothers, who had originally dismissed *Typee* as a fiction. Melville remained on good terms with Duyckinck, though subsequently the two fell out for a time when Melville thought his friend failed properly to appreciate *Moby Dick,* as did every other critic, a blow from which Melville the writer never fully recovered.[62]

Typee was not the first text that John edited to appease religious readers. Margaret Fuller wrangled with John and Duyckinck over the content of her contribution to the Library of American Books, *Papers on Literature and Art*. Fuller, an early women's rights advocate, was an odd match indeed for John, and their relationship suggests John's readiness, to a degree, not to let personal religious convictions stand in the way of editorial judgments, at least when it came to the Library's mission to promote American literature.

Fuller was important, and John knew it. She offered a series of "conversations," or lectures, in Boston, from which emerged her women's rights manifesto, *Woman in the Nineteenth Century*, and she was the first editor of the Transcendentalist journal *The Dial*, all in the 1840s. A friend to prominent New England intellectuals, she probably also played a role in bringing Lydia Marie Child, Caroline Kirkland, and Lydia Sigourney, her friends and fellow activists, to Wiley. Horace Greeley hired Fuller at the New York *Tribune* as literary critic, and it was this work that found its way into Duyckinck's series in 1846—but not before Duyckinck instructed Fuller that "Mr. Wiley" would like her to omit "all other matters of a controversial character or likely to offend the religious public." John had probably seen Fuller's review of *Typee* in the *Tribune* in which she encouraged women who belonged to sewing societies which raised funds for missionaries to read the book

PROFILE

EDGAR ALLAN POE

Born in Boston to traveling stage actors in 1809, Poe was orphaned at age three and was raised by John and Frances Allan of Richmond. As a young man, he was something of a ne'er-do-well, dropping out of the University of Virginia and then the army, twice. His first book of poems, *Tamerlane* (1827), was not a success. In the mid-1830s, however, he became editor of the *Southern Literary Messenger*, and his reputation grew. Other editorships, such as a highly successful stint with *Graham's Magazine,* followed, as did book deals, including a London reprinting by Wiley & Putnam of his *Narrative of Arthur Gordon Pym.*

Poe was a poet, a journalist, and a master of the horror tale, and he is often credited with inventing the detective story. *The Raven*, published in the *New York Evening Mirror* in 1845 and reprinted the same year by Wiley & Putnam, brought him national attention. "The Murders in the Rue Morgue" and "The Purloined Letter" are among his most famous detective stories.

*E*dgar Allen Poe

In 1836, Poe married his 13-year-old cousin, Virginia Clemm. She became an invalid a few years later; after her death, his struggle with alcohol and drugs deepened. He suffered from depression, attempting suicide in 1848. He died in 1849 after a mysterious delirium that left him in a Baltimore gutter.

"and make inquiries in consequence, before going on with their efforts." In the end John cut Fuller's book from two volumes to one, and Fuller threatened to "publish an account of this transaction . . . to expose the restrictions upon mental freedom which threaten to check the progress of genius or of a religious sentiment worthy of God and man in this country."[63]

Wiley's relationship with Edgar Allan Poe could also be strained. In 1838 Wiley & Putnam reprinted Poe's *Narrative of Arthur Gordon Pym*, and the relationship continued in 1845 with two books in the American series—a selection of Poe's short stories, titled *Tales*,

and *The Raven and Other Poems*. Poe complained bitterly about Duyckinck's selections, however, describing them as not "fair play." Fair or not, the editor's judgment was probably better than the author's, and *Tales* sold 1,500 copies in just five months. Duyckinck had chosen "The Gold-Bug" and "The Fall of the House of Usher," which met immediate critical acclaim and remain classics today. "We could hardly introduce our friends to a more pleasant *compagnon du voyage*—or for that matter, *compagnon du shade*—than this volume," wrote one reviewer. Poe's poem *The Raven* was also an immediate commercial and critical success and one of the decade's

TALES

BY

EDGAR A. POE.

LONDON:
WILEY & PUTNAM, 6, WATERLOO PLACE.
——
1846.
[ENTERED AT STATIONERS' HALL.]

THE RAVEN AND OTHER POEMS.
————————

THE RAVEN.

Once upon a midnight dreary, while I pondered, weak and weary,
Over many a quaint and curious volume of forgotten lore,
While I nodded, nearly napping, suddenly there came a tapping,
As of some one gently rapping, rapping at my chamber door.
" 'Tis some visiter," I muttered, " tapping at my chamber door—
⠀⠀⠀⠀⠀⠀⠀⠀⠀⠀⠀⠀⠀⠀⠀Only this, and nothing more."

Ah, distinctly I remember it was in the bleak December,
And each separate dying ember wrought its ghost upon the floor.
Eagerly I wished the morrow ;—vainly I had sought to borrow
From my books surcease of sorrow—sorrow for the lost Lenore—
For the rare and radiant maiden whom the angels name Lenore—
⠀⠀⠀⠀⠀⠀⠀⠀⠀⠀⠀⠀⠀⠀⠀Nameless here for evermore.

And the silken sad uncertain rustling of each purple curtain
Thrilled me—filled me with fantastic terrors never felt before ;
So that now, to still the beating of my heart, I stood repeating
" 'Tis some visiter entreating entrance at my chamber door—
Some late visiter entreating entrance at my chamber door ;—
⠀⠀⠀⠀⠀⠀⠀⠀⠀⠀⠀⠀⠀⠀⠀This it is, and nothing more."

top sellers. Its opening lines—"Once upon a midnight dreary, while I pondered, weak and weary"—are among the most memorized in American verse.[64]

⠀⠀⠀Wiley & Putnam also tried, without great success, to become the publisher of choice for the New England Transcendentalists. Henry David Thoreau declined their offer to publish *A Week on the Concord and Merrimack Rivers* at the author's risk. Finally published by a consortium of Boston, New York, Philadelphia, and London publishers in 1849, the book sold fewer than 300 of the 1,000 copies printed, prompting Thoreau to write in his journal that he had a library

of 900 books, 700 of which he wrote himself. Ralph Waldo Emerson also turned the company down despite Duyckinck's practiced flattery, the series' solid reputation, and the appeal of New York as a place of publication, not to mention a royalty of 20 percent. "You make me a very liberal offer," Emerson told Duyckinck, "yet it does not in fact promise me the advantage I had expected."[65]

⠀⠀⠀Disappointments aside, Wiley & Putnam had much to be proud of. Charles Wiley had helped launch the careers of Washington Irving and James Fenimore Cooper, the first generation of American writers. His son's firm had done the same for the next. The firm's letterhead proclaimed: "English, French, German and American Publications In Every Department of Literature. Particularly Theology, the Classics, the Arts and Sciences, History, Biography &c. Choice Editions of Standard Authors. Public Libraries and the Trade supplied on the best terms. Foreign Books Imported for Universities and Private Libraries free of Duty." Far from niches, this list implied a broad net. Owing to the efforts of John and Duyckinck in New York and Putnam in London, Wiley & Putnam had become one of the most well-connected publishing firms in America. Editor John O'Sullivan and poet James Russell Lowell served as its quasi-acquisition editors, soliciting authors for manuscripts. None other than Emerson himself had served as a go-between for the firm with Carlyle. Similarly, the eminent British geologist Charles Lyell linked Wiley to the world of science. Lyell's *Travels in North America*, published by Wiley in 1845, rendered a refreshingly unbiased, even scientific, view of the nation.[66]

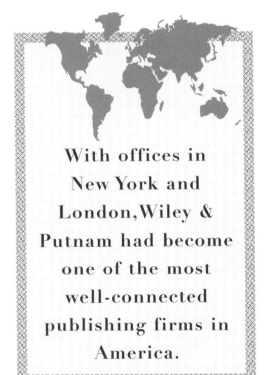

With offices in New York and London, Wiley & Putnam had become one of the most well-connected publishing firms in America.

Clearly, Wiley & Putnam was an outstanding critical success, its two Library series "far-famed." Even *Maga* took notice. But the series' moment atop the U.S. publishing scene would be short-lived. In September 1846, though he remained a Wiley & Putnam investor, Duyckinck left the editorship of the two libraries to edit *Literary World*, a joint Wiley–Appleton weekly newsletter that kept him in close contact with the firm into 1847 as the final titles in his two series appeared. Why then did Wiley & Putnam shutter the series?[67]

One problem was that Duyckinck, the ostensible Democrat, cared more about quality than quantity and held an undeniably elitist understanding of the book market. His books were superb in every way but sold too few copies to turn a profit on very thin margins. The two libraries got the craft side of publishing as right as they got the business side wrong. Another problem was that some Americans bristled at the shrill nationalist views of Young Americans like Duyckinck and his fellow Columbia alumnus (and Wiley author) Cornelius Mathews, a young New York attorney nicknamed "The Centurion." Mathews' rhetoric in particular was abrasive and divisive. What John and Putnam thought of Mathews is not known. John and Putnam may have grown wary of the fire that Duyckinck and the other Young Americans began to attract. *The North American Review* in Boston and the Young Americans' nemesis, the *Knickerbocker* in New York, began ridiculing them, the latter calling them the "Mutual Admiration Society" because they usually reviewed each others' books favorably. The *North American* showed less mercy, denouncing Duyckinck and his followers as "would-be men of letters, noisy authorlings, and noisy in proportion to their diminutive size."[68]

The company's advertising efforts certainly were not to blame for the demise of the series. By the early 1840s, Wiley was marketing its lists with the annual publication and distribution of a substantial and informative catalog and with a monthly newsletter. The catalogs were well thought out. The 1845 edition not only listed titles but also provided their tables of contents, pre-publication blurbs, and snippets from reviews. "Lively, entertaining

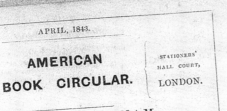

and instructive," *The Atlas* called Daniel Kidder's *Empire of Brazil*. "A work of rare interest and value," the *New York Courier* added. When reviews were not available, the catalog tried a fine line between description and promotion. For example, it called *The Art of Weaving* "altogether the most complete work on the subject ever published." The catalog offered detailed coverage of Putnam's own book, *American Facts*, including a review by Duyckinck from the *Democratic Review*.

Nor do the two series appear to have spread the company too thin, for innovations in other areas continued. In 1847, for instance, John made efforts to tap the education market, unveiling a "District School Library priced at $10." In the end, the firm's two ground-breaking series faltered because they were premature; America's legal environment did not yet support such ambitious endeavors.[70]

The Fight for International Copyright

The root problem for the demise of The Library of Choice Reading and The Library of American Books series was external to the company: The key legal infrastructure essential for the healthy development of American literature was not in place and would not be for a long time to come. In Abraham Lincoln's words, copyrights, like patents, provided "the fuel of interest to the fire of genius." America did not have, but badly needed, an international copyright law. John was keenly interested in copyright and with his partner Putnam was a leading advocate of international copyright reform. Their company was involved in the international copyright debate on several levels. Putnam and Duyckinck were among the earliest advocates, and the company published two of Cornelius Mathews's books on the subject, though Mathews' extreme views probably alienated as many as they convinced.[71]

Wiley published another more persuasive writer, Francis Lieber, a Prussian émigré who taught

In an era in which reviews could make or break a book's success, Wiley's 1843 catalog was actually reviewed. It is "unquestionably the most convenient one we have ever met with," proclaimed *Brother Jonathan: A Weekly Compend of Belles Lettres and the Fine Arts*, "and will be an excellent guide" for purchasers because "the works are admirably arranged under appropriate heads, classified in subjects, with the prices affixed."[69]

history and political economy at South Carolina College in Charleston. Lieber had arrived in the United States in 1827 and immersed himself in the editorship of the *Encyclopedia Americana*, which put his name before America's intelligentsia. His cogent analyses attracted the attention of Supreme Court Justice Joseph Story (1779–1845), arguably America's most important jurist after the death of John Marshall in 1835. Deeply

interested in international jurisprudence, Lieber drew up notes for Senator Robert Preston of South Carolina to use in congressional debates on the copyright issue, and though they arrived too late for the purpose he published them through Wiley & Putnam in pamphlet form at his own risk and expense. Appearing in 1840, Lieber's *On International Copyright* crystallized arguments in favor of reform.[72]

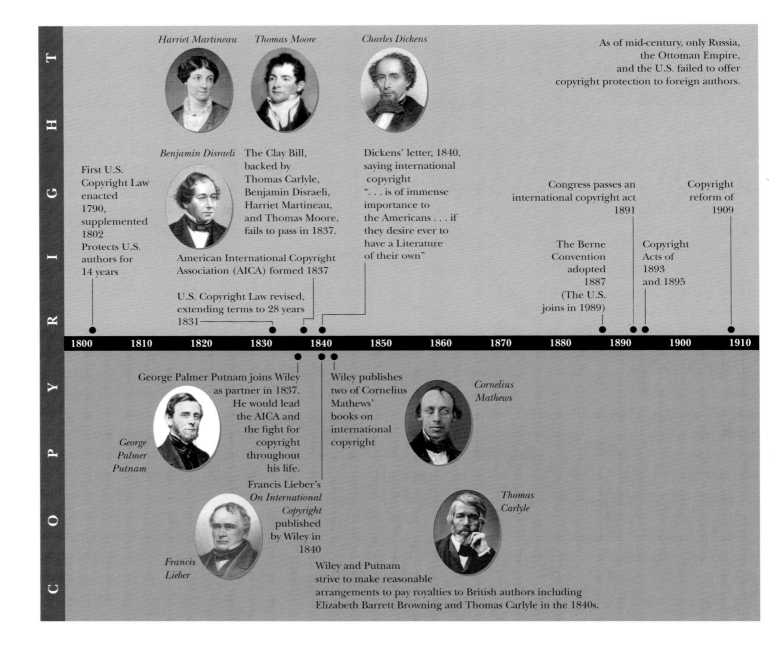

COPYRIGHT

Harriet Martineau *Thomas Moore* *Charles Dickens*

As of mid-century, only Russia, the Ottoman Empire, and the U.S. failed to offer copyright protection to foreign authors.

Benjamin Disraeli

First U.S. Copyright Law enacted 1790, supplemented 1802 Protects U.S. authors for 14 years

The Clay Bill, backed by Thomas Carlyle, Benjamin Disraeli, Harriet Martineau, and Thomas Moore, fails to pass in 1837.

American International Copyright Association (AICA) formed 1837

U.S. Copyright Law revised, extending terms to 28 years 1831

Dickens' letter, 1840, saying international copyright ". . . is of immense importance to the Americans . . . if they desire ever to have a Literature of their own"

Congress passes an international copyright act 1891

The Berne Convention adopted 1887 (The U.S. joins in 1989)

Copyright Acts of 1893 and 1895

Copyright reform of 1909

1800 1810 1820 1830 1840 1850 1860 1870 1880 1890 1900 1910

George Palmer Putnam joins Wiley as partner in 1837. He would lead the AICA and the fight for copyright throughout his life.

George Palmer Putnam

Wiley publishes two of Cornelius Mathews' books on international copyright

Cornelius Mathews

Francis Lieber's *On International Copyright* published by Wiley in 1840

Francis Lieber

Thomas Carlyle

Wiley and Putnam strive to make reasonable arrangements to pay royalties to British authors including Elizabeth Barrett Browning and Thomas Carlyle in the 1840s.

Literary property, Lieber contended, was a Lockean natural right, not the gift of government. It was in fact the purest form of property because it emanated solely from the mind of its creator, but paradoxically it was one of the easiest types of property to steal because the author/owner could not possibly monitor it. The physical book and the words expressed in it were distinct and separate. So an owner of a book could do what he wanted with his particular copy—burn it, give it away, mark it up—anything but copy it. Though widely reviewed, the pamphlet had no discernible effect on policymakers. Lieber was in good company here, as Charles Dickens, arguably the most important English-language novelist of the nineteenth century, also failed to change American policy, despite concerted efforts.[73]

As it then existed, U.S. copyright law effectively prevented American publishers only from stealing the work of American authors. In February 1831, Congress overhauled the basic law, enacted in May 1790 and supplemented in 1802. The new version extended initial copyright from 14 to 28 years. In addition, though like the original law it limited the optional extension to 14 years, the new law extended the privilege of extension to an author's heirs. The new act remained in force until July 1870.[74]

Like the original, the new law, which had been shepherded through Congress by Wiley author and congressman Gulian C. Verplanck, did not afford any copyright protection for foreign authors. Foreign books, in other words, remained fair game. Without fear of criminal or civil prosecution, American publishers could appropriate any foreign work without receiving permission from, or making payments to, the original author or publisher. At mid-century, of the world's major nations,

only Russia, the Ottoman Empire, and the United States failed to protect foreign authors.[75]

Protectionists, neo-mercantilists, and nativists—people who put America and its products and interests first—might support such legislation because it appeared to aid the United States, but this appearance was deceptive. In fact, the arrangement pitted book manufacturers and readers against American authors. It also split the publishing industry in two and for a time even split the New York literary community.

The failure of U.S. copyright law to protect the interests of foreign authors hindered the development of American literature in two ways. The British reciprocated and afforded no reliable copyright protection to American authors. (Although Great Britain began the process of reciprocal relationships with other countries in the 1840s, it had no agreement with the United States.) By one estimate, British publishers appropriated some 600 American titles between 1800 and 1836. Between 1841 and 1846 alone, British publishers reprinted 382 American books. About one in every dozen new titles offered for sale in Edinburgh or London in the antebellum period was American in origin. Most of the American authors of those books received, in Putnam's words, not "a farthing" for their work.[76]

The biggest losses for American authors, though, came at home. The business logic was impeccable if perverse. Why publish unproven new works by American authors who had to be paid when market-tested British titles could be reprinted and their authors paid nothing? Many American firms took the easy course by specializing in reprinting British works. Reprinting was easy only up to a point, however. As

> The failure of U.S. copyright law to protect the interests of foreign authors hindered the development of American literature.

competition intensified, prices fell and profits dwindled. Being first to pirate a book conferred transient advantage at best, as new editions of the same works by other reprint specialists promptly came to market often only a few days, or even hours, later. The cost of buying or stealing proof sheets from British printers, or running multiple print shops throughout the night, to gain such a slight advantage ate away the incentives of all but the most efficient reprinters.[77]

By the 1830s and 1840s, pirating had reached such absurd heights that some publishers began to sense they might be better off paying royalties if they could enjoy the same monopoly on publishing that they did with domestic works. They joined with American authors to agitate for the United States to join the growing list of nations that protected foreign authors. Others—those most efficient in the pirating game—demurred, as did printers, compositors, pressmen, binders, papermakers, and everyone else who made a living by physically manufacturing books. Readers eager for good but inexpensive books also saw little reason to support international copyright protection.[78]

The first serious movement for international copyright protection in the United States came, interestingly enough, from 56 eminent British authors, including Thomas Carlyle, Benjamin Disraeli, Harriet Martineau, and Thomas Moore. Sponsored by Senator Henry Clay and Congressman Churchill Cambreleng in February 1837, their bill died in the House. The Senate moved ahead with another bill that would have extended the Copyright Act of 1831 to include works by British, Irish, and French authors. To appease book manufacturing interests, the bill gave protection only to books physically

Copyright proponents argued that American publishers, readers, and authors stood to benefit.

manufactured in America, not to those imported from abroad. Despite the vigorous support of a small group of authors, intellectuals, and a few publishers, the Senate bill, too, failed to pass. Out of the effort, however, was born the American International Copyright Association (AICA). From its formation in 1837 until his death in 1872, Putnam led every major international copyright movement mounted in the United States.[79]

Supporters of international copyright appealed to nationalism, arguing that an international copyright law would aid American authors financially and thereby strengthen American cultural and literary independence. Intense competition from foreign authors kept remuneration for American authors at a bare minimum, and with rare exceptions like Irving, Cooper, and Longfellow, American authors could not live by writing alone. Because they had to take other jobs, they wrote less than they otherwise would have, or less well.[80]

Proponents of reform also argued that American publishers and readers, not just authors, stood to benefit. Publishers would benefit from the end of cutthroat competition among pirates. Readers would benefit from higher quality and greater value in the books they bought: no more productions hastily thrown together by pirates driven to beat other pirates to market, no more mutilated texts—a common practice that shaved costs and supposedly made foreign works more palatable to domestic readers—no more strange hybrids of Thackeray and Dickens.[81]

Opponents of reform contended that copyright was a statutory, not a natural, right, which rendered the central issue merely political, not moral. Even domestic copyright extended only to language or the mere "clothing" of books; facts and ideas, or the "body" of writings, were, upon publication, "the common property of all mankind." Many books took liberally from that common stock of knowledge and only added value in the packaging, in the style of the clothes. Philadelphia publisher Henry C. Carey went so far as to argue that "the whole tendency of the existing system is to give the largest reward to those whose labors are lightest, and the smallest to those whose labors are most severe."[82]

> Authorship, . . . opponents said, was a form of public service, not a means to wealth.

Authorship, properly understood, opponents said, was a form of public service, not a means to wealth. True scholars labored for long years with little or no remuneration. Those who sought international copyright essentially stole from those hardworking scholars by popularizing their ideas and discoveries for a mass audience. Copyright was a form of "literary monopoly," a tool used by self-aggrandizing authors to raise prices at the expense of the reading public. Republication ought to be seen as an honor that often led to substantial subsidiary revenue streams, like lecture fees. Text mutilation was rare, the opponents continued, and was punished by the market.[83]

Opponents protested vehemently the alleged devastating impact of international copyright on the American book trades. Reform would throw tens of thousands of laborers out of work, they claimed, many of them women and children, and it threatened capital. "In the Manufacture of Books in this country there is now employed a capital of probably thirty millions or more of dollars in the various departments of Paper-making,

Paper-dealing, Printing, Bookbinding, Stereotyping, Bookselling, Newspaper and Periodical publishing, and collateral branches," an 1837 petition claimed. That capital had been invested with the expectation that the United States would not adopt an international copyright law. To change the rules in midstream would heap uncertainty onto injustice and drive investors from the industry.[84]

For more than fifty years the debate continued, sometimes hot and sometimes cold but always along lines so well worn that reprints of old pamphlets were brought out for each new round. The reformers failed to catch the attention of legislators increasingly embroiled in the prolonged recession that began in 1837, then in westward expansion and the Oregon question, then war with Mexico and, above all, the slavery issue. Addicted to cheap books, Americans bought the opponents' arguments. Meanwhile, the reformers deluded themselves that "the conviction is rapidly growing and spreading itself through this country, that its literature is not, has not been Equal to its wants nor its desire." But few really cared. When it came to fiction, at least, cheap books seemed more important than American books.[85]

Attempts to secure a more modest goal, a reciprocity treaty with Britain (a favored cause of Dickens), also failed, in large measure owing to the diligence of Carey and his friends in Washington. Not until 1891 did Congress pass an international copyright act, and then only a weak one at the last minute. The United States did not join the much more stringent Berne Convention of 1887 and would not do so for another century.[86]

Shift and Split

Although law and economics conspired to dampen the profitability of publishing American fiction, as John gradually recognized, other valuable niches still existed. The absence of international copyright protection did not destroy American authorship completely. In 1830, about 60 percent of books published in the United States were of British origin and 40 percent were American. Between that year and 1842, the percentages reversed. In 1853, when 733 books were published in the United States, 420 were original American works and only 278 were reprints of English books (the other 35 were translations of foreign language texts). Other estimates give higher totals but similar proportions. American publishers also appropriated Spanish, German, and French books but, interestingly enough, mostly for export to foreign markets.[87]

> As Putnam slowly proved, it was possible to build a publishing empire based on American literature, but the task was long and not immediately profitable.

Given the lack of an international copyright agreement, why did antebellum U.S. publishers still print more books by American than British authors? The answer lies in the kinds of books published. Aside from light literature, especially fiction, the international copyright issue did not matter much. Most British books found no market in America at all, nor did British authors cater to the U.S. book market. They generally did not write about U.S. history, geography, geology, and a host of other subjects, so there was nothing British to reprint. Second, books for specialized or small markets were not worth reprinting. With high fixed costs to overcome, they were more cheaply imported than reprinted, especially if nothing prevented a second pirate from entering the market. Despite occasional agitation to raise tariffs on imported books, duties stayed relatively low and did little to protect U.S. printers. To keep prices low, books could be imported "in sheets," that is, unbound and on cheaper paper, if so desired. Increasingly fast, reliable, and cheap transatlantic shipping made importing even more economical. So while Wiley found little profit in importing *Maga* or popular novels, importing specialized books did pay. According to one observer in 1844, the "main business" of "numerous houses in New-York, Philadelphia and Boston" was "the importation of foreign books."[88]

British publishers likewise found it unprofitable to pirate small-market books, which meant the playing field was relatively level. A one-of-a-kind or otherwise exceptional scientific or technical book could win both markets; a competitive one was likely to own the home

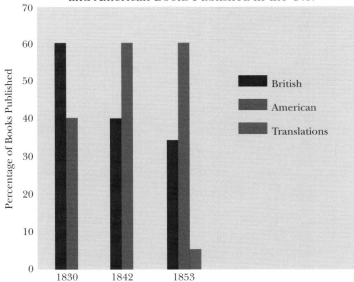

Changes in the Proportion of British and American Books Published in the U.S.

market. As one British observer noted in 1844, "There are many scientific works which are never republished here, which are more essential than all the narratives and poems that England has produced for the last century." Little wonder, then, at the common observation that American scientific and technical works were far advanced over American fiction.[89]

Such were the economic realities behind Wiley's shift, under John, toward the technical, scientific, nonfiction side of the market. Probably with frustration and regret, John saw how copyright failure crippled his beloved cause of American literature. He also understood that America offered Wiley bigger opportunities. Industrialization, urbanization, and the fever of technology-fueled economic growth were sparking demand for scientific and technical books of all sorts. The appeal of fiction was subjective and notoriously tricky to judge: What makes readers prefer one novel over another? Calculating the appeal of scientific and technical literature was simpler: What was it that people needed to know?[90]

Wiley's business soon shifted in another way, too. The London branch, at best only moderately successful, began causing tension between the two partners. John was "a clear-headed and shrewd business man," Putnam's son later recalled, and worried about the London operation, particularly Putnam's expense accounts. Moreover, Putnam was eager to return to New York and start out on his own. In March 1848, the partnership formally dissolved. Putnam's son later lamented the breakup with a memorable backhanded *bon mot*: "Every well-organized publishing office needs in its direction at least one persistent pessimist." That would be John.[91]

> As John predicted, American nonfiction, especially of a technical turn, grew strong indeed.

John and Putnam had not made a bad pair, however, and on some important publishing matters the two were nicely matched. Both believed in quality over quantity. "Be ambitious about the quality rather than the quantity of your publications," Putnam told young publishers in 1863, "remembering that two or three well-considered, thorough, and permanent works of high character, and suited to the market, are a better investment, and are better for the community, than fifty tame or indifferent volumes, which will bring neither reputation, usefulness, nor profit." Both partners also believed, again in Putnam's words, that publishers should "study independence of the world financially as far as practicable; avoid entanglements with responsibilities of others; don't spend all your profits on the brokers and note-shavers of Wall Street; and don't spend your money in any way faster than you make it."[92]

The partnership ended amicably. John kept the shop at 161 Broadway, the London office, and the rights to the nonfiction titles, while Putnam opened a shop three doors south, at 155 Broadway, and took on the fiction. So Putnam got Cooper and Irving, though in an exception John held on to Dickens (he put out *David Copperfield* in "an elegant form"). Ultimately, both men succeeded in their own ways. As Putnam slowly proved, it was possible to build a publishing empire based on American literature, but the task was long and not immediately profitable. Unprotected from British titles, American fiction languished until the end of the century, as pirates continued to infest the trade. And as John predicted, American nonfiction, especially of a scientific and technical turn, grew strong indeed. Others, including David Van Nostrand,

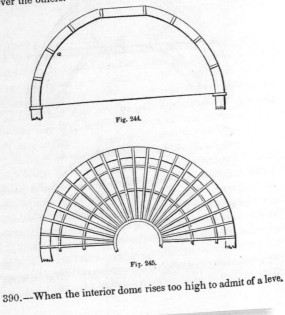

the tie-beam in both. Two trusses of this kind, (*Fig.* 242,) parallel to each other, are to be placed one on each side of the opening in the top of the dome. Upon these the whole framework is to depend for support, and their strength must be calculated accordingly. (See the first part of this section, and *Art.* 356.) If the dome is large and of importance, two other trusses may be introduced at right angles to the foregoing, the tie-beams being preserved in one continuous length by framing them high enough to pass over the others.

Fig. 244.

Fig. 245.

390.—When the interior dome rises too high to admit of a level.

ne of Wiley's successful titles was R. G. Hatfield's *American House Carpenter*, first published by Wiley & Putnam in 1844 but reprinted by Wiley in 1850, 1852, and numerous times thereafter. The book commanded its field, its prose the epitome of "simple clearness" and with "300 very good wood engravings." This type of book—practical knowledge packaged for a specific audience—would soon become a Wiley mainstay.[93]

who started a bookselling and publishing firm in New York in 1848, came to the same conclusion at about the same time.[94]

Post-Putnam Wiley had about it the air of a good but not exactly top-line effort. Something was missing. In March 1850, Cooper informed his wife that "Wiley has failed." It was said that Putnam's rivalry hurt him badly. Cooper was wrong, and rumors of Wiley's business death were once again exaggerated. But John's

decision to move his residence, though not his business, to East Orange, New Jersey, in 1851 may have been prompted in part by financial considerations. John managed to keep the company together by concentrating on reprints of tested titles and new material by established authors. *Scientific American* noted in 1850 that John was at work on a construction-architecture list, with R. G. Hatfield's elementary text backed by a reprint of George Wightwick's more advanced treatise, *Hints to Young Architects*, bolstered by a chapter from Andrew Jackson Downing, "a name well known in our country."

John also worked hard on his import and domestic bookselling businesses, retailing and wholesaling far more titles than he published. When still in partnership with Putnam, he had invested heavily in the bookselling side of the business. He had physically reorganized the retail portion of the company's New York store, arranging its books alphabetically within broad subject headings including Science; Natural History; Useful and Fine Arts; History, Biography, and General Literature; Greek and Latin Classics; Philology; Theological Literature; and Medical Literature. To extend its reach into the hinterland, Wiley & Putnam teamed up with W. C. Little of Albany and other local booksellers and established a new wholesale department located on John Street. It also expanded its international business, offering for sale at cut rates in 1847 an extensive "List of English Books" that ranged from Thomas Haines Bailey's comedic *Weeds of Witches* to Thomas Croker's *Popular Songs of Ireland* to Francis Kugler's *Hand Book of the History of Painting* to the anonymous how-to *Hints on Husband Catching, or, A Manual for Marriageable Misses*. "Having established a regular correspondence with the principal booksellers in London, Oxford, Birmingham, Manchester, Edinburgh, Glasgow, Paris, Leipzig, and Brussels," the company boasted, "W&P are now prepared to execute orders for British, French, and German publications, on the most favorable terms."[95]

In the 1850s, John continued to position himself as a major international book merchant, advertising in the *New York Times* that he offered a full range of English and French titles plus Bibles and other religious books, "by the single copy or in quantity." He made two buying trips to England and promised to supply to city or country booksellers on cash or credit the books of leading publishing houses, including Blanchard & Lea, H. C. Baird, Lippincott, Ticknor, Derby & Miller, D. Appleton, Harper & Brothers, and his erstwhile partner G. P. Putnam. John also engaged in the resale of "Old, Rare, and Curious Books" in sundry foreign languages and "Galleries of Engravings, English and French." Violins, stationery, and stereoscopes reflected additional diversification. By 1855, his letterhead ran the gamut: books and periodicals for the trade, for public and school libraries, and for private collectors, catalogs furnished gratis.

In October 1855, John sent a printed circular letter to publishing-industry leaders, soliciting both advice and subscribers and broaching ideas for a book fair. Ironically, the week-long fairs to be held in Philadelphia, Boston, and New York were supposed to replace the trade-sales system that his father Charles had helped to establish almost exactly thirty years earlier. One innovation was that the new system would use posted prices rather than auctions, and publishers would commit to selling a minimum number of copies if demand for each title proved sufficient at the posted price. Another change was that publishers at the fair promised not to sell on more favorable terms to non-attendees within six months of the fair's close. John thought the fair idea would help bookmen forge more personal relationships in an industry that was becoming increasingly large and geographically dispersed. He hoped the

John Wiley, in his barely legible hand, corresponded with Henry C. Carey about books sent to Liverpool and returned. John started out in publishing selling books in New York for Carey's father, Mathew, the Philadelphia publisher who worked and competed with John's father. In 1855 publishing was still a business characterized by lasting relationships among a relatively small number of people.

system would also help publishers to support their price points by avoiding auctions, where *"sacrifices* in consequence of sales *at an untimely hour"* were frequent. And he thought the fairs a way to save on commissions and other expenses. John's motivation here is unclear. According to the *Monthly Trade Gazette*, the 1855 trade auctions in New York had been "gratifying" and even "increasingly useful."[96]

Despite a change in family residence, Wiley remained firmly rooted in New York. As the booming metropolis spread northward, subsuming Greenwich Village and streaming toward present-day midtown, the city's publishers leapfrogged with it. Wiley migrated ever northward up Broadway with the rest, relocations made easier by the fact that publishers and booksellers almost always leased rather than owned their shops. The size of Wiley's bookstore in this period is not known, but some stores were sizeable. In 1863, Leggat Brothers advertised that it owned almost 130,000 titles. Judging the size of the two bookstores by their purchases from

Wiley & Putnam began to publish the works of German chemist Justus von Liebig in 1841 introducing American farmers to scientific agriculture, which encouraged the use of chemical fertilizers. Liebig's laboratory at the University of Giessen in Germany was an early teaching institution. Many American chemists were trained in Germany, and the teaching of chemistry in Germany, as with engineering and architecture in France, had a major impact on the teaching of chemistry in the United States.[97]

Boston's Ticknor & Fields, Wiley's bookstore was quite a bit smaller. Yet Wiley was bigger than most of the stores the Boston publisher deemed worthy of credit. Clearly, Wiley was nothing like the multitude of petty booksellers peddling "decayed school books" and "a cheap line of soiled novels." One contemporary source juxtaposed such dingy outfits with "the splendid Broadway importations of those choice antiquarian bookstores, of Wiley and Putnam, and Bartlett and Welford." [98]

In January 1856, John took as partner a distant relative, Robert Halsted, and began publishing a monthly newsletter. The partnership did not change the basic nature of the business but it did allow John to travel to London in May of that year. It also may have allowed for the publication of more titles. The publication program remained small, however, in quantitative terms. The types of books that Wiley published through the 1850s indicated John's strengthened focus on useful knowledge. Works by Mahan (*Industrial Drawing*, 1852) and Downing (*The Fruits and Fruit Trees of America*, 1856; *Hints to Persons About Building in the Country*, 1859; *Landscape Gardening*, 1859) remained solid. New titles like *Elements of Electro-metallurgy* (1852), *On the Application of Cast and Wrought Iron to Building Purposes* (1854), and *Principles of Agricultural Chemistry* (1855) suggested the emerging specialization of knowledge and how Wiley would cater to it. John Blyth's translation of Justus von Liebig's *Letters on Modern Agriculture* (1859) was a good example, as it foreshadowed Wiley's increasing interest in science and technology, which would lead after the 1996 acquisition of Verlag Chemie (VCH), a leading German chemistry publisher, to Wiley becoming one of the largest chemistry publishers in the world. All these publications shared simple guidelines, however, which must have

come from John: to be compendious, clear, practical, and complete. [99]

The partnership with Halsted ended in March 1859 when John bought out Halsted's interest and advertised that he would "continue the Bookselling, Publishing, and Importing business as heretofore." He also began promoting himself as a textbook publisher and wholesaler and retailer of books and stereoscopic pictures in the leading trade journal, *American Publishers' Circular and Literary Gazette*. That same year, Wiley reprinted David Stevenson's *Sketch of the Civil Engineering of North America*, of which a reviewer wrote: "I think the matter exceedingly well arranged and the subject so clear and popular . . . as to make it interesting even to me who know nothing about it." [100]

In 1865, John's eldest son, Charles, began working for the firm. Neither the coming of the younger generation nor the coming of the Civil War much energized the publishing program, however. It remained small, though consistent with the 1850s' turn toward useful knowledge, as in John S. Hittell's *Mining in the Pacific States* (1862) and Zerah Colburn and D. K. Clark's *Locomotive Engineering* (1864). Except for two titles by Mahan on guard outposts and military engineering, Wiley published no war-related titles, while competitors like Van Nostrand squeezed profit from every wartime opportunity.

John survived the war by another twenty-five years, but in 1865 his company, though solvent, looked stagnant, more likely past its prime than still waiting to flourish. Total profits must have been far less than those of Ticknor & Fields, which netted just shy of $173,000 between 1843 and 1863. John had laid the foundations, but if the House of Wiley was to rise further it would require editorial and business expansion. [101]

> **John had laid the foundations.**

Thomas Alva Edison's lab in Menlo Park, New Jersey (founded in 1876), was devoted to the invention of useful and profitable devices and machines, ranging from the light bulb to mining equipment to the phonograph.

And Sons: Transition to Modern Publishing 1865–1925

Chapter Four

✸

Wiley and Edison at Menlo Park

Wiley the publisher grew up, found its legs, in the Gilded Age. That was how Mark Twain (not, alas, a Wiley author) dubbed the first post–Civil War decades in America, that time when prodigious—rapacious, some said—energies transformed an agrarian republic into the world's premier industrial power. Historian Vernon Parrington captured the spirit of the times with the phrase "The Great Barbecue," where genuine entrepreneurs and brazen con men, often one and the same, created, conjured, or stole unheard-of economic wealth. Matthew Josephson famously called them "Robber Barons." Allan Nevins preferred "Captains of Industry." Whatever one's perspective, the facts were much the same. Incomes rose. Injustice flourished. The nation chewed up the western frontier and with it the native peoples who lived there. The South remained the nation's poor stepchild; its immense population of former slaves little better off than Russian serfs. Railroads ran everywhere. The steel mills of Pittsburgh and Chicago eclipsed those in the British Midlands and the Ruhr area of Germany. Cities grew dense, polluted, enticing.

The "Second Industrial Revolution" is how economists and historians describe this same period of time, to distinguish it from the "first" one, which they think of as a largely eighteenth-century affair, centered in England and driven by textile mills.

coal mines, and steam engines. The second had technology at its heart, too, but was bigger and moved faster. The timing of two technologies illustrates the difference between these two revolutions. Railroads, invented toward the end of the first industrial revolution, climaxed with the second and then soon declined. Electricity, experimented with by the Franklins and Faradays of the eighteenth century, found no economic application at all until late in the nineteenth century. Indeed, the full impact of electricity, both as a source of energy and as a tool for communication, would wait until the twentieth.

Business success rests in part on a sensitive nose: how to discern markets early and then organize to serve them. The Wileys in the Gilded Age proved they had nose. Under John's sons Charles and William H., the company left the publishing of literary art largely to others and fixed its future on publishing useful knowledge: things that people needed to know in order to get on in life and to teach others how to get on in theirs. There was precedent here. Wiley had published scientific and technical works before the Civil War. After the war, Wiley would focus on science and technology. In the context of the Second Industrial Revolution, useful knowledge increasingly meant knowledge of technology. It was a seller's market, where demand far outpaced supply. Technology subjects abounded, and publishers had to scramble to find authors who understood and could write about them.

No name quite summons the spirit of the era like Thomas Edison, the "Wizard of Menlo Park" and a friend of the Wileys. Menlo Park was a whistle-stop in then-rural New Jersey until Edison built his laboratory there in 1876, devoted to the invention of useful and

Thomas Alva Edison, 1877.

profitable devices and machines ranging from the light bulb to mining equipment. Unlike the Smithsonian Institution, which was dedicated to pure science, Edison's lab was all about applied science and technology. Its relation to the great corporate industrial laboratories of the twentieth century was only loosely transitional; Alexander Graham Bell can be better described as father of what we think of as the modern research lab. Nevertheless, the fecundity of the place fixed it at the very center of Americans' enduring romance with invention and inventors. Henry Ford, it was said, sifted the ground outside where Edison tossed the refuse of his experiments, searching for relics.

Though Edison moved his lab to another location after five years, Menlo Park was where the facts and the legends of Edison the Inventor all were established. There the tousled-headed figure with the air of a mere mechanic, then in his early forties but still looking like an overgrown schoolboy, nursed the triumphs that made him famous: the telephone, the phonograph, and the incandescent light. Edison hated to share glory and didn't really need to. Alexander Graham Bell indeed may have invented the telephone, at least according to the patents, but it was the forever self-promoting Edison who sparked the industry based upon it. Edison's successful search for a system of practical electrical lighting sparked another, after predecessors like Sir Humphrey Davy, who had demonstrated arc lighting in 1801, and Michael Faraday, who built the first dynamo, had reached their own dead ends. With the phonograph, Edison had no precursors at all, experimenting first with a diaphragm attached to a stylus and a revolving foil-covered cylinder. Mother Goose's "Mary Had a Little Lamb" were the words he first recorded, an ironic triumph in sound for a man who was himself largely deaf. For all his hayseed/wizard image, Edison was emphatically not deaf to the ways of big businesses that drove the Second Industrial Revolution. He kept company with the A-list of robber barons and captains of industry of the age: Jay Gould, J. Pierpont Morgan, Henry Ford.

The Wileys moved, albeit less eccentrically, in the same knowledge world as Edison, and as the nineteenth century moved toward its close they firmly affixed their publishing fortunes to this world. For the Gilded Age was also an age of professionalization, where the skilled and the educated organized societies to promote and develop their disciplines. Many of these societies launched their own journals, and universities vied to sponsor them. A handful of societies, such as the American Chemical Society (founded in 1875), would become significant publishers in their own right. Oddly, while Europeans continued their long tradition of society publishing, Wiley eschewed journal publishing until after World War II. William Halsted Wiley, the "Major" for his service in the Civil War, joined the company in 1876, the year of America's centennial and the same year Edison set up shop in Menlo Park. He had a degree in civil engineering from Rensselaer Polytechnic Institute, had attended the Columbia University School of Mines, and for the rest of his career (he died in 1925) cultivated a vast network of contacts in the engineering world for the purpose of acquiring technical manuscripts for Wiley. He was a founding member of the American Society of Mechanical Engineers and a member of several other engineering societies, and he served as agent and correspondent for the London-based journal Engineering. The Major's connections brought books to Wiley, and enough influence to himself to be elected to a seat in the U.S. House of Representatives early in the twentieth century.

Wiley's direct connection with Edison came through the Major's brother Osgood, who also worked for the family firm, briefly. Osgood's chief passion was electricity. He spent the first years of his career at Western Union, and then, after repeated requests to

Osgood Wiley, 1855–1903. Osgood, who once described his occupation as electrician, was John's youngest son. He worked for a while at Wiley, but then secured a job with Thomas Edison in 1888. He was fired in a dispute over his expenses. Osgood found electrical engineering work at some big New York electrical companies and managed a power plant in New Jersey. He died at age 48 after a year-long illness.

join Edison, Edison finally relented and hired him in 1888. The Major, who was well known to Edison, had his own interest in the inventor: He longed for a manuscript. Though no book ever materialized, Edison did publish, via the Major, an article in Engineering, which also ran the Major's description of Edison's operation at Menlo Park. Edison dispatched Osgood on a mission to London to promote one of the Wizard's less than stellar inventions, an ore separator and milling machine. Osgood took it on for a share of the royalties, if there were any. There weren't. There were expenses, though, which the younger Wiley seems to have abused—for which Edison promptly sacked him. Edison was deaf to the Major's pleas to give his brother a second chance, and Osgood never worked for Edison, or for Wiley, again. When he died young, he was running a power plant in New Jersey.

Edison did not hold the Osgood episode against the Major, whom he recommended glowingly for the position of Commissioner General of the United States at the Paris International Exposition of 1900. Edison outlived the Major by six years, but their lives had intersected at a critical point. Edison, and thousands and thousands of lesser Edisons, vastly increased the supply of useful knowledge about how things worked and what people needed to know to make them work: an enduring American enthusiasm. This stimulated other equally creative types like the Wileys, who had a nose for markets and who mediated supply and demand to build enduring knowledge businesses.

The timbers needed to build the House of Wiley arrived in due time, in the form of smart and sturdy sons whom John lived long enough to see grow to maturity and become valuable business partners. In 1865, John's eldest son, Charles (1835–1916), joined him in partnership with a 25 percent stake in the firm. The company now styled itself "John Wiley & Son." Charles took the title of vice president and treasurer and was to concentrate on sales and finance. He drew $30 per week plus allowances for coal and commuting.[1]

John certainly needed the help. The publishing industry continued growing at breakneck speed, especially in Manhattan. The Wileys may have lived in New Jersey, but they knew that New York was the place for their business. They had not yet quite worked out all the balances, however. Wiley's publishing program was impressive in

Writer and poet Sarah King Wiley, only daughter of William Halsted Wiley (the Major) and his wife Joanna Clark. In 1893, Wiley published *The Yosemite, Alaska, and the Yellowstone*, a "beautifully printed" travelogue penned by Sarah and her father. "The joint authors are of the wide-awake kind," a reviewer in the *New York Times* noted, "and describe all that they saw in a capital manner." Sarah married, acted as her father's hostess when he

Charles Wiley, 1835–1916. At age thirty, Charles joined his father as a partner in the newly named John Wiley & Son.

quality, but it was also, since the break with Putnam, small. It was likely too small to cover the company's fixed costs (the necessary costs of running a business regardless of its scale). The cash flow from the bookstore may have helped, but Wiley, like other technical publishers, discovered that the retail and import businesses were a distraction and eventually divested them. Wiley exited slowly by forming a subsidiary, "John Wiley's Sons," which was devoted solely to importing books and journals from Europe to order. That business, too, along with Wiley's retail outlet, faded completely over time.[2]

In 1876, Wiley's publishing business got the boost of a second son, William Halsted (1842–1925), and henceforth was called "John Wiley & Sons." William H. had graduated from the College of the City of New York in 1861. He served in the Union army during the Civil War and was brevetted major for his gallantry. He finished a degree in civil engineering in

was first elected to Congress, and died young, of peritonitis, without children. Her poems and plays were published by the Macmillan Company.[3]

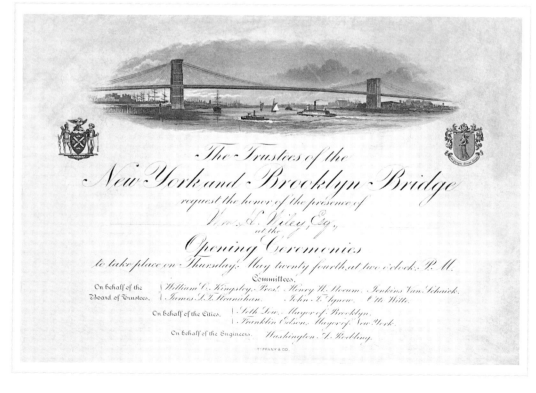

William Halsted Wiley, a civil engineer, received an invitation to the official ceremonies commemorating the opening of the Brooklyn Bridge in 1883. The work of two generations of Roeblings—John Augustus and his son Washington Augustus—the bridge took 15 years to complete and was admired by engineers and poets. A "literal and genuinely religious leap of faith," observed John Perry Barlow, speaking of its builders' belief in technology. For poet Hart Crane ("To the Brooklyn Bridge," 1930), the bridge was a magnificent, even prophetic backdrop to a sometimes troubled city.

PROFILE

JOHN RUSKIN

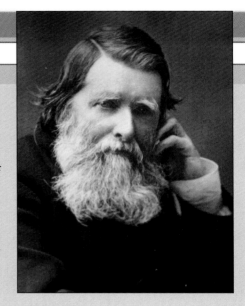

John Ruskin (1819-1900), British writer, critic, scientist, poet, artist, environmentalist, and philosopher, was the most important art critic of his time. His *Modern Painters* (1843) rescued J.M.W. Turner from obscurity. His *Seven Lamps of Architecture* (1849), written after trips to France and Italy, examined Gothic architecture as indicative of moral values. *The Stones of Venice* (1851) followed. As chair of fine arts at Oxford University, and through his many books and essays, Ruskin was the arbiter of artistic opinion in the Victorian era. He championed the Gothic Revival style and the Pre-Raphaelites, and his interest in the moral influence of art and architecture led him to decry the consequences of industrialization and the "dishonesty" of machine-made products. Like William Morris, he believed that handwork and craftsmanship brought dignity to labor, and in 1871 he founded a utopian arts and crafts community.

Ruskin's name in gilt on the cover of *Modern Painters* and his letter to John Wiley (shown at right) in which he responds to John's request to be recognized as Ruskin's publisher in the United States.

1866 at Rensselaer Polytechnic Institute, attended the Columbia University School of Mines, and spent almost a decade working as an engineer in New York, Chicago, and Ohio. Major Wiley, the first Wiley to hold that rank since Jack Wiley during the Revolution, began his stint with the firm as a "traveler" who concentrated on sales and acquisitions. A third son, Osgood (1855–1903), also worked briefly for the firm but apparently never became a partner.[4]

Though to what degree is hard to tell, John oversaw the business activities of his sons, which grew more extensive in the 1870s and 1880s. More Wileys in the company clearly meant more Wiley books. The scale of Wiley's publishing business, as measured by the number of brand new or substantially new editions published each year, trended upward, but it was not until John's death in 1891 and the sons' emergence from their father's conservative influence that the publication program accelerated.[5]

Ruskin began work on *Modern Painters* in 1842 as a defense of the painter J.M.W. Turner but expanded it into a general survey of art in five volumes, the last published in 1860. These engravings of art by Ghirlandaio and Claude Lorrain are in Part V, *Of Mountain Beauty*.

PREFACE.

I WAS in hopes that this volume might have gone its way without preface; but as I look over the sheets, I find in them various fallings short of old purposes which require a word of explanation.

Expansion did not happen all at once, of course, and for a number of years after the Civil War Wiley remained something of a house divided, publishing in the categories of both literature and useful knowledge. Literature continued to include the books on religious subjects that interested John and in America sold so well. But Wiley also published and reprinted a variety of literary titles, including the children's tales of Danish author Hans Christian Andersen and some fifty volumes by England's leading art, architecture, and social critic,

John Ruskin. In 1874, the *New York Times* noted that "Messrs. Wiley & Son, of Astor Place, appear to have almost entirely monopolized the publication of Mr. Ruskin's works in this country." Wiley kept Ruskin's highly regarded *Seven Lamps of Architecture* (1849) in print for decades, for example, and republished most of his other works. Yet it paid no royalties to a recalcitrant Ruskin, who refused to deal with the company because he loathed America, especially New York City, and refused to relinquish artistic control of any of his work.

Some Wiley editions of Ruskin were acquired by the British Museum in 1889. The importation of pirated editions into Britain and their placement on the shelves of one of Britain's premier libraries of course caused quite an uproar. In 1890, Ruskin at last authorized the publication of his works in the United States, but by Charles E. Merrill & Co., not Wiley.[6]

An Industrialized Economy

Slowly but surely Wiley shook off John's old enthusiasms and reoriented itself toward the Second Industrial Revolution. His sons embraced the new economy, becoming arbiters of the new science and technology.

New processes for steel production made better, faster, safer rail transportation possible, and in the course of the nineteenth century railroads increased by a factor of ten the average speed at which people and goods routinely moved (from 5 to a swift 50 miles per hour). In the East, rail networks begun before the Civil War grew more dense and efficient. In the West, new lines stretched over vast spaces where as yet no markets were. The first transcontinental line was completed in 1869; the last in 1893. Steam locomotives, fueled by coal, crossed this vast landscape; on the seas steamships, also made increasingly of steel, increased the tonnage of goods that could travel at faster speeds as well.[7]

Railroads were not just engineering feats but, compared to their antebellum predecessors, were large and complex organizations that called forth new ways of doing business and a new science of management. The manufacturing sector followed their lead as concepts like formal hierarchical authority and control, cost-benefit analysis, cost accounting, horizontal and vertical integration,

> **Americans were overwhelmingly literate and ever more of them were becoming educated as well.**

and mass production came into use. The steel industry was the archetype. The Bessemer process, which came to the United States from England in 1865, assured steel's triumph over mere iron, and by the 1880s Andrew Carnegie, a Scottish immigrant who started as a telegraph operator, was on the way to making America the world's leader in steel, the material upon which rested much of the physical infrastructure of modern life.[8]

Reduced information costs accompanied transportation and manufacturing innovations. First the telegraph, then the telephone, made information flow between parties not in earshot, more or less instantaneously. Even with continuous engineering refinement, however, the telegraph remained ill suited for widespread use in homes or smaller businesses, as messages had to be funneled through a telegraph office. The telephone was different because it could be placed right in the home or business. Though the basic concept emerged almost simultaneously from different sources in 1876, with Edison adding crucial improvements, Alexander Graham Bell and his partners would control the patent, the glory, and the profits as they began the Bell Telephone System. By 1900, some 3,000 subsidiary patents for everything from call bells to switchboards had improved the telephone's performance and convenience and brought down its cost.[9]

Bell, Carnegie, and the great railroad barons personified the technological and business dynamism of the age. But no one captured its spirit quite like Thomas Edison, the man who gave the age a new form of energy. Edison spearheaded the inventive side of the electrical revolution, his three greatest claims—the incandescent light bulb, the phonograph, and the Projectoscope, an early motion picture projector—alone changed the lives of millions and created immense economic wealth. So did a multitude of other inventions of the era: sewing machines, synthetic dyes, steam harvesters, typewriters, X rays, indoor plumbing, central heating, refrigeration, and the internal combustion technology that led to the automobile and the airplane.

The Second Industrial Revolution fed, and was fed by, an expansion of basic science that constituted a revolution in knowledge about how the physical world worked. By the mid-nineteenth century the tinkering and the trial and error that had produced the first Industrial Revolution had given way to controlled exper-imentation, precise measurement, logical analysis, and advanced mathematical treatment of practical problems. The word "scientist" was first widely used in the 1840s, and soon professional scientists, most employed by univer-sities, corporate research centers, or the government, sup-planted independent and amateur gentleman-scientists. With professionalization came the genesis and explication of powerful ideas such as the laws of thermodynamics and of gases, electromagnetism, the theory of evolution by means of natural selection, and atomic, cell, genetic, kinet-ic, light, and germ theories. By the early twentieth cen-tury, Pierre and Marie Curie had discovered important properties of radioactivity; Albert Einstein confounded understandings of the nature of time and matter; and Niels Bohr, Werner Heisenberg, and Erwin Schrödinger probed the nature of atoms.[10]

In America these advances in science and tech-nology had a broad impact. Americans lived in an open society where information moved easily and economic incentives encouraged the application of new knowl-edge to the production of goods and services. Americans were overwhelmingly literate and ever more of them were becoming educated as well. The Morrill Land Grant Act of 1862 promoted colleges and universities across the land and propelled more and more Americans, some 350,000 per year by 1900, toward higher education. The knowledge revolution determined what they learned there, as colleges and universities turned from classical subjects toward technological and

Wiley installed its first telephones in 1888. It never had its own telegraph equipment, though it did have its own cable address, "JONWILE."[11]

scientific curricula, some emphasizing basic research. In the latter half of the nineteenth century, the universi-ty did not make science, science made the university. Technically focused institutions prospered—Rensselaer Polytechnic Institute, Massachusetts Institute of Technology, Rochester Institute of Technology, Lehigh, Lafayette, and a host of less elite public institutions. Older colleges—even Princeton, Harvard, and Yale— had to adapt or risk producing only "lawyers and dilet-tante[s]," warned a critic.[12]

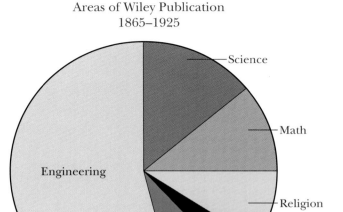

Areas of Wiley Publication
1865–1925

Science
Math
Engineering
Religion
Business
Chemistry

Scientific Wiley: Its Market and Competitors

Together the Second Industrial Revolution and the knowledge revolution fueled a third—a revolution in the market for books and periodicals. In this era, science and technology became Wiley's specialty. As early as 1870, Wiley's listing in the directory of booksellers announced: "Wiley, John & Son, 15 Astor Place & 138 Eighth Street (See advt., page 256.) Scientific & Misc. Bk. P[ublisher] & B[ookseller]." The "advt." cited practical books on subjects from agriculture and assaying to shipbuilding and ventilation. Of the 1,500 or so new or substantially revised editions that Wiley published between 1865 and 1925, the vast majority were titles in basic fields such as chemistry, mathematics, biology, and mineralogy and in applied fields such as architecture, construction, engineering, metallurgy, mining, and railroads. Miscellaneous, religious, and Ruskin titles accounted for only about 5 percent of the total, and most of those were published before 1900. Titles in some other smaller fields, including aeronautics, accounting, business, and economics, appeared on Wiley's list only after 1900; these were the growth fields that would become important during the company's fourth generation.[14] Even the business list, begun at the instigation of William H., remained small until after his death. Taking book publishing as a whole, Wiley still remained a minor player. In 1903, for example, 6,977 books were published in the United States, 5,621 by American authors and 1,356 by foreign authors, mostly British. Wiley published only 40, or less than 1 percent, of those new editions. In its own chosen niche of science and the "useful arts," however, Wiley published nearly 9 percent of a total 457 new editions in 1903. In the first half of the 1910s, Wiley sustained its

Germany proved to be a particular influence. American students who had been educated at German universities and went on to play important roles in academia borrowed freely from their university experience. Johns Hopkins, though an exception when it was founded in 1876, "was the most impressive example of the German university's ideals of advanced scholarship and Ph.D. programs being transplanted to the United States," according to one historian of higher education. The number of specialized engineering schools grew from just 6 before the Civil War to 85 by 1880 and 126 by 1917, when the United States entered World War I. By that time many high-technology corporations, such as AT&T, General Electric, Alcoa, and DuPont, had established heavily funded and expertly staffed science-based laboratories of their own as the demands of their fast-evolving businesses pressed hard against the boundaries of academic knowledge.[13]

> **Science and technology became Wiley's specialty.**

28 RENSSELAER POLYTECHNIC INSTITUTE.

Rules and Directions.

ADMISSION TO THE INSTITUTE.

All applications for admission to the institute, or for special information concerning it, should be addressed to the DIRECTOR OF THE INSTITUTE. Copies of the ANNUAL REGISTER may be obtained on application, either to the Director, or to W. H. YOUNG, Treasurer of the Institute, 8 First Street, Troy, N. Y,

The proper time—that is the *best* time—for entering the Classes of the Institute, is at the beginning of the scholastic year in September. Students are admitted, however, at the opening of the summer session, or at any other time in the year; but if not fully prepared on the previous work of the class, they are then obliged to make up their deficiencies by *extra efforts* during the session.

It is earnestly recommended to those who contemplate entering upon either of the courses of the Institute, to commence with the studies of Division D, rather than attempt those of Division C by means of an incomplete or superficial preparation. The requirements for entering Division D may be readily met; after which, with due attention to the studies of the class, a degree of disciplinary culture may be reached, not only sufficient for fully meeting the prescribed requirements for entering Division C, but peculiarly well adapted for *introducing* the student to the studies of this class.

EXPENSES.

Institute Fees.—In the general courses, the fees for instruction, use of astronomical and field instruments, use of consumable materials, chemicals, etc., are $75 for each semi-annual session; and in the partial courses, they are in the same proportion for the time of study. These Fees must be paid to the Treasurer in advance for each session. The Graduation Fee, including the Diploma, is $18, and must be paid to the Treasurer at least two weeks before the time of graduation. There are no extra charges.

Living Expenses.—Members of the Institute find b[…] with respectable private families in the city. The pr[…] and furnished lodgings vary, at the present time, [...] per week. The total living expenses, which inclu[…] lodgings, laundry, fires, lights, and attendance, vary [...] $350 for the scholastic year.

RENSSELAER POLYTECHNIC INSTITUTE. 29

For those parents or guardians desiring it, funds may be placed in the keeping of the Treasurer of the Institute, who will disburse and render an account of the same, (charging a commission of two and a half per cent. on the amount of his disbursements,) either to the order of the student directly, or to that of the President, Director, or other officer of the Institute. It is always liable to be injurious, unless the student be accustomed to habits of self-control, to allow him too free command of pocket money. There is little necessity for spending much money during the student's life at the Institute; and the supply of any more money than what is sufficient for his proper wants is very apt to be *worse than useless*.

STUDENT'S FURNISHINGS.

Drawing Instruments.—The instruments used at the Institute are the Swiss,—which are preferred both for their general excellence and moderate cost. These instruments, with the materials for geometrical and topographical drawing, cost from $15 to $35. The student is advised to defer his purchases of drawing instruments and materials until he comes to the Institute, when he will have the advantage of procuring them under the direction of the professors of drawing.

Chemical Instruments.—A blowpipe, platinum wire, certain re-agents, bottles, test tubes, etc., are required by each student for the courses in practical chemistry, and can be obtained at the cost of about $8.

Text-Books and Stationery.—The text-books, etc., used at the Institute, may be purchased at the city bookstores. The student is advised, however, to bring such scientific books as he may possess.

Field Service and Excursions.—All who come here are advised to bring or provide themselves with a suit of heavy and substantial clothing, boots, etc., for field service, and for the botanical and geological excursions.

SESSIONS AND VACATIONS.

The scholastic year is divided into two sessions. The first or winter session consists of twenty-one weeks, and is followed by a vacation of one week. The second or summer session consists of twenty weeks,

Above, pages from the 1864–1865 Rensselaer Polytechnic Institute catalog, the year before William Halsted Wiley took his degree in civil engineering. Right, a surveying class in civil engineering from 1862, around the time that William Halsted Wiley would have studied surveying. RPI conferred its first civil engineering degree on four students in 1835—the first such degrees granted in the United States or Britain. Williams' nephew, surrogate son, and future Wiley president, Edward P. Hamilton, graduated from RPI in 1907.

PROFILE

DAVID VAN NOSTRAND

David Van Nostrand (1811–1888) won high honors in school before joining the house of New York publisher and bookseller John P. Haven in 1826. In 1834, he joined in partnership with William Dwight, putting out a few religious tracts before the concern folded in the aftermath of the Panic of 1837. Van Nostrand then moved to New Orleans, where he developed a taste for military and scientific subjects and made important contacts with military engineer J. G. Barnard and future Union generals William Tecumseh Sherman and Philip Sheridan. In 1848, Van Nostrand returned to New York and began publishing and retailing scientific and technical books under his own name, including Washington Roebling's *Long and Short Span Railway Bridges*, which has a detailed description of his masterpiece, the Brooklyn Bridge. In the early 1900s, Van Nostrand Co. was one of the four big scientific and technical publishers (with John Wiley & Sons, McGraw-Hill, and Prentice Hall). In the late 1960s, having merged with Reinhold in 1969, it was later sold to Thomson. Van Nostrand remained a major Wiley competitor until 1997, when it was acquired by John Wiley & Sons.

*D*avid Van Nostrand was only ten when his father, a New York merchant, died.

A "Catalog of Scientific Books," advertising the publications of D. Van Nostrand. In the 1850s and 1860s, Van Nostrand was the largest dealer of technical and scientific books in New York. After the Civil War, D. Van Nostrand and Wiley competed head to head. Over a century later, D. Van Nostrand had become Van Nostrand-Reinhold, and John Wiley & Sons acquired it in 1997.

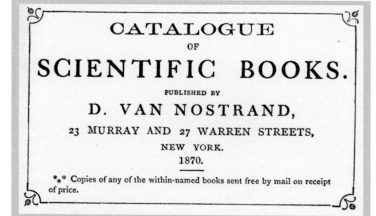

CATALOGUE
OF
SCIENTIFIC BOOKS.
PUBLISHED BY
D. VAN NOSTRAND,
23 MURRAY AND 27 WARREN STREETS,
NEW YORK.
1870.

** Copies of any of the within-named books sent free by mail on receipt of price.

position in this field, supplying around 7 percent of new titles.[15]

In the 1850s and 1860s, Wiley's primary competitor in technical and scientific fields was David Van Nostrand, a New York book dealer who began publishing and retailing scientific and technical books under his own name in 1848. Unlike John Wiley, Van Nostrand took advantage of the Civil War to expand his list significantly. After the war, the two companies went head-to-head in fields like chemistry, engineering, and railroads. Van Nostrand pioneered the cheap scientific pocket book series, putting out some 127 titles, at $.50 to $.75 each, between the 1870s and 1902. The company survived the death of its founder in 1888 by incorporating and buying out Van Nostrand's widow. In addition to continuing its importation business, the company published important titles in architecture, construction, chemistry, the industrial arts, and civil, electrical, and mechanical engineering.[16]

McGraw-Hill emerged as another important Wiley competitor, and a formidable one at that. Before 1906, the separate McGraw and Hill publishing companies concentrated on technical and business periodicals; they regularly referred authors with book ideas to Wiley or Van Nostrand. But Wiley's and Van Nostrand's success with books induced McGraw and Hill to form book units of their own. When McGraw and Hill merged in 1909, a technical book publishing legend was born. (The periodical businesses remained separate entities until 1916 when they, too, merged after the death of John Hill.) Though a newcomer to the book field, the McGraw-Hill Book Company had much experience with publishing technical authors, and Wiley immediately felt the pressure. First, sales of McGraw-Hill's *American Machinists' Handbook* overtook those of Wiley's handbook; then its *Manual of Engineering Drawing*, by Thomas French (1908), overcame Wiley's manual as well. Successes followed rapidly. Between 1909 and 1919, McGraw-Hill expanded from a staff of 12 to 86, supported by annual sales of 650,000 units, up from 73,000. Wiley, by contrast, had sales of only $757,633 in 1920. That meant that for every dollar Wiley brought in, McGraw-Hill sold a book, most priced at well over a dollar each. It seems that McGraw-Hill was besting Wiley at its own game. During World War I, McGraw-Hill filled an order for 150,000 technical books for the educational wing of the American Expeditionary Force in France in just 10 days, learning much about modern management, production, and distribution in the process.[17]

Macmillan, a corporate offspring of the great British publisher of the same name, was another major competitor. In addition to bestsellers like *Richard Carvel* (1899), by Winston Churchill (the American writer, not the British politician), and Jack London's *Call of the Wild* (1903), Macmillan published many high-quality scholarly books. It was, in short, what Wiley might have become had John Wiley and George Palmer Putnam not split. Newcomer publishers also competed against Wiley titles, though few

The McGraw Book Company at 239 West 39 Street, New York, 1911. Roger Burlingame, *Endless Frontiers: The Story of McGraw-Hill* ©1959 McGraw-Hill.

survived for long. University presses, too, entered the scientific and technical publishing field, and college professors sometimes had their notes printed locally and sold them directly to students. On a grander scale, the government competed by publishing and distributing technical pamphlets through the Government Printing Office, which after the Civil War became the largest publisher in the country. The better textbook publishers also occasionally entered Wiley's space. Ginn and Company published some books in mathematics and general science that competed with Wiley titles. And general-trade publishers tried to tap the lower end of the market. Houghton, Mifflin Company's Riverside Science Series targeted

*M*other and daughter reading, Mt. Meigs, Alabama, 1890.

the general reader who wanted to stay abreast of the latest findings.[18]

Scientific and technical book publishers like Wiley responded to competition in various ways. They worked harder and accepted lower profits. They also tried to differentiate their products in terms of quality, length, content, and price. In 1923 and 1924, Wiley, McGraw-Hill, and Macmillan all came out with college texts on industrial management, or "management engineering." Of the three, Wiley's *Industrial Management* by Richard Lansburgh was the longest, at almost 500 pages, but at $4.50 it was more expensive than the McGraw-Hill book and $1.75 more expensive than the much slimmer Macmillan title. At this time books over $4 were hard sells, so the Wiley title probably ended up primarily at the better schools, where high prices and page counts mattered less. It also caught on in business schools, just then being established.[19]

Competition called for alertness to multiple opportunities and markets. Some publishers, including Wiley, took to selling ads in books. Its *Catskill Water Supply of New York* (1913), by Lazarus White, contained a half-page advertisement by the East Jersey Pipe Co. of Paterson, New Jersey. East Jersey Pipe, like advertisers in other media, undoubtedly wished to catch the attention of people interested in its water pipes. For publishers, however, accepting advertising in books was a risky proposition because they could never guarantee the number of books that would be sold or even the timeliness of publication. Wiley, like other publishers, often advertised their own lists at the back of their higher-volume titles.[20]

As early as 1870, Wiley advertised an extensive list of books for schools and colleges. These were both primers and more advanced texts. Wiley's edition of classic texts, The Ordo Series, was aimed to give students "real and substantial help," not "injurious relaxation." Wiley also appealed to teachers, noting that its books would "relieve" their "anxiety and labors." As a business strategy, the school business was probably seen as a good hedge against times when publishing more generally slumped.[21]

The primary and secondary school markets did not loom large for Wiley under John's sons, which was probably just as well given the graft and censorship problems that periodically plagued them. Wiley's higher education business, on the other hand, flourished. The rapid growth of the higher education sector, from 563 institutions, 5,500 faculty members, and 52,000 students in 1870 to 961 institutions, 36,480 professors, and 355,000 students in 1910, was a boon to Wiley and other well-positioned publishers. Even though members of this sector represented less than 2 percent of the population at the end of the nineteenth century, 100 percent of them needed textbooks and scholarly monographs.[22]

Library sales were a big and growing business. In the 1850s, the Harvard library, among the country's largest, held only some 75,000 volumes. By 1861, even before the higher education boom, American collegiate libraries owned some 1.2 million volumes. By 1868, New York State Free Lending Libraries, which doubled as school-district libraries, had more than 3 million volumes. (It was the Germans, not the Americans, who led the field, though: In the 1850s, the library at the University of Göttingen contained 360,000 volumes.)

Guided by faculty requests, professional librarians selected titles for purchase with the aim of achieving a balanced collection that did not duplicate those of nearby institutions. Local agreements arose, such as one in Worcester, Massachusetts, under which Wiley sold mostly to Clark and Worcester Polytechnic and hardly at all to the American Antiquarian Society, Worcester County Law, or Worcester Public. A similar agreement in Chicago meant that Wiley sold all its titles to John Crerar Library but almost none to Chicago Public, the Newberry, or the library of the Chicago Historical Society. (Not until the 1920s would the interlibrary loan system allow patrons of one library to access the collections of a geographically enormous network of other institutions.)[23]

Of course not every library bought every book, and Wiley sold its publications more and more to academic and research libraries. Between 1875 and 1925, American academic libraries grew five to ten to twenty times larger. Again German institutions, primarily academic libraries, with their emphasis on building highly specialized collections to provide research libraries for professors and students, helped shape the American academic library. Then too there were important governmental research libraries, such as those of the United States Coast and Geodetic Survey, the Weather Bureau, and the Geologic Survey. Full-time library staffing began to appear in the 1870s, though specialized training was rare for several more decades. Libraries professionalized their operations after Melvil Dewey established a school of library economy at Columbia in 1887.[24]

Nonacademic libraries also modernized in this period. Rental libraries survived into the twentieth century, numbering at least 25,000 by 1930, but encountered much competition from the ever more numerous public libraries, thanks in part to Andrew Carnegie's generosity. Specialized libraries for corporations and professional societies also appeared in the early twentieth century; Edison, characteristically, helped to pioneer the form, building impressive libraries at his research facilities. Public libraries tended to stress popular fiction, trying to balance the best books with the "best that people will read." English literature remained popular, but Wiley published very little in this field. Nor were public libraries much interested in what Wiley now published, for all but the largest found it "impossible to buy to any great extent . . . in special fields such as technical, law and medicine, [and] highly specialized technology." Nevertheless, Wiley tracked trends in public libraries closely, and even published, in 1869, a volume devoted to their history in Britain, France, Germany, and the United States.[25]

Practical Knowledge and Engineering

The market for Wiley's books was wider than just libraries, professors, and students. It included practicing professionals in need of knowledge now; people who did not just think about knowledge but who were paid to apply it in jobs where, in addition to reputation, money and often lives were at risk. The America of Charles and William H. was a heyday for engineers. And of course the Major himself was one, trained at RPI and Columbia and active throughout his life in professional societies for mechanical, civil, mining, and electrical engineers. Engineering as a field of study had developed

pragmatically and for years had little connection with higher learning. Most engineers learned their skills on the job. Graduates of West Point and RPI's engineering programs were an exception. The Major's sort of formal training exemplified the progressive acceptance after the Civil War of engineering as a course of university study, which followed from the growing complexity of technology and engineering practice. So did the sequence of the Roeblings, father and son, designers of the Brooklyn Bridge. John Augustus had studied engineering in Berlin, but his knowledge of steel cable came out of his practical, on-the-job experience. His son, who took over construction of the Brooklyn Bridge

A Heyday for Engineers . . .

*E*lectrical engineering students at Ohio State University in 1907. Ohio State was founded in 1870 as a land grant university.

following John Augustus's eventual death from an injury on the site, was an RPI graduate who also studied in Europe.

In post-Civil War America, engineers were needed. Settlement of the trans-Mississippi West, depending as it did on the development and application of new skills in transportation, communication, mining, and agriculture on a grander scale than ever before, increased the demand for engineers and accelerated their rise to full professional status. The Morrill Land Grant Act of 1862 specifically promoted colleges for the benefit of agriculture and "the mechanic arts" (which meant engineering). By codifying the nation's

need, it broadened opportunities in engineering education. The year it passed, America counted fewer than two dozen engineering schools. Ten years later there were seventy.[26]

Professions have literatures, for present and future practitioners, and as the body of engineering knowledge grew, so did the need to publish it. Wiley laid its foundations well in this key field. John Trautwine had been writing for Wiley for years. His two books from 1851, *Field Practice of Laying Out Circular Curves for Railroads* and *Method of Calculating Cubic Contents of Excavations and Embankments*, sold well over time. Trautwine bridged the old world of mechanical engineering to the new one

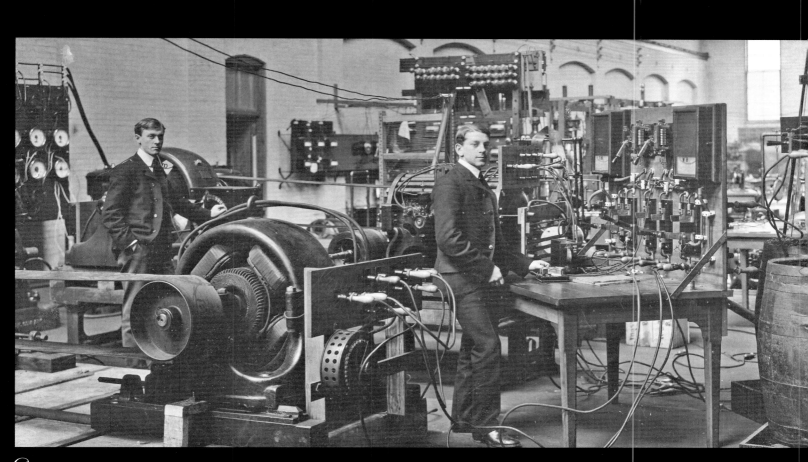

*E*lectrical engineering class, dynamo lab, at Massachusetts Institute of Technology, 1905.

tied to chemistry and electricity. With no formal education, he began his career in the office of Philadelphia's chief engineer and architect. His abundant in-the-field experience included work on ports and railroads at home and abroad. (He laid out the railroad across the isthmus of Panama.) Like the Roeblings, Trautwine exemplified the transformation of engineering from practice to profession, a trend with which the Major

firmly aligned his family's company. The number of engineers in America leapt from 7,000 in 1880 to 136,000 in 1920, a market that devoured Wiley's many pocket books, "catechisms," and handbooks. The company published more than 80 such books in this period, beginning in 1880 with William H. Searles's *Field Engineering: A Hand-Book of the Theory and Practice of Railway Surveying*, *Location and Construction*, and Trautwine's own *Civil Engineer's Pocket-Book*, which sold over 23,000 copies.[27]

One of Wiley's most important authors in this period was Mansfield Merriman, a civil engineer who published 22 books with Wiley between 1881 and 1915. A generation younger than Trautwine, Merriman was educated at Yale's Sheffield Scientific School and then moved from the U.S. Corps of Engineers to Lehigh University to the U.S. Coast and Geodetic Survey. The enlarged second edition of his *American Civil Engineers' Pocket Book*, which ran to 1,475 pages and included 1,200 illustrations and 500 tables, retailed for $5.00. The total issue numbered 15,000. Wiley also published eight books by legendary mechanical engineer

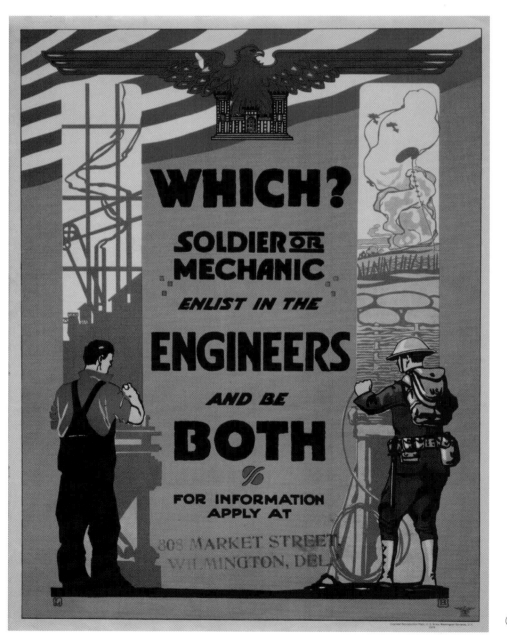

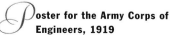
Poster for the Army Corps of Engineers, 1919

PROFILE

JOHN CRESSON TRAUTWINE

John Cresson Trautwine (1810–1883) authored *Civil Engineer's Pocket-Book*, a Wiley bestseller. Trautwine's career models the evolution of civil engineering in the United States. He started out in an architect's office in Philadelphia in 1828, where he designed and supervised the construction of Penn Township Bank and assisted in the construction of the U.S. Mint in Philadelphia. He worked on the first railroads in the 1830s and on the construction of the Canal del Dique in Colombia in the 1840s. He surveyed for the Panama Railroad in 1850, returned to work on U.S. railroads, surveyed another canal route in Honduras in 1857, designed a dock system for Montreal in 1858, and retired from practice in 1864 to write books for Wiley and others. A member of several professional societies, he wrote for numerous journals. By this time, to be an engineer one had to start with university study, and Trautwine's publications for Wiley helped transform engineering into a profession.

Wiley's many pocket books, "catechisms," and handbooks were its biggest sellers. John Trautwine's *Civil Engineer's Pocket-Book*, for example, sold over 23,000 copies.

Illustration of a late 19th-century level from *The Civil Engineer's Pocket-Book*

Robert H. Thurston; nine by Dennis Hart Mahan, a civil engineer who taught at the U.S. Military Academy and was the father of Alfred Thayer Mahan, the famed naval strategist; eight by electricity expert William Henry Timbie; and twelve by engineer S. Edward Warren, who taught upriver at RPI.[28]

The Major was a founding member of the American Society of Mechanical Engineers in 1880. His passion for railroads probably matched his father's passion for Ruskin, and his engineer's mind shaped a publishing program that gradually pushed all nontechnical titles to the sidelines. Wiley's pocket books were typically praised for their combination of small size and comprehensiveness: what you needed to know, organized in a manner easy to grasp and communicate. The *New York Times* called *The Cost of Cleanness*, for instance, "small in size but big in importance" because "each sentence is a bullet for compactness and energy

120

PROFILE

MAJOR WILLIAM HALSTED WILEY

A former Civil War officer, the Major joined the company in 1876, the year of America's centennial and the same year Edison set up shop in Menlo Park. He had a degree in civil engineering from Rensselaer Polytechnic Institute, attended the Columbia University School of Mines, and for the rest of his career cultivated a vast network of contacts in the engineering world for the purpose of acquiring technical manuscripts for Wiley. He was a founding member of the American Society of Mechanical Engineers and member of the American Society of Civil Engineers, the American Society of Mining and Metallurgical Engineers, and the American Institute of Electrical Engineers, and he served as agent and correspondent for the London-based journal *Engineering*.

The Major was a Republican who served as East Orange, N.J., City Council president and president of the Seventh Regiment War Veterans. In 1898, he helped to establish the People's Telephone Company of New York. By then he had matured into a very distinguished-looking gentleman possessed with what *Publishers' Weekly* called an "unusually winning personality" in an era in which distinguished Civil War service was political gold in the North. When New Jersey received two additional congressional seats in 1902, the GOP tapped him to fill one of them. The Major accepted the nomination, carried the election in 1902, and was re-elected in 1904, partly for the good press he continued to receive for stopping a serious train wreck some thirty years earlier, and partly for the benefits he brought home to his district. In 1906, he lost the Republican nomination to Henry Gottlob, who in turn lost the general election. The Major returned to the U.S. House of Representatives in 1908 in a landslide. In 1910, however, he lost again, his opponent riding the coattails of Democratic gubernatorial candidate and future president, Woodrow Wilson. The Major traveled to Europe, India, Japan, and the Philippines at a time when Wiley books were reaching overseas markets. Whether he conducted business in his travels remains unclear.[29]

*T*he Major died on May 2, 1925, after a short illness. Obituarists recalled a man attentive to business and good at human relations. Old soldiers and employees loved him.[30]

*A*t right are the newspaper article announcing Major Wiley's candidacy for a new seat in Congress and a congratulatory telegram after his election.

of propulsion." Published in 1908, and written by Ellen H. Richards, a faculty member at M.I.T. widely known for her investigation of "sanitary science," the book "brought the light of science to bear" on that long-time scourge of humanity known as dirt. Sales reflected usefulness: By its ninth edition, William Kent's *The Mechanical Engineers' Pocket-Book* (1916) had sold 113,000 copies, more than five times the sales of its leading competitor. That title and Frank Kidder's *Architects' and Builders' Handbook* were probably Wiley's biggest sellers during the period. By the 1890s, the firm's technical publishing program was far enough developed to merit separate scientific circular catalogs that were organized by category: the materials of engineering (including elasticity and strength); bridges, roofs, and trusses; hydraulics and hydraulic engines; and (probably William H.'s personal favorite) steam engines, boilers, and locomotives.[31]

Carvel (Macmillan, 1899) sold hundreds of thousands of copies in their first year; *Carvel* eventually sold over two million. Even more modest popular novels from long since forgotten authors, like Mary Cholmondeley's *Red Pottage* (Harper, 1899), could sell in the range of 50,000 copies. In contrast, print runs on most Wiley titles were 250 or 500. "Printing of 1,000 copies," one employee later recounted, "was considered a large order." Binding orders were separate and even lower, in the range of 100 to 250 copies. (It was thought imprudent to go to the expense of binding books that might never sell; books were still sometimes shipped to customers, wholesale or retail, unbound.) As at Van Nostrand, a scientific book that sold 5,000 copies in a year was considered a bonanza. The (relatively) big sellers on a publisher's list buoyed the smaller ones. Wiley's net sales in 1914 were $313,000 (gross sales minus returns of just over 2 percent). Sales of the top 28 titles, a tiny fraction of the list and composed mostly of technical pocket books, amounted to about $118,000, or about 38 percent of the net.[32]

Wiley's total output under the Major must be seen relative to the rapid growth in American book production generally: Some 2,000 new titles appeared in 1881, more than 11,000 in 1910. In an industry tabulation of new titles produced in 1914, Wiley's chief competitors in scientific books, Van Nostrand and McGraw-Hill, turned out 95 and 50 volumes respectively; Wiley managed 5. On the other hand, lean output reflected winnowing of what it meant to be a publisher. Books published had come to mean books originated; developing and then publishing a book was a long, complex process. The reprinting and/or pirating of existing titles ceased with the passage of an international copyright law in 1891. Gone, too, were the days when reputable publishers like Wiley would throw the risk of publication onto authors, an activity henceforth consigned, derisively, to "vanity publishers." It also became rare for publishers to purchase the rights to books outright, without a provision for authors to receive royalties of some form or another.[33]

What no doubt looked from the inside to be exciting and was by any objective measure a decisive shift from old interests to new should be kept in perspective, however. Wiley's handbooks sold well, though in comparison with other types of books from other publishers the numbers look small. By the end of the nineteenth century, commanding bestsellers like Edward Noyes Westcott's novel *David Harum: A Story of American Life* (Appleton, 1898) and Churchill's *Richard*

THE Printing craft

THE LINOTYPE AND SMYTH SEWING

Like the world around it, publishing at Wiley in the third generation participated in the technological innovations that also fed its lists. The printing process continued to improve in the second half of the nineteenth century, especially after the introduction of the Linotype. Using this machine, an operator depressed keys on a keyboard to fill molds with hot metal, usually lead, that were used to create a line of type. By 1900, 5,000 Linotype machines were in use in the United States. These, combined with rotary presses capable of printing 70,000 pages an hour, caused the efficiency of American printing to soar. In 1843, to put to press 100,000 copies of a certain book took fifty days. Using an early mechanized press, it could be done in five days. By 1888, with a Hoe perfecting machine, the work could be done in five hours.[34]

Improvements were not always synchronous. Huge increases in page output created a bottleneck at the back end, in binding. At first, binders continued to work by hand but then responded to competitive pressures by switching from the ancient "boarding" technique to the more efficient "casing-in" method. The latter, in which the case and the book were made separately and then joined via pasting, was amenable to machine processes. In the late nineteenth century, machines increasingly replaced people in the binding process, first in the rolling, pressing, or "beating" of the pages, then in the backing process, then in the folding, then in the sewing or stitching of the pages, and by the century's last decade, in the production of the cases. In 1903, the Smyth Company introduced a machine that joined the bound pages and the cases into finished books. About the same time, an automatic gathering machine finally made obsolete the scads of "factory girls" who walked miles each day around tables gathering and collating the signatures that started the whole process.[35]

Whether collated by hand or machine, the paper used in those books came cheaper than ever before as mechanized wood-pulp mills completely supplanted earlier ones based on handicraft methods and expensive

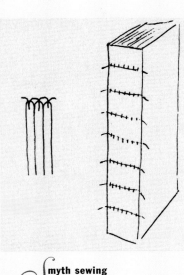

Smyth sewing

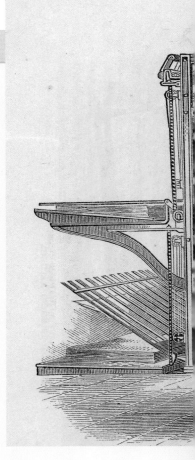

Hoe rotary press

cotton rags. By the end of the nineteenth century, the United States was one of the world's leading exporters of machine-made paper. Chromolithography and methods of cheaply reproducing photographs—photomechanical line engraving, halftone engraving, photogravure, rotogravure, collotype, and photolithography—also proliferated widely in the second half of the nineteenth century and the first decades of the twentieth century, much to the benefit of Wiley and other firms that published books with numerous graphics and illustrations.[36]

Since Charles gave up his print shop in the early nineteenth century, Wiley had used numerous printers and binders. In the late nineteenth century, it used George W. Alexander as its binder. To spread the risk of damage due to fire or other catastrophe to its

offices, the firm kept its unbound stock with Alexander. In the first half of the twentieth century, Wiley used F. H. Gilson Company for most of its book-printing needs. That company formed about 1900, after Wiley's previous primary print shop, G. J. Peters, went out of business following a disastrous fire. (The fear of fire in the book trades has always been strong, even though fire insurance was available by the early nineteenth century.) Gilson, which had other clients but pretty much relied on Wiley for its existence, was proud of its record of providing "what Wiley needed when it was needed." The company also printed some titles with Scientific Press. By the early 1920s, Wiley also sometimes used Braunworth & Company for printing. For reasons that are not clear, Wiley had its printers destroy manuscripts after the books came out.[37]

*L*inotype machine, 1886

Working at Wiley

Work life in the offices of the early twentieth century was not unlike office life today. A division of labor appeared in upper management. The Major was president, Charles was vice president and treasurer, and in 1890, Charles's son William O. added a new generational layer by joining the company as secretary. His cousin, Edward Hamilton, son of Alice, the Major and Charles's sister, came aboard in 1914. The Major appears to have handled most of the editorial contacts while Charles focused on sales and marketing. Even while William H. still lived and continued to make the top-level decisions, William O. found himself in charge of much of the day-to-day operation, though not all of it. He professed to know little, for example, about the details of the various series which the company established in the 1920s. That was Hamilton's territory.[38]

Assignments were becoming compartmentalized and positions hierarchical. In 1914, Wiley employed about two dozen men. Long-time employee Samuel E. Norris had gradually evolved into a production manager, responsible for ensuring that the manufacturing of Wiley books ran smoothly. (He later became a member of the board of directors and vice president.) There were three bookkeepers, two billing and three shipping clerks, two assistants, an advertising man, two stenographers, and at least five men with "roving assignments." Wiley hired its first female employee, a telephone operator, in 1917. Thereafter, women became an increasingly important part of the company, though at first they were restricted to gender-specific clerical functions. By 1924, Wiley had added an in-house copy editor, "for the purpose of uniformity in regard to spelling, compounding of words and abbreviations." The number of employees sometimes exasperated the old Major: "What are we going to do with them all? There are so many they are stepping on one another's toes!"[39]

Official work hours were a little longer than they are today: 8 to 5 during the week and 8 to 3 on Saturdays, with shorter hours during the summer. Then, as now, occasional pranks punctuated workplace decorum. In 1915, for example, someone somehow replaced "gofer" Charles Musgnug's winter underwear with garbage. Musgnug and his wife, who thought she was the butt of the joke, were not amused. The guilty party was never found; employees called it the "overnight mystery of the missing drawers." In the 1920s, workers took an exercise and deep-breathing break every afternoon—a predecessor, of sorts, to today's coffee breaks and yoga classes. "Travelers" (the designation for men who visited schools seeking sales and manuscript proposals) could also have fun. Frank Hayden snuck the following into one of his trip reports, which the typist dutifully copied: ". . . and [a reviewer] thinks that the authors have been a little brief in their treatment. For instance in the chapter on Manure Pits there is no depth given."[40]

Throughout his tenure, the Major personally screened books and courted authors. He had to, because the staff was so small, but he was also good at this difficult job. Demands on his time were enormous, as many manuscripts were unpublishable and each year at many presses hundreds were returned to authors unopened. According to one story, the Major sent away one genius wannabe who had written a huge manuscript on "Squaring the Circle" with the suggestion that he would find a publisher in Daniel Appleton, a keen rival at that time. For years thereafter, the story goes, Appleton and William H. enjoyed wasting each other's time with such backhanded recommendations. The Major traveled coast to coast in search of manuscripts, bookstore sales, and course adoptions. As he went, he cultivated a network of friends and acquaintances that helped with acquisitions, previews, sales, and reviews. Stories of the Major's yearly wintertime excursions through the South in a chauffeur-driven Pierce-Arrow to pay calls at Virginia Military Institute and the Citadel, where he sometimes met up with old Civil War adversaries, are part of company lore.[41]

The Need for More Space . . .

Wiley moves uptown: John Wiley opened a bookstore at 161 Broadway (top two illustrations) in 1834 where he was joined by his new partner, George Palmer Putnam, in 1836. In 1848 Wiley and Putnam ended their partnership. Putnam moved three doors to 155 Broadway. A later office, possibly 15 Astor Place (lower left), where Wiley was located after 1870. And 440 Fourth Avenue (lower right)—later renamed Park Avenue South—where Wiley moved from 432 Fourth Avenue in 1924 after William H. Wiley complained, "There are so many [employees] they are stepping on one another's toes."

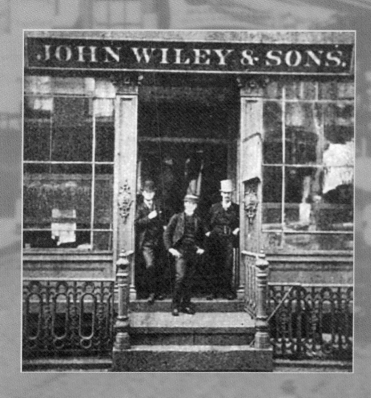

We know that the Major was responsible for many of Wiley's books in the third generation, though increasingly acquisitions became the work of a number of editors. In the preface to the first edition of his *Mechanical Engineers' Pocket-Book* (1895), William Kent noted that the book was assembled "at the request of the publishers." Beginning in the 1890s, William O. also contributed to the company's list, but, a classicist by training, he stumbled at first. In 1892, the Major chided him for signing up another book from an author whose previous works had not sold well. Worst of all, the major reminded his nephew, the company would have to pay for the author's numerous drawings. Thus the old Wiley sensibility for books of literary merit but questionable profit, as in the time of the first Charles and of Evert Duyckinck, gave way, under the Major and the Wileys who followed him, to strict business sense.[42]

The Art of the Textbook Trade

In the 1910s and 1920s, Wiley first began to employ travelers, breaking what had been something of a family monopoly in creating goodwill with customers and authors and in soliciting titles. These men would canvass colleges across the country each year, gathering information and seeking to secure course adoptions for existing titles and manuscript submissions for courses that lacked a Wiley text. They interviewed faculty members and remitted their notes back to the home office in New York. On a visit to the University of California at Davis in April 1922, for example, a Wiley traveler recorded the following:

> *MR. H. L. BELTON:* Received a copy of Foster & Carter's Farm Structures. Thinks it good. . . . Is thinking somewhat of writing a text on Structures adapted to conditions in California. . . .
>
> *PROFESSOR S. H. BECKETT:* Received a complimentary copy of Powers & Teeters, and considers it a decided improvement over the other texts that are now used. . . .

> *PROFESSOR L. J. FLETCHER:* Now giving a special course in Tractors and is going to work his material into book form.
>
> *MR. R. C. INGRIM:* He is now writing a Shop text. . . . Said that he expects to have his mss. finished by May 20th. . . . Will deal with Forging.[43]

The role of these travelers was critical, because textbook acquisitions up front had to be matched with course adoptions at the end. After publication, Peter Austen's *Notes for Chemical Students* (1896), for example, was immediately adopted at the author's school, the Polytechnic in Brooklyn, and De Volson Wood's books on bridges were adopted not only at his own University of Michigan but also at Iowa University, Iowa Agricultural College, Illinois Industrial University, Sheffield Scientific School, the Cooper Institute, and the Polytechnic in Brooklyn. By the early 1920s, Wiley was soliciting recommendations for changes in its textbooks from professors who used the books in class, a technique that publishers employ to this day. It was an important practice because, as Ohio State University professor F. W. Ives put it, "things were not as apparent in reading it as they are in the teaching from it." The practice also gave the commentators a sense of ownership in the book, increasing the likelihood that they would not readily abandon it for another. Any hint that an important professor who taught large classes might drop a book caused considerable consternation, and when sales actually fell off the company did everything it could to get out an improved edition. In one instance it even considered destroying its existing stock of first editions.[44]

To ensure course adoptions and widespread professional interest, Wiley sought authors from among the top names at the best schools, specialists who commanded national attention. Whenever it could, Wiley also solicited promotional blurbs from recognized authorities. Of course these were also the busiest people and often not easy to get.[45]

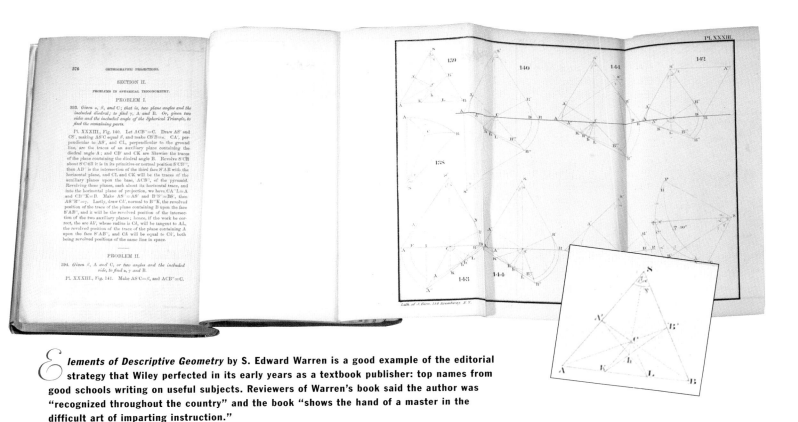

Elements of Descriptive Geometry by S. Edward Warren is a good example of the editorial strategy that Wiley perfected in its early years as a textbook publisher: top names from good schools writing on useful subjects. Reviewers of Warren's book said the author was "recognized throughout the country" and the book "shows the hand of a master in the difficult art of imparting instruction."

But being at the top of one's field did not guarantee one a book published by Wiley. To secure a contract, one had to have a marketable idea and some writing skill. Wiley was seasoned in discerning the right combination, and for the most part readers and reviewers praised Wiley's textbooks for their authority, comprehensiveness, clarity, and overall usefulness. S. Edward Warren's *Elements of Descriptive Geometry* (1874) won praise from one reviewer for its "excellent" classification of "the problems by which the whole science is elucidated." R. G. Hatfield's *Theory of Transverse Strains* (1877) "ought to be popular with students," its reviewer predicted, because it provided "a practical example . . . to elucidate every rule" and even "appended questions of a practical nature, and at the end of the work the answers to these questions are given."[46] Writing for the textbook market was not as easy as it looked. In 1951, Edward P. Hamilton described the following conversation:

I recall once saying facetiously to Professor William H. Timbie, "Writing of elementary books seems easy for you." With characteristic vehemence which I shall not attempt to reproduce, he replied that this type of work was the very hardest to write and that he devoted much effort to rewriting and polishing before he was satisfied that he had an understandable result which was at the same time accurate.[47]

Textbook and reference work reviewers assessed usefulness. Although De Volson Wood's *A Treatise on the Resistance of Materials* (1871) was called "a thorough investigation" written by "an author of distinguished ability," it was chided for its lack of an index. "This, while it matters little in a work used solely as a text book," the reviewer noted, "limits the usefulness of the treatise as a work of reference." Reviews of many Wiley books, like DeWitt Eggleston's *Auditing*

Procedure, indicated that the books could serve dual roles, as guides for practitioners and as textbooks.[48]

When reviewers complained, Wiley put the comments in context, advising its series editors and authors to pay little heed to superfluous criticisms, which they called "inevitable and not important." In 1922, for example, it told a series editor to ignore a reviewer who had complained that "there was not enough devoted to structures for potato storage." Indeed, the potato storage section had been trimmed by the editor "to keep the size of this book down," one of the thousands of choices that authors and their editors, then as now, have to make when confronted with the harsh reality of opportunity cost.[49]

Editors and Authors

Many Wiley authors and editors clearly formed close personal bonds, the kinds of relationships on which knowledge publishing depends. Repeat authors were, of course, known quantities, involving less risk than a first-time author. After a few books, authors could be promoted as important in their field, and the possibility that their works would sell for decades increased. For example, one of Mahan's books, *Ordnance and Gunnery*, remained in print from 1891 until the 1950s. Two of

iley's list included "evergreen" titles that sold for decades: *Field Engineering* (70 years in print); *Textbook of Geology* (40 years in print); *Ordnance and Gunnery* (60 years in print); MacCord's *Practical Hints for Draftsmen* (a page with curves used in engineering is at right); several electricity books by William Henry Timbie, in print for several decades. Timbie, professor of electrical engineering and industrial practice at the Massachusetts Institute of Technology for many years, was one of Wiley's all-stars. By 1954, eight of his books had sold an incredible 711,841 copies. The same two books he had on Wiley's 1914 list—*Elements of Electricity* (page 199 of which is shown at right) and *Essentials of Electricity*—were still doing extremely well after four decades. "Following his death, Timbie's daughters contacted John Wiley & Sons concerning their father's contractual arrangements. A search revealed, somewhat to everyone's surprise, that none existed. William O. and Timbie apparently just made a verbal agreement, smiled, and shook hands to cement an amicable and highly profitable relationship that eventually produced over three-quarters of a million books."[50]

Timbie's books on electricity, first published before World War I, were still formidable sellers in the 1950s. Other notable Wiley "evergreens" included *Field Engineering* by William Searles and Howard Ives, which went through 22 editions between 1880 and 1949, and *Textbook of Geology*, which went through numerous editions (and authors, beginning with Louis Pirsson and Charles Schuchert) between 1915 and the mid-1950s. In 1917, Wiley published *Engineering for Dams* by William Creager and Joel Justin, an important work that was printed eight times, the last in December 1965.[51]

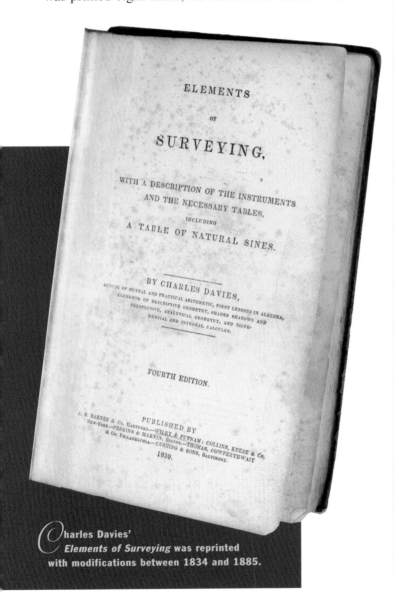

*C*harles Davies'
Elements of Surveying **was reprinted with modifications between 1834 and 1885.**

Of course, not all editorial decisions turned out to be good ones. Some titles failed; others got passed by but succeeded wildly elsewhere. Wiley passed on Dexter Kimball's path-breaking *Principles of Industrial Management*, which McGraw-Hill then brought out in 1913. Wiley also failed to secure some important books that became evergreens. Ginn and Company's *Elements of Calculus* by William Granville, first published in 1904, long dominated the elementary calculus market; Wiley failed to break its dominance for sixty years. In 1905, Wiley published *Concrete, Plain and Reinforced* by Frederick Winslow Taylor, the leader of the highly influential school of scientific management. In addition to what one reviewer called "an acute analysis of concrete construction," the book contained chapters "on time study and valuable tables of unit times determined in accordance with the Taylor methods." For reasons now unknown, however, Taylor published his later books elsewhere. Partly in an attempt to minimize such occurrences, Wiley in the early twentieth century established a number of monograph series edited by scholarly experts. One of these, the agricultural series, is described later in this chapter.[52]

Marketing Books

By century's end, the business side of publishing at Wiley was becoming as important as the craft side. None of the Wileys was as yet an economist, but they did pay close attention to some of the business fundamentals. How much to charge, for instance: What will the market bear? What must the seller earn in order to stay in business? Scientific publications always seem to cost too much. Printing alone was expensive. In 1912, it cost the company about $80.00 to print 1,000 copies of a 320-page book. In 1922, mathematician R. C. Archibald called the prices of mathematics books and periodicals a form of "extortion." At $4.65 for a 368-page book and $9.00 for 526 pages, or $51.16 and $99.03 in 2003 dollars, those prices look to be in the same range as today's for specialized technical works. When it came to the prices of its books, Wiley was unapologetic. The economics of publishing, like the economics of most goods, is best placed in the context of the interaction between supply and demand. Producers (authors and publishers) supply knowledge (books, journals); readers (individuals, institutions) demand it. The desires of the two parties conflict. Producers want high prices, readers low ones. The relative economic power of both parties determines the going price for a particular book or piece of knowledge. Prices are relatively low when there are many producers or many readers and are relatively high when there are few producers and/or few readers. The allegedly "high" prices of scientific and technical books and journals stem from the last-mentioned dynamic, a paucity of both producers and consumers. The simple fact is that few people (relatively) read scientific knowledge and fewer still can produce it, so specialized books will never be as low-priced as works of light literature that many more people can produce and many more yet choose to read.[53]

Book marketing also changed, in the trade generally and within Wiley's brand of it. After the Civil War, fiction publishers sold aggressively as population grew and wealth increased, thus enlarging their markets. The problem was, as always, how to get the information out, how to broadcast the availability of new titles. Many volumes were moved by "the army of book agents numbering many thousands who skirmished through every city, town and hamlet" knocking on people's doors and otherwise hawking their literary wares like pots and pans. By the twentieth century, bookstores proliferated and roving agents nearly disappeared. General and drug stores also began selling the most popular books, much to the chagrin of those in the "regular" book trade.[54]

Some publishers returned to selling books by subscription. Over time, the practice shifted mostly to sets of fairly expensive books, presumably because that was where the risk of misjudging demand was most

grave. Other publishers went in the opposite direction with cut-rate editions—paperbacks priced at from $.10 to $.50—but passage of the international copyright law and the severity of the late-nineteenth-century business cycle proved their undoing.[55]

Book clubs were considered ready audiences, attracting members through personal solicitations but mainly through advertising and direct mail. Their ability to "make" a book by assuring a large quick sale and much publicity gave the clubs considerable buying power. Other innovations did not catch on. An early book-vending machine was a complete flop, mostly because the novelettes it contained were of pathetic quality. In the early twentieth century, Booklovers Library Incorporated, a Philadelphia-based company, went public to raise $2.6 million that it invested in a nationwide book rental business. For $2 down and $2 per month for a year, customers of its "Tabard Inn" service received 24 books and a case. They could exchange any or all of those books for others at any time for $.05 per volume replaced. Allegedly, some 500,000 "well-to-do (reading) families" waited to be signed up. This early version of today's DVD rental services quickly spread to Canada and Britain. By 1905, though, the innovative conglomerate was in receivership, its stock of books dumped at "slaughter prices."[56]

Wiley published no light reading, however, and few of its customers were interested in rentals. They wanted to own volumes of knowledge useful to them in their professions and businesses. Finding these readers was Wiley's greatest challenge. For decades after the Civil War, Wiley continued to advertise in mass-media publications and to encourage them to review, or at least notice, their books.

As late as 1891, The *New York Times* reviewed Wiley's *Problems in Direct Fire*, a manual for artillerists. It became increasingly difficult, however, to obtain coverage for such narrow works in general publications. "Publicity is the great thing nowadays," an observer lamented in 1899.

"To be sold, it must be shouted." At the same time, paid advertising in general-interest publications became less efficient, as European book publishers had long experienced. Low-margin, low-volume books simply could not compete for advertising space in major outlets with a flood of consumer goods: food, liquor, tobacco, housekeeping supplies, and, in time, home appliances and automobiles. In 1926, of nearly $140 million spent on advertising in 32 leading magazines, book publishers purchased ads worth only about $3.8 million, or less than 3 percent of the total. Most of that money was spent by the big trade houses.[57]

So Wiley targeted, advertising selected titles in *Publishers' Weekly*, the leading journal of the book trades, and in the appropriate technical journals. In 1924, for example, it advertised Walter G. Whitman's *Household Physics*, a book written "for elementary college students in Household Arts courses, and for high school classes of girls," in the *Journal of Home Economics*. Wiley also ran advertisements and lists of related titles in its own books and experimented with "free examination" copies: Anyone could receive the book, examine it for 10 days, and then either pay for it or return it in good condition. Teachers got better terms: 60 days to review and a 20 percent discount on purchases. Wiley apparently had offered all its books to teachers and professors on

CLEARANCE CATALOGUE

OF A VALUABLE SELECTION OF

RARE AND STANDARD BOOKS,

OFFERED AT THE EXCEEDINGLY LOW PRICES AFFIXED BY

JOHN WILEY'S SONS,

15 ASTOR PLACE, NEW YORK.

1884.

easy terms since shortly after the Civil War, though the technique did not become industry best practice until about 1909. Cheap postal rates for books made the practice viable; the dearth of bookstores willing to fill shelf space with extensive inventories of scientific and technical titles made it necessary.[58]

The problem with such "on-approval" or "no-risk" policies, of course, was that sometimes books came back. In 1922, a fussy member of the department of agricultural economics at the University of Wisconsin, Henry Keller, returned a Wiley book on farm buildings because it said "nothing . . . about the position of the buildings." As it happened, Keller was wrong: 10 pages of Chapter 26 did address the topic. Wiley took the book back as promised but not without directing Keller to the section he evidently missed and pointing him to yet more detailed material elsewhere. Despite such risks, the on-approval policy made sense because it got books into the hands of likely buyers, even though some of them did not buy. Wiley also had no qualms about sending complimentary or free "review" copies to strategic persons and publications. Knowing who were the right recipients, however, was never certain.[59]

Direct mailings were another source of sales, especially after the reduction of postal rates for books

INSIDE THE BOOKS

The Wiley Colophon

Wiley, like other publishers, also adopted a colophon, an emblem or trademark placed on the title page of its books and on its letterhead. The notion was to create a brand image, to link the symbol to good thoughts in the minds of readers and authors. Wiley's colophon in the early twentieth century was a large, broad letter "W" crossed on the left with a "J" and on the right with an "S" while "& INC" filled the void created by the middle triangle of the "W."

JOHN WILEY & SONS, INC.

SCIENTIFIC PUBLISHERS

to $.01 per pound in 1885. Wiley's mailing list is thought to have been more extensive than those of many other publishers of the time. All U.S. publishers in the early twentieth century used direct mail to some extent, but the principle that direct mail sales worked best for specialized books aimed at specialist readers determined the effectiveness of the method. Specialized books for specialist readers defined Wiley by the turn of the century, and it invested accordingly.[60]

Word of mouth, every parsimonious publisher's dream marketing tool, also worked, and sometimes quite well. Wiley expected J. C. Wright's *Automotive Repair* (1921) to have even greater success "when more people have had a chance to consider it." The expectation

proved true, and Wright's work soon developed into a full line of books, some for the shop, others for the classroom. Wiley also promoted forthcoming books at conferences, with mixed responses. However its books were marketed, each eventually carried on the title page a colophon: a graphic emblem meant to associate the publisher with what it published and to build the Wiley brand.[61]

The company's array of marketing tools was not unusual for the time. The simple fact was that it was not at all clear why some books sold well and others flopped. "It is almost amusing how one publisher takes up such a book," Charles Scribner wrote in 1895, "after so many others have declined and confirms what we all know, that publishing is very far from an exact science," even if the book was about science. If anything, Wiley had fewer marketing options open to it because of the technical nature of its list. Gimmicks never did sell chemistry handbooks or calculus texts. Toying with titles could be a dangerous game too, and many experiments proved to be expensive mistakes. Sometimes, though, the timing was right, as when Wiley brought out Asa C. Chandler's *Animal Parasites and Human Diseases* just in advance of the influenza pandemic of 1918–1919.[62]

Connections Abroad

Like many growing American companies between the Civil War and World War I, Wiley was largely preoccupied with meeting the demand of an immense and fast-growing domestic market. The United States was the equivalent of a vast free-trade area almost continental in scope, where American managers and entrepreneurs learned the ways of doing business on an unprecedented scale. There was nothing like it in Europe. The knowledge revolution associated with the Second Industrial Revolution, which Wiley's list reflected, was no American monopoly, however. America was challenging the established European leaders in science and technology, and the knowledge that flowed from Europe to the United States in the nineteenth century was refined and augmented in the United States before being sent back to Europe in the form of books. The prospect of exports beckoned Wiley abroad for the second time.

When John Wiley sent George Palmer Putnam to London in 1836, Putnam went largely in the hope of bringing British literature to the United States,

> **Specialized books for specialist readers defined Wiley by the turn of the century.**

Americans still believing that American books offered little that would sell beyond their shores. By the end of the century opinion had shifted, especially in the realm of scientific and technical publishing. This subject matter was largely transnational: Railroads needed to be built in Russia, India, and Africa, too. After the Civil War, Wiley at first cautiously tested foreign publishing connections, serving as the agent of Samuel Bagster & Sons Bibles and the London Tract Society's publications. It also occasionally published books with Trubner of London, one of the successor firms that filled the lacuna created by the closure of Wiley & Putnam's London office, and with other London publishers, including the publisher of *Engineering*. Gradual reform of the international copyright regime also opened channels and improved incentives for doing business abroad.[63]

The copyright acts of March 3, 1891, March 3, 1893, and March 2, 1895, increased international cooperation in the book trades by extending U.S. copyright protection to foreign authors under certain circumstances, including domestic printing. To secure copyright in both countries, it was necessary that a book be published in both countries simultaneously, a provision that encouraged American publishers to form close associations, especially with British publishers. In 1895, Wiley broke the old pattern of dealing with numerous European agents in favor of consolidating its business with Chapman & Hall of London, which had published Dickens but also had scientific and technical ambitions.[64]

Further copyright reforms in 1909, which provided much more leeway in publication dates, increased the benefits of association with foreign, especially British, publishers, and the Wiley-Chapman partnership took on an air of permanence. Wiley listed

Chapman & Hall on its letterhead, in its advertisements, and in other marketing materials, and Chapman & Hall was well pleased with an arrangement that linked its name to the latest scientific and technical publications. "The market for Wiley books throughout the British Empire and on the Continent," wrote Chapman & Hall managing director Arthur Waugh, "was increasing with great rapidity from year to year." Demand grew so quickly during World War I that Chapman & Hall retained a management consultant to help it handle increasing transactions and also to contend with customs officials who thought the importation of books during wartime the height of folly.[65]

Though Wiley did not establish foreign offices until later, this foray abroad was more penetrating than the company's earlier ventures. By 1900, it was becoming clear that many of Wiley's texts and handbooks appealed to a global market, prompting the company to sign distribution agreements with booksellers as close as Montreal (Renouf Publishing) and as far as Shanghai and Manila (Philippine Education Co.). As they traveled, Wiley books began to appear in languages other than English. *Rational Geometry* (1904) by George Bruce Halsted, one of America's first American-born and -trained mathematicians of note, was translated into French, German, and even Japanese. It is true that this was export business and far from "global" business as a later generation would come to understand cross-border capital flows and trade in all manner of goods and services. But such exports were how many a latter-day global company got started far from home. Wiley was no exception.[66]

Exports were how many a global company got started far from home.

Wiley Series Books: A Case Study

Lively markets at home and abroad proved the pervasiveness, at least across the western and northern hemispheres, of the Second Industrial Revolution. As inventors and scientists discovered and accumulated knowledge, publishers like Wiley transmitted it through books to engineers, managers, and other professional practitioners—and to students—who would soon put that knowledge to work. Once begun in earnest in the latter half of the nineteenth century, knowledge publishing self-propelled itself forward. Scientific and technical knowledge was cumulative, as one generation recorded and handed off its best to the next. For knowledge publishers, linear and cumulative meant more and more books.

Perhaps Wiley's most important contribution to the knowledge publishing of this era came from its series rather than from its individual titles. In the early twentieth century, series of books in specific fields edited by top scholars became major undertakings; series editors were even given their own customized Wiley letterhead. The Wiley Mathematical Monographs series (1896–1921) was the first, winning praise for creating "an interest in some of the rich fields of modern mathematics." Edited by Mansfield Merriman and Robert Woodward, the math series in 1906 and 1907 alone put out 13 quality studies priced at just one dollar each.[67]

Wiley also published an important series of books on agricultural science. Improvements in agricultural efficiency underlay the economic transformation and modernization of America. One way, in fact, to look at the nation's growing cadres of engineers, scientists, professors, publishers, and factory workers was as displaced farmers, people whose labor was no longer needed on the land. When the first Major Wiley returned from his service in the Revolution, nine Americans were needed to feed ten. By the time the second Major Wiley died, about 150 years later, just five Americans fed twenty, and a growing number of foreigners as well. Such numbers testify to the enormous productivity wrought by mechanization and chemical fertilizers. Between 1870 and 1900, employment in agriculture grew by just 53 percent, while in manufacturing it was up 182 percent, in professional services 254 percent, and in clerical services 279 percent. Between 1900 and 1930, employment in agriculture flattened, while in manufacturing employment almost doubled, in professional services it nearly trebled, and in clerical services it grew more than fivefold.[68]

As agriculture became less labor-intensive and more capital- and knowledge-intensive, Wiley established its presence in this field. The firm had occasionally published agricultural titles, including *Manual of Cattle Feeding* (1880), *Practical Farm Drainage* (1882), and *A Handbook for Farmers and Dairymen* (1897), but it lacked in-house expertise. So, following the model of the math series, Wiley in 1918 turned to Arthur K. Getman from the New York State Education Department and Carl E. Ladd from the Cornell School of Agriculture to edit a Wiley farm series for high school students. In 1921, Wiley signed Professor Jay Brownlee Davidson from Iowa State College and Professor L. W. Chase from Penn State University to co-edit a new agricultural engineering series.[69]

A voluminous correspondence flowed between Wiley and its new series editor (Chase, it appears, soon dropped from the picture) in the early 1920s. The letters

> Scientific and technical knowledge was cumulative, [and that] meant more and more books.

reveal Wiley's focus on the connection between content and its utility to particular audiences of readers, and on books of useful knowledge that met its own business tests of publishing. Wiley quickly dropped manuscripts, such as certain laboratory manuals, that did not promise to stimulate sufficient demand. It bluntly told Davidson that "we believe that it would not pay to publish the Curtiss book, especially at the present time," and declined to consider another book because it appeared to be too close to Harry C. Ramsower's *Equipment for the Farm and the Farmstead* (Ginn and Co., 1917). Wiley also rejected a manual for the American Society of Agricultural Engineers because that professional society insisted on a loose-leaf form. Wiley had learned through experience with loose-leaf manuals on materials testing and chemistry that this format "does not pay at all" except on a very large scale.[70]

Just as decisively, Wiley took on projects that did promise to pay. From the beginning, the company had a clear notion that it wanted the agricultural engineering series to "stick pretty closely to textbooks." When ideas arose for professional titles, though, it considered them, too, but always on their business merits. Wiley appreciated the nuances of its market. It considered, but ultimately rejected, a book on farm machinery written specifically for the South, and reflected on whether specific books should lean toward texts or reference works. It also tried to ascertain the appropriate content for textbooks in emerging fields whose technologies and courses were still developing. For example, it debated whether tractors should be treated in a separate book or included in more general books about farm power or farm machinery. It also pondered a text's degree of difficulty, searching for the safe middle ground between the too elementary and the overly technical. What did readers want? What would the market bear?[71]

PROFILE

JAY BROWNLEE DAVIDSON

Jay Brownlee Davidson (1880–1957) chaired the department of agricultural engineering at what was then called Iowa State College in Ames from 1919 until 1946. A tall man from rural Nebraska, Davidson worked hard to build his department into one of the best. In addition to editing a series for Wiley, he authored or co-authored with a variety of publishers numerous books, including *The Durability of Prepared Roll Roofings* (1932), *Machinery for Growing Corn* (1940), *Life, Service, and Cost of Service of Farm Machinery* (1929), *Farm Machinery and Farm Motors* (1908), *Planning and Adorning the Farmstead* (1912), *Farm Poultry Houses* (1912), *Agricultural Engineering* (1913), and many others. He was considered by many the father of agricultural engineering

and the founder of the American Society of Agricultural Engineers, and his series, books, and teaching were an important part of the continuing agricultural revolution. The engineering building at his school, now Iowa State University, was named in his honor in 1975.[72]

In 1915, the annual meeting of the Society for the Promotion of Engineering Education was held at Iowa State College in Ames. A Wiley representative was in attendance specifically to talk with Davidson, who seemed the right person, in the right place, to develop a new Wiley series in agricultural engineering. On July 20, Davidson and Professor L. W. Chase from Penn State University agreed to co-edit a new agricultural engineering series.[73]

At left, Jay Brownlee Davidson is shown kneeling (on the far right) to examine the soil behind a cultivator at Iowa State College in 1934. Iowa State was the nation's first land grant institution and became Iowa State University in 1959. Above, students at Pennsylvania State College (now Penn State University) observe the mechanical harvesting of potatoes in 1934.

Readers would want, for example, an answer key, and when author Frederick Wirt refused to write one for his *Laboratory Manual in Farm Machinery* (1917), Wiley approached Davidson about finding someone else who might "care to do the job." And when it heard that Wirt might write a book on farm machinery for another company, Wiley made known to Davidson that it remained in earnest about getting such a book out of Wirt. The same letter reveals a concern for list development, proposing that the Wirt book "might form a very good combination with the one that Prof. Blasingame is now preparing on Tractors." (Wirt and Blasingame later did team up on a textbook and laboratory manual.)[74]

Wiley was astute in reading the market, and its responses were swift. Whenever a major course adopter threatened to drop an existing text, Wiley pressed the author and series editor to come out with a suitable new edition as soon as possible to save the account. In 1921, its sales manager, F. E. Mee, noted that there was a strong demand for a book on farm motors. The company implored Davidson to "do something to get one started," even if it meant co-authoring the title himself. Early in 1922, it urged John T. Bowen, an employee of the U.S. Department of Agriculture, to finish his manuscript on dairy engineering by July so the book would be ready for the International Dairy Congress in October 1923. Despite help from Davidson, Bowen was several chapters short at deadline time. After he had begun working, moreover, he wrote too much. Worse, he produced text that had to be trimmed by editing throughout rather than by cutting whole chapters, because nobody could decide what exactly should be cut, electricity or milking machines. Davidson finally called in a dairy expert to help with the revisions, and ultimately the Major himself had to get involved. Bowen's book did not appear until 1925, and its troubles, fueled by suggestions from potential course adopters, continued right up to the moment that typesetting began. "If we heeded the recommendations of all of the people who offer us

suggestions," Wiley noted, "many of our books would be nearly twice their present size, and would consequently be too unwieldy to have any sort of a sale." As final deadlines pressed, Wiley often resorted to express mailing of galley proofs to keep things on schedule.[75]

When promising proposals came in, Wiley searched out expert readers and simultaneously prepared estimates of manufacturing costs. When the costs rose, Wiley drove hard bargains with Davidson and his authors, capping author royalties at 12 percent and editor royalties at 3 percent. The proximate cause of the change in royalties was the loss incurred with selling Wirt's *Laboratory Manual* at $1.50: With higher printing costs and an 18 percent total royalty, Wiley lost money on every copy sold. It also asked Davidson if he thought raising the price of the manual to $2.00 would hurt sales. Davidson said it was Wiley's call, but thought probably not. Davidson also advised Wiley that in his view a large book on dairy engineering would sell readily at $4.50.[76]

Wiley later standardized series royalties at 3 percent on all copies for the series editor, and 10 percent for the author on the first 2,000 copies and 12 percent thereafter, down from the 15 percent after the first 1,500 copies for Wiley contracts in which there was no series editor to be compensated. No evidence of advances exists, but the company hinted that it would consider better royalty terms if an author showed signs of turning to a competitor. Wiley never promised much, however, making clear that it could only "slightly modify" terms and urging Davidson to stress to authors the higher quantity their books would sell as part of a series. In Wiley's standard contract, authors were expected to furnish a table of contents and an index. Wiley by this time considered an index essential and believed the author better qualified to prepare it than anyone else. Author-prepared indexes also saved the company money.[77]

Wiley also had to be cautious. When the preface of one manuscript suggested that the author may have unwittingly violated copyright, the company stopped the publication process and warned Davidson:

"If you reprinted any matter from any other copyrighted publication verbatim, the mere fact that you give credit in your manuscript does not give you the right to use the material." Author and publisher must give permission first, Wiley further explained, though "if you have received merely helpful suggestions from reading the books listed, and have not made direct quotations there can be no objections." And it was sometimes difficult to read the market. In the 1910s, Clarence Hirshfeld and Tomlinson Ulbricht co-authored two books, *Steam Power* (1916) and *Gas Engines for the Farm* (1913). The former title sold poorly because it was written for secondary school students, most of whom did not take courses relevant to the book. The latter, in contrast, did well. When Hirshfeld and Ulbricht approached Wiley in 1922 with a proposal for "Modern Gas Engines," the company hesitated, fearful that the new text would be unsuitable for agricultural colleges and too elementary for mechanical engineering programs. Davidson concurred.[78]

As manuscripts progressed toward completion, the company selected a few for special prepublication promotion in its bulletin. In 1921, it picked W. A. Foster and Deane G. Carter's book on farm buildings because of its illustrations. (Wiley in this period began to render artwork for authors, much to their delight.) "If you have any additional information about it, or points to stress," Wiley told Davidson, "we shall be glad of them." The book on farm buildings was a good choice, and its initial printing was gone in a year.[79]

As much as the letters between Wiley and Davidson reveal Wiley's seriousness about the business side of publishing, they also confirm its enduring instinct for the craft of books. In 1920 and 1921, it paid careful attention to the text and illustrations in a manuscript on drainage. After painstaking editing, in 1922,

> The letters between Wiley and Davidson . . . confirm [their] enduring instinct for the craft of books.

Land Drainage, by W. L. Powers and T. A. H. Teeter, was published. "I am very much pleased with the job of printing," Davidson wrote Wiley after perusing the finished product. "We had so much trouble with this book it is rather gratifying to have it turn out so well." Similarly, Wiley and Davidson made George R. Chatburn revise his manuscript before publishing it in 1921 as *Highway Engineering, Rural Roads and Pavements*. Foster and Carter had to rewrite and rename their "Farm Structures" manuscript before Wiley published it in 1922 as *Farm Buildings*. Wiley and Davidson made Bowen cut his book on dairy engineering drastically, then persuaded him to cut some tedious mathematical sections.[80]

Not all manuscripts made it to print. Professor Blasingame could not get his manuscript on tractors into shape, so Davidson signed Edward Wiggins, editor of the *Chilton Tractor Journal*, to set it right. Wiggins made progress, but the book was never published. Some authors did not complete the manuscripts they were under contract for, sometimes because they were too busy to get started or because their titles were superseded by books in other Wiley series or other publishers' lists before theirs were ready. Professor Musselman gave up on his book on farm mechanics, admitting that he "had not time and is no book writer." Yet he proposed to write another book, on "farm conveniences." Not quite sure what he meant by conveniences, Wiley wisely let the matter rest. Many manuscripts died at the proposal stage because Wiley was selective, and strict editorial standards kept series small. Accident also intruded: One manuscript on tractors and tractor plows burned up in a fire.[81]

Even relatively strong proposals, if they came from novice writers, got treated coolly. A handbook on architectural design proposed by two of Davidson's Iowa State colleagues never appeared despite an elaborate proposal containing a detailed table of contents and a draft foreword that argued the book filled a growing gap in the literature on farm buildings. An outside reader wanted to see even more, given that the would-be authors had no writing track record. Both Davidson and Wiley were uncomfortable with writers whose drafts might require much work in editing. Conversely, they made allowances for seasoned writers whose work they could depend on being complete, well-prepared, and on time. Wiley wanted professionals, not apprentices.[82]

Pedagogical considerations mattered, too. Davidson pulled back from F. N. Kranich's manuscript on farm machinery because it was not written "from the standpoint of an educator and does not have the organization of a good textbook." Because Wiley needed a book on the subject, Davidson suggested that Kranich get help from a co-author. When this arrangement fell through in 1923, Davidson said he would write the book himself, if Wiley was willing to wait. It was, and *Agricultural Machinery* finally appeared in 1931.[83]

Davidson was an ideal series editor—tactful and prompt in his dealings with authors and prospective authors, a politic liaison between Wiley and series authors, and a constant source of market information. In 1924, for example, he pointed out that a book on dairy engineering could sell to the nation's 25,000 creameries in addition to the relatively few classrooms where the subject was taught. With that new information, Wiley went ahead with publication. Davidson was patient in pursuit of authors; it took a full decade from his first contact to get Orson Israelsen's *Irrigation Principles and Practices* (1932) into print. And when Davidson advised to hold off on contracting, Wiley listened.[84]

Wiley paid Davidson a $25 honorarium for reviewing a manuscript, but he was more than an acquisitions editor, as he followed the production process through to approving sample pages and reviewing proofs. He had much leeway in matters of size and nature of illustrations. For these services he received $25 to $50, depending on the length of the book. The company also sent him two copies of published books, one bound for his personal use and a second unbound "press" copy to be used to keep track of changes for future editions, a service that Davidson also performed as series editor.[85]

Under Davidson, the Agricultural Engineering Series was so successful that it spawned spinoffs. In 1922, J. G. Lipman, dean of Rutgers University's college of agriculture, assumed editorship of The Wiley Agricultural Series, and in 1924, A. K. Getman and C. E. Ladd began co-editing The Wiley Farm Series, which had a more vocational emphasis. Wiley encountered some difficulties in finding suitable outside editors for those series because editors had to be in high-profile positions yet not "too busy to do the work." Moreover, Wiley believed that they had to be "very broad minded . . . not tied up too much in any one field." Davidson was hard to duplicate. Though Lipman was a good choice, the two new series almost immediately began to conflict with Davidson's. In addition to causing confusion among readers, authors began to wonder which series was most appropriate for their work and if the existence of the other series would hurt sales.[86]

Between Family and Firm

The talent and labors of men like Davidson won Wiley an enviable editorial reputation, but from a business perspective the company was less successful. No one other than the Wileys owned any significant part of the firm, and only a Wiley or blood kin played any role in managing it. In 1904, Wiley restructured itself as a corporation under New York State law. Charles, William H., William O., and accountant William F. P. Conner took up all the shares, $50,000 worth in all. (Conner was included at least in part because one of the incorporators had to be a resident of New York and the Wileys all lived in New Jersey. He received only 1 of the 500 shares issued.) There was no initial public offering of stock, and the company remained a closely held family corporation. No new money was raised. The decision to incorporate did, however, secure the advantage of perpetual and separate legal existence for a concern that owned about $150,000 worth of assets. Wiley was still a small family business, though, due to the nature of what it did, knowledge publishing, a small business linked to large worlds. Its influence was disproportionate to its size, which meant that its potential for growth was greater than its principals may have recognized.[87]

> Wiley was still a small family business [but] its influence was disproportionate to its size.

The new corporation did well at first, paying dividends of 6 percent and salaries as high as $40,000 per year to the Major and Charles. It was just at this point that generational weariness set in, as the Major continued to be involved in both his political career and the company's top management. By the end of the new century's first decade, the company's performance sagged despite continuing editorial successes, including, in 1909, Joseph G. Coffin's path-breaking *Vector Analysis* and the *Elements of Metallography* translated by Yale's C. H. Mathewson. Salaries were slashed and, uncharacteristically, Wiley borrowed heavily. World War I boosted sales

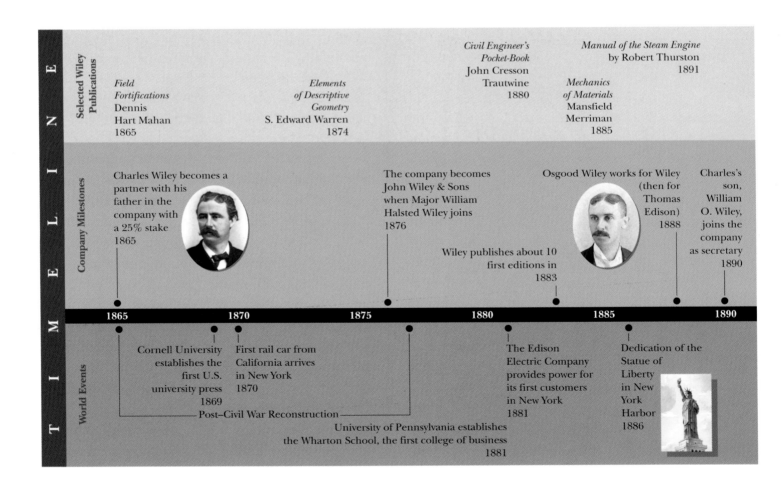

TIMELINE

Selected Wiley Publications

Field Fortifications
Dennis Hart Mahan
1865

Elements of Descriptive Geometry
S. Edward Warren
1874

Civil Engineer's Pocket-Book
John Cresson Trautwine
1880

Manual of the Steam Engine
by Robert Thurston
1891

Mechanics of Materials
Mansfield Merriman
1885

Company Milestones

Charles Wiley becomes a partner with his father in the company with a 25% stake
1865

The company becomes John Wiley & Sons when Major William Halsted Wiley joins
1876

Wiley publishes about 10 first editions in
1883

Osgood Wiley works for Wiley (then for Thomas Edison)
1888

Charles's son, William O. Wiley, joins the company as secretary
1890

1865 — 1870 — 1875 — 1880 — 1885 — 1890

World Events

Cornell University establishes the first U.S. university press
1869

First rail car from California arrives in New York
1870

——— Post–Civil War Reconstruction ———

University of Pennsylvania establishes the Wharton School, the first college of business
1881

The Edison Electric Company provides power for its first customers in New York
1881

Dedication of the Statue of Liberty in New York Harbor
1886

and reinvigorated exports, but the next generation of Wileys was still not ready, or not allowed, to assume a major decision-making role even after Charles's death in 1916. Only the company's past successes saw it through the slow transition to the fourth generation.[88]

The old Major stayed on at Wiley nearly to the end, though as the years passed he delegated more and more responsibility to William O. and Edward Hamilton. The Major left the company by early 1925, and died on May 2 of that year, after a short illness. The business continued among signs that the next generation was eager to push ahead quickly. W. O. and Hamilton increased the number of new titles by more than 25 percent in their first five years. The company needed to grow in order to survive, but the Major had resisted necessary moves like increasing the payroll. Salaries

slashed in the 1910s crept back only slowly after the war. In 1921, the company paid the first bonuses since 1904. Sales grew from $519,700 in 1918 to $869,687 in 1925, but in relative terms Wiley continued to lose ground to McGraw-Hill and other powerful competitors.[89]

The market, though changing, brimmed with potential. Despite the coming of new diversions and technologies such as the phonograph, movies, and the radio, the public appeared as hungry as ever for books. Nonfiction more than held its own against fiction, due in some part to the need-to-know knowledge revolution that created those very technologies. As the fourth generation of Wileys finally took full control of the company, however, it was not at all clear that Wiley was sufficiently unified or energized to tap the burgeoning demand for knowledge books and to sustain itself.[90]

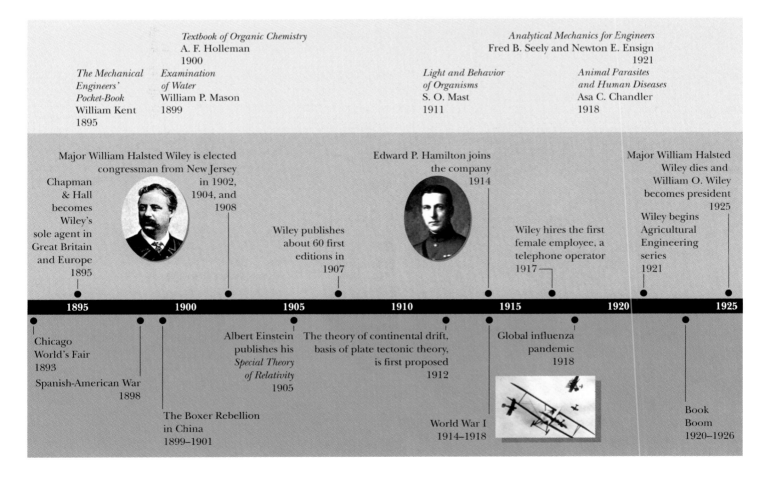

Textbook of Organic Chemistry
A. F. Holleman
1900

Analytical Mechanics for Engineers
Fred B. Seely and Newton E. Ensign
1921

The Mechanical Engineers' Pocket-Book
William Kent
1895

Examination of Water
William P. Mason
1899

Light and Behavior of Organisms
S. O. Mast
1911

Animal Parasites and Human Diseases
Asa C. Chandler
1918

Major William Halsted Wiley is elected congressman from New Jersey in 1902, 1904, and 1908

Chapman & Hall becomes Wiley's sole agent in Great Britain and Europe
1895

Wiley publishes about 60 first editions in
1907

Edward P. Hamilton joins the company
1914

Wiley hires the first female employee, a telephone operator
1917

Major William Halsted Wiley dies and William O. Wiley becomes president
1925

Wiley begins Agricultural Engineering series
1921

| 1895 | 1900 | 1905 | 1910 | 1915 | 1920 | 1925 |

Chicago World's Fair
1893

Spanish-American War
1898

The Boxer Rebellion in China
1899–1901

Albert Einstein publishes his *Special Theory of Relativity*
1905

The theory of continental drift, basis of plate tectonic theory, is first proposed
1912

World War I
1914–1918

Global influenza pandemic
1918

Book Boom
1920–1926

Assembly line workers inside the Ford Motor Company factory in Dearborn, Michigan, March 1, 1928.

The Cousins:
Conservative Change
During the Fourth Generation

1925—1956

Chapter Five

✽

The Cousins
and Their Times

Wiley, in the Roaring Twenties, that enduring caricature of American urban life in the 1920s, remained a staid scientific publisher. But it could not help being swept up in the social, and especially economic, tumults of the age. In 1925, when William O. Wiley and his cousin Edward P. Hamilton took over the company on the death of their uncle William Halsted Wiley, Manhattan exuded, in the words of F. Scott Fitzgerald, "all the iridescence of the beginning of the world. . . . this was the greatest nation and there was gala in the air." The war to end all wars was over. Advances in technology and business administration portended great things to come. In the stock exchanges at the island's foot, prices responded, slowly at first, then with an irrational ebullience. In midtown, busy offices like John Wiley & Sons clanked and jangled with typewriters and telephones. At the top of Manhattan, New Yorkers, black and white, snuggled in smoky clubs, drank illegal booze, and heard a whole new music being born: Louis Armstrong played the trumpet and Bessie Smith sang the blues. Across the river in the Bronx, fans cheered Babe Ruth's home runs in a brand new Yankee stadium, opened in 1923.[1]

Edward Hamilton, the great grandson of Wiley's founder, fancied horses and dude ranches, not baseball, and he preferred opera to jazz. In this era of giddy experimentation,

Female employees of Boeing stitch fabric onto the top wing of a Boeing-built Thomas Morse MB-EA Army pursuit plane in 1922.

Wiley preferred tradition. Hamilton wore dark suits to the office, white shirts, and club ties. While new publishing houses were bursting into being—Norton, Simon & Schuster, William Morrow, Viking Press, John Day, Vanguard Press, Random House, all in the mid-1920s—Wiley remained unperturbed, steadily focused on serious publications, technical manuals, and textbooks, still a small, family enterprise. Hamilton and his cousin William O. Wiley took the time to nurture authors and customers in a way that, even then, in the go-getting 1920s, was beginning to seem old-fashioned. In the shadow of America's corporate behemoths—General Electric, General Motors, U.S. Steel—Wiley seemed quaint.[2]

Quaint or no, Wiley knew what it was doing. Outside the windows of its midtown offices one would have noticed the city soaring upward, in a relentless vertical development that would create the most famous skyline in the world. At the corner of 42nd and Lexington rose—four floors a week—a skyscraper that would be the world's tallest, at least for a year. The Chrysler Building, named for the automaker who built it, was mightily impressive—an example of engineering on the edge. Art Deco in style, it also boasted automobile motifs. The corners at Floor 31 spouted radiator caps; at Floor 61 perched eagles, replicas of Chrysler's 1929 hood ornaments. Where the masonry ended and the soon-to-be-illuminated dome began, giant stainless-steel hubcaps spun skyward. On October 23, 1929, when a 185-foot spire, erected in secret within the building, was hoisted above the hubcaps in just 90 minutes, New Yorkers thrilled at the spectacle and surprise. The Chrysler Building, says architectural historian Christopher Gray, "presents like a Machine Age product." It was surely the symbol of an era.[3]

Three years later in 1932, Wiley produced a landmark of a different sort, Architectural Graphic Standards for Architects, Engineers, Decorators, Builders and Draftsmen. As originally authored by Charles G. Ramsey and Harold R. Sleeper, Architectural Graphic Standards was published in its eleventh edition in Wiley's bicentennial year. With more than one million copies sold, it is one of the best-selling titles in Wiley's history, in some years representing 10 percent of the company's gross income. It has become the architect's bible: "Every architect loves it, wears it out, and keeps it within arm's length." The book doesn't call attention to itself, unlike the Chrysler Building, but as a star in Wiley's book program, it is every bit as much a symbol of the age. The manuals, technical treatises, and textbooks that Wiley published were just what the Machine Age needed and wanted. In 1927, Wiley's list numbered a thousand books, on the various branches of engineering, chemistry, mathematics, geology, biology, agriculture, forestry, and other subjects, as well as accountancy, economics, and business administration, and the growing fields of electrical sciences, aeronautics, management science, telecommunications, and the social sciences.[4]

The week after the Chrysler Building unveiled its spire, stock prices began a painful descent, portending what we now know as the Great Depression. But in 1929, Wiley posted $1 million in sales for the first time. It lost ground during the 1930s but persevered by focusing on its traditional core strengths: Books of a utilitarian character that helped people build and rebuild, make and make do, account and account for, communicate, and accomplish, a list that would allow sales to soar to new heights during World War II, a war won as much by engineers, manufacturers, and scientists as by soldiers, sailors, and marines.

The Chrysler Building was the tallest building in the world from October 23, 1929, when the 185-foot hidden spire was hoisted into position, until May 1, 1931, when the Empire State Building was completed.

The Cousins Come into Their Own

Cousins William O. Wiley (1862–1958; known as W. O.) and Edward P. Hamilton (1883–1977; hereafter Hamilton) both grandsons of John Wiley, represented the fourth generation of the House of Wiley. Already Wiley far exceeded the life expectancy of most family firms, and there was no reason to believe it would not continue. W. O. sired two daughters. Hamilton was a bachelor, presenting the problem of finding a male heir who could be a successor in this unquestionably patriarchal age. W. O. and Hamilton turned to William Bradford Wiley, grandson of the mysterious Osgood Wiley. Brad would join his second cousins in 1932. What challenged the cousins, though, were not family matters but business dynamics. Externally, the economic environment soon served up disruptions at which few could have guessed. Internally, tensions simmered between old and new approaches to publishing.

W. O. became president of the company in 1925, and Hamilton became vice president and treasurer. In 1941, W. O. became chairman of the board and Hamilton assumed the presidency, the post he held until 1956. Together, the two men, aided by considerable input from their younger family protégé, Brad, worked to make Wiley grow, expanding the company's workforce and its list. They navigated the Roaring Twenties, the Crash, the Great Depression, World War II, and the postwar textbook publishing boom. They wrestled with rising costs, low prices, and anemic profits. Ever searching for new sources of revenue, they expanded exports and began a sustained effort to set up Wiley offices overseas.

PROFILE

WILLIAM O. WILEY

A reluctant starter, W. O. thought several times before giving up a sales job in the woolen business that paid a solid $1,800 per year to join the family's book business in 1890 for less than half as much. How Major William Halsted Wiley, his uncle, managed to persuade the young man is unknown. He probably convinced his nephew there was a good future in publishing, if one had patience for the long haul. Wiley's future, the uncle might have said, lay with scientific and technical books. He may have also presented working in the family firm as a challenge because W. O.'s formal education—a master's degree in Greek and Latin from Columbia—prepared him for technical publishing in only the broadest sense. However cajoled, the nephew did his duty and became a businessman in publishing. He gained experience running the company's daily operations and found himself in nominal charge well before the Major's death in 1925. Like his uncle, the classical scholar became professionally active particularly in the field of engineering, serving on the board of directors of the Society for the Promotion of Engineering Education for 35 years and forging, like his uncle, close, mutually beneficial ties between engineers and the company. W. O.'s service in Theta Xi, an engineering fraternity born at Rensselaer Polytechnic Institute in 1864, landed him in its hall of fame, "The Order of the Unicorn." Other connections abounded. His name was in the *New York Social Register* and on the membership rolls of numerous professional associations.

William O. Wiley (1862–1958) maintained ties with his classical education, for many years meeting every Friday at the Columbia University Club with Nicholas Murray Butler, who would become president of their alma mater, to chat, eat oysters, and down martinis.

PROFILE

EDWARD P. HAMILTON

Edward P. Hamilton (1883–1977) was the son of the Major's and Charles's sister Alice (1845–1893), who married Edward Parmalee Hamilton in 1870. Orphaned in the 1890s, Hamilton moved into the Major's household and in practical terms became his adopted son. After graduating from Rensselaer Polytechnic Institute in engineering in 1907 and spending several years in the construction business in Cuba, Hamilton joined the company in 1914, when it had a staff of twenty. Hamilton quickly began to share management responsibilities with W. O., his cousin. Hamilton was also a soldier, his early Wiley years interrupted by duty on the Mexican border, where he chased Pancho Villa with General John "Black Jack" Pershing in 1916, and then, in 1917, with the American Expeditionary Force in France. He was captured while serving as a forward artillery observer, and anxious telegrams from the Major to the Red Cross about his fate confirm a deep and lasting affection for the young man. Smart pictures of Hamilton in uniform—puttees, riding crop, and all—show him every inch the dashing cavalry officer. Later in life, Hamilton donned the crisp dark suits of a Wiley executive, and when, in the 1950s, Brad appeared in the office in a blazer and gray flannels and *loafers*, Hamilton was not amused. He never married, but for years cut a tall handsome figure with New York hostesses at dinner and the opera. He also fancied horses and seemed equally at home at the Dublin Horse Show or a Wyoming dude ranch.

About these men and the company they led between the world wars, there is an unmistakable backward-and-forward quality. The company strove to modernize, but it moved with deliberate speed and not without debate. Quietly but steadily, the company grew, even in tumultuous times. It was posting sales of more than $5 million when the GIs came back home from World War II and then, courtesy of the GI Bill, headed off to college—where their need for textbooks spiked demand for Wiley's professional and higher education titles. Knowledge publishing was what Wiley had done for many years, and under the cousins its focus got stronger and broader. Wiley books would help reshape the future for just about everyone. In the spring of 1940, ahead of the postwar consumer curve, Wiley published a book by two RCA executives and scientists on the subject of, as the jacket copy put it, "radio's newest development: *Television.*" Most Wiley titles were both up to date and destined for long lives, some through generations of editions for generations of readers.[5]

The years of the cousins were marked by tradition and innovation, a mid-course in the fast-changing publishing world. Wiley was slow to advertise, for example, even when it began to publish titles for the general reader. Other publishers of trade titles, like the young Simon & Schuster, took out full-page newspaper ads and even enclosed cards in its books to solicit reader response. Nor did Wiley launch publicity campaigns, as trade publishers aiming to create bestsellers did. From its offices at 440 Fourth Avenue (later renamed Park Avenue South), Wiley retained its small company culture. But out of necessity in a company approaching $1 million in sales, W. O. and Hamilton were joined by a cohort of professional managers. W. O. and Hamilton continued to know their authors. These authors weren't billed as stars; they were ordinary academics and government and industry technocrats. Wiley liked to talk of the "Wiley family" and meant by it not the descendants of the first Charles alone. The cousins talked of a "Wiley spirit" shared among staff, editors, and authors that was more than cheap sentiment. Perhaps this was because W. O. and Hamilton were also the company's owners with much at risk in the effort to master change and make the company succeed.[6]

> The first order of business was to expand without sacrificing quality.

After the Major's death, W. O. owned 36.6 percent of the company's stock, Hamilton 40 percent, his sister Elizabeth 10 percent, and two other close relatives 6.7 percent each. Of the five shareholders, only the cousins were active in management, and far from squabbling over titles and preferment, they worked well together over the years. Editorially and administratively, they pursued a strategy of controlled growth and incremental change. "Hasten slowly" was the phrase that a company editorial manual used to describe the process for transforming a manuscript into a book. It described Wiley's business

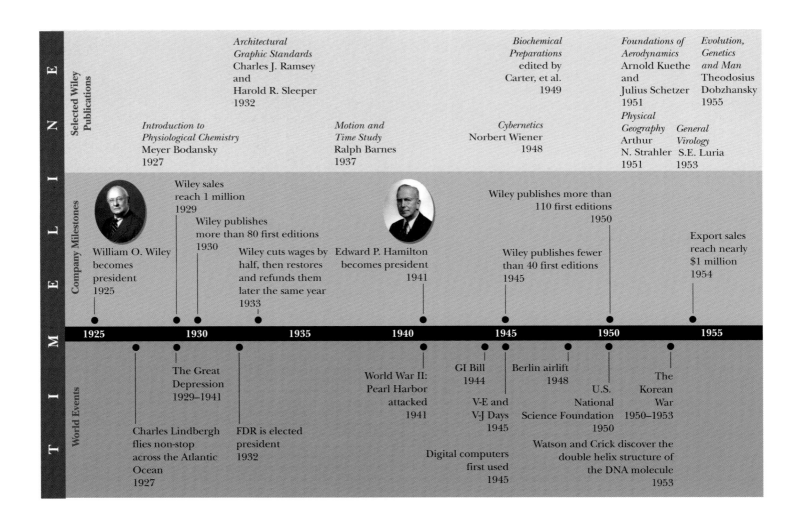

TIMELINE

Selected Wiley Publications

Introduction to Physiological Chemistry Meyer Bodansky 1927

Architectural Graphic Standards Charles J. Ramsey and Harold R. Sleeper 1932

Motion and Time Study Ralph Barnes 1937

Cybernetics Norbert Wiener 1948

Biochemical Preparations edited by Carter, et al. 1949

Foundations of Aerodynamics Arnold Kuethe and Julius Schetzer 1951

Physical Geography Arthur N. Strahler 1951

Evolution, Genetics and Man Theodosius Dobzhansky 1955

General Virology S.E. Luria 1953

Company Milestones

William O. Wiley becomes president 1925

Wiley sales reach 1 million 1929

Wiley publishes more than 80 first editions 1930

Wiley cuts wages by half, then restores and refunds them later the same year 1933

Edward P. Hamilton becomes president 1941

Wiley publishes more than 110 first editions 1950

Wiley publishes fewer than 40 first editions 1945

Export sales reach nearly $1 million 1954

| 1925 | 1930 | 1935 | 1940 | 1945 | 1950 | 1955 |

World Events

Charles Lindbergh flies non-stop across the Atlantic Ocean 1927

The Great Depression 1929–1941

FDR is elected president 1932

World War II: Pearl Harbor attacked 1941

GI Bill 1944

V-E and V-J Days 1945

Digital computers first used 1945

Berlin airlift 1948

U.S. National Science Foundation 1950

Watson and Crick discover the double helix structure of the DNA molecule 1953

The Korean War 1950–1953

Wiley First Editions, 1926–1956

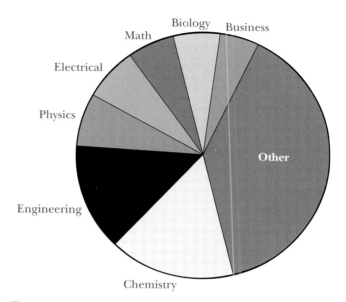

Wiley First Editions by Category, 1926–1956

Source: OCLC; Wiley catalogues.

This chart illustrates the ups and downs of the firm's editorial fortunes from the boom years of the 1920s through the Great Depression, World War II with its paper shortages, and the post-war publishing take-off driven by government expenditures in education and research.

This pie chart shows the relative importance of each area of publication during the fourth generation. Engineering and chemistry remained the company's bread and butter, with biology, the electrical sciences, physics, and mathematics also making impressive contributions to the list. Just behind them in quantitative importance were the accounting, business, and economics titles and the agricultural books. The balance of the list, a full third of it, was composed of titles in newly emerging fields, as well as some old fields on the wane.

policy as well, even though the cousins, alert to the threat from rapidly growing competitors like McGraw-Hill, also knew that their company must grow or be lost.[7]

The first order of business was to expand without sacrificing quality. As soon as they assumed control, the cousins increased the number of new and substantially revised editions Wiley published. Wiley's active list grew from 869 titles at the end of World War I to 1,231 at the beginning of World War II. These numbers hardly put Wiley in the front ranks for size, but the company was not marginal, either.[8] Its average annual output of 40 new titles exceeded that of the average publisher of 5 or more titles, though its output dropped during the Depression.[9]

During the fourth generation, Wiley's editorial strategy continued that of the Major's era. Wiley's editors and their academic counterparts, aided by travelers, worked on series, professional books, technical books, and textbooks, with the addition of titles for the general reader starting in the 1930s. W. O. or Hamilton themselves served as editor for many of those volumes. The company's officers made rounds, too, and were widely engaged in professional and social activities, partly for their own sake and partly to enhance the network of acquaintances and friends that attracted more manuscripts and generated more name recognition and ultimately more sales. The focus remained on tapping the experts at top schools.[10]

Publishing for Established Fields

ROCKS AND ROCK MINERALS

A MANUAL OF THE ELEMENTS OF PETROLOGY WITHOUT THE USE OF THE MICROSCOPE

FOR THE GEOLOGIST, ENGINEER, MINER, ARCHITECT, ETC., AND FOR INSTRUCTION IN COLLEGES AND SCHOOLS

BY

LOUIS V. PIRSSON

PROFESSOR OF PHYSICAL GEOLOGY IN THE SHEFFIELD SCIENTIFIC SCHOOL OF YALE UNIVERSITY; GEOLOGIST, U. S. GEOLOGICAL SURVEY; ASSOC. EDITOR AMER. JOURNAL OF SCIENCE, ETC.

FIRST EDITION
TOTAL ISSUE EIGHT THOUSAND

NEW YORK
JOHN WILEY & SONS, Inc.
LONDON: CHAPMAN & HALL, Limited
1915

QUALITATIVE ORGANIC ANALYSIS

AN ELEMENTARY COURSE IN THE IDENTIFICATION OF ORGANIC COMPOUNDS

BY

OLIVER KAMM

Scientific Director, Parke, Davis & Co. Formerly Assistant Professor of Chemistry, the University of Illinois

SECOND EDITION

NEW YORK
JOHN WILEY & SONS, Inc.
LONDON: CHAPMAN & HALL, Limited

THIN SECTIONS OF ROCKS AS SEEN UNDER THE MICROSCOPE.
(U. S. Geological Survey.)

A star of the Yale Geology Series: Rocks and Rock Minerals by Louis V. Pirsson (1915).

Oliver Kamm's Qualitative Organic Analysis, first published in 1922, went through several editions and sold well into the 1950's.

In knowledge publishing, where audiences were well defined and intellectually critical, books of less than top quality had no chance of success. Wiley under the cousins consistently understood this connection. Remarkable books resulted. Meyer Bodansky's *Introduction to Physiological Chemistry* (1927) and Ralph L. Shriner et al.'s *Systematic Identification of Organic Compounds* (1935), two highly influential and market-leading textbooks, became long-lived classics. So did Fred B. Seely and Newton E. Ensign's *Analytical*

Mechanics for Engineers (1921) and the series of statistics texts acquired with the guidance of H. T. Scovill of the University of Illinois in the 1920s and edited after World War II by Walter A. Shewhart of Bell Telephone Laboratories. In 1932, Wiley published Hardy Cross and Newlin Morgan's *Continuous Frames of Reinforced Concrete*, which the *Journal of Engineering Education* praised as the greatest ever contribution to the theory of indeterminate structures. The Yale Geology Series marked up similar critical and sales success. Oliver

Kamm's *Qualitative Organic Analysis* (1922) exposed an entire generation of scientists to the systematic nature of organic chemistry. Horace Deming's *General Chemistry* began its long run of sales in 1923. In engineering, important new Wiley offerings included Fred Seely's *Resistance of Materials* (1925) and John Monypenny's *Stainless Iron and Steel* (1926). Even though Wiley was but one of 63 major publishers of accounting texts, its books were widely acclaimed as among the most important, and Wiley also continued to dominate in architecture and construction.

Wiley under the cousins devoted a full third of their publications to coming fields like aeronautics, management science, education, the earth sciences, telecommunications, and various social sciences. The six editions of Ellsworth Huntington's *Principles of Human Geography* (1921–1956), which argued for climatic determinism in human development, sold almost 140,000 copies. John Morecroft's *Principles of Radio Communication* (1921) beat the best competitor Van Nostrand had to offer. Wiley pioneered with Edwin Wilson's *Aeronautics* (1920) and Kenneth Williams's *Dynamics of the Airplane* (1921). In telecommunications, Wiley published Vladimir Zworykin's *Photocells and Their Applications* with E. D. Wilson, 1930; his *Television* with G. A. Morton, 1940; and *Electron Optics and the Electron Microscope* (Zworykin et al., 1945). Zworykin was the RCA vice president who, as an RCA executive, oversaw the development of the electron scanner, iconoscope, and orthicon tube, which made television possible on a large scale.[11]

Reviews of Wiley's books, however diverse their subject matter, had a common theme: They told of comprehensive, readable volumes of great practical worth. The *New York Times* called Rudolph Duncan and Charles Drew's *Radio Telegraphy and Telephony* (1929) a "very comprehensive treatise . . . discussed in such a way as to make it invaluable as a handbook . . . while the

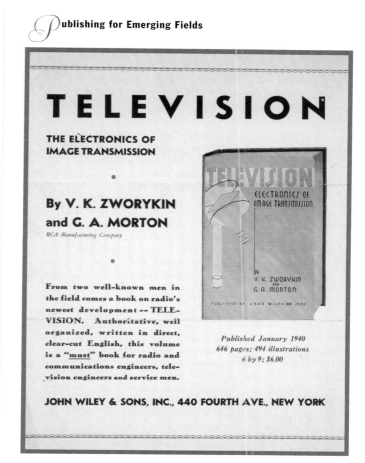

Publishing for Emerging Fields

TELEVISION

THE ELECTRONICS OF IMAGE TRANSMISSION

By V. K. ZWORYKIN and G. A. MORTON
RCA Manufacturing Company

From two well-known men in the field comes a book on radio's newest development -- TELEVISION. Authoritative, well organized, written in direct, clear-cut English, this volume is a "must" book for radio and communications engineers, television engineers and service men.

Published January 1940
646 pages; 494 illustrations
6 by 9; $6.00

JOHN WILEY & SONS, INC., 440 FOURTH AVE., NEW YORK

Vladimir Zworykin was one of the pioneering authors in telecommunications. *Television* was one of three titles he wrote with co-authors for Wiley.

language employed will make it understandable to both novice and technician." Another reviewer called Frank Arnold's *Broadcast Advertising*, published by Wiley in 1931, a clear and concisely written view of a rapidly changing field. Reviews in the *Times* were coveted and rare; such general-interest outlets managed to cover only about 15 percent of all new science titles and less than 30 percent of other books in the "useful arts." Reviews were abundant and reliably positive, however, in specialized journals and technical magazines. Combined with reliable sales, such reviews endorsed the wisdom of Wiley's specialized, high-quality program.[12]

New People, Ideas, and Practices

Increased output and sustained high quality required more hands and heads to do the work, something the Major had resisted. W. O. and Hamilton expanded the shop prudently but readily. The company grew to about 65 employees by 1930 and, despite a rollback during the Depression, to 90 by 1940. It attracted and retained good people because of its reputation as a pleasant place to work. Wiley also had a reputation for generosity. When times were good, employees received attractive bonuses of between 10 and 20 percent of base salary. Wiley also nurtured a large network of outside readers across all fields, academics and other authorities who combed manuscripts for problems of fact, interpretation, and organization.[13]

On the business side, by far the most important newcomer was Martin Matheson, a polymath who earned a bachelor of science in English literature from Colgate University in 1917 by taking *science* courses instead of Latin and Greek. Matheson, or "MM" as he was affectionately known about the office, was an innovator who came to Wiley in December 1924 after service in World War I and a four-year stint with the U.S. Rubber Company, where he learned the basic principles of sales and marketing. At Wiley, he took on the challenge of a much-neglected advertising department and quickly transformed it. In addition to marketing, he designed books and authored some himself. So clear was his value to the company that W. O. and Hamilton invited him onto Wiley's board of directors in 1930, and he became a vice president in 1941. In 1956, the first nonfamily member to join the board, he was named senior vice president and secretary of the corporation. He remained influential until his retirement in 1960, and continued beyond that as a consultant.[14]

> **Growth called forth systematization and standardized procedures.**

Growth called forth systematization and standardized procedures. By the early 1920s, Wiley had grown large enough to need its own author's manual. Wiley's was proposed by traveler F. E. Mee, who got the idea from a professor impressed with guidelines put out by McGraw-Hill. Wiley's production manager, Samuel E. Norris, another important senior manager, saw the creation of a similar book as an opportunity to "enable the [Wiley] author to produce a more attractive book, eliminate vexatious delays, and reduce the expense of author's corrections" and save himself some vexation, too. In early 1924, a little over a year after Mee's report about the McGraw-Hill manual reached headquarters, a 39-page book, largely the work of Norris, appeared as *The Manuscript: A Guide for Its Preparation.* Shortly thereafter, an abridged glossary of publishing terms was printed and distributed with the book. In 1927, Wiley brought out an enlarged edition, which ran to 56 pages due to the glossary and other additions.[15]

Manuscripts, according to the *Guide*, were to be typed; handwritten manuscripts, "if very legible" and in ink, were accepted but not encouraged. The typing had to be double-spaced, with 1- to 1.5-inch margins, single-sided on white bond paper. Pages were to be numbered consecutively in Arabic numerals, as were notes and equations. Notes were to be footnotes, placed at the bottom of the page on which the superscript appeared or directly under the superscript. Underlining, one to three times, indicated italics, small capitals, or large capitals; a wavy underline meant boldface. Illustrations went on separate pages. The author was to retain a carbon. For the authors of scientific and technical books, Wiley advised text subdivisions for easier classroom use, with subheads breaking "the monotony of the closely printed page." For engineering subjects, authors were to submit

PROFILE

MARTIN MATHESON

Martin Matheson (1895–1972), who joined Wiley in 1924, had a knack for discovering what professionals in various fields needed and then convincing able authors to turn out practical how-to texts that matched. His coup was Ramsey and Sleeper's *Architectural Graphic Standards*, but he had many successes, including Keith Henney's *Principles of Radio* (1929), which was designed for technical institute students but was widely used in college classrooms. A cigar smoker, "MM" was the only employee exempted from the company's "no smoking" ban of the 1930s. He was resolute and devoted to Wiley, a tactful man who worked to make peace between Wiley's traditionalists and innovators while mentoring the next generation of managers, including Brad Wiley. In the 1950s, his assistant recalled him as a lucid, succinct writer, and a good friend: "a helluva leader and a counselor to all of us, really." He was an important innovator in marketing and sales. Matheson, one of Wiley's first professional managers, represented the growing importance of professional management in a firm whose scope of activity demanded more than leadership from family members. He retired as a senior vice president and member of the board of directors in 1960.[16]

*M*artin Matheson, "MM" to his colleagues at Wiley, had a B.S. in English from Colgate University. After serving in World War I, he worked for the U.S. Rubber Company for four years.

*T*he Manuscript: A Guide for Its Preparation, **by Samuel E. Norris, was Wiley's first author's manual. Norris saw the need for such a manual for Wiley authors and published this 39-page book. Norris was head of production for 16 years and a member of the board of directors at Wiley for thirty years until his death in 1948.**

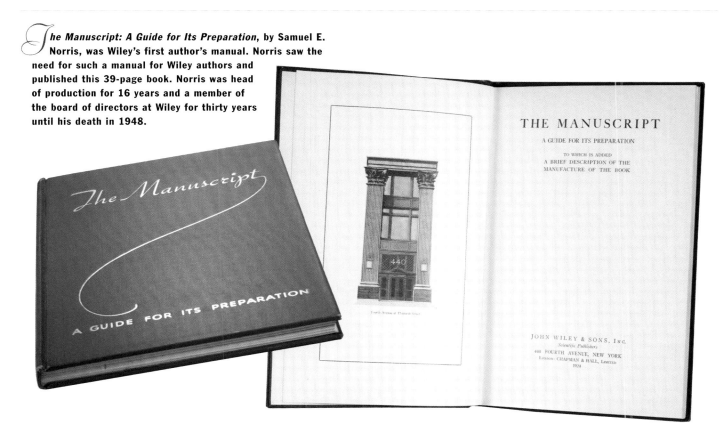

THE MANUSCRIPT

A GUIDE FOR ITS PREPARATION

TO WHICH IS ADDED
A BRIEF DESCRIPTION OF THE
MANUFACTURE OF THE BOOK

JOHN WILEY & SONS, Inc.
Scientific Publishers
440 FOURTH AVENUE, NEW YORK
London: CHAPMAN & HALL, Limited
1924

*B*y the 1920s, most authors used typewriters or hired a typist to prepare their manuscripts. This practice continued through the latter part of the century.

pencil sketches of artwork, which would be rendered into engravings by in-house illustrators.[17]

Wiley stipulated no particular authority on matters of spelling, punctuation, abbreviations, scientific symbols, and style but did urge authors to be consistent and pointed them to various style sheets. Its own editor, of course, checked for accuracy and consistency and made stylistic changes as necessary. From the galley-proof stage onward, however, Wiley authors in this period dealt directly with the printers, except for the index, which the company edited before forwarding to the printer.[18]

The Manuscript makes it clear that Wiley wanted its books to be useful to readers. Running heads—chapter title on the left and topic or subhead on the right—were a guide to content. This preference ran counter to the common practice of using the book's title as a running head: "It is to be assumed," said *The Manuscript*, "that the reader knows the title of the book he is reading." Typefaces were limited to those that had

the mathematical symbol sets required in many Wiley books. Good book design to Wiley meant harmonious arrangement of all the elements: little in Wiley books was merely decorative; everything had a purpose.[19]

The Manuscript explained the importance of the preface and warned authors not to "ding off an inadequate Preface at the last moment." Matheson was such a great admirer of prefaces that he put out a pamphlet called "In Praise of the Preface," a frank "plea for the return of the dignity and importance of the preface." Prefaces, he argued, were important marketing tools and a means of staving off criticism in reviews.[20]

Wiley urged equal care at the back of the book, instructing authors to make their indexes "as full and complete as required by the nature of the subject." The company never wavered on this point, Hamilton telling librarians in the 1950s that "a good index can add a great deal to the value of a book—a poor one can be exasperating in the extreme." Wiley contracts offered authors the choice of providing the index themselves or paying the press to have it done professionally. Wiley preferred author indexes, however. It later produced an additional short guide titled, "Notes on Indexing," in which it patiently explained why an entry such as "Algae, characteristics of" was more useful than "Characteristics of Algae."[21]

Everywhere—front matter, back matter, and in between—Wiley worried about mistakes and explained to authors that mistakes cost money. Moreover, authors could not make extensive changes with each new printing. Wiley's printers printed not from type but from electrotype plates, a more efficient and modern form of stereotype plates. Though it was possible to make changes, it was expensive and physically weakened the plate. In most cases, the company explained, it made economic sense to fix only the errors, reserving substantial revisions for a subsequent edition.[22]

Books and Reading Between the Wars

In the 1920s—surely in contrast to the 1820s—Americans had more leisure. As the economy boomed and wealth increased—per capita GDP rose from $486 in 1900, to $711 in 1929—work hours decreased and vacations lengthened. In fact, "leisure" was something of a new concept: regular periods of hours and even days freed from toil, especially as farming declined as a line of work and white-collar occupations rose. The 1920 census revealed that for the first time most Americans lived in urban places of 2,500 or more. Reading habits changed and with them publishing markets, which now allowed for the mass publication of serious nonfiction and difficult fiction works. No publisher thought that Americans, given their unmatched levels of wealth and education, read as many books as

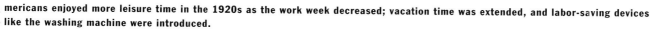

Americans enjoyed more leisure time in the 1920s as the work week decreased; vacation time was extended, and labor-saving devices like the washing machine were introduced.

they could or perhaps should, but many publishers shared a belief that "good and serious books" enjoyed a wider sale than ever before. By 1929, a very large percentage of the 10,000 or so new titles published in the United States were nonfiction.[23]

The Great Depression, which, at its nadir in 1933 saw official unemployment rise to 25 percent and per capita income fall to $5,061 from a 1929 high of $7,105, threatened to permanently reverse America's economic fortunes, publishing fortunes too. As big players like McGraw-Hill shuddered, worry spread among publishers about the effects of the downturn on their highly competitive industry. To get some sense of what had happened and where to head next, the National Association of Book Publishers (NABP) commissioned an economic study of the publishing industry, the first of its kind in America. The external challenges of the times were obvious, but the NABP study laid bare internal failings just as frightening. The author of the NABP's report, O. H. Cheney, a New York lawyer and banker, criticized inadequate management and control throughout the industry and was scathing about waste. Record-keeping was primitive, most of it hand work. The book distribution system was particularly inefficient: "It's all a gamble and guesswork." Cheney thought he had an answer, or at least something modest to try. The industry's goal should not be to find the next blockbuster but to transform the titles that sold 1,000 or 1,500 copies into ones that sold 4,000 or 5,000 copies and to turn those mid-list titles into books that sold in the 10,000 to 25,000 range. Wiley saw the sense in that and likely influenced the study. The company had joined the NABP in 1927, probably because its major competitors, McGraw-Hill, Van Nostrand, and a newcomer that Wiley would later purchase, the Ronald Press, had done so.[24]

For pessimists, threats to books came from all directions—the movies, radio, the automobile. But good data on the number and preferences of book buyers were scarce. Cheney tried to fill some of the information gap, estimating book readership in each state in the country by examining per capita rates of literacy as defined by the census, numbers of urbanites, professional occupations, school attendance rates for those 18 or older, library usage, periodical reading, disposable income, automobile ownership, and retail sales of necessities and luxury items. It is not surprising that the North in general and New York in particular emerged as the major center of book readers. Surveys offered other random glimpses but little in the way of patterns. One showed that about 80 percent of young bank executives in the sample read at least one book over a period of 11 days. Fewer than a quarter, though, read more than three books in that span. Figures for the clergy and other religious professionals were similar. When disaggregated by gender, the female members of a religious group read more books on average and were also more likely to be readers. It was no surprise that library patrons turned out to be "the most voracious" readers.[25]

At the state level of aggregation, book buying was closely and positively correlated with the number of automobiles that cost over $1,000, but not at all associated with the number of automobiles that cost less than that. So socioeconomic class was clearly an important determinant in book readership, but the price of books was not the limiting factor. Book prices were low, generally $2 or $3, and hence affordable to millions of Americans who spent as much for other diversions. About one-fifth of a cent of each consumer dollar went to books, compared to 1.4 cents for candy and 19 cents for automobiles and their upkeep.[26]

Why were there so few book readers overall? By the time people were old enough to be making choices among cars, movies, or books, it was already too late, Cheney argued. He blamed the school system, which tried hard but not always effectively to teach reading. By the late 1920s, over 80 percent of Americans attended elementary and middle schools; over 40 percent went to high

*B*uster Keaton's eloquent face looks out in a New York movie house in the 1920s. Below, Evelyn C. Lewis, Miss Washington of 1921, listens to the radio. She tunes in by adjusting the condenser. Books had to compete with film and radio as they became increasingly popular in the 1920s.

school; about 10 percent attended college. Reading instruction was not handled well at any of those levels, however. Elementary schools pushed reading on students who lacked adequate preparation, with the result that those who survived early drubbing later resented books and literature. The typical adult American, Cheney claimed, had the education of a 12-year-old, yet was expected to quickly read and comprehend books written for Ph.D.s. Charles Judd, director of the School of Education at the University of Chicago, agreed. Average people read less from desire than from necessity, and poor training had made most of them slow readers even into the college years. Too many too often

associated reading not with leisure or self-edification but with work.[27]

For those who were inclined to read, booksellers and publishers tried to make book buying an easier, more pleasant experience. By 1930, book prices were often marked on the inside of the wrapper so purchasers need not ask the clerk for the price and could rest assured they were not paying over list. Advances in binding, particularly the adhesive process called "perfect" binding, combined with newspaper-style rotary-press mass printing, made possible the paperback revolution of the 1930s. Still, many Americans did not wish to buy any books at all, even quality ones with clearly marked low prices.[28]

THE Printing craft

INNOVATION AND THE DRIVE TO EFFICIENCY

During the cousins' reign, printing technology continued to advance apace. Even ink improved in ways mysterious to the lay observer. Other advances involving improvements in the chemistry of printing were equally important and only slightly less mysterious. By 1930, deeply etched lithographic plates coated with gum and ammonium dichromate had largely displaced plates coated with albumin, a water-soluble protein made from egg white. After World War II, the new technology gave way to even newer presensitized litho plates.[29]

Printing presses also improved. Web-offset printing was introduced in the United States in the early 1930s but was not widely used for book production until the 1950s, and then only on runs in excess of 50,000. Gigantic four-color Hoe and ATF-Webendorfer presses cost about $1 million each; some models even came equipped with their own ovens and dryers. One million dollars was a small fortune, but the mega-machines

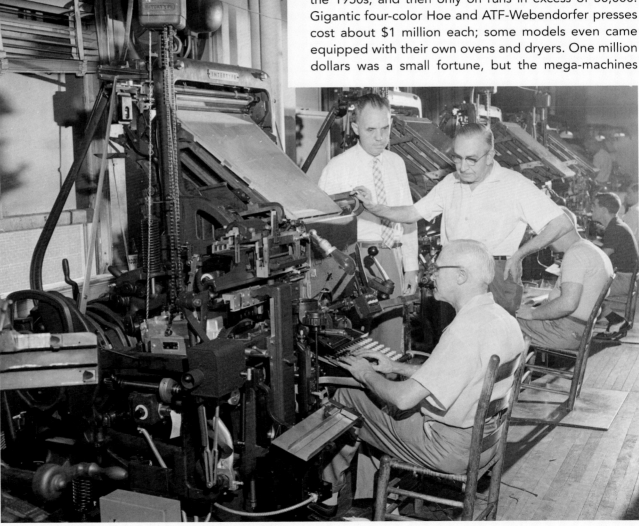

paid for themselves over time due to their increased efficiency. "Perfect" binding, a way of using glue to bind loose pages into books that was far from perfect in the usual sense but was relatively fast and inexpensive, became common after the war. (Adhesive binding began in the late nineteenth century but got off to a slow start.)[30]

Typesetting made great strides too. By 1935, a double-decker Linotype with 642 characters ranging in size from 5 to 36 points became available. In 1929, a phototypesetter capable of setting 7,000 characters per hour was first marketed in the United States. (From that machine eventually arose the Photon, of which more in Chapter 6.) After World War II, teletypesetting on perforated tape allowed printers to outsource typesetting to lower-cost, usually non-union, areas.[31]

Such innovations helped publishers and readers but harmed craftsmen in all three major stages of printing—composition, plate-making, and presswork. In the latter part of the nineteenth century, fast typesetters were known as "swifts." Printers boasted of their accomplishments and even staged public races to prove that their man could best their competitors' swifts. Over time, machines completely displaced these humans. Into history also faded "tramp" printers, highly skilled and experienced craftsmen who scoured the country, and sometimes foreign lands, in search of temporary work. Between World War II and the late 1970s, continued rapid technological innovation and thin profit margins conspired to further de-skill workers in the printing trades. Though craftsmanship was not completely eradicated after World War II, printing, like publishing, of necessity became increasingly business and efficiency oriented.[32]

*L*inotype operators, shown here in 1955, were highly skilled. The machines composed type molds into lines from which solid slugs or lines of type were cast. Corrections were made by resetting and recasting the entire line, so authors were urged to make corrections that affected as few lines as possible. The letters on linotype keyboards were arranged in decreasing order of frequency in the English language; the first two columns were usually ETAOIN SHRDLU, a phrase that has occasionally made its way into print.

In other industries, advertising might have helped to promote sales, and advertising was surely big business in the 1920s. In 1929, American corporations spent more on advertising than Americans spent on formal education. Bruce Barton's *The Man Nobody Knows* (1925) famously portrayed Jesus as an ad man. But books were different from Ford automobiles, Listerine, and Kodak film. Consumer information relating to them was extremely poor; neither publishers nor retail booksellers had much idea who purchased which books or why. Some publishers did not even know the month in which their books sold. Public and rental libraries had no better information. All that the trade knew for sure was the numbers of copies sold, and this piece of data was jealously guarded. Ignorance about their audiences made any sort of targeted advertising difficult for general interest publishers. Books were custom-made, not mass-produced, and they came out not on an assembly-line schedule but each in its own good time.[33]

If uncertainty shrouded the who and when of book buying, the why was total guesswork. Why did people buy this and not that? Why did one title exceed expectations, another disappoint? Even if data had been available, the cost of analyzing them in this pre-computer age would have been prohibitive. In the absence of market analysis, therefore, publishers and booksellers relied on gut feelings, instincts, hunches. "The good publisher," Cheney quipped, "is the one who guesses wrong least." (He undoubtedly picked this line up from Stanley Unwin's classic book on British publishing, *The Truth About Publishing*, which had appeared a few years earlier.) Publishers did not just take risks, they gambled and, like other gamblers, watched each other carefully.[34]

Publishers understood supply better than demand. When times were good, even the most pervasive market inefficiencies mattered less. When they weren't, every little thing counted, and publishers could face serious difficulties. The book industry responded to the Depression by severely curtailing the number of new

159

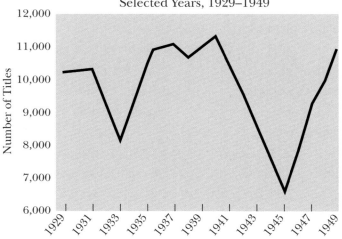

New Titles Published in the United States, Selected Years, 1929–1949

Source: William Miller, *The Book Industry* (New York: Columbia University Press, 1949), 141.

titles. Competition for scarce consumer dollars became so intense that some publishers, especially newer and smaller ones, simply gave up. Others merged with bigger companies. Yet others cut quality and cheapened their imprints, a short-sighted policy that sometimes doomed them later on.[35]

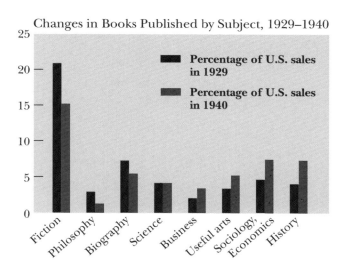

Changes in Books Published by Subject, 1929–1940

- **Percentage of U.S. sales in 1929**
- **Percentage of U.S. sales in 1940**

Source: William Miller, *The Book Industry* (New York: Columbia University Press, 1949), 141-2.

*N*ote the reduction in number of literary and general titles and the increase in business, the useful arts, and social sciences.

Wiley Weathers the Great Depression

Wiley shared some of the industry's shortcomings, but was spared the worst consequences because it served defined markets in education, research, and the professions, and thus knew more about its buyers than trade publishers knew about theirs. During the Depression, it fared better than many. The year of the Crash, 1929, was Wiley's best to date, with revenues of $1.1 million topping the previous high, 1928, by almost $150,000. In the first three quarters of the Depression's first full year, 1930, revenue grew before things soured, and the company ended the year just a few thousands in revenue ahead of the previous year. *Publishers' Weekly* attributed Wiley's relative success to the fact that it had recently broadened its list to include business, education, and social science titles and even "a growing number of books of interest to the general reader," so it was well-hedged. Wiley was in the right niches. While publishers in the humanities, philosophy, religion, and biography suffered relative declines in the 1930s, books in sociology and economics, business, science, and technology all improved their relative positions. Most of Wiley's books, moreover, were professional necessities, not discretionary luxuries. Scientists had no choice but to stay abreast of changes in their fields. As long as they had jobs, they bought books and journals.[36]

Even so, Wiley slumped along with everybody else, its sales falling to as low as approximately $700,000 in 1933. The company trimmed its workforce, cut back the hours of those who remained, and reduced wages by half. However necessary, layoffs pained the paternalistic Wileys, who relented as soon as they could, which wasn't long. In December 1933, the company brought workers back, restored hours, and not only restored salaries but refunded lost wages. Just a year later, it actually paid a bonus. By 1941, with war spending finally reviving the economy, Wiley posted revenues of nearly $1.7 million.[37]

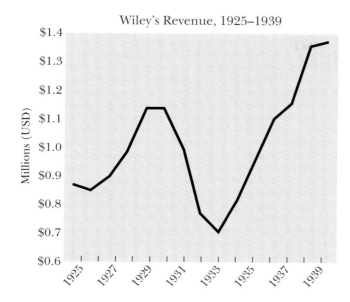

Wiley's Revenue, 1925–1939

Source: Martin Matheson's Little Black Book, JWSA.

This graph of Wiley revenue shows some resilience against the U.S. Depression and a quick rebound owing to the broadening of the list.

Wiley understood the value of timeliness and was quick to offer books likely to appeal to people during hard times: James Davis and J. C. Wright's *You and Your Job* (1930), Warren Persons's *Forecasting Business Cycles* (1931), and Maurice Parmelee's *Farewell to Poverty* (1935). Institutional economist John R. Commons praised the last title in the pages of the *American Economic Review* for its bold attack on the "profit motive," which was one way to get attention. *The Menace of Overproduction* (Scoville Hamlin, ed., 1930) took on another demon of the Depression. Another Depression-related title included George F. Warren and Frank A. Pearson's *Prices* (1933), which argued that tying the price level to gold caused periods of uncontrollable inflation and deflation that destabilized business conditions, societies, and governments. "An impressive and

disturbing story, told with gusto and conviction," one reviewer described it. Dense with graphs, it sold especially well in Washington, D.C.[38]

Records are thin, and it is hard to know exactly where publishing revenue went, though we do have industry averages: of every dollar, about 36 cents went to manufacturing, 2 cents to editorial costs, 17 cents to royalties, 7 to selling, 12 to advertising, 2 to shipping, 18 to overhead, and 6 to bad debts and profits. During the Depression, every cent spent had to count. The biggest area of budgetary discretion was advertising, and Wiley's efforts there reveal its approach to propping up demand. Wiley followed the general rule that advertising could not rescue a book that was not selling but could make a difference for a book that was moving slowly. In 1931, for example, it took out a full-column ad in *The World Tomorrow*, a Christian socialist bimonthly put out by New York's Fellowship Press, for Charles Hodges's *The Background of International Relations*. The ad, which offered the book on a five-day free examination basis, boldly asked readers "Does America Lack Foreign Consciousness?"—not quite street corner conversation but, among readers of Wiley books a timely topic as the country pondered isolationism. Excerpts from reviews touted the book's strengths, which were by now classic Wiley: comprehensive, detailed, timely, accurate, yet readable and visually stimulating.[39]

Advertising could also help big sellers that were slowing down. So Wiley advertised Warren and Pearson's *Prices* in 1934. The ad emphasized that the book was in its sixth printing and that after 14 months it continued "to be the guide of those who want to understand the administration's policy on money, gold, and prices." Wiley also supported its books with fliers distributed largely by mail. For series, it put out pamphlets. In one example, a 1938

> Advertising could not rescue a book . . . but could make a difference for a book that was moving slowly.

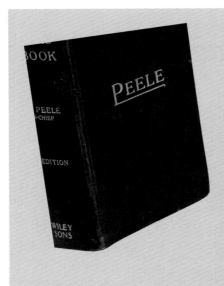

The flier for the third edition of Peele's *Mining Engineers' Handbook*, which came out in June 1941, was exquisitely done in black, white, and blue. The first page of the flier provided a list of the major selling points. The inside showed a full-sized photograph of one of the pages so that prospective buyers could see the improved typeface, layout, and illustrations. The flier also provided a detailed table of contents and the photographs and brief biographies of all 46 distinguished contributors. The back page was reserved for review blurbs that reinforced the selling points on the front and that basically said, "This is the miner's bible, new and improved."[40]

pamphlet advertising the company's engineering handbook series, a man gazes up at the first five volumes in the series, twice his own height. "Answers Thousands of Questions In Your Field of Work"—and of course worth every dime of the $25 plus that it cost.[41]

Wiley had built up years of goodwill that paid off handsomely during the Depression. Its travelers were warmly received, and they continued to be crucial in finding new authors and fresh course adoptions.

Unflagging demand in the college textbook market certainly helped. In 1929, about 1.1 million students were enrolled in U.S. colleges and universities. By 1933, the figure had dropped only slightly, to 1.05 million. That same year, total college textbook sales were roughly $6 million of the $109 million book market. (Wiley's share of the college market is unknown but with total text and professional sales of around $700,000, it was not a significant percentage.)

Enrollments (and textbook sales) rebounded in 1934 and grew annually thereafter, to 1.3 million by 1939, thanks in part to $93 million in federal aid paid to college students between 1935 and 1943.[42]

Growing college enrollments also meant that the supply of potential authors remained strong. The number of college faculty dipped slightly in 1932–33, but on average recovered fully by the start of the 1935 school year. Professors at many schools took pay cuts but typically far less than deflation and the losses suffered by most other professional groups. Their purchasing power actually increased. New courses in ever greater variety—which drove demand for new textbook titles—continued to be developed. In 1931, a student at the University of Nebraska might ramble through courses in early Irish,

American English, third-year Czechoslovakian, football, and sewerage. Almost every college course needed some sort of text.[43]

It has been argued that during the Depression, most retail booksellers were carried financially by the publishers and the publishers by the book manufacturers. There is no evidence that anyone other than its own customers and employees carried Wiley. During the worst years, however, Wiley did leverage long-standing relationships with its suppliers. It continued printing with Braunworth, which billed itself as "builders of books, book manufacturing in all its branches." Braunworth also direct-shipped books for publishers in quantities ranging from one to a carload. (After Braunworth closed in July 1941, Wiley shifted some of

*T*he Iowa State campus in 1926. Iowa State was one of many institutions of higher learning that saw growth after World War I.

PLANT OF THE QUINN & BODEN COMPANY

RAHWAY, N. J.

Quinn & Boden: Long-time
Wiley printer.

its plates and much of its printing to Quinn & Boden in Rahway, New Jersey.) The company also continued to use F. H. Gilson and one of its spinoffs, Technical Composition Company. Wiley was the company's major customer, and the typesetter always aimed to please. For brass dies to stamp covers, Wiley went to Becker Brothers Engraving of New York from 1885 through at least 1951. For its paper needs, Wiley often tapped W. F. Etherington & Co.[44]

Celebration, Cooperation, and Competition

Loyalty to trusted vendors was less about history than about good business practice, but Wiley in the early 1930s was conscious of history too, its own and the publishing industry's. *The Manuscript* contained the firm's first narrative of its past, which was updated in 1940 in a separate booklet, *The House of Wiley*. Both were pieces of historical advertising designed to keep some thousands of professors, scientists, technologists, librarians, book dealers, and retail customers abreast of the company's recent history and remind them of its venerable tradition.[45]

Wiley celebrated its 125th anniversary in 1932, Depression or no, with a dinner at New York's University Club and with publication of Henry Walcott Boynton's *Annals of American Bookselling, 1638–1850*. Boynton was a well-known author, editor, and reviewer, who had written a biography of James Fenimore Cooper. Boynton's *Annals* was a lively summary history of American publishing including sketches of important figures, such as John Wiley and William Halsted Wiley. The book and the party generated gratifying notices, with a spate of letters and wires from Wiley authors marking the event. Vladimir Karapetoff of Cornell University, veteran author of *Experimental Electrical Engineering* (rev. 1927), wrote that he had a "warm place" in his heart for Wiley "and all its members." William H. Timbie, one of the company's most successful authors ever, noted that "it was indeed a happy chance that led me to your office over twenty years ago with a manuscript under my arm."[46]

Authors were loyal because Wiley valued quality, but this commitment was not without perils. Quality could retard growth. Wiley's engineering books, for example, were only used at the top-tier schools because of the sophistication of their mathematics. McGraw-Hill, meanwhile, was posting big numbers selling lesser but still respectable "Grade B books." One indisputable advantage of quality, though, was longevity. Wiley put out several important evergreens in this period, including *Architectural Graphic Standards*, but it also sought fresh subjects. Wiley entered the field of modern statistics in 1930, with Mordecai Ezekiel's *Methods of Correlation Analysis*. It also stepped up its publishing program in home economics and psychology. An introductory psychology text edited by Edwin Boring, Herbert Langfeld, and Harry Weld did particularly well. In 1931, Wiley entered into an arrangement with

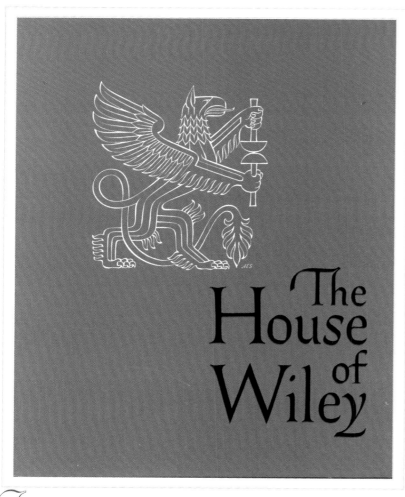

The House of Wiley, first published in 1940.

General Electric (GE) for two series of books, one of textbooks and the other of handbooks, written exclusively by GE authors. The goal was to "make available to the profession at large General Electric's contributions to basic engineering knowledge, in a form adapted for advanced study and reference use." All turned a profit. After GE terminated its contract with Wiley in 1959, Wiley kept many GE series books in print and continued contracting regularly with GE employees. The GE series was a model, and in the late 1940s, Wiley entered into a similar agreement with Westinghouse.[47]

In 1937, Wiley forged a different agreement with the university press of the Massachusetts Institute of Technology (MIT). For the next twenty-five years, Wiley and MIT published under a joint imprint more than four score scholarly books under a joint imprint, including Norbert Wiener's *Cybernetics* (1948), which sold almost 24,000 copies in its first five years and generated high praise: "provocative," "deeply original," "seminal," "comparable in ultimate importance to" Galileo or Malthus or Rousseau or Mill. Some of the volumes in the Wiley–MIT series sold only a few hundred copies, but others, like *Magnetic Circuits*, easily breached the five-figure mark. Social science authors included Charles P. Kindleberger, W. W. Rostow, Karl W. Deutsch, and George P. Schultz, who served as Secretary of Labor, Treasury, and State. In 1962, Wiley calculated that the series subsidized MIT and thought it best to allow the press to go it alone, but with its usual touch of class the company threw a gala dinner in Boston to celebrate the press's independence and to commemorate the critical success of the joint series. Brad Wiley remained on the MIT Press's board for a number of years thereafter. Beginning in 1949, Wiley also teamed up with Harvard University Press to publish a series of monographs in

INSIDE THE BOOKS

Architectural Graphic Standards

If Wiley books helped define professions, *Architectural Graphic Standards*, originally written and illustrated by Charles George Ramsey and Harold Reeve Sleeper in 1932, is one of Wiley's most successful and definitive titles. Wiley traces its architectural publishing back to the work of Andrew Jackson Downing, whose *Cottage Residences* (1842) helped define gracious living at a time when semi-rural homes foreshadowed the rise of suburbia. Ramsey, an Irish immigrant draftsman, and Sleeper, a Cornell-educated architect, worked for the New York architectural firm of Trowbridge and Ackerman. Frederick L. Ackerman was known for

thoughtful consideration of the need for low-cost housing and the interplay between the use of new materials and the impact of standardization on those who manufactured standardized products. Through constant revision—*AGS* is now in its eleventh edition—this title has been the faithful companion of architects, designers, engineers, draftsmen, and builders around the world as it helped shape architecture's new directions.

From its first publication until the end of 1963, *AGS* sold more copies—333,199—than any other Wiley book except Joseph Henry Keenan and Frederick G. Keyes's *Thermodynamic Properties of Steam*, a hot title if ever there was one, which sold 372,498 copies after its first publication in 1936. The Keenan and Keyes book has since run out of steam, but *AGS* continues to motor along. The

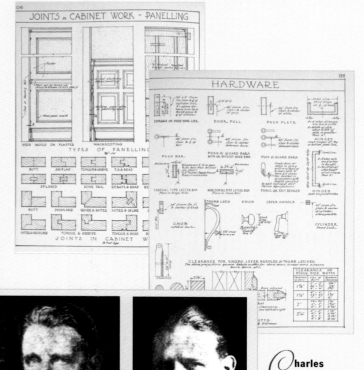

*C*harles Ramsey and Harold Sleeper, authors, with pages from the first edition.

book became so important to the architectural profession that its main professional body, the American Institute of Architects (AIA), assumed editorial responsibility for it in 1964. In 1989, the AIA honored Wiley and Brad by announcing that the book "is, and always will be, an irreplaceable tool for improving the practice of architecture and the quality of the built environment." As predicted, *AGS* remains a strong Wiley brand to this day. "It is a monument," said Wiley CEO (1979–1989) Andrew Neilly, "to the kind of publishing concept that really works. If we had ten of those, we could have stopped everything else."[48]

*R*enowned architect Philip Johnson helps launch the tenth edition of *Architectural Graphic Standards*.

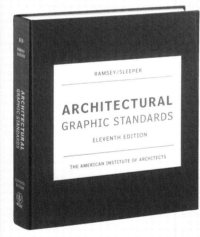

88 **ELEMENT B: SHELL** **SUPERSTRUCTURE**

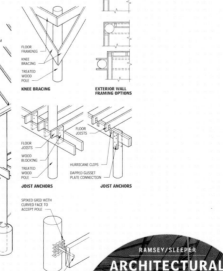

*A*GS celebrated its 75th anniversary in 2007 with a new look and a more robust companion product—*AGS* 4.0 CD-ROM.

applied science. At about the same time, Wiley contracted to publish the monographs of the University of Chicago–based Cowles Commission for Research in Economics.[49]

American university presses did not come into their own until the great expansion of the university system after World War II, but Wiley's early affinity with them seemed natural: They shared the same intellectual neighborhood. Increasingly university presses ceased being school print shops and began acting as nonprofit knowledge publishers of faculty-produced research. Between 1920 and 1970, an average of one new university press formed in the United States each year. They became a new source of competition, often subsidized and not required to produce a profit, poaching authors from Wiley and other scientific and technical publishers. Yet as late as 1937, when Wiley and MIT first teamed up, it was thought necessary to publish a book, *Some Presses You Will be Glad to Know About*, to publicize their very existence.[50]

The books published by knowledge publishers like Wiley almost all found their way into great research repositories, where they supported additional research that in time was also published. The small size and lack of sophistication of the reading public put important limitations on public libraries as markets for knowledge publishers like Wiley. Though the scale was huge—libraries in America were so numerous that good penetration of the library market was all that was needed to meet the cost of publication—the market was thin for high-toned books. Of the more than 7,000 public library systems in the United States by the 1940s, most had tiny budgets and could purchase only a small percentage of the new titles published each year. Scholarly and scientific libraries

> **Research libraries had as their purpose the purchase of knowledge, which meant acquiring as many Wiley titles as possible.**

were different, and during the interwar years they came into their own. They were natural Wiley markets. Centered in America's best and largest cities, corporations, and universities, these research libraries had as their purpose the purchase of knowledge, which meant acquiring as many Wiley titles as possible. Their users expected to find Wiley titles on the shelves, and their reputations depended on it.[51]

In 1900, no U.S. library had more than 1 million volumes. The Library of Congress was just shy of that mark, and Harvard made it only by counting pamphlets as books. By 1934, some 13 U.S. research libraries had passed the million-volume mark. In that year, there were 77 research library centers of 50 miles' radius or less containing one or more libraries with at least 500,000 books. The largest were New York, Washington, Boston, Chicago, Los Angeles, Philadelphia, and Cleveland, in that order, which together housed over 50 million volumes. All told, the research centers were home to 138.9 million volumes. In research volumes per capita, the Far West and Northeast far outdistanced the other sections of the country. These were also the geographical centers for "special" or technical libraries, which brimmed with Wiley-friendly readers and librarians. In 1909, there were about 50 independent technical libraries in the United States. By 1935, there were more than 1,800. Secondary-school libraries were less important to Wiley until compulsory education became standard and pedagogy more flexible, as instructors taught from a variety of books instead of adhering to a single text. As a result, school libraries expanded enormously, and some Wiley books were well suited to high school libraries. By 1934, school libraries in the United States had a total of 28.33 million volumes.[52]

Family Matters

In a small, closely held family firm such as Wiley still was, continuance depended, obviously, on succeeding in the business but also on the offspring. Were they suitable? What were their aspirations? Fathers judged sons; uncles, nephews; in time, mothers and daughters came into play. The young people weighed the prospect of life in the family firm against other opportunities. The elders worried that what they had inherited they might not be able to pass on.

The fourth generation of Wileys produced a smaller fifth. W. O. had two children who survived to adulthood, but both were daughters and despite gaining voting rights, women were generally not regarded as potential business leaders. Cynthia Darby, one of W. O.'s daughters, did make sales calls with him for a time, but only at women's colleges, before becoming a landscape architect.[53] Hamilton was a bachelor without an heir, who satisfied his paternal instincts by helping underprivileged boys and young men. Who, then, would run the company next, the cousins wondered?[54]

William Bradford Wiley (1910–1998), or Brad for short, was the answer. Brad's grandfather was Osgood Wiley, John's electrician son who had worked briefly for Thomas Edison as well as for Wiley. Osgood had three sons; one of them, William Carroll Wiley, married Isabel LeCato in 1909, and together they had four children, of whom Brad was the eldest. Brad was both a great-grandson of John Wiley and a cousin to Hamilton and W. O. The cousins recruited Brad, who was planning to enter the insurance industry like his

illiam Bradford Wiley, 1950s

father, just as he was graduating from Colgate University in 1932. Growing up in a publishing family was no guarantee of suitability, though Charles Scribner Jr. claimed it had prepared him "to take over the family publishing business." The Wileys had raised and trained their successors: John had certainly learned something from Charles, the founder; the second Charles and the Major learned from John, and W. O. and Hamilton learned from the second Charles and particularly from the old Major. Brad was not part of that intergenerational university, however. The cousins told him that if he showed no promise they would not hesitate to let him go.[55]

The caution turned out to be unnecessary. After a stint in the office and minimal training, Brad became a traveler, eventually for the southern and then western territories. That kept him on the road every year between September and June, save for the two-week Christmas break. His wife, Esther ("Esto") Wiley (1912–1989), née Booth, traveled with him. Brad settled into the home office in 1937, but still made frequent trips to train new travelers. In time, he would act as editor-in-chief, sales manager, and human resource director.[56]

To the tension between tradition and innovation, Brad, working as the assistant manager of the educational department, would add a new dimension. In the late 1930s, he and Matheson pressed the old guard, particularly Hamilton and Rudolph Triest, Brad's manager, to consider books written by professors at second-tier schools. Hamilton had hired Triest, an engineer and a friend, in 1923. Progressively head of the educational department (1925), assistant secretary (1927), director (1928), secretary (1941), and vice president (1943),

COLLEGE TRAVELERS

"The college travelers who visit our offices," wrote professor Edmond L. Volpe of New York's City College in 1970, "are anxious, of course, to sell texts. But they are just as anxious to buy ideas. If their ambition is to become editors," he continued, "they have to prove that they can estimate what the market needs and will need; they have to be receptive to new ideas, and they have to be good enough at judging people to know which professors can transform ideas into texts." Volpe knew what he was talking about. College travelers were both salespeople—men until 1969 when Anita Constant and Deborah Wiley, Brad's daughter, joined the sales force—and the eyes and ears of the editors, who spent most of their time in the office. Throughout the United States, travelers identified and signed authors and spotted textbook trends and changes on college campuses in the United States. And at many publishers, the cream of today's travelers became tomorrow's editors. Rinehart traveler Bill Hackett, for example, went on to become an editor for Holt, Rinehart & Winston, and then to found the college division of Bobbs Merrill and later his own philosophy imprint, Hackett Publishing Company. In 1949, Oxford University Press elected its erstwhile traveler, William Oman, Vice President. Wiley, too, regularly recruited its own travelers into its editorial and later managerial ranks.[57]

Wiley's first sales force concentrated on the textbook market, visiting professors and college bookstores. Travelers usually found professors hospitable to their visits (as long as they did not show up unannounced, an hour before final grades were due). No foot in the door needed here because most professors enjoyed talking about their research and writing ideas. And for those who did turn an idea into a book, the traveler could be an ally in convincing the home office to give it a go. The traveler's sales angle, too soft to be called a pitch, could come later, as a natural part of the conversation. At the more teaching-oriented schools, professors often welcomed travelers as founts of information on new

Bradford Wiley (right) with William F. Merril, then a Houghton Mifflin traveler, during summer vacation at North Amherst, Massachusetts (1937).

products of potential classroom use. "The first question of professors," travelers reported to publishers, "is 'What are you bringing out this year?'" Even those interested in neither scholarship nor pedagogy could get their fill of gossip.[58]

Though now called "college representatives," they were aptly named college travelers because when colleges were in session, they were on the road. Increasingly, they wandered about in automobiles, but the first travelers necessarily took the train when trains went everywhere. By the early 1950s, Wiley claimed that its travelers regularly visited every college and university "of consequence throughout the United States and Canada," including those in Alaska and Hawaii. They could do so because there was a small but growing cadre of them and visiting colleges was all they did.[59]

Triest was a conservative influence. Brad prevailed, however, appealing to numbers that did not lie. By 1939, enrollments at public colleges and universities almost matched those at elite private ones, Wiley's preferred source of authors, and would soon surpass them. The company would still publish only what Brad called "books of caliber"—but recognized that such books could just as well come out of the University of Cincinnati as from MIT. By the time America entered World War II in 1941, Brad was an integral part if junior member of Wiley's leadership team. His cousins still ran the company. Hamilton assumed the presidency in 1941, and W. O. retired from day-to-day control but remained as board chairman. Brad enlisted in the Navy, serving in its publication division from 1942 to 1945.[60]

In some ways, the Hamilton years looked chaotic. Wartime, and then a flood of returning GIs heading for education under the GI Bill kept demand for Wiley books high, but material and labor shortages and higher production costs presented tough challenges. Hamilton himself was a stabilizing presence and a hands-on manager unafraid to make a surprise inspection of the warehouse. He also articulated a clear vision for the company's editorial and business policies. "The key to a publisher's success," he argued, "is the ability to subject personal hunches and snap judgments to the most

> **By 1939 enrollments at public colleges and universities almost matched those at elite private ones.**

> **Wartime, and then . . . the GI Bill kept demand for Wiley books high, but material and labor shortages and higher production costs presented tough challenges.**

objective and factual scrutiny." Legend has it that the Major ingrained that notion by dismissing him whenever he used the word "guess." "Come back when you 'know,'" the old Major would say.[61]

A gentle, humorous man, Hamilton was a philosopher of scientific publishing, who thought long and hard about the attributes of the ideal technical book. His musings ranged from practical—keep prefaces short when paper is scarce—to comical. Some dedications, he whispered, were "bribes to abused wives" who suffered during the "gestation and borning period" of the book. He also had thoughts about the ideal author: a hard-working scholar-teacher who left little for the publisher to do except issue a contract and offer sage advice about book design and marketing, all of which the grateful author would accept quickly and completely. The ideal publisher, in Hamilton's mind, was an enthusiastic listener willing to spend hours becoming acquainted with each manuscript. He was also an operations expert who made sure "that every phase of the project is covered in detail." He must be firm with authors who would destroy the profitability of their own books with cost-prohibitive demands like "six or eight four-color inserts." The publisher's goal was to produce books that sold well at the start and then kept on selling, evergreens that would last twenty, thirty, even forty years.[62]

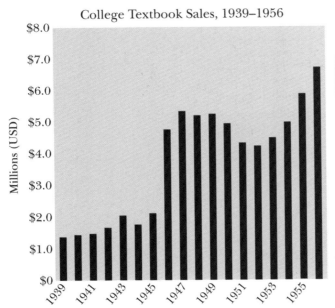

College Textbook Sales, 1939–1956

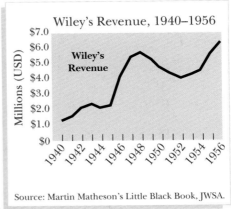

Wiley's Revenue, 1940–1956

Source: Martin Matheson's Little Black Book, JWSA.

Source: M. Frank Redding and Roger H. Smith, *Revolution in the Textbook Industry* (National Education Association of the United States, Occasional Paper No. 9, 1963), 4.

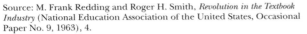iley's sales mirror the trends in textbook sales during the war and postwar years.

The Big War

Wiley was fortunate to have Hamilton as president during World War II, which was a boon to publishers. "Any book would sell as long as it contained either words or pictures," said one jokester. Wiley didn't publish "any book," but the market for books expanded exponentially during the war. In 1939, U.S. publishers had printed 177 million copies of books of all kinds. By 1945, that number stood at 429 million.[63]

Publishers of scientific and technical books did especially well. From rebuilding the naval base at Pearl Harbor to building the atom bomb, from water purification to bridge building to automobile, aircraft, and ship repair, technical know-how in a wide range of fields was at a premium. Military training programs soon produced record demand for new titles, and old ones were called back into service. Scientific publishing was instantly more important.[64]

The military training programs, termed "The University of War," were massive undertakings.

Between October 1940 and June 1945, the federal Engineering, Science, and Management War Training program (ESMWT) administered 227 programs that offered 42,568 courses to 1,795,716 students. The vast majority of the courses (31,465) and students (1,337,225) were in engineering, but chemistry, physics, radio skills, and production supervision were also taught. Textbook sales rose from $13.4 million in 1939 to $16.3 million in 1942 to $20.8 million in 1945. Wiley almost doubled its revenue between 1940 ($1.4 million) and 1945 ($2.5 million). The largest single order Wiley received to that time was from the Navy—for 10,000 copies of Hubert Lesley's *Airplane Maintenance* (1940).[65]

During the war, Wiley pushed its time and motion study books especially hard. "When both men and materials are so hard to get, it would help, wouldn't it" to be able to "get 17 men to do the work of 27," one of its ads asked rhetorically. "You don't need elaborate new equipment," the company promised, just its books. One of the books advertised, Ralph Barnes's *Motion and Time Study*, was a classic engineering text in the emerging field that would later become known as human factors and ergonomics. It was among the twenty or so books that Wiley published during its third and fourth generations that sold over 100,000 copies during their time in print. Most of Wiley's top titles consistently sold in the hundreds or low thousands of copies per year, for decades.[66]

Less visible but still important were the books used to train civilian workers, many of them women,

*D*eclaring that "Books Are Weapons in the War of Ideas," this poster was featured in bookstore windows during World War II. It was issued by the Office of War Information (OWI), an arm of the federal government.

new to the labor force. Increasingly, technical titles were geared toward these workers and not just their foremen or supervisors, inducing retail bookstores to increase the size and profile of their technical departments. Retailers who had long relegated technical titles to the back shelves now put them in the front windows.[67]

As one of technical publishing's biggest players, Wiley gained immensely from the war dynamic. But so did other, newer entrants. The promise of high profits induced dozens of firms to crowd the technical publishing field. Some were new and small, but others were established general publishers who simply switched from sonnets and novels to electricity. Nor was all competition "published." Rather than assign a textbook, many professors mimeographed and circulated copies of their own notes.[68]

Some battles for market share Wiley lost, but others it won. The best choice among competing titles depended on each reader's individual needs. Take, for instance, *Basic Radio Principles*, a McGraw-Hill title published in 1944, and *Fundamental Radio Experiments* by Robert Higgy, a Wiley book that came out about the same time. The McGraw-Hill title cost more ($3 vs. $1.50) but was meatier (271 pages vs. 95). It was also more forbidding: "at first a little rough on the new student," as one reviewer put it.[69]

Along with hotter competition, wartime brought government regulation to the book trade. Instead of allowing goods to clear on price as usual, which would have invited inflation, the federal government rationed goods by quantity. That meant that people and businesses could buy rationed items only if they had both the money and a ration allotment. One of the strategic items rationed was paper, and book publishers thought their allotments were never enough. Some publishers actually responded by turning away bestsellers. Others decreased the quality of

Scientific and Technical Evergreens

Introduction to Physiological Chemistry and
Heat Power Engineering Sales

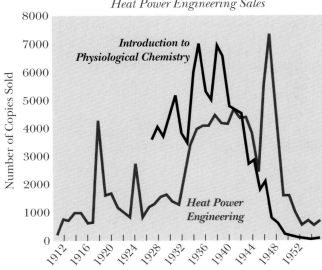

Number of Copies Sold (y-axis, 0 to 8000)

Introduction to Physiological Chemistry

Heat Power Engineering

Years (x-axis): 1912, 1916, 1920, 1924, 1928, 1932, 1936, 1940, 1944, 1948, 1952

Source: "JWS Records: Sales by Title, 1912–1959," JWSA.

By midcentury, large numbers of Wiley books had sold more than 20,000 copies. Timbie's Elements of Electricity (1937) was a big seller, eventually passing the half-million mark. William Kent's Mechanical Engineering Handbook sold over a quarter of a million copies in all editions; originally published as a pocket book in 1895, this title was rewritten as a handbook in the 1920s and was updated in its eleventh edition in 1936–1938.

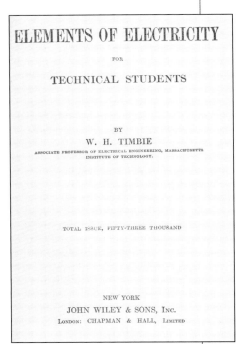

ELEMENTS OF ELECTRICITY

FOR

TECHNICAL STUDENTS

BY

W. H. TIMBIE

ASSOCIATE PROFESSOR OF ELECTRICAL ENGINEERING, MASSACHUSETTS
INSTITUTE OF TECHNOLOGY.

TOTAL ISSUE, FIFTY-THREE THOUSAND

NEW YORK
JOHN WILEY & SONS, INC.
LONDON: CHAPMAN & HALL, LIMITED

Heat-Power Engineering, by William Barnard, Frank Ellenwood, and Clarence Hirshfeld (first published 1912), came out in a third and most successful edition in 1926. Other evergreens followed other patterns. Meyer Bodansky's Introduction to Physiological Chemistry, first published in 1927, stayed strong for twenty years before taking a nosedive after the war.

Wiley published for the occupational market, such as these Goodyear Girls working on airplane maintenance, a market it would persue periodically in the future.

WILEY...TECHNICAL BOOKS

Those names just naturally go together.

We have technical books by the hundreds — in fact we published nearly a hundred new books and new editions last year. In 1942 we will publish even more.

From experience we know the kind of books technical men need. For many years we have been publishing books on aviation, radio, mechanical engineering, drawing, metallurgy, structural engineering, mechanics, electrical trades, mathematics, chemistry, physics, etc.

If you are located in a community devoted to war industries, you will want to take advantage of the tremendous boom for technical books.

Come in and talk to us when you are in New York for the ABA Convention. We will be pleased to see you, and to make recommendations about Wiley books. If you cannot visit us, write us and we will answer you promptly.

JOHN WILEY & SONS, INC.
440 FOURTH AVENUE, NEW YORK, N. Y.

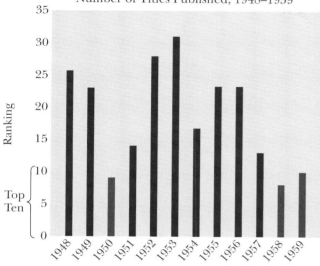

Wiley's Rank Among U.S. Publishers by Number of Titles Published, 1948–1959

Source: *Publisher's Weekly* data as compiled in Martin Matheson's Big Black Book, JWSA.

their books by using inferior papers or by putting more words on each page, as Wiley did by moving to smaller margins. The paper shortage became so acute that the War Production Board, the agency responsible for setting the quotas, granted publishers extra paper in the second half of 1943. Wiley's additional allotment was 28,020 pounds, a tiny fraction of the over 9 million additional pounds made available to the industry as a whole.[70]

Wartime constraints reduced every firm's room to maneuver and called for patience. During the war, few publishers sought higher price points. In fact, the average price for nonfiction books peaked at $4.10 in 1930, trended lower throughout the Depression, then in 1943 dropped steeply to $2.61, 13 cents *cheaper* than the average fiction title. Another constraint occurred in writing and revising, as many authors joined the fight overseas or passed the war years in government offices or corporate labs. Most authors found writing difficult in the best of times; it became almost impossible in wartime, and many titles were delayed or scrapped entirely. Uncle Sam's appetite for statisticians, for example, was so voracious that Wiley's statistics series dried up.[71]

Postwar Bonanza

The great flashes over Hiroshima and Nagasaki that ended the war in August 1945 bespoke the awful power of science and foreshadowed continued federal involvement in scientific research in the 1950s. America experienced an unexpected jump-start thanks to the influx of talented Jewish refugees just before the war and then, in an ironic twist, from a cohort of captured former Nazi scientists just after it. Together, they helped make the United States the world's undisputed leader in science and technology. (In 1946, two of these Jewish refugees, one from Germany and one from Holland, founded Interscience Publishing Company, which would have a profound impact on Wiley 15 years later.) The National Science Foundation (NSF), formed in 1950, helped too, by supplying about 10 percent of all federal funding to science by the mid-1960s.[72]

It was the right atmosphere to feed growth, and Wiley soon went back to building its list. In terms of the number of titles published, Wiley had become one of the nation's larger publishers. Usually ranked in the top 30 and occasionally in the top 10, Wiley never came close to Doubleday, Harper, Oxford, Macmillan, or arch competitor McGraw-Hill. However, it was closer in size to another major competitor, Prentice Hall, and in this period always published more titles than the Ronald Press and Van Nostrand, whose interests still coincided very closely with Wiley's. In terms of revenue, Wiley was in the top 10 percent of publishers that, combined, published over 85 percent of all American books.[73]

In 1945, Wiley's staff numbered 7 officers, 99 full-time employees, and 2 part-timers. By the end of 1946, there were 151 full-timers. By 1948, the staff had expanded to 229 and the sales force from 11 in 1946 to 30. Revenue rose from $4.3 million in 1946, to $5.6 million in 1948, but then sagged. By 1948, the organization was divided into two editorial departments: an educational division charged with developing and revising textbooks, and a science and industry division that developed reference books, monographs, handbooks, and manuals for the use of scientists, engineers, and other technical professionals. The advertising department's job was to create demand, and a sales department and export division charged with the actual sale of Wiley titles to trade and college bookstores, to library, industrial, and government purchasers, and to individuals. The company also had production and manufacturing departments, plus the usual back-office operations in accounting, orders, credit, and traffic and shipping. Wiley added two new administrative functions after the war. Richard Fiske joined in 1949 to handle advertising production, and Carolyn Harwood was hired to edit Wiley's house publications, *Footnotes* and *The Wiley Bulletin*.[74]

In 1949, Wiley also made extensive changes to its headquarters at 440 Fourth Avenue to handle the crush. Improvements included more private offices with daylight exposure and a spacious library and conference room. New furniture, pastel tones, light woods, and indirect lighting made things cheerful. The company upgraded the lobby in 1954, and added air conditioning throughout, an especial boon for in-house draftsmen who for years had dripped sweat onto their summer work. The mailing and shipping departments remained at 601 West 26th Street, by the Hudson River docks.[75]

Generating new titles was becoming more difficult. First, writers of scientific works were not, as a group, as fluent as they once had been. According to Wiley's senior copyeditor, the authors of nineteenth-century technical treatises "had a real grasp of the grammatical framework of their sentences" and could even handle participles correctly. "On the whole," she told Hamilton, "they wrote as one might expect intelligent, well-read men of good general background to write." By the end of World War II, however, most technical writers needed help. "The insistent problem now," Hamilton asserted, "is to find the author with technical competence who is also a good expositor." This concern reflected a general worry that the war

had brought on a more highly commercialized publishing culture and that quality was on the decline. Critics reported that 1946 "was the most arid year in literary production" in three decades. There was no consensus on the best productions of the year, only a general feeling that all were mediocre.[76]

Second, Hamilton believed that the acquisitions process was growing more difficult because the war had accelerated the pace of scientific discovery and competition was feverish. Rather than wait for writers to approach them, big publishers began to do what Wiley had been doing for decades, sending scouts in active search of writing talent at universities and corporations, traditionally Wiley country. Wiley developed a nationwide information-gathering system spearheaded by its

*T*he reception area at 440 Fourth Avenue, with two receptionists and operators of the PBX system, the private branch exchange telephone system.

travelers, aiming both to increase its contact time with prospective authors and to identity which areas of research were most important, which were dying. Wiley then pursued the best writers it could find in emerging areas.[77]

Wiley snagged George T. Trundle Jr.'s *Managerial Control of Business* (1948) through such aggressive tactics. A Wiley executive researched Trundle, decided he was the best person to write a book summarizing the overall philosophy of management engineering, and convinced him to take on the task. Trundle accepted the project straightaway but soon found that writing a book was hard work. He learned from it, though. The writing process compelled Trundle and his colleagues at Trundle Engineering to organize their thoughts, sift through their data, and outline procedures and courses of action more thoroughly than ever they had imagined.[78]

Wiley concentrated acquisition efforts in the emerging fields, even when it thought sales demand might at first be light. This strategy was essential for preserving Wiley's reputation as a leader in technical and scientific publishing, but it was risky. Edmund Berkeley's *Giant Brains or Machines That Think*, published in 1949, followed Norbert Wiener's more influential *Cybernetics*, which Wiley co-published with MIT Press in 1948. In the postwar years, Wiley launched a series in nuclear physics, including titles by a number of authors, well-known because of their role in the Manhattan Project (which had led to the development of the atomic bomb). J. Kenneth Maddock, the head of the Science and

> **Wiley concentrated acquisition efforts in the emerging fields, even when it thought sales demand might at first be light.**

Industry Division, initiated the series with Hans Bethe's *Elementary Nuclear Theory* (1947). Among the 17 titles was Francis O. Rice and Edward Teller's *The Structure of Matter*. Bethe and Teller were leading members of the Manhattan Project, and Teller would go on to become known as the father of the hydrogen bomb. Series editor Donald MacPherson, according to Brad, "virtually single-handedly tracked down all the authors in the nuclear science field."[79]

That was a slight exaggeration. Before the war, Brad had corresponded with Niels Bohr, the Danish physicist whose work contributed to the development of the atom bomb, and John Wheeler, his Princeton colleague, about a possible book. In 1943 Bohr, a step ahead of the Nazis, crossed from Denmark to Sweden in a small boat, was flown to England in the bomb bay of a plane, a trip during which he almost froze to death, and then entered the United States, where he joined the Manhattan Project under the pseudonym Nicholas Baker. During the war, the Bohr-Wheeler project file disappeared from the Wiley office after Brad ran

Niels Bohr

into Bohr on a train to Washington. The file, Brad speculated, was probably taken by a government agency curious to know if he and Bohr were in contact. In 1958, Wiley finally published a Bohr book, *Atomic Physics and Human Knowledge*.[80]

Other Wiley series included the Structure of Matter Series, an interdisciplinary series (physics, chemistry, biology, geology) under the editorship of Maria Mayer of the University of Chicago; the Biological Research Series, headed by the Wiley Advisory Board in Biology; the Biochemical

$\mathcal{P}$ROFILE

NORBERT WIENER'S CYBERNETICS

CYBERNETICS

OR CONTROL AND
COMMUNICATION
IN THE ANIMAL
AND THE MACHINE

Norbert Wiener
PROFESSOR OF MATHEMATICS
THE MASSACHUSETTS INSTITUTE
OF TECHNOLOGY

THE TECHNOLOGY PRESS
JOHN WILEY & SONS, INC., NEW YORK
HERMANN et CIE, PARIS

$\mathcal{N}$orbert Wiener's *Cybernetics*, one of the Wiley/MIT Series. Wiener at his classroom desk at MIT, approximately 1937. The story of the complicated publishing deal between Hermann et Cie in France and MIT led to one of the most "memorable and influential" works of the twentieth century according to *American Scientist*.

Born in Missouri in 1894, Norbert Wiener received a Ph.D. in mathematics from Harvard at age 18. In 1919, after postdoctoral work at Cambridge University under Bertrand Russell, he took an instructorship at M.I.T. He taught there for over forty years and became a legendary figure, the subject of numerous anecdotes, stories, and jokes, some true, but many apocryphal. "In the stories," relates one student, "he comes out as absent-minded, nearly blind, brilliant, elliptical, savagely moral, egotistical, and insecure." Bespectacled with coke-bottle lenses and conversant in any number of languages, he was nothing short of a mad scientist and absent-minded professor.

In one oft-repeated story, Wiener forgets that he moved his family to bigger digs. He returns to his old house only to find it empty, then realizes that he left the address of the new house back at the office. Thinking quickly, he flags down a little girl, identifies himself, and asks her if she knows where he now lives. "Mommy thought you'd forget, Daddy," the little girl responds. The only way to get a book out of him, another story goes, was to pay photographers to snap pictures of the differential equations he scrawled on the board before he erased them. The photographs were then arranged and published!

Wiener agreed to publish his book with M. Freymann, a Mexican immigrant who was head of the well-known Parisian scientific publisher, Hermann et Cie. According to Weiner, "the MIT authorities" insisted that his book be published in the United States first. After many transatlantic phone calls, The Technology Press, MIT's imprint,

MIT's co-publisher John Wiley & Sons, and Hermann all put their names on the title page. Wiener's path-breaking book, *Cybernetics* (from the Greek for helmsman), was definitely not a compilation of photographs. The eccentric genius exuded what Edmund O. Wilson would later call "consilience," the unity of knowledge, and his book was part mathematical treatise, part biological probe, part sociological exploration, part economic history, part psychological study, part engineering wonder, and much more besides. The book was reviewed in a remarkable range of journals, including *Time, Business Week,* the *Journal of the Operations Research Society of America, Science, Land Economics, Journal of Symbolic Logic, Annals of the American Academy of Political and Social Science, Philosophy of Science, Economic Journal, American Anthropologist,* and *Journal of Philosophy.* And it all arose out of Wiener's attempts to predict the movements of Nazi bomber planes during World War II. Wiener had a bomb of his own to drop: "If the seventeenth and early eighteenth centuries are the age of clocks, and the later eighteenth and nineteenth centuries constitute the age of steam engines, the present time is the age of communication and control." We wrestle yet with the implications of that profound insight, as Wiener did. "Before modern electronic computers existed," wrote well-known physicist Freeman Dyson, "these books [Wiener's] predicted with some degree of accuracy the economic and political effects of computer technology on human societies."

Cybernetics's influence is more easily described than measured. Type "Wiener Cybernetics" into the search box of JSTOR, the premier full-text searchable online database of articles published in the English-speaking world's most important social science journals, and a whopping 1,009 hits appear. Items include belated respect from Marxists in the Soviet Union and a seemingly endless train of knock-offs, explications, and simplifications, some published by Wiley. Like any great artist's, Wiener's death in 1964 only heightened the appreciation of his work.[81]

Preparations Series, another interdisciplinary series of interest to biologists, chemists, chemical engineers, and medical researchers edited by a board of internationally prominent scholar-practitioners; two chemistry series, two mathematics series, two agricultural series, and others in aeronautics, home economics, and the social sciences, which included subseries in economics and psychology. The editor of the social sciences series, Henry Pratt Fairchild, was a leading sociologist at New York University. Series editors continued, as before the war, to receive only a token royalty on each copy sold, but for a large, successful series the income could quickly add up. One series editor reported receiving almost $30,000, or about $300,000 in today's dollars, in Wiley royalty checks over the life of his series.[82]

Postwar Changes and Challenges

In publishing, as in most businesses, almost nothing sells itself, and marketing efforts are seldom cheap or easy. "Many people can write books," marketer Matheson put it, "[and] it's no great trick to manufacture an attractive book; but it takes a lot of doing to *sell* a book." Under Matheson's leadership, Wiley kept refining whatever was needed to move books. For trade titles, it was important that jackets be laden with advance praise and blurbs by leading experts. Costly mass-media advertising was rare, and, given the targeted audience for its books, the benefits were low. Direct mail worked better, and Wiley maintained 29 different direct-mailing lists, with hundreds and in most instances thousands of names and addresses of interested recipients in every subject from accounting to sociology. It mailed as often as eight times a year. Circular advertising was much more important to Wiley in this period than magazine advertising. By the late 1930s, the company was mailing about 1.3 million pieces a year. In 1950, it dispatched over 6 million.[83]

Advertisements in professional journals were efficient because their audiences were well defined. A

Wiley headquarters at 440 Fourth Avenue (later Park Avenue South), approximately 1950, with an interior office shown at right.

full-page ad for *Conservation of Our Natural Resources* by Guy H. Smith, appeared in the June 1950 *Professional Geographer*, while one for a German-English dictionary for chemists appeared in the *Journal of Chemical Education*. For titles of broader interest, like A. B. Hollingshead's *Elmtown's Youth: The Impact of Social Classes on Adolescents*, Wiley took out a full-page ad in *Publishers' Weekly* aiming at retail booksellers, not consumers. New forms of cooperative advertising also evolved by the early 1950s. General Electric and National Anilines, for example, featured Wiley books in some of their in-house advertising. Exhibits at professional conventions were another sales and marketing outlet. Wiley had discovered this opportunity in the late nineteenth century when it became the first exhibitor at the annual conference of the Society for the Promotion of Engineering Education. In 1949, Wiley employees displayed several hundred of the company's titles at more than forty academic conferences, including the meetings of the American Association for the Advancement of Science, the American Psychological Association, the American Chemical Society, and the Econometric Society. At industrial meetings, where display space was more expensive, Wiley books appeared

CHAPTER FIVE

181

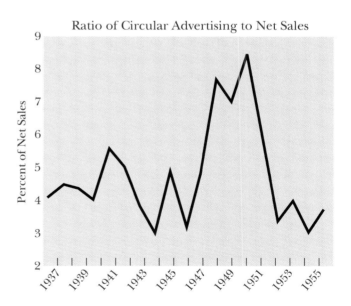

Ratio of Circular Advertising to Net Sales

Source: Martin Matheson's Little Black Book, JWSA

courtesy of specialist firms like the Conference Book Service and the Combined Book Exhibit.[84]

Marketing could get showy, too, at least when it came to bookstores specializing in technical works. J. W. Stacey's in San Francisco, for example, kicked off the publication campaign for the fourth edition of Harold Pender's *Electrical Engineers' Handbook* in 1949, with an elaborate window display that featured a sign proclaiming that "Wiley Books Are All High Voltage!" next to Wiley volumes surrounding a model of a new Pacific Gas and Electric Company power substation and transmission-line towers. Stacey's was one of only 50 or so large retail outlets in midcentury America and was by far Wiley's largest account, annually selling hundreds of thousands of dollars worth of Wiley books, some retail but most wholesale, as it also served essentially as Wiley's western distributor.[85]

By the 1950s, the old "examination copy" system had given way to the "complimentary copy" system, whereby Wiley sent out textbooks gratis to likely professors in hopes of course adoptions or some constructive feedback detailing why another text better suited the needs of the professor's students. This arrangement was not cheap. In 1955, Wiley budgeted to give away $70,000 worth of books, almost as large a budget item as travelers' expenses ($95,000) or the salaries of advertising department personnel (about $99,000). The need to distribute free copies varied over time and subject. To gain market share in mathematics alone, it was necessary by the 1950s to give away as many as 3,000 copies.[86]

All of Wiley's marketing, regardless of form, drilled home the message that Wiley books were reliable. This message was true across the list, from specialized classics like Theodosius Dobzhansky's *Evolution, Genetics,* and *Man* (1955) and the Alloys of Iron

> All of Wiley's marketing . . . drilled home the message that Wiley books were reliable.

Monograph Series, also from the 1950s, to the company's occasional general-interest titles with a how-to slant, such as the Sleepers' *House for You,* Mary Lou Glass's *Recipes for Two,* and Janet Lane's *Your Carriage, Madam!* Publicity personnel liked to push such lighter items hard: They were fun and probably a relief from the usual heavier fare. They arranged book signings across the country for Harold and Catharine Sleeper, authors of *House for You,* a humorous discussion of the average person's difficulties in obtaining good housing. (Harold Sleeper was also co-author of *Architectural Graphic Standards.*) They also helped to arrange publicity in the Homes section of The *New York Times* for Lenore Sater Thye, co-author of *Household Equipment.* The *New York Herald Tribune* could not resist running a story about Melvin Calvin, a Wiley author who predicted the creation of food factories that would artificially reproduce the photosynthetic process, making vegetable matter out of raw materials "in the same way that Detroit turns out automobiles."[87]

Two words summed up the biggest publishing stories of the postwar period: textbooks and exports. Volatility in the first pushed Wiley and other scientific and technical publishers toward the second. After the war, demand for textbooks soared with enrollments, thanks to the GI Bill, which paid for returning servicemen's education. Happily for Wiley, both reference books and required texts qualified for reimbursement under the law. The market became a rollercoaster, however. Wiley did well in it because it had a very clear idea of what constituted a high-quality textbook and never wavered.

For decades, the company had intentionally blurred the distinction between textbooks and professional titles, hoping to sell the same book into both markets. By the 1950s, however, textbooks and professional

A Wiley advertisement in *Publishers Weekly* (January 31, 1948).

features, extensive illustration programs, and supplements. Hamilton felt strongly that good texts were logical, gave the topic adequate coverage, were clearly written, and avoided jargon—and that they were teachable with the inclusion of pedagogical tools like definitions, glossaries, illustrations, worked-out examples, and good study questions. Good beginning-level texts usually included chapter summaries; advanced ones often provided an extensive bibliography. Definitions of key terms had to be dead on, neither too wordy nor too short. Good textbooks were readable throughout, written in direct, simple language and never showy.[88]

Hamilton suggested that even subjects like mathematics and physics could be made more comprehensible by inclusion of similes, examples, and even metaphors—so long as they weren't mixed. Textbook authors who wanted to be as successful as Timbie, he cautioned, should be prepared to expend much time and effort honing their words as well as their ideas. Of course, the publisher stood ready to help by editing and producing

books had followed different paths. The content of the former was ratcheted down while design was livened up; the latter remained highly technical, formidably studded with equations and stark black and white graphs. Wiley began to differentiate between the two genres and divided its editorial staff accordingly. The distinction was especially notable for the junior college and freshman markets, where books evolved from exposition-dense main titles to learning tools complete with pedagogical

M any World War II veterans went to college after the War, thanks to the GI Bill, causing an increase in textbook sales. Above, students at the University of Iowa, April, 1947.

attractive books. Textbooks in the past had all pretty much looked alike, but by the late 1940s, publishers competed on content plus appearance. Good design and illustrations that actually illustrated, not decorated, were essential. The same general rules applied to reference books as well, though without, of course, the pedagogical aids. The result was hard to quantify, but Hamilton knew it when he saw it, the intangible "inner vitality" that made a book stand apart, the quality that "in a race horse is class; in an athlete, form; in a human being, personality."

The late 1940s witnessed a pedagogical innovation in which Wiley was one of the leaders: the creation and sale of supplementary materials designed for classroom discussion. Emerging out of intense research on learning styles, "visual education" became a buzzword among faculty scrambling to include more visuals in their classroom presentations. Wiley responded quickly, appointing Ned Reglein its visual aids director. Reglein, who held an Ed.D. from Indiana University, helped the company and its authors to develop slides, films, and filmstrips that supplemented books and classroom lectures in biology, botany, chemistry, geology, and psychology. Each package, which included hundreds of color slides and several films and filmstrips, cost schools or their faculty between $65 and $100 dollars per set.[89]

Amid such lively and growing markets, Wiley and other quality textbook publishers should, it would seem, have made hefty profits between the end of World War II and the beginning of the Korean War. Because book prices did not keep pace with inflation, they did not. The cost of producing books had soared since the beginning of the World War II. Technical books were hit especially hard because the cost of preparing and printing illustrations, mathematical symbols, and tables (which were still hand-set) rose faster than the cost of words. Instead of the break-even point being 1,500 copies, as it was before the war, publishers like Wiley now had to sell 5,000 copies to cover costs. "This means that many worthy and badly needed books will

never be published," Hamilton lamented. "A technological society which can develop an atom bomb cannot forever be stymied by the printing industry." Although plastic printing plates, new typesetting machines, quality paper coatings, and other innovations produced modest savings, these were offset by the costs of composition, which rose steeply as the material being composed grew ever more technical and difficult. Manufacturing costs soared from 36 percent of publishers' costs in 1930, to 45 percent by the end of 1948. Editorial and shipping costs also took a bigger share than they had when O. H. Cheney wrote the NABP report at the outset of the Depression. Those added costs ate up royalties, advertising, and profits.[90]

In the face of cost pressures, it would have been rational to push up prices, but there were constraints. Wiley, like other textbook publishers, believed that doubling prices would only lead to students' sharing books before they would pay more. Book readers other than students had also been hurt by inflation, publishers believed, and would resist higher prices by purchasing less. Trade publishers feared that if book prices went too high, their readers would depart in droves for movies and television, never to return. For Wiley, as for Van Nostrand and other technical publishers, high foreign and industrial sales, combined with high college enrollments for a time eased the low-price conundrum because it allowed the publishers to make up for low margins with high volume. When college enrollments dropped off as the GI Bill ran its course, however, the low-margin, high-volume strategy no longer worked. The pain caused by the end of the GI surge can be traced in the stories of individual books. Roger Adams's eight-volume *Organic Reactions* was one victim. According to Matheson, sales of this major reference work dropped precipitously because few GIs went on to graduate school. In the end, textbook publishers, including Wiley, did increase prices and armed their travelers with sharp-looking charts created by the

American Textbook Publishers Institute that showed how textbook price increases were long overdue.[91]

The Korean War might have helped the armaments industry, but publishers understood it would cut college enrollments further, as young men went to Asian battlefields. Near panic set in at Wiley. Bonuses disappeared, dividends dropped, and workers who left were not replaced. The company reduced staff by about 20 percent in 1950. In 1951, profits plummeted to a mere $23,000, and with its secondary reserve of $235,000 of U.S. Treasury bonds long used up, Wiley was forced to borrow to meet its August royalty payments. As revenues bottomed out at $4.1 million in 1952, the company even considered moving its editorial operations out of Manhattan to Stamford, Connecticut.[92]

To combat higher costs, the company tried to keep a lid on hiring until it absolutely needed extra personnel. Some winnowing might have been good, however. The 1950 downsizing was popular with older workers who thought many of the newcomers let go had been incompetent loafers. Afterward, Wiley intensified its efforts to hire only the finest employees. One way was to promote from within, and so travelers often moved into editorships. In 1947, Wiley had moved its Midwest traveler, Walter G. Stone, into an engineering editor position and installed James Helming, its New England traveler, as a social science editor. Both went on to develop outstanding textbooks, handbooks, and monographs in their fields. By 1954, Wiley's editorial department was headed by John Snyder. Stone covered all phases of engineering (aeronautical through mining) with help from another former traveler, Charles Stoll, who was

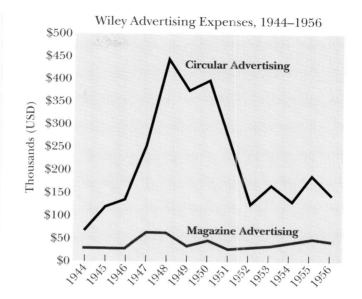

Wiley Advertising Expenses, 1944–1956

Source: Martin Matheson's Little Black Book, JWSA

*D*uring the college textbook downturn of 1949-1952, Wiley kept a close eye on its advertising and marketing expenses. One figure it tracked was the ratio of circular advertising to net sales. As the graph shows, the cost of circular advertising had clearly gotten out of hand by the late 1940s and had to be brought to heel.

*C*harles B. Stoll, 1948

a Princeton graduate and Marine Corps veteran. William Grimshaw, with help from Robert Polhemus, yet another traveler and later vice president, handled the physical sciences, while Kendall Getman covered the biological sciences as well as economics, mathematics, and statistics. Gordon Ierardi handled some economics too, along with business, political science, psychology, and sociology. J. Kenneth Maddock was charged with industrial and professional books, while Russell Fraser, whom Wiley hired away from McGraw-Hill, concentrated on books for junior colleges, technical institutes, and general education.

Meriam's *Mechanics*

In the 1950s, Wiley textbooks began to evolve from exposition-dense main titles to learning tools complete with pedagogical features, extensive illustration programs, and supplements. *Mechanics*, written by J. L. Meriam and published in two volumes, *Statics* and *Dynamics*, was a prime example, emphasizing accuracy, rigor, clarity, and applications. After decades of success, Lath Meriam recast *Mechanics* as a "new" book with a greater emphasis on practical, real-world problems for students in the 1970s, many of whom had never seen heavy equipment or machines up close—let alone designed or operated them. He renamed the book *Engineering Mechanics*. Now in its sixth edition, with long-time co-author L. G. Kraige, it remains a respected leader in its field.

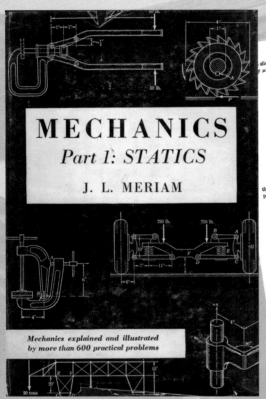

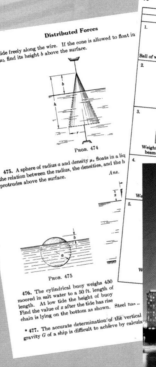

The cover and selected pages of the first edition of Statics, *copyright 1951 and 1952, alongside the sixth edition, published in 2006.*

Wiley's Illustration Department, 1948.

Footnotes
NEWS OF INTEREST TO WILEY AUTHORS

New York — April 1949   No. 1

Vol. I

What is 'Footnotes'?

FOOTNOTES is something new. Therefore, we would like to tell you briefly how it came about, and what its purposes are.

You are a Wiley author, or a prospective author, and there are many of you scattered all over the world—in the United States, Britain, Australia, and New Zealand, to mention only a few places. Like your fellows, you write not for prestige or profit alone, but principally to put before others the knowledge and experience you have accumulated in your particular specialty.

Since John Wiley & Sons are your publishers, you look to us to see your books competently manufactured and distributed. On the other hand, we depend on you for many of our ideas, projects, and plans, and for their execution. So together we constitute a special group—the Wiley associates, if you like.

We feel that the membership of this "association" is especially close-knit, because our common endeavors lie almost exclusively in fields of technology and the sciences. And we submit that FOOTNOTES will strengthen this group by keeping its members in closer touch with one another.

We have outlined a plan for FOOTNOTES which we think will prove valuable in several ways. First, this new publication will bring you news of your fellow-authors—their achievements and recognition in projects other than writing. It will also keep you in touch with those of us here in New York and acquaint you with members of the Wiley staff, with our long-range plans, and with highlights among our publishing projects in fields besides your own.

Through FOOTNOTES' columns we plan, from time to time, to discuss technological developments that promise changes and improvements in the book manufacturing process itself.

Finally, FOOTNOTES will gather together news of the technical publishing world, and will reprint or discuss current articles of special interest to you as a writer of technical books.

Since we are just launching FOOTNOTES, we are especially interested in your reactions to it. What aspects of the plan appeal to you most? Do you like our proposed features? If

W. O. Wiley Begins 60th Year in Publishing

Board Chairman Recalls Varied Experience

Many Wiley authors are frequent visitors to the offices on Fourth Avenue, and others have met Wiley representatives on their campuses, in their offices, and at professional and scientific meetings throughout the country. But, because of the limitations of time and distance, a far greater number are acquainted with our staff only through correspondence. For this reason, we feel that introductions are in order.

We shall begin by introducing William Ogden Wiley, chairman of the board of directors of John Wiley & Sons since 1941. It should first be noted that the Wiley firm is not only one of the oldest publishing houses in this country, but that it is actually the oldest publishing business in America that has remained uninterruptedly in the hands of the founding family. Charles Wiley founded the business in 1807, and in the hundred-and-forty-odd years of the firm's existence, at least one, and usually more, of the members of the Wiley family has been active in its management. William O. Wiley, a great-grandson of the original Charles, has been associated with the House of Wiley for fifty-nine years.

Mr. Wiley graduated from Columbia College in 1882, at the age of twenty. And many years later, in 1945, a college classmate, Nicholas Murray Butler, presented to him the University's Alumni Medal, which described him as "persistent in good citizenship; long conducting the work of an important publishing house; devoted son of alma mater." While at Columbia, young Wiley was an enthusiastic student of the classics, majoring in Latin and Greek. His bachelor's degree acquired, he went on to receive his master's degree in 1887.

Rather than go directly into the publishing business, Mr. Wiley preferred to gain some business experience elsewhere before joining the firm. His father, Charles Wiley, and his uncle, Major William H. Wiley, who were running the business, agreed wholeheartedly to this plan. They wanted the young classical scholar "to be of some use to them." Mr. Wiley

W. O. Wiley

commission basis. Mr. Wiley emphasizes that the smallness of the firm enabled him to obtain a variety of valuable experience.

So Mr. Wiley came to John Wiley & Sons in 1890 with a good basic understanding of how a business actually operated. He recalls that his starting salary was $5.00 a week, and that his first duties consisted of running errands and helping to move the offices, including every book, to a new location at 53 East 10th Street. The new offices were in a private house which the firm rented, and Mr. Wiley remembers well when someone left a faucet running, flooding Major Wiley's private office and ruining a large portion of the stock of books.

Major Wiley had served in the War Between the States, had then studied engineering at Rensselaer Polytechnic Institute and practiced engineering for several years before joining the family business. It was he who recognized the great need for and the possibilities of developing a technological and scientific literature in America, and he was largely responsible for effecting Wiley's swing toward publishing technical books. By 1890,

The first issue of "*Footnotes*," the first Wiley newsletter for authors, begun in 1949.

experience that publishing was no longer a gentleman's game; it was a business. Wiley knew that the industry had changed and that it would have to change as well. That did not mean, however, that it had to forsake all its old family ways for new corporate ones. Striving to maintain a small company feel, in 1949 the company had begun *Footnotes* to disseminate news of interest to Wiley authors and prospective authors. As the first number explained, Wiley authors were spread around the globe, in Britain, Australia, and New Zealand as well as the United States. The newsletter's stated goal was to keep the Wiley "association" of publishers and authors "especially close-knit" by providing readers with news about Wiley, the publishing industry, and science and technology generally. *Footnotes* was also designed to encourage Wiley authors to keep George Lovitt, Wiley's publicity director, up to date. "If we are kept informed of your activities," Lovitt noted, the company could help to create tie-ins with local bookstores and media outlets that helped to move books. Everything, even the nice things, came down to business.[94]

To help reward and retain such talent, Wiley in 1952 began offering its employees life, accident, and hospitalization coverage via a group policy underwritten by the Home Life Insurance Company, one of the industry's best; there was no deduction from salary for these policies. Wiley's travelers, of course, received expense reimbursements that basically doubled their salaries. In 1955, the company set up a pension trust plan. In 1956, it switched to a performance-based bonus system. All those changes were consistent with the best practices of leading U.S. firms at the time.[93]

The industry and the company weathered the storms of the early 1950s, but it was clear from the

The Search for Overseas Markets

Wiley's editorial reputation helped the company make inroads into markets outside the United States, the second big publishing story of the postwar years. The United States emerged from the war with its economy unscathed and dominant, while its aid programs, such as the Marshall Plan in Europe, eased American reentry into pre-war markets and the opening of new ones. Growth in Wiley's export business was important for two reasons. First, foreign sales could help to smooth out revenues by offering a hedge if economic, demographic, or other shocks hit the U.S. book trade. Such a hedge was particularly important for Wiley because, unlike general trade houses, it did not earn much revenue selling subsidiary rights for cheap editions, movies, and the like. The foreign-sales hedge was imperfect, but it worked. For example, Wiley's sales in Japan, mostly through Maruzen in Tokyo, jumped from less than $100 in 1949, to more than $13,000 in 1950, a year when U.S. revenues were down. Exports to Mexico, Venezuela, and Uruguay also increased dramatically in 1950, helping to reduce some of the sting of the domestic slump.[95]

Second, the export market was potentially enormous. Europe and Japan may still have been a postwar shambles, and the rest of the world relatively poor, but partly thanks to American help they would not be in ruins or poor forever. Wiley and other publishers shrewdly sent books to restock Europe's burned-out libraries via CARE, a charity that used donations to buy books from publishers at a steep discount and remit them overseas. Though selling books at cost was not profitable,

the publishers received good publicity at home and extended their name recognition and contacts abroad, helping to prime demand for American technical and scientific works when the time was ripe. By 1949, there was enough levity in the air that an employee at a German periodical could write to Wiley:

> We read your ad and accept your offer,
> Send us the booklet that you proffer.
> Send us your brochure and without delay,
> That you assure us will pave the way
> To wealth and wisdom if we but read it.
> From your description we guess we need it.[96]

To increase international sales as well as scout new authors, Hamilton traveled widely. In May 1945, with the war in the Pacific not yet over, he visited Australia, New Zealand, and sundry smaller Pacific islands at the behest of the Book Publishers Bureau, the successor of the National Association of Book Publishers. Charged with gathering information that would help U.S. publishers to distribute their books in that region, he co-authored, with his traveling

*T*he ruins of a library in England, October 1, 1940. Wiley helped replace books destroyed during World War II.

companion, Whitney Darrow of Charles Scribner's Sons, a detailed report of his journey. More than a month of meetings with Australian and New Zealand authors, booksellers, educators, government officials, librarians, and publishers revealed some intriguing differences in the book trades of North America and the South Pacific. Most important, book selling and publishing had not diverged as completely in Australia and New Zealand as it had in the United States. These countries appeared to be about 25 years behind the U.S. publishing industry. Due to the goodwill generated by the common war effort against Japan, Australian and New Zealand book buyers and textbook adopters did not discriminate against American books, as evidenced by the fact that American books similar in price, quality, and content sold just as well there as their British competitors'. Distribution difficulties were numerous, especially for

limited-sale books like most of Wiley's. Hamilton, however, found that situation promising. Wartime demand for technical books had been strong and he saw signs of a rapid growth in scientific, technical, and business education after the war. Moreover, the market, though small, was a high-quality one due to extremely high literacy rates.[97]

As soon as the war ended, Wiley set up an export division. In 1948 and 1949, Hamilton (who had learned Spanish while working as an engineer in Cuba) visited Latin America, spending six weeks studying the need for and availability of U.S. technology books in the region. Hamilton concluded that, while it was important to plant the seeds for future growth, the immediate prospects were limited because of a dearth of English-language skills, differences in nomenclature and measurement units, and an unfavorable dollar exchange rate, not to mention high

Wiley and Foreign Markets, 1945–1950

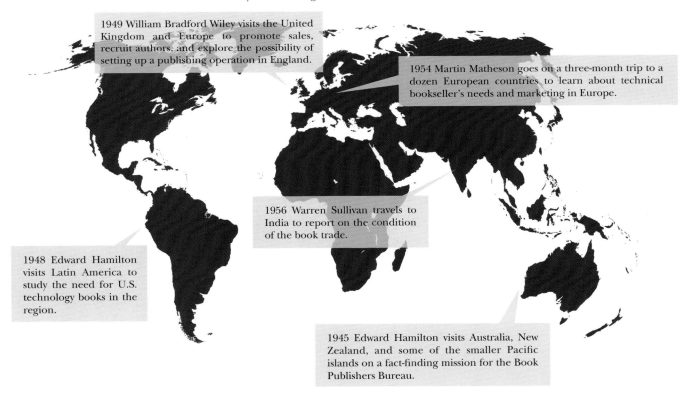

1949 William Bradford Wiley visits the United Kingdom and Europe to promote sales, recruit authors, and explore the possibility of setting up a publishing operation in England.

1954 Martin Matheson goes on a three-month trip to a dozen European countries to learn about technical bookseller's needs and marketing in Europe.

1956 Warren Sullivan travels to India to report on the condition of the book trade.

1948 Edward Hamilton visits Latin America to study the need for U.S. technology books in the region.

1945 Edward Hamilton visits Australia, New Zealand, and some of the smaller Pacific islands on a fact-finding mission for the Book Publishers Bureau.

This map shows the series of trips taken between 1945 and 1950 by Edward Hamilton, William Bradford Wiley, and Warren Sullivan to promote sales overseas.

trade barriers designed to protect local economies against foreign domination of domestic markets. Hamilton stayed abreast of international developments, writing detailed articles about the efforts of U.S. publishers to penetrate international markets. The activities of rival McGraw-Hill, which had begun probing Latin American markets in 1943, were of particular interest to him.[98]

Wiley tried to do its part to promote international scientific exchange. When it could, it translated and published foreign works. It also arranged for the translation and publication of its own English-language works, especially into Spanish for Latin American markets. It even toyed with the idea of publishing books originally written in Spanish, but feared that Spanish-language publishers would take affront and that manufacturing costs would prove too high. To protect the reputation of its books and authors, the company sold translation rights only to established and reputable technical publishers, of which there were few.[99]

Many "exports" in this period were in fact sales made to U.S. information centers established by the State Department. There librarians helped local people—numbering in the hundreds of thousands in some places—to find answers to questions regarding everything from buses to cows to labor relations to tuberculosis. The fact that the information centers were often inundated with patrons suggested to Hamilton and other publishers that foreign demand for U.S. books was high. The increased course adoption rate for American technical books in foreign universities was another good sign, as was the fact that overseas scientists and technical professionals required access to U.S. books if they were to remain up to date in their fields.[100]

To reach European markets, Wiley joined the United States International Book Association, which hired two employees in Amsterdam to promote the sales of American books. To promote sales overseas, Wiley used many of the same advertising and marketing techniques it practiced at home. In other countries, including

Germany, India, and the Philippines, arrangements with local distributors ensured the physical presence of Wiley books at important meetings where potential Wiley authors and customers thronged. Chapman & Hall, Wiley's British partner for more than 50 years, displayed Wiley books in Chapman & Hall booths at professional meetings and conferences in the U.K. This kind of marketing was expensive but effective. The company also started several foreign mailing lists, the four largest of which covered foreign bookstores (635 addresses), college libraries (1,296), public libraries (1,095), and professional societies (398). By the late 1940s, these efforts had begun to show results as Wiley daily shipped "thousands of books" around the globe. The sale of foreign rights also increased dramatically as soon as the war ended.[101]

In 1948, Brad Wiley was given responsibility for carrying out a European strategy, which was to focus on sorting out Wiley's long relationship with Chapman & Hall and then move on to setting up publishing and distribution operations in the U.K. or Europe. Both W. O. and Hamilton had visited London in the 1930s, but no Wiley had visited British or European booksellers for decades. When Brad informed Jack McDougal, the head of Chapman & Hall, of Wiley's plans, McDougal came to New York but neglected to tell Brad that Chapman & Hall had been acquired by Methuen & Company, another British publisher with whom Wiley had a co-publishing arrangement. In 1949, Brad and Esther sailed for Europe aboard the *Queen Mary*. Brad's many interviews with officials from the British Board of Trade, which would have to rule on whether Wiley could set up a subsidiary in the U.K., were frustrating. He was passed from bureaucrat to bureaucrat, each one dressed in the traditional dark jacket and striped pants, only to finally be told that Wiley could set up a publishing operation in the U.K. only if Wiley agreed to have every book it sold in the U.K. and Europe printed in the U.K.[102]

That left Brad with no alternative but to reestablish Wiley's agency relationship with Chapman & Hall. After visiting a few bookstores with James Durrant, the assistant to Chapman and Hall's sales manager, Brad insisted that Chapman & Hall keep a ready supply of Wiley books on hand rather than continue its traditional practice of restocking only when a title was exhausted. (Durrant would later join Wiley as marketing director when the company finally set up its local operation in 1960.) Working with colleagues at Methuen, Brad visited author prospects at Cambridge and Oxford and then took off for the Continent where he visited universities and met with a wide range of publishers, bookstore owners, and distributors. In Copenhagen, he met the elusive Niels Bohr. Bohr had become an advocate of sharing the secret of nuclear weapons in an attempt to head off an arms race. Burgess Whiteside was hired to represent Wiley in Europe after Brad returned to New York.[103]

Brad and Esther continued to travel to Europe on a regular basis, attending the Frankfurt Book Fair for the first time in 1956. Even then, six years after its resumption in 1949, Frankfurt's Fair was a modest event housed in Quonset huts with straw mat flooring. "Not long after the fair opened," Brad recalled, "everyone was hacking, coughing, and sneezing because of the dust that seeped up from the dirt floor through the mats."[104]

Despite setbacks, Brad's hard work paid off, and 1953 turned out to be the best sales year for Wiley's Export Division. Requests for translations also increased, as did reports of pirating, especially in countries behind the Iron Curtain. But the company, which clearly understood that it needed exports and, wrote Brad, "*big selling* reference books for the low points in the textbook cycle," continued to look for ways to expand its foreign sales. In 1954, it sent Matheson to a dozen European countries for three months to identify the needs of technical booksellers. In 1956, Warren Sullivan, who had joined Wiley as Matheson's assistant in 1949, set off to India to report on the condition of the book trade there and to dig into the credit rating of the Asia Publishing Company, which had begun helping to market Wiley books in India in 1947, four years after its formation.[105]

All the while, Matheson carefully tracked Wiley's foreign sales and the aggregate exports of other U.S. and British publishers, to give the company a good idea of where it stood in the market. In 1950, for instance, Wiley was responsible for 24 percent of U.S. book exports to Belgium and Italy, 16 percent to Siam, 15 percent to Norway, 12 percent to France and Turkey, and 9 percent to Uruguay and Holland. Other markets, including Africa, Canada, Germany, and Lebanon, it barely reached. Export sales increased from just under $1 million in 1954, to just over $1.5 million in 1957. Both figures represented just over 20 percent of Wiley's revenues, which in 1955 placed exports second only to college bookstores as a vital Wiley distribution channel.[106]

Old to New

Even as things got bigger, busier, and more spread out, it is worth noting that Wiley still was a family business and one that treated its family well. The cousins' correspondence is filled with chatter about fancy cars, dinners, and apartments. Ownership in the company had widened to include Elizabeth Wiley Darby and Julia Wiley Gilbert, W.O.'s daughters; Randolph Runyon and his wife Mabel; and other silent family partners. The largest blocs of shares, however, remained in the hands of W. O., Hamilton, and his sister. Julia Gilbert, for one, was thrilled with her dividend checks. "How proud and pleased you must be with the way things are going," she wrote. The Wileys had few illusions of grandeur, however. With so much tied up in the company, they worked hard, consistently remembering the little things that kept their company's customers happy. A letter from William Scalsky, the proprietor of a small bookstore called Shelley's that opened in 1947, suggests their old-fashioned attentiveness:

Over the past seven years our service from Wiley has been so consistently on a high level we thought that we might make a small mention of it formally. . . . Every time we have had occasion to consult Wiley the answer has been prompt, courteous and satisfactory. We needed credit; we got it. Promptly. We needed time in several cases to bring our account up-to-date. Time was granted. To a small store these are more than just incidents in the conduct of business; literally, they are a small store's life blood. . . . I think that the service that they give would be more appreciated if one were to make the rounds of other publishers' city trade desks, as I do, and make a comparison.

At a time when publishers and booksellers seemed to be waging war on one another, this was strong testimony that the Wileys were different. Booksellers typically complained that publishers were dilatory in filling orders and that they reneged on promises, used high-pressure sales tactics and worked at the margins of ethics. Publishers retorted that booksellers were mere order-takers, and slow-paying ones at that. Some went so far as to claim that bookstores were so poorly run that they actually alienated more customers than ever they sold to.[107]

The Wileys had strong incentives to keep their house in order. One problem that was gradually resolved was the long-running tension between tradition and innovation. By the late 1940s, the old school at Wiley was almost gone. Samuel E. Norris, who joined the

Rudolf Triest

Samuel E. Norris

Elmer A. Smith

Brad Wiley Sr.

John Snyder

J. Stetson Barnes

Francis Lobdell

Edward P. Hamilton

The "Traditionalists" and the "Progressives" of Wiley. Rudolf Triest (retired 1951), Samuel E. Norris (with Wiley since 1885), and Elmer A. Smith (1905–1953) were all traditionalists; William Bradford Wiley Sr., John Snyder, J. Stetson Barnes, and Francis Lobdell, progressives. Edward P. Hamilton evolved into a progressive.

company in 1885, retired in 1943, after serving as production manager for 16 years, vice president for 2 years, and a director for 30 years. Wiley's treasurer, Elmer A. Smith, died in December 1953. A member of the board since 1921, Smith had joined the company in 1905, serving in a number of positions of responsibility before becoming vice president and treasurer in 1942. Smith's death led to the immediate promotion of four who looked to the future: Brad became vice president and treasurer; John Snyder was promoted to vice president and manager of the editorial department; J. Stetson Barnes, a former traveler and a graduate of Cornell University, moved up to full vice president and manager of manufacturing; and Francis Lobdell moved from office and personnel manager to become company secretary. Lobdell was also selected to fill Smith's position on the board. Rudolf Triest, the last of the traditionalists, retired in

1951. "My resignation seems the only logical step," he said on retiring, in a long handwritten letter to Hamilton, communicating that an era was passing.[108]

Hamilton himself evolved into a new-schooler. Under his leadership, the early 1950s were a forward-looking time for the company. Hamilton realized that venerable institutions like Wiley were sometimes lulled into a "dozy complacency," and he went to some lengths to ensure that it stayed awake. He made it a fundamental policy that "the age of our institution is something we must never emphasize in our thinking." No publisher of science and technology books could afford to feed off its past.[109]

Hamilton believed that publishers were more than mere intermediaries or "middlemen" who linked authors to readers. The publisher's most important function is to help authors craft their books to reach as many

Wiley's 1955 Net Sales by Outlet

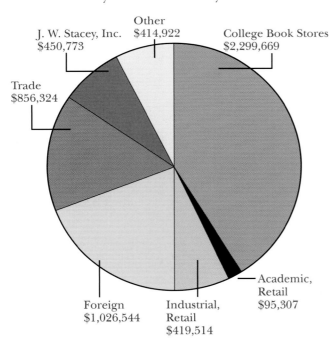

Source: "Net Sales by Outlet," 1954, 1955, Martin Matheson's Little Black Book, JWSA

Unit Sales of Seelye's *Foundations* by Sales Outlet, 1956–1957

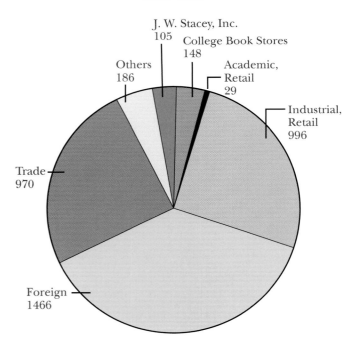

Source: "Breakdown of sales on Seelye's FOUNDATIONS," 1957, "JWS Records: Sales by Title, 1912–1959," JWSA.

iley kept detailed information on book sales in the 1950s. As these charts of sales information for Elwyn E. Seelye's *Foundations: Design and Practice* (1956) show, foreign sales were important for a typical technical work at Wiley.

people as possible, doing so by providing authors, who supply the text, with the context of the publishing business through long experience of what works and what does not work in various fields. A publisher's knowledge of the market, such as knowing the number of college courses a particular book might be suitable for, makes the author's arduous task of writing easier, less risky, more certain of success. Only rarely did it happen that an author could anticipate future needs and write a pioneering textbook that would reshape course development at universities, and the high cost of such pioneering efforts usually made Wiley steer clear. Publishers, Hamilton explained, essentially served as proxy audiences for authors, allowing them to try out their ideas before expending the considerable time necessary to actually write their books. That is why Wiley liked to work closely with authors as early as possible in the book-development process and why it often approached authors with ideas rather than the other way around.[110]

To make such claims about market expertise seriously, Wiley could not rely on guesswork as the publishers that Cheney berated in the early 1930s had done. It had to have facts, and the more the better. But information came at a high cost, so the company had to obtain its information strategically, as business conditions, personnel, and the state of technology allowed. By 1949, for example, the company looked anxiously at weekly sales figures, hoping to see double-digit increases over the previous year's figures. It also distinguished between retail and wholesale orders. The first overall company budget was drawn up in 1951. Also by 1951, the company recognized the way in which multivolume works fueled demand for themselves. The sales of Volume 1 of *Organic Reactions*, for instance, increased with the publication of successive volumes: 85 percent with Volume 2, 110 percent with Volume 3, and 25 percent with Volume 4.

> Brad Wiley, . . . the heir apparent, helped to extend this managerial revolution.

In 1952, the first detailed comparative analysis of sales and costs appeared. In 1954, the first outside consultants were brought in, internal accounting controls were implemented, and budgets were for the first time tied to performance. In 1955, the company was making a range of predictions (conservative, medium, and optimistic) about future sales three years into the future. Those predictions were based on the number of agricultural scientists, biologists, chemists, metallurgists, earth scientists, engineers, mathematicians, physicists, and other scientists employed in the United States, and the percentage of those devoted to research and development work, as well as on college enrollment projections. That same year Wiley developed its first strategic plan and made its first allocation for product research and development. By 1956, Wiley had reasonably detailed information about how its books sold.[111]

Brad Wiley, who emerged as the heir apparent, helped to extend this managerial revolution. In June 1953, during the publishing industry slump, he sent three mid-level executives—Snyder, Barnes, and Lobdell—to the Harvard Business School's Advanced Management Program. Brad attended in 1954. The recommendation came from a graduate of the program, an employee at McGraw-Hill. The Wiley executives returned from their studies with a new understanding of their business and encouraged other managers to attend; more, including Warren Sullivan, would attend in later years. During the decade after the end of World War II, Wiley's senior management team, which now included a cadre of both old and new senior managers, worked hard to adjust the company's traditional publishing practices and culture to the needs of the modern business world. At the same time, Wiley, at a remarkable rate for what was still a relatively small, privately-held family business, extended its reach around the globe.[112]

When the Soviets launched the first man into space in 1957 in the *Sputnik* rocket, a year before the Americans, the United States realized that it was no longer the unchallenged leader in the world of science and technology. Wiley's publishing program was shaped by new research funding and the educational reform movements that were triggered by *Sputnik*.

William Bradford Wiley: The Transition to Professional Management 1957—1979

Chapter Six

✣

Sputnik Launches a New Era

In 1956, William Bradford Wiley, John Wiley's grandson and the son of William O.'s and Edward P. Hamilton's cousin, followed Hamilton as president of the House of Wiley. Brad had gone to work for the company fresh out of college in 1932 and over the years had some big ideas. He once tried to convince his cousins to move Wiley from New York City to Washington, D.C., destined, he believed after his wartime experience there, to become the global capital of an increasingly English-speaking world. His seniors were dismissive, however, and so Wiley stayed in New York. But it was the sort of big thought typical of a man alert to change and anxious to position his company on an optimal path.

In 1957, Wiley marked its sesquicentennial, a remarkable milestone that the company duly celebrated with the publication of a commemorative volume and festivities in Europe, Asia, Australia, and America. There was much to celebrate: In the 25 years since Brad had joined the firm, sales had grown from less than $1 million to $8.8 million. While maintaining Wiley's reputation in the domestic market as a quality publisher, Hamilton, Brad, and their colleagues greatly enhanced the company's reputation overseas. The anniversary included a black-tie dinner in New York City, where Henry T. Heald, president of the

THE FIRST ONE HUN-
DRED AND FIFTY YEARS

A History of John Wiley and Sons, Inc.

Bradford Wiley speaking at the celebration of Wiley's 150th year in 1957. Brad succeeded his cousin, Edward P. Hamilton (left), as president the year before. Hamilton remained as chairman of the board. Below, Brad and his wife, Esther, aboard ship en route to Europe.

Ford Foundation and a man who knew how to make an audience of publishers and authors purr, delivered the keynote address. Books, he said, were "nourishment for the thinking man," and the real danger to America—at just what we now know was the height of the Cold War—came not from subversion by bad ideas but from the impoverishment of too few ideas. The more books the better. Publishers like Wiley, who engaged in the risky but noble business of packaging and marketing ideas, were freedom's true defense.

When Heald spoke in May, such sentiments may have had the appearance of pandering. Before Halloween of that same year, however, his words seemed prophetic. The Soviet Union's launch of Sputnik in October 1957 shocked the world, and it propelled the United States into a burst of spending in the sciences and engineering and a reevaluation of education in these fields. From that investment and subsequent revolutions in the command and organization of information ran the thread of one technology for which Wiley was an early and lasting enthusiast. The ideas of Wiley authors, including Norbert Wiener, swirled through post–Sputnik organizations like the Department of Defense's Advanced Research Projects Agency (ARPA) where the computer was developed into a communications as well as a data processing tool. Wiley's connections to this world were deep and lasting. J.C.R. Licklider, who served on the company's Research and Development Committee in the 1980s, regularly attended Wiener's famous brainstorming dinners at MIT. In 1957, Licklider experimented with a transistor-powered computer, the TX-2, which featured a screen with which he could interact and write code. Three years later, Licklider published a landmark paper combining the latest ideas on computing and artificial intelligence into a vision (foreshadowing the Internet) of humans and machines linked worldwide in a supercommunity of networked computers. In the 1960s, he headed up ARPA's Information Processing and Techniques Office, a post–Sputnik creation of the Department of Defense, where he collaborated with ARPA head Robert Sproull, the author of Modern Physics: A Textbook for Engineers (Wiley, 1956, 1963). In 1965, Sproull joined Wiley's board of directors.[1]

Though no technologist, Brad showed an early enthusiasm for computers. Many of his neighbors in suburban New Jersey worked at Bell Labs, and one of them, an IBM salesman whose henhouse could be seen from the Wiley family's kitchen window, persuaded Brad to install a computer in the Wiley office. More importantly, by the early 1960s Wiley was considering the impact that computers would have on education. The company's greatest challenge was how to grow fast enough to keep pace with the country's expanding investment in education and research in the post-Sputnik world. To do this, Wiley acquired Interscience Publishers in 1961. The company's first acquisition would vault Wiley to sixth place among American publishers and secure its reputation among the very strongest in the field of scientific texts, references, and books. The merger also prompted recapitalization of the company, which meant the end of Wiley as a privately held family company, while preparing the company to expand and diversify in the years ahead. Brad had already proved to be an eager internationalist, visiting Europe on a regular basis starting in 1949. As the Cold War slowly thawed, Brad, often accompanied by his wife Esther, traveled widely, cheerleading at Wiley subsidiaries and lobbying on behalf of the American publishing industry everywhere (for the cause of copyright, for example, an old Wiley favorite). They even traveled to Moscow before the Cold War ended and to Beijing after the United States reestablished diplomatic relations with China.

$\mathcal{T}$he formidable TX-2 computer at MIT in 1962. Inset, J.C.R. Licklider.

The Right Wiley

William Bradford Wiley (1910–1998) became president and CEO of the company in June 1956. When Brad assumed the presidency, W. O. Wiley finally left the board after 68 years of company service. Hamilton became chairman and served ten more years, leaving day-to-day operations to Brad and a team of managers. Increasingly aware that they could no longer manage all aspects of the growing company, the Wileys under the cousins had begun to cultivate a cadre of professional managers without relinquishing their control of the firm. By the time Brad began to think about succession, it was unclear whether any member of the family was ready, willing, and able to assume top-level responsibility. The company's gradual transition from a closely-held firm owned or run by family members to a modern public joint-stock corporation managed by professionals from top to bottom would prove at times trying, but time and the family ultimately sustained it.[2]

Brad stayed in command a long time, and under his management the evolution in publishing practices begun during the cousins' final years gained momentum. He remained president until 1971, CEO until 1979, and chairman of the board of directors until 1993. Under the cousins, Wiley had survived the Depression and wartime, and they had groomed a successor for the next round of challenges. On Brad's long watch, Wiley grew dramatically, transcending its reputation as a small, quality publisher to become a major player in the emerging global knowledge publishing business.[3]

Brad could not have succeeded, though, without a capable team of senior managers, men like John S. Snyder, J. Kenneth Maddock, J. Stetson Barnes, Walker Stone, and Gordon Ierardi. Snyder had joined Brad on Wiley's three-person sales force in 1935, moved on to become head of educational publishing in 1946, and then in 1958 was appointed vice president and head of all editorial staff. Maddock, too, started out as a traveler, becoming head of professional publishing in 1944.

Barnes also began as a traveler but returned after World War II to a job in production, a department he ended up running. He eventually became a vice president and a member of the board of directors. Stone, another traveler hired in 1938, was, according to one of his colleagues, "a very interesting guy" with a "real knack . . . for smelling out what was likely to be important and for making contacts." He was an architectural engineer who became an editor and then in 1958 publisher for technical books for engineers and scientists, an important area for the company. Hired in 1940, Ierardi became one of Wiley's most renowned editors, responsible for building the company's social science list.[4]

Three post–World War II hires also had a profound impact on Wiley. Warren Sullivan, or "Sully" as he was known, was Brad's closest protégé, particularly after he assumed a greater role in the 1950s in the international arena. Sullivan was destined for great things, though he never headed Wiley. After stints in the military and the University of Rochester, Andrew H. Neilly Jr. joined Wiley in 1947 and quickly rose through the ranks, eventually reaching the top post, the first non-Wiley to head all publishing operations. The third member of the postwar triumvirate, Princeton graduate Charles Stoll, became a traveler in 1946 and then an editor in 1950. Over the next 40-plus years, Stoll would serve in many capacities: head of the college and international divisions, managing director of Wiley's British subsidiary, and member of the board of directors.[5]

Wiley's reputation as a good employer enabled it to attract top talent from competitors and build a quality team. In the late 1950s and early 1960s, editors from Holt, Irwin, and Van Nostrand joined the Wiley firm. The reputation of Wiley editors rested on the quality of the books they brought in. In 1957, 24 Wiley books made R. R. Hawkins's list of "The 100 Most Essential Books for the Scientific and Technical Shelf," two more than McGraw-Hill. Wiley also had two titles on the "Best Business Books" list that year. Nine out of every

PROFILE

WILLIAM BRADFORD WILEY SR.

Beyond his role at Wiley, Brad was an important industry leader. In 1970, Brad was a founder and the first board chairman of the Association of American Publishers (AAP), the body created by the merger of the American Book Publishers Council and the American Educational Publishers Institute. In this role he battled publishing's two greatest foes, copyright violations and censorship. Domestically, the spread of inexpensive photocopiers in the 1960s threatened to make widespread duplication of copyrighted materials economically feasible.

Internationally, publishers like Wiley were victims of their own success. Books sold abroad were copied illegally, often by large sophisticated operations, sold in local markets, and even exported back to the United States. For 15 years publishers, including Wiley, pressured Congress to strengthen U.S. copyright law, unchanged since 1909. As president of the AAP, Brad was integral to the publishers' eventual success in fortifying copyright law in late 1976. Among other things, the completely revamped Copyright Act, which took effect in January 1978, codified "fair use," a doctrine the courts had developed as a defense to infringement to permit the limited copying of copyrighted works, including published books, for purposes such as research, scholarship, and teaching. For example, fair use would allow students or library patrons to photocopy limited portions of published works. But by creating such an exception, the new Copyright Act made clear that any systematic, large-scale photocopying of copyrighted materials is illegal. In 1983, Brad received the prestigious Curtis G. Benjamin Award for Creative Publishing, in part for his strenuous efforts on behalf of copyright reform. Internationally, Brad traveled extensively—including

William Bradford Wiley Sr. (1910–1998): Publisher, internationalist, copyright champion, and industry leader. The great grandson of John Wiley, Brad was CEO of John Wiley & Sons from 1956 to 1979, and chairman of the board from 1966 to 1993.

trips to the Soviet Union and Romania—to campaign on behalf of the international copyright law.[6]

In 1967, Brad was one of the leaders of a large, ad hoc committee of publishers who took out a full-page advertisement in the *New York Times* calling on President Lyndon B. Johnson to "END THE WAR IN VIETNAM NOW." He also stood up to government censors. The war and social unrest at home made the Nixon administration more than usually fearful of criticism, and when CBS broadcast a piece called "The Selling of the Pentagon" on February 23, 1971, the administration reacted fiercely. Brad, via the AAP, sprang to the defense of CBS and the First Amendment. He did so again when first the *New York Times* in June, and then the *Washington Post* and Beacon Press published *The Pentagon Papers*, a top-secret 7,000-page inquiry into U.S.–Vietnam relations since 1945 that had been commissioned by Secretary of Defense Robert McNamara in 1967. The government's injunction against publication of the papers was overturned when the U.S. Supreme Court voted six to three in favor of the publisher's right to print them without restraint under the First Amendment.[7]

THE SECRET HISTORY
OF THE VIETNAM WAR

THE COMPLETE AND
UNABRIDGED SERIES
AS PUBLISHED BY
The New York Times

THE PENTAGON PAPERS

BASED ON INVESTIGATIVE REPORTING
BY NEIL SHEEHAN.
WRITTEN BY NEIL SHEEHAN,
HEDRICK SMITH, E. W. KENWORTHY
AND FOX BUTTERFIELD
WITH KEY DOCUMENTS
AND 64 PAGES OF PHOTOGRAPHS

In the 1960s, the Vietnam War and the resulting exposés of how and why it came about led to government actions that threatened First Amendment rights. Brad Wiley was an active supporter of the industry's right to publish controversial views and information.

PROFILE

WARREN "SULLY" SULLIVAN

On the last day of 1946, Warren "Sully" Sullivan joined Wiley as a traveler, with a territory extending from Virginia to Florida. Then-president Edward Hamilton, who wintered in Florida, provided him with some expert, if niggardly, on-the-job training. (Hamilton was famous for living on $3 per day by sleeping in cheap hotels and eating small lunches.) In 1949, Sullivan moved up to sales manager and assistant vice president of marketing under Martin Matheson, responsible for sifting through travelers' field notes and supplying travelers with data, advice, and instruction.[8]

A great "people person" with numerous friends, and a graduate of Harvard's Advanced Management Program, Sullivan had both the hard and soft skills necessary to thrive in publishing management. In 1957, Wiley promoted him to a vice presidency and made him director of marketing, with a specialty in international marketing. In 1961, after playing a crucial role in the negotiations to acquire Interscience Publishers, he left Wiley to serve as president of Macmillan, by then a subsidiary of Crowell–Collier, which was losing value under the leadership of the son of storied but aged publisher George Brett. In 1966, after righting Macmillan, Sullivan became president of Barnes & Noble. He returned to Wiley in 1971 to head the company's new Halsted Press, an important operation that under his leadership grew rapidly in psychology and the life sciences. He was also put in charge of professional book marketing. "Sully," remembered Charles Stoll, "was the kind of guy who said this was [like the story of] the emperor's clothes; . . . His activities were very effective for us."[9]

Warren "Sully" Sullivan was born in New York in 1922. He graduated from Dartmouth in 1943 with specialties in history, economics, and political science and then went off to the Navy, where he served as one of the original "frogmen."

ten books that Wiley published were written at the request of one of the company's editors, while the average professional publisher built 20 percent of its list from unsolicited manuscripts.[10]

Many of Wiley's senior managers came from the editorial side of the company with limited business experience. When Wiley's performance was poor in the early 1950s, Brad recognized that modern business practices were needed if Wiley was to expand in the new publishing environment. To build the necessary human capital internally, he dispatched Snyder, Barnes, Sullivan, and Francis Lobdell, the company's chief financial manager, to the Advanced

J. Stetson Barnes was head of production in the 1960s. He also served on Wiley's board of directors.

Management Program at Harvard, following them himself within six months. As Stoll, a later graduate, remembered, Brad was "enthusiastic, business-oriented, hard-nosed, and determined to concentrate his full energies on the financial aspects of publishing"—to the degree that he hired Kenneth Andrews from the Harvard program to help with modernizing the company's financial analysis and reporting and with the writing of the company's first strategic plan. Andrews taught that a firm's structure had to follow from its strategy—that is, from its plans for the "long-term health of the enterprise," in the words of Alfred D. Chandler, another proponent of strategic thinking. Andrews urged companies to assess their strengths, weaknesses, opportunities, and threats, in what came to be known as SWOT analysis. Andrews went on to join the Wiley board in 1966.[11]

These new approaches to the business aspects of publishing led to other changes, such as the first use of revolving credit to smooth cash flows in an overdue recognition that sales varied widely from month to month. This pattern was tied to the seasonality of the higher education market, which was by far Wiley's most important. In 1958, Wiley also for the first time seriously discussed the advantages and disadvantages of tapping outside sources of capital. That same year, it established an information center charged with collecting market research data and making sales forecasts and reports. In 1960, computers began to handle billing and payroll. During this period the company also developed its first pension plan and for the first time tied bonuses to performance instead of to rank and seniority. So in December 1957, for example, Wiley paid Sullivan a bonus of $5,833.33, but Neilly, who was also an officer and joined Wiley at almost the same time, received only $4,000.[12]

Babies, *Sputniks*, and Publishing

Demographics in part determined the new publishing environment to which Brad and his team were adapting. After World War II, the American birthrate rose, producing what became known as the "baby boom generation." The number of live births per 1,000 women aged 15 to 44 years increased from its Depression low of about 80 to over 120 by the late 1950s before trailing off to around 90 in the late 1960s. Scholarly consensus on the reasons for this relative fecundity remains elusive. Cultural explanations are ad hoc, and economic explanations are equally unsatisfactory because as a nation's per capita income rises, its birthrate usually falls as children cost more and become financial liabilities rather than income producers. But in the United States in the 1940s through the 1960s, birthrates and per capita income grew in tandem. In 1950, per capita income was $11,672; by 1970, it stood at $18,395. As the baby boom generation grew up, college enrollment rose, from around 2 million in the late 1940s and early 1950s to almost 10 million by the end of the 1970s. Part of that increase was directly due to population growth but part was also due to increased rates of college attendance.[13]

Two major shifts in U.S. education account for the increased rates. First, education came to be seen as an investment rather than an expense. Second, the emphasis moved from teaching to learning, from a teacher- to a student-centered model. As a result, Americans in all regions and of all classes and ethnicities were spending more time in school and while there were reading more widely than ever. Textbooks remained the staple pedagogical tool, supplemented

John Wiley & Sons Sales by Month, 1945–1959

Wiley's sales varied widely from month to month, tied to the seasonality of the higher education market.

Source: Martin Matheson's *Big Black Book*, JWSA.

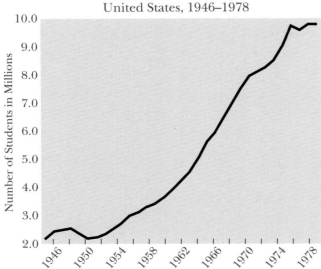

Total College Enrollment in the
United States, 1946–1978

Source: *Digest of Education Statistics*, 1980, 89.

*B*etween 1950 and 1980, the population of the United States increased from 151.33 million to 226.54 million. The number of college students also soared, from around 2 million in the late 1940s and early 1950s to almost 10 million by the end of the 1970s. Part of that increase was directly due to population growth but part was also due to increased rates of college attendance.

with workbooks, problem sets, trade books, slides, records, films, and tapes. In higher education, engineering enrollments increased from around 200,000 in the early 1950s to almost 400,000 in the late 1970s, but clearly did not keep pace with overall enrollment growth. Other scientific, technical, and business majors experienced such strong growth, however, that by the mid-1960s observers predicted (some lamented) the demise of the liberal arts. Growth in the number of graduate students of all types was strong, with enrollments increasing from 315,000 in 1960 to 1.3 million in 1976. At the entry level, community college enrollments grew at an astounding pace, doubling during the 1950s

*S*tudents flooded college campuses in the late 1960s and early 1970s. Their needs—and sometimes their demands—changed higher education curricula and publishing in the United States.

*T*he spike in the birthrate during and just after World War II known as the "baby boom" drove the increased demand for textbooks in the 1960s.

Enrollment of Young Americans (18–24) in College

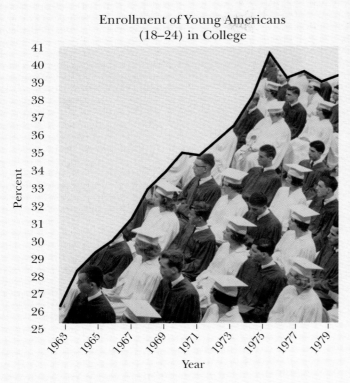

Source: *Digest of Education Statistics*, 1980, 87.

Students at Southwest Texas State College have a discussion after the school was integrated in 1963.

The Nuclear Age

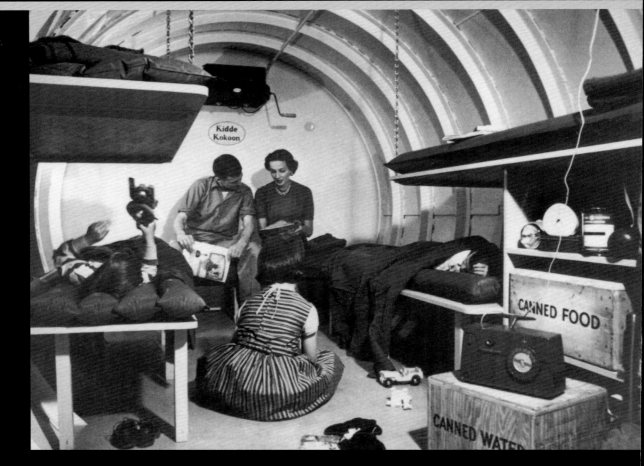

The Cold War between the United States and the Soviet Union created an environment of real and imagined fears. Fearing a Soviet nuclear attack, public air raid shelters became ubiquitous, air raid drills were common, and some families built their own fallout shelters.

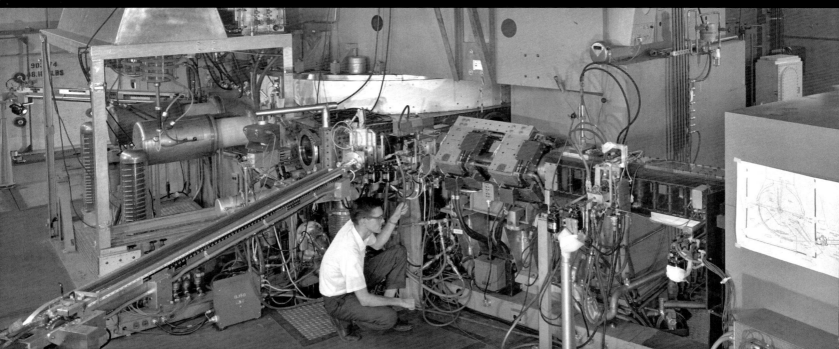

The Cyclotron at Lawrence Berkeley National Laboratory at the University of California, Berkeley, in 1961. The first cyclotron was invented by Ernest O. Lawrence at the University of California, Berkeley, in 1930. Cyclotrons, used in high-energy physics experiments, have led to important developments such as magnetic resonance imaging and radiation therapy for cancer. Wiley not only published some of the classic works in nuclear physics but also produced major physics textbooks, such as David Halliday and Robert Resnick's *Physics*, first published in 1960, which became a leader in the field.

and then growing five times over in the next decade—all of which meant a dramatic increase in access to higher education for lower-income Americans. The number of faculty members tripled in public institutions between 1939 and 1963 and nearly doubled in private schools. By the end of the 1960s, the country's professoriate numbered nearly half a million.[14]

Geopolitical developments, chiefly the Cold War, also prompted growth in education and publishing. The Cold War's seemingly endless arms race was fueled by a technology race. Americans had emerged from World War II and entered the atomic age convinced that they had a technological edge over the Soviets, and at first they did. But the Soviets soon caught up and dramatically so in October 1957, launching *Sputnik* and beating the Americans into space.[15]

In response, federal dollars soon poured into scientific research and education. The National Defense Education Act of 1958 richly subsidized higher education, support that jumped to $7.4 billion by 1962. Industry and business also stepped up, especially with aid to higher education. A *New Yorker* cartoon captured the mood of the moment: a legion of scientists, white lab coats, pocket protectors and all, marching in formation while chanting to the tune of the Marine hymn, "From the cyclotron of Berkeley to the labs of M.I.T., We're the lads that you can trust to keep our country strong and free."[16]

Libraries, an important market ($261 million of the $2 billion domestic book market in 1966) for Wiley and most other publishers, were also caught up in the Cold War. In the early 1950s, libraries were hurt by anti-communist initiatives and McCarthyism. Some librarians

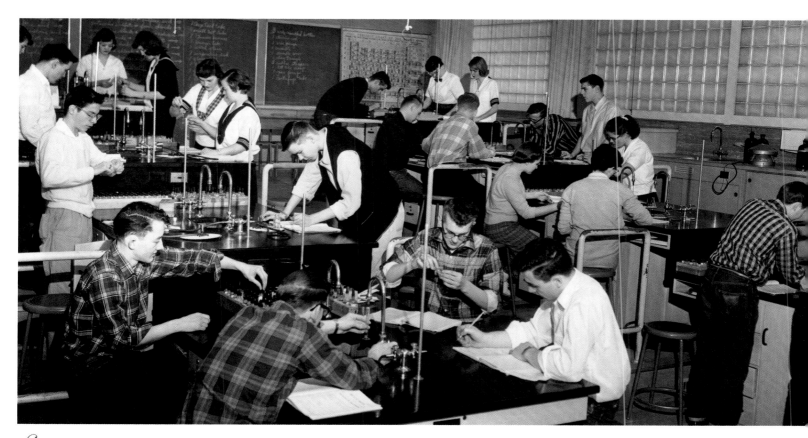

*S*tudents conduct experiments in a science laboratory.

New Main Library of Indiana University under construction. The library, which was completed in 1969, was partially funded by the federal government. The 1960s were boom years for educational institutions, leading to the construction of libraries, laboratories, classroom buildings, and even entirely new campuses.

were fired for their political activities and collection development decisions. When the American Library Association upheld Americans' "right to read," the American Legion quickly identified the ALA as a "Red front," an outpost of communism in the United States. At the same time, many leaders realized that a strong economy was the nation's best defense against communism from both within and without, and they believed that a strong public library system could help to strengthen the economy while simultaneously fostering a politically engaged citizenry. So Congress in 1956 passed the Library Services Act and extended its life in 1960 in the wake of the *Sputnik* shock. In 1961, the United States boasted 8,250 public libraries, up from 6,909 in 1939. Local and state funding was vastly improved, and circulation figures approached 500 million per year nationwide. Two years later, President John F. Kennedy hailed libraries as one of the doors that would lead the American people "to the richest treasures of our open society." That same year, the National Educational Improvement Act increased subsidies to libraries, even the nonrural ones that had been neglected during the Depression. Later in the 1960s, the federal government bestowed yet more funds on libraries as part of President Lyndon Johnson's Great Society programs. "American libraries," Johnson argued, "have a key role to play in the war against poverty."[17]

Big public libraries such as the New York Public Library were important to Wiley, but so too because of their large numbers were the smaller ones. To this day, for example, the shelves of the 26 public libraries of Montgomery County, Pennsylvania, a part-suburban, part-rural county just north of Philadelphia, are home to 57 Wiley titles published between 1950 and 1959, inclusive. The titles are a testament both to the diversity of the county and to Wiley's broad list, ranging from the *Dictionary of Architecture* to *Theories of Personality* to *Partial Differential Equations* to *Logical Design of Digital Computers*. Those libraries also still house 176 Wiley books published between 1960 and 1970, including *Principles of Refrigeration, Behavior Therapy, Biology of Cells,* and *America, Russia, and the Cold War.* (Their shelves seem to sag with recent Wiley books, but the number of earlier titles that they deaccessioned is unknowable and so their relative importance to the company's sales cannot be readily ascertained.)[18]

Academic and industrial research libraries were more important to Wiley in this period, and they too expanded. Under the Farmington Plan of 1948, developed by an advisory committee to the Librarian of Congress, an academic research library could place a so-called blanket order with a book dealer for books in the library's areas of interest. Richard Abel and Company, for example, sent all scholarly books on particular topics published in North America, the United Kingdom, continental Europe, Australia, New Zealand, and South Africa to participating small and mid-sized academic libraries on an approval basis. To the extent that they were in place, blanket orders made life easier for sales representatives, who could focus attention on a few book suppliers rather than thousands of librarians. For librarians, the outsourcing of collection development helped to relieve the strain on library staff gasping for breath during the heady postwar and post-*Sputnik* growth surges. "New, large, library buildings appeared on almost every campus," recalled Warren Haas, onetime president of the Council on Library Resources. "The challenge for libraries," he reported, "was to grow fast enough and to spend effectively rapidly rising annual budgets." Massive government subsidies helped to cover the costs of the blanket agreements and the new buildings, programs, and acquisitions, but librarians said it was not enough and Wiley did not demur.[19]

Industrial and other types of corporate libraries were ubiquitous by this time. By the late 1950s, the United States alone was home to over 3,000 corporate libraries, up from 1,000 at the end of World War II. Though highly specialized and relatively small—the largest was probably Bell Telephone Laboratories'100,000-volume, 2,000-periodical library—most were large enough to require the services of at least one librarian. General Electric needed a staff of 16 to handle its 23,000 books and 25,000 pamphlets, but even relatively small companies like the Armstrong Cork Company of Lancaster, Pennsylvania, needed a librarian to manage their expanding collections. An estimated $3,000 to start and $10,000 per year were required to begin and build a decent collection, a sum many companies found to be a bargain, although salaries and overhead were extra. Good industrial librarians were rare because most were better equipped in the humanities than in the sciences, but that did not dampen corporate America's increasing lust for libraries, the number of which continued to grow in the 1960s and 1970s, to the point that it was virtually mandatory for big corporations to have at least one (and by the 1970s, most had several) professionally staffed library or "information center." In aggregate, American companies and industry organizations spent millions on their libraries because they increasingly came to realize the business value of knowledge. In addition, much of the investment was tax deductible.[20]

> By fostering basic and applied research, . . . federal expenditures . . . indirectly increased the demand for, and the supply of, Wiley titles.

Not all of the government's appropriations for science and technology helped Wiley. Public Law 480 subsidized the sale of American grain in developing countries, such as India and Pakistan, in local currencies. The U.S. government used the funds to buy locally published books, especially technical and financial ones, which were given to American research libraries. Wiley was able to mitigate the negative effects of this additional competition by seeking out local publishing partners. In any event, these negative effects paled compared to the positive effects for Wiley of other government programs. By fostering basic and applied research in atomic physics, for example, federal expenditures on the Argonne National Laboratory indirectly increased the demand for, and the supply of, Wiley titles. A direct outgrowth of the Manhattan Project, Argonne National Laboratory

was one of the premier nuclear reactor development laboratories in the world in the 1950s and 1960s.[21]

The intrinsic vigor and excitement that characterized the scientific community during Brad's tenure provided strong impetus for Wiley's growth. Important breakthroughs in econometrics, computing, game theory, genetics, jet propulsion, manned space flight, nuclear energy, plastics, psychology, radar, silicon, sociology, space flight, telecommunications, and transistors created intense industrial, public, scholarly, and student interest that Wiley strove to tap. Connecting these breakthroughs with book sales, however, was not always easy

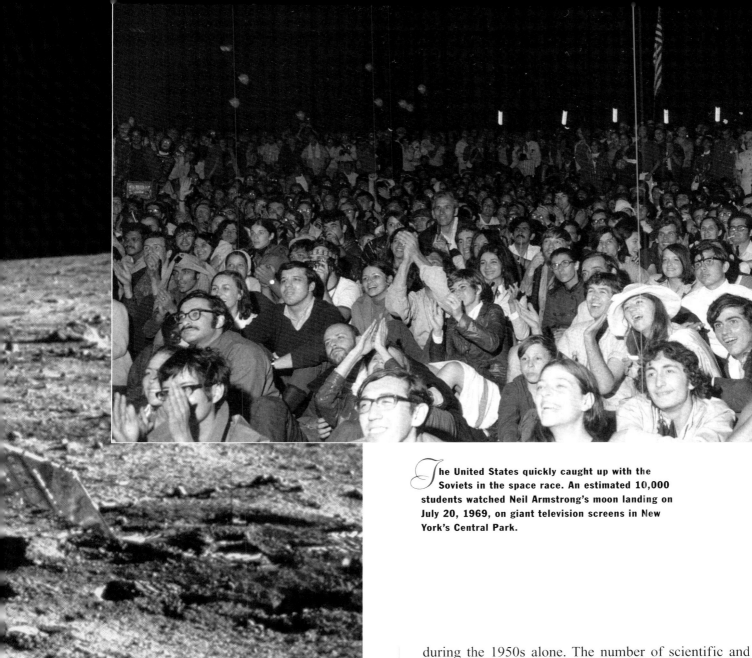

The United States quickly caught up with the Soviets in the space race. An estimated 10,000 students watched Neil Armstrong's moon landing on July 20, 1969, on giant television screens in New York's Central Park.

during the 1950s alone. The number of scientific and technical titles published in the United States soared from 865 in 1950 to 3,170 in 1966. College textbook sales hit $85 million in 1958 and continued strong thereafter. In Wiley's chosen subject areas, American higher education was a Wiley world. In 1957, the year of its sesquicentennial, Wiley's revenue was $8.8 million. Five years later, it was $16 million.[23]

When Brad took over Wiley in 1956, its pretax earnings were $741,700, but after-tax earnings totaled only $340,000. Within a year, Brad had boosted those figures to $983,000 and $450,000, respectively, on sales of over $7 million. Higher prices for science and technology

in a nation in which only a relatively small percentage of the public consistently read books.[22]

Even so, the United States was a very large country, and the numbers could be impressive. Americans read 60 million newspapers daily and 270 million magazines annually, and book sales doubled

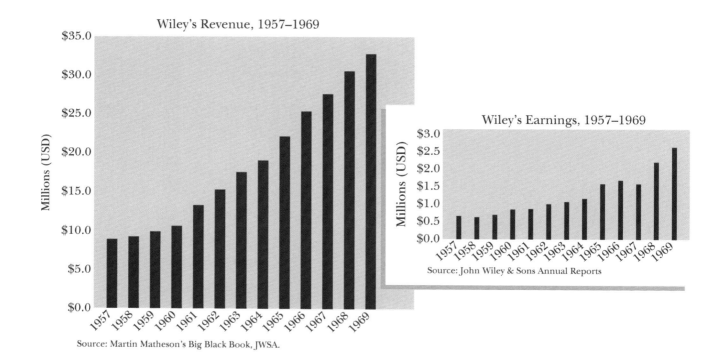

Wiley's Revenue, 1957–1969

Wiley's Earnings, 1957–1969

Source: John Wiley & Sons Annual Reports

Source: Martin Matheson's Big Black Book, JWSA.

books, which roughly doubled between 1949 and 1962, certainly helped the company, but much of the credit goes to Brad and his emerging management team.[24]

The growth of Wiley's list, its stock of titles in print, between 1958 and 1978 was impressive by any standards. Between 1958 and 1968, Wiley's catalogue of in-print books leapt from 1,239 to 2,778 titles. Just ten years later, in 1978, Wiley's catalogue contained an astonishing 6,743 titles. The number of Wiley series and periodicals also increased dramatically, from 128 and 11, respectively, in 1968 to 263 and 33 by 1978. Many Wiley books were published in series edited by scholarly researchers, continuing the programs begun under the cousins. Some series did well both critically and economically. Others, like *Advances in Plasma Physics*, barely broke even but further enhanced Wiley's reputation in fast-growing fields.[25]

Equally striking was the development of the list, from one with relatively few subfields in 1958 to one suffused with specialties by 1978. Consider sociology. Not only did the number of titles increase from 13 (1.05 percent of the total list) in 1958 to 63 (2.27 percent) in 1968 to 247

(3.66 percent) in 1978, but the list developed ten subfields in just a decade. History, political science, and other social sciences similarly matured. Part of the increased complexity of the social science list was due to the increased complexity of the social sciences, which in fields like anthropology manifested itself in specialization, or what Curtis Benjamin of McGraw-Hill called "the twigging phenomenon." Part, however, was due to a thickening of the company's list, to its conscious attempt to exploit each market niche as it emerged.[26]

Brad and company also shifted Wiley's list, traditionally weighted toward math, science and engineering, toward the social sciences, humanities, and business, which increased from 22 percent of the list in 1968 to 38 percent in 1978. Much of that gain came from the relative decline of titles in the physical and life sciences, which decreased from almost half of Wiley's list in 1968 to under 40 percent in 1978, and in the applied sciences, which dropped from 28 percent to less than 21 percent of Wiley's list over that same decade. Whatever the mix, however, Wiley clearly remained a knowledge publisher. Its publications helped

Americans to eat, sleep, work, and understand everything from atoms to anomie, from materials to machismo, from the elasticity of plastics to the elasticity of demand.[27]

Under Brad, Wiley's stable of authors boasted a fair share of thoroughbreds. Michael Holt was one of the most important historians of antebellum American politics. In geography, Allan Pred was a major force. Political scientist Adam Przeworski was another well-known name. Albert Bandura and Jerome Kagan, psychologists, were famous for theories about modeling and psychological development, respectively. In economic history, Robert Higgs was top tier. Henri Theil did important work in econometrics, as did Edward Altman in finance and investments. Theodor Adorno was one of the premier social philosophers of the twentieth century. In the sciences, Wiley could claim numerous Nobel laureates, including Selman Waksman (medicine, 1952), William Shockley (physics, 1956), Glenn Seaborg (chemistry, 1951), Salvador Luria (medicine, 1969), Geoffrey Wilkinson (chemistry, 1973), Paul Flory (chemistry, 1974), Paul Dirac (physics, 1933), Herbert Simon (economics, 1978), David Baltimore (medicine, 1975), Maria Goeppert-Mayer (physics, 1963), Ilya Prigogine (chemistry, 1977), and Nikolaas Tinbergen (medicine, 1973). Wiley authors won other prestigious prizes as well. William Feller, for instance, was awarded the National Medal of Science. Henry Eyring, the author of six Wiley books, won the Priestley Medal of the American Chemical Society. "We start looking for geniuses early," a Wiley executive remarked in 1957. In 1975, another executive noted that Wiley editors served as "the *intellectual companions* of young and developing teachers."[28]

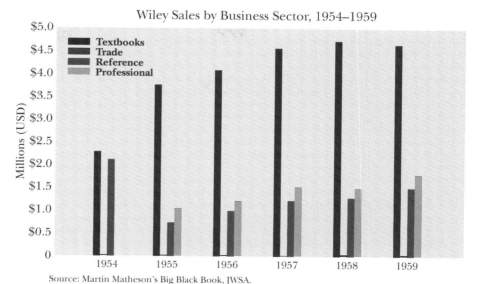

Wiley Sales by Business Sector, 1954–1959

Textbooks
Trade
Reference
Professional

Source: Martin Matheson's Big Black Book, JWSA.

How did Wiley's list grow so quickly? Superficially, the rate of new titles Wiley added on average greatly exceeded the number of titles retired each year.[29] By paying close attention to markets, to the expressed needs of customers, and then cultivating authors willing and able to write books that fulfilled those needs, Wiley strengthened its list. Increasingly, other publishers adopted this model, which was intrinsically less risky than the traditional method of accepting books "over the transom" and then trying to find markets for them.[30]

Brad and his team worked hard to keep up with developments in the textbook, trade, and professional/reference markets. In what he called his Big Black Book, Martin Matheson kept track of Wiley's growth by publishing sector between 1954 and 1959. Over this period, textbooks grew from 52 to 58 percent of sales, while reference publishing shrank from 48 to 13 percent between 1954 and 1955 and then grew gradually to 19 percent in 1959. Matheson also tracked trade sales, by which he meant the sale of technical and professional titles through retail outlets. In 1959, trade sales accounted for less than 1 percent of total sales.

The Textbook Revolution

During the 1950s, Wiley more than ever became a text-book publisher. Due to the rapid expansion of knowledge in most areas, textbooks needed to focus more on principles and basic science and less on comprehensive coverage of a subject. Hamilton worried about too many highly specialized projects, which, however good for Wiley's reputation, drained its resources. Wiley was just then, in 1958, in the process of adding important but not very lucrative series in Publications in Operations Research (in conjunction with the Operations Research Society of America, or ORSA) and in space technology. In February 1959, at a special board meeting in Skytop, Pennsylvania, Wiley decided in a significant shift that it needed to publish more basic textbooks and fewer specialized titles. The viability of specialized titles and/or research monographs would remain a preoccupation for years.[31]

By the early 1960s, some observers pointed to a nascent pedagogical revolution that drove rapid changes in the textbook industry. A massive increase in sales—which nearly doubled between 1956 and 1961—was linked via the *Sputnik* scare to a profound qualitative change. This exciting time had peripatetic acquisition editors moving from conference to conference, briefcases bulging with new manuscripts and proposals for "new media" pedagogical aids, including educational television programs, films and filmstrips, even teaching machines.[32]

Wiley duly expanded its publishing program to include introductory textbooks and upper division books designed for use at second- or third-tier schools. As part of that effort, Wiley began to develop or "carpenter" textbooks, hiring "depth" (later developmental) editors with pedagogical experience and skills to help textbook authors turn their manuscripts into effective learning tools. Like its competitors McGraw-Hill, Macmillan, and Prentice Hall, Wiley also produced a wide range of ancillary materials designed to help sell textbooks. For example, it provided language professors with free copies of master tapes for lab use and charged the cost of the tapes to its language textbook sales.[33]

McGraw-Hill had long developed textbook series that covered a subject like psychology from general introductory text to advanced titles in each of the major subfields such as clinical, abnormal, developmental, and experimental. With college enrollments and textbook sales growing but increasingly uncertain, Wiley too wanted the best chance at selling something to as many students as possible and adopted McGraw-Hill's approach, following it in the realm of textbook design. Wiley had never ignored book design, but like the rest of the industry only began to stress its importance in the first decades of the twentieth century. By Brad's time, the company had grown very sensitive to design issues. Before its postwar boom, Wiley published mostly advanced textbooks that contained little if anything in the way of colorful graphics or other pedagogical devices. That changed as students changed and as the company moved down-market to freshman-level texts. Wiley's first four-color text appeared in 1959. The new breed of textbook featured numerous high-quality illustrations as well as attractive jackets and better typography.[34]

One important question that emerged was whether textbooks should "wear cloth or appear in paper." Paper was cheaper—less expensive and less durable—but most of the cost of a textbook was in the creation of the words and pedagogical devices, not its packaging. So for a new book, the price differential between a "quality" paperback and a hardbound edition was relatively small and not clearly advantageous given the rugged use that textbooks typically received. Nevertheless, as early as 1970, Wiley considered publishing textbooks in paper.[35]

Reaching as many college students as possible meant tracking trends in majors. In the 1960s, about 25 percent of U.S. undergraduates took degrees in engineering and the natural sciences, while the other 75 percent opted for majors in business, the humanities, and the social sciences. Not surprisingly then, in addition to moving downstream to more basal texts, Wiley also sought to expand its offerings in the social sciences and humanities, becoming a full-fledged higher education publisher.

INSIDE THE BOOKS

Schifferes' *Healthier Living*

*W*iley textbooks stressed high-quality illustrations, using beautiful color and attractive design to support learning. The company's first color book, *Healthier Living* by Justus J. Schifferes, published in 1959, was very successful and sold in various versions for 10 years. Illustrations from one of those versions, *Essentials of Healthier Living*, also by Schifferes, first published in 1963, are shown below.

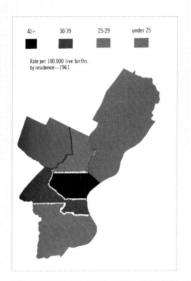

40+   30-39   25-29   under 25

Rate per 100,000 live births by residence—1961

AIR POLLUTION

	Heavy	Med. heavy	Med. light	Light
WINTER	75	55	35	25
SPRING	60	40	25	15
SUMMER	50	35	20	10
FALL	65	45	30	20

Average seasonal values of "settled dust" (tons per sq. mile per month)

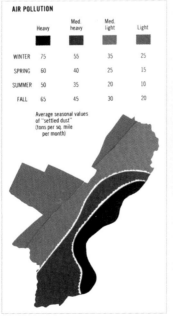

PLATE

V

Appendix (7)
Auditory (Eustachian) tube opening into pharynx (8)
Bile duct (12)
Brain (22)
Cerebellum (28)
Cerebrum (29)
Corpus callosum (33)
Diaphragm (37)
Frontal sinus (53)
Gallbladder (55)
Hepatic (liver) artery (58)
Hepatic (liver) veins (59)
Intestine, large (colon) (69)
  a. Cecum
  b. Ascending colon
  c. Transverse colon
  d. Descending colon
  e. Sigmoid colon
  f. Rectum
Intestine, small (70)
Larynx (75)
Liver (76)
Lung (77)
Mesentery (85)
Nasal turbinates (88)
Omentum, lesser (91)
Pituitary gland (101)
Pons (103)
Portal vein (104)
Sphenoid sinus (125)
Stomach (131)
Thigh muscle (137)
  a. Rectus femoris
Thyroid gland (141)
Tongue (142)
Vena cava, inferior (151)

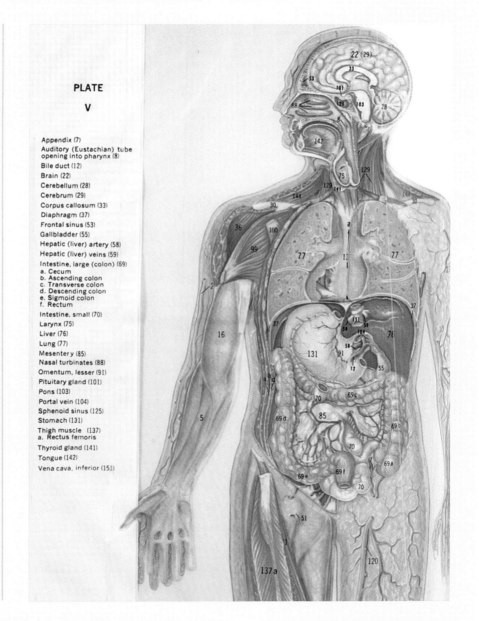

The Urge to Merge

As it became clear in the years immediately after *Sputnik* that the market for typical Wiley books was surging and that educational publishing presented exciting new possibilities, the company's leaders were challenged to find a way to meet the increasing financial demands of a growing marketplace. In 1958, in terms of the number of new titles published per year, Wiley was still far from the top tier of publishers—Doubleday, Harper, Macmillan, McGraw-Hill, Oxford, and Prentice Hall. But at 148 titles and growing, it was only a few titles behind Random House and slightly ahead of Simon & Schuster; Pocket Books; Houghton Mifflin; Little, Brown; and Harcourt, Brace. Of course, it was way ahead of most other publishers, who were tiny. In 1958, only 32 U.S. publishers out of the more than 11,500 houses that published at least 5 titles per year put out 100 or more titles each.[36]

To publish 100 titles in a year required editorial expertise, logistical efficiency, and, most basically, financial power, especially if the books were for classroom use. Publishers spent up to a million dollars, a monstrous sum before the Great Inflation of the 1970s, to develop big textbooks or series of texts designed, if all went well, to dominate their respective fields for a generation. Such texts might take five or more years to come to fruition, and they required capital.[37]

Businesses grow in different ways. One is to start small, from the savings of a family or a couple of individuals, and to grow slowly by plowing profits back into the business. Wiley and most other publishers pursued this route until World War II. The experience of wartime publishing demonstrated that production and distribution of books on a massive scale was feasible and could be profitable. As growth became the watchword of the postwar industry, financing expansion from retained earnings alone became too slow, especially for technical and textbook publishers who needed big cushions of working capital. Brad saw this new situation clearly and described it forthrightly: Wiley intended "to grow apace with the vast, expanding needs for educational materials of all kinds that accompany the scientific and technological explosion of our times." To keep pace, Wiley acquired Interscience Publishers in 1961. As a result, revenue grew from $8.9 million in 1957 to $15.2 million in 1962. Wiley continued to grow, thereafter acquiring a number of smaller publishers and related businesses by going public and selling shares *twice* on the open market.[38]

Mergers were not unknown to the publishing industry. In fact, the early publishing partnerships, such as Wiley in several incarnations, might be seen as mergers of an elementary sort. But these partnerships were transient affairs between gentlemen. Modern mergers, where two companies join on a permanent basis, were not common in publishing until the intense merger wave that occurred between 1885 and 1890 led to the creation of American Book Company and other early giants. By the early twentieth century, publishing legend Frank Nelson Doubleday (1862–1934) could point to the merger successes of Doubleday and Houghton Mifflin as "the quickest and most surely successful method of developing a fine business." "Quickest" could be relative, however, for mergers depended on the availability of willing partners. Not many came to market, and it could take years to broker a deal.[39]

Another problem with mergers and acquisitions was the size of the sums required. Most of the time, publishers sold out when they wanted cash (or its near equivalent). That forced acquirers, whose capital was tied up in books (just like the sellers' capital), to sell securities or borrow in the capital markets. Some firms remained private and sold only bonds, but many sold equity shares to the public. Unlike bondholders, stockholders did not receive fixed quarterly interest payments but rather participated in the publisher's profits if there were any, accepting both the risks and rewards of publishing books. The disadvantage of going public was that stockholders, unlike bondholders (assuming the interest on their bonds was being paid as promised), could vote for directors. Publishers, however, learned ways to minimize stockholder influence and generally preferred sales of stock over bonds.[40]

Before World War II, such financing in publishing was rare, the big exception being McGraw-Hill, which went public soon after its acquisition of business book publisher A. W. Shaw of Chicago. The transaction came at a very propitious time, as the stock market neared its apex in early 1929, ensuring an easy sale at high prices. (The price of McGraw-Hill stock, like the price of all stocks, declined in the secondary market during the Depression, but the company had already pocketed large sums from its initial public offering [IPO], almost a full year before the Crash.) By the late 1950s and early 1960s, however, economic pressures persuaded over a dozen major publishers to go public: American Heritage Publishing; Ginn; Harcourt, Brace; D.C. Heath; Richard D. Irwin; Pocket Books; Random House; Row, Peterson (later Harper & Row); Scientific Research Associates; Scott, Foresman; Webster Publishing Company; Western Publishing Company; and John Wiley & Sons.[41]

Analysts believed that market growth and *Sputnik* helped to drive the movement, especially among textbook publishers, who found they had to quickly produce record numbers of textbooks of higher quality. Hungry Wall Street investors and their bankers also smelled opportunity in noteworthy numbers. In 1955, 750 million copies of 12,589 titles were sold for a total of $800 million in revenue for U.S. publishers. In 1965, U.S. publishers put out 28,595 titles that produced sales of 1.25 billion copies worth about $2 billion in revenue.[42]

The government's response to *Sputnik* certainly induced Wiley to seek out more capital, but the proximate cause of its first foray into the capital markets was its desire to merge with Interscience, a well-respected

publisher that had begun operations in 1940. Interscience was one of a number of scientific, technical, and medical (STM) publishers that emerged during and after World War II. Interscience was a so-called refugee house because founders Dutch bookseller Maurits Dekker and German chemist Eric Proskauer had fled Europe for America in the 1930s. In 1960, it had revenue of about $3 million and significant pretax earnings. In December of that year, Brad and Sullivan began courting Dekker and Proskauer over Dulce gin at the Netherlands Club of New York. The merger occurred in June 1961, both parties agreeing that Interscience would retain considerable editorial autonomy under Proskauer's direction. As part of the agreement, in spring 1962 Wiley went public, selling 150,022 shares to employees and outsiders in an offering underwritten by a syndicate of investment banks led by White, Weld & Company. The shares sold for $15.00 on the basis of a prospectus that touted Wiley's gross revenue of $13.1 million and net earnings of $822,817 with a nearly 50:50 balance between textbook and professional/reference sales. The prospectus also presented Wiley as the fourth largest textbook publisher in the country, with about 6 percent market share. Ownership of most of the company's stock would remain safely in the hands of the Wiley, Dekker, Proskauer, and allied families. As an additional safeguard, stockholders were urged to offer any shares they wanted to sell to other stockholders or the company itself. The IPO financed the merger by allowing Wiley to create new shares. Interscience exchanged its shares for 19.29 percent of Wiley's shares.[43]

The Wiley-Interscience merger belonged to a larger trend. The period between November 1959 and March 1962 witnessed 28 major publishing mergers. Farrar, Straus and Company acquired Noonday Press. McGraw-Hill swallowed up F. W. Dodge Corporation. Random House seized Alfred A. Knopf—a merger that made the front page of the *New York Times*—Pantheon Books, and others. World Publishing took over Meridian

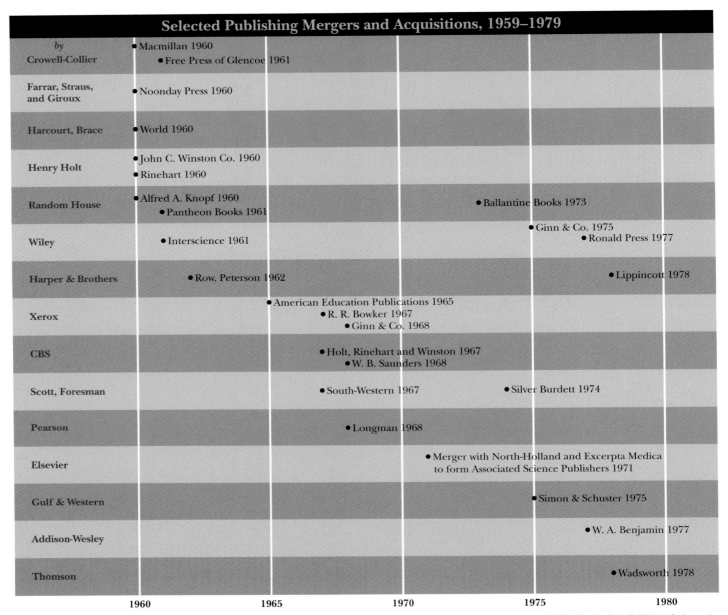

Selected Publishing Mergers and Acquisitions, 1959–1979

	1960	1965	1970	1975	1980
by Crowell-Collier	Macmillan 1960 / Free Press of Glencoe 1961				
Farrar, Straus, and Giroux	Noonday Press 1960				
Harcourt, Brace	World 1960				
Henry Holt	John C. Winston Co. 1960 / Rinehart 1960				
Random House	Alfred A. Knopf 1960 / Pantheon Books 1961			Ballantine Books 1973	
Wiley	Interscience 1961			Ginn & Co. 1975 / Ronald Press 1977	
Harper & Brothers		Row, Peterson 1962			Lippincott 1978
Xerox		American Education Publications 1965 / R. R. Bowker 1967 / Ginn & Co. 1968			
CBS		Holt, Rinehart and Winston 1967 / W. B. Saunders 1968			
Scott, Foresman		South-Western 1967		Silver Burdett 1974	
Pearson		Longman 1968			
Elsevier			Merger with North-Holland and Excerpta Medica to form Associated Science Publishers 1971		
Gulf & Western				Simon & Schuster 1975	
Addison-Wesley				W. A. Benjamin 1977	
Thomson				Wadsworth 1978	

Sources: *A History of Book Publishing in the United States, Volume IV, The Great Change 1940–1980*, by John Trebbel. Clock & Rose Press, 2003. *The Academic Publishing Industry, A Story of Merger and Acquisition*, by Mary H. Munroe. Prepared for the Association of Research Libraries (website).

Books, and Macmillan acquired the Free Press. While some analysts ascribed the mergers to the prospect of a doubling of the textbook market, Wiley wanted Interscience for more specific reasons. For one, Interscience would add balance to the company's publishing portfolio, which was increasingly focused on the text market. In addition, Wiley gained the editorial expertise of Eric Proskauer, who was highly regarded in both the United States and Europe. Proskauer had a knack for persuading scientists with good but unmarketable ideas to expand their focus and enlarge their audience. Like Ierardi, Proskauer also knew when to turn

Dr. Eric S. Proskauer was a German chemist who fled to the United States during the Nazi era and founded Interscience Publishers with Maurits Dekker in 1940. Wiley bought Interscience as its first acquisition in 1961. Proskauer and Dekker introduced Wiley to European-style journals publishing. Proskauer managed Wiley's Interscience division and served on the board of directors.

Interscience's strong list of 10 scientific journals included the *Journal of Polymer Science*.

authors away: "Ja, an editor's first job is to say no, you could always say yes later." He did his best work, it was said, at his weekend house overlooking Lake Peekskill, scotch on the rocks close at hand, his sailboat nearby. Interscience's other editors, all ten of them, were equally high caliber. Three held Ph.D.s; three were women.[44]

At the time of the merger, Interscience had a solid track record of success in the form of 650 titles, almost all of which were still in print. Wiley wanted that backlist and Interscience's technical encyclopedias, which included the Kirk-Othmer *Encyclopedia of Chemical Technology*. Interscience employed about 65 people and maintained an international web of professional contacts, scientists who did everything from oversee series to edit books to peer-review manuscripts. Finally, the merger yielded Wiley good press in the publishing industry, which began to speak of a Wiley "empire."[45]

For its part, Interscience gained access to Wiley's distribution network, which was relatively well developed owing to the company's heavy reliance on textbook sales. "Rather than publish third-rate textbooks of our own," Dekker said, "we decided to solve the problem by joining a first-class textbook house." Interscience also benefited from Wiley's back-office computer and warehouse systems. Interscience maintained its identity, becoming an independent division within Wiley, which promised to phase out Interscience's service departments gradually. The merger also served the estate planning needs of Interscience's founders by making their equity more liquid.[46]

An added benefit of the merger, one that Wiley realized but did not immediately capitalize on, was Interscience's strong, though small, list of ten scientific journals. These included the *Journal of Polymer Science*, which was highly respected in its field and generated revenue of about $300,000 a year. Wiley had published a few journals in the nineteenth century (long-forgotten titles like *Literary and Scientific Repository* and *Whig Review*) and at the time of the merger had a short list, but was hardly known for them. Like Van Nostrand, Wiley was in the book business and cool toward journals. The Interscience merger did not immediately change that; Wiley seemed to think that the seven years it took a journal to become profitable was a bit too long to wait. In 1975, Wiley's position on journals was still bearish. By that year, it published 22 journals in the United States and Great Britain. The journals' subscription base ranged from 750 to

> **Wiley family control of the bulk of the stock made the company resistant to takeovers and less sensitive to the vagaries of the market.**

3,000, and seven titles were "marginal or worse" from a profit standpoint. Nevertheless, by getting Wiley back into the journal business in a serious way, the Interscience merger laid the foundation for the company's later push into an arena of scholarly publishing that it had long underestimated.[47]

An unanticipated benefit of the merger and public offering was improved governance. Before the acquisition of Interscience, the Wiley board was made up of insiders. The by laws stipulated between five and nine directors "who need not be stockholders of the corporation." In the years immediately prior to the merger, Wiley's directors included Brad and Hamilton for the family and Matheson, Snyder, Barnes, Lobdell, and Sullivan for senior management. Meetings were pro forma affairs. The merger immediately brought new blood—Proskauer and Dekker—and ideas, onto the board. In the years following the merger, Wiley, like other publicly traded American companies at the time, began adding true outside directors, experts in various fields related to publishing who did not work for the company or own much of its stock. The outsiders—attorney Charles Lieb, Interscience's outside counsel; William Eiseman of Morgan Guaranty Trust; Merck's Antonie Knoppers; Cornell's Robert Sproull, who would later become president of the University of Rochester; and Harvard Business School professor Kenneth Andrews—challenged some of Wiley's conservative views of its industry and taught its executives "a lot of things about how to run a business." Some, however, thought the board did not function as effectively as it could because it appeared to be divided into first- and second-class directors, with the second class allegedly being ignored by the first class. Others believed that the outside board members were not proactive enough and that the inside ones were too deferential to Brad. Nonetheless, the board was substantially improved over the pre-public days. Andrew Neilly once claimed that "the best thing that ever happened to us [after the company went public] was having an outside board of directors."[48]

Publicly traded stock led to new channels of information about how the market viewed a company's performance. If stockholders disliked a move, they sold their stock, depressing its price. If they liked what management was doing, they tried to buy more shares, bidding up its price. Through that mechanism, many practices peculiar to publishers, contemporary expert Dan Lacy claimed, were quickly eradicated at publicly traded companies as executives, fearful of being taken over if their stock price dipped too low, worked hard to please investors resistant to takeovers by providing them with timely information and profits. Wiley's managers were also concerned about keeping stockholders happy, but Wiley family control of the bulk of the stock made the company resistant to takeovers and hence less sensitive to the vagaries of the market. Nevertheless, the possibility that the company could be bought out still existed, and Brad used that possibility to encourage productivity. In 1968, for example, he told employees that the company had to keep costs down, increase efficiency, and search out profitable new areas. "Wiley intends to remain an independent company," he reassured employees, but it was clear that if the company was to do so, everyone was going to have to work harder and smarter than ever before.[49]

Knowledgeable analysts judged the combination with Interscience a good one. Editorial programs complemented each other, with little duplication. Wiley was strong in textbooks and Interscience in journals and scientific monographs. The merger created what *Publishers'*

> The merger [with Interscience] created . . . the sixth largest publisher in the country.

Weekly considered "perhaps the largest combination of science publishing in the world" and the sixth largest publisher in the country. Reynolds Research recommended the company's stock "as an attractive issue for income and growth."[50]

The merger was largely amicable, yet Wiley knew that personality and cultural conflicts might erupt. The two organizations were different. Interscience was closer to a cottage industry, with its founders still very much in charge. Interscience was also loosely organized in its daily routines. It was rather like Wiley before World War I. Aware that Wiley faced a steep learning curve, especially in marketing, the company assigned one of its best copywriters, Rosamund Fowler, to work with the Interscience editors to help publicize titles. This task posed challenges because of both the books' extremely technical nature and their large quantity—55 titles in 1963 alone. Each required three major pieces of promotional writing—jacket copy, file card, and a circular—as well as small write-ups such as journal advertisements and various library periodical blurbs.[51]

A post-merger conflict did arise and eventually involved the U.S. Supreme Court. Workers at Wiley and most of the rest of New York's publishing houses were not unionized, but Interscience was. The legal issue here was whether the successor employer (in this case, Wiley) was obliged to fulfill the labor contracts of the predecessor. As a general rule, nonconsenting successors (Wiley) are not bound by old (Interscience) agreements. But in *John Wiley & Sons, Inc., v. Livingston*, the Supreme Court held that a nonconsenting successor employer could be forced to arbitrate an existing collective bargaining agreement if there was substantial continuity of the enterprise after the transfer of ownership. The case caused more stir among jurists than at Wiley,

Wiley moved in 1962 to 605 Third Avenue, where it remained for 40 years.

which as usual did so well by its employees, even its adopted ones, that the arbitrators awarded Interscience employees very little. Wiley hired a Harvard business school professor to help clear up the situation. While most former Interscience employees found a home at Wiley, one of Interscience's principals did not. Dekker was not assigned a clear role in the merged company and soon left it to establish one of his own.[52]

In 1962, Wiley's net sales were around $15 million, 80 percent of which came from its backlist. (Compare that with Harcourt, Brace, which in 1959 got almost 95 percent of its school revenue, as well as 80.3 percent of its higher education revenue, from its backlist.) Wiley's stated goal was to achieve "balanced sales"— that is, about half its revenue from textbooks and half from reference books, monographs, journals, and a few trade titles. It also wanted healthy revenue from different distribution channels and markets. Wiley largely succeeded in the years 1960, 1961, and 1962, when about a quarter of its revenue came from foreign orders, about 10 percent from direct mailings, about 20 percent from trade distribution channels, and 45 percent from educational orders. In 1961, for example, Wiley's revenue (including that from Interscience) consisted of 48.5 percent from textbooks, 47 percent

from professional/reference books, and 4.5 percent from journals and abstracts. By outlets, 42.6 percent of sales came via college bookstores, 21.4 percent through trade outlets, 11.4 percent via direct mail, and 24.6 percent via foreign sales.[53]

Thanks to the Interscience merger and increased editorial work, Wiley's output in 1962 soared to 478 titles, putting it sixth on the list, ahead of Oxford and McGraw-Hill. Its revenues and earnings also soared during this period. Growth was so rapid that Wiley found it necessary to expand to 440 Park Avenue South and then move from Park Avenue South to larger quarters at 605 Third Avenue. As Brad explained, "We were so crowded that if you got up you lost your chair, and we had no conference room unless someone went on a trip." The move allowed the company to consolidate its expanding editorial and business offices. By the mid-1960s, the company employed some 500 people, including 30 travelers. The idea of moving to Stamford, considered in 1952, was never raised again, as Wiley, like most publishers,[54] found Manhattan was as much the place to be in the mid-twentieth century as it had been in the nineteenth.[55]

Reorganization

The Interscience merger prompted Brad and his colleagues to reorganize the business—and reorganize it again—in an effort to more carefully align the types of books published with their markets. After the merger, editors were grouped into three main subject areas: the physical sciences, headed by Proskauer; engineering/math, led by Walker Stone; and the social sciences/humanities, under Gordon Ierardi. Each area was responsible for developing textbooks, handbooks, and research monographs. In 1964, however, targets were being missed, and the company reorganized its editorial program into three functional divisions, more or less the same three that it has today: textbooks (higher education), headed by Charles Stoll; professional/reference (professional/trade), led by Stone; and Interscience (science, technology, and medical), controlled by Proskauer. Each division head became a vice president, and a fourth vice president, William Suter, was appointed head of a marketing division devoted primarily to textbooks. In 1966, Suter headed up a new division, the schools division, and Robert E. Wilson, who started with the company as a traveler in 1956, took over the marketing department.[56]

Stone's Professional and Reference Book Division was by 1965 composed of a team of nine editors, five based in New York, and one each based in the West, Midwest, East, and Southeast regions of the country. Proskauer's Interscience Division had seven editors: two for the *Encyclopedia of Polymer Science and Technology*, two for the *Encyclopedia of Industrial Chemical Analysis*, one for the *Kirk–Othmer Encyclopedia of Chemical Technology*, and two for monographs in

PROFILE

GORDON S. IERARDI

In 1958, Gordon Ierardi was Wiley's lead social science editor. He joined Wiley in 1940 but was quickly whisked off to Europe to fight in the war. When he returned, he served as a traveler but was soon appointed to serve as an editor under J. Kenneth Maddock in the Science and Industry Division. He worked under Walker Stone in engineering until 1953, when he took on the job of building the company's social science list after the departure of James Helming. Building up the social sciences was no mean feat, given that Wiley was still largely perceived as a science and engineering specialist. With associate editor Al Richards, Ierardi quickly built a list of over 150 titles, including many important psychology books. In fact, he was soon considered "one of the foremost psychology editors in the nation." The key, he claimed, was signing up some prestigious and influential, though unremunerative, books early on. "Authors," he noted, "like to think they're in good company." And with Wiley, they were.

Following a long Wiley tradition, Ierardi believed that quality trumped quantity every time, and he lamented the fact that some of the company's competitors—whom he did not publicly name—put out substandard books because they knew that they could grab a share of the rapidly expanding market. "Frankly," he said, he spent "about as much time discouraging authors as trying to sign them up." Those he did sign had so much respect for him that they threw a surprise party in his honor—a truly unusual event in the knowledge publishing world. As reported in the *New York Times* in 1964, 50 leading psychologists, from Stanford to Northwestern to Toronto, attended the party at the Players Club to honor Ierardi for the 60 Wiley titles that dominated the *Harvard List of Books on Psychology*. According to contemporaries, Ierardi could "get the best out of authors" and had given publications in psychology "a sense of style." Wiley's social science list suffered a heavy blow in February 1966, when Ierardi, just 48, died of a heart attack in his office. Wiley later paid for the education of his children, one of whom, Laura, worked for the firm as a designer for eight years in the late 1970s and 1980s.[57]

Gordon Ierardi (1917–1966) was a Harvard man, born in Nova Scotia. He was Wiley's most famous editor in the post–World War II era. Hailed by America's leading psychologists, Ierardi was a "member de facto of the psychological profession, maker of our books, messenger, and good friend." At just 48, he died of a heart attack in his office.

PROFILE

CHARLES STOLL

Charles Stoll was an editor for Wiley's engineering books in 1958. His duties were to "build a list of books that will sell widely, to keep these up to date through continuous mild harassment of his authors, and . . . to anticipate how things will be done in the college five or ten years from now." He was also charged with reminding textbook authors that they were supposed to write for students and "not for the amazement of their colleagues." Stoll joined Wiley as a traveler in 1947 after graduating from Princeton, and he became an editor in 1950. He served with the Marines during World War II and the Korean War. As an editor, he sought out a few good men to author textbooks in areas that he and Snyder, his boss, thought would blossom. That required much travel and patience. Sometimes, Stoll heard about prospective authors when they were still graduate students. He tracked them for years until they were ready to make a contribution, and then he rescued them from competitors. Sometimes he won, sometimes he lost. Sometimes he got a little help, as when he signed one title that he had pursued for years solely because the author enjoyed sailing with one of his Wiley colleagues, Robert Polhemus! Stoll was remembered as a quiet man with a keen sense of humor who earned the respect of Wiley's top brass as well as his colleagues throughout the publishing industry.[58]

*C*harles Stoll, Princeton graduate, would serve Wiley in many capacities over 40-plus years: traveler, editor, head of the college and international divisions, managing director of Wiley's Canadian and British companies, and finally member of the board of directors. Brad Wiley and Andrew Neilly, his successor, frequently turned to Stoll to troubleshoot and analyze situations that needed change. Stoll died in 1994, remembered for helping to establish Wiley as a global company.

mathematics, physics, earth science, chemistry, and chemical engineering.[59]

By 1966, Brad had four direct reports: Francis Lobdell of Controls and Services, which oversaw customer service, data processing, distribution, and finances; J. Stetson Barnes of Production, which managed copyediting, book design, illustration, and manufacturing; Andrew Neilly of Marketing, which covered sales,

promotion, public relations, and international ventures in London, Mexico City, and Australasia; and the editorial executive committee. Brad himself chaired this committee, composed of the top editors in special projects and the social sciences, science, engineering/math/physics, and professional departments.[60]

In 1967, the textbook division became the College Division. The following year it became an autonomous publishing unit under Stoll with its own editorial, marketing, and production units. Meanwhile, Interscience formally joined forces with the old Wiley professional and reference division. In 1968, the Wiley-Interscience Division was created. As with the College Division, Wiley-Interscience assumed full authority for all its publishing operations, including marketing and overall control of its budget. Proskauer was vice president and general manager, and Stone vice president and executive officer. As part of its 1968 restructuring, Wiley also created Marketing Services to handle advertising and book publicity, trade, library, and direct-mail sales, conventions and exhibits, and other marketing

activities for the School, College, and Wiley-Interscience Divisions and International Marketing. In another significant 1968 change, Snyder became vice president of Wiley's New Media Department, which was charged with identifying new technologies, products, and markets. By 1976, the department was engaged in numerous feasibility studies for in-house editing terminals, optical character recognition, databases, print-on-demand, automatic indexing, and various audiovisual and video projects.[61]

Michael Harris was named a vice president and general manager of the Wiley-Interscience Division in 1969. He succeeded Proskauer and Stone, both of whom assumed other duties.

PROFILE

MICHAEL HARRIS

Michael Harris, who began his career as a CIO labor organizer and later held posts with the Allied High Commission in Europe, the Marshall Plan, and the Ford Foundation, was known as a manager and negotiator. During 11 years with John Wiley & Sons, he was instrumental in integrating professional and reference publishing, played a major role in drafting the 1976 copyright law, and was instrumental in the creation of the Copyright Clearance Center, serving on its board of directors for many of its early years.

Harris followed Eric Proskauer as head of the Wiley-Interscience Division (later known as the Professional Group) in 1969 and ran it until 1980. In 1969 that division reported sales of books, encyclopedias, and journals totaling $11.4 million. Eleven years later, as Harris relinquished control, sales had reached $48.7 million. Under his administration, the number of journals published by the Professional Group doubled, and an ever-increasing number of books were published for users of mainframe, mini-, and microcomputers. What was a relatively small division in the early 1970s grew into a smooth-running organization that rivaled the larger Educational Group.

In May 1981, Harris received a special award from the Association of American Publishers in recognition of his service as an AAP board member and especially for his work done on behalf of the industry on copyright law. At the time of his death in 1981, Harris was a senior vice president of the company.

Michael Harris came to Wiley from the United Steelworkers and the Marshall Plan. He headed Wiley's Professional and Reference Division after Eric Proskauer's retirement but died unexpectedly in 1981 at a young age.

Expansion Through Acquisitions

After it went public, Wiley was widely recognized as "an energetic publisher" with aggressive long-term goals. Having successfully integrated Interscience and begun the process of reorganization, Wiley turned to Morgan Guaranty Trust for a loan of $3.25 million for six years at 5 percent, which it used to pursue additional acquisition targets. In educational publishing, the company aspired to increase the number of disciplines for which it published, reaching beyond the college market into the high school and industrial training markets. In late 1965, it bought Great Society Press, which several schoolteachers had established the year before to publish short self-teaching pamphlets for disadvantaged high school students and "reluctant readers." The move made sense in two ways. First, President Lyndon Johnson's Great Society programs and urban unrest prompted both the government and the private sector to play a more active role in the inner city. Second, Wiley began to experiment with "programmed instruction," a learning technique developed by behavioral psychologist B. F. Skinner, which, via computer or nonlinear books, rewarded users for learning new concepts and provided remediation when they stumbled. At first as a subsidiary renamed Portal Press, Great Society Press was folded into the company proper in 1969 after Wiley lost faith in its founders' ability to manage the operation. The enterprise had lost so much money in 1966 that it actually stalled Wiley's earning growth.[62]

The Great Society purchase fit with the decision to test the elementary and high school markets. William Sutter established an "el-hi" department in math and science in 1965 and a full-blown School

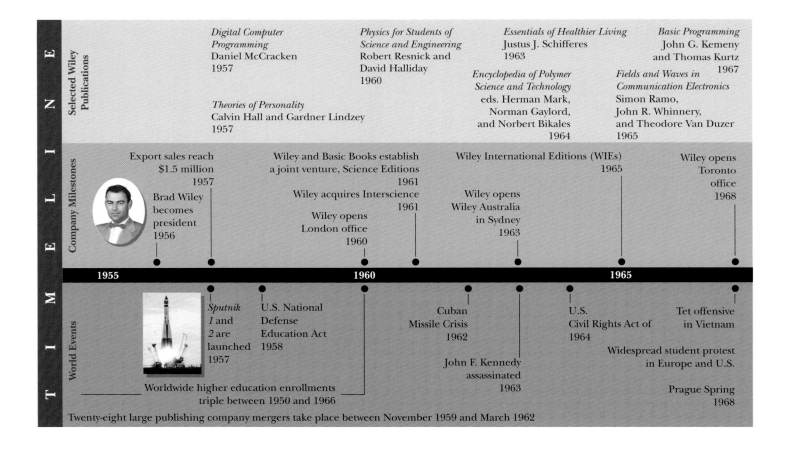

TIMELINE

Selected Wiley Publications

Digital Computer Programming
Daniel McCracken
1957

Theories of Personality
Calvin Hall and Gardner Lindzey
1957

Physics for Students of Science and Engineering
Robert Resnick and David Halliday
1960

Encyclopedia of Polymer Science and Technology
eds. Herman Mark, Norman Gaylord, and Norbert Bikales
1964

Essentials of Healthier Living
Justus J. Schifferes
1963

Fields and Waves in Communication Electronics
Simon Ramo, John R. Whinnery, and Theodore Van Duzer
1965

Basic Programming
John G. Kemeny and Thomas Kurtz
1967

Company Milestones

Export sales reach $1.5 million
1957

Brad Wiley becomes president
1956

Wiley opens London office
1960

Wiley and Basic Books establish a joint venture, Science Editions
1961

Wiley acquires Interscience
1961

Wiley opens Wiley Australia in Sydney
1963

Wiley International Editions (WIEs)
1965

Wiley opens Toronto office
1968

1955 — **1960** — **1965**

World Events

Sputnik 1 and *2* are launched 1957

U.S. National Defense Education Act 1958

Cuban Missile Crisis 1962

John F. Kennedy assassinated 1963

U.S. Civil Rights Act of 1964

Tet offensive in Vietnam

Widespread student protest in Europe and U.S.

Prague Spring 1968

Worldwide higher education enrollments triple between 1950 and 1966

Twenty-eight large publishing company mergers take place between November 1959 and March 1962

CHAPTER SIX

226

Division in 1967. The company thought it could, over time, tap the market for math, science, social science, and vocational-technical education titles for grades 7–12 because that market's traditional publishing pattern was shifting away from books that had served for decades toward a more flexible situation that resembled the college market.[63]

Despite the problems of the Great Society Press, the market responded favorably to Wiley initiatives. In 1967, through White, Weld & Co., Wiley sold 50,000 new shares of common stock at $34 a share. Inside shareholders sold 50,000 shares at that price as well. The offering was oversubscribed, indicating that investors thought $34 a good price for Wiley stock at that time. This financial picture darkened quickly, however. The company made a careful study of its situation, and its travelers and authors urged it forward, but

it never committed enough capital to make headway in a market dominated by 11 big and highly focused players. Poor management and a misreading of the el-hi market may also have been to blame. In 1969, the company sold the division's products and commitments to another publisher. In the mid-1970s, Wiley again considered moving into schoolbooks, but Brad resisted, noting that this market was "well covered and it would be hard to break into it" unless the company purchased a publisher with established market share.[64]

The Great Society foray was not quite a total loss because in the 1970s Wiley introduced a series of self-teaching guides, some of which, like *Quick Calculus*, proved highly popular with students. By 1976, Wiley's self-teaching guides, which sold primarily through some 700 college and chain bookstores, were ahead of expectations on sales and profit contribution

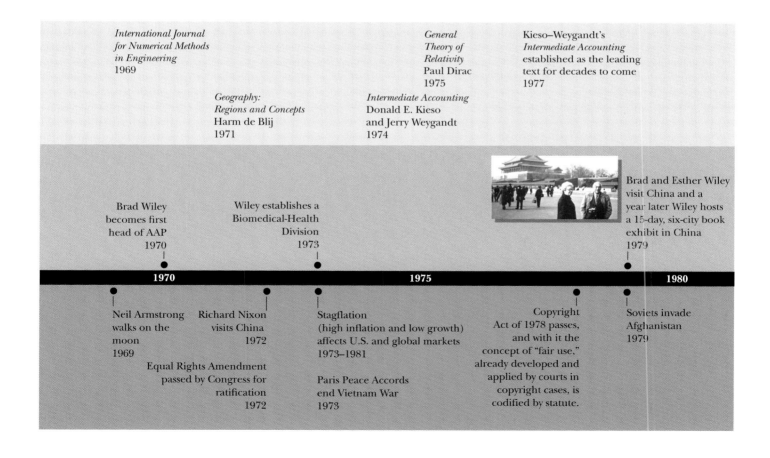

International Journal for Numerical Methods in Engineering
1969

Geography: Regions and Concepts
Harm de Blij
1971

General Theory of Relativity
Paul Dirac
1975

Intermediate Accounting
Donald E. Kieso and Jerry Weygandt
1974

Kieso–Weygandt's *Intermediate Accounting* established as the leading text for decades to come
1977

Brad Wiley becomes first head of AAP
1970

Wiley establishes a Biomedical-Health Division
1973

Brad and Esther Wiley visit China and a year later Wiley hosts a 15-day, six-city book exhibit in China
1979

1970   **1975**   **1980**

Neil Armstrong walks on the moon
1969

Richard Nixon visits China
1972

Equal Rights Amendment passed by Congress for ratification
1972

Stagflation (high inflation and low growth) affects U.S. and global markets
1973–1981

Paris Peace Accords end Vietnam War
1973

Copyright Act of 1978 passes, and with it the concept of "fair use," already developed and applied by courts in copyright cases, is codified by statute.

Soviets invade Afghanistan
1979

but struggling to achieve the scale necessary to compensate for their relatively low margins. Great Society and the el-hi experiment, however, turned out to be only the first in a series of acquisition errors.[65]

In 1969, Wiley bought Contemporary Systems Corporation, a one-year-old developer of seminars for business and industrial training. Wiley paid almost $400,000 and renamed it Wiley Systems. Brad thought that the acquisition was a logical extension of Wiley's programs in textbooks and professional and scientific works into another growing educational field and hoped that with an infusion of an additional $400,000 or so Wiley Systems would develop profitable new seminars, publications, and services in information sciences, systems design, data processing, advanced computer technology, and mathematics for managers. It was not to be. Though renamed Wiley Learning Systems to reflect a renewed emphasis on pedagogy, by 1976 the enterprise had cost Wiley over $900,000, with losses growing. It, too, was sold off.[66]

In 1969, for 12,000 shares Wiley acquired a small provider of professional services and systems to libraries called Becker & Hayes. The principals of the firm, Joseph Becker and Robert Hayes, were Wiley authors, but the results were unsatisfactory; the operation lost so much money in 1972 it actually caused Wiley's profits to decrease. In 1973, Wiley set up Melville Publishing in Los Angeles to take over the book-related parts of Becker & Hayes's business and to tap the growing information and library sciences areas with an integrated program of textbook and reference materials. A plan to spin off the rest of Becker & Hayes as Urban Systems, a supplier of geodemographic information and software, came to nothing. The subsidiary tried hard, even attempting to enter the Soviet market, but it continued to founder, and Wiley disposed of it in 1976.[67]

> **Wiley had made the classic error of optimists.**

In 1971, Wiley acquired James E. Freel Associates of Palo Alto, California, specialists in the community and junior college markets, with high hopes. By 1970, junior college enrollment had reached 1.6 million, and California, which had built the most extensive community college system in the nation, was the logical place to set up shop. Wiley believed that most enrollment growth would consist of part-time or nondegree students seeking to enhance occupational or vocational skills. Such people needed specially written and designed textbooks of their own. But correct assessment of the market was not followed by performance, and Wiley sold Freel at a loss in 1973. The same year, with the same audience in mind, Wiley formed Hamilton Publishing, named to honor Brad's predecessor. Based in Santa Barbara, the enterprise developed core text materials for a wide range of college courses but eventually found that its editorial group was competing with the one in New York. So Hamilton, too, was shuttered.[68]

More successful was the establishment of an occupational division in 1971. Robert Douglas, who had succeeded Stoll as head of the College Division, turned to Alan B. Lesure, a young editor who joined Wiley in 1971. "My editorial program was largely engineering (sans computers) and comprised lots of solid old warhorses," Lesure recalled. "Engineering enrollments were shrinking in the early 1970s, and it was clear that if my programs were to grow, revenues would have to be found in new markets." A group of researchers at San Jose State University had identified one new market, which they described as an "invisible" student population made up of working adults looking for vocational training. Vocational courses could be found at community colleges and proprietary (for profit) schools, which were just moving from the "mom and pop" stage to one where some of them would become larger, more sophisticated corporations. "American industry was being badly beaten by the quality of the competition from Japan and Germany," according to Lesure. "Community colleges responded quickly to this concern with new programs and content that emphasized changing technology and an increased concern with product and process quality."[69]

The vocational market was dominated by Gregg/McGraw-Hill and Southwestern, followed by Prentice Hall, Delmar, and Glencoe. The publishing process itself differed from that of a standard textbook; it was "characterized by publishers who had as much to say about a book's content as did the book's authors." Occupational launched its first efforts in criminal justice, a new and rapidly growing field, with a series of texts designed by the editor for each volume in the series. Chapters were written by carefully selected instructors and then significantly rewritten by the volume editor and Wiley's developmental editor.[70]

There was a logic to Wiley's acquisition and new subsidiary strategies: They were an effort to hedge against erosion of its traditional college textbook revenue, which, though still growing, had fallen short of expectations because of the development of the used textbook market, campus turmoil, student resistance to purchasing required texts, declining enrollments in historic Wiley disciplines such as engineering, and growing concerns about fluctuations in student enrollments. Disappointing results suggested, however, that Wiley had made the classic error of optimists in acquisitions: underestimating start-up costs and overestimating management's ability to integrate and sustain these new operations. Ultimately, the results were a wash; none of these acquisitions helped the company much, nor did they inflict grave harm.[71]

Wiley's appetite for acquisitions decreased somewhat in the early and mid-1970s, for four reasons. First, it was not a propitious period for mergers and acquisitions because the bargains were gone. To make a good buy, one had to move fast and bid competitively. Second, Brad was generally content with the company's size and profitability. Third, the company was again dedicated to financing its growth primarily from profits. Fourth, an internal report revealed that Wiley's revenue had on average grown faster than that of its competitors, but its profits had grown much more slowly than average, suggesting that the company had grown too fast and that it was time to focus on the costs of running the business.[72]

Despite the setbacks, Wiley experienced some successes, beginning in 1975 with its acquisition from Xerox of Ginn & Company's extensive list of textbooks, which was a real shot in the arm for revenue. In 1979, Wiley paid $200,000 to purchase St. Clair Press, a respected Chicago-based textbook publisher of business and financial books. These books would become the basis for a highly successful list of business texts that would be launched in the 1980s.

Exploring Opportunities in Professional and Trade Publishing

In an expansive mood, Brad and his team began in the early 1960s to search out new publishing lines, even new businesses. The company had long been concerned

*T*rade sales representative Nettie Bleich reorders fast moving titles with Tim Pletscher, buyer at the McGraw-Hill bookstore in New York, 1979.

The American Voter by Angus Campbell, Philip E. Converse, Warren E. Miller, and Donald E. Stokes was a "must-read" in 1960. A classic theoretical study of voting behavior, it has become a standard reference in the field.

about maintaining a balance between textbook and professional/reference sales, with texts in the early 1960s accounting for about 60 percent of revenue. Increasingly, however, the company came to see the virtue of yet more diversification and decided at this time on trade publishing with an emphasis on the types of books that aligned with Wiley's educational and professional titles. The company showed no interest in fiction, of course, or in popular trade titles, such as biographies or autobiographies of high-profile individuals, whether politicians or Hollywood celebrities. Some experienced trade publishers argued that trade books tend to be anti-cyclical because, as Bennett Cerf once explained, "when everything goes to hell, books become one of the cheapest forms of pleasure." Yet trade publishing was fraught with risk; trade publishers lost on six out of every ten books they published, and discounts approached 50 percent. Trade, therefore, accounted for about 15 percent of total book industry sales in the United States, but only 12 percent of profits. Nevertheless, Wiley began to view trade titles as another revenue stream, something to keep the money coming in if the professional or, more likely, the textbook market weakened, a very real fear. The move toward trade publishing had the side benefit of getting Wiley titles reviewed in publications like the *New York Times*; its popular titles on childcare, geopolitics, business and economics, education, child psychology, and food garnered publicity rare for a textbook and scholarly monograph publisher.[73]

In 1961, Wiley and Basic Books established a joint venture called Science Editions, which published high-quality paperback reprints of well-known titles. The books were simultaneously published in Britain by Wiley, Ltd., and distributed in Canada by General Publishing of Toronto. The list was a very good one indeed, including titles by Sigmund Freud (*The Interpretation of Dreams*) and Edward Teller (*The Structure of Matter*). The titles fit well with Wiley's image as a high-quality publisher of serious content. Some of them could be sold to college bookstores both for general readers and as supplementary reading for courses. Timing, too, appeared propitious, as quality paperbacks were all the rage following the success of Doubleday's Anchor Books. Moreover, since 1955 the Basic Book Club had proven that it could move large numbers of books in its Library of Science by direct-mail order. Book clubs had been around since the 1920s but like so many other aspects of publishing did not really grow in importance until after World War II. They relied on habit and honesty—members (customers) who got used to receiving books every month would, bet the club, get used to paying for them. By the early 1960s, the book-club craze subsided, and though acclaimed, the Science Editions venture never took off. Wiley bought out Basic Books' interest in early 1963 and shuttered the project in 1968 for more than a decade.[74]

Wiley's own trade titles included Angus Campbell et al.'s *The American Voter* (1960), which promised to answer the questions: "Why do we vote as we do? Is it the Man or the issues?" It advertised that title and Richard Neustadt's *Presidential Power* (1960) in the *New York Times* with the assurance that such "'must' reading for every thinking voter" could be found "at your bookstore." There were trade how-to books too, such as David Clurman and Edna Hebard's *Condominiums and Cooperatives* (1970), which a *New York Times* reviewer called an important work for anyone who lived in or was thinking of buying such a property. At first, Wiley sold to bookstores via an outside company called Trufant Foster. Soon after the introduction of its agency plan, which increased discounts to booksellers, Wiley hired a sales representative away from Foster. Nevertheless, ambivalence among senior managers about trade publishing held back its growth. Sullivan supported it, but Brad was more tentative because he valued the relatively low discounts and high predictability of textbooks and professional/reference titles. According to Simon Michael Bessie, one of the founders of the prestigious Atheneum Press, Brad, who was a good friend, turned him down flat when he offered to sell Atheneum to Wiley.[75]

Wiley looked at other publishing possibilities. In 1965, for example, a team of managers investigated the market for law, medicine, and psychiatry books. Nothing came of the efforts. Wiley under Brad remained selective, turning away many projects it felt unsuited to pursue. In 1966, for example, two scientists approached Wiley with a proposal for a controlled-circulation journal, *The Scientific Observer*. Martin Matheson thought the sample well done but questioned whether it could compete with *Scientific American* or *International Science and Technology*, a young magazine with "big names on the editorial board" that struggled for four years to obtain adequate advertising revenue. "I doubt that this is for us," Matheson concluded. "This type of journal," he explained, "requires the know-how and the staff of big companies like McGraw-Hill, Reinhold, Penton, Chilton, etc. These outfits," he argued, "have experienced advertising solicitors and long managerial experience. The learning process for us might be quite painful."[76]

At other times Wiley turned away promising ideas because it was clear that the scientist, engineer, or

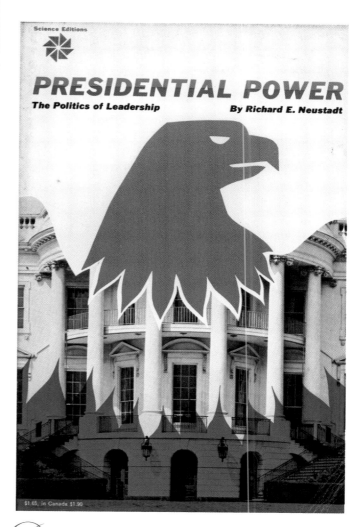

*A*fter Wiley published *Presidential Power* in 1960, Richard Neustadt became an advisor to John F. Kennedy and Lyndon B. Johnson, and many years later to Bill Clinton.

technician had ideas but simply did not have the requisite writing skill. The nonprofessional technical writer was the bane of Wiley, McGraw-Hill, and other technical publishers in another way too. Because they wrote for personal satisfaction or professional prestige rather than for their livelihood, they often took years to complete manuscripts, if they finished at all. Other potential Wiley authors were good writers but not technically or pedagogically astute. To protect its long-standing, hard-won reputation, Wiley refused to emulate a competitor's practice of publishing a large number of texts in one area, letting the marketplace evaluate them, and then backing the winner. Instead, Wiley's editors refrained from publishing until they found a high-quality product capable of really cracking the market. The company was known to wait years for the right manuscript from the right author.[77]

The most significant move for the Professional and Reference Division was the establishment in 1973 of a Biomedical-Health Division under Niels Buessem. Medical publishing doubled in size in the five years between 1971 and 1976 and was growing at 15 percent per annum, which made expansion in this business very attractive to Wiley. Buessem pulled together Interscience's medical titles and some high-level textbooks published by the educational division, aiming his program at clinical practitioners as well as the nursing and allied health professions. Among the program's successful publications were the Learning Experience Guides, or LEGS, a multimedia learning system for nurses. The LEGS titles sold well at 75 nursing schools, which represented about 25 percent of the market. In 1978, Wiley took a 16 percent stake, and an option for the rest, in Patient Care Publications (PCP) for $600,000. Based in Darien, Connecticut, PCP published *Patient Care*, one of the world's leading clinical medicine journals. A

> **Medical publishing was very attractive to Wiley.**

bi-monthly publication with a circulation of over 100,000 to doctors in the United States alone, it was supported entirely by advertising. Unlike many controlled-circulation publications, however, the periodical enjoyed an exceptional reputation. Wiley, however, decided not to exercise its option and sold its share in the 1980s. The medical program grew steadily, outpacing the competition while quadrupling in size between 1975 and 1980.[78]

In another development, Warren Sullivan returned to Wiley in 1977 to set up Halsted Press, named for Phoebe Halsted, the mother of Charles Wiley. It was designed to import and distribute in the United States books and journals from overseas publishers and to arrange for small American presses to market and sell their books through Wiley's overseas offices. By 1973, Halsted was collaborating with more than 50 publishers from Tokyo to Jerusalem, helping them to sell small quantities of books designed for specialized audiences. Just five years later, Halsted's client list exceeded 200. The Halsted operation evoked John Wiley's various import businesses, the first with George Palmer Putnam in the 1830s and 1840s, and then on his own in the 1850s.

Two important acquisitions in professional publishing contributed to Wiley's growing reputation in two categories, business and accounting. In 1977, Wiley bought Ronald Press for $5 million. After the acquisition, Wiley renamed the Interscience Business and Social Science Book Department for the Ronald Press. Though small, Ronald's backlist, especially its *Montgomery's Auditing*, a title first published in the nineteenth century, nicely complemented the newly acquired Professional Publications, Inc., a publisher of CPA review course materials in Florida. Both of these publishers served professionals, but the Ronald acquisition in particular would provide Wiley a platform for launching a highly successful business trade list in the 1980s.[79]

Andrew Neilly and Nonfamily Professional Management

In an organization that was growing in size and complexity, with no Wiley family member in position to succeed Brad, it was necessary to continue developing publishing managers who were at least as good as the competition's. Brad and Esther had three children—William Bradford Jr. in 1941, Peter Booth in 1942, and Deborah Elizabeth in 1946—but only Deborah worked for the company. In the 1970s, she was systematically exposed to a variety of jobs, including business manager of the College Division and manager of industrial sales, but she was not ready to run the entire company. Neilly, who had been moving up through the ranks for a quarter century, showed all the signs of a true leader. In 1971, he became president and chief operating officer, a clear signal that he was Brad's heir apparent.[80]

With his appointment as president and chief operating officer, Neilly agreed to the management

In May 1970, a group of Wiley employees celebrated the fashion of the 1960s with a lighthearted fashion show.

Laurie Schacher at front left, Ronnie Strafella at front middle and Jo Bacchi second from right; top row middle: Diane Gillis with Ellie Tracey on her left; just behind Ronnie, partially hidden, Eileen O'Grady.

Wiley cultivated in-house talent in the 1970s not only through its human resources practices but also through its book team awards, recognizing the group effort needed to produce successful books. Shown from left are winning textbook teams with their awards: Ellen O'Neill, manufacturing; Madelyn Lesure, design; John Balbalis, illustration; Deborah Herbert, copyediting; Len Kruk, editorial; Bill Kellogg, supplements; Nina Lewis, editorial; an unidentified team member; Dennis Sawicki, marketing; and Anita Kahn, production.

*D*eborah Wiley's presence on the staff, where she held a variety of managerial roles, sent a strong signal that women were ready to play a larger role at Wiley.

*R*ita Irons, corporate manager, Human Resources, helped transform Wiley's personnel department into a modern human resources department.

team's turning to an outsider to assess the team's development. In 1972, James F. Gillespie, a corporate psychologist with close ties to the company and a neighbor of Neilly's, ran a group therapy meeting designed to elicit critical comments from the top managers. Gillespie did what amounted to a SWOT analysis, identifying the major leadership problems to be inconsistency, lack of clear corporate direction and purpose, and lack of confidence in subordinates. Gillespie concluded that Neilly's authoritative management style was impairing the effectiveness of the organization and he was admonished to engender "a more participative style of management" across the organization. Neilly continued to retain Gillespie, and Gillespie went on to help Neilly transform Wiley's personnel department into a modern human resources department, which included the hiring of Rita Irons, trained in human resources management, as corporate manager, Human Resources. Gillespie helped Neilly in the 1980s launch a full-scale experiment in participatory management.[81]

The change from family to professional management led to the creation of new structures, such as the Corporate Management Group (CMG). Composed of corporate officers and the director of analysis and planning, the CMG met every other Wednesday morning to coordinate the company's long-term planning efforts, especially those projects that entailed "unusual risk or commitment," and to review other matters. In one October 1976 meeting, for example, the CMG discussed the compensation packages of officers and middle managers, stock options, and employee benefits, including complaints about small pensions and the lack of dental coverage. The group also considered better ways to develop the company's human resources potential, including more formal training and job performance programs. Most important, the CMG was responsible for succession planning, identifying a pool of talent that could be groomed to assume leadership of the company when the time came for Brad, and later Neilly, to step down.[82]

In his attempts to modernize Wiley, Neilly faced another challenge: the role of women in the company. Before the 1960s, the company had employed many women but not in positions of authority. Clotilda Lowell, for example, was, according to Neilly, a "very smart maiden lady who was very good" at direct-mail marketing. She joined Wiley in 1934 and in the 1940s became Martin Matheson's right hand before smacking her head on the glass ceiling. Finally, in 1962, she was promoted to assistant advertising manager. She retired in 1970, having established a reputation for her

_M_ arianne Orlando, a former Interscience editor, became assistant vice president and director of International Marketing.

encyclopedic knowledge of the company and its books and her knack for training young employees in the art of advertising.[83]

According to Lizanne Stoll, Charles Stoll's wife and Wiley's first important, if informal, female leader, Brad's wife, Esther, believed women should play a bigger role in publishing and had made this opinion plain to her husband. Deborah Wiley's presence on the Wiley staff also sent a strong signal. By the late 1960s, Marianne Orlando, who came from Interscience, was an assistant vice president and director of international marketing reporting directly to Neilly. Her role grew in the 1970s and 1980s. By the mid-1970s, Beatrice Shube, who began work as a secretary and then worked for a decade as an editor in physics, mathematics, and statistics, had become a publishing vice president. Also by the mid-1970s, Wiley had in place an affirmative action program designed to ensure that qualified female and minority job candidates received the opportunities they deserved, and in keeping with its liberal disposition, Wiley provided a tolerant environment for homosexual employees. Perhaps not coincidentally, Interscience published a number of psychiatric studies at a time when the psychiatric community was abandoning the idea that homosexuality and other forms of sexual expression represented deviant behavior.[84]

Wiley Goes Global

For Wiley outside the United States, the first decade after World War II proved to be a period of expansion and frustration. Overseas markets for college textbooks were large and growing, with the number of students enrolled in institutions of higher education worldwide tripling between 1950 and 1966. As Japan, for example, rebuilt its economy and began to catch up with the developed world, the number of students enrolled in institutions of higher education per 100,000 people increased from 471 in 1950 to 1,285 in 1966. Countries in the developed world also witnessed rapid gains but still had ample room for growth. Brad had visited Europe several times, beginning in 1949 with the aim of opening a subsidiary in England and increasing the distribution of Wiley titles there. He took naturally to an assignment that was both business and pleasure. He and Esther loved to travel and enjoyed serving as ambassadors for their company and country. Due in part to their globetrotting ways, Wiley would become a major player in the emerging global market for knowledge, and under Brad's leadership Wiley would establish itself squarely on four continents.[85]

By the late 1950s, international contact was constant. In 1959, Frank Forkert of Wiley's overseas department toured Asia and the Middle East, stopping at universities and bookstores in Japan, South Korea, Hong Kong, the Philippines, Indonesia, Singapore, Malaya, Burma, Egypt, Lebanon, and Turkey. Other areas of the globe at first knew Wiley only by representation: Chapman & Hall in Britain, Asia Publishing House in India, Antonio Carpinteiro in South America, Fred Nicdao in the Philippines, Philip Creswell in Australia and New Zealand, and Burgess Whiteside in continental Europe. It became increasingly clear, however, that to fully tap international markets Wiley would need its own offices. In international operations, Wiley was neither in the industry vanguard nor in the rear. Establishing foreign subsidiaries was the thing to do for major U.S. publishers in the 1960s, and that is what Wiley did.[86]

Starting in 1949, Brad had explored the possibility of establishing a subsidiary house in Britain but was put off by British red tape and insistence that Wiley manufacture locally all the books it sold in Britain. Brad continued to be frustrated by Wiley's historic relationship with Chapman & Hall, which proved to be more a hindrance than a help as Chapman & Hall resisted suggestions about how to market and sell Wiley books more effectively in Great Britain. Additionally, Chapman & Hall's discount and exchange rates made the price of Wiley's books higher than the competition. In 1958, Brad was warned by a director at Methuen, Chapman & Hall's parent company, that Brad would have to bring the issue to a head. Accompanied by Sullivan, who was promoted to vice president and director of marketing in 1957, Brad surveyed the publishing scene in Britain in October 1958 and then visited Chapman & Hall. Together they inspected the operations of several British houses, including Angus Robertson and Longmans, Green, as well as the British operations of several of Wiley's American competitors—observing and probing, weighing the strengths and weaknesses of each house as they eyed possibilities for some new arrangement. When Longmans, Green suggested that it was the best house to work with Wiley in Europe and the rest of the world, Wiley agreed, provided that Wiley absorb Longmans, Green's New York operation. "They saw the point," Sullivan noted in his report, "and that is the end of negotiations between us."[87]

Sullivan and Brad also visited McGraw-Hill's struggling new London operation, where they heard McGraw-Hill used direct mailing to overcome the passivity of English booksellers. They tried to find out more about Van Nostrand's new independent operation and learned that textbook publisher Prentice Hall was going on its own in England in the spring of 1959. They also investigated Interscience, which operated in New York, London, and Germany and would soon become a Wiley acquisition, as previously discussed.[88]

Sullivan and two representatives from Chapman & Hall also visited more than a dozen of Wiley's best bookstore accounts, including H. K. Lewis, a technical bookstore near the University of London and the heart of the city's medical district; Dillon's University Bookshop; and the world-renowned The Economist Bookshop. H. K. Lewis, which included a bookstore, export business, and lending library, was Wiley's largest account, but Dillon's, a new store with a large glass frontage directly across from the university's student union, was coming on strong. The Economist Bookshop kept Wiley's social science titles well stocked. The entourage also visited Frank E. Stokely, "the dean of technical booksellers in England," a man so thoroughly conversant with his market that he disdained returns. Sullivan concluded from these meetings that the "great loyalty" that existed between British book buyers and their retailers was advantageous to Wiley, which could easily service Britain itself simply by attending to the needs of the top 25 or so of these large technical accounts. Close attention to its British bookselling customers would clearly offset what McGraw-Hill thought was passivity. Rather than try to buck the system, Sullivan suggested, Wiley should leverage it.[89]

Sullivan also met with Morgan Guaranty Trust, one of Wiley's preferred banks, which informed him that restrictions on the establishment of branches of American companies in England would soon be lifted. The bank suggested forming a limited company and promised to help out with loans if Wiley chose not to use its own cash to fund the start-up. It also warned Wiley away from 50:50 partnerships with British companies. British companies, explained the bank, thought and acted so differently that combinations with American partners usually ended badly. In a meeting at Chapman & Hall, Sullivan and Brad ascertained that their British colleagues feared that Wiley would start an original publishing program in Britain, which would compete with Chapman & Hall. Brad explained that

View of the Corn Exchange before work commenced.

Work starts

*W*iley's Chichester office in the historic Corn Exchange. Wiley moved from London to Chichester in 1967, taking over an abandoned corn exchange where farmers once sold their crops to grain merchants. Chichester's Michael Colenso recorded his first impressions: "The building was derelict except for a substantial population of pigeons demonstrating their habitual incontinence and a number of warfarin-immune [rat poison–immune] rodents of spectacular size."

this was not their intent. Rather, they wanted and needed, for business and prestige reasons, to have a production and editorial base in London—with a London imprint on the title page—to adapt American textbooks for the British market. At that point, Brad and Sullivan were intent on continuing their co-publishing arrangement with Chapman & Hall if the company's proposal to improve their working relationship proved acceptable. When the proposal arrived in New York, however, it was found wanting. Brad informed Chapman & Hall that their relationship of more than half a century was over, and that Wiley would open its own publishing office in London.

In November 1959, John Wiley & Sons Ltd., a wholly-owned subsidiary of Wiley, was registered in London. On August 29, 1960, after months of careful preparation of new employees, advertising, mailing lists, warehouse, and back-office operations, the subsidiary officially commenced business in London. For the first time since the days of John Wiley, London would appear as a publishing location on a Wiley title page. [90]

Led by Burgess Whiteside, the new managing director, and James Durrant, the marketing director, the subsidiary was charged with publishing and distributing books in Great Britain and the entire sterling area of the world. Durrant had come from Chapman & Hall looking for greater career opportunities. Whiteside had helped to set up Macmillan of New York in London, so Sullivan considered him the prime choice. Wiley Ltd. was also charged with publishing local student editions of Wiley textbooks and keeping some 60,000 volumes in stock for immediate shipment. The new company's broad goal was to expand the sale of Wiley titles in Britain, Europe, Africa, and the Middle East and to implement a new shipping system designed to improve customer service. [91]

The company's first subsidiary got off to a rocky start. The new IBM system caused problems that negatively impacted cash flow, and employee morale was equally negative. In addition, editorial director Ronald Watson found himself saddled with Interscience's European list, which he thought might help jump-start the British venture but was composed

PROFILE

OVE STEENTOFT

Ove Steentoft, a Danish bon vivant , raconteur, and salesman extraordinaire, represented Wiley in Europe, Africa, South Africa, South Asia, and the Middle East for over thirty years. He told the following story about a trip to the Middle East.

> Having taken off from Karachi in the evening—en route to Bahrain via the Sheikdom of Qatar—on a GF Tristar, we managed to get about twenty minutes' flying out of Karachi when the captain announced, "Please do not panic. There is no reason for panic, and I am sure we will get the flaps repaired." After half an hour's flying . . . we did actually land . . . [and] I was offered the chance of boarding another, but rather small, plane . . . I was hurried on board and into the small cabin where only one seat was left . . . After a few minutes the rest of the passengers started boarding. I was indeed honoured because they were all of them princes from the Sheikdom of Qatar with an entourage of falconers. They brought with them their 79—repeat—79 falcons . . . They were placed wherever there was space in the cabin. Hence I had seven falcons under my feet, four above my knee, one by my left arm, and four above my head. Although the falcons did have those lovely little masks over their faces, they had no masks or 'containers' fastened to their nether ends . . . The falcons were rather nervous and reacted violently by perpetually dispensing with what had become superfluous matter in their stomachs.[92]

Ove Steentoft, Wiley global sales representative extraordinaire.

mostly of professional and reference books already past their prime and, Watson thought, "difficult and expensive to produce and almost impossible to sell." Wiley Ltd. also unwisely rented expensive offices in Stag Place, a prestigious London location it could ill afford. The New York parent had to intervene, and Whiteside, instead of joining the New York office as planned, was let go. Watson took his place, and Neilly and Francis Lobdell began to give the operation more personal attention. Slowly, the subsidiary righted itself with help from sales representatives like Michael Colenso, a South African; Michael Foyle, who was fluent in Russian; Ove Steentoft, a former Danish resistance fighter; Mike Coombs, another South African; and Jamie Cameron.[93]

Though wholly owned by the Americans, Wiley Ltd. remained indubitably English. Eventually, it launched its own highly successful publishing program on the editorial backs of Watson and a band of talented eccentrics: Ossian Goulding, an Irishman said to be capable of charming the birds out of the trees; Paul Resbane, an Austrian who spied for the Allies during the war; Marjorie Redwood, one of the first women to play a senior role for Wiley; and Jamie Cameron from sales, who had helped spread Wiley's name far and wide in Europe. Watson, a wounded veteran, was disorganized and always seemed slightly out of touch. Cameron stalked the office in stocking feet listening to recordings of classical music. Goulding drove an automobile that looked like a space ship.[94]

In the early days, Wiley Ltd. turned out no blockbusters but produced enough solid hits, books that sold 2,000 to 6,000 copies over a few years, to prove itself a viable business. High rents and high employee turnover in London, however, compelled relocation to Chichester, in West Sussex, in 1967. Competitors at first scoffed at the move, and Wiley employees wondered whether the decision to relocate was based on Brad and Esther's infatuation with this charming new locale. But within a few years, even McGraw-Hill had also fled the metropolis for cheaper quarters. It was clearly the right move. Out of commuting distance from London but close to the major port of Southampton, Chichester offered an adequate and stable labor supply and long-term leases at a fraction of London rents. In 1968, the subsidiary employed 109 people and put out 27 titles of its own.[95]

In the 1970s, the British operation grew at a rapid pace. Between 1972 and 1975, for example, sales more than doubled growing from £2 million to £5 million. At the beginning of the decade, Wiley Ltd. published only one journal, *Numerical Methods in Engineering*, a highly regarded one at that. In the 1970s, Chichester's journals program, driven by editorial director Jamie Cameron, grew quickly, with new titles coming out every year. To its standard fare of Wiley International Editions (WIEs) new journals, and new STM books, Chichester sold titles brought to them by Halsted Press, Sullivan's operation in New York, which arranged for Chichester to promote and sell on behalf of smaller American publishers, such as Ballinger, Jai Press, and Ann Arbor Science. In 1976, Watson retired as managing director and was replaced by Adrian Higham. When Higham arrived, he found a company with six journals and hundreds of titles selling £3 million worth of product a year with all of its profitability derived from

Wiley moved abroad steadily and carefully, exploring a range of relationships from subsidiary offices to joint ventures.

Numerical Methods and a second journal, *Software Practice and Experience*. That situation would improve dramatically in the years ahead.[96]

Wiley looked at the possibility of acquiring either a British or European company. Brad showed particular interest in Blackwell Publishing, the Oxford-based company belonging to the family that owned Oxford's most famous bookstore. On a regular basis, Brad would court Chairman Richard Blackwell over dinner at the Frankfurt Book Fair. Having listened to Brad's overtures for a number of years, Blackwell at one point felt compelled to respond that the best way to solve Wiley's problem was for Blackwell to acquire Wiley. According to Neilly, Brad was not amused.[97]

Wiley moved abroad steadily and carefully, exploring a range of relationships from subsidiary offices to joint ventures—whatever increased the sale of U.S. product and/or presented local publishing opportunities. Essential to Wiley's overseas mission was the ability to price according to the standards of the local economy. The developing world was still very much just that: in the earliest stages of modernization. And though developing countries like India were investing aggressively in higher education, their students could not afford American textbook prices. The same was true in Europe as it recovered from World War II destruction. In the 1950s, Wiley began to experiment with low-priced reprints of American textbooks and then turned in the early 1960s to Toppan, the large Japanese printing company, to produce similar texts for Japan, India, and Southeast Asia. In 1965, Wiley launched Wiley International Editions (WIEs), a full-blown series of paperback textbooks. Printed in

Tokyo, Hong Kong, Singapore, and the United States, WIEs were eventually published simultaneously with the North American texts and proved a successful way of reaching university textbook markets in Europe and the developing world.[98]

With product to offer, Wiley began to accumulate foreign addresses. In 1962, Wiley entered into a joint venture called Editorial Limusa-Wiley, with a syndicate of five Mexican publishers and booksellers. The company translated English-language scientific and technical books into Spanish and also published original Spanish-language works. The reason for the creation of Limusa was clear. Earlier arms-length arrangements with Spanish-language publishers simply had not gone well because the publishers had either taken too long to arrange for translation and publication—which was death for scientific books—or had contracted with non-technical translators who did sub-standard work. A few translators even pirated Wiley books. Mexican law required that at least 51 percent of the company be locally owned, so Wiley was a minority owner in Limusa. At first all went well—too well in fact. Wiley recouped the start-up costs by 1965 but complained that the venture was growing too fast, well ahead of schedule. The problem was that the enterprise was sacrificing profit and reputation for size. The arrangement did, however, keep Brad and sometimes Esther on the road in Latin America, where they became close friends with the Noriega and Trillas families, the leading shareholders in Limusa-Wiley. Brad and Esther made new contacts, gathered information, generated publicity, and sometimes even collected debts.[99]

In late 1962 and early 1963, Wiley established John Wiley & Sons Australasia PTY., Ltd., a proprietary limited company based in Sydney that did business in

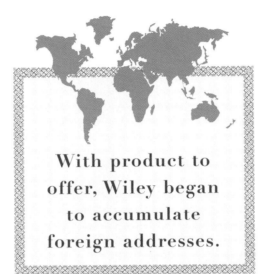

With product to offer, Wiley began to accumulate foreign addresses.

Australia, New Zealand, the Philippines, Japan, India, and South Africa. The Australian market was then ripe because the country's educational leaders were in the process of jettisoning the British system in favor of the American one and there was no used book market to speak of. As in Britain, the subsidiary began cautiously, as a marketing and distribution arm, before evolving into a complete publishing center. It published textbooks for all levels of the education markets, growing organically and through the acquisition of Jacaranda Press for $1.375 million (U.S. dollars) in September 1976. Established in 1952 by an enterprising teacher and later acquired by Reed International, by the mid-1970s Jacaranda was one of Australia's largest elementary/ high school publishers, but a troubled one. The acquisition was attractive, since organic growth of Wiley Australasia had all but ceased and losses loomed. Although it was technically the acquiring company, John Wiley & Sons Australasia essentially folded itself into Jacaranda and its Brisbane offices. After some debate, the new company was renamed Jacaranda Wiley.[100]

Some markets remained tougher to penetrate. In 1963, Whiteside, Forkert, and George Rappole, manager of sales in the Near East and Africa, toured Africa, where cultivating and nurturing customers could lead to some fascinating adventures, many related by Ove Steentoft in his inimitable style.

India was a different story. Wiley entered the subcontinent in the usual way, at first only selling, later selling and publishing. Established in 1962 to avoid a bad situation that had sprung up with its agent and to tap into grants under the joint Indo-American Textbook Program (U.S. Public Law 480, the Food for Peace program), Wiley Eastern Ltd., in New Delhi, published reprints of U.S. titles as well as original Indian publications, some in English, some in Hindi, and sold Wiley exports in India and neighboring Burma and Sri Lanka. In 1970, the enterprise became a true joint venture company in which Wiley held a 40 percent stake. With some 150 universities and 1,500 affiliated colleges and the world's second largest population, India possessed huge numbers of book readers even though its literacy rate was less than 50 percent. Profits came easily, at first.[101]

In 1968, Wiley began another Latin American joint venture, this one in Brazil for Portuguese-language publication. The Rio de Janeiro–based firm, Livros Tecnicos e Cientificos Editora, S.A., was substantially enlarged in 1972, following a two-week fact-finding visit by Brad that revealed a booming book market in Brazil fueled by the country's growth in population, literacy, and income. Wiley's joint ventures in Latin America were expected to produce impressive results, but hopes far surpassed performance. Limusa, the Mexican joint venture, showed some promise at first but then soured amid deteriorating economic conditions in Latin America. Poor infrastructure, mail theft, trade restrictions, unpredictable government policy, and even an earthquake plagued the Mexican endeavor. By the late 1970s, competitive pressure came from McGraw-Hill, Harper, Prentice Hall, Houghton Mifflin, and Addison-Wesley. Wiley found itself at a further disadvantage because it did not offer integrated English/foreign-language programs in Latin America, a fundamental problem that it took some time to discover.[102]

In other markets, Wiley trod more lightly and stopped short of forming subsidiaries or joint ventures. In 1957, it arranged with Charles E. Tuttle Company of Tokyo for the publication of Modern Asia Editions, low-priced English-language technical and scientific books published in Japan. This move was designed to combat the losses from local piracy: nine titles were illegally copied in 1957 alone. Partly in response to continued pirating by local booksellers, Wiley completed an agreement in 1963 with Toppan Printing

*B*rad Wiley, Sr. and Jr., at the Frankfurt Book Fair in 1962.

Company, Ltd., allowing it to reprint Japanese editions of Wiley textbooks and to sell them at one-third the price charged in the United States. "We hope to sell books in the Asian market which we could not reach otherwise," Brad explained. Wiley books sold equally well in Japanese and English. Professors may have wanted the English version to check the translation, and students to help them learn the leading language of science. Wiley considered joining Toppan in a joint venture, but mutually amicable terms could not be agreed upon.[103]

In 1971, the company set up John Wiley & Sons, GmbH, Frankfurt, Germany, to co-publish German-language editions of its books. Minimally capitalized at just DM12,500, the paper enterprise was established in part to tap into a science renaissance in continental Europe. The big competitors were British publisher Blackwell, Dutch publisher Elsevier, German publishers Springer-Verlag and Georg Thieme Verlag, and a number of small, specialized houses. Wiley considered acquiring one of these houses or establishing its own publishing houseca, but decided in favor of co-publishing. German publishers were at first interested but later thought it best to simply purchase translation rights and take on all of the risk, and reward, of publishing themselves. It would take more than two decades for Wiley to become a truly European publishing house with the acquisition of Verlag Chemie in 1996.[104]

In 1968, the company opened an office and warehouse outside Toronto, Canada, for the sale of American textbooks and a smaller number of professional titles. The first Canadian publishing program was launched in 1974 with a series of paperback science titles for the high school market. Wiley Canada also took over the sale of Charles Scribner's Sons' titles for the local market, a lucrative arrangement given the strength of Scribner's backlist, which included famed American authors, such as Ernest Hemingway. In 1976, Geoff Dean was appointed president of the Canadian operation. Working with James Rogerson, editor-in-chief for the Elementary and High School Division, he shut down the science series due to lack of profitability and shifted emphasis to new titles in business and law.[105]

In 1978, in response to increased interest in scientific and technical books in the Middle East, Wiley announced the launch of Wiley Arabooks, Arabic-language translations and original works. The venture was fraught with difficulties from the beginning, largely due to Interscience's Jewish heritage and a seeming affront over a dozen years earlier. In 1965, three Arab directors of Franklin Books Program, a nonprofit international publishing venture founded in 1952, had

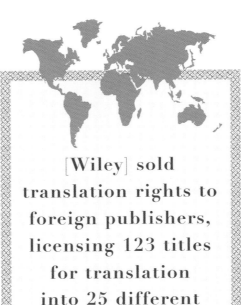

[Wiley] sold translation rights to foreign publishers, licensing 123 titles for translation into 25 different languages in 1965 alone.

protested vigorously because Brad, then Franklin's president, had invited an Israeli delegation to a cocktail party ostensibly hosted by Franklin rather than by Brad personally. Ever the diplomat, Brad managed the situation as best he could and further ameliorated the tensions by traveling to Cairo to announce the Arabooks launch in person. It was not enough, however. The program successfully translated major higher education titles like James Brady and Gerard Humiston's *General Chemistry* (1975) and Saturnino Salas and Einar Hille's *Calculus* (1974) but could not induce Arabic-speaking students to buy many of them. Wiley sold the translations to the Jordan Book Centre in 1990.[106]

By the late 1970s, Wiley's overseas presence had grown dramatically. There were new offices in Canada, Latin America, England, Australia, and Asia supporting a broad spectrum of publishing arrangements. Wiley was in the import and export business and was exploring the possibilities of local publishing. The company also sold translation rights to foreign publishers, licensing 123 titles for translation into 25 different languages in 1965 alone, eight years after it began to push for more translation fees. Whatever its form, international publishing was rife with challenges, and not all of Wiley's overseas forays in this period were easy conquests. In some regions, printing technologies and book distribution channels rivaled those of the United States; in others they were primitive. Some countries placed oppressive tariffs on foreign books; others imposed a bewildering array of nontariff barriers that raised the cost of importation by creating red tape. The Cold War itself probably presented one of the toughest challenges.[107]

Exploring Behind the Iron Curtain

In 1962, Brad and M. R. Robinson of Scholastic led a delegation of American publishers from the American Textbook Publishers Institute and the American Book Publishers Council (the two organizations that would merge to form the Association of American Publishers) on an exploratory visit to the Soviet Union to discuss scientific and technical book publishing exchanges under the cultural exchange program Washington had negotiated in March of that year. The attraction was clear: The Soviet Union was a huge market, highly literate, book-minded, and technologically astute, as *Sputnik* had proved. Moreover, Wiley had known since at least 1959 that the Soviet Union and some of its Eastern European satellites had published some excellent scientific and technical titles of interest to scientists in the West. The group issued a report called *Book Publishing in the U.S.S.R.* urging the Soviets to become a party to the Universal Copyright Convention (UCC), which the United States joined in 1955 as an alternative to the Berne international copyright agreement. (Many countries, including the United States, could not sign the Berne Convention because of manufacturing clauses in their national copyright laws. Supported by the American printing industry, the U.S. manufacturing clause dated from the 1891 U.S. International Copyright Act and stated that all copies of a work written in English must be printed in the United States, or from plates made in the United States, even if the copyright was held by a foreigner, in order to receive copyright protection.) In 1973, after Brad participated in a second delegation, the Soviets

The Soviet Union was a huge market, highly literate . . . and technologically astute.

joined the UCC, a move at once heralded by American publishers who had long been the victims of Soviet book pirates. Wiley's important role in the Soviets' decision was later cited by a Soviet official who joked that Brad had "coerced us" into signing. In his retirement years, Brad had lunch with Boris I. Stukalin, the head of the Press Committee of the Council of Ministers, which controlled Soviet publishing in 1962. At that lunch, Stukalin acknowledged that, as the Americans suspected, he was a KGB officer. Stukalin was wrong, however, in his assumption that Brad was a member of the CIA.[108]

A gap between intention and behavior soon became clear, however, and de facto implementation of the terms of the treaty would be slow and incomplete because Soviet publishers had little experience with such matters and no easy way of obtaining the foreign exchange needed to pay royalties to European and American authors and publishers. The UCC was a major step forward, but far from a sign that the Soviets were willing to expose their population to a free flow of information. Indeed, the Soviets repeatedly banned books from the annual Moscow Book Fair in the late 1970s. Nevertheless, Brad, Esther, and Michael Foyle, Wiley's marketing director at Chichester, visited Moscow and Leningrad in September 1974 to try to drum up business. The Soviets doted over the Wiley entourage and set up an exhibit featuring 300 Wiley titles that included selections from all areas except, of course, politics and history. They even offered to provide Wiley with the exclusive publishing rights to the Hermitage, the Soviets' world-class art museum in Leningrad. After some initial excitement about the possibilities, Brad turned his hosts down,

THE WILEYS AS AMBASSADORS

*B*rad Wiley receives the Department of Commerce's E for Export Award from President Lyndon Baines Johnson in 1965. Two years later, Brad would become a member of the executive committee of Publishers for Peace in Vietnam, which called for an end to the war through negotiations.

*B*rad Wiley and Esther Wiley in 1966 with Secretary of State Dean Rusk, and managing directors of the Franklin Book Program from Pakistan and Nigeria. Brad served as the chairman of the board of the Franklin Book Program, which encouraged indigenous publishing in the developing world, especially in Muslim countries.

referring them to Harry Abrams, the American art book publisher. Discussions of translation rights, royalty payments, typesetting, and the like were complicated by differences between Soviet and American publishing, business, and legal practices. Matters at first looked hopeful, but the Soviets did not even know the intent of letters of intent. Over the next few years, Wiley found it difficult to meet with Soviet officials and even more difficult to get its questions answered. Slow mail, Soviet bureaucracy, and language barriers did not help matters. As encouragement, Brad sent Soviet officials books and glowing thank you letters and hosted a visit to Wiley's offices by a Soviet delegation.[109]

Some good did come of courting the Soviets, as several top Soviet scientists joined the editorial staff of Wiley's *International Journal of Circuit Theory and Applications*. And by 1978, Wiley billed itself as the "leading publisher of Russian-language textbooks in the United States." The market was small, however, with fewer than 28,000 students enrolled in Russian-language classes in the United States in 1977. The leading first-year textbook, Wiley's *Introductory Russian Grammar* (1972) by Galina and Leon Stilman and William E. Harkins, sold 7,000 copies per annum. Wiley also attempted to tap other markets behind the Iron Curtain. In 1965, Brad headed a delegation to Romania,

*B*rad Wiley and Townsend Hoopes, president of the Association of American publishers, sitting with a delegation of American publishers at the Writer's Union in Moscow in September 1976. Standing from left, Ted Vendenbempt; Michael Foyle (later managing director of John Wiley & Sons Ltd); Don Jones, Addison-Wesley; Robert Bernstein, Random House; Chester Brooks Kerr, Yale University Press; Mead Stone, McGraw-Hill International; Lawrence Hughes, president of William Morrow and Company; Martin Levin, New American Library; Peter Neumann, Addison-Wesley; Leo Albert, chairman of the board of Prentice-Hall International Publishers.

a prime candidate owing to its Romance-based language, independent stand vis-à-vis the Soviet Union, and close ties to Germany. In Bulgaria, Wiley sent books to a socialist-style book fair in 1968; Brad also explored publishing connections in Hungary and Yugoslavia.[110]

Attempts to cooperate with the Soviet Union and other Eastern European countries brought little in the way of profits, however. Sales of scientific and technical books, as some observers predicted, were never large because the Soviets' own technical books were heavily subsidized and hence cheap, if they could be found. For their troubles, American publishers sometimes drew heavy fire from Cold Warriors.[111]

The International Corporation

By the mid-1970s, Wiley's international strategy appeared to be working, as international sales accounted for about a third of Wiley's total revenue, protecting the company from periodic downturns in the U.S. market. Though reliable industry statistics for export sales were lacking, the company believed—likely accurately—that it enjoyed "one of the highest export percentages of any scientific and technical U.S. publisher." Perversely, success sometimes brings with it a penalty. In November 1974, the U.S. Department of Justice brought an antitrust suit against Wiley and 20 other

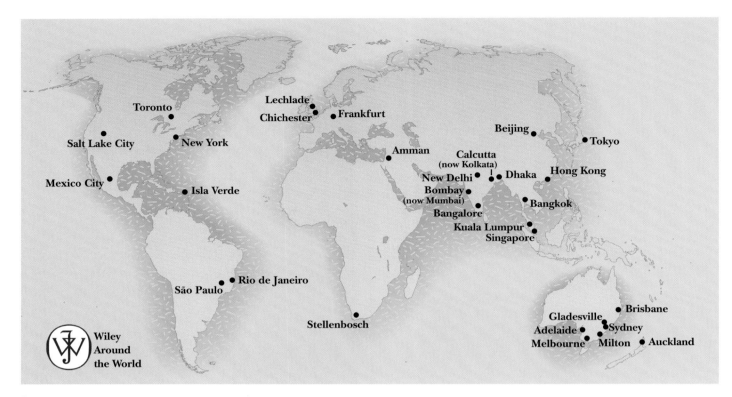

Wiley's Global Reach, 1976. Wiley sales offices, subsidiaries, and other locations in 1976 included Singapore, Dhaka, Chichester, Toronto, Salt Lake City, New York, and Frankfurt.

American publishers, alleging that they conspired with major British publishers to divide up world markets in violation of the Sherman Antitrust Act. Wiley denied the allegations, which seemed directed at U.S. and U.K. publishers that did a mostly domestic business. How things seem can be as important as how things are, and Brad promptly instructed Wiley Ltd. to withdraw from the British Publishers Association and its Traditional Market Agreement (TMA), the organization and contract at the heart of the government's suit. Wiley Ltd. had signed the TMA in 1966 without its parent's knowledge. By February 1970, the Chichester office expressed concern that the Publishers Association and its agreement might be considered collusion, a fear that the association argued was groundless. The matter ended when the U.S. publishers, which included all the large ones, signed a cease-and-desist consent decree in

1976. The Publishers Association also revoked the TMA, a move that most publishers conceded was inevitable and desirable. There were no fines or admissions of guilt, but legal fees were, of course, high. Signing the TMA in the first place, Brad later admitted, "was a pretty costly boner."[112]

As on the domestic front, Brad acted abroad not only for Wiley but for the larger book industry. He was chairman of the Book Industry International Trade Committee, sat on the Council for the Advancement of Technical Writing, and was a member of the Science Information Council of the National Science Foundation. In 1962, he became one of the initial members of the U.S. Government Advisory Committee (GAC) for International Book and Library Programs, which helped, among other things, to reduce book piracy in Taiwan. In 1964, Brad went from director to chairman of the Franklin Book Program, succeeding Thomas Wilson, director of the Harvard University Press. Franklin secured translation rights from the American proprietor, then contracted with a local publisher and translator. Franklin paid for the translation, special editorial work, the introduction, and artwork. The local publisher usually paid for paper, printing, and binding and also agreed to pay Franklin ten percent of the local selling price. Franklin books were in Arabic, Bahasa, Farsi, Peshtu, Urdu, Bengali, Spanish, and Portuguese. In an at times tortuous journey, Brad and Esther toured Franklin's facilities worldwide, visiting Argentina, Nigeria, Egypt, Lebanon, Iraq, Iran, Afghanistan, Pakistan, Malaysia, and Indonesia, some of the world's poorest and most unstable countries. The Nigerian prime minister was assassinated soon after the Wileys' visit; Iraqi officials restricted their visitors to a brief sojourn in an airport hangar; and inflation was so high in Indonesia that Brad's second cup of coffee at dinner cost more than the first, or so he claimed. When the president of McGraw-Hill took over the chairmanship

from Brad in 1966, Franklin was well respected internationally and thriving.[113]

In 1974, Brad described Wiley as "a true international organization," saying that the company's foreign subsidiaries operated with a "high degree of independence and flexibility in decision making." Despite its size, Wiley was perhaps the most international of all the American publishing houses.

Moving Books, Managing Information

In 1958, Wiley published some 155 new books in 30 separate fields. By 1975, the company operated more than 20 product lines, comprised 15 "companies" (the parent, foreign and domestic subsidiaries, divisions, or joint ventures) with separate profit and loss statements, had 7 domestic and 6 international selling units, distinguished 86 different categories of customers, and ran a publishing program that covered 60 major subject areas. The company was one of the 11 big publishers that accounted for a full half of the total U.S. publishing market.[114]

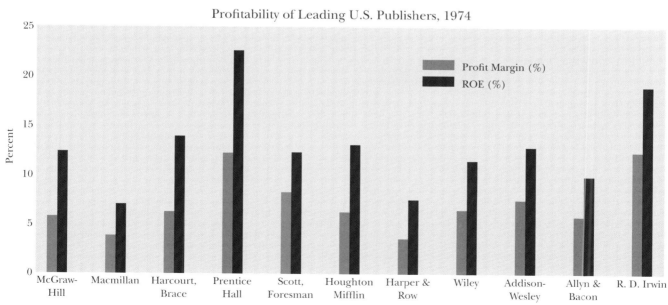

Profitability of Leading U.S. Publishers, 1974

Source: "Summary of Five Year Plans, Fiscal 1976–1980," 10 December 1974, JWSA.

Computers and Wiley

*I*van Sutherland was one of the important innovators in the first years of the computer age. In 1963, he experimented with a digital sketch pad (top right). Wiley published books about computers starting after World War II, introduced computers into the business in the 1950s, and began to consider their impact on book publishing in the 1960s. Ivan's brother, Bert, made significant contributions to Wiley's transition from print to a digital environment as a member of CEO Andrew Neilly's Research and Development Committee and later the board of directors.

*W*iley published *Digital Computer Programming* by Daniel McCracken (below), an early, classic computer title, in 1957.

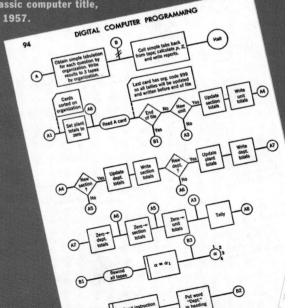

Wiley was able to expand geographically, acquire other businesses, grow its lists organically, and partner with publishers at home and abroad because professional managers ran the company. These individuals knew both business and books and understood the value of information. Publishing was still part craft, but its mystique receded under the influence of business and economic theory and computerization. Personal hunch in editorial decisions was giving way to market research. Other aspects of publishing, ranging from advertising to production to distribution, were similarly transformed. In the late 1950s, Wiley converted its manual billing system to an IBM 650, which served authors, booksellers, and retail customers even faster and more efficiently. The system also created detailed sales analyses "by subject, book, territory, and sales outlet; lists of best-sellers; discount analyses; up-to-the-minute inventories; stock evaluations; and a host of smaller pieces of useful data."[115]

Wiley was among the first publishers to embrace such technology. Brad had learned about computers during the war, and Wiley of course published some of the first books about them. A positive feedback cycle began whereby, partly as a result of its use of computers, Wiley began to publish more books about them, including early classics such as Daniel McCracken's *Digital Computer Programming* (1957) and McCracken, Harold Weiss, and Tsai-Hwa Lee's *Programming Business Computers* (1959).[116]

Wiley understood that to function efficiently it needed information, carefully crafted data combined with expert opinion. Increasingly, the company conducted internal studies designed to elucidate key aspects of its business. In March 1961, it engaged in its earliest long-range planning efforts, setting a target of 15 percent annual growth over the next five years. In 1964, the international sales department conducted a historical quantitative analysis of Wiley's exports since the end of World War II. The goal was to identify trends and to analyze sales fluctuations by looking for a correlation between sales to a given country and its per capita output, electrical energy consumption, exports, and other appropriate economic indicators. Wiley hired McKinsey, the management consulting firm, to help with certain information management problems, such as predicting and tracking a book's profitability. According to Neilly, McKinsey stirred things up. For continuing help, Wiley hired William Diefenbach away from McKinsey as an internal consultant with the job of improving administrative performance. He helped develop a book management system used into the 1990s, which in modified form is still used to this day. He also helped the company to strengthen, though not perfect, its management-by-objectives and strategic planning programs. By 1970, Neilly could write that the company had "firm control of expenses and indirect costs" and sales and all the other major variables that affected the bottom line.[117]

Better information and better managers meant better decisions about the timeless questions facing publishers: how many copies of a particular title to print, what list price to assign to each title, how and how much to advertise and otherwise market each book in its list, and how much publicity to seek for the company itself. Most of Wiley's top sellers were introductory textbooks; by the early 1960s, a good introductory text could be counted on to sell 10,000 or more copies a year. More advanced texts and technical reference books could sell more than 5,000 copies a year. The downside was that the market for textbooks was naturally limited, as few nonstudents ever bought them, so none in this period came close to selling 100,000 in a single year. By the early 1970s, the hottest textbooks, notably Gideon Nelson, Gerald Robinson, and Richard Boolootian's *Fundamental Concepts of Biology* (1967, 1970, 1974), which sold more than 75,000 copies, and Calvin Hall and Gardner Lindzey's *Theories of Personality* (1957, 1970, 1978), which sold over 50,000 copies, had higher sales levels but still

Halliday and Resnick Define Physics

The first edition of David Halliday and Robert Resnick's *Physics* (1960) was hailed for its content, organization, and pedagogically superior use of art. David Halliday (right) in 2001, standing next to the accumulated paper— manuscript, edited manuscript, galleys, and page proofs, all atop one of the competing books—prepared for the 5th edition of *Physics*, now coauthored with Kenneth S. Krane.

Halliday · Resnick
Physics
Parts **I & II**

*R*obert Resnick and David Halliday

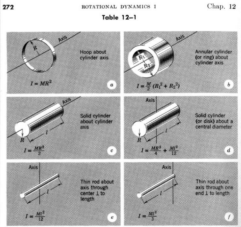

272 ROTATIONAL DYNAMICS I Chap. 12

Table 12–1

Hoop about cylinder axis
$I = MR^2$ (a)

Annular cylinder (or ring) about cylinder axis
$I = \frac{M}{2}(R_1^2 + R_2^2)$ (b)

Solid cylinder about cylinder axis
$I = \frac{MR^2}{2}$ (c)

Solid cylinder (or disk) about a central diameter
$I = \frac{MR^2}{4} + \frac{Ml^2}{12}$ (d)

Thin rod about axis through center ⊥ to length
$I = \frac{Ml^2}{12}$ (e)

Thin rod about axis through one end ⊥ to length
$I = \frac{Ml^2}{3}$ (f)

Solid sphere about any diameter
$I = \frac{2MR^2}{5}$ (g)

Hoop about any diameter
$I = \frac{MR^2}{2}$ (i)

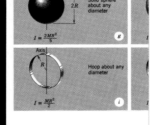

Fig. 13–6 A diver leaves the diving board with arms and legs outstretched and with some initial angular velocity. Since no torques are exerted on him about his center of mass, $L (= I\omega)$ is constant while he is in the air. When he pulls his arms and legs in, since I decreases, ω increases. When he again extends his limbs, his angular velocity drops back to its initial value. Notice the parabolic motion of his center of mass, common to all two-dimensional motion under the influence of gravity.

where L_z is the component of the angular momentum along the rotation axis and I is the rotational inertia for this same axis. It is possible for the rotational inertia I of a rotating body to change by rearrangement of its parts. If no net external torque acts, then L_z must remain constant and, if I does change, there must be a compensating change in ω. The principle of conservation of angular momentum in this case is expressed as

$$I\omega = I_0\omega_0 = \text{a constant.} \quad (13\text{–}8)$$

Equation 13–8 holds not only for rotation about a fixed axis but also about an axis through the center of mass of the system that moves so that it

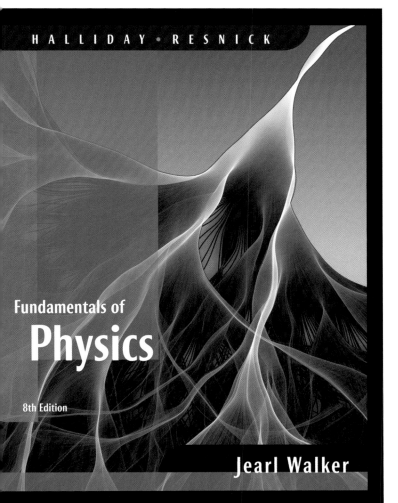

earl Walker

David Halliday and Robert Resnick's *Physics* (1960) redefined the teaching of introductory physics and became the dominant text in the market almost immediately after publication. It hit the million-copy mark in the early 1970s. A more accessible version of the book, titled *Fundamentals of Physics*, was published in 1970. With Jearl Walker, who became the author as of the fifth edition, *Fundamentals* today is still the most widely used physics textbook in the world. *Physics* and *Fundamentals of Physics* combined have sold well over 3 million copies.

faced enrollment ceilings. Only through careful cultivation for many years could titles like David Halliday and Robert Resnick's *Physics* (first published in 1960) and *Fundamentals of Physics* (1970, 1978) hit the million-unit mark. Careful cultivation also yielded franchise titles in geography, where titles by the teams of Harm de Blij and Peter Muller and of Arthur and Alan Strahler dominated the field for decades.[118]

It was impossible to tell beforehand whether a book would succeed, so decisions about the number of copies to print were tricky. The trade-off here is clear. The cost *per copy* decreased as print runs increased, but of course *total* costs rose with print runs so there was no safety in numbers: print too many and the publisher ended up with a warehouse full of unsold books and high indebtedness. "Forecasting sales of an individual title," Matheson reminded Neilly in a 1965 memo, "is a very hazardous undertaking." "One can come pretty close in forecasting total sales for the year," he noted, "but it is different to make accurate 'guesses' on individual titles. We must admit that it is kind of crystal gazing at best." Matheson suspected "that most estimates are tossed off rather casually" because creating good estimates was hard work and there were bound to be major estimation errors on the inevitable titles that did unexpectedly well or poorly. Nevertheless, he thought that better estimates could be made if editors and marketing managers carefully studied "the contents of the editors' folders" rather than making "estimates according to a hunch and their general experience with similar books." There was a floor, of course. Scientific and technical books could be expected to sell several hundred copies to domestic libraries and several hundred more to libraries overseas. Beyond that, though, it was a guessing game.[119]

The optimal number of copies of a book to print is largely dependent on the book's price, a variable over which publishers have surprisingly little control. Book prices are a function of the actual costs of manufacture and distribution, both of which in turn are a function of technological and economic development

Wiley and Geography

THE WORLD TODAY

Concepts and Regions in Geography

THIRD EDITION

H. J. de Blij • Peter O. Muller

Geography: *Regions and Concepts* (1970) by Harm de Blij, was known for the quality and effectiveness of its map program. *Regions* remains a market leader today in its 13th edition, and reviewers still cite the quality of its maps as a compelling competitive distinction. Now co-authored with Peter O. Muller, the author team has also produced the concise regional geography book, *The World Today*.

Harm de Blij

Peter O. Muller

Arthur and Alan Strahler, father-and-son writing team, wrote a combined total of over 20 textbooks with multiple revisions in physical geography, environmental science, Earth sciences, and geology. Together they have reached hundreds of thousands of students. The first text, *Physical Geography*, written by Arthur Strahler and published in 1951, established the Strahler reputation for scholarship, accessibility, clarity, and artwork, a reputation carried forward through an extraordinary five—now nearly six—decades of publications. Shown here are the 3rd edition of *Physical Geography* (2005) and the first edition of *Introduction to Physical Geography* (1965).

and the decisions of others. The remuneration for authors must also be taken as a given by publishers. That leaves only advertising, marketing, and publicity costs, as well as general overhead, and it is here that publishers traditionally struggle to control their fates. Yet despite the pervasive complaint that books are "too expensive," they are on average perfectly priced, allowing publishers just enough profit to justify staying in business in the long run.[120]

Scientific and technical titles cost more than comparable trade books in part because trade books are much more likely to create revenue through the sale of movie, translation, or other rights. Wiley had so little chance of making any money from movie rights that it even joked about it in *The Wiley Bulletin*. David Kritchevsky's book *Cholesterol*, the *Bulletin* claimed, tongue firmly in cheek, would be a blockbuster movie if it came out with a title like *Across the Liver and into the Spleen* or *The Old Man and the Sterol*.[121]

Wiley reviewed the prices of its books annually and made adjustments where necessary. A 1965 internal study indicated that Wiley books were on average priced like those of McGraw-Hill and Van Nostrand, in the middle of the road, considerably lower than those of Prentice Hall but higher than those of Macmillan. Such studies, though imperfect, were much better than the company's earlier efforts, when competitive analysis entailed nothing more than the travelers sitting around the office in the summers going through other publishers' catalogues.[122]

The company's books cost less than the books of some of its competitors because Wiley did not use expensive sales tactics. Unlike World Book and some other encyclopedia publishers, for example, it did not have to run credit checks on individuals, sell its products in installments, pay the expenses of door-to-door salespeople, and the like. Wiley could also charge less at times because it had a better idea of each book's profitability at different prices. Unlike editors at trade houses like Random House, Wiley editors eventually had to have more than a hunch about a book; they had to have data. That made sense given that it was easier to measure a technical book market than a trade one. McGraw-Hill's Curtis Benjamin put it this way: "No one can tell how many general readers are likely to be interested in an absorbing new book on Lincoln's doctor's dog, but the publisher of a new book on physical optics can estimate with accuracy the number of his potential customers." By 1971, Wiley used a computer program, pushed by William Diefenbach, that allowed editors to try out different combinations of contract terms, designs, and prices in just a few minutes. By 1974, the company used the program to calculate the required return on investment on every book project. The program could not divine how many books would be sold, but, rather, spit out scenarios based on judgments of likely sales ranges. The program, which Wiley sold to other publishers and which soon made its way into textbooks about publishing, was very sophisticated. It even discounted cash flows.[123]

Sales were also a function of advertising, marketing, publicity, and company reputation. Here the company's record was mixed. That is not to say that Wiley did not expend considerable sums on advertising and marketing, but only that its expenditures were lower than those of some of its competitors. Wiley's executives knew, no doubt from their Harvard courses, about famous Philadelphia retailer John Wanamaker's comment about his company's advertising: "I know I'm wasting half my money, but I don't know which half." Spending just the right amount on a book was another of publishing's vagaries that Wiley sought to make more rational. Spending in just the right way was important, too. Television advertising can effectively move books,

> Availability, not price, was a major factor in the purchase of books

but for most the expense is far too high to bear and the target market too narrow. Authors could, of course, be demanding when it came to promoting their titles. One author wrote to Beatrice Shube, a Wiley-Interscience editor, that he had checked with "all my colleagues and have confirmed that neither they nor I have ever seen any advertising for my book." But like all scientific, technical, and medical (STM) publishers, the company persisted with a targeted approach to promotion.[124]

Bookselling in the United States in the 1950s and 1960s was much as it had been in the early 1930s when O. H. Cheney castigated it as inadequate in absolute terms and undeveloped compared to Europe. Though more numerous in absolute terms than during the Depression, booksellers had not grown as fast as the nation, its economy, or its publishing sector. Neither book retailing nor wholesaling was an easy or a particularly profitable business, and not surprisingly it was still controlled by small, privately held, and personally managed businesses. But Wiley anticipated change. Perhaps the right people read the 1959 survey by the New York University Graduate Institute of Book Publishing, which revealed that "availability was a major factor in the purchase of books." Urged on by Sullivan, Wiley adopted a new "agency" incentive program for retailers. In exchange for standing orders and display space, Wiley gave retailers extended discounts, to 32 percent, on reference and trade books. This was a smart way to counter retailers' complaints that they simply could not afford to sell, let alone stock, most titles because publishers' discounts were too small to allow them a profit. The new program was so successful—producing nearly a 50 percent increase in the number of stores stocking Wiley titles—that competitors soon copied it. Few Wiley books were blockbusters, but thanks to the agency program, which evolved over the years, many did sell through regular trade channels, including emerging chains such as Walden's and B. Dalton's.[125]

Many booksellers found that keeping Wiley's and others' technical titles on hand was a good idea for their bottom line. "A bookshop, in order to be good," one contemporary wrote, "must have a large stock of books for which there is not likely to be a great demand but for which there will be an occasional demand." Those who would be good booksellers noted, however, that to get a good stock cost at least $1,000, a major commitment (before the Great Inflation of the 1970s) for businesses so slight of capital. Moreover, technical books, which tended to be in a small format and relatively expensive, were prime targets for shoplifters. For that reason, they were often kept close to the cash register. Booksellers found that it was worthwhile to deal with Wiley and its major competitors when they offered discounts of between 20 and 40 percent. Wiley books in the earth sciences, computers, mathematics, and architecture proved especially good to stock.[126]

The biggest change in bookselling took place in Wiley's largest outlet—college bookstores. Companies such as Barnes & Noble used their campus stores to buy books back from students after they were used. Already by the mid-1960s, the used book market had become, according to economist Paul Horvitz, "an efficient, well-developed one, with books being transferred rapidly from one section of the country to another to take advantage of changes in adoptions." Technology made it easier and cheaper for the used book distribution system to function at even higher levels of efficiency. The MBS Textbook Exchange, for example, upgraded its business practices in the late 1970s by computerizing its inventory and providing its customers (bookstores) with toll-free telephone customer service.[127]

The local monopolies known as college bookstores were no help. The bookstores were happy to sell a new book at, say, $50, buy it back at the end of the semester for $25, and resell it the next term for, say, $37.50. (This was the usual spread—sell at 100 percent of list, buy back at 50 percent, and resell at 75 percent). The margins for used books, therefore, were generally higher than those for new ones. New and used textbooks were not exact substitutes—the used book might be marked up or otherwise damaged; a newer edition might appear—but they were close enough. Students (and their parents), more strapped for cash than ever due to rising tuition rates in public institutions in the 1960s and 1970s, were happy to save a few dollars if a used copy was available. By the 1970s, Wiley managers were keeping a wary eye on the used book business as it ate into their sales.

Under Brad, Wiley's marketing division consisted of both sales and advertising people. A battery of copywriters wrote the promotional materials, while layout artists did the design work. The in-house printing operation churned out several million pieces a year. In 1960, Wiley devised an in-house manual for its in-house advertising copy writers. Hook and praise blurbs, short descriptions of books for use in catalogues, dust jackets, and advertising, were important to get just right. Often authors were asked to draft them, but publishers always tweaked them—not too wordy, no clichés. To aid in the process, publishers began to ask authors to fill out extensive questionnaires, which also helped tap micromarkets, the author's areas of influence—hometowns, alma maters, professional societies—and made certain to hit all the journals, magazines, and newspapers likely to write reviews.[128]

Reviews, as ever, were a blessing and a danger. When reviews carried the reviewer's signature, the reviewer more often put some energy into reviewing, which by all accounts is not an easy process. Unsigned reviews, and a surprising percentage of signed ones, were usually bare summaries, sometimes of nothing more than the dust jacket copy. Getting books reviewed at all in general publications was difficult. Even the *New York Times* reviewed only about 20 percent of all new trade titles. Many a book that won a National Book Award went unreviewed in major national journals.

Little wonder, then, that some observers believed that by the early 1960s book reviews had lost much of their prewar cachet.[129]

Spontaneous word-of-mouth advertising was by far the best in cost-benefit terms, but as the *Wiley Bulletin* once noted, "the publisher cannot arrange such things. They just happen." (This laissez-faire attitude made authors cynical about publishers.) When book sales did not "just happen," the publisher had to decide how much to spend on advertising. As Wiley tried to explain to its authors in 1958, book advertising was different from other forms of advertising because each title was a singular product: "If we manufactured clothes-pins, there would be no question as to our profound faith in continuous promotion of the product. But the book publisher has not one product, one book. He has a hundred or more products, each requiring a special kind of promotion if it is to be sold successfully." Wiley was wary about advertising too much. Reviews, personal recommendations, and works by the same author ranked much higher in questionnaires about why people bought particular books than advertising. Moreover, the effectiveness of direct-mailing promotion was much easier to measure.[130]

Wiley found that when it came to the international market, group promotion was superior to promotion

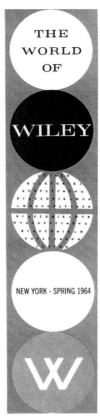

The Unity of Human Knowledge *Niels Bohr*

The question alluded to in the title for this address is as old as civilization itself, but has acquired renewed attention in our days with the increasing specialization of studies and social activities. From various sides concern has been expressed with the widespread confusion arising from the apparently divergent approaches taken by humanists and scientists to human problems, and in this connection there has even been talk about a cultural rift in modern society. We must, however, not forget that we are living in times of rapid developments in many fields of knowledge, reminiscent in such respect of the age of European Renaissance.

However great the difficulties of liberation from the medieval world view were felt at that time, the fruits of the so-called Scientific Revolution are certainly now a part of the common cultural background. In our century the immense progress of the sciences has not only greatly advanced technology and medicine but has at the same time given us an unsuspected lesson about our position as observers of that nature of which we are part ourselves. Far

from implying a schism between humanism and physical science, this development entails a message of importance for our attitude to common human problems, which — as I shall try to show — has given the old question of the unity of knowledge new perspective.

The pursuit of scientific inquiry with the aim of augmenting and ordering our experience of the world around us has through the ages proved fertile, not least for the continual progress of technology which to so great an extent has changed the frame of our daily life. While early developments of astronomy, geodesy, and metallurgy in Egypt, Mesopotamia, India, and China were primarily directed to serve requirements of the community, it is in ancient Greece that we first meet with systematic endeavours to clarify the basic principles for the description and ordering of knowledge.

In particular, we admire the Greek mathematicians, who in many respects laid the firm foundation on which later generations have built. For our theme it is important to realize that the definition of

The World of Wiley was introduced in 1963 as a replacement for the *Wiley Bulletin*, emphasizing the company's international presence. *The World of Wiley*, mailed to authors, customers, and others interested in the company, featured articles by well-known Wiley authors.

of individual titles. A month before publication, it listed its products in its monthly preview, which was distributed to 10,000 foreign bookstores and libraries. Books were also promoted via appropriate international mailing lists. In 1960, the company revamped all its mailing lists. Just three years later, though, Matheson suggested reducing the number of mailings to the chemistry list, which, at over 100,000 names, created "a formidable strain" on Wiley's promotion budget. Matheson's suggestion was to split the list into six: analytical, biochemistry, inorganic, organic, physical, and polymer chemistry. He further recommended that instead of maintaining highly specialized lists of industrial chemists, it would be better to buy such lists whenever Wiley published a treatise in applied chemistry, which included topics ranging from cosmetics to insecticides to paints. Nonetheless, direct mail remained one of the most effective ways of selling knowledge products such as Wiley's professional and reference books, which were also touted at numerous association conferences.[131]

Wiley also spread its fame via several periodicals devoted to its activities and those of its authors. In 1958, it split *Wiley Bulletin*, now almost 40 years old, into two: a new Science and Industry Edition geared toward working scientists, engineers, and managers, and an Educational Edition with a focus on higher education. In 1963, it ended the venerable publication, replacing it with *The World of Wiley*. The changed name helped to emphasize the company's rapidly growing international presence as well as its place in the world.[132]

Make, Buy, or Ally?

A key issue for publishers, as well as for other business-people, is what to do in house and what to outsource to other firms. Because publishing is ultimately an entrepreneurial venture, everything except the financial risk of putting out a book can be delegated to specialized companies. Wiley followed a middle path. It internalized its editorial and marketing departments and found it was also best to maintain its own art department and distribution facilities. The actual manufacturing of their books, on the other hand, went outside, as it had since Charles Wiley gave up printing in the company's first generation.[133]

By the mid-1960s, Wiley printed more than three million volumes annually and in a peak month shipped as many as 450,000 copies. Especially in the textbook market, where timely delivery is absolutely essential, an efficient warehouse system was both a money-saver and a business builder. Prospective authors knew they would not lose sales due to poor execution: Wiley was known in the industry to be very fast, typically filling orders within 24 hours of receipt.[134]

Wiley's shipping department occupied 40,000 square feet in the landmark Starrett Lehigh Building at 601 West 26th Street, but the slowness of the mails hampered timely processing from any single location. The solution was to establish regional warehouses. The first publisher to establish them was Macmillan, which by 1949 had warehouses in New York, Boston, Chicago, Dallas, and San Francisco. Wiley ultimately settled on Salt Lake City to service the western part of North America and the

Australasian business. That warehouse, which supplanted J. W. Stacey of San Francisco as Wiley's gateway to the West, opened in June 1962. In 1967, Wiley also opened up a new distribution center in Somerset, New Jersey, to avoid the expense and congestion of Manhattan. The 150,000-square-foot facility also housed Wiley's IBM 360-30 computer.[135]

Most orders, over 60 percent in fact, were for single copies of single titles. Most of the books that were shipped, however, were big orders for booksellers, wholesalers, and libraries. Orders came in by phone, mail, and, in this period, telex. Once received, they went into the computer for record keeping, credit checking, and inventory analysis, and finally to the warehouse for physical fulfillment, packaging, and shipment.[136]

Publishers' distribution systems were doubly challenging because they also had to work in reverse. Unlike many industries, where customers, retailers, or wholesalers could return only damaged or defective goods, in publishing books could be returned in resalable condition if they were unsold or unwanted. As noted earlier, Wiley had long allowed individuals to take books on a trial basis, many of which came back. Like other publishers, it had also long allowed retailers and wholesalers to return books for credit on their accounts. The return policy arose and persisted for the good reason that it made sense given the uncertain demand for many titles. Without it, bookstores and book wholesalers would have been fewer and/or smaller. The return system kept the risk with the publishers.

Of course, returns caused endless logistical and financial headaches for publishers, who never knew for certain how many books that left the warehouse might be back. For Wiley, however, returns were never of the magnitude faced by many trade houses. In 1957, $640,582.83 worth of books, or 8.78 percent of gross sales, came back to Wiley. By 1959, the absolute figure had risen to $844,325.98, but the relative figure had dropped slightly

PROFILE

JOHN BALBALIS

Authors loved John Balbalis for his extraordinary knowledge of all kinds of subjects and his ability to make art meaningful to students. His work combined accuracy, clarity, and beauty to reveal the science in each subject. His office was testimony to the range of his skills. There he had a rendered skeleton and a small painting of a baboon's head with the most exquisite reds and blues on its face and nose, every detail and each hair so precise that only close inspection would reveal it as a painting, not a photograph. There were also perspective charts and ellipses. A ball-and-stick chemistry model served to provide perspective in the 3D rendering of chemistry structures. Balbalis, who had studied chemistry at New York University, established illustration styles for various books; for priority titles, he provided each figure with detailed instructions for the artist. He also rendered many of the realistic figures himself. He later created a library of art on different subjects that could be used for multiple projects. His talents were not limited to illustration, however, as he also mounted a solo exhibit of abstract paintings in a New York gallery. He loved opera and gladly gave away issues of *Opera* magazine.

John Balbalis, Wiley "illustrator extraordinaire" (at left) reviews illustration specs with John Durbin, author of *College Algebra and Trigonometry* (1984), in 1979.

to 8.32 percent of gross sales. Until the mid-1960s, Wiley returns hovered around the 10 percent mark, while industry averages ranged from 35 to 55 percent. By the 1970s, in part due to the growth of the second-hand textbook business, returns started to move upward. Many returns were remaindered and sold for a pittance the following year, often to purchasers in developing countries. Warehousing costs rose and tax and accounting considerations encouraged publishers to shred their returns.[137]

Illustration was another area where Wiley could ill afford delays or mistakes. Wiley formed its own art department in 1942 to reduce reliance on freelancers of uncertain quality. By the mid-1950s, it turned out more than 14,000 illustrations annually. Headed by George Flohn and 25 draftsmen, the Wiley art department was known for its quality. Setting the standard was John Balbalis, who, like Wiley's other illustrators, turned authors' rough sketches into professional illustrations. For some books, like Edwin Colbert's *Evolution of the Vertebrates*, extensive face-to-

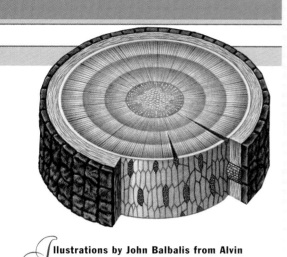

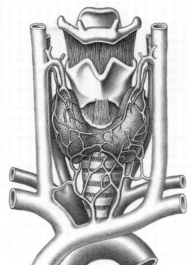

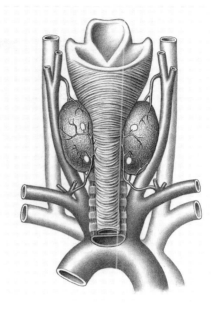

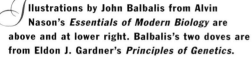

Illustrations by John Balbalis from Alvin Nason's *Essentials of Modern Biology* are above and at lower right. Balbalis's two doves are from Eldon J. Gardner's *Principles of Genetics*.

Fantail

Bluette

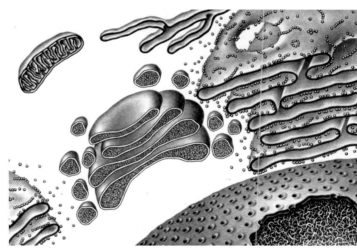

face coordination between author and artist was necessary. For others, a few sketches were sufficient and efficient. By the late 1950s, Wiley, unlike many other publishers, had given up hand lettering on illustrations in favor of type stamping. The result was more consistent and legible captions, legends, labels, and the like.[138]

Although computers played an early role in information management, their impact on book production came more slowly. Early electronic word processing programs had their uses, but book publishing was generally not among them. Xerox copy machines, which greatly reduced the cost of photoduplication, proliferated in offices of all types, including publishing houses, but mostly as an aid to the administrative and business side of publishing, not for most companies as a substitute for the printing press.[139]

The first change came in typesetting. By the late 1950s, Wiley's outside compositor, the Machine Composition Company of Boston, began using the Photon, a new computer-driven electromechanical-optical typesetting machine that Wiley had helped to design.[140]

THE *Printing craft*

THE COLD TYPE REVOLUTION

Photocomposition was the first real breakthrough in composition since the Linotype and Monotype machines. Sometimes called "cold type" in contrast to the hot metal (cast metal type) used in Linotype machines, photocomposition swept the industry in the 1970s. The technology evolved rapidly; by the 1980s, hot metal was obsolete in the publishing industry, although it was still used for some specialty typesetting.

*S*egmented discs holding type fonts on a DYMO Pacesetter photocompositor.

Initially, photocomposition was driven through phototypesetters, which were film-output versions of the old Linotype machines. A beam of light was projected through a film negative image of an individual letter and collected on film. The earliest photocomposition machines of the 1950s, such as the Photon, Mergenthaler VIP, and Harris-Fototronic TxT, used photomechanical processes. The Photon, for example, used a standard typewriter keyboard for input. The machines employed a variety of mats, drums, and discs holding character negatives, moving them into position to project the type onto the photographic material. These early machines could not change text size and font very easily, and their speed was limited by the mechanical action to about 20 characters per second. As the machines evolved, the mechanical processes began to be replaced by electronic ones, and the speed improved dramatically.

By the 1970s, photocomposition machines such as the VideoComp and Fototronic 7000 used cathode ray tubes, or CRTs, to project images onto photographic paper or film. The images were composed of dots or line strokes, which varied in degree of resolution. These machines were capable of astonishingly high speeds, ranging from 6,000 to 10,000 characters per second. Some machines used a computer to control hyphenation and line justification.

The results were printed on galleys, long columns of text alone, without photos or illustrations in place, which could be proofread before page makeup began. Pages were created by cutting up the galleys and pasting them onto boards. The boards were photographed, negatives produced, and film negatives of art work cut into place. Individual pages were then taped together to form signatures (groups of pages) for plating and printing. Over the years, technological improvements resulted in greater sophistication and speed.

Photocomposition systems not only increased the speed of typesetting but also allowed for easier corrections and easier storage of composed type for later revision. They also permitted more flexibility in design, as art, tables, and other text elements could be positioned by a makeup person using positive film. The big *business* advantage of the Photon and other phototypesetting equipment was that they reduced the cost of typesetting heavily illustrated books or books containing complicated mathematical formulas.[141]

The pace of change in printing technology was slower. Some improvements had taken place in the manufacturing of books in long press runs, but since the early twentieth century nothing had occurred for the short-run book. For short runs, books in the 1950s, 1960s, and 1970s were printed directly from type, whether composed on Linotype, Monotype, or a modern photocompositor. For longer runs, offset printing was common: Type was used to create plates, which increasingly were made from cheaper and lighter plastic or rubber rather than metal. Images (words and art) are burned onto plates, which are then dampened by water and then ink. The ink adheres to the image area and the water to the non-image area. The image is then transferred to a rubber blanket and from the rubber blanket to the paper. Gravure printing was (and is) more common for very long runs. In gravure printing, ink is collected in wells etched into printing cylinders. The ink is transferred directly to the paper. About 80 percent of Wiley books are printed by offset.[142]

The reel stand of the Sunday 3000 web press, which splices one roll of paper to the next at full speed without stopping the presses. Courtesy of RR Donnelley in Jefferson City, Missouri, and its employees, who have printed this book.

Gravure web press (below)

Through the 1960s, the Photon and other photocomposition machines had little impact on the time between the final manuscript and the arrival of the book in the warehouse; it still took at least nine months. Estimating length and cost generally took a month, as did design, composition, author proofing and indexing, printing, and binding. Correction of type generally took only two weeks, but unexpected delays anywhere in the process—a dilatory author, insufficient paper supplies, a new editor—could easily delay publication another month or two. Brad lamented the time it took to get a book into print. "Too long," he complained. Too many books were obsolete by the time they were published.[143]

Wiley had no production facilities for paper, cloth, or ink of its own; instead it sourced goods and services from over 20 major suppliers in the late 1950s. Outsourcing production to specialized firms usually

> The Great Inflation of 1968–1981 caused the prices of everything, from paper to labor to borrowed money, to jump unpredictably.

paid off but at a risk. In 1966, for instance, shortages of paper, cloth, and printing presses caused delays. The Great Inflation of 1968–1981 caused the prices of everything from paper to labor to borrowed money to jump unpredictably. Relative prices were even less predictable than the rise in average prices. So in 1974, for instance, paper prices soared 40 percent, printing costs jumped 15 percent, and binding went up by 12 percent, but composition costs rose hardly at all. Such volatility made it difficult to plan far ahead or to minimize the overall production costs of any given title. Unlike the situation just after World War II, however, publishers found for a time that they could raise prices to keep pace without injuring unit sales (the number of books sold).[144]

An essential part of the production process that proved especially resistant to outsourcing was editing. Wiley's authors' guide, *A Guide for Wiley-Interscience*

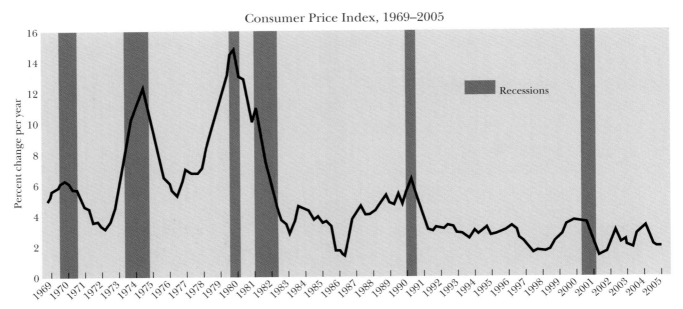

Consumer Price Index, 1969–2005

Source: Bureau of Labor Statistics, Macroeconomic Advisors.

Guidelines for Corrections 85

FIGURE 34 *Keyboarding manuscript and making corrections in photocomposition. (a) Initial keyboarding of manuscript. (b) Reading proof against manuscript. (c) Keyboarding author's corrections on video display terminal. (d) Stripping in corrections on reproduction proof. Note that this step requires handwork.*

tions seem to be exceeding your 15 percent allowance, we check the proofs against the edited manuscript, determine the cause of the corrections, and send you a letter advising you that they appear to be excessive.

HIGH COST OF PROOF CORRECTIONS The typesetter bills us for proof corrections on a time basis, thus making them disproportionately expensive. Even the smallest change requires a number of intricate and exacting steps. In photocomposition—the most common typesetting method—a typical way of making a correction is to keyboard the line or lines that need correcting on a perforated tape together with the necessary codes for typeface, type size, and line length (see Figure 34). The operator loads the photocomposing machine with the appropriate type fonts and runs the tape. The material is then exposed on film, which is developed and proofread. Next the pasteup artist locates the line or lines that are being corrected, cuts them from the galley or page, and pastes in the newly set correction.

GUIDELINES FOR CORRECTIONS To prevent unnecessary changes that might exceed your alteration allowance, we suggest the following guidelines for proof corrections.

■ Confine your corrections to errors.

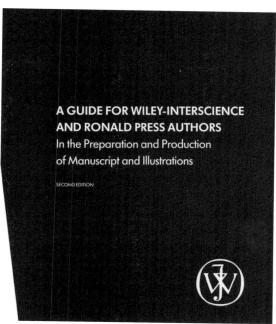

A GUIDE FOR WILEY-INTERSCIENCE AND RONALD PRESS AUTHORS
In the Preparation and Production of Manuscript and Illustrations

SECOND EDITION

Guide for Wiley-Interscience and Ronald Press Authors: In the Preparation and Production of Manuscript and Illustrations laid out the basic guidelines for preparation of the master manuscript, including everything from paper to page numbers, headings to tables and figures, and footnotes to bibliographies.

and Ronald Press Authors: In the Preparation and Production of Manuscript and Illustrations (2nd ed., 1979), the direct descendant of the original *The Manuscript: A Guide for Its Preparation* described in Chapter 5, captured the company's production values. By the end of Brad's time, the 134-page document, the work of over a dozen Wiley employees and outside counsel, was being sent routinely to all its authors. It laid out the basic guidelines for preparation of the master manuscript, including everything from paper to page numbers, headings to tables and figures, and footnotes to bibliographies. Joseph Pulitzer's famous admonition suffused it: "Put it before them briefly so they will read it, clearly so they will appreciate it, picturesquely so they will remember it, and, above all, accurately so they will be guided by its light."[145]

*D*ebbie Herbert, head of the copyediting department, facing the camera.

Transition

Despite the company's overall strong domestic and international growth and improved operations, Wiley experienced a certain amount of unease as it watched house after house go public only to become conglomerates or be swallowed up by one: D. C. Heath fell to Raytheon in 1966 and Xerox purchased Ginn & Company in 1968. Publishing stocks soared as investors and corporate suitors sought them out. (Much conglomeration would be undone in later years; Wiley, for instance, bought Ginn, Xerox's textbook division, in 1975.) Corporate managers had been induced to find growth, even at the expense of profits, and so many of them did. It took two decades for this cycle of the conglomeration movement to play out, and until it did Wiley employees could only wonder if Wiley might be next, either to become a conglomerate or be purchased by one.[146]

By 1971, Wiley had $2.5 million in net income on sales of $35 million: no giant but not small either.

> Wiley watched house after house go public only to become conglomerates or be swallowed up by one.

Not just the size of the company but its complexity demanded change. John Wiley had been able to restart his father's business while hardly yet a man. In 1968, when Brad was 58, family succession did not look promising, at least in the short term: daughter Deborah had just joined the company as a secretary (the kind who answers phones and types letters), and sons Brad II and Peter were starting their own publication on the West Coast. The situation would begin to change in the next decade. Deborah became progressively a traveler, a social sciences editor, a financial analyst, and a business manager. She was elected to the board in 1978, where she was joined by Brad II the next year.[147]

Brad wanted to end the intergenerational uncertainty and malaise that gripped Wiley every three decades or so. Trained in management at Harvard, long known for its attention to the past, Brad was a student of history and politics. (He majored at Colgate in economics and literature and minored in history and politics.)

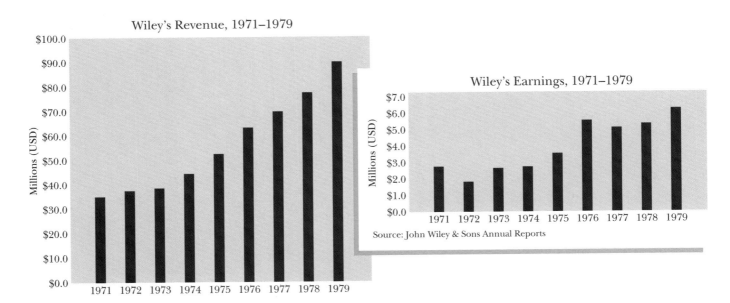

Wiley's Revenue, 1971–1979

Source: John Wiley & Sons Annual Reports

Wiley's Earnings, 1971–1979

Source: John Wiley & Sons Annual Reports

He realized that family ownership and control was fraught with risks. An untimely death—too early but also too late—or the absence of an heir apparent, or any number of other family-related issues could destroy the company, as it had come close to doing several times in the past. He also knew that companies like Wiley's long-time competitor Van Nostrand that remained one-man shows were doomed. So as early as the 1950s, he had fostered professional management, anticipating that highly trained and trusted professionals would manage the company's day-to-day operations while the family would retain ownership and ultimate control. At the time, he and Hamilton had written their wills and set up a series of trusts that would ensure that ownership would remain in family hands. What role his children might play in the future remained unclear at this point. What was clear was that Wiley should remain a family firm, but a family firm with a very sophisticated team of senior managers.[148]

Brad's vision more or less became reality. All three of his children came to play crucial roles in Wiley, but unlike their father or other forebears, they would not run the company themselves on a daily basis. It had simply grown too large, too complex, and too valuable to leave to the fate of family. When Neilly became chief executive officer in 1979, he became the first non-Wiley to head the company.

The era during which Brad served as CEO witnessed the most dramatic changes in Wiley's history. The Interscience acquisition and the resulting recapitalization of the company marked the end after 155 years

of Wiley as a privately held family enterprise. Wiley's successes in the capital market precipitated an aggressive acquisitions strategy, which, though occasionally successful, for the most part produced disappointing results. However, the company's underlying strength in its core publishing areas was such that it continued to grow at a fast enough pace that the company's shareholders benefited from Brad's and his team's ambitions. Wiley had moved aggressively and successfully into educational publishing, with student enrollments growing at a healthy pace—for a while. The Interscience acquisition was transformative, but most efforts to reach out to new markets, whether by moving into high school publishing or acquiring a training company (Contemporary Systems) and a provider of information for the library market (Becker & Hayes), were not. In an expansive era, Brad and his colleagues were willing to take the risks and suffer the consequences, which they did while building the underlying business. Internationally, the company grew at an extraordinary pace, setting up subsidiaries, forming joint ventures, opening sales offices, and exploring new possibilities in every corner of the globe. The decade and a half after the launch of *Sputnik* in 1957 was a uniquely bountiful period for publishers. If you published a good book, it was going to sell. In 1957, Wiley sales were $8.9 million. By 1979, they had reached $90.4 million. Over more than two decades, Wiley had grown at 11.1% per annum. As Wiley approached its one hundred and seventy-fifth year, the prospects for publishers would darken.

> **Wiley and Hamilton set up a series of trusts that would ensure that ownership would remain in family hands.**

A Turbulent Decade: Experimentation and Survival 1979–1989

Chapter Seven

❋

The Challenges Ahead

The year 1979 was a historic turning point for John Wiley & Sons. Bradford Wiley, the sole member of the fifth generation of the family to work at the company, and the sixth Wiley to run the business, stepped aside as president and chief executive officer to be replaced by Andrew H. Neilly Jr. After 172 years, Neilly was the first nonfamily member to hold this senior position.

In New York, Wiley's senior managers looked out at a world that at times appeared threatening, at times full of promise. The city itself was recovering from near bankruptcy in 1975. Central Park wallowed in neglect, as did many of the city's poorest neighborhoods. When, on December 8, 1980, Beatles member John Lennon was slain by a delusional stalker outside his apartment building on the Upper West Side, it reinforced the view that crime in New York was ubiquitous. Racial violence suffused the city's very atmosphere. Crack, a potent and cheap variant of cocaine, was ruining the lives of countless young people even as the AIDS epidemic was killing at a frightening rate and draining the city's coffers. Against this troubled social backdrop, New York was experiencing a painful shift from an industrial and commercial economy to a more fluid service- and technology-based postindustrial economy. Many of the city's old-line businesses, especially in its manufacturing districts, were disappearing. At the same time, however, these major changes also brought renewal. In neighborhoods like SoHo and Tribeca, artists began to turn the husks of

former manufacturing lofts into fashionable dwellings. New York, despite its problems, remained a center of creativity and a haven for the literate and the literary—which, of course, was good for publishing, and particularly a publisher like Wiley, which planned to benefit from the knowledge needs of a shifting economy.

The U.S. economy in the late 1970s and early 1980s was battered by stagflation, a confounding combination of inflation and economic stagnation.

Still, the U.S. and global economic situations remained disheartening. In the United States, the aftershock of the Vietnam War led to the curtailment of public spending for education, libraries, and research laboratories, the same institutions that had fueled the expansion of publishers like Wiley since the launch of Sputnik in 1957. Following the war with Israel in 1973, the Arab world began to use oil as a weapon, triggering global inflation. In 1979 alone, oil prices would double. With economic growth limping along, economists talked of the twin dangers of stagflation—a perverse combination of rising prices and rising unemployment.

Anyone consulting the proverbial tea leaves would have come away perplexed. On the first day of 1979, the United States and the People's Republic of China signed documents calling for the normalization of diplomatic relations after 30 years of estrangement, but six weeks later China attacked Vietnam. And what about Japan? Was it a strategic partner of the United States, or had it become a new, menacing economic hegemon? What would Wiley make of the Four Tigers, as the newly emerging economies of Hong Kong, Singapore, South Korea, and Taiwan were called? After Islamic revolutionaries

deposed the Shah of Iran, the Ayatollah Khomeini announced the formation of a new ruling body known as the Council of Islamic Revolution. In November of that year, Iran's Republican Guard surrounded the U.S. embassy in Tehran, taking its occupants hostage. Saddam Hussein had just come to power in Iraq. And four months before the Iranians seized the American embassy, President Jimmy Carter signed the first secret directive providing aid to the opponents of the pro-Soviet regime in Afghanistan. In a classic case of what became known as blowback, some of those funds and tons of weapons would make their way into the hands of such groups as the Taliban and Osama Bin Laden's al Qaeda network.

At Wiley, things started off well enough in this economically turbulent decade. Revenue and earnings grew steadily through fiscal year 1982, with record sales of $137 million producing record profits of $10 million. That same year the company celebrated its 175th anniversary in high style, with numerous parties culminating in a gala dinner party at the American Museum of Natural History in New York. The guest list was a Who's Who from Wiley, the publishing world, and scholarship generally. Publishers Weekly offered a nice write-up: "The doom and gloom one often picks up elsewhere along Publishers' Row," the PW reporter remarked, "is nowhere apparent at Wiley in the summer of 1982." The family patriarch, Brad Wiley, was quoted as saying: "I guess you can say that we Wileys are survivors."

The company published a new book on its history, accompanied by a pamphlet titled "Two Thousand and Seven," in which leading experts guessed what their fields might look like a quarter century into the future. The most prescient line in the pamphlet, which predicted numerous advances that have not yet come to pass, came from the nuclear physicist and Wiley author Herman Feshbach: "Only fools and knaves provide predictions with apparent confidence." He was talking about nuclear physics, but he could just as well have been talking about the predictability of Wiley's future.[2]

In the 1980s, the entire enterprise system of the United States was in flux, book publishing no less than other traditional industries. Another wave of media conglomeration in the 1980s brought an end to the independence of many publishers, including several family firms of fame and long standing. Wiley presented a tempting target, too, and there were times when many wondered whether Wiley would in fact survive. Meanwhile, the company's largest market was shifting, as a precipitous slowdown in the rate of college enrollments hit hard at textbook sales. Wiley responded with what would

prove to be an overzealous diversification strategy. Best-laid plans proved hard to implement. A tough former General Electric manager hired in the late 1980s to turn the company around quickly ran athwart of Wiley's many-layered collegial culture and was replaced. But in the end, Wiley possessed enough assets—a strong backlist, a superior reputation, skilled employees, and family owners devoted to maintaining organizational as well as editorial independence—to right itself and press on.

175th Anniversary Party
at the American Museum
of Natural History

269

175 YEARS OF
1807 $\bigcirc$ 1982
PUBLISHING

Facing Uncertainty

Wiley's authors were legends, its books prizewinners that sold in aggregate millions of copies each year. Even the indexes of its books won awards. Quality joined quantity in a company that seemed to have it all. Brad Wiley, who remained as chairman of the board after Andrew Neilly's appointment as president and CEO, said in 1979 that it would not be hard for Wiley to double in size in five years. He was right, and it did, though in large part because of inflation. It was a real worry, at Wiley and elsewhere, whether economic growth would ever again be as robust as it had been for most of the period following World War II.[3]

By the end of the 1970s, the creeping "normal" inflation (under 3 percent) of the postwar period had accelerated to 11.28 percent per annum (in 1980, it spiked to 13.48 percent), forcing up interest rates, crimping investment, and making it harder to forecast costs and revenues. Facing stagflation, everyone from Jimmy Carter to Henry Ford II proclaimed that the days of sustained economic growth were over. The new Federal Reserve chairman, Paul Volcker, slashed the money supply in 1981, taming inflation but inducing American's deepest recession since the 1930s. To most people and corporations alike, the medicine was worse than the disease.[4]

As a newly minted Wiley CEO, Neilly faced some daunting challenges. Neither he nor his colleagues could do anything about stagflation, but Neilly recognized its impact on publishing, particularly textbook publishing, and would struggle to deal with it. Beyond inflation was the problem of college enrollments. During the 1960s, the years that Wiley moved aggressively into educational publishing, student enrollments grew at a healthy pace. Suddenly, in 1975, the curve turned downward, bounced back for a year, and then flattened, recovered, and fell again for three years in the 1980s before recovering its upward momentum in 1986.

Publishers like Wiley faced an ever-changing and increasingly difficult competitive terrain. The 1980s

proved to be an era of unprecedented consolidation among book publishers and media firms more broadly conceived. The consolidation that began in the late 1950s and introduced new players, including both media conglomerates and their nonmedia counterparts, into the industry in the 1960s and 1970s, continued into the next decade. Prentice Hall bought Appleton-Century-Crofts; Random House bought CRM. American Express failed in its bid to buy McGraw-Hill, but Thomson, then a Canadian newspaper company, was able to buy up Chilton and Litton's publishing assets. Bertelsmann, a German publisher, bought Bantam in 1980 and Doubleday in 1986. Holt, Rinehart & Winston, with its strong business imprint, the Dryden Press, went to the Von Holtzbrinck Group, another German concern, in 1985. In that same year, Reed, a British firm, acquired R. R. Bowker, and Time bought Scott, Foresman. In 1986, Harcourt Brace Jovanovich purchased the CBS book division. International Thomson absorbed South-Western Publishing, and Gulf & Western acquired Silver Burdett. In 1987, Australian Rupert Murdoch's News

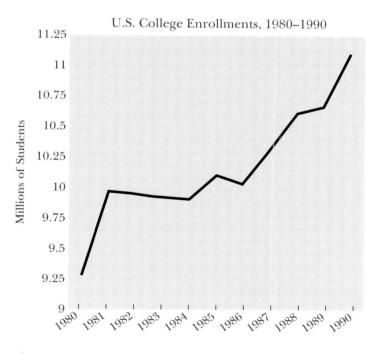

U.S. College Enrollments, 1980–1990

Source: U.S. Census Bureau, Table A-7. College Enrollment of Students 14 Years Old and Over, by Type of College, Attendance Status, Age, and Gender: October 1970 to 2004

Selected Publishing Mergers and Acquisitions, 1979–1989

Company	Events
by Advance Publications	• Random House 1980 • Times Books 1984 • Crown 1988
Bertelsmann	• Bantam 1980 • Doubleday 1986
Thomson	• Delmar 1981 • South-Western 1986
Gulf & Western	• Ginn and Co. 1982 • Prentice Hall 1984 (merged with Simon & Schuster 1985) • Silver Burdett 1986 • Renamed Paramount Communications 1989
Von Holtzbrinck	• Holt, Rinehart and Winston (trade) 1985 • Scientific American (including W. H. Freeman) 1986
Reed	• R. R. Bowker 1985
Time	• Scott, Foresman 1985 (merging with Time's Little, Brown) • Time merges with Warner 1989
Harcourt, Brace Jovanovich	• CBS book division (W. B. Saunders and Holt, Rinehart and Winston) 1986
Wolters Kluwer	• Kluwer and Wolters–Samsom merge to form Wolters Kluwer 1987
News Corporation (founded 1980)	• Harper & Row 1987 • Harper & Row merges with William Collins & Sons, forming HarperCollins 1989 • HarperCollins acquires Scott, Foresman and Little, Brown (from Time Warner) 1989
McGraw-Hill	• Random House higher education 1988
Pearson	• Addison-Wesley 1988
Wiley	• Liss 1989
Maxwell Communications	• Macmillan 1988 • Jossey-Bass 1989
	1980 1985 1990

Sources: *The Columbia Electronic Encyclopedia 6th edition, 2006* Columbia University Press (website)

Mergers, Acquisitions and Access: STM Publishing Today, by Kathleen Robertson. Library and Information Services in Astronomy IV July 2-5, 2002

Company websites.

The Academic Publishing Industry, A Story of Merger and Acquisition, by Mary H. Monroe. Prepared for the Association of Research Libraries (website)

Corporation bought Harper & Row; and in 1988, Hachette, a French publisher, bought Grolier, and Pearson, a British firm, picked up Addison-Wesley.

New to the acquisition scene were foreign publishers, such as Bertelsmann, Reed, and Von Holtzbrinck, all of them angling for a piece of the world's largest English-language market. The American market first drew the attention of European publishers in the years after World War II. In a striking parallel to the thinking of Brad and his colleagues in the 1940s about research in the postwar world, Springer-Verlag, the German publisher, decided at the same time that "the shift of research centers to the Anglo-Saxon region, especially to the United States, had made the English language the lingua franca of the scientific world." After discussing possible co-publishing arrangements with Wiley-Interscience and other publishers, Springer opened an office in New York's Flatiron Building in 1964 from which it sold its new English-language journals. Springer began keeping records of books published in the United States in 1977 (1,873). By the end of the 1980s, that number had increased to 10,285, while journal production grew from 1,731 to 7,176 issues in the same period.[5]

Larger and larger firms generated more cash to invest in publishing projects, posing a clear competitive threat to Wiley, which remained relatively small in a world of media giants. In January 1988, Brad II listed the threat of "globalized competition" as a major concern. There was also a proliferation of new players, such as CRM Books, before it was sold to Random House; Boyd & Fraser; Dellen; PWS-Kent; Warren, Gorham & Lamont; and a new textbook publishing operation set up by the Times Mirror newspaper company from Los Angeles.[6]

The proliferation of publishers made publishing decisions in all markets much more complex than previously, when Wiley needed only to track the doings of firms like Addison-Wesley, Harper & Row, Houghton Mifflin, Macmillan, McGraw-Hill, Prentice Hall, and Scott, Foresman.[7] The gentlemanly days of a cozy publishing club, where most people knew one another, where the competition was less likely to challenge a company in its dominant subject areas, and where the poaching of authors was deemed bad form, were gone. Now, Wiley, with its increasingly diverse list, had to contend vigorously with dozens of nonfiction English-language publishers.[8]

After the government's tight money policies finally broke the back of the Great Inflation in 1982, the economy would expand for the next seven years. As financing became easier, companies in traditional industries either would continue to undergo major restructuring or would disappear under the pressures of global competition. In contrast, for publishing houses, leaner academic and corporate library budgets and lower per capita personal expenditures on books would take their toll. Although public libraries survived—nearly 15,000 were in operation in the United States in 1990—funding to acquire new books, especially less popular titles, would shrink to the vanishing point. And although the United States possessed over 3,000 college libraries, their rate of book buying would also fall precipitously.[9]

Finally, there was the question of what impact technology, something that Wiley had watched carefully since the 1950s, would have on the publishing business. In 1979, Steve Jobs, one of Apple's founders, made his famed visit—the so-called daylight raid—to Xerox PARC in Palo Alto, California, leading to Apple's commercialization of product research, which Xerox never took advantage of. In 1981, when IBM announced that it would run Microsoft DOS exclusively in its latest PC, the market for personal computers was still small and fragmented,

> New to the acquisition scene were foreign publishers.

Time Magazine's 1982 "Man" of the Year was the computer.

but growing quickly. The next year, *Time* nominated as "Machine of the Year" the computer, which in exaggerated Time-speak the editors claimed had "beeped and blipped [its] way into the American office, the American school, and the American home."[10]

To the external uncertainties had to be added an important internal question for Wiley—the matter of managerial succession. Neilly was the first nonfamily member to head the firm, but he had already worked at Wiley for 37 years, and though he was just beginning his term as CEO, he wouldn't be there forever. As chairman, family patriarch Brad, who had been at Wiley a decade longer and was now 69 years old, was responsible for governance. He spent the rest of his time on industry affairs and international aspects of the business, including

the possibilities of a new publishing venture in China. Was Neilly to serve as a placeholder for the next family CEO? Deborah Wiley was taking on additional managerial responsibilities, which many saw as part of her grooming to succeed Neilly. If not, then how would the devolution of management authority from family to hired professionals work? And if the Wileys were to withdraw, employees might well wonder what would become of the company's long history of independence.

Neilly took on his new post just as upbeat stories in high-profile venues like *Barron's* touted Wiley's good fortunes. An August 1978 Wiley press release announced record sales and earnings, to which someone affixed (for internal circulation) a cartoon of a tycoon surrounded by bags of cash. "Now what?" he wondered out loud with clear self-satisfaction. What, indeed?[11]

In what could be read as a harbinger of the next decade, on the eve of Neilly's appointment as CEO, Wiley was confronted by the first test of the paternalism that had characterized the company's relations with its nonprofessional employees. Nationwide, many industries were enduring their worst labor problems since the Great Depression. Living conditions for average workers worsened as relentless price increases for basic household expenses rose, along with a spike in energy prices. The appearance of rising corporate profits looked to workers less like a sign of economic security than of management and shareholder greed. In late 1978, hourly workers, represented by the Teamsters Union in Wiley's Eastern Distribution Center (EDC) in Somerset, New Jersey, demanded a cost-of-living increase. An anonymous letter directed to Wiley's senior management described the workers' frustration. "Just in case you may have forgotten how it feels to be on the bottom instead of the top, employees who feel they are underpaid, underbenefited, and not cared about will not perform for their employer as they would if they were," the letter said. "The dollar is steadily decreasing, prices [are] increasing *every* day and we are still paid the same amount." Wiley's management responded that its compensation package—wages and benefits—was competitive. It was not a winning argument.[12]

Negotiations failed to produce a collective bargaining agreement, and on March 20, 1979, 68 of the EDC's approximately 150 workers declared a strike. Supporters picketed and interrupted shipments by hurling bottles, nails, and obscenities, frightening both suppliers and customers, and driving some nonunion employees to quit. The union's representatives stopped negotiating and stormed out of meetings. In the months-long waiting game that followed, back orders and extra expenses piled up. New York employees were diverted from their usual duties to help out at the warehouse. Wiley's Western Distribution Center in Utah picked up some of the slack, but the company lost valuable editorial and administrative time, and its reputation with some authors and distributors suffered. Finally, in December 1979, Wiley brought the strike to an end by delivering an ultimatum to the striking workers: either work or be fired. Some quit; others were terminated for misconduct. A reliable group of 17 workers were asked to orient new hires, and a private security firm was engaged to protect the facility from further violence. In the final analysis, the troubles at the EDC were part of an industry trend. The Teamsters, in particular, redoubled their efforts to unionize the distribution centers of other publishers, as the industry, along with the nation, was forced to cope with mounting labor unrest. With the strike ended, Neilly and his team could again focus on the business of publishing.[13]

Neilly's Imprint

Neilly inherited a company organized into four entities: Educational, Professional, Medical, and International. In 1979, together they generated $90,365,000 net sales. The

> To the external uncertainties had to be added an internal question . . . the matter of managerial succession.

Educational Group, which published for the college and occupational markets (described by Wiley as the junior college and nonclassroom continuing-education markets), accounted for 53 percent of its total sales. The Professional Group came next, followed by a small Medical Division. Thirty-five percent of what Wiley as a whole published was sold outside of the United States.[14]

As Wiley recovered from the strike, Neilly was determined to place his own imprint on the firm. He would work with Brad to reshape the company's board, adding Nils A. Kindwall, senior vice president and chief financial officer of Freeport Minerals Company; Robert Sproull, Wiley author and president of the University of Rochester (Neilly's alma mater, where he now served on the board); and Allen Fernald, Neilly's friend and an experienced publishing executive, who had moved from college publishing to ownership of Down East Publications in Maine.

Two years into his tenure, in April 1981, Neilly and his senior managers unveiled a strategic plan for fiscal year 1982 (May 1, 1981, to April 30, 1982), a document that summed up their intentions. Among the plan's major assumptions were that:

- high worldwide inflation would continue
- college enrollments in the developed world would "decline in total, but remain stable in Wiley's strongest subject areas"
- the number of highly trained specialists would increase, with a "related rise in the demand for training materials"
- "new technologies," such as electronic dissemination of information, would "initially complement hard copy publishing," but would "begin to erode growth in the period and may replace some traditional methods"
- "buyer resistance to high prices of books" would accelerate, "especially as alternatives become more economical"[15]

PROFILE

ANDREW H. NEILLY JR.

Andrew H. Neilly Jr. was a bridge between the family-run Wiley and the professionally managed company that had begun to take shape with the ascendancy of the fourth generation of Wileys beginning in the 1920s. Kindly and book-loving, with a wide range of intellectual interests, Neilly also rose in the ranks as Wiley managers became more businesslike in their approach to publishing. As CEO, he inherited a company that was established in its ways but aware that changing times would require new approaches to knowledge publishing.[16]

Neilly was hired by Wiley in 1947 as a traveler; after two years in that role, he joined the New York office as an assistant sales manager. By 1955, he was manager of college sales. He attended Harvard Business School in 1964, and in 1968, after stints in advertising and marketing, he was named executive vice president. In 1971, he became president and chief operating officer.[17]

Like Brad, Neilly was an industry presence. He served as chairman of the Association of American Publishers and was on the board of Columbia University Press. He was a member of the International Publishers Association, eventually becoming president; and was the first chairman of the Book Industry Study Group, an organization that brought together publishers, retailers, distributors, libraries, and industry service providers to promote and support research in and about publishing.

Andrew H. Neilly Jr. was born in Baltimore but grew up in Rochester, New York. In 1947, after a stint in the service, Neilly graduated from the University of Rochester with an English degree. On the advice of his vocational advisor, he left Rochester, whose labor market was dominated by Kodak and other optical behemoths that hired mostly science majors, and headed for Manhattan. Between examinations and graduation, he landed a job with Wiley.

Textbook sales for the industry were projected to grow at 7 to 8 percent for the rest of the decade, while industry sales of professional books were projected to grow at 16 percent until 1985 and then decline for the next five years, to 11 percent. In comparison to these numbers, the plan called for Wiley's sales to grow at 16 percent per annum. All numbers included 8 percent inflation. Wiley revenues had grown at 14 percent from fiscal year 1976 to 1981; and when measured against its eight major competitors, Wiley consistently ranked either third or fourth among its class of publishers in sales, profits, and return on shareholders' equity. The plan called for:[18]

- investing in the educational and professional markets while divesting low-growth or low-profit segments

- improving profit margins and return on income to "the levels of our more successful competitors" and providing "the financial strength to fund entry into new businesses"

- initiating "modest investments in faster growing technology-based domestic and international information and educational businesses, which complement our present market strengths"

- increasing investment levels "using funds generated from harvesting lower growth traditional product lines," as the use of new technologies expanded

*N*eilly's leadership team, shown here in 1982, consisted of (from left) Robert T. Douglas, vice president, Educational Group; Kenneth Collins, vice president, Professional Group; Edward Reynolds, vice president, Finance and Administration; Robert Hauck, vice president, Corporate Development and Planning; Neilly; and Charles Stoll, vice president, International.

The plan acknowledged a gap of $28 million in revenue between levels projected for fiscal year 1986 and the stated goal of $250 million in sales for that year. "The gap will be filled," according to the plan, "by such new businesses as personal computer software, subscription-based publishing services, industrial training, and others." Wiley was "willing to accept dilution of earnings in order to achieve [its] long-range goals."[19]

Although Wiley's balance sheet was robust enough to support reasonably priced acquisitions, Neilly was still concerned about Wiley's ability to move forward. There were questions of predictability: change might be more rapid than expected; technology might not have the impact envisioned; profit erosion might be greater than anticipated, leaving insufficient resources for developing and acquiring as planned. The final, and perhaps most important, question was: Did management have the capability to execute the plan?

Given his sense that technology was both a threat and a new opportunity, Neilly assembled a high-profile advisory group known as the Research and Development Committee to serve as an internal think tank. Chaired by J.C.R. Licklider, an eminent M.I.T. computer science and electrical engineering professor and Internet visionary, the committee also included Peter Jensen, an engineering professor from the Georgia Institute of Technology, and William R. (Bert) Sutherland, a consultant who had directed research at Xerox Research Park in Palo Alto. The R&D committee's mission was to provide Wiley with advice about how new technologies would impact research, education, and business while offering ideas and support for the development of publishing tools and new products that would employ technology. The committee reviewed new product developments, guided Neilly and his team about investments in the company's electronic infrastructure, and reviewed—and in Sutherland's case also provided guidance for—the management of new media projects.[20]

The 1982 plan was the platform from which Neilly and his team would launch an effort to remake Wiley, an effort vastly more ambitious than what Brad's team (with Neilly as a leading member) had undertaken in the 1960s, when Wiley acquired Interscience, expanded its textbook business, experimented with trade and high school publishing, and made numerous other acquisitions. There were some striking similarities, however: a commitment to sustain and expand the company's core businesses, the resolution to use the company's experience as a college textbook publisher to move into related educational markets, and the determination to engage with new technologies. In the 1960s, the new markets had been remedial education, the high schools, and corporate and library training. In the 1980s, they would be vocational and technical education; corporate and industrial/technical training; electronic delivery of journal content; and software, interactive media, and authoring tools.

Unlike the early 1960s, the 1980s began as a less promising era. The economy was shaky, Wiley's traditional markets looked less than robust, and technology equaled both opportunity and threat. The two eras were also marked by a significant difference in the scale and scope of Wiley's investments and in the risk associated with their execution.

In early 1982, the company plunged into an entirely new business, corporate training, when it acquired the Wilson Learning Company. A year and a half later, Neilly announced a comprehensive corporate reorganization into what he described to the board as "a headquarters company with four major components": a book publishing company, an international company, an

Higher education was experiencing demographic changes . . .

In the 1980s, Wiley collected information about the number of nontraditional students enrolling in institutions of higher education. These included older and working students, some of whom were returning to school to be trained for new types of work, such as data processing.

industrial training company (quickly renamed the Learning Group), and an information publishing company. All the book publishing units now reported to vice president Robert C. Douglas, who also sat on the board with three other of the company's vice presidents: Marianne Orlando, Charles B. Stoll, and Deborah E. Wiley. Reporting to Douglas were Serje G. Seminoff (College Division), Kenneth B. Collins (Professional Division), Robert B. Polhemus (Interscience), Andrew E. Ford Jr. (Medical Division), and Adrian Higham (International Group). Wiley's new commitment to "lifelong learning" was manifested by its new Learning Group, which included the Occupational Division, headed by Alan B. Lesure; the Wilson Learning Corporation (industrial training), headed by W. Mathew Juechter; and the newly formed Wiley Learning Technologies (technical and engineering training products), under Deborah Wiley. Information Publishing, initially headed by Robert Hauck, vice president of Strategic Planning and Business Development, would oversee the development of audiotapes, databases, compact disks, and software.[21]

the rise of the secondhand book dealer, and . . .

USED

The largest college textbook distributors in the 1980s included Nebraska Books, Missouri Books, and Folletts.

increasing investment in ancillaries.

One of the huge book/supplement packages common in college publishing in the 1980s. Faculty often considered the size of the supplement packages as a key factor in their adoption decisions. Texts that had once been accompanied by only an instructor's manual and a student study guide now came with a full complement of teaching and learning aids: transparency acetates and/or slides for classroom projection, test banks, solution manuals, workbooks, and more.

The Higher Education Market

To move onto new terrain as envisioned in the 1982 strategic plan and symbolized by the acquisition of Wilson, Wiley had to sustain, even build, its core businesses. Textbook publishing was Wiley's largest business, its "traditional bastion of strength," a business that had posted a remarkable 25 percent increase in sales in 1981. As the company entered the 1980s, changes in the textbook market were already under way. Sheer demography was a challenge; a long period of robust growth in textbook sales had been the direct result of the postwar baby boom, and now it was no longer possible to sell more books simply because incoming freshmen automatically outnumbered graduates. The college market had become increasingly unpredictable, as reams of data published by the federal government each year testified. Some thought that college enrollments would decrease; others that the rate of college attendance would actually increase more than the decrease in the absolute number of potential candidates, meaning enrollments would continue to rise.

Another factor to be taken into account was the hard-to-predict number of nontraditional students, working adults who might enroll in college on a part-time basis.[22]

Educational publishing had reached an important decision point. The Carnegie Council on Policies in Higher Education warned in 1981: "It is no longer enough to look just at the size of the age cohort, or at changing high school graduation rates, or at private rates of return in the labor market on investments in a college education, or at long-term historical trends." Only 40 percent of students were "hard-core," that is, the children of college graduates, the report explained. The other 60 percent were first-generation attendees or nontraditional students (adults, often with full-time jobs) with high dropout rates and highly variable enrollment rates. The percentage of high school graduates enrolling in college trended upward through the 1980s, from just less than 50 to just over 60 percent, in a fluctuating pattern. Similarly, over the entire decade total enrollments rose almost 2 million, but almost no growth took place between 1981 and 1986, and there was a small but notable decline between 1981 and 1983.[23]

Another challenge was how to assess demand elasticity—how much prices could be raised before unit sales fell. The secondhand market had gobbled up 20 percent of the textbook market; the percentage of students who bought required textbooks new was trending downward but, again, unpredictably. Used book distributors like the Nebraska Book Company, the Follett College Book Company, and Missouri Books (later renamed MBS Textbook Exchange) made sure that used books got on the shelves and reached buyers. Throughout much of the 1980s, used book distributors could fill orders more promptly than the publishers themselves. The low shipping costs of books, long a matter of U.S. social and postal policy, made the market national.[24]

Adding insult to injury, the academics, who were the core constituency of textbook publishers, continued to sell their complimentary copies to the used book market (publishers routinely gave away thousands of copies of textbooks in the hopes of securing large adoptions). Publishers responded by marking these "complimentary books," but retailers could simply replace the covers. Aware that such practices and the used book market eroded royalties, professors might hesitate to create a good textbook in the first place, thus making it that much more difficult for textbook editors to sign high-quality authors.[25]

By the late 1980s, somewhere between 25 and 80 percent of sales of any edition of a textbook were used ones. Sales of introductory texts, both new and revised, regularly dropped 40 to 60 percent in the second year, largely due to sales of used books. Wiley's return rate—books ordered by the bookstore but then returned to the warehouse—continued to hover at disturbing levels. In 1985, a number of publishers including Wiley and Houghton Mifflin considered entering the used book business. According to Neilly, a number of the publishers thought this would be inappropriate. The costs of setting up a parallel organization with campus bookstores and warehousing would be prohibitive. Authors might complain about publishers making "a second profit without benefit to them." The alternative,

Neilly concluded, was to pay more attention to quality, frequent revisions, and required supplements.[26]

For its part, Wiley turned to both raising and lowering prices. Prices were raised to offset inflation. Often the increase in prices reflected increased investment in new or revised editions. In fact, many texts were the core product in a package of ancillaries (teacher's guides, test banks, transparencies, etc.) that were "given away" with the book, meaning that their cost was added to the price of the textbook. Wiley also experimented with lower prices, offering paperback and "black and white" editions that sold at about half the usual list price. These experiments ultimately failed. Students might not like the higher prices, but their professors, the people actually selecting the text to be bought, preferred the fancier packages to cheaper editions. The wave of mergers in the industry meant that the larger companies, especially those headed by media companies, brought their marketing expertise into higher education bookselling and changed its nature forever.

Wiley executives understood all this. They had been keeping a close eye on the textbook business for years. "We worried about the growing sentiment against textbook prices," Neilly explained.

They were a required purchase often irrelevant to the courses; [we heard] many complaints from students and faculty. It was not much fun to be accused of overcharging or of passing off an inferior product, which soon would be replaced. Nobody seemed to realize how many faculty spent years creating and lovingly revising their textbooks, not for the income in most cases, but because they were dedicated teachers. We came to regard the college market as cyclical. Enrollments went up and down. We had the leading title in physics for a season, and then Prentice Hall or McGraw-Hill would invade our market share the next. Some years, we held our own or dominated a market, say in math, but it usually did not last unless we could build an empire via a title like Halliday and Resnick's Fundamentals of Physics. *But these were few and far between.*

Still Wiley—and others—persisted.[27]

What accounted for the persistent attractiveness of textbook publishing? In the short term, each wave of consolidation led to rising prices and profits. High profits tempted new entrants—often editors who bravely abandoned their corporate positions to start their own publishing businesses. Profits shrank accordingly. The rise and disappearance of publishers was a highly dynamic process, and at any one time each of the major book publishing markets contained hundreds of small houses eager to make their mark. With the exception of introductory textbooks, the costs of entry were low, especially in niche markets, and the telecommunication and computerization revolutions of the 1980s made entry into publishing even easier.[28]

Each textbook subject area had a dynamic of its own. In business and economics, Wiley had to contend with R. D. Irwin, McGraw-Hill, Prentice Hall, Harper & Row, Scott, Foresman, and Random House's Dryden Press. In biology and earth sciences, competition most often came from W. C. Brown, Wadsworth, McGraw-Hill, Prentice Hall, Macmillan, Van Nostrand Reinhold, and Harper & Row. In chemistry and physics, there were Saunders, Prentice Hall, Freeman, Benjamin Cummings, Addison-Wesley, and Holt, Rinehart and Winston. Engineering was still dominated by Wiley, along with McGraw-Hill, Prentice Hall, and Addison-Wesley, with the significant exception of the introductory courses, where there were as many competitors as in the sciences. Mathematics, home economics, and psychology, too, were highly competitive. In architecture, Van Nostrand Reinhold had a strong list. By the late 1980s, competition was so ferocious in basic textbooks that one Wiley college representative complained that all he had to offer was "just one more in the 'pile' of titles from which . . . adopters may whimsically choose." Competition was less intense in upper-division textbooks, but still keen and growing more so each year.[29]

College curricula also were changing, following the student activism of the 1960s and the rise of postmodernism in the 1970s, both of which called into question the view that reason, science, and technological

> **Curricular changes also hurt Wiley's lists.**

progress promoted human welfare. Required courses fell before a plethora of electives, which was not good news for Wiley's core lists in math, science, and engineering. Curricular changes hurt Wiley's lists in the social sciences and the humanities, as well. The company had moved into the history field at a particularly unpropitious time, when mainstream history was shorn of its title as the queen of the social sciences and took a hard turn toward the humanities. The linguistic shift snapped several empirical moorings, causing history to drift into what one critic called "fertile ground for scandal and controversy." It was a hard field to assess. In 1975, Neilly had predicted that history was moving "toward quantification." It seemed so then; but while an energetic group of economist historians was developing a field called cliometrics (the use of statistical methods to analyze historical data), most historians would remain wedded to the word. Literary studies, too, came under attack as being detached from reality, and hence expendable, in an increasingly "vo-tech" environment. A curricular battle over the old canon diverted the focus of textbooks, as the great works of Western literature were displaced by texts that included newer voices.[30]

Throughout the 1980s, another disturbing downward trend continued to hit Wiley's core science and engineering lists. Every year almost half a million students would leave high school planning to major in science or engineering in college. Sixty percent of them would change their plans while in college, a dropout rate that alarmed universities and science publishers alike. Explanations were easy to come by—students simply were drifting from more demanding to less demanding courses; or students resented the authoritarian and competitive science and engineering cultures; or they burned out on the relentless problem-solving approaches. One popular explanation was that the lure of financial careers became so strong during the decade that students listened to that siren call and heard no other. Effective plans to reverse the dropout rates were not easy to come by.[31]

Kieso and Weygandt and Wiley Accounting

Wiley's strong backlists proved to be critical to the company in the turbulent 1980s, and its array of publications in accounting were among its strongest titles. Their strength came as something of a surprise. Wiley had published accounting texts since the beginning of the century, but few had sold well. Donald E. Kieso's 1969 textbook *Intermediate Principles of Accounting*, for example, suffered from disappointing sales. "The intermediate course at most schools was two or three semesters, but the book was geared for a one-semester course," then accounting editor Donald Ford later recalled. "No wonder it didn't sell." The 1974 edition, *Intermediate Accounting*, co-authored with one of Kieso's former students, Jerry J. Weygandt, received positive reviews in accounting magazines and journals; and with a stepped-up marketing effort, sales increased dramatically. When the next edition appeared in 1977, *Intermediate Accounting* was the top-selling book for intermediate accounting and has remained so ever since. "Not only is their book refreshingly well written," William L. Stephens of the University of South Florida explained in *The Accounting Review* (1978), "but the best written chapters are usually those covering the most difficult topics." The book was Wiley at its best, and its commitment to this discipline was clear: it regularly updated the must-have FASB (Financial Accounting Standards Board) and GAAP (Generally Accepted Accounting Principles) content that the market needed. In 2007, Kieso and Weygandt remains the market leader in intermediate accounting, with a market share of over 70 percent. Today, *Intermediate Accounting* is in its twelfth edition, and it has held the number-one spot since the third edition.[32]

Other Kieso-Weygandt titles followed the 1977 edition, including *Accounting Principles* in 1987, *Financial Accounting* in 1995 (the second, third, and fourth editions have each held the number-one position in financial accounting), and *Managerial Accounting* in 1999. Paul D. Kimmel, of the University of Wisconsin–Milwaukee, first joined as an author for the fifth edition of *Accounting Principles*.

Terry D. Warfield, from the University of Wisconsin–Madison, became part of the team for *Intermediate Accounting* on the tenth edition. By 2007, these texts had sold millions of copies since 1974.[33]

The development of texts was complemented by the acquisition and development of professional accounting materials. With the 1977 Ronald Press acquisition came *Montgomery's Auditing*, published initially in 1912. Its author, Robert Montgomery, was one of the first inductees into the Accounting Hall of Fame in 1950. Later editions were authored by teams

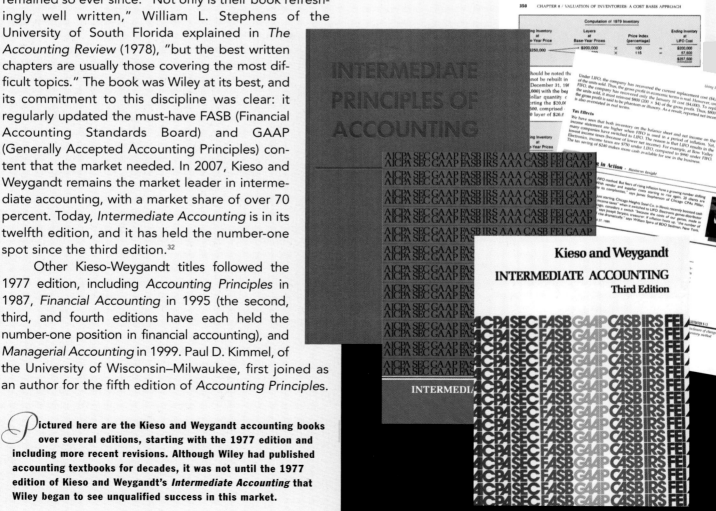

*P*ictured here are the Kieso and Weygandt accounting books over several editions, starting with the 1977 edition and including more recent revisions. Although Wiley had published accounting textbooks for decades, it was not until the 1977 edition of Kieso and Weygandt's *Intermediate Accounting* that Wiley began to see unqualified success in this market.

from leading accounting firms, and *Montgomery's* became the model for a new series of titles also authored by teams from prominent accounting firms. In 2007, *Montgomery's* was in its twelfth edition. *Accountants' Handbook*, first published in 1923 and in its tenth edition in 2007, and Victor Z. Brink's *Modern Internal Auditing*, in its sixth edition in 2007, also came to Wiley via Ronald. In 1980, Wiley further strengthened its accounting program by acquiring *CPA Examination Review*, the market-leading review text for CPA candidates. Under publisher Richard Lynch, the *Review* became an example of a successful early effort to publish in various media. By 1986, Wiley was offering the *Review* in print, video, audio, and software versions. In the same year, Lynch reported that Wiley had increased the *Review* products market share from 70 to 80 percent.[34]

Bradford Wiley with Jerry Weygandt (center) and Donald Kieso (right), 1978. Below, Kieso and Weygandt center front, with Wiley team in 1990.

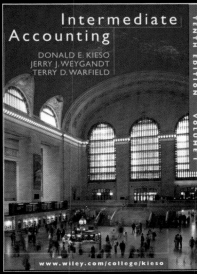

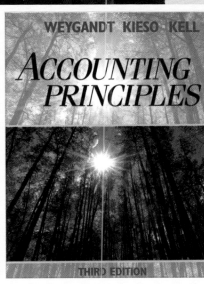

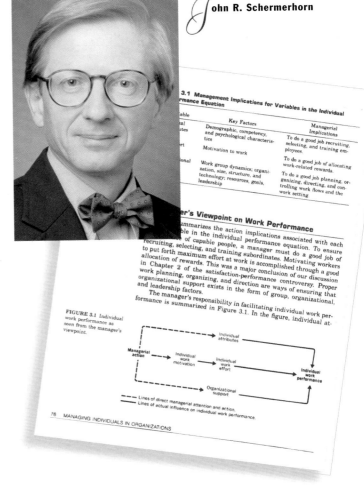

*J*ohn R. Schermerhorn

*T*he first edition of *Managing Organizational Behavior* by
John Schermerhorn, James Hunt, and Richard Osborn was
published in 1982 and marked the beginning of Wiley's
powerful push into the business textbook market.

Wiley reacted to changes in student enrollments in various disciplines and in the student population as a whole just as it had in the 1960s: by exiting some subject areas and moving into new ones. In 1981, it sold off its nascent list of literature and composition titles to Scott, Foresman. "It was a good list," Brad explained, "but not number one, or anywhere close to it." To offset its shortcoming in its traditional disciplines, Wiley bought St. Clair Press's business list in 1979 and made it the basis for a new list of business textbooks. According to Rick Leyh, an editor and manager who led this effort, business "was seen (rightfully so) as the one remaining area for Wiley to grow in Higher Ed that was consistent with market trends, enrollment growth, careers, and where we had a very small position." Leyh and his colleagues published *Managing Organizational Behavior* by John Schermerhorn, James G. Hunt, and Richard N. Osborn in 1982, selling 10,000 units in its first year. A second Schermerhorn title, *Management for Productivity*, sold 33,000 units in its first year, 1984. (Both titles were going strong in their ninth editions in 2007.) The list was strengthened by the acquisition of Grid Publishing (which published marketing, management, and general business titles) in 1984. The Schermerhorn titles along with the acquisition of Grid put Wiley on the map as a major business publisher.[35]

Eager to adapt to the introduction of personal computing on college and university campuses in the early 1980s, which began to impact selected disciplines and courses, Wiley was one of the first higher education publishers to set up a software division in 1983 (before the Apple Macintosh appeared). This group began to develop educational enhancement software for direct sale to students. The differences between book publishing and software publishing became obvious very quickly: the time-honored system of an author writing a book with the help of an editor was replaced by a film production model whereby faculty and professional programmers, graphic designers, quality assurance experts, and project managers worked together. The sale of individual books gave way to site licenses. The differences in marketing books versus software were too long to list. Software purchasing decisions, too, were made differently than textbook adoption decisions, often by administrators rather than faculty. A new business had moved in with an old one, and methods, styles, and even languages often clashed. Wiley managers soon decided to integrate the two businesses rather than have them coexist, shutting down the separate software division in the mid-1980s. Thereafter, each member of a book team redefined and broadened his or her role to include new media, most commonly called "hypermedia" at the time, a term that soon gave way to "multimedia." Computers did not revolutionize either college campuses or publishers but did change them forever. Each campus innovated at its own pace, ranging from those that became trendsetters to those that lagged behind. Each publisher did so as well, and both trendsetters and laggards paid a dear price, for the market for educational software developed slowly.

Despite difficult and shifting market conditions in some traditionally strong areas, Wiley continued to find success in accounting, physics, geography, chemistry, and earth science. By the end of the 1980s, Wiley was the market-leading college text publisher in both physics and geography, the second-leading publisher in college chemistry, and the third in earth science. Best-selling science authors David Halliday, Robert Resnick, Harm de Blij, James Brady, Graham Solomons, and Brian Skinner continued their creative and productive quarrels with their editors (as *New Yorker* founding editor Harold Ross once said, editing is the same as quarreling with writers). The physical science and geography lists were still relied on for their accuracy in artwork and content as well as for their upper-level publications. By the end of the 1980s, they were also becoming known for their pedagogical innovations.

> **Wiley was one of the first higher-education publishers to set up a software division in 1983.**

To reach the nontraditional students described by the Carnegie Council, Wiley began in the 1970s to move into educational markets outside of four-year colleges. It set up the Hamilton Publishing Company in Santa Barbara, California, and started an Occupational Education subgroup under Alan Lesure within its College Publishing Division. The aim was to develop educational materials for community and junior colleges; technical, trade, and vocational schools; and industrial training programs, with texts designed to provide students with practical, marketable skills.[36]

In the 1980s, Wiley's Occupational Group was firmly committed to publishing for the market in life-long learning. The Group published books in automotive repairs, machine tool manufacturing, civil engineering technology, secretarial training, and professional cooking. Secretarial training, for example, offered intriguing possibilities, but it required Wiley to work closely with faculty members because of the impact of the computer on a typical secretary's job. While employers were interested in graduates with training in word processing and data processing, "faculty were afraid of these courses and were trying to turn their backs on them to teach typing and stenography," according to Lesure. Following an approach pioneered by Autodesk, the maker of AutoCAD, architectural design software that was hellishly difficult to use, Wiley began to train faculty to teach word processing. To bulk up the business, Wiley acquired Milady, the leading publisher of materials for the cosmetology market, in 1985. One of the Occupational Group's most successful titles was Wayne Gisslen's *Professional Cooking* (1983). Occupational came to be seen as an important new growth area in educational publishing.[37]

Educational publishing continued to grow through the end of fiscal year 1984; but at the end of the next fiscal year, the College Division, having budgeted for a 10 percent increase in sales, showed a decline of 17 percent. In June 1985, Neilly reported that he had moved the New York company from contingency budgeting to "a real sense of crisis." A select committee was appointed, which after intensive study recommended a review of responsibilities in editorial and marketing, terminations for performance reasons, staff reductions, new job descriptions, and new appointments, plus "a new set of rules which will change the way we manage the business." Wiley wasn't alone in its poor showing. Citing enrollments and the secondhand book market, other publishing houses with college divisions, such as McGraw-Hill, also reported less than stellar results, although not as dramatic as Wiley's. The Book Industry Study Group estimated that for the industry as a whole, domestic dollar sales of college texts increased 4 percent while unit sales fell by 4.6 percent.[38]

Wayne Gisslen's *Professional Cooking* and other titles became a mainstay of Wiley's Occupational list and was later moved to the Professional and Trade list.

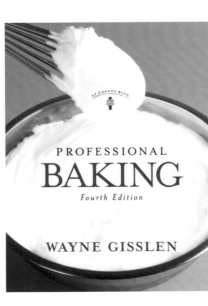

Some titles from the Professional Group in 1979.

Professional Publishing

In 1979, the Professional Group under Michael Harris was producing primarily scientific books and journals, and some books in business and the social sciences under the Wiley, Wiley-Interscience, Ronald Press, Halsted Press, and Self-Teaching Guides imprints. Also in the Professional domain were the Interscience journals acquired in 1961, plus a handful of start-ups, making a total of 26. At the time, Wiley U.K. in Chichester was responsible for 10 additional journals. Wiley's Professional business had quadrupled in size over the previous decade. The books part of this program stretched back to Wiley's earliest days as a science-technical publisher in the nineteenth century. Wiley's 1979 annual report featured such wide-ranging titles as Frank Arthur Patty's *Industrial Hygiene and Toxicology*, a major reference work whose first edition dated back to 1948; *The Effective*

Woman Manager by Nathaniel Stewart; and *Solar Heating Design* by William Beckman, Sanford Klein, and John Duffie. Titles that indicated Wiley's new interests were *BASIC for Home Computers* by Robert Albrecht, LeRoy Finkel, and Jerald Brown, and *Doing Business with the People's Republic of China* by Bohdan and Maria Szuprowicz. The same report described professional publishing as "one of the fastest-growing areas in our industry."[39]

In 1981, Harris was forced to retire due to the onset of cancer. Sadly, this brilliant manager, who seemed to have such a promising future at Wiley, died shortly thereafter. He was replaced by Kenneth B. Collins, who pushed for rapid growth despite concerns about funding for research and libraries. These were the early years of the Ronald Reagan administration (1980–1988), and the academic research community was anxious about Reagan's known antagonism toward the University of California, which he saw as a hotbed of student

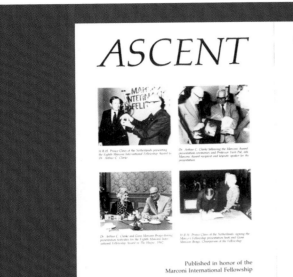

A rthur C. Clarke, author of science fiction classics and Wiley's *Ascent to Orbit*, published in 1985.

activism. Reagan, however, turned out to be a strong advocate for increases in research spending. Libraries did not fare as well, but Wiley compensated by exploiting new markets: focusing the Self-Teaching Guides on personal computing, publishing trade paperbacks for small-business people and PC users, collaborating with Wilson Learning on a number of book projects, and establishing a legal publishing program in 1981 and a software and database operation in 1983. The law program, set up in Colorado Springs, Colorado, aimed to publish current and updated materials for practicing attorneys in the areas of taxation, trial practice, federal litigation, and business law. Edited by lawyers, these publications differed from those offered by most other law publishers by containing fewer volumes at much lower prices and selling primarily by direct mail rather than by field staff.[40]

At the same time, new editors were hired with a view toward producing trade titles for retail outlets. Two successful titles, both published in 1984, were Arthur C.

Clarke's *Ascent to Orbit* and Stephen T. McClellan's *The Coming Computer Industry Shakeout*. Clarke was none other than the author of *2001: A Space Odyssey*, and one of the Big Three of science fiction. McClellan's book sold 14,193 copies in two months, while Clarke's book sold slightly fewer in five months. And in an indication of things to come, Interscience's renowned *Kirk-Othmer Encyclopedia of Chemical Technology* went online, also in 1984.[41]

Journals Publishing

Harris, and then Collins, pushed for expansion in Wiley's journals business, which was managed by Alan Wittman, who came to Wiley from *Scientific American*, and later by Mary E. Curtis, starting in 1982. The acquisition of Interscience in 1961 introduced Wiley to journals publishing. Although Wiley U.K. had an active journals program, it took more than two decades for the New York company to fully embrace this important medium. By the beginning of the 1980s, Wiley was one of the world's largest producers of English-language academic journals, though with just 45 active titles its output lagged far behind that of front-runners Elsevier and Pergamon. The principal markets for journals were still the United States, Europe, and Japan, and Wiley was competing in these markets with global players, most of which were European.[42]

Journals publishing could be a more profitable and reliable business than textbook publishing. Research was growing, and scientists relied on journals to disseminate results, earn tenure, and increase their prestige and salaries. According to a practice established decades, even centuries, before by professional societies, publishers did not pay for content, and journals were sold on a subscription basis with payment in advance. Journal subscriptions had high renewal rates, making sales predictable. By the early 1980s, hundreds of thousands of manuscripts were submitted to scientific journals each year, necessitating about 1 million reports by peer reviewers or referees. That sounds expensive, but at that time the vast majority of peer reviews were provided gratis. Of course, there were other publishing expenses, such as editorial and administrative work, production (design, paper, typesetting, and printing), distribution, marketing, sales, subscription solicitation, and maintenance. There was also the risk associated with starting new journals, some of which took years to become profitable, while others fell by the wayside. On the demand side, journal purchases to an extent crowded out book purchases, as libraries struggled to meet increasingly tight budgets in the 1980s and beyond.[43]

In New York, Wiley launched a number of new journals, including *Medical Ultrasound, Medicinal Research Reviews,* and *Mass Spectrometry Reviews*. Professional also increased its publication of business journals, adding the *Journal of Futures Markets* and the *Journal of Policy Analysis and Management*. In 1982, in a first for Wiley, the Journals Department announced the online distribution of the *Harvard Business Review*'s bibliographic and full-text database via Dialog Information Services, Inc., an early provider of online content.

*I*nterscience head **Robert Polhemus (standing center) and Ken Collins (far right) in the 1980s.**

The Knowledge Explosion

The company was confronted with an interesting paradox during the Reagan years: as student enrollments wavered, academic research funding grew. In fact, academic research in the 1980s grew faster than in any previous decade. "No brief account," wrote educational historian Roger L. Geiger, "can do justice to the enormous progress of basic academic science during the era of the 1980s." This new funding inspired breakthroughs in areas such as optoelectronics, materials science, supercomputers, and biotechnology. Funds were also dispersed beyond the traditional elite research universities, at the same time corporate funding flowed into academia to back applied research. Funding for other types of research grew even faster—with a significant portion going to the Department of Defense for weapons development, to support Reagan's challenge to the Soviets. What came to be known as the Star Wars missile defense system was a direct result of this research. At universities, an increased emphasis was placed on applied research, in areas such as biotechnology, with a clear message "to disseminate that knowledge as expeditiously as possible." All these developments meant good things for journals publishing.[44]

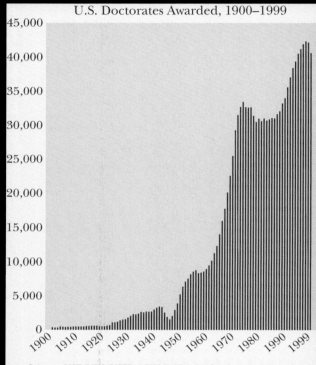

U.S. Doctorates Awarded, 1900–1999

Sources: NSF/NIH/USED/NEH/USDA/NASA, Survey of Earned Doctorates and Doctorate Records File (1920–1999); U.S. Office of Education annual reports (1900–1919).

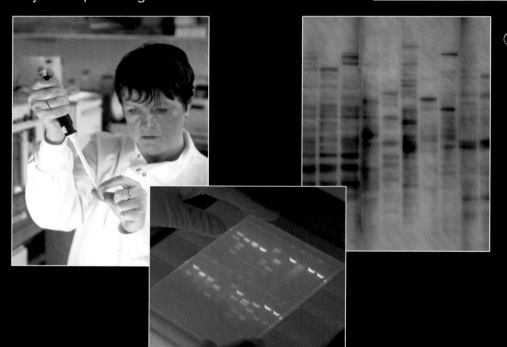

The 1980s saw the development of several techniques to analyze DNA, including the polymerase chain reaction, electrophoresis gel, and genetic fingerprinting, as well as the development of genetically engineered food.

U.S. Doctorates Awarded by Major Field, 1920–1999

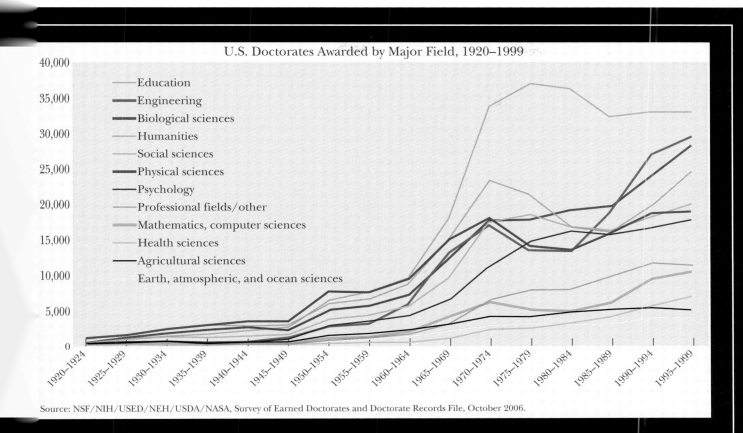

- Education
- Engineering
- Biological sciences
- Humanities
- Social sciences
- Physical sciences
- Psychology
- Professional fields/other
- Mathematics, computer sciences
- Health sciences
- Agricultural sciences
- Earth, atmospheric, and ocean sciences

40,000
35,000
30,000
25,000
20,000
15,000
10,000
5,000
0

1920–1924, 1925–1929, 1930–1934, 1935–1939, 1940–1944, 1945–1949, 1950–1954, 1955–1959, 1960–1964, 1965–1969, 1970–1974, 1975–1979, 1980–1984, 1985–1989, 1990–1994, 1995–1999

Source: NSF/NIH/USED/NEH/USDA/NASA, Survey of Earned Doctorates and Doctorate Records File, October 2006.

Superconducting materials were developed, and we learned more about Earth, including the growing ozone hole over Antarctica. The space shuttle *Columbia* was launched, and the *Magellan* orbiter mapped Venus.

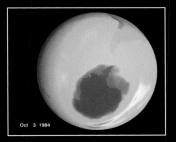

Oct 3 1984

The year 1984 was a particularly busy one. Wiley acquired Scripta Technica, a Washington, D.C.–based firm that specialized in the translation of Russian and Japanese scientific journals. Wiley also acquired the journal and newsletter publishing program of longtime rival Van Nostrand Reinhold (VNR). Journals vice president Curtis suspected that VNR had entered the journals business after seeing that Wiley was aggressively pursuing new titles: Her boss had spotted a VNR colleague furiously taking notes at a presentation that Curtis made at a professional-society meeting just before VNR went into the business.[45]

Curtis recalled "a lot of pressure to do different things," in this case experimenting with magazine publishing, another first for Wiley in the twentieth century. In 1984, she negotiated a deal with Hewlett-Packard (HP) to launch *Personal Computing*. HP was working on a laptop with a touch screen and was planning to use it to get into the personal computing market. HP promised Wiley marketing support, but then decided not to go into personal computing, leaving Wiley high and dry. Consequently, the magazine quickly began to lose money and was sold.[46]

During the first half of the decade, Wiley strove mightily to catch up with its larger European competitors, increasing the number of its journals to 138 titles. Senior management, however, remained skeptical about the future of Wiley's journals program and the future of the journals business in general. "There was huge ambivalence in New York about whether we should have journals at all," Curtis remembered. Wiley's senior managers were all book people now that Eric Proskauer, Interscience founder and former head of the Professional Division, was retired, and did not understand the journals financial model. "Everything was measured by profitability," Curtis explained. She was questioned about the profitability of journals when the more significant number was cash flow. Because of the minimal up-front investment, cash flow was significant, and the return on investment was very high. Perhaps symbolic, Curtis suggested, was that when the company's headquarters at

605 Third Avenue became overcrowded, the journals department was moved across the street. "My division was like a separate little company," Curtis said. And there was no effort to link book publishing to journals publishing. "Wiley should have followed the European model, in which editors are paid to publish both books and journals," Curtis explained. Instead, Wiley's book editors "were not rewarded for publishing journals" and journal editors did not pursue book opportunities. Several meetings were set up to explore editorial coordination with Wiley U.K., but there were few results. The U.K. operation, like all subsidiaries, according to Curtis, "was worried about being managed by the center. I think they wanted to remain at arm's length as long as they were doing what they were supposed to be doing and could justify it to the parent company."[47]

Medical Publishing

All the market signals—increased funding for medical research and higher enrollments in nursing and medical schools—indicated that Wiley's fledgling Medical Division should also prosper in the 1980s. Wiley first identified itself as a medical publisher in 1973. Declaring that it wanted to be "a dominant force in the life sciences," the company combined the medical publishing activities of Wiley-Interscience and the nursing publication program of the College Division with the intent of focusing on this fast-growing segment. The move would also reduce Wiley's exposure to the vagaries of the textbook market and maintain balance across its publishing programs. The division grew at the rate of 29 percent per annum between 1976 and 1981, astounding even when corrected for inflation. Yet the program suffered through fits and starts. After eight years as a separate division, Medical was still not profitable. By 1981, division head Niels Buessem was facing another serious problem: He had to scramble just to keep good staff members on board.

These problems did not stop Medical from acquiring Houghton Mifflin's medical program, which

*A*ndrew Ford, the head of the Medical Division in the 1980s (left), with James Brady (far right), author of a successful series of introductory chemistry texts.

International Expansion and Contraction

Wiley's 1979 annual report described a network of subsidiaries and affiliates on five continents, including subsidiaries in the United Kingdom, Canada, and Australia, with joint ventures in Mexico, Brazil, and India. "Each of these subsidiaries," it was pointed out, "is locally staffed and managed. Local direction, we believe, allows each company to identify and respond most effectively to changing demands and opportunities in its own markets." The year before, the International Division under Marianne Orlando, the company's most senior female executive, had established Wiley Arabooks in Jordan. Arabooks published texts in Arabic, both originals and translations of Wiley titles. Two of Wiley's subsidiaries, Canada and Jacaranda Wiley in Australia, published for elementary and high school students. In 1982, Wiley opened a warehouse in Singapore to serve Asia from India to Korea and Japan.[48]

The pivotal 1982 strategic plan called for Wiley's International Division to continue "building or buying publishing strength on a foundation of mature and aggressive international marketing." The plan divided global markets by product. Educational materials, in Wiley's low-priced international editions, were to be sold in Europe as well as in the developing world, which was defined as Southeast Asia, Africa, India, China, the Middle East, and Latin America. Professional and reference materials, including journals, were destined for "regions [and countries] that are industrially and scientifically advanced (Europe, Japan)." The plan called for "coordination of publishing strategies" and "improvement of effectiveness in international marketing and distribution." Naturally enough, it also called for higher profit margins, which were expected to come from investment in local publishing programs that would produce higher margins than imports. Finally, the plan warned, "*Reduction of investment* will be undertaken on a selective basis in areas of less than satisfactory return, by

included three clinical journals, clinical reference and diagnostic handbooks, a loose-leaf update service in general surgery, and other assets. Three years later, Wiley sold its *Current Series* in neurology, nephrology, pulmonology, gastroenterology, hematology, and medicine to Year Book Medical Publishers. The same year Wiley also purchased a New York–based niche publisher, Park Row Publishers, for $1.75 million plus "incentives." Established in 1979, Park Row published books, pamphlets, magazines, symposia, teleconferences, audiovisual materials, computer software, and exhibits for big pharmaceutical companies. Over the next four years Medical would launch a controlled-circulation journal for osteopathic physicians, numerous nursing titles, and paperback series for nurses preparing for their licensing examination, for critical care nurses, and for specialists in pathophysiology. In 1986, Wiley bought Harwal Publishing. Founded by James Harris in 1977, the company specialized in reference books and texts for those primarily involved in hospital technologies and administration, along with educational materials for medical and nursing students, including the successful *National Medical Series*, which students used to prepare for National Board exams.

Books for Global Markets

By 1981, over 400 WIEs, or Wiley International Editions, were available, making Wiley's name as well known outside the United States as it was inside. These three versions of *Advanced Engineering Mathematics* by Erwin Kreyszig are, from top to bottom, the WIE, a translated version, and the original edition.

termination of programs, sale of properties, or inviting shared investment."[49]

"The world changes and we adapt," John Collins, managing director of Jacaranda Wiley, wrote in 1989. Despite the serious problems Wiley confronted overall, its international operations stayed the course in the early 1980s, vindicating the time and resources the company had expended since the 1940s to cultivate foreign markets. As the 1980s wore on, life in Wiley's International Division, too, became more challenging, particularly in Latin America where devaluation undermined two key investments. Over time, it would become apparent that, as local publishing grew at overseas operations, notions of local autonomy so deeply engrained in the global business practice established by Brad and his colleagues would have to be revisited before Wiley could move ahead more effectively.[50]

The depreciation of foreign currencies, which became commonplace after the demise of the Bretton Woods system of fixed exchange rates in the early 1970s, proved to be a special challenge for Wiley's international operations. Early in the 1980s, the strong showing of the U.S. dollar against all currencies hurt the company by increasing the price of its books for foreign purchasers and reducing the value, in dollar terms, of the company's overseas assets. Rather than make a systematic attempt to hedge,[51] which was not a common practice, the company picked exchange rates to be used for internal budgeting over the next year and hoped for the best—which often was not very good. In 1985, for instance, Wiley budgeted the Australian dollar at 84 cents to the U.S. dollar. By September, it was at 70 cents. The pound sterling was budgeted at $1.10 that year. By September, it stood at $1.38 and changed every few seconds. Even so, Wiley's international operations generally performed as it was hoped they would: that is, in some cases their profitability made up for the lack of profits in the domestic market. In 1981, some 400 Wiley International Editions (WIEs) titles were available. They sold well, and in 1982 international sales accounted for about 30 percent of the company's revenues.[52]

In the 1980s, Wiley Ltd. in the United Kingdom, under managing director Adrian Higham, continued to grow as a publishing center second only to New York, with particular emphases on professional, scientific, technical, and medical books and the related journals business. In 1982, Higham replaced Marianne Orlando as head of International in New York; Charles Stoll moved to Chichester to become interim managing director for one year until Michael Foyle was appointed to the position, effective July 1, 1983. Foyle had his work cut out for him. The worldwide economic downturn of the 1970s persisted into the 1980s in England. High unemployment and low growth led to austere budgets for education and public libraries.

The book program was the largest part of the British offering, representing 70 percent of sales at the beginning of the 1980s. To enhance its collection of science and engineering reference works, Wiley Ltd. acquired Research Studies Press in 1981. Chichester also started a computer book club, but it did not survive.

U.K. editorial under Jamie Cameron was divided into six teams: engineering, molecular and physical sciences, psychology, life sciences, social sciences, and medical. Wiley U.K. developed a particular emphasis on medical publications, building relationships with the European pharmaceutical industry. It also published for the Ciba Foundation and the Dahlem conferences in Germany, named for a Berlin neighborhood in which were clustered a number of academic institutions and research centers. The conferences provided a forum for interdisciplinary discussion of issues such as "Pain and Society."

Chichester was also aggressively growing its journals program. John Jarvis was hired away from Elsevier in 1979 to head the medical team specifically because of his experience in the journals business. Chichester soon began launching several new journals a year—four in 1981. That same year, Chichester acquired Heyden & Son, which published books as well as 16 journals. The acquisition more than doubled the size of the U.K.'s journals program. In early 1986, Wiley Ltd. bought Media Medica, a British publisher of sponsored journals, drug information booklets, and reports on medical proceedings. With that acquisition, Chichester overreached, however, and Media Medica was sold a few years later. Despite this setback, by 1988, Wiley Ltd. published almost half of Wiley's 130 journals.[53]

Encouraged by New York's willingness to experiment with new technologies, Wiley Ltd. developed a computerized composition system that facilitated short print runs of specialized publications at a low cost and

)))iley's international leadership team meeting in Chichester in the 1980s. From left, Dennis Hudson, Michael Foyle, Adrian Higham, Jamie Cameron, Robert Hauck, Marianne Orlando, Charles Stoll, Harry Newman, John Collins, Dan Rubin, and Thomas Cassidy.

*G*eoff Dean (left), head of Wiley Canada, with Adrian Higham, head of Wiley Ltd., and John Collins, head of Jacaranda Wiley, 1979.

formed a joint venture to produce an interactive videodisc called *Interactive Science Laboratory*. In line with other Wiley start-ups in database publishing, Chichester launched its first digital product, the *Directory of Medical Research*, in 1983. The company also toyed with the idea of entering the European software market.[54]

Chichester also took advantage of the 1982 Wilson Learning acquisition by putting together the first collaboration between a Wiley publishing unit and Wilson's European sales force. In 1984, for a British pharmaceutical company that was about to launch a new antibiotic, Chichester's editors published technical information about the drug, which their Wilson colleagues used to train the sales force. In another collaboration, Chichester and Wilson published biomedical manuals for sales representatives working for Hoechst, the German pharmaceutical company.[55]

Michael Foyle, who spoke several languages, including Russian, was a true internationalist. Among his contributions was mentoring the next generation of leaders in Britain—John Jarvis, his publishing director, Robert Long, international sales manager, and Peter Ferris, who started in Wiley's British warehouse at the age of 16 and would become information systems and

distribution director. With sales of U.S. $37 million in 1989, Chichester employed over 250 people.[56]

Some of the subsidiaries did especially well in the 1980s. Australia's Jacaranda Wiley, under John Collins, invested heavily in its renowned school atlas program and launched the school editions of the *Macquarie Dictionary*, Australia's teaching dictionary. In 1988, Jacaranda Wiley acquired a local high school list, Brooks Waterloo, with revenues of $1.9 million in Australian dollars. The discounted cash-flow return on investment was a very strong 22 to 25 percent for most of the decade, and profits frequently exceeded plan. At the end of 1988, Collins explained that Jacaranda Wiley's success stemmed from its local publishing program, which amounted to 100 titles per year by the mid-1980s, from the availability of Wiley International Editions, and from a print brokering operation in Hong Kong, where quality printing could be had relatively cheaply compared to printing in Australia. In 1989, Jacaranda Wiley employed 124 people, and its sales were U.S. $14.4 million.[57]

Wiley Canada provides an interesting example of the interplay between New York's International Division and a subsidiary during the volatile monetary exchange climate of the 1980s. The subsidiary had originally been set up in 1968. In the early 1980s, Geoff Dean, who became its president in 1976, continued to build Canada's already successful high school publishing program. He and editor-in-chief James Rogerson launched a business education program designed for a new curriculum in the Ontario school system. In 1980, the high school division won a unique competition to provide texts for the British Columbia Junior Secondary Science Program. By 1988, the High School Division had 72 titles in print, a staff of 21, and sales of U.S. $4 million. The 1980s, however, proved to be a trying time. High school sales were flat, the exchange rate with the U.S. dollar was unfavorable, and price resistance was strong. The market for college textbooks also proved difficult. Canada adapted its first American college text for the local market, Kieso and Weygandt's *Intermediate Accounting*, in 1982. As for imports, however, New York, negatively impacted by unfavorable exchange rates, insisted on maintaining high profitability targets, which made Wiley texts more costly in Canada than those of the competition.[58]

Dean also explored trade publishing. In 1980, the company became the distributor in Canada for Charles Scribner's Sons, which Dean saw as an opportunity to become a major player in the Canadian trade market. Most of Scribner's list did not sell well in the Canadian market, but Wiley sold thousands of copies every year of titles by Scribner's two most renowned authors, Ernest Hemingway and F. Scott Fitzgerald. The Scribner relationship helped Dean to attract other agency arrangements representing U.S. and U.K. publishers and to start a modest trade program. In 1980, Canada published *Take My Family . . . Please* by *Toronto Mail* humor columnist Gary Lautens. The book, which won the prestigious Stephen Leacock Memorial Medal for Humour, sold 100,000 copies, 50,000 as a Wiley hardback and another 50,000 in a paperback licensing arrangement. These were very impressive numbers in the small Canadian market. Another title, *Ogilvy on Advertising*, by David Ogilvy, turned out to be a classic, cited for years in marketing and communications literature.[59]

In 1985, Canadian sales reached U.S. $13 million, but the next year sales declined, in part due to the loss of the Scribner agency when Scribner's merged with Macmillan. Dean left Wiley Canada in that year, and Charles Stoll, ever ready to help out, took over until Dean was replaced by John Dill in 1986. Stoll urged Wiley to let Dill have the chance to turn Wiley Canada around, but under strict supervision. "If the new [high school] publishing program fails to meet reasonable checkpoint performance criteria," he cautioned, "phase it out as gracefully as possible" and turn the subsidiary into a distribution facility or close it altogether and service Canada directly from the United States. This advice was rejected, not without doubts, and Wiley

Canada carried on. Dill's first move was to reorganize, shifting from a functional to a market-focused divisional structure. He then turned to rebuilding the management in High School, Higher Education, Professional & Trade, and Human Resources. Two years of change and uncertainty followed. Given Stoll's recommendation, Dill's major preoccupation was to demonstrate to the parent company that all of Wiley would benefit from a Canadian subsidiary with a mandate to publish locally as well as market U.S. products in Canada. In 1989, there were 83 people working for Wiley Canada, generating U.S. $12.8 million in revenue.[60]

Canada's publishing initiatives were an inspiration for the formation of an International Management Group in the early 1980s. "It was a good opportunity to discuss problems and opportunities," said Dean. Foremost on the minds of subsidiary heads was how to correlate their local publishing efforts with New York's expanding publishing program. This rudimentary form of global coordination proved helpful for the British publishing program, but less so for Canada and Australia, where the indigenous programs were "much more locally focused."[61]

In Mexico, Limusa-Wiley prospered in the 1960s and 1970s, and all of its profits were plowed back into the joint venture. Later, that arrangement became difficult for Wiley when the Mexican government defaulted on its foreign debt, devalued the peso, and nationalized the banking system in 1982. The resulting inflation drove the value of the Mexican peso down from about 26 per dollar in 1982 to more than 2,200 per dollar by the end of 1987, a depreciation of over 8,000 percent. Wiley watched helplessly as the dollar value of Limusa-Wiley plummeted, too, even while the venture continued to thrive operationally, putting out 120 titles in 1985 alone. However, this arrangement began to lose its appeal for Wiley as profits from Mexico declined while profits were already fading away at home. In late 1985, after exploring sundry suboptimal ways to reduce its peso exposure and receiving discouraging reports of government corruption and looming macroeconomic instability, Wiley decided to sell its stake in Limusa to the two remaining Mexican partners for U.S. $1.25 million, far less than Limusa should have been worth under normal circumstances. The Noriega family, one of the partners, bought out the other, the Trillas, at the same time. When the deal took effect on February 15, 1986, Wiley wrote off a loss in excess of $1.9 million. It was a sad situation in every sense. Soon after the sale, Editorial Limusa became the third largest textbook publisher in Spanish Latin America. It was still thriving in 2007, in part due to its strong co-publishing relationship with Wiley.[62]

At the same time that it sold Limusa, Wiley sold its stake in Livros Tecnicos e Cientificos Editora, its Brazilian joint venture, for the same basic reasons. As late as 1978, Livros was the largest university textbook publisher in Brazil. But, hammered by that country's hyperinflation, Brazilian college students began photocopying rather than purchasing textbooks; so even if Wiley had successfully hedged its exposure to Brazilian currency, it would not have done well. Wiley sold its share to the Koogan Lorch family, owners of Editora Guanabara Koogan. Wiley's co-publishing arrangement with Guanabara also continued into the twenty-first century.

Wiley did not entirely regret its expansion into Latin America and in fact continued to do well there through its co-publishing arrangements and by selling translation rights to third-party publishers. In the Middle East, however, Arabooks was struggling, so much so that by 1985, Wiley began to look hard at its continuance. In 1990, Wiley sold its list to the Jordan Book Centre.[63]

Wiley Eastern, the company's joint venture in India, also faced difficulty in the 1980s. It was growing fast—7 offices, 65 to 70 original books a year, and 76 employees by 1988—and needed additional capital. The company's Indian partners balked, refusing even to guarantee loans due to conflicts with the company's management. Moreover, the interest rates charged by the local banks hovered around a punishing 17 percent per year. The Indian currency was devalued heavily, which seriously impacted the book trade. Most of the importers were unable to pay the publishers and defaulted on payments. Indian retailers were similarly strapped, so they could not order significant quantities of books or be counted on to remit in a timely fashion. The Indian Government Institutes, a major customer, was also very slow to pay. Worse, in 1985 the government raised taxes to punitive levels. In 1987, a serious drought and a strike by university professors created a crisis. Debt was also a factor, for Wiley Eastern owed $450,000, including arrears on royalties to authors and payments to Wiley for books imported through Singapore, most of which were Wiley International Editions. Worse, Wiley Eastern's plans to pay down the debt were based on "little more than guesstimates," in part because the subsidiary had no control over its inventory. If its managing director were forced out, Wiley concluded in late 1988, it would have to pull out of the venture.[64]

In April 1989, after several months of turbulence at the subsidiary, Wiley threatened to withdraw its 40 percent stake in the joint venture. Wiley backed away from the threat when its Indian partners also threatened to pull out, which would have sunk the local company. Moreover, Wiley's managers realized that they could not easily transfer the company's Indian business to its Singapore office, if only because its information processing system was inadequate to handle so massive a transfer of account information. Singapore would have needed at least a midsized IBM AS/400, like that used in both Chichester and Toronto. Wiley finally came to an agreement with its Indian partners by granting Wiley Eastern a "concessional existence" that would last as long as it paid down its debt.[65]

As the years passed, Wiley Southeast Asia, based in Singapore where it was managed by John Lee, grew in size and importance, especially with the expansion of two-year English-language colleges designed to help Asian students gain admission to schools in the United States and the United Kingdom. The subsidiary was transferred to the control of Jacaranda Wiley in mid-1987. In 1989, Asian sales through Singapore reached U.S. $10.3 million, and there were 31 people in the office and warehouse.[66]

As Japan's economy moved from basic manufacturing to the production of more sophisticated consumer goods featuring innovative uses of technology, such as automobiles, it developed into a significant market for Wiley books and journals. In the early 1980s, Wiley Japan, with eight employees, was still small. Hiroshi Tsukabe managed the import business with the help of two colleagues, while a separate college textbook operation staffed by five people recruited Japanese authors to write textbooks and translate English-language texts into Japanese. But Wiley faced a problem: The Japanese returns system, which allowed retailers to return books for up to one year, required abnormally high investments in inventory, resulting in extreme uncertainty about actual sales levels. In 1984, the textbook program was shut down after translating 18 titles. Wiley's efforts to sell its books directly into the Japanese market were also stymied by the limited amount of Japanese-language promotional material produced by Wiley's small office there. Wiley Japan's total revenue was just over $2 million in 1984, with less than half coming from the sale of journals. Although sales had increased to $3.9 million by 1989, Wiley's managers expressed concern that Wiley was falling behind the competition.[67]

If publishing in the developing world was a challenging proposition in the 1980s, even more challenging were the Soviet and Chinese markets. In the early 1980s, Wiley's revenues from the Soviet Union hovered around $250,000 per year from the sale of both publishing rights and a few thousand book units. Wiley also made money

[P]ublishing in the developing world was a challenging proposition in the 1980s . . .

selling books by Soviet authors to a Western audience. Among these were the *Theory of Quantized Fields* by N. N. Bogoliubov and D. V. Shirkov, and *Fundamentals of Plasma Physics* by Viktor Golant and colleagues. Encouraged by changes implemented by the reform-minded Soviet leader Mikhail Gorbachev beginning in 1985, Wiley stepped up its efforts in the Soviet market. In 1988, the U.S. Book Store opened in Moscow. In this cooperative venture, publishers like Wiley rented display space for their books and Russian clerks took orders in "hard currency" (dollars or sterling). The store, which displayed about 4,000 titles in exchange for a rental fee of $30 to $40 per book, was not without problems but was vastly better than nothing.[68]

Also in 1988, Wiley and Nauka, the publishing house of the USSR Academy of Science long courted by Wiley, explored the possibility of co-publishing. At the 1989 Moscow Book Fair, a representative from the Academy of Science approached Rudi Weiss of the Wiley subsidiary Scripta Technica, which translated Russian journals into English, about a possible joint venture to be called Wiley-Nauka Scientific Publishers. After visiting Moscow and Leningrad for several weeks in September 1989, Andrew Neilly reported that his discussions with Soviet publishers were "open, frank, and friendly" and that almost all of them looked forward "to establishing a market economy for books and journals, greater freedom to deal with publishers in the outside world, and to joining the IPA [International Publishing Association] as soon as conditions permit." He noted too, however, that Nauka was still hobbled by regulations requiring it to publish books that had extremely limited market potential. An agreement would finally be reached in summer 1991, just before the attempted coup against Gorbachev. The coup failed, but it caused the cancellation of the Moscow Book Fair that year and rattled publishers. These events, combined with the striking revelation that Nauka was not as well thought of as Wiley believed, caused the company to rethink its strategy in the Soviet Union.[69]

Wiley did not hesitate to take the lead when it came to entering the China market, which Wiley forecast would become a major market for English-language books because English was rapidly becoming China's second language. To this had to be added the growing demand for Chinese-language editions of technical and scientific works. After mainland China fell to the communists in 1949, Chinese nationalists established the Republic of China (Taiwan) on the island of Formosa. Taiwan soon became home to major reprinting companies that had both the will and the way for piracy. The will sprang from both a culture foreign to copyright and an early twentieth-century treaty that granted then-Imperial China the right to translate and reprint U.S. books without permission from the copyright holder.

During the Cold War, the United States recognized the Taiwanese as the lawful government of China, which to the Taiwanese meant recognizing the old treaty. The way to piracy came with possession of some of the world's best offset printing technology and the skill to use it.[70]

By the mid-1970s, the geopolitical situation was changing. Though still communist, mainland China, having shunned the Soviet Union for more than a decade, warmed to the United States while beginning to show signs of economic reform after Mao Tse-Tung died in 1976. Western companies sensed great possibilities on the mainland. Having forged relations with government officials and publishers in the Soviet Union, Brad was eager to do the same in China. His son, Peter, introduced him to Henry Noyes, owner of China Books and Periodicals in San Francisco. Noyes, a committed Maoist, was licensed by the U.S. Treasury to import books and periodicals from China. Noyes advised Brad to approach the Chinese through their embassy in Canada. Noyes also advised Brad not to go to the Canton Trade Fair, warning him he

Goodwill was generated by a series of Wiley book exhibits in China starting in 1979. Inset: Brad Wiley Sr. with Patricia Wang, a Wiley trainee who later became the first editor of the Chinese-language edition of *Elle* magazine.

Brad and Esther Wiley's second visit to China, 1979. Esther Booth Wiley, "Diary of 2nd Visit to China with WBW, November 25 . . . to December 15, 1979."

22
Dec. 4 —
The great day has arrived — the Wiley reception at the national Gallery. About 200 people in attendance — U.S. Ambassador Wood- cock, John Thompson of the Embassy (PAO), editors of the different publishing houses, professors from the universities, mrs fong (our interpreta in April who is now working for the national academy of science screening young people to go to U.S. to study), the vice-chairman of Education etc. etc. The books were well arranged (only 15 missing), tables spread with goodies (cakes, hors d'oeuvres, duck, moutai, red wine + orange juice for drinks. Excellent signs on the outside of the China national Gallery with Wiley colophon antous.

Esther Booth Wiley
Diary of 2nd visit to China with WBW. — November 25 (to Japan - Tokyo until Nov. 30) to December 15, 1979
Accompanied by Charles Stoll of John Wiley + Sons (international v.p.) and Tom Cassidy marketing manager. Occasion - opening of exhibition of 1,000 Wiley titles in 7 cities of China — first american publisher to have won exhibition (Peking, Shanghai, Foochow, Changsa, Wuhan, Chungking and Hofei (a city destined to be the center of industrial research).

would "lose face" by doing so. Thus, in the mid-1970s, a salesperson was sent in his place. In 1979, probably thanks to an introduction by Noyes, Brad and Esther were invited to visit China before the arrival of a larger delegation from the Association of American Publishers. They became the first noncommunist American publishers to visit that country since the revolution in 1949.

Wiley became, in Charles Stoll's words, "very excited about" doing business in China. "It looked like something," he later recalled, "that was really opening up." By the end of 1979, Wiley had set up a 1,100-title, 15-day book exhibit in six important cities and, as a gesture of goodwill and to seed the market, donated all the exhibited books to Chinese libraries. The strategy, which involved supplying libraries through purchases funded by the World Bank, combined with a Wiley training program for Chinese book editors and marketers, worked wonders for sales. In

Wiley in the 1980s became the largest foreign supplier of books to China.

fact, Wiley in the 1980s, represented by Martha Avery, became the largest foreign supplier of books to China, selling some $1.25 million worth of books there at its peak. The training program, though, came to a sudden end after the Tiananmen Square massacre in 1989.[71]

Establishing a local publishing presence in China, where scientific research was still relatively backward and book prices were low even by the standards of other developing countries, proved more difficult. Wiley tried to form a joint venture with China's Science Press but could not agree on a proper business plan. It also tried forming joint ventures with China Academic Publishers and Shanghai Scientific and Technical Publishing Company (SSTP), but again, after much effort, little came to pass. "They were very eager to talk about these things," Stoll noted, "but then when it came down to actually pinning them down to a business proposition, they and their

*C*o-publishing ventures with China's Science Press, such as *Physical Geography of China*, by Zhao Songqiao, solidified Wiley's relationships in China. A delegation from the People's Republic of China State Education Commission toured Boston in 1988 as Wiley's guests and talked to publishers. Charity Robey (second from right) hosted.

[superiors] really didn't have much heart for it." Prices so low that they ruled out profitability and a lack of copyright protection undercut Wiley's ambitions. Ultimately, the best Wiley could do was to reach a co-publishing arrangement with SSTP. Wiley's own books continued to fall victim to pirates. By 1988, at least 350 Wiley titles were being pirated in China, and the estimated total number of these units sold far exceeded the company's legitimate sales. Perhaps worse, many unauthorized translations were so poorly done that Wiley and its authors worried seriously about the long-term negative effects on their reputation in China.[72]

Despite Wiley's best efforts, the pirating of foreign books in China continued apace, and the practice in South Korea, Pakistan, and other countries remained a serious problem as well. Even so, Wiley, in 1983, established an exclusive agency agreement with Kumi Trading Company in Korea. The agreement, which bound Kumi to purchase at least $300,000 of Wiley books per year, worked reasonably well but nonetheless was abandoned in 1987 because Kumi did not deal in textbooks, which Wiley knew from other Korean booksellers were in demand. The company also licensed United Publishing and Promotion Company there, to reprint about 40 of its textbooks. After making an initial payment, however, United Publishing neglected to report its activities. Even when it did, a basic problem remained: "One cannot believe the print numbers," reported Adrian Higham after a trip to Korea. If the low numbers were true, then United Publishing was not selling enough Wiley books. If they were false, then it could not be trusted. Either way, Wiley had to walk away from these relationships.[73]

Internationally, Wiley's overseas investment showed an understandable pattern, given the global economic situation. Wiley did better in some developing country markets than in others. In this part of the world, the decade of the 1980s was definitely a period of retrenchment. The company backed out of joint ventures in Brazil and Mexico and came close to shutting down its Indian operation. The one exception was the company's aggressive posture in China.

But Wiley lacked strategic and operational coordination overseas. Brad Wiley had set up a regimen by which the American company gave local managers ample room to run their own businesses and fit them to local circumstances. The results were mixed. Even Brad admitted as much, saying in his unpublished memoir about New York's relationship with Chichester, the company's second-largest publishing center and a place where he and his wife spent many days each year: "Essentially, we were trying to work out the correct relationship between our New York publishing programs and the publishing program of an autonomous subsidiary." There were efforts at coordination, first in journals and later with the establishment of the International Management Group, but the results were minimal. Meanwhile, local managers felt compelled to defend their autonomy and their indigenous publishing programs, particularly when the parent company, with the acquisition of Wilson Learning, appeared to be headed off in a new direction about which some knew very little and others were not sympathetic. One managing director was a belligerent defender of local autonomy against the inroads of front-office imperialism. Another built a publishing program financed by the import of Wiley books but constantly delayed payment for their sale, while a third traveled extensively, cutting deals with distributors without regard for financial performance. But the days of such extravagant autonomy for country managers were waning. Brad Sr., the family patriarch, offered a new vision of Wiley International in a 1987 speech when he argued that the company had "outgrown thinking and acting 'domestic' and 'foreign' to thinking and acting '*global*.' We have a *global* strategy and a *global* presence." There was still a wide gap, however, between vision and execution that would be closed only by new CEOs in the 1990s.[74]

NEW CHALLENGE TO COPYRIGHT

In 1978, a group of publishers, authors, and users, including Wiley's Michael Harris, established the Copyright Clearance Center, Inc. (CCC). It was created in response to several suggestions in the legislative history of the U.S. Copyright Act of 1976 that a collective licensing organization, like those that already existed in Europe, be formed to address the growing availability of photocopy machines in American businesses and universities. CCC, a not-for-profit organization located first near Wiley's offices in New York and later in Salem and Danvers, Massachusetts, was initially funded by bank loans guaranteed by seven publishers, including Wiley.[75]

By 1992, the CCC was representing more than 8,500 publishers and other copyright holders in licensing photocopy rights to more than 1.5 million titles, through both transactional and repertory licensing services, and was distributing more than $6.1 million per year in royalties to those copyright holders. By 2006, the CCC's annual distributions from all its licensing services (which had expanded beyond photocopying) had climbed past $110 million (on total revenues of about $150 million), of which Wiley received more than $3.6 million. Cumulative distributions to all copyright holders had surpassed $1 billion, all net bottom-line revenue to those copyright holders.[76]

In addition to its early participation in loan guarantees, Wiley's contributions to the CCC included advocacy for the collective licensing model and a strong and continuing commitment of senior executive time. Michael Harris served on the CCC's board of directors for many of its early years. Brad Wiley served as the chairman of the center's board during the 1980s; and Wiley's general counsel, Richard Rudick, served on its board beginning in the late 1980s, and served many years as vice chairman and as a member of the Executive Committee. Other Wiley executives also served on various CCC committees. In 2006, Wiley legal director Roy Kaufman joined Richard Rudick on the CCC's board of directors.[77]

> Prominent copyright [cases] defined the parameters of copyright "fair use" . . .

In the early 1980s, Wiley and other major publishers—including McGraw-Hill, Elsevier, Blackwell, Springer-Verlag, Butterworth, Pergamon, and Academic Press—renewed their guarantees of CCC's bank loans to allow the center to build a repertory licensing service enabling large corporations to acquire annual copyright licenses and thereby ease the administrative burden of copyright compliance. Wiley's participation helped convince major R&D-oriented industries to obtain CCC licenses. This increased royalties to publishers and other rights holders, expanded copyright compliance in Wiley's customer markets and in U.S. business in general, and ultimately created extensions of the photocopy licenses, first into the academic coursepack market and later into licenses of digital (e-mail and intranet) uses in American businesses. These licensing services, with Wiley's help, were so successful that within a few years the CCC not only had paid off its bank loans but also had paid off all back-due royalties to participating rights holders, including Wiley.[78]

Through its substantial participation in both the Association of American Publishers (of which Brad Wiley was an early chairman of the board) and the CCC, Wiley also galvanized publisher lawsuits against prominent copyright infringers, including several large universities in the early 1980s and Texaco in 1985. Publishers litigated and won the prominent copyright case known as *American Geophysical Union v. Texaco Inc.*, 60 F.3d 913 (2d Cir. 1994), which essentially defined the parameters of copyright "fair use" in the corporate environment. This motivated much of corporate America to obtain CCC licenses. At roughly the same time, Wiley and another group of publishers litigated and won another important case, *Basic Books, Inc. v. Kinko's Graphics Corp.* (decided in a New York district court in 1991), which clarified copyright holders' entitlement to be paid for use of their works in university coursepacks. As a result of the *Kinko's* case, the CCC created (and still maintains) a licensing service expressly for the academic coursepack market (later extended to the "electronic coursepack" market). Wiley's participation in those services helped make them the standard for copyright compliance in academia and helped produce a steady stream of royalties for copyright rights holders, while simplifying the copyright compliance process for professors, librarians, and copy shop owners.[79]

In the international arena, Wiley continued its efforts to limit the impact of piracy while proselytizing about the virtues of effective and robust copyright laws in the People's Republic of China. Brad urged the Chinese to join the Berne Copyright Convention or the Universal Copyright Convention. These treaties require member countries to enforce copyright of foreign authors of member countries within their territory. In 1983, Brad and Charles Stoll met with a number of officials in Beijing concerning copyright and the piracy of textbooks. In 1985, Brad lectured before various Chinese interest groups about the importance of instituting strong domestic copyright laws and joining international copyright treaties. He also met with key players behind the scenes explaining that "copyright proponents always have a tiny constituency, even in developed countries such as the United States." In 1986, Charles Stoll and corporate counsel Richard Rudick explained to a Chinese copyright delegation some of the finer details of contracts ranging from permissions to full reprints to co-publishing. The Chinese, like the Americans and Russians before them, moved slowly, only in 1992 signing a copyright enforcement reciprocal agreement with the United States. Later that year they joined the Universal Copyright Convention and, effective January 1, 1993, the Berne Convention. The United States itself had finally joined Berne only a few years before, in March 1989, following the congressional testimony of Neilly, among others, who spoke strongly in favor of the move. Other U.S. publishers also supported Berne, but Wiley was a driving force in the movement, effectively counteracting what Rudick described as the "inaccurate and incomplete" materials distributed by Berne's opponents.[80]

Wiley Learning Technologies and the Promise of Wilson Learning

In the United States, Wiley's management had long sensed the danger of overreliance on the higher education market. The company's acquisition strategy in the 1960s had been designed to address this issue, but its acquisitions in adjacent markets, such as library technology and training, did not prove successful, and the textbook business actually grew as a percentage of sales. In the 1980s, diversification by acquisition appeared to offer better possibilities.[81]

America's fast-growing service economy created new market opportunities for corporate training that looked attractive. The United States still manufactured more than it ever had, but inexpensive imports, many from Japan, were undermining basic industries. Beginning in the 1960s and accelerating in the 1970s and 1980s, the nation's leadership eroded in such industries as steel, automobiles, textiles, and consumer electronics, leaving the communities in which manufacturing had been predominant depressed. The children of former factory workers, and sometimes former industrial workers themselves, moved into service occupations. Some were low-paying jobs—colloquially, "McJobs," in reference to those at McDonald's, which often paid its entry-level employees minimum wage— but many were highly paid positions in management, business-to-business sales, healthcare, and consulting, which required considerable education, experience, and training. Declining productivity was also becoming "one of the critical issues for American industry in the 1980s," consultant James Gillespie told Wiley. Articles and books extolling the virtues of Japanese-style capitalism and providing wisdom on business practices flooded the business book market. Wiley wanted to position itself atop this sea change in the economy, much as it had ridden the waves of industrialization beginning in the nineteenth century.[82]

Taking a cue from McGraw-Hill, which had acquired Tratec in 1978, and Prentice Hall, which had bought Deltak in 1979, Wiley entered the corporate training business, which was growing at 20 percent per year, anticipating synergies between training and its educational publishing programs. It was an exciting time. Training, or, more broadly conceived, "lifelong learning," was a market in which, it was argued, technology—meaning electronic delivery of digital content and related assessment tools—was going to play a big role. Then, in February 1982, Wiley purchased the Wilson Learning Corporation for $15.5 million plus a "substantial contingent payout based on Wilson's future performance." Headquartered in Eden Prairie, Minnesota, a Minneapolis suburb, Wilson posted revenues of about $15 million, and had a staff of 210, 20 offices in the United States, and operations in 15 other countries, including Japan. It sold seminars, classroom instruction, and products such as workbooks, audiocassettes, videotapes, and computer programs with a particular emphasis on sales and sales management training. Wilson's management appeared to be imaginative and entrepreneurial, which had garnered the company a reputation for being a high-quality, high-end business, much like

Wiley. As Peter Wiley recalled, "Wilson was building the content and the tools that would enrich the usual seminar-based training programs." Even more important, Wilson would help Wiley jump-start the entrepreneurial culture Neilly was trying to foster among his managers.[83]

To some, Larry Wilson was a charismatic presence. He had founded Wilson in 1965 after stints as a high school teacher and a life insurance salesman had left him convinced that "motivated people, not products, are the key to an enterprise." Now he was looking to sell, not to cash out but rather to ensure that his company could play on a wider stage and not simply be swallowed up by too large a corporate suitor. For this reason, Wiley looked more attractive than other, larger houses that were also interested.[84]

The price tag, a big number for Wiley, was met through a sale of Wiley's shares. Wilson was the company's biggest acquisition since Interscience some 20 years earlier. Following a string of smaller acquisitions, Neilly put it this way: "It's too expensive to dabble these days. We want to be an important factor in whatever area we enter." With Wilson, Neilly told a reporter that "we are just at the tip of the iceberg now." But "iceberg" would turn out to be an unfortunate metaphor. Just before the deal closed, in a memorable incident that signaled trouble ahead, Wilson and his managers greeted Brad and the visiting Wiley managers in Eden Prairie with bear hugs. Brad was known to his board members as "The Mandarin"; nobody, recalled board member Alan Fernald, would ever dare to hug The Mandarin.[85]

Wilson was to be the core of the new Learning Group announced in Neilly's post-acquisition reorganization of the company. To extend the reach of the group's training programs and build on the company's strength in engineering, Wiley in 1983 formed Alpha-Omega, a division dedicated to the production of technical training materials, particularly for software and manufacturing engineers. The division was renamed Wiley Learning Technologies (WLT) and placed under the direction of Deborah Wiley. In fiscal 1985, WLT successfully

Wilson Learning president Mathew Juechter (left) with Larry Wilson, the company's founder.

Wilson Learning's Pecos River Conference Center in New Mexico and Wiley participants in the team-building exercises that Larry Wilson ran at the center.

completed pilot tests for a program titled *Managing Software Development: Solving the Productivity Puzzle* conducted at General Dynamics and Paradyne Corporation. The program's brochure described "an active learning environment designed to match how adults most effectively learn," which would be "interesting and engaging, with touches of drama and humor." The program was divided into ten modules that could be presented by a moderator ("a working software developer") or used on an individual basis. Combining classroom instruction with videos, workbooks, and various learning aids, the prize-winning program sold quickly to IBM, Grumman, GTE Government Systems, Rolm, Lockheed, General Electric, and NASA.[86]

Wilson was seen as a source of growth that traditional publishing lacked. A high-level committee including Neilly and Wilson president Mathew Juechter worked with Larry Wilson to set up a "skunk works" known as Interactive Technologies in Santa Fe, New Mexico, in 1984. Interactive was charged with producing a library of interactive training programs on videodisc to supplement Wilson's seminar products. Wiley's R&D advisory committee tapped Bert Sutherland, one of its members, to help oversee progress at Interactive, which then produced a "state of the art digital training program." It was a remarkable piece of work. The trainee was presented with videos of different personality types—as defined by psychologist Abraham Maslow—among whom the would-be salesperson had to maneuver to make a sale. The disc also provided assessment of a trainee's progress.[87]

About the same time, Wilson Learning formed the Wilson Alliance for Research and Development with the University of Minnesota to study how adults learn, with particular emphasis on how new technologies could aid the learning process. In November 1984, Wiley bought Assessment Designs, Inc., a 52-employee company based in Orlando that developed employee selection and performance evaluation systems and training programs designed to measure competencies. (In a notable reversal, Wilson divested its South African subsidiary in 1985, to protest apartheid.)[88]

Wilson was moving quickly to become a full-service training firm, and the company's prospects looked bright. Its sales in 1983 increased 44 percent, to $23.8 million, at a time when Wiley's total sales were increasing from $137 million to $167 million. By 1984, Wilson Learning counted over 250 of the Fortune 1000 companies as clients and again contributed substantially to Wiley's total sales growth.

> The software market . . . was "hard to define and harder to reach."

"Wiley's entry into new technology businesses and markets via internal development and acquisitions" while taking responsibility for the company's digital archive, editing, and production tools projects. Wiley was already selling the *Harvard Business Review* and the *Kirk-Othmer Encyclopedia of Chemical Technology* online. The company had also put its catalog online and was testing new book production tools, including electronic copy editing, developed by board member Sutherland and his associate, Robert Sproull Jr., the son of board member Robert Sproull. Typical projects Johnson and his colleagues would become involved with were a joint venture with the National Bureau of Standards to publish a mass spectral database and a series of cooperative seminars with the American Chemical Society to train chemists in how to use the ACS's online journals and the online *Kirk-Othmer Encyclopedia*. The mass spectral database proved to be successful, logging year-on-year revenue growth throughout the decade. The software

New Technology from Existing Product Lines

Consistent with senior management's view that the technology wave would begin to surge in the mid-1980s, Wiley moved into the software business while building or attempting to acquire computer-based tools that would add speed and efficiency to the publishing process. Software was already a $4.9 billion industry, but Wiley approached it with a small number of programs, such as grade management tools for instructors and self-teaching guides, which were designed to tie in with Wiley's college and professional book lists. In 1984, Neilly hired Richard O. Johnson as the new head of Corporate Development. In his first report to the board, Johnson explained that his department would plan and implement

Cliff Mills, science publisher in the College Division, with Wiley Learning Technologies' *Managing Software Development: Solving the Productivity Puzzle.*

market, in contrast, was "hard to define and harder to reach." In 1984, Johnson cut spending on professional and college software programs. Other publishers that had entered the market likewise backed off. After consultations with the R&D committee, Johnson decided to focus more on product development than on the sale of existing product.[89]

Audio technology seemed yet another promising field. In 1986, Wiley entered audio publishing with the launch of Wiley Sound Business Cassettes, products based on current or backlist Wiley titles in the general area of business. The idea was not to simply record versions of books but to provide audio adaptations that complemented books. "Conversations with an Expert" was the program's subtitle, and the format consisted of an introduction by the series host followed by a text interspersed with short vignettes to dramatize key concepts. The first titles—*The Creative Mystique* by advertising executive John M. Keil, *The Entrepreneurial Life* by venture capitalist A. David Silver, *Win-Win Negotiating* by arbitrator Fred Jandt and Paul Gillette, and *Excuses* by clinical psychologists C. R. Snyder, Raymond L. Higgins, and Rita J. Stucky—were chosen on the basis of their potential for entertainment as well as education. Wiley Sound also created a line of language and culture tapes aimed at business travelers plus successful Wiley books, such as William E. Mitchell and Thomas R. Ireland's *Common Stocks for Common Sense Investors* and Russell Ackoff's *Management in Small Doses*, released in audiobook editions. There were discussions about turning out "audio first, book second" products, but as the market matured it usually worked the other way around. A particularly innovative product was an interactive videodisc, *The Puzzle of the Tacoma Narrows Bridge Collapse*, by Robert G. Fuller, Dean A. Zollman, and Thomas C. Campbell, which helped engineering students understand structural physics. The disc was geared to students at three different levels of mathematical aptitude and contained problems for each level to solve.[90]

1985: A Pivotal Year

Although the 1980s proved to be a tumultuous decade in publishing, Wiley fared well in the early years. By 1985, its list—books and other learning technologies—encompassed a wide swath of human knowledge, with 7,586 books, 111 journals, 12 software packages, and 179 audio and video discs. Growth had continued both organically and by acquisition, some of the latter through the purchase of established lists or entire companies. The atmosphere was charged with excitement; Neilly and his team had steered Wiley into new fields and new technologies. In 1985, however, there was a dramatic shift in confidence. The company, after three years of free spending, would quickly reverse field, reducing costs and shuttering or selling off nonproductive assets to raise cash. Fortunately, Wiley was able to offload unwanted assets at good prices because the media industry was caught up in a wave of conglomeration, which inflated values and made publishing companies, or parts of them, hot commodities.

A report by Charles Stoll, the vice president in charge of strategic planning, painted a sobering picture: Wiley's revenues and profits were up largely because of higher prices associated with the inflation of the early 1980s. In "real" terms, the number of books actually sold was flat, dropping in most of Wiley's subject areas. (This was partially offset by growth in business/economics, computers/data processing, and occupational titles.) The inescapable fact was that the company was selling fewer copies of most of its titles. A bold strategic plan had been developed but had not been sufficiently implemented. Wiley was not alone in this situation. "The industry had masked results for some time with inflationary price increases," said Robert Wilder, who was head of finance in the Publishing Group at the time and later chief financial officer. "This, combined with lax inventory management techniques and poor [management] development efforts, placed many [companies] in jeopardy. "Our execution," Neilly wrote to Charles Stoll in 1985, "has often been faulty, and the world is changing faster than we know."[91]

In December 1984, Neilly had already offered the board an alarming description of his concern that management had not been sufficiently attuned to the markets: "*Schizophrenia* is defined as a psychosis characterized by loss of contact with one's environment and by disintegration of personality. We are reasonably certain that loss of contact with our environment (markets) is a contributing factor to the poor performance in some of our publishing programs. As to the second element, only time will tell." "Our sales estimates were far too optimistic," Brad Wiley added, "and we failed to pay attention to what our sales reps had been telling us from the marketplace." Bigger, well-heeled publishers like Houghton Mifflin, Macmillan, Random House, Harper & Row, and others were invading "Wiley territory" in engineering, mathematics, and computer science, often with better books than Wiley's. For a knowledge publisher of long standing, this development might have been fatal. Wiley was "not getting the good books," Brad complained. Wiley was also burdened by some editors who were "long of tooth," said Rick Leyh, the acquisitions editor assigned to building a new business list. "These editors were living off the backlist, revising the list with very little new blood through the early 1980s. . . . Worse, editorial management supported this approach. There was cronyism with authors and reviewers alike, leading to a few backlist bestsellers that would churn the dollars to support an entire program." There was also a tendency to sign prestige authors; do minimal developmental work, including manuscript review; and then cut corners to save costs on the supplements package. With cuts in marketing and development, the quality of Wiley's textbooks had slipped far enough by the mid-1980s that industry observers no longer considered Wiley one of the Big Six college textbook publishers.[92]

> "The world is changing faster than we know."

Another corporate reorganization was announced in December 1984, effective January 1985. Through it, all domestic publishing came under the direction of Robert Douglas and was organized into six groups: College, under Serje Seminoff; Occupational, under Alan Lesure; Journals, under Mary Curtis; Scientific and Technical Books, under Myer Kutz; Medical, under Andrew Ford; and Business, Law, and General Books (BLG), under Stephen Kippur. Kenneth Collins, who had headed the Professional Group, had been let go in the fall of 1984.[93]

Wilson had been acquired to offset the problems of a sluggish higher education market. But even Wilson, after a brilliant start, was contributing to Wiley's slack performance. And there were other problems as well. In the seven years since Neilly had become CEO, the company had more than doubled in size, averaging double-digit growth each year. Acquisitions, of course, contributed to that growth. But costs grew faster still, eroding earnings in 1983, 1985, and 1987 through 1990. A banner year in 1984 made up for a profit dip the previous year, but in 1985 profits plummeted some $5 million. From then until 1990, profits fell year after year, bottoming out at $2.7 million in 1990.

Wilson's rapid growth had been deceiving because its revenues increased but not its earnings. Moreover, as Wilson expanded, its traditional products were debased. Staff cuts, new leadership, tight control of expenses, surveys: none of it worked, or so it seemed, until Wilson turned a healthy profit in fiscal 1987, largely owing to the performance of its international subsidiaries. Still problems persisted. Once-hoped-for synergies between Wilson's training capabilities and Wiley's educational expertise did not materialize, despite strenuous efforts. Wilson's offerings became a cluster of "highly imitated, not very well differentiated, premium priced, not easily adapted, tailored, or translated set of generic off-the-shelf courses," reported Gary Quinlan, who had

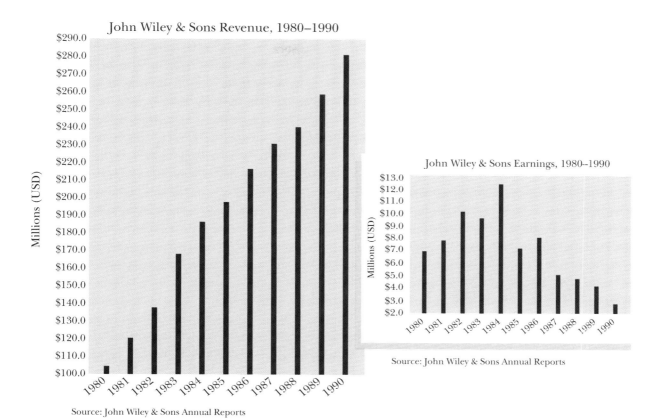

John Wiley & Sons Revenue, 1980–1990

Source: John Wiley & Sons Annual Reports

John Wiley & Sons Earnings, 1980–1990

Source: John Wiley & Sons Annual Reports

been promoted in 1986 to replace Mathew Juechter, the Wilson CEO. By early 1988, feedback from participants and instructors made it clear that Wilson was not doing well even in the seminar room, where it was supposed to be most at home.[94]

Wilson's management had asked for, and had gotten, considerable operating autonomy. More oversight on Wiley's part might have revealed that Wilson's salespeople, compensated on gross sales rather than on the profitability of the products and services they sold, were motivated to push large quantities of low-margin, easy-to-sell products instead of the higher-margin, more custom-tailored seminars. In time, the sales representatives lost their confidence as they found it increasingly difficult to make forceful sales pitches or even to justify Wilson's benefit to customers. "These people [customers] have expectations," one noted, "and I can't honestly tell them that this course will meet those expectations."[95]

As competition in management training was growing ever more intense, and the situation at Wilson deteriorated, low morale and high turnover were inevitable. Wilson's "folks are really disgruntled, personal fulfillment is not being found and . . . lots of folks are talking about leaving," according to a 1987 survey of Wilson employees. Neilly set up a special committee to provide greater oversight, replacing Wilson's CEO twice, but to no avail. Wiley's senior staff continued to assess the roots of Wilson's failure. Some pointed to Larry Wilson and the inherent weaknesses of the company. Wilson employees laid the blame on Wiley, arguing that it had "substantially killed the spirit of Wilson Learning." Others concluded that Wiley had done too little to integrate Wilson into its own corporate culture, a view also held by Juechter. What Juechter had apparently learned from his experience, who went on to establish a consultancy to help companies better integrate their acquisitions, was that Wiley might have done well to form a transition team that included members of both companies' top leadership. This was an important lesson for Wiley, one that would be applied to later acquisitions.[96]

Wilson's numbers continued to worsen. Wiley in the meantime had received feelers from potential buyers but brushed them off. Neilly was open to discussion, but Brad was adamant: "Wilson is not for sale." A meeting with investment bankers, Brad argued, would be like "letting the fox into the hen house!" meaning that such a discussion could lead to others about whether all of Wiley was for sale.[97]

Neither Wiley Learning Technologies (WLT) nor Interactive Technologies, the businesses designed to

complement Wilson, fared well either. Despite WLT's promising start, the important question of markets remained: Who, precisely, was going to buy these products? Most corporate purchasing agents were operations people with little or no training experience. And rather than being organized hierarchically like traditional companies, both software firms and corporate software departments were organized around projects or programs, making the identification of key decision-makers difficult. Where Wilson had a sales force calling on human resources departments, WLT had none, making it difficult to reach line managers who controlled training budgets. The greatest resistance came

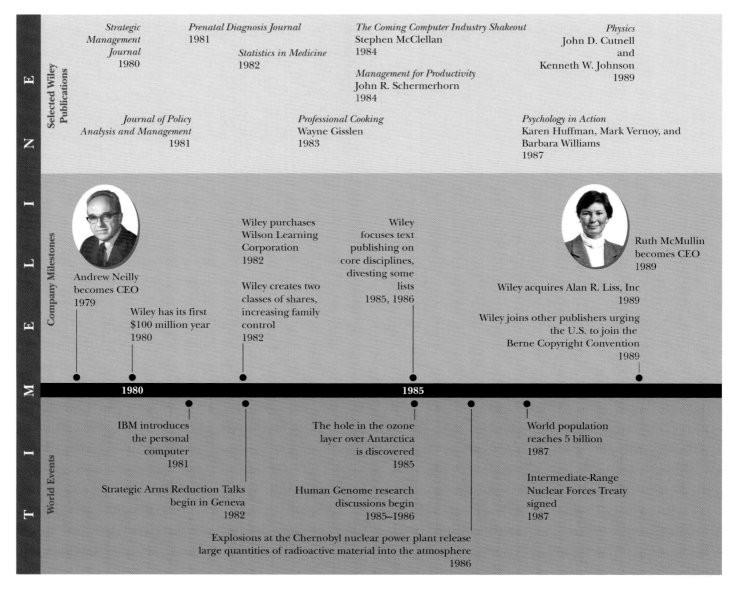

TIMELINE

Selected Wiley Publications

Strategic Management Journal 1980

Prenatal Diagnosis Journal 1981

Statistics in Medicine 1982

The Coming Computer Industry Shakeout Stephen McClellan 1984

Management for Productivity John R. Schermerhorn 1984

Physics John D. Cutnell and Kenneth W. Johnson 1989

Journal of Policy Analysis and Management 1981

Professional Cooking Wayne Gisslen 1983

Psychology in Action Karen Huffman, Mark Vernoy, and Barbara Williams 1987

Company Milestones

Andrew Neilly becomes CEO 1979

Wiley has its first $100 million year 1980

Wiley purchases Wilson Learning Corporation 1982

Wiley creates two classes of shares, increasing family control 1982

Wiley focuses text publishing on core disciplines, divesting some lists 1985, 1986

Ruth McMullin becomes CEO 1989

Wiley acquires Alan R. Liss, Inc 1989

Wiley joins other publishers urging the U.S. to join the Berne Copyright Convention 1989

1980   **1985**

World Events

IBM introduces the personal computer 1981

Strategic Arms Reduction Talks begin in Geneva 1982

The hole in the ozone layer over Antarctica is discovered 1985

Human Genome research discussions begin 1985–1986

Explosions at the Chernobyl nuclear power plant release large quantities of radioactive material into the atmosphere 1986

World population reaches 5 billion 1987

Intermediate-Range Nuclear Forces Treaty signed 1987

from technical managers who did not—or could not—see how training could help them solve business problems. Under these circumstances sales became time-consuming and costly.

Interactive Technologies' first videodisc, *The Versatile Organization,* faced the same problem. Interactive booked sales to IBM, Pacific Bell, US West, and others, but these sales to early technology adopters did not provide sufficient growth to cover the large up-front investment. A digital, interactive training program requiring a $15,000 Sony videodisc player proved to be significantly beyond what most companies were ready to invest in at this stage in the development of computer technology.[98]

Neilly reported to the board, in December 1984, that senior management had introduced "draconian measures to control expense budgets." Layoffs loomed. The New York staff shrank from 989 at the end of April 1984 to 944 at the end of April 1985. This was a 5 percent cutback, a significant number anywhere but especially at a paternalistic firm like Wiley, which during the Depression had let people go but then hired them back, with back pay. In the same period, Wilson shrank approximately 15 percent, with 17 jobs eliminated and 18 converted to part-time. Lists of further cuts were assembled. The efforts to protect the bottom line proved counterproductive, however, compromising both the quality and sales of Wiley's traditional products. In the College Division, the layoffs eliminated marketing managers and developmental editors; the vaunted illustration department was cut to the bone. While Neilly and his managers pushed for special revenue-enhancing projects, their cuts had the opposite effect, and the company spiraled downward.[99]

By 1987, the list of expensive investment projects, which produced insufficient amounts of revenue, ranging from Interactive

> The efforts to protect the bottom line proved counterproductive.

> The list of expensive investment projects, which produced insufficient amounts of revenue . . . were bleeding the company.

Technologies and WLT to various software endeavors, were bleeding the company. In addition to these problems, a drop in computer book sales, and the poorly executed installation of the National Distribution System (NDS), the company's new computerized order system, added to the sense of crisis. The downturn in computer book sales was more than a little ironic, because Wiley had just published Stephen McClellan's bestseller, *The Coming Computer Industry Shakeout.* Moreover, a quiet but significant public library budgetary crisis continued, while relentless growth of the used-book market and a rash of returns caused in part by the NDS debacle made things even worse.[100]

Searching for New Leadership

The 1982 strategic plan noted that "competent management" was the key to reaching Wiley's ambitious goals. Neilly, working with his personal consultant, James Gillespie, and with Rita Irons, the first head of a human resources department, tried numerous ways to build a team that could master a plan calling for movement into an entirely new business and emphasis on technology. Neilly radically reorganized the company a year and a half after the Wilson purchase and then again in 1985. Although having been nurtured in a patriarchal culture, where Brad Wiley was clearly the first among equals, Neilly hoped to create a more participatory, incentive-based culture. He broadened his senior leadership team and encouraged open discussions. Neilly even experimented with sending groups of managers to Larry Wilson's Pecos River Conference Center in New Mexico, where they discussed strategic issues and action plans while engaging in Outward Bound–type team-building exercises, climbing walls and soaring out over canyons in rope and harness. Neilly, the man identified by his consultant as a would-be authoritarian in the 1970s, had seen the Wilson acquisition as an opportunity to flatten the company's organizational structure while encouraging participatory management. Ironically, the decision-making process had become "too egalitarian," according to Richard Johnson. Management meetings had become exercises in "stalling for time," poor substitutes for decisive action.[101]

There was also conflict and confusion about the future of management at Wiley. Would it be led by one of the Wileys or would the company continue to be run by professional managers? In 1985, it became clear to Neilly that none of the sixth generation of Wileys, Brad's children, aspired to become the company's CEO when Deborah Wiley informed Neilly that she would not pursue the top job. When Neilly and Irons could not identify an internal candidate to be developed as his successor, they began to look outside Wiley for a possible replacement. Meanwhile, Brad II was beginning to play a more active role in succession discussions with leading board members, such as William Eisman, Nils Kindwall, and Bert Sutherland. The board urged Neilly to find a chief operating officer who could be groomed as his successor.[102]

A plan evolved to bring in a chief operating officer for a few years to prepare him or her for the role of CEO. Several candidates were interviewed, and in August 1986, Neilly made an offer to an individual with outstanding publishing credentials. The candidate and his wife flew to New York to meet the Wileys and others as a final gesture before signing a contract. The candidate's wife balked at the idea of moving to New York, however, and the candidate withdrew. Wiley reopened the search, but no desirable candidates emerged.[103]

Ruth McMullin, Wiley CEO from April 1989 to March 1990.

Neilly and Irons continued to look, eventually finding a number of possible candidates. One was Charles Ellis, who was managing Elsevier's operations in North America. Brad Sr. interviewed Ellis but did not think he was qualified to become a successor for the CEO position. "This was a great disappointment to me," Neilly recalled. "And in retrospect the extent of the costly mistake we made at that time is hard to exaggerate." Rather than go back into the publishing pool, Neilly and Brad II both preferred to look for a business executive—someone with the interest, experience, and education to manage the company's far-flung empire. Other big publishers, including Houghton Mifflin, had enjoyed substantial success after turning their administrations over to businesspeople. Moreover, a candidate with substantial business credentials, Ruth McMullin, had joined Wiley's board of directors in June 1986, after being introduced to Neilly by corporate counsel Richard Rudick.[104]

A history major with an MBA and a master's in public and private management, McMullin began her career at McGraw-Hill in the early 1960s. In 1979, after stints as an editor, business manager, and treasurer at Doubleday and audiovisual publisher Weston Woods, she joined the corporate strategic planning staff of General Electric. By 1985, she was senior vice president of GE Capital Markets Group, Inc., working on leveraged buyouts and leasing. A bright, numbers-oriented director at Wiley, McMullin quickly emerged as a candidate for Wiley's COO job.[105]

In a two-hour interview conducted in March 1987, Neilly and McMullin discussed the company's recent history, McMullin's publishing experience, and the company's current strengths (authors, editors, reputation) and weaknesses (marketing, finances, staff training). Neilly came away from the meeting excited and confident that McMullin could improve the company's performance without eroding its editorial ("human capital") resources or its "colophon integrity." Brad II met with McMullin and then went to Neilly to express his concern about her leadership capabilities, a concern shared by Irons, who noted that she had never managed more than ten people. When Brad asked Neilly to consider continuing the search so that they could compare her with another candidate, Neilly opposed the idea.[106]

McMullin agreed to become Wiley's executive vice president and chief operating officer, effective June 1987. She realized from the outset that it was a high-risk move on her part, so as part of the arrangement, in addition to a healthy six-figure salary, six-figure bonus potential, and stock options, she negotiated a "golden parachute" severance package that included retirement benefits plus two years of full pay. The agreement stipulated that she could leave with the severance package if she did not become Wiley's CEO on or before October 1, 1991, or on Neilly's death or retirement, whichever came first.[107]

Simultaneously, Brad II initiated an effort to work with family members to communicate with the board about the problems the company faced and the family's expectations for the transition years ahead. In an unprecedented exchange, the family, starting from a draft written by Brad II in August 1987, prepared a memo for Neilly and McMullin. The memo explained that the family was drafting "a set of guidelines" to be discussed with Neilly and McMullin and then the board. "In the interim," read the memo, "we want to urge that your highest priority ought to be the rapid development of top management at Wiley through the use of the Wiley family, the Executive Compensation and Development Committee, and all necessary headhunters." The family went on to say that they were eager to see: "1. the hiring of a vice president for domestic publishing as quickly as possible; 2. staff quickly put in place that can handle management information systems, planning, budgeting, and research and development." In January 1988, the family wrote to the board offering

their "contribution to a continuing discussion involving top management, the board, employees, and the family about how to make John Wiley & Sons a healthier company." Emphasizing that they understood the company to be professionally managed, with one or more members of the family in top management and represented on the board, they stated that "active family participation in the business is essential to keeping the company independent." Also essential, they said, was "a strong, active, and critical board of directors." To achieve a turnaround, the family urged the board and management to address the following, in addition to "renewal of top management":

- renewal of the basic businesses
- a more precise understanding of the role of Wilson Learning
- an informed investigation of other markets and product formats relative to "lifelong learning" so that Wiley could consider new investments in the next five years

The memo concluded with a list of financial guidelines for the period 1988–1997: 12 percent revenue growth per annum, 6 percent growth in the net profit/sales ratio, 10 percent equity growth, and 15 percent growth in return on investment.[108]

After McMullin became COO, she and Neilly started to make changes in the senior management team. Robert Douglas, head of the Domestic Publishing Group, was let go, as was the head of educational publishing, with McMullin temporarily taking his place. Charles Ellis was brought in to head professional and reference publishing and was quickly moved to head all publishing operations. Stephen Kippur took over the leadership of Scientific and Technical Books in addition to Business, Law, and General Books. Mary Curtis of Journals left of her own accord and was replaced by Timothy B. King, an experienced publisher with stints at McGraw-Hill, Pergamon, and Springhouse. King went on to become senior vice president of planning and development, playing a key role in such acquisitions as Alan R. Liss, VCH, Hungry Minds, and Blackwell Publishing.

Attempted Turnaround

McMullin had a mandate, and the family had laid out their priorities, which were supported by the board and followed, at least with regard to hiring new managers, by McMullin. Soon after her appointment as COO, she received a letter from Brad II that portrayed Wiley's management style since World War II as inherently conservative, "based on asset maintenance, incremental enhancement of product, performance, etc." The company was good at acquiring active publishing businesses, he accurately stated, but not as good at start-up activities, especially those involving new technologies. "If this behavioral pattern is in fact prevalent," Brad II continued, "it needs to be downed." He also encouraged McMullin to revamp the company's approach to management of its personnel, including more "raiding" of other publishers for high-quality people and greater mobility within the company. Neilly also encouraged McMullin to understand that she had considerable latitude to make the company healthy.[109]

The state of affairs would most certainly require some tough decisions. Neilly had already begun the sale of underperforming assets while he, Douglas, and later Seminoff worked to refocus the college publishing operation on Wiley's traditional strengths. In 1985, Neilly set up a finance group headed by Robert Wilder inside the Publishing Group, which compiled a list of divestment candidates, proposed closing the Western Distribution Center, and began cost cutting in production and manufacturing. In 1987, the College Division sold its health, physical education, and recreation list to Macmillan for $1.1 million, a good price for a slow-growth sector in which Wiley had been unable to develop a "critical mass" of sales. Macmillan also bought Wiley's college lists in sociology, political science, education, and home economics for $3.2 million. (Macmillan's chairman confided to Neilly during the negotiations that Macmillan's college division was "dead in the water.") Next Neilly proposed downsizing the Medical Division.[110]

In her first communication to the board, McMullin reported that senior management (actually, Wilder's finance group) had "made a comprehensive review of the company's asset base to identify those investments which will not produce results at performance levels required to meet our standards." First on the list was the shuttering of Wiley Learning Technologies, with a write-off for product development assets of $2.7 million. Wiley exited medical publishing, selling off various medical texts including nursing and allied health; references; the Park Row imprint; Harwal; and the prized three-volume *International Dictionary of Medicine and Biology*, which had been nurtured for ten years at a cost of $2 million. Occupational and Milady also went on the block. And in 1989, Wiley wrote off its $8.3 million investment in Interactive Technologies. McMullin had also suggested selling the College Division but was dissuaded by a report written by Stoll with the assistance of Brad II, which described the division as badly flawed but fixable.[111]

The market for media content was, at the time, both buoyant and none too selective, with the likes of Rupert Murdoch and Robert Maxwell competing for just about any publishing property. "A lot of people then were buying just about any junk," McMullin remembered, "and boy, did I have junk to sell." Wilder had to fight hard to make sure that McMullin didn't include any valuable people and products in the sell-off. Still, there were some gems, properties such as Occupational, whose sale was regretted as Wiley returned to the same publishing areas at a later date. All together, these sales generated $60 million before taxes.[112]

In July 1987, Wiley wrote off $10 million and trimmed 141 staff positions by closing the Western Distribution Center in Salt Lake City, Utah, a move long overdue. More efficient use of space at the formerly troubled Eastern Division Center (EDC) had increased its capacity by 1.1 million units, and an improved computer system, together with decreased cost and increased

The Turnaround Sours

In August 1988, Brad II advised the family that McMullin was ready to assume control, which she did on April 30, 1989. Neilly's departure began in stages on January 1 of that year. He stayed on the board as vice chairman and became president of the International Publishers Association. McMullin moved quickly to replace Neilly's staff, hiring a chief financial officer, head of Human Resources, and chief information officer (a newly created position). She also tightened budget and accounting controls, invested more in employee training, and invested in $2 million worth of the latest management information technology. McMullin then restructured the company around the triad of education, professional and trade, and training, taking on the job of head of the College Division herself.[115]

The time and place were right for someone new, but McMullin was not the right person. Partly it was style. Her aggressiveness might have been effective at one of Wiley's competitors, but at Wiley her hard-charging, GE approach to management grated at every point with the company's soft-spoken, collegial culture. Wiley employees were in the habit of being nurtured, not assessed according to the standards championed by GE CEO, Jack Welch. And although McMullin had begun her career at Wiley's largest competitor, McGraw-Hill, it was widely believed within Wiley that she never quite understood publishing, its traditions, its jargon, or the business itself. For example, she incessantly discussed "returns" even in contexts where it was not clear to Wiley managers and employees whether she meant return on investment, where high is good, or retailers sending books back to the publisher, where high is bad. Though cautioned about her confusing use of terminology and warned by the Wiley family that her "shortness" and "presentation style" undercut her ability to be an effective leader at Wiley, she could not or would not adjust. Still, despite the mismatch between her personality and Wiley's culture, McMullin did set out to do what she had been hired to do: turn the company around.[116]

*T*homas Vernon was the project manager for the acquisition of Harper & Row's college titles in 1987.

efficiency in the telecommunication and transportation industries owing to deregulation, now allowed the EDC to handle the business of the entire country. Wiley retained warehouses in Australia, the United Kingdom, and Singapore.[113]

With cash on the balance sheet, Wiley continued to acquire. The sale of selected college lists was offset by the acquisition in 1987 of Harper & Row's college accounting, astronomy, computer science, electrical engineering, and physics lists, which included nearly 100 published titles and some 60 projects in production or under contract. The exchange allowed Wiley to refocus on engineering, business, science, and mathematics, which proved wise. Sales of humanities and social science titles lagged significantly behind those in subjects Wiley acquired. Science, long so important to Wiley, now figured larger than ever in the company's plans.[114]

In the view of some observers, parts of the domestic publishing operations were already moving in the right directions when she arrived, but overall what McMullin found upon her ascension was a company in need of general management discipline. The company's administrative apparatus, she wrote, was an uncoordinated collection of "enclaves, fiefdoms, and niche operations," far too internally focused and underinvested in external market intelligence. What passed for corporate planning, she said (echoing Neilly's earlier analysis) was "the rhetoric of strategy, short on any real strategy, and shorter still on execution." Financial controls were loose, and a consulting report had concluded that Wiley's overhead expenses had soared out of control.[117]

The problem for McMullin was that she was unable to link divestitures, write-offs, and downsizing to the perception by Wiley employees that they were necessary and good. Too many employees, chafing at the suddenness of the changes, concluded that McMullin caused the problems she claimed merely to have unearthed. In the College Division, where she was running the day-to-day operations, "it was clear that she knew very little about managing people and most important very little about publishing," recalled Rick Leyh. "We lived with consultants [hired by McMullin] strapped to our hips . . . and [were] totally bogged down in self-analysis and scrutiny that clearly took managers' eyes off the ball and the marketplace." McMullin required that new book proposals have a breakeven of six to eight months, depending on the expense level. "This," said Leyh, "was practically impossible for any first-edition textbook. . . . It indicated that she did not understand the basic core business."[118]

The sheer speed of the reforms was profoundly upsetting. Overly sanguine about the company's short-term prospects, McMullin raised expectations higher than she could ultimately satisfy. And by pressing for quick results, she inflamed Wiley's rank and file, who complained that the firm's old family feel was gone and that senior managers had turned cold and aloof. Why did she move so quickly? Partly, because it was what she knew. Speed was the norm at Jack Welch's high-performing GE. What worked well in many companies, however, did not work in all, and certainly not in knowledge publishing—or not at Wiley at least.[119]

In retrospect, some of McMullin's changes might have made sense in the hands of a different manager. But a more baleful character mismatch is hard to imagine. Wiley had its ways and habits—a culture deeply rooted in its long history—with which she could not mix. In one example of the mutual frustration that marked those times, in 1988, as COO, she tried to launch a $1 million internal "venture fund" to help the company develop new approaches to how it did business. "So make your case for getting some of that money," she challenged Wiley's senior executives, expecting them to leap. "This is an amazing company," she flattered them. Their response underwhemed McMullin. She could not figure out Wiley's employees, who, she acknowledged,[120] were miserable. Beyond anxieties about the company's future, most of the angst at Wiley was due to the clash of styles. At Wiley, nobody ever told anyone else that they were stupid or a dead weight; McMullin had no such qualms. Her employee assessment letters were not gentle. "I can't remember one bit of positive feedback in six months against a deluge of negative, disrespectful, or insensitive feedback," one target of her wrath complained. Her own hires received much more favorable reviews than did Wiley's old guard, which in the estimation of pre-McMullin executives seemed fantastic. To those outside her inner circle, McMullin appeared constantly angry and irritable. What she considered tough and forthright, others thought rude and mean-spirited.[121]

In the rough and tumble of a world where a new breed of blunt, performance-demanding managers was becoming the norm, and where layoffs and firings were becoming commonplace, Wiley, despite the turmoil of the previous five years, remained a business where creative talent was supported and nurtured, not reviled and abused. At many companies, corporate cultures were changing dramatically and swiftly. Decision makers and anyone else not deft enough to adapt were replaced. That did not, and could not, work at Wiley, if only because its corporate culture rested on a durable pillar, the Wiley family.[122]

The mood did not improve. The head of Human Resources lamented that a "we versus they" atmosphere plagued the company. A 1990 consulting study put the problem this way: Wiley's management was in thrall "almost wholly to quantitative data," to the exclusion of "the strategic context of that quantitative data." Even worse, a tendency to engage in "group think," where assertions and the people making them went unchallenged for too long, had resulted in an unhealthy weeding of personnel. "People who don't conform" were more likely to be forced out than listened to.[123]

Stockholders were not so sure either about the direction Wiley was taking. Fueled by takeover speculation, Wiley's stock hit approximately $70 per share in September and October 1989, and then plummeted to $39.50 by the end of April 1990.[124] Now the markets, too, were registering displeasure. With talented employees leaving along with those underperformers weeded out by McMullin and her staff, there was a growing atmosphere of rebelliousness. The challenge for Brad II—who was clearly the board's de facto leader while his father struggled with Esther's death in August 1989—was to help the board understand how the senior publishing managers felt about Ruth and her staff. "There is beginning to unfold a sharp . . . conflict between publishing and corporate-type management over objectives and methods of operating the business," Brad II wrote in one memo. "[F]or the family to assume disinterest in or detachment from remediation of this situation would," he went on, "damage the leadership role and reputation of the family in the eyes of the board, management, staff, publishing, and financial communit[ies]." In short, it was time to act. At the board's March 1990 meeting, an ad hoc committee was formed to address the situation. It collected evidence and deliberated extensively before deciding, on

May 18, that McMullin had to go. It was Brad Sr. who carried the news, "in a friendly manner," he recalled, assuring McMullin that her golden parachute would open fully.[125] When she left, her staff quickly followed.[126]

Whatever the pain and suffering, McMullin did continue the turnaround initiated by Neilly and his associates. She also left behind one indisputably positive legacy. In hiring Charles Ellis, she and Neilly helped to solve the leadership problem for the next decade. Ellis assumed operating management of the company on June 1, 1990. He was the one viable option among Wiley's senior personnel; there were no other obvious internal candidates, no publishing industry executives who were right for the job, and no desire on the part of either the board or the Wileys to hire from outside the industry. Deborah Wiley had observed that Ellis's management style "probably would *not* be as aggressive" as that of his predecessor, which for Wiley's employees was an important point. Difficult times and hard work still lay ahead, but under Ellis's day-to-day leadership and the Wileys' watchful eyes, the 1990s happily proved to be different for the struggling, midsized family publishing house that in the turbulent 1980s had bucked prevailing industry trends.[127]

Ellis was personally responsible for one of the most encouraging signs of new life at Wiley during this otherwise dark period. In 1989 Wiley bought Alan R. Liss, a scientific, technical, and medical (STM) publisher, for $38 million. The sale was engineered by Ellis, who had been hired as head of all publishing at Wiley. Ellis was an experienced STM publisher and a personal friend of Liss, who had founded his company in 1971 and built it into a force in scientific journals publishing. By 1989, the Liss company had a staff of more than 200 and was publishing about 140 books and 60 journals annually. Wiley, in both New York and the United Kingdom, had continued to invest in new journals, and with the Liss acquisition it was once again regarded as a force in the world of STM journals. With an experienced STM publisher overseeing the acquisition, Wiley faced none of the

*E*ric A. Swanson began his publishing career at Alan R. Liss, Inc., in 1974 and came to Wiley when Liss was acquired in 1989. At Wiley, he led the Liss Division and then became vice president and general manager, Scientific, Technical, and Medical Publishing in 1991 and senior vice president and general manager, STM Publishing, in 1996. He was appointed senior vice president, Wiley-Blackwell, in 2007 when Wiley acquired Blackwell Publishing. From 1996 to 1998, Swanson was chairman of the Professional and Scholarly Publishing Division of the Association of American Publishers. He served as the first chairman of *CrossRef,* the international publishers' reference-linking organization, from 2000 to 2002, and as chairman of the International Association of Scientific, Technical, and Medical Publishers, from 2002 to 2005.

problems that had marked the acquisition and integration of Wilson. Wiley closed some of Liss's extensive back-office operations (Liss had done almost everything in-house) while absorbing its core publishing, marketing, and editorial functions. More than half of Liss's personnel departed after the acquisition, but several key people remained. One was Eric Swanson, Liss's executive vice president, who managed the transition and then Liss as a division of Wiley. He went on to become responsible for Wiley's global scientific, medical, technical, and scholarly business, known as Wiley-Blackwell. Others included Reed Elfenbein, who became vice president, Wiley-Blackwell sales and marketing, Brian Crawford, and Eileen Cudlipp. Alan Liss joined the Wiley board until his health made it impossible for him to continue.[128]

As the newly installed CEO, Ellis moved with dispatch to divest Wilson Learning. By 1990, Wilson was struggling to achieve a 5 percent operating profit, while comparable companies were returning between 10 and 20 percent. Wilson's market share was just 0.4 percent and showed no sign of improvement in a field in which competition was increasing from institutions of higher education, as well as from internal training programs at major corporations. On August 31, the new Wiley senior management team advised the board to put Wilson on the block. It was sold to Shozo Mori, president of Wilson's Nippon Wilson Learning subsidiary, and a group of Japanese investors, for $30 million and a 2 percent stake in Nippon. At that price Wilson Learning was basically a wash financially, but the experience had handed Wiley "a big beating," said corporate counsel Richard Rudick.[129]

There was one other sign of new life: the growth, under Stephen Kippur, of Business, Law, and General Books (BLG), an organization that would grow into Wiley's highly successful professional and trade business over the next two decades.

Kippur was appointed head of the BLG division in 1985 during the reorganization of the Professional Group, and after the departure of its vice president when it was becoming clear that 1985 was going to be a disastrous year. Kippur, a Ph.D. historian and largely self-taught publisher, came from Praeger in 1979. With management's attention focused elsewhere, Kippur had an unsought but valuable advantage: He was largely left alone to develop the business publishing section, expand the law program, and renew the company's interest in trade publishing. "Flying," as he remembered, "largely under the radar," the expanded BLG operation started out with just 22 people and revenues of $13 million. Kippur's first editorial hire, Jeffrey Brown, managed the accounting list; Gwenyth Jones became his first production manager, and Katherine Schowalter was hired as a production manager. All three would develop into leaders of the business. By the late 1980s, BLG was growing steadily at about 10 percent per year, with gross

$\mathcal{S}$tephen A. Kippur joined Wiley in 1979 as an editor, after having briefly worked for Praeger Publishers. Prior to that, he received a Ph.D. in Western Cultural and Intellectual History. He was appointed head of a new division, the Business, Law, and General Books Division in 1985. This was retitled Professional/Trade in 1988. He led the effort to reestablish Wiley's reputation as a professional publisher while building Wiley's extensive trade publishing program and overseeing the development and growth of its brands, franchises, and alliances. He is currently executive vice president and president, Professional/Trade. In addition to the company's global Professional/Trade publishing business, he is also in charge of John Wiley & Sons Canada, Ltd.

Worklife at Wiley in the 1980s

Although centralized mainframe computers were in use well before the 1980s, it was not until the second half of the decade that the new technology began to impact the daily worklife of Wiley colleagues. "When I came in 1985, acquisitions editors were still using manual type-writers to record contract information on index cards," recalled Jeffrey Brown, an editor at the time in the newly formed Business, Law, and General Books Division. "There really wasn't much difference between 1985 and 1935. Yes, you could get a computer-generated report, but it would be about six inches thick, printed out on accordion-fold paper with perforated edges. The PC was viewed as an expensive luxury, and you'd have to make a very strong case to have one. But all of that changed very quickly, and by 1990, we had made the transition to a computer-driven work style."[131]

As PCs became cheaper, variations on this scenario played out across the company. "In the Higher Education sales organization, we used a 'comping' tool, a printed list with the names of professors on one side and textbook titles on the other, each with a three-digit code," said Susan Elbe, who joined the company as a sales representative in 1980. "You would write the appropriate code next to the name of a professor who wanted a comp [complimentary] copy for review. The information would be punched into the computer at USDC [Wiley's U.S. Distribution Center], and the book would be sent out; that's the way we did it through the '80s. But sometime around 1986 or 1987, one of the regional managers set up a system on his own PC to track sales rep activity, including sales, expenses, and comps. He did it entirely on his own initiative, and we all used it. He spent hours and hours at the end of every month, inputting data to print out a report. There were people who thought it was a waste of time, but he was very forward-looking, a real data guy who found a way to put it into useful form. Today, the reps carry wireless tablet PCs; they can do their record-keeping on the fly and transmit things like comp requests directly into our system."[132]

margins around 65 percent. Thomas Conter oversaw an increase in sales of law books and subscription products in real estate and accounting. Theresa Zak achieved a $1.5 million sales increase in microcomputer trade books, while Brown generated an extra $400,000 through sheer productivity increases as executive editor of Wiley's accounting, finance, banking, and investment books. David Sobel matched Brown's productivity with sales of Wiley Science Editions, the reappearance of Wiley's list of science books for the educated lay reader that had been started in the 1960s. Ellis found himself at the beginning of his career surrounded by colleagues old and new from BLG and the Liss acquisition, who would later take Wiley to higher levels of achievement than could ever have been imagined in the 1980s.[130]

THE *Publishing craft*

FROM HANDWORK TO COMPUTERS

By the late 1970s, even first-generation photo compositors were disappearing from the industry, increasingly supplanted by second-generation photo compositors that utilized digital inputs in the form of coded paper, magnetic tape, or floppy disks. Yet the craft of book design and layout continued to be practiced in a fairly traditional way. "For a book cover," explained Madelyn Lesure, a senior designer in Higher Education, "you would trace the letters of the words you needed from type specimen books onto vellum, a heavy tracing paper. Then you would cut out the strips containing the

words and position them as needed on the layout, and send the results out to a typesetter. When you got back the set type, you would cut and paste it onto a mechanical, which would go out to another vendor to be rendered as a color cel. Finally, you'd place that over the cover photo and mat it, and do your presentation."[133]

During the 1980s, some aspects of design operations did begin to benefit from automation. New computer programs allowed for the storage of type and artwork as bit-mapped images, or data. After John Warnock and Chuck Geschke, founders of Adobe Systems, introduced PostScript, data could be

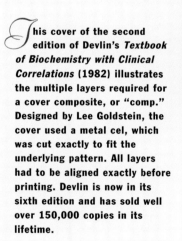

This cover of the second edition of Devlin's *Textbook of Biochemistry with Clinical Correlations* (1982) illustrates the multiple layers required for a cover composite, or "comp." Designed by Lee Goldstein, the cover used a metal cel, which was cut exactly to fit the underlying pattern. All layers had to be aligned exactly before printing. Devlin is now in its sixth edition and has sold well over 150,000 copies in its lifetime.

In production, the computer was used ever more effectively as a means of transmitting manuscripts, as a copyediting tool, and finally in conjunction with a laser printer or second-generation photo compositor as a camera-ready copy output device. Wiley was quick to follow this trend. CEO Andrew Neilly Jr. took great

pride in Wiley's experiments with computer-assisted typesetting and electronic delivery of journals. By early 1983, Brad Wiley was already talking publicly about receiving manuscripts "almost instantaneously" over telephone lines. By then, Wiley had not one but two IBM 4341 mainframes, a powerful minicomputer called the

Apple's $2,195 Macintosh computer on the left, with the Atari imitator Jackintosh computer ($900 approximately) on the right, January 1, 1985.

used to generate pages with art and photos in place. These pages could be sent directly to an imagesetter, which would plot the entire page. Negatives could be output from the imagesetter; eventually the machines could even output imposed flats, ready for plating.

Soon desktop publishing (DTP) systems, which merged copy preparation and composition as never before, also allowed a designer working on a PC or a Mac to create a page, proof it on a local printer, and use the same files to output high-resolution pages for printing. Among the earliest DTP systems were PageMaker, launched in 1985 by Aldus (later acquired by Adobe), and Ventura Publisher, launched in 1986 by Ventura Software (later acquired by Xerox), which incorporated the use of style sheets. The launching of QuarkXpress in 1987 by Quark, Inc., took DTP to a new level.

Simultaneous with the launching of desktop publishing systems was the development of digital drawing programs, such as Adobe Illustrator and CorelDRAW. These programs created digital images, allowing the typesetter to incorporate illustrations directly into files without having to shoot originals and create negatives. During the same period, typesetters began to move away from shooting photographs to produce negatives, using scanners instead. Drum scanners and, later, flatbed scanners allowed for faster scans and the ability to incorporate those scans into an individual page. Programs such as Photoshop made it possible to manipulate photographic images.

At Wiley, explained Jean Morley, an Interscience P/T design manager, "We worked with the people in IT in '86 or '87 to develop a complete data system on the mainframe for book interior specs, the typographical and layout information that determines appearance." Previously "we'd been doing it all with pen and paper," she recalls. "This was revolutionary."[134]

Hewlett-Packard 3000, a Wang VS80 system hooked to a 50,000-page-per-day laser printer for word processing, and more than 60 PCs.

Computerization made everything move faster. Neilly became known as the "three-month-book man" because he continually pressed to reduce the time from

submission to warehouse. In 1986, 23 titles were brought out on average 50 percent cheaper and five weeks more quickly through the use of preproduction planning and a computerized composition system and standardized coding developed by Wiley. Authors who created electronic manuscripts cut production time and

Worklife at Wiley, 1980s

Jennifer McKenna, Robert Fletcher, Carol L. Beasley, and Lisa Culhane with the classic *Architectural Graphic Standards*, eighth edition, produced a year ahead of schedule.

College engineering group with (back) Susan Elbe, Cliff Robichaud, Charity Robey, (seated) Wayne Anderson, Brad Wiley II, and Steve Elliot.

costs further, especially on short-run academic monographs, as they literally became their own compositors. By the end of 1986, more than 250 Wiley authors were preparing their manuscripts electronically. They liked the control they retained; editors liked the flexibility; and of course production people appreciated the savings.[135]

Bypassing several production steps, authors' electronic submissions were sent to a compositor, which generated pages. There were technical difficulties, of course, many stemming from a lack of standardization. "The multiplicity of formats," one Chichester wag noted, made "the problems of the Tower of Babel look simple." Desktop publishing at Chichester was neither publishing nor, in that age of huge footprints for PCs, monitors, printers, and their cables, was it exactly doable on one desktop. Eventually P/T head of production Ruth Greif was successful in reducing production cycles on many trade books to three months—far less time than Wiley's or the industry's standards, which had ranged from 8 to 14 months from receipt of the final

manuscript. During the 1980s, Wiley also investigated the digital production of journals.[136]

At the same time, some changes during the 1980s had nothing to do with technology. "When I started in '83, we didn't have book proposal meetings the way we do now," recalled George Telecki, then STM acquisitions editor for electrical engineering. "I'd just give my proposals to Bob [Robert B]. Polhemus, the vice president, and he'd generally say, 'okay, this looks good.' That all changed around the time of the Liss acquisition in 1989. The process became more formal, with the marketing manager, marketing director, editor, publisher, and someone from production all meeting to evaluate every proposal. It's still done that way today."[137]

There were ways in which the Wiley culture was distinctly ahead of the curve. "I had a six-month-old child when I started," recalled Jean Morley, who came on board as an Interscience design manager in 1985, "and I was one of the company's first telecommuters. Debbie Wiley had just adopted her two children, and she was very supportive; we used to have a weekly mothers' brown-bag lunch, along with two or three others. Wiley was one of the first companies, as far as I know from friends in the industry, to provide this kind of support."[138]

Wiley Remains Independent

New York publishing was a close-knit, gossipy—some would say inbred—community, and the troubles at Wiley quickly became public. During the 1980s, Wiley's stock fluctuated widely, surging to almost $40 in 1982–1983 before dipping below $30 in mid-1985. It oscillated dramatically thereafter, as Wiley became an object of takeover speculation. After the stock market crash of 1987, Wiley's stock price dipped below $25, then rose steeply before falling off again after McMullin became CEO. To some extent, the company's stock price reflected internal as well as external uncertainty. Commenting on the acquisition environment at the time, Brad Sr. argued that many of the deals were consummated for the enrichment of shareholders while "not [contributing] to the advancement of publishing," a view of the business that might have seemed quaint to the now far more financially driven leaders of many of his competitors. In 1984, First Boston Research proclaimed that John Wiley & Sons was the "best value" in the publishing industry, followed closely by Harcourt Brace Jovanovich and McGraw-Hill. That judgment was based on what the analysts saw as Wiley's earnings potential, which greatly exceeded its current stock price. To be undervalued was to be highly vulnerable in a takeover environment.[139]

The family, however, was a formidable barrier to a tender offer, and even though it was relinquishing its claim to the CEO's office, it had already arranged for its continuing control over policy decisions. On September 13, 1982, following some creative analysis and discussions with First Boston, the company was recapitalized, creating in the process two classes of stock, A and B, with the B shares having the greater voting power. The impetus behind this move was to enable the Wiley family to retain control of the company, even

while expanding the shares available to the public. Class A shareholders, which included Wiley insiders as well as general investors, elected 30 percent of the board of directors. Class B shareholders elected the rest of the board. Some 66 percent of the Class B stock was owned directly by Brad Sr. and Esther or was held in trusts, of which Brad Sr., Brad II, Peter, and Deborah were the beneficiaries. For all other matters, Class A shareholders commanded one-tenth of a vote per share, while Class B shareholders held one full vote per share. Class A shares were created to help the company raise new funds in the capital market. (To pay down the debt it incurred to buy Wilson, for example, Wiley in July 1983 sold 418,000 shares of Class A stock. The issue, which was oversubscribed, netted $13.6 million.) Effective July 16, 1985, Class A shares, which were much more numerous and liquid than Class B shares, traded on the top-tier NASDAQ National Market System; because Class B shares were much less liquid, they traded only on the regular-tier NASDAQ National List. Over time, the Wileys were able to persuade a number of Class B shareholders interested in liquidating their shares to sell to them or trade for the more liquid Class A shares.[140]

The two classes of stock did not deter the advances of many would-be new owners in an era of corporate consolidation. Robert Maxwell, who had morphed from the British STM publisher who founded Pergamon Press into a media baron, claimed to have amassed a huge fund with which to buy American publishing properties. In 1986, he approached Brad Sr. at the Frankfurt Book Fair and suggested that Wiley and Pergamon join in partnership because, as Brad reported, "Wiley was not and would not be sufficiently capitalized to accomplish whatever our long-range missions were." Brad, who abhorred Maxwell, declined. The following year, Longman, a subsidiary of Pearson since 1968, made an overture, offering to allow Wiley to "seek cover" under Pearson's more benevolent corporate umbrella. In October 1987, Sterling & Company of Los Angeles offered to broker a sale to an unnamed English company. In April 1988, Sterling wrote again, offering to pay cash for Wiley on behalf of one of its unnamed clients of long standing, a "large, private

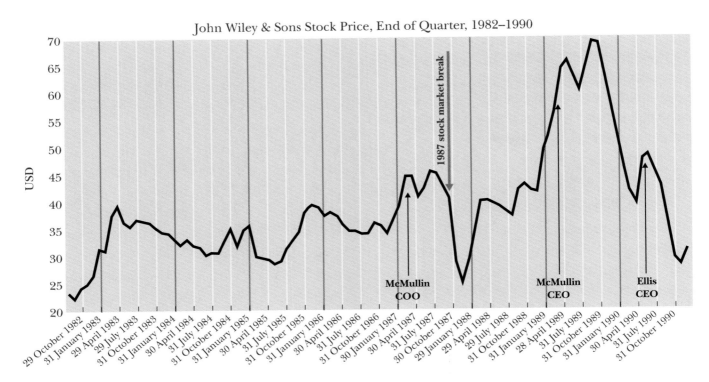

John Wiley & Sons Stock Price, End of Quarter, 1982–1990

Source: Center for Research in Security Prices

investment partnership" that was "very active in *friendly* management buyouts of public companies." Before circulating copies of either missive to his children and the company's top two executives, Brad made some angry scrawls at the bottom: "No answer" and "He will *not* receive a reply!!" Just a month later, International Thomson called, with similar results. The phone continued to ring in 1989, but Brad deflected the blandishments of Harper & Row, Butterworths/Reed International, the Times Mirror Company, and others with the same emphatic "No."[141]

In 1989, *Forbes* called Brad Sr. the "stubborn patriarch" of the publishing business. If he was stubborn, it was for good reason, if one believed that the conglomerates were more interested in making a fast buck at the expense of long-term profitability based on a strong backlist and a reputation for quality. "After we were bought," one family publisher lamented after selling his company to a conglomerate, "I never had time to see authors; I spent all my time in meetings with various corporate execs and 'selling' our imprint within the parent company." Another complained that headquarters

wanted quantity, and quality be damned. "They want us to do more books," he said, "and we keep telling them there may not be any more books of real merit that we can do justice to." Charles Scribner Jr. explained that he, too, valued independence because it conferred "an important business advantage, the opportunity to take the long view." Independence also allowed people at Scribner's "to follow our own judgment." "When you have someone pulling up the plant to check its roots," he concluded, "the plant simply will not grow." This was before Scribner's was merged into Macmillan in 1984. In short, even if Wiley was not quite hanging on for dear life, Brad Sr. was hanging on to a way of life in publishing that was foreign to the spirit of the moment. But how much longer could the company afford to hold out? "The company's independence will probably end when the elderly chairman dies, if not before," said *Forbes.* "The market is betting that a takeover has become inevitable," it said, "so, the vultures circle."[142]

What was and is inevitable is that journalists will forecast blithely, with utmost certainty, and often wrongly. There was nothing "inevitable" about Wiley's future. The Wileys agreed among themselves that there was no offer that could persuade them to sell. They also agreed that they should focus on turning the company around within three to five years and make it profitable. It was not so easy, however, to persuade Wiley's executives that they meant it, as managers grew edgy and asked for special severance agreements in the event of a change of control. One investor, Theodore L. Cross and his associates, unsuccessful bidders for Harper & Row in 1987, accumulated over 20 percent of the company's Class A shares by late 1989. Shortly thereafter, a German publisher offered to join the Wiley family in a voting trust that would have left the family's "prerogatives" intact.[143]

As it turned out, Wiley was not only more financially valuable as an independent company; it may have also been right about the economics. Concentration in publishing is neither inevitable nor always desirable. Industries that depend on individually created products, that do not have large, inflexible capital investments, and that face highly unpredictable markets are prone to periods of concentration followed by periods of intense competition. Publishing fits that theoretical mold, and the history of publishing conforms to the expected pattern. Most of the conglomerates formed in the 1960s and 1970s, especially those that brought electronics companies and book publishers together, quickly foundered, if only because the anticipated changes that computers were supposed to bring to education simply did not materialize or did not come as quickly as expected.[144]

Three things would keep Wiley off the auction block as the "stubborn patriarch" became increasingly inactive. The first was the Wiley family. The Wileys knew that they could never be hands-off owners of the company, because the managers could, at some point, go off in their own direction. So they made it clear that they understood the company as being professionally managed, with one family member, Deborah, playing an active role in senior management and Brad II learning more about the business as an editor in the College

Division, a job he had taken in 1987. Meanwhile, four Wiley family members remained active on the board, which Brad Sr. chaired until 1992. They also indicated their interest in bringing members of the next generation of Wileys into the business.

The company's second saving grace was its employees. During dark times, some employees left because they felt poorly compensated, uncomfortable with Neilly's new strategy, beleaguered by red tape, or disrespected by McMullin and her staff. But many stayed, loyal and appreciative of the goodwill the Wileys had generated over the years. Accustomed to working and playing together, Wiley employees possessed affinity and cohesion. "I respect John Wiley as a firm" was a mantra that often prefaced and softened complaints. Acquisitions editors continued to secure high-quality manuscripts; production people turned them into books; marketing and sales people sold them; warehouse workers got them out the door; and those in the back office collected the sums due. In 1990, despite all its troubles, Wiley published 726 new titles and 154 new editions.[145]

In a 1987 memo to the staff, Brad Sr. explained that the company had "much to do to improve Wiley's

*W*iley remained independent in an era of consolidation. Charles Ellis, the newly installed CEO, is seated at left with Brad Wiley Sr. and Deborah Wiley. Standing are Brad Wiley II (left) and Peter Booth Wiley.

traditional publishing business," to expand its position in industrial training and continuing education, and to "explore and invest in appropriate new businesses," all, of course, with an eye toward increasing profitability. The staff responded. In the warehouse, the company looked for both cost efficiency and quality service. It began to reduce inventory. With the company's computerized National Distribution System (NDS) fixed by July 1986, Wiley now offered the Wiley Express—a promise to 2,000 college stores guaranteeing 24-hour order fulfillment or free shipping. In 1989 alone, the warehouse shipped more than 581,000 books free—to induce professors to adopt them—at an investment cost, including freight, of over $3 million.[146]

The Domestic Publishing Group, at that time composed of the College, Periodical, Business/Law, Scientific/Technical, Occupational, and Medical Divisions, slashed its costs by $900,000 in fiscal 1987 alone. With urging from Brad, Wiley editors worldwide were enjoined to "exert more controls over what authors write (e.g., 300 pp. of succinct information vs. 1000 pp. of 'stuff')." Yet Wiley acquisitions editors never forgot the old adage that "it isn't what you know, it's who you know," and they strengthened their circle of authors, agents, readers, reviewers, and other editors.[147]

To help with its computerization initiative, Wiley joined the Applied Information Technologies Research Consortium (AITRC), which included some major universities as well as computer-intensive organizations like the online information services CompuServe and OCLC (the Ohio College Library Center, now Online Computer Library Center). By investing $250,000, some of it paid in cash and some in books, Wiley was able to leverage its investment by participating in common research and the development of industry standards while obtaining information and technologies developed by the AITRC.[148]

The third saving grace was the backlist. Bennett Cerf, a co-founder of Random House, once declared that his backlist was like "picking up gold from the sidewalk." That was a bit of an exaggeration; nevertheless,

PROFILE

BEATRICE SHUBE & TED HOFFMAN

Editors like Beatrice Shube and Ted Hoffman spent decades nurturing authors and producing high-quality manuscripts. Shube signed, among other titles, *General Theory of Relativity* (1975) and *Directions in Physics* (1978) by Nobel Laureate Paul Dirac. She also signed H. J. Tichy's *Effective Writing for Engineers, Managers, Scientists* (1966), which sold 62,000 units over its long and successful life. Shube once told a new editor that her secret for managing difficult authors was to be "the iron fist in the velvet glove."

Ted Hoffman edited two of the top books in graduate and reference chemistry, Jerry March's *Advanced Organic Chemistry* (1985) and Albert Cotton and Geoffrey Wilkinson's *Advanced Inorganic Chemistry* (1962) through multiple editions. Despite declining demographics in his markets, Hoffman's books sold more than $2 million in 1984 alone.[149]

PROFILE

STELLA KUPFERBERG

In the photo illustration business, few names evoke a stronger image than that of Stella Kupferberg, manager of Wiley's Photo Department. During her career, Kupferberg trained, bargained with, charmed, edited, and/or commissioned a virtual *Who's Who* of the industry.

As the baby boomers went to college and the textbook industry shifted toward more visual presentation and use of color, Stella became a driving force behind the creation of the photo illustration industry in New York City. Over the course of her 33-year career at Wiley, she worked with a galaxy of major authors, illustrating forces and motion with David Halliday and Robert Resnick, and with John Cutnell and Kenneth Johnson; exploring psychology with Gerald Davison and John Neale; mapping the world with geographers Harm de Blij and Peter Muller; demonstrating chemistry with James Brady and John Holum; and so much more. Stella's work helped to build Wiley's reputation for engaging, accessible, and technically correct visuals in its leading texts. She and her colleagues built a vast photo archive over the years and shared it with all Wiley divisions. Quick to see the benefits of technology, she built one of the first electronic photo databases from that photo archive.

Although Stella worked long hours and demanded the best of others, she embraced life, friends, and ideas, combining them all with her love of good food and wine. Well informed and well read, she was lively in her conversation, impatient with mediocrity, and good-humored in her outlook. She died in 1996; her impact lives on in many texts and in the work of her colleagues.

Stella Kupferberg began working for Wiley in the 1960s; but when asked exactly when, she usually replied "around the turn of the century" or "since 1807." She was hired as an editorial assistant, which at the time meant logging manuscripts and galleys in and out, typing letter after letter with carbon copies, and running to get coffee for her boss. In those days, the editors were all men, and the assistants, women. There was no such thing as a stock photo business or publisher photo research department. Books, in fact, carried few images.

backlists are the backbone of quality publishers. One of the most important reasons for Wiley's staying power was simple. "People trust the Wiley imprint," noted Teresa Zak, an editor who came to the company in 1986. Not every Wiley book lived a long economic life, however; the value of many titles eroded during the 1980s. Still, key evergreens buoyed Wiley even as external threats and internal dissension threatened to sink it. One of the most important was Kieso and Weygandt's *Intermediate Accounting*: Wiley's CPA business was an extremely valuable property. J. L. Meriam's *Engineering Mechanics* was another. First published in 1952, Meriam's work was still going strong in the 1990s. David Halliday and Robert Resnick's 1960s *Physics* textbook went through multiple editions. By 1982, the

title had sold 1.9 million copies. Translated into 15 languages, it brought in over $18 million and controlled almost 50 percent of its market. Charles P. Jones's *Investments: Analysis and Management*, first published by Wiley as *Essentials of Modern Investments* in 1977, was in its ninth edition in 2007. One astonishing evergreen was more than a century old: James Dwight Dana's *System of Mineralogy*, the second edition of which Wiley published in 1844. (The first edition came out in 1837 under the imprimatur of Durrie & Peck and Herrick & Noyes of New Haven.) The eighth and most recent edition of *System*, often hailed as "a veritable bible to the mineralogist," was published by Wiley in 1997. Since 1932, *Architectural Graphic Standards* by Charles Ramsey and Harold Sleeper (celebrating its seventy-fifth year in 2007) has remained an essential book for every architect. And Daniel McCracken, who first published with Wiley in 1957, kept writing new books on computers and on programming in FORTRAN and other now ancient computer languages. After their successes in the 1970s, Wiley's Self-Teaching Guides, which included titles like Dinah Moché's *Astronomy*, faded in the early 1980s but revived late in the decade, especially those in the computer field for both novices and experts.[150]

In the end, the Wiley family and Wiley's loyal employees found a way to save the company from itself. Mark Twain is alleged to have said that history doesn't repeat itself; it rhymes. The songs of the 1980s were similar to the songs of the 1960s. Those of the 1960s were played by a chamber orchestra; by the 1980s, Wiley thought itself capable of performing with a full orchestra plus chorus. The ambitions were remarkably similar: expand beyond Wiley's core businesses into new, related, faster-growing fields, such as corporate training, while leveraging technology to deal with the threats and promises of the computer age. Some of the best, most respected minds in publishing threw themselves into these efforts. Brad II remembered the period as one with "a positive appetite for what was for the most part uncontrolled experimentalism ahead of the curve." Wiley, to use a phrase common in the dot.com era, was on the "bleeding edge of change." Execution, as everyone acknowledged, was the problem.[151]

In a hurry to correct course, Neilly and the board hired a new CEO who turned out to be the wrong choice. She continued the course correction begun by Neilly and his colleagues, but could not figure out how to lead a collection of highly creative individuals who, while steeped in Wiley traditions, needed positive reinforcement to

Daniel McCracken's *FORTRAN* was one of the earliest and best-selling programming-language books in publishing history.

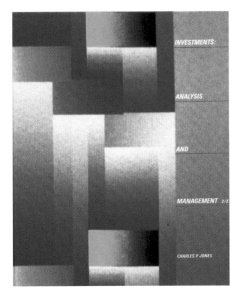

*I*nvestments by Charles P. Jones, first published as *Essentials of Modern Investments* in 1977, was in its ninth edition in 2007.

move beyond the past and perform at their best. Even this negative experience had its positives, according to Brad: "I think the shock and distaste for her leadership style . . . encouraged all of us to understand the value of dumping much of the pre-McMullin behavior, the patriarchal, loyalty- and tradition-based culture and operating style that McMullin and Neilly, each in their own way, tried to wrestle with." Brad and his colleagues, he assured, came away from the experience ready to substitute "more disciplined publishing and management attention to the assets and people in our charge while maintaining the collegial affection for one another and the industry we worked in."[152]

Neilly and McMullin, as noted above, made one very important hire: Charles Ellis as head of all publishing operations. Ellis then hired William J. Pesce, who was charged with reviving the College Division. Ellis with Pesce would run Wiley for the next decade and a half. Ellis also engineered the acquisition of Liss, which would bring on board more talent and leadership. Moreover, a fortuitous reorganization of the Professional and Reference business opened the doors to a new generation of leadership in this area as well.

The Wiley family and Wiley's loyal employees found a way to save the company from itself.

A man stands on top of the Berlin Wall, November 12, 1989, as East Germans flood into West Berlin at Potsdamer Platz.

Renaissance: Rebirth as a Global Company 1989 and Beyond

Chapter Eight

✻

A New World

For Wiley, 1989 marked the beginning of an era of rapid transformations, the first of which was the restoration of Wiley's reputation as a world class publisher. The company's textbook operation required radical reorientation, while the Scientific, Technical and Medical (STM) and the Professional/Trade (P/T) businesses were more in need of the support and investment that would permit them to continue to build already successful programs. Central to sustained growth was the generation of sufficient cash to make larger and larger acquisitions and effectively integrate the acquired publishing programs into the Wiley portfolio. The Liss acquisition, consummated in 1989, was only the first step. As growth accelerated, Wiley became a truly global enterprise with a fully realized capability to deliver the content of books and journals via the World Wide Web.

In the world beyond Wiley, 1989 was a tumultuous year. The most striking events took place in the Communist world, as citizens' movements in Czechoslovakia, Hungary, Poland, and Romania swept Communist regimes from power. In November the German Democratic Republic announced it would allow its citizens to cross through the checkpoints in the Berlin Wall. In an extraordinary outburst of popular sentiment, Germans east and west joined hands to tear down the barrier that had kept them apart for nearly thirty years. In China,

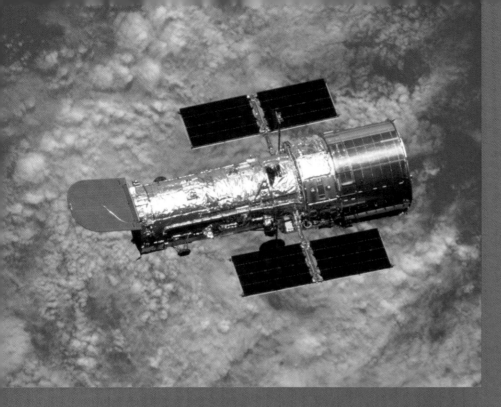

NASDAQ Composite of the dot.com bubble, 1988–2004

Value @ Close

6,000
5,000
4,000
3,000
2,000
1,000
0

31 December 1988
31 December 1990
31 December 1992
31 December 1994
31 December 1996
31 December 1998
31 December 2000
31 December 2002
31 December 2004

Copyright © 2005 www.NYSE.TV

students occupied Tiananmen Square, but their hopes for democracy were crushed by tanks. In Afghanistan, the Soviet withdrawal left a wasteland of despair and violence that would breed a new global enterprise called al Qaeda.

For a time the U.S. economy appeared to be recovering from the Black Monday stock market collapse of October 1987, only to be rocked again in October 1989, by the Friday the Thirteenth mini-crash, thought to have been brought on by the excesses of junk bond dealers. Other events, however, propelled the U.S. economy into giddy expansion. "The essential background to growth in the 1990s," wrote London School of Economics historian Nicholas F. R. Crafts, "was the unprecedented extension and intensification of globalization in terms of the international integration of capital and product markets." Global merchandise exports grew at an unprecedented rate. More impressive, according to Crafts, was "the surge in international capital mobility." Underlying these trends were technological changes in the worlds of information and communications worthy of comparison to the steam engine and electricity.

In 1989, Oxford graduate Timothy Berners-Lee, working at the particle physics laboratory of the European Organization for Nuclear Research (CERN), wrote a proposal for an Internet communications tool, which connected Internet browsers to servers, called the World Wide Web. The next year, using a NeXT computer as a server, he wrote the first Web browser code. On August 6, 1991, Berners-Lee made the Web publicly

*H*ubble Space Telescope (above), launched 1994.

*N*asdaq tumbles, Nasdaq offices, New York, January 5, 2001 (left). The Nasdaq Composite Index plunged 159.18 points, or 6.20 percent.

available for the first time. Two years later CERN announced that the World Wide Web would be free to everybody. A new information exchange system and a new industry were launched on a global basis. The World Wide Web forever changed the nature of communication and with it the very nature of publishing, which soon began the greatest transformation since Gutenberg invented a press that used movable type in 1448.

The World Wide Web pulled together the most remote corners of the global economy, ultimately benefiting every country. The economic consequences of globalization were another story. The United States experienced a decade of expansion, while Japan suffered through a decade of minimal growth, as did Europe, Africa, and Latin America. In what Crafts described as "the most dramatic arrival on the world scene since that of Japan in the 1960s," China's economy grew at a staggering pace, with India following not far behind.[1]

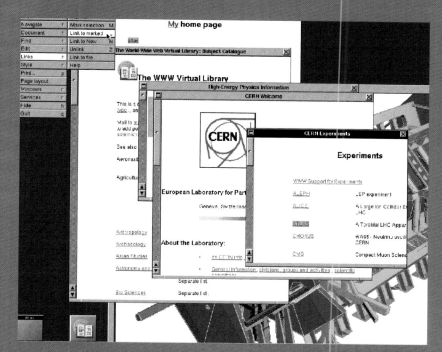

Tim Berners-Lee's original World Wide Web browser in 1993.

Tiananmen Square, China, June 5, 1989

New Leadership, New Energy

Efforts to refocus and realign Wiley's core businesses began under Andrew Neilly and continued under Ruth McMullin, but signs of a true renewal were not evident until Wiley found a new leader in Charles Ellis, a publisher with extensive international experience who initiated Wiley's transition to a truly global company. Under Ellis, Wiley regained its reputation as an outstanding publisher of quality content. Ellis dedicated the first half of the 1990s to renewing and restoring Wiley's basic publishing skills. The introduction of a planning process that tied plans to results was essential to this renewal. Next, Ellis, and after him Will Pesce, who succeeded Ellis in 1998, turned to acquisitions to enhance Wiley's position in the global publishing community. In 1996, Wiley bought the VCH Publishing Group, the publishing house of the German chemical and pharmaceutical societies, an acquisition that drove STM management to take further steps toward global planning and integration. Three years later, Wiley bought Jossey-Bass, a well-known professional house with an important presence in education, psychology, and leadership. In a particularly bold move in 2001, Wiley, now led by Pesce, acquired Hungry Minds, and with it a collection of brands—Betty Crocker, CliffsNotes, For Dummies, Frommer's, Webster's New World Dictionaries—known far and wide. This acquisition, and specifically the acquisition of For Dummies, accelerated Wiley's globalization. For Dummies came with publishing operations in Australia, Canada, and, four years later, Germany. For Dummies would enhance local publishing programs in these countries and England, leading to the beginnings of global planning in P/T.

The combined efforts of Ellis, Pesce, and their colleagues were impressive. In May 2003, the company reported that its revenue had grown at the rate of 11 percent per year from $282 million in fiscal year 1990 to $854 million in fiscal year 2003. Between 1992 and 2002, Wiley's Class A stock had appreciated in value at a compound annual rate of 27 percent. Wiley's shares split four times in the 1990s. To put it another way, a person who invested $100 in Wiley in 1993, designated Wiley's turnaround year by Ellis, would have seen the investment swell to about $793 in 2003. Wiley shares had outperformed those of the publishers with whom it is usually compared. Wiley had become not only larger but more profitable and far more attractive to investors.[2]

Charles Ellis: Focus and Renewal

When the time came to replace McMullin, the board saw Ellis, who had been hired to run Professional and Reference Publishing in 1988 and was promoted to president of the Publishing Division in 1989, as the logical in-house candidate. He had a successful track record, having overseen the Liss acquisition, and a feel for the mindset of colleagues, authors, and customers. Ellis accepted the assignment "as perhaps the most interesting" one in all of U.S. publishing and served as Wiley's CEO from June 1990 until May 1998. Gracious and diplomatic, he fit well with the Wiley culture. Ellis brought "joy and laughter everywhere," according to Brad Wiley Sr. "including meetings of board committees."[3]

With the departure of McMullin, Ellis replaced her staff with talent from within the company. Robert Wilder became CFO, William Arlington, head of Human Relations, and Timothy King, head of Planning and Development. Will Pesce remained as head of Higher Education (Higher Ed) and Stephen Kippur as head of Professional and Trade (P/T). Eric Swanson, former executive vice president at Alan R. Liss, Inc., became head of the Scientific, Technical, and Medical Division (STM), reporting to Stephen Kippur but working directly with Ellis on journals and electronic publishing. John Collins, head of the Australian company, and Michael Foyle, head of the British company, also

PROFILE

CHARLES ELLIS

Charles Ellis was a publisher by temperament and by trade. He came to Wiley in 1988 after successful stints in executive positions at Pergamon Press, D.C. Heath, and Elsevier. He had proved to be a skilled manager, revivifying the Dutch publisher Elsevier's troubled North American operations in the early 1980s at a time when Wiley was experiencing the beginnings of intense global competition. Before Wiley, Ellis had spent a decade in Europe, giving him valuable international experience.[4]

During McMullin's tenure, Ellis was hired to run Professional and Reference Publishing, which included a Scientific, Technical, and Medical division (STM) and Business, Law, and General (BLG) Books. He improved performance there while encouraging Stephen Kippur to build Wiley's trade list. He also played the leading role in the acquisition of Alan R. Liss, which occurred after he was appointed president of the Publishing Division in 1989.[5]

Ellis served as Wiley's CEO from June 1990 until May 1998. He tended to industry activities, serving, for instance, as chair of the Association of American Publishers (AAP) from 1992 until 1994 and promoting the efforts of the Copyright Clearance Center (CCC) in copyright protection. Ellis was an avid supporter of the Digital Object Identifier (DOI), a code embedded in digital content that would facilitate the tracking of content use and the enforcement of copyright laws. With his industry contacts, he was influential in promoting the essential nature of the DOI and later served as the first chair of the DOI Foundation.[6]

*F*rom a modest background, Ellis graduated from Princeton thanks to a scholarship offered by the DuPont family. He taught at a preparatory school and then worked for Bertrand Russell, the British philosopher and peace activist. To support a growing family, he forsook his initial ambition to earn a Ph.D. and teach, in favor of a business career. But "if I went into a business," he recalled, "it would have to be a business in which I placed some value upon the product or the service." Publishing fit that criterion perfectly, a blend of the intellectual life with the practical concerns of making a living. He gravitated toward educational publishing at first but then broadened his interests to all areas of knowledge publishing, including the journals business.[7]

reported to Ellis.* Richard Rudick remained as corporate counsel. Appointed in 1978, he was responsible for all company legal and secretarial functions, including corporate governance as well as acquisition and litigation matters. He kept Wiley's contracts and copyright notices up to date, comprehensible, and sensible. He pursued pirates and promoted improvements in copyright laws in

the United States and around the world. Rudick was very much of the Wiley mold, promoting these issues in various industry leadership roles.[8]

In 1992, Josephine Bacchi became corporate secretary. Bacchi had been at Wiley longer than any of her colleagues, having signed up as a secretary when there *were* secretaries, in 1966, at 19 years of age. She served as Brad Wiley Sr.'s assistant for 24 years until she was appointed corporate secretary, at his request, when he retired as chairman in 1992.

Both Charles Ellis and Eric Swanson, *before* coming to Wiley, questioned Wiley's need for an

---

* The names of Wiley's three *core* businesses changed in the 1980s and early 1990s, although their publishing programs remained consistent. In this chapter, the authors use the names of Wiley's businesses as of 2006. In 2007, STM became Wiley-Blackwell or STMS.

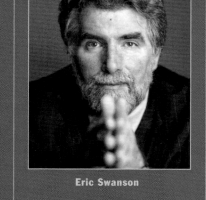
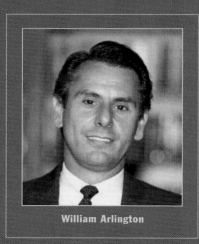
International Division. Ellis once described the division as akin to the Colonial Office in the British Foreign Office—that is, a remnant of the past. Since its formation in the 1960s, the division had been the connective tissue between Wiley's home office and its overseas subsidiaries and joint ventures, which were seemingly remote outposts that required servicing in an era before faxes and email. To Ellis's way of thinking, it was a barrier rather than an aid to global coordination. Accordingly, one of Ellis's first steps was to eliminate the International Division. As an STM publisher with extensive international experience and contacts, he knew that the worlds of research and related publishing demanded closer, more direct relationships, and that this community, with the growth of the Internet and the invention of the World Wide Web, was becoming increasingly global.[9]

Planning for a Renewal

Ellis argued that Wiley needed to turn its attention to what he saw as the company's most important, but neglected, asset—its core businesses. Management's fascination with Wilson Learning and the prospects for creating new lines of business, he believed, had resulted in serious underinvestment across the board—in new products, marketing, management, and technology. The sale of Wilson Learning allowed him to focus all his attention on Wiley's publishing strengths. The company was reorganized into two major reporting groups. Higher Education continued to publish textbooks while Professional/Trade published trade books for general readers and books and subscription products for professionals. Scientific, Technical, and Medical published books, journals, reference works, and some high-level texts. With the Liss acquisition and the steady growth of the P/T lists, P/T and STM accounted for more than half of the business.[10] Almost all of Wiley's profits came from STM and some of the international operations. The trade part of P/T was a growing and promising business, but small. Higher Ed presented the most daunting challenge: its pipeline of new projects had gone dry and had to be meticulously refilled, morale had plummeted, people had left or been forced out, and the marketing department had been shut down.[11]

To renew and grow these businesses, Wiley needed a planning process that linked plans to execution. The challenge, as Ellis and his team saw it, was to remain focused and agile at the same time. Wiley had been through a dizzying period when the industry was consolidating, great houses were disappearing or changing hands, competition was growing more cutthroat, and Wiley's largest business, textbooks, was being undermined by the used book business. When a 1988 memo suggested a radical reorganization of the company as a means to improving the implementation of strategy, Ellis disputed the memo's key assertion, that "organization [necessarily] follows strategy." The basic task, he believed, was to get the planning process right—to relate plans to changes in the market, communicate them effectively, and motivate managers to execute them consistently. This was no small feat at a time when some publishing experts were arguing that long-term forecasting was "of very limited value in an era of rapid technological change."[12]

Between 1991 and 1995, Wiley's strategic plans consistently identified five core strategies that were central to Ellis's approach to recovery and growth:[13]

- increase Wiley's revenue, earnings, cash flow, and return on equity by investing in the development of Wiley's core businesses organically and through acquisition
- grow internationally
- emphasize subscription and "continuity products" over unique, "one-off" books in the STM and P/T businesses

- pursue acquisitions to take advantage of the fact that Wiley's infrastructure (warehouse, information technology systems, financial and human resources systems, etc.) could support a larger business
- apply new information technologies to existing and new assets.

The judicious application of technology provided a particular opportunity. By 1990, 105.2 million computers were in use worldwide, 51.3 million in the United States alone, foreshadowing a market not just for software but also for books about software, computing, and even an emerging "cyber culture." The World Wide Web, launched in 1991 and made freely available two years later, opened up even more possibilities. Wiley was poised to take advantage of the commoditization of PC, CD-ROM, and DVD technologies, the growth of the World Wide Web, and the explosion of e-commerce.[14] The company was already offering a sampling of electronic products ranging from academic journals to online databases to CD data supplements; computer software applications in accounting, chemistry, and other scientific disciplines; and computerized test banks as textbook ancillaries for professors. Although some of Wiley's early experiments with technology had failed, the experience was cumulative. In 1992, the Boston Consulting Group urged Wiley to ride along the cutting edge of digital publishing technology. Wiley, having already suffered the consequences of this type of journey, was determined to let customers set the pace this time around.[15]

With board support for its five core strategies, Ellis and his team mandated fiscal 1993 as the turning point for Wiley. Success was defined as record revenue and profits, driven by the expected turnaround of Higher Education by April 30, 1993. "To put it bluntly," Ellis explained to one of his overseas managers, if the company's financial performance did not improve by then, "management will lose all credibility . . . and the future of Wiley as an independent company [will be] very seriously

Improvements at Wiley's U.S. Distribution Center

In the atmosphere of continuous improvement inspired by Charles Ellis and carried out under the direction of Robert Wilder and Clifford Kline, who joined Wiley in 1996 as vice president of Customer Service and Distribution, changes were introduced in the Wiley warehouse. For example, picking and packing areas of the warehouse, shown here, were reorganized to increase efficiency and reduce work stress.

at risk." Thus Ellis established a deadline to improve people's "basic blocking and tackling skills," as he liked to say, and to rebuild the company around "quality assets and quality people."[16]

Ellis's way of setting "reasonable goals," mixing urgency with charm, was a welcome change from the hard-nosed tone of the McMullin years. He knew that publishing was a creative profession in a rough-and-tumble industry, but it had to be made more efficient. That Wiley remained a pleasant place to work was due to the time-honored belief that the work was worthwhile and the renewed feeling that Wiley was a very decent place with a future, for both employees and authors. Robert Wilder, the new CFO, working with Peter Clifford, senior vice president of Finance, corporate controller, and chief accounting officer, reorganized Wiley's financial operations, a move essential to restoring transparency in financial reporting and reassuring the investor community about the validity of Wiley's

numbers. Wilder then turned his attention to bringing the company's distribution system (centered in the United States at the New Jersey warehouse) up to and beyond industry standards. Confidence and the right kind of jokes returned, too: "If we don't have a good year this year," said Robert Long, a U.K. marketing executive, "I shall eat my catalogue." It was all part of a steady shift in Wiley's corporate culture. Ellis's exhortations worked wonders for morale. Human Resources senior vice president William Arlington worked with Ellis to foster workplace improvements and job satisfaction among all Wiley employees. Employee turnover dropped, thanks also to a revamped compensation program.[17]

Wiley's plans over the decade grew more sophisticated and detailed. In 1993, STM began to work with a new planning methodology, which would replace the traditional planning methods that Wiley had employed in previous decades. The new methodology, "multiple scenario planning," assumed that the future would not be a linear projection of past or present observable trends. Instead, this broader approach brought the larger socioeconomic environment into the center of the process while keeping managers alert to the possibilities for change. One company in particular, the Global Business Network (GBN), was gaining recognition for its work with varied clients such as Royal Dutch Shell and South Africa's African National Congress, which had turned to GBN to help fashion a strategy for post-liberation economic development. Timothy King met with GBN's Lawrence Wilkinson and then approached Eric Swanson, who was running Wiley's STM business and was willing to experiment. Swanson explained his affinity for scenario planning this way: "You cannot chart the future. You can antici-pate it, you can prepare for it, and, with luck, you can survive it." He was attracted to the idea that one might "pin the corners" of alternative futures and then develop and implement plans that would serve Wiley well in a variety of possible circumstances. Further, he knew that the introduction of the World Wide Web had the poten-tial to change the way research was published, either undermining Wiley's essential journals business or pro-viding a tremendous opportunity for growth. Scenario planning offered the opportunity to think about how to prepare for unpredictable change.[18]

Scenario planning employed by Wiley's STM called for an analysis of possibilities, looking at critical uncertainties such as the competitive environment, the quality of demand, and importance of copyright. Within this construct, the following questions were explored: What might happen in an environment where customers were willing to pay in an industry charac-terized by a rush of new products and services, new business models, and new entrants? What might hap-pen when customers were willing to pay with the industry remaining more or less static, yet competitive? What might hap-pen in a world where customers were price-resistant under conditions where new entrants rushed in, provid-ing new channels of distribution and new business models? What might happen if online delivery of con-tent led to a demand for free content and widespread violation of copyright laws? Finally, what might hap-pen under conditions of price resistance in an industry where revenue barely covered costs?

The exercise enabled STM to position itself to remain successful under all four of those "what if" scenar-ios and everything in between. For example, the process enabled planners to consider how STM should respond if U.S. copyright laws were undermined by the Web, or

if scientists bypassed publishers and self-published their research online, or if massive new research funding for government and university laboratories became available, as well as many other possibilities.[19] As a result, STM's business-level plan provided that it would increase its capabilities to "incorporate technology into the publish-ing process as much as possible." It would champion the need to safeguard copyright protection, strengthen its relationships with authors and journals, participate in new technology projects, and develop new products in tune with the changing marketplace. Through the 1990s, implementation required energetic devotion to keeping up with technological and market innovation; getting closer to customers and their needs; reducing costs wherever possible to enable greater investments to increase productivity in administra-tion, production, and distribution; increasing global integration; and seeking out partners to compensate for areas of weakness.[20]

In 1994, Ellis and his cor-porate staff embraced the scenario-planning methodology used first by STM, as, eventually, would Higher Ed. P/T carried on with its own proven strategy, carefully extending and refining its category management approach and broadening its publishing for each category into related lines of publishing—"straight ahead," said Tim King—without any loss in momentum. The results, across the board, were increasingly impressive, largely because the plans tracked the larger market realities and were effec-tively implemented. Scenario planning became essential to Wiley's strategic thinking and contributed to the men-tal agility required to adjust quickly to changes in mar-ket realities. At a time when all publishers were becom-ing more efficient and competitive, Ellis articulated a new theme for Wiley: "reasonable progress, not instant success." Making it work was key—the mantra became "blocking and tackling." Implementation of strategic

> Scenario planning
> offered the
> opportunity to . . .
> prepare for
> unpredictable change.

plans had been Wiley's Achilles' heel. Ellis and his team were determined that this would no longer be the case. Indeed, Wiley did make its turnaround goals, posting double-digit increases and market share growth in every division at the end of fiscal year 1993.[21]

In executing their strategies, Wiley's business managers had several things working in their favor. Recent divestitures had left the company with excess capacity in its infrastructure; it could add more published content by growth or acquisition without increasing back-office operations. In addition, more and more of Wiley's publishing lines, led by the growing journals program, were generating the cash flow with which to pay down any debt needed in an acquisition. Building on funds that Wiley had accumulated from several divestitures, including Harwal, which was sold soon after Wilson Learning, Ellis built an acquisitions war chest to augment Wiley's organic growth, while Tim King and his staff put together a list of potential acquisitions and updated it constantly.[22]

The business environment helped. Demographic and macroeconomic variables became more favorable after the 1990–1991 recession, as the United States resumed a briefly interrupted surge of economic growth. The markets for Wiley's new technology products grew rapidly throughout the decade, as computers and the Internet changed the way people got their information. The technological revolution also boosted the traditional book market, despite fears to the contrary, through the online sale of books, especially technology books, and enrollments in electrical engineering and computer science courses. College enrollments also nudged upward again, from the so-called "baby boom echo" and the increase in nontraditional students. Such favorable developments made Ellis's job easier, but they did not guarantee success. Success came from Ellis and his

> Ellis's team and their colleagues delivered one of the most impressive records of financial performance in Wiley's long history.

team's ability to mobilize a staff demoralized by McMullin. It was not just a question of working harder, but of working smarter in ever more competitive markets. Ellis hired and led an impressive group of publishing professionals, and this team and their colleagues delivered one of the most impressive records of financial performance in Wiley's long history.[23]

As operating efficiencies and net income improved, the company managed to repay all of its long-term debt by 1995, freeing itself from interest rates and covenants that might put a brake on further expansion. During Ellis's tenure, Wiley's revenue and earnings were restored to a pattern of consistent and robust growth, generally meeting the ambitious targets he set in his plans. From 1991 through 1998, the year Ellis turned the reins over to Will Pesce, Wiley's revenue increased nearly twofold, from $237 million to $467 million, growing at 11% per year. Net income grew from $4.1 million in fiscal year 1991 to $27 million in fiscal year 1998, while net income per share increased appreciably during that same period.[24] As a measure of Ellis's and his team's achievements, the *Financial Times* in 1998 ranked Wiley as the world's 27th most respected company, tied with Dell, Honda, and Japan Railway East, and the only publisher on the 40-company list. What was fascinating about the survey was how well known Wiley was among Asian CEOs. Ellis, who spoke modestly to the board about the company's "increased resilience," had every reason to take pride in his achievements. Without the renewal led by Ellis, Wiley might not have been able to survive as an independent company. With the renewal, the company was poised for even greater accomplishments. The board acknowledged his achievements, noting that "his personal respect for the Company's traditions of independence, integrity, and quality enabled him to survive a period of organizational confusion about the competitive meaning and value of these principles," and that "he brought us the intellect, vision, energy, and discipline, as well as a wealth of publishing experience, needed to improve our financial performance, expand and focus our business, prepare us for the digital world, and restore to the staff its pride in the industry and the firm."[25]

An article in the *Financial Times*, November 30, 1998, naming Wiley the 27th most respected company in the world.

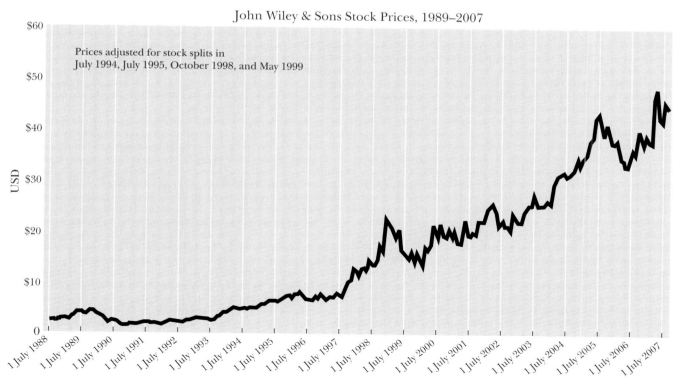

John Wiley & Sons Stock Prices, 1989–2007

Prices adjusted for stock splits in July 1994, July 1995, October 1998, and May 1999

Source: Yahoo! stock prices at finance.Yahoo.com

Will Pesce: Vision and Execution

Brad Wiley Sr. passed away on February 3, 1998, in his 88th year. He had been chairman emeritus since 1993 and for decades Wiley's most earnest ambassador to the world, pressing hard to the end his belief that China was the next great publishing horizon. He missed the transition between Ellis and his successor by three months. Wiley lost a great publisher, but was soon benefiting from the ascendancy of a talented new leader.

Will Pesce, who became Wiley's tenth president and CEO on May 1, 1998, was a seasoned publisher and a healthy blend of the old and new. The hand-off was orderly and sophisticated. Ellis and William Arlington, senior vice president of Human Resources, had developed a careful succession-planning process that stretched down into the ranks of the organization, identifying at least one successor for every manager. As Ellis approached his sixty-third birthday and the anticipated end of his contract, the process produced its first successor at the very top of the organization. Pesce had been primed for the position by increasing the span of his responsibilities: in 1996, he was named executive vice president of Educational and International Publishing, and in 1997, he became chief operating officer. The transition was smooth in other ways. Pesce retained Stephen Kippur, Eric Swanson, John Jarvis, Stephen Smith, and Peter Donoughue in senior publishing positions. Bonnie Lieberman became the new head of Higher Education in 1996, and William Arlington, Timothy King, Richard Rudick, and Robert Wilder continued as Pesce's staff. Wilder retired as CFO in 2001, to be replaced by Ellis Cousens; Rudick retired as corporate counsel in 2004, to be replaced by Gary Rinck.[26]

Pesce's appointment as CEO represented a matured understanding of the sort of leader that this publicly held, family-controlled knowledge publishing company required. Building on Ellis and Arlington's successful efforts to restore morale, Pesce was committed, as he had been since his arrival, to making Wiley "the place to be." By this he meant a working culture committed to ethical behavior, openness, mutual respect, deliberative career planning, the extension of performance-based compensation deep into the organization, and the understanding that people at Wiley, while asked to give 100+ percent at work, had a life beyond the office.

Pesce never forgot what Wiley had been like in 1989 when he arrived, a time when the perilous consequence of great plans poorly executed was most evident and the ranks of first-rate managers very thin. He saw how far an honorable but poorly led organization could slip away from simple principles and sound strategies and get tied up in its own visions. From the moment he was chosen for Wiley's top job nine years later, he resolved that the company would not go in directions where it couldn't turn words into actions and do the job well. Pesce was chosen to succeed Ellis precisely because he had not only the craft and business skills required of successful publishing executives but also a nice touch with people. He believed that leaders had to inspire followers to succeed, so he set out to win the trust of those he served at Wiley. For Pesce, Wiley was and had to remain a people-centered business. "Unlike other companies," he would explain to the company's shareholders, "we have not forgotten that this is still a business built on the strength and character of human relationships."[27]

As Wiley navigated an ever-changing publishing environment with Pesce at the helm, he identified three overarching goals. He put Wiley as *the place to be* at the top of the list. The next two goals sounded ordinary enough, though hardly easy: to sustain long-term relationships with customers and to increase the firm's profitability, cash flow, and return on investment. Charles Ellis had led a successful effort to restore the vitality of Wiley's core businesses while moving Wiley well along one of the paths toward globalization and the digital future. Pesce wanted to build on that momentum by exploiting Wiley's global positions and brands, and by improving collaboration across organizational and geographic boundaries and so improve the quality of

PROFILE

WILLIAM J. PESCE

After a couple of years in the pharmaceutical industry, Will Pesce joined CBS, where he stayed for ten years, eventually becoming president of W. B. Saunders, the medical publisher. "Those were the glory days at CBS," Pesce said, recalling a time when he personally presented Saunders' strategic plan to the legendary Bill Paley. Pesce started at CBS in financial analysis, then moved to planning and development, including work in acquisitions and new media. As president of Saunders, Pesce steered through the shoals of intense industry competition, sluggish sales, and increasing costs. After recruiting a new management team, introducing formal strategic planning, restructuring marketing and sales, and sharply cutting costs, he was able to improve Saunders' market position to the point where it was one of the most profitable companies in medical publishing.[28]

In 1987, after CBS divested its publishing operations to Harcourt Brace Jovanovich, Pesce departed to start MediVisuals, a venture staffed with medical illustrators who created demonstrative evidence to support the testimony of experts involved in malpractice, personal injury, and product liability litigation. After successfully launching the company, he realized he missed the interaction with diverse groups of people in corporate life. When a search firm called, offering to introduce him to Charles Ellis at Wiley, he responded out of more than curiosity. After many discussions with Wiley executives about taking on a turnaround challenge, he joined the company in September 1989 to lead Higher Education along with Wiley's Canadian operations. "I joined Wiley because it is a great brand," Pesce later recalled. "I had a high level of confidence that the Wiley family was in it for the long haul. And I had a lot of faith in Charles and the people around him. I thought that we could actually get this right."[29]

After leading a successful turnaround effort, Pesce became Wiley's chief operating officer in 1997 and Wiley's president and CEO on May 1, 1998.

A native of New Jersey from an Italian immigrant neighborhood, Pesce was the son of a functionally illiterate plumber. As a youngster, Pesce was fascinated by books, which quickly expanded his insular world. He had few opportunities for travel, so he read. His father encouraged his education, and he graduated from William Paterson University in 1973. The first in his family to earn a college degree, he financed his studies by paving roads and working at a local supermarket. A campus activist, Pesce was also a participant in student government. In 1975, he received an MBA in finance from New York University, leaving with self-confidence and "an approach to problem solving and critical thinking" inspired by his mentors. Years later, Pesce took a seat on the NYU Stern School's Board of Overseers and the William Paterson University Board of Trustees.

Wiley's products and its service. His strategies also included pursuing partnerships and alliances with highly regarded organizations around the world that would add content and capabilities to Wiley's portfolio of businesses. In addition, Pesce aimed to build on the company's record of growth by pursuing acquisitions that made strategic and financial sense, then integrating them into Wiley according to best practices. Finally, he advocated engaging technology to improve service to customers and increase internal productivity.[30]

Pesce started out with a simple yet fresh insight: Wiley must be guided by inclusive decision making and reject what he called "either/or" thinking. The company did not have to choose between satisfying stockholders or sustaining a superior work environment for colleagues. It did not have to choose between being financially driven or author-friendly. Conventional wisdom held that such objectives were naturally at odds. Pesce disagreed, viewing the interests of stockholders, employees, and authors as intertwined. Trained in finance, but a people-oriented person, he knew intuitively, as well as from his extensive experience in both STM and educational publishing, that people served customers most effectively by working collaboratively. When collaboration improved, financial performance improved as well.

Building and maintaining long-term relationships with customers was vital to success. It was time to make collaboration a priority. Customers did not care whether Wiley content was published by Higher Education, P/T, or STM; turf battles were the very human results of group allegiances and competitiveness. Pesce attacked this problem by setting up a series of collaborative cross-divisional teams that could sell content published in one business into another business's market, publish material that crossed organizational boundaries, and exploit skills found in one business for application in another. If collaboration could work within a business, then why not across businesses, or for that matter across international boundaries? To ensure progress, this approach was backed up with monetary incentives tying collaboration objectives to compensation. Still, old habits die hard and change came gradually.

To begin, Pesce reorganized Wiley's businesses into Higher Education, Professional/Trade (P/T), and Scientific, Technical, and Medical (STM). Bonnie Lieberman was appointed Pesce's successor in Higher Education. STM, still led by Eric Swanson, was separated from P/T, which was still managed by Stephen Kippur. The three-business portfolio clarified reporting responsibilities.[31]

John Wiley & Sons, 1989–2007

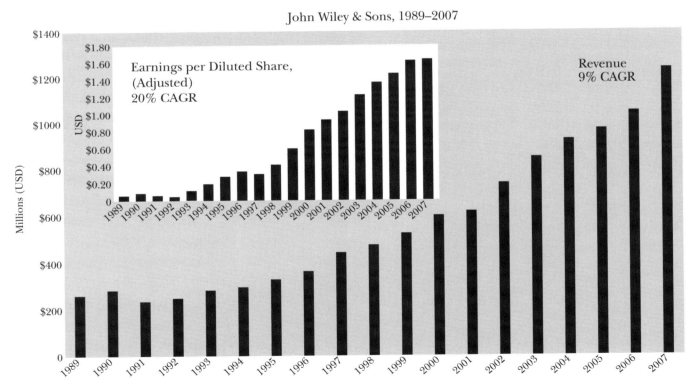

Source: John Wiley & Sons Annual Reports.
CAGR stands for Compound Annual Growth Rate.
Adjusted for stock splits, for illustrative purposes.

Higher Education

In 1989, the Education Publishing Group, once known as College and after 1998 as Higher Education, was no longer Wiley's largest business as it had been for half a century. The prized backlist authored by well-known academicians had atrophied. The marketing staff had been the victim of cost-cutting. Morale was terrible. "The company had not been investing competitively in new product acquisitions," recalled Pesce. The higher education business "was in such bad shape," Ellis said, "that we used to wonder whether it could be resuscitated."[32]

The textbook industry was "in the midst of . . . rapid and traumatic change." Eight companies controlled 80 percent of the U.S. market, and the battles for market share were fierce. The market was plagued by a variety of ills, including college "funding cutbacks and the aging of the baby boom generation." As prices rose, students were seeing less and less value in textbooks. The frustrations of a larger, more diverse, and less affluent student body were exacerbated by a sharp rise in tuition and other costs of education, especially as more and more states passed legislation modeled after California's 1978 Proposition 13, which limited increases in property taxes, a major source of funding for public education. As tuition and fees rose faster than inflation, students turned increasingly to the used book market. At the same time, consolidation in the college distribution channels—as the likes of Barnes & Noble and Follett were taking over college bookstores and as independent stores were forming buying consortia—was shifting pricing power to these sales intermediaries. Some students bought no textbooks at all. Toward the end of the decade, students began to turn to Internet-based Amazon.com, a new player in the book distribution business. Amazon offered new and used textbooks on its Web site.[33]

Not all the news was negative. By 1992, higher education enrollments were expanding, thanks in part to strong growth in the number of nontraditional students,

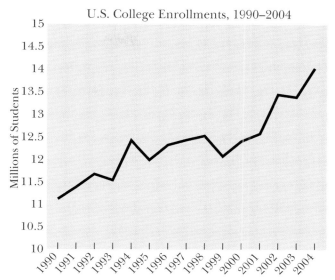

U.S. College Enrollments, 1990–2004

Source: U. S. Census Bureau. College Enrollment of Students 14 Years Old and Over, by Type of College, Attendance Status, Age, and Gender: October 1970 to 2004

particularly working adults seeking to improve their skills and credentials. Distance education and for-profit career colleges, such as DeVry (established in 1931) and the University of Phoenix (established in 1976), became major features of the educational landscape in the 1990s. These institutions, through online courses, geared their programs to people in the workforce seeking two- and four-year degrees, mostly in business and technical disciplines. The prospects for publishers in a market once served by the divested Occupational Division were bright.[34]

There were new possibilities in the publishing of electronic media, too. At first, Wiley looked forward to producing video and digital simulations on compact disks to supplement (rather than replace) textbooks. By 1996, as faculty and students were migrating to the Internet, it would become increasingly possible—and necessary—to bypass intermediaries and deliver content plus learning and teaching tools to the ultimate customer via the Internet. The challenge, though, was that the educational community would need time to feel comfortable in the new digital environment.[35]

Yes, there were problems in higher education and textbook publishing, but when Pesce was hired to

Successful Higher Education Revisions

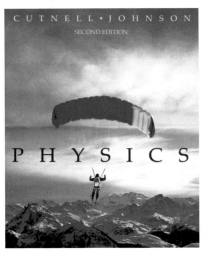

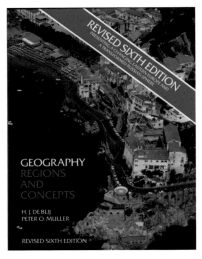

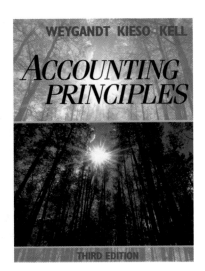

turn the Higher Ed business around in 1989, he emphasized that "most of Wiley's problems in higher education were internal, not external. The market was sluggish, but there were opportunities to grow. We just were really not executing." In addition to its diminished pipeline of new titles, its weakened backlist, and its lack of marketing, Higher Ed was poorly structured for competitive growth. As Pesce observed, "Higher Education was not organized and led in a way that supported a collaborative publishing model, i.e., editorial, production, marketing, and sales working together to launch new products and revisions." Instead, publishing decisions were editorially driven, then handed off to production and sales without much input.[36]

Higher Ed's fortunes depended on a new leadership team, one that could return Wiley to the ranks of quality publishing. Pesce hired Bonnie Lieberman initially as a publisher and eventually to lead all product development, and Steven Kraham to lead marketing. Pamela Fleisher joined Wiley to manage the business's finances shortly before Pesce's arrival. James Nye came on board first as a publisher, then moved over quickly to lead sales. They met and coordinated their efforts as a team, enhancing the effectiveness of the total business.

In his first presentation to the board of directors in 1989, Pesce made some startling statements: He promised to deliver three years of *declining* revenue and profits, saying that he was proud of his proclamation. "Wiley," Pesce explained, "had to prune the list while rebuilding and investing in the future." Pesce set the end of fiscal year 1993 (April 30, 1993) as the deadline for the revitalization of Higher Ed and the delivery of record financial results.[37]

To start, Higher Ed began to exploit one of Wiley's traditional strengths—its almost familial ties with authors such as Howard Anton (calculus), Harm de Blij and Peter Muller (geography), Donald E. Kieso and Jerry J. Weygandt (accounting), and T. W. Graham Solomons (organic chemistry), to name just a few—inducing authors to make the substantial revisions in existing texts required to increase the likelihood of sales. The team's approach to revisions followed the new, collaborative process, in which editorial, production, marketing, and sales worked together at every stage of the publishing process, including planning, development, product launch, and closing adoptions. Two revisions in particular symbolized Higher Ed's commitment and capability to tackle the intensely competitive introductory

Karen Huffman

Howard Anton

*J*ohn Cutnell and Kenneth Johnson, Harm de Blij and Peter Muller, Donald Kieso and Jerry Weygandt, Karen Huffman, and Howard Anton are just a few of the authors whose successful revisions, in highly competitive introductory markets, factored into the Higher Ed turnaround.

markets and demonstrated the effectiveness of the collaborative process: the second edition of *Psychology in Action* by Karen Huffman, Mark Vernoy, and Barbara Williams, and the third edition of *Accounting Principles*, by Jerry J. Weygandt, Donald E. Kieso, and Walter G. Kell.[38]

The second edition of *Psychology in Action*, published in 1991, reflected a shift from the conventional textbook formula, with its traditional, static content supported by extensive pedagogy, to a dynamic, student-centered learning environment. The theme of active learning, which motivated student involvement with the material and was embraced by the academic community as a meaningful educational philosophy, was the centerpiece of the new edition. As Steve Kraham recalled, the goal of the second edition paralleled the promise of Higher Ed to "help teachers teach and students learn." Editorial and production ensured that the active learning theme was highly visible throughout the product in part by incorporating feedback from student focus groups. Marketing developed a compelling message linking active learning and student motivation, reflecting that message in the book's cover and reinforcing it with an innovative promotional campaign. The sales strategy

revolved around organizing faculty workshops throughout the academic community. The workshops, conducted by Karen Huffman, focused on methods of integrating active learning techniques into classroom presentations. The result? The book took its place among the leaders in the introductory psychology market, with sales of the second edition more than tripling first-edition sales. The collaborative process became rooted as the basis for producing quality products and successful sales results. Books like this reestablished Wiley as a major college publisher.[39]

The third edition of *Accounting Principles*, by Weygandt, Kieso, and Kell, also demonstrated the effectiveness of the collaborative process. With this title, Higher Ed committed to doubling its market share in the principles of accounting market and devoted the resources to make that happen. According to Susan Elbe, senior marketing manager at the time for business and economics, the third edition was completely revised and revamped with a stunning design, eye-catching photographs, and rewriting of chapters. The theme of "Breaking Through to a New Perspective" was used throughout with a ground-breaking marketing and advertising campaign. A true segmentation strategy was

The Higher Ed pipeline began to fill with first editions, such as *Information Technology for Management: Improving Quality and Productivity* by Efraim Turban, Ephraim McLean, and James Wetherbe and *The Sciences: An Integrated Approach* by James Trefil and Robert Hazen.

employed, with sales and marketing strategies tailored to different segments, such as prior users, four-year colleges, or two-year colleges. Workshops around the country were devoted to teaching critical thinking skills in accounting. Published in 1993, the book surpassed its ambitious goal, achieving 250 percent of prior-edition sales.[40]

These and other results were striking. In August 1992, Pesce, with James Brown's "I Feel Good" playing in the background, described some of Higher Education's early successes at a rowdy sales meeting. The revised edition of de Blij and Muller's *Geography: Realms, Regions, and Concepts* sold 36,000 units and Solomons' *Organic Chemistry* sold 28,000 in an equally short period, while the second edition of John Cutnell and Ken Johnson's *Physics* sold 36,000. At the end of fiscal year 1993, Higher Ed exceeded every major financial goal. At the August 1994 sales meeting, Pesce reviewed Higher Ed's successful turnaround. Between May 1990 and April 1994, the business grew at a rate of 12 percent per year. The industry, in comparison, grew at 3 to 4 percent. Operating income grew at an annual rate of 30 percent.

The cumulative operating income over four years was a staggering 14 percent over budget.

Pesce was equally proud of his hiring and retention record. When he arrived, Higher Education had been plagued by the highest rate of involuntary turnover that anyone could remember at Wiley. He had promised his colleagues at his first sales meeting in 1989 that his most important personal challenge was "to create an environment in which quality people will thrive." By 1994, Higher Ed had promoted 100 colleagues and hired 150 people away from the competition.[41]

An active program of first editions helped diversify Higher Ed's offerings and expand its market presence during this period. *Information Technology for Management: Improving Quality and Productivity*, by Efraim Turban, Ephraim McLean, and James Wetherbe, was supplemented by software and computerized texts. *The Sciences: An Integrated Approach*, by James Trefil and Robert Hazen, signed by publisher Kaye Pace, created a new course and was developed with a preliminary edition, to incorporate student feedback into the publishing process.

Embedded in the Curriculum Reform Movement

While nurturing its backlist and publishing successful first editions, Higher Education again involved itself in a curriculum reform effort as it had after the Soviets launched *Sputnik* in 1957. This movement was initiated in 1986 at a meeting in Washington, D.C. hosted by the National Science Foundation's National Science Board. Among the NSB participants was Dr. Warren Baker, a civil engineer and president of California Polytechnic State University, who became a member of Wiley's board of directors in 1995. "The major thrust of the meeting," Baker later recalled, "was a growing concern that the undergraduate engineering curriculum was not addressing things like design, manufacturing processes, and reliability, quality control, project-based and hands-on learning and had become increasingly focused on analysis and science. There were some discussions that this was in part responsible for our declining ability to compete internationally (read Japan)." More and more students were entering four-year institutions ill prepared for or turned off to math, science, and technology. The results were alarming: the country was no longer educating the scientists and technicians needed to sustain its economy. Instead, colleges and corporations were turning to foreigners to fill the gap.[42]

In the early 1990s, the NSF funded a number of coalitions made up of six or more engineering schools working together to develop new curricula and new ways of teaching and learning engineering. The goals were to attract and retain more minorities and women and to make engineering more appealing to all. Following the NSF mandate that coalitions partner with publishers, Wiley's Higher Education engineering group joined the Synthesis Coalition in 1991. Wiley's responsibility was to help the coalition develop and distribute new teaching tools based on the latest technologies. Publisher Wayne Anderson worked with professors at Cornell, University of California Berkeley, Stanford, California Polytechnic State University at San Luis Obispo, Iowa State, and Hampton University.[43]

This partnership did not lead to any immediate publishing opportunities, but it did mark the beginning of a relationship with Stanford Professor Sheri D. Sheppard, who co-authored two mechanical engineering titles with Berkeley Professor Benson H. Tongue in the early 2000s. Moreover, Wiley learned a great deal about what worked and did not work in the engineering classroom and how professors used and did not use new technologies in teaching. One of the Synthesis Coalition's projects was to develop a database of "units of learning" that professors around the world could access through the Internet and use in their teaching. The coalition spent a great deal of time and NSF money developing "Internet Navigator," a Web browser that became useless when Mosaic (eventually released as Netscape) became available and captured the early Web browser market. But the effort turned out to be Wiley's first exposure to ideas about the development of modular digital content that could be customized into a series of unique products.

In the mid-1990s, Wiley and the coalition sponsored an annual award for a faculty member who developed the most innovative and useful new technology product for teaching and learning. Wiley built a few of these products, but most had limited success because many instructors were not yet comfortable using new technology products in their teaching. "This project got us thinking about what new technology tools we should be developing for teaching and learning," according to Anderson.[44]

CALCULUS REFORM

Ruth Baruth, a newly minted math editor in her first months at Wiley, found out about the Calculus Consortium at Harvard by accident on a visit to the University of Arizona in 1990 to make routine calls on math professors. The project, aimed at improving calculus instruction, had been launched two years earlier with a $2 million National Science Foundation (NSF) grant. Consortium members had just met with publishers at the annual Joint Mathematics Meeting, but they had not invited Wiley. They assumed that, since Wiley already published a number of traditional math titles, the company would not be interested. The members, who hailed from a diverse range of schools, from Harvard to the University of Southern Mississippi to a Massachusetts high school, were not pleased with the publishers' proposals. When Baruth found this out, she scrambled to visit every project member on their respective campuses, something competing publishers neglected to do. With encouragement from Bonnie Lieberman, head of Higher Education publishing, and Wayne Anderson, her publisher, and with Will Pesce's participation, Baruth submitted a proposal, which was accepted in January 1991.

The publishing process was an unusual one. A second draft of the Consortium's first title, *Calculus*, by a group of authors headed by Deborah Hughes-Hallett and Andrew M. Gleason, was already being class tested when Wiley inked the contract. Because of Harvard's cachet, reform-minded instructors were on the lookout for this new title. After class testing, a draft version was circulated to a limited number of professors, which only increased the buzz. The marketing effort, led by Susan Elbe, played on this scarcity principle. A preliminary edition, published in 1992, sold 93,000 units. The first edition, which followed a year later, sold 120,000 units. "It was the best-selling first-edition calculus book ever published. Twenty thousand units was considered . . . good for a first edition," Baruth recalled. Three other titles followed: *Multivariable Calculus* in 1994, *Applied Calculus* in 1995, and *Functions Modeling Change: A Preparation for Calculus* in 1996.[45]

The Consortium's slogan was "A pump, not a filter," by which the authors meant that calculus was filtering too many students out of engineering and science. *Calculus* was designed to push students through calculus so that they could move on to degrees in these disciplines. The NSF had charged the Harvard Consortium with dissemination of their reform curriculum. To help faculty understand this new approach to teaching calculus, Higher Education published a newsletter and hosted a series of annual summer conferences on the teaching and learning of calculus. The authors of competing texts were invited to participate. The conferences were supplemented by workshops on individual campuses.

*R*uth Baruth, math editor (top); Nancy Prinz, senior production editor (middle); Rob Meador, copy chief, Advertising & Promotion, and Susan Elbe, senior marketing manager (bottom).

The Harvard calculus titles further enhanced Wiley's reputation as a major publisher in math and contributed significantly to the turnaround effort of Higher Ed.[46]

Leveraging Technology

Participation in the NSF coalitions was a formative experience for Higher Education. For the first time, Wiley *partnered* with authors and institutions of higher education to shape content, develop new uses for technology, and reform the curriculum. From his first days at Wiley, Pesce insisted that, unlike established practice, his colleagues needed to pay attention to what students had to say about textbooks. Focus groups with students became a way of doing business in Higher Education. Students—with their concerns about the effectiveness of textbook pedagogy and the uses and price of content— also contributed to Wiley's thinking about technology. Technology over the 1990s came to be seen as central to the teaching *and* learning experience. Higher Ed was entering the most innovative phase of Wiley's history as a textbook publisher. Unlike STM, where research behaviors and library buying practices were somewhat predictable, the nature and consequences of changes in teaching and learning in a digital environment were less apparent.

As the first generation of students to grow up with computers hit college campuses in the 1990s, Higher Ed began to incorporate digital technology into its products in a variety of ways. As with any new medium, the process included a certain amount of trial and error. A strategy emerged by the end of the decade in which technology was no longer regarded as a support for printed text, but was seen as a delivery system for integrating content with essential learning and teaching activities, as embodied in *WileyPLUS,* the educational platform introduced in 2005.

Soon after Will Pesce took over the leadership of Higher Ed in 1989, he appointed Susan Saltrick as technology "guru." In those days, according to Pesce, he and Susan had to bribe colleagues to attend new media discussions by providing a free lunch. "Initially she had no staff," recalled Bonnie Lieberman. "The idea was really just to get technology on our radar screen." Early efforts focused on the sciences and were carried out with various vendors and partners. "We were approached by SmartBooks in 1991," said Kaye Pace, publisher for the sciences, "with a proposal to do an electronic version of our Halliday *Physics* text. It was very advanced, with hyperlinked text on a CD. They released it and we distributed it, but they went out of business, which ended the venture. We did get some traction with the concept, however."[47]

In 1992, Wiley teamed up with IntelliPro, a New Jersey-based interactive multimedia development company, to build software simulations supplementing a new edition of Michael J. Moran and Howard N. Shapiro's *Fundamentals of Engineering Thermodynamics,* delivered on Windows-compatible CDs. Two years later, Wiley purchased an equity interest in IntelliPro.[48] The creation of ancillaries, such as test banks and teachers' guides, had greatly increased the cost of the textbook package. Digital ancillaries provided a binary solution: they provided tools that would help students and faculty while reducing the cost of texts. The IntelliPro alliance was a useful step in the migration of printed text to electronic media that supplemented print and then, finally, to electronic media that would supplant print. In the short term, the alliance provided Wiley with cost reductions for a number of ancillaries. More than a dozen were published, mostly in engineering and mathematics, but the market uptake was not sufficient to justify the investment. IntelliPro foreshadowed one aspect of Wiley's emerging technology strategy: learn from a partner until the learning process suggests the next steps—whether to acquire the partner and its skills, continue to work on the same basis, or seek a new partnership.[49]

Another early effort targeted a specific student and instructor need. Students complained that they were paying for textbook content they never used, while instructors were looking for flexibility when selecting materials for a course. Rather than assign the entire text, professors were in the habit of bringing selected content to shops where it was copied and bound for sale to students, often at a price lower than for a typical textbook. Although they posted notices warning against violations of the copyright law, copy shops, by and large, did not insist on the need to get permission to reproduce multiple copies of a text. To find a solution that worked for faculty, for students, *and* for Wiley, Wiley first had to take on the illegal activities of copy shops, like Kinko's, that proliferated around college campuses. Kinko's activities clearly violated U.S. copyright law, but publishers were reluctant for a time to move legally against the company for fear that the professors who made buying decisions for students would view the action negatively. In 1991 Wiley and a number of other publishers successfully sued Kinko's, substantially reducing the amount of illegal copying while creating both a market and an obligation to replace what Kinko's had produced.[50]

Evolving Technology in Higher Education

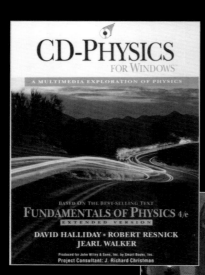

*C*D-Physics for Windows, based on *Fundamentals of Physics*, fourth edition, by David Halliday, Richard Resnick, and Jearl Walker, was developed for Wiley in 1999 by Maris Technologies. In 2002, Wiley acquired Maris, run by a team of Russian software engineers, many of them from the Russian space program, and renamed it Training and Educational Services (TES).

*J*uly 24, 2002, at the Boris Godunov restaurant near Red Square (Moscow, Russia). Members of the Wiley and Maris teams dine together as Wiley does due diligence prior to acquiring Maris's Russian software development operation. From left to right: Gregory St. John, Vadim Karpov, Andrew Townsend, Fedor Terlov, Alexander Schetinnikov, Frank Lyman, Eugeny Drozdov, Deni Auclair, Tatiana Chernosvitova, Scott Penny, Deirdre Silver, Irina Vsanova, Julian Clayton

At the time, many professors of introductory engineering were teaching without textbooks, preferring to assemble their own instructional material. Executive editor Charity Robey developed an electronic interface that allowed professors to browse chapters from Wiley's introductory engineering titles on a CD and select what they wanted, adding their own content if desired, and then order the resulting custom book electronically through their college bookstores. The program was launched in the fall of 1993 as the Wiley Custom Publishing System; it was not large enough to be self-sustaining, but it was perhaps the most technologically advanced custom publishing solution at the time. Nevertheless, Higher Education was moving gradually toward the idea of fully customized content.[51]

Some projects showed where *not* to go. "In 1998, we made a significant commitment to a multimedia project out of the University of California at Berkeley that was funded by the National Science Foundation," said Kaye Pace. "The plan was to develop

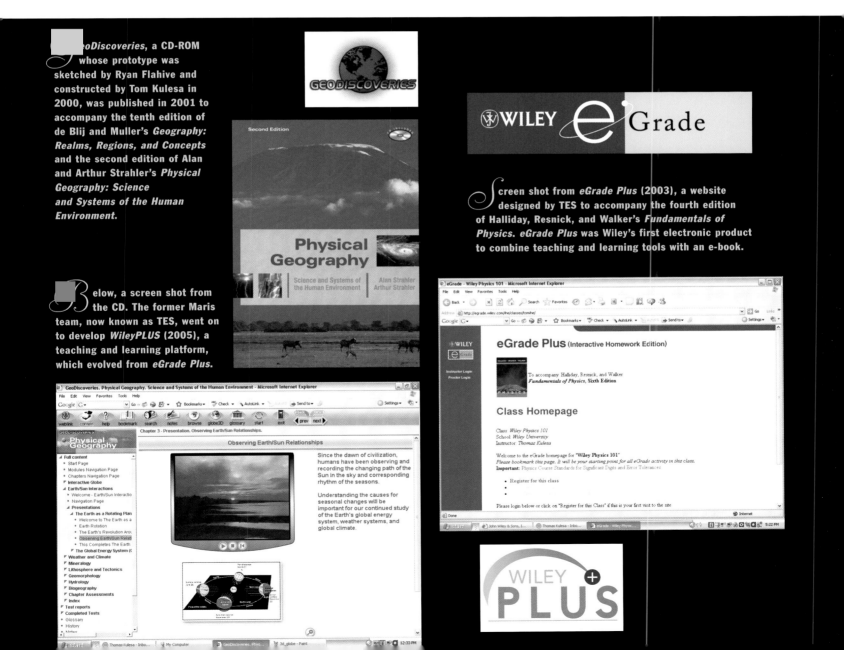

eoDiscoveries, a CD-ROM whose prototype was sketched by Ryan Flahive and constructed by Tom Kulesa in 2000, was published in 2001 to accompany the tenth edition of de Blij and Muller's *Geography: Realms, Regions, and Concepts* and the second edition of Alan and Arthur Strahler's *Physical Geography: Science and Systems of the Human Environment.*

elow, a screen shot from the CD. The former Maris team, now known as TES, went on to develop *WileyPLUS* (2005), a teaching and learning platform, which evolved from *eGrade Plus.*

creen shot from *eGrade Plus* (2003), a website designed by TES to accompany the fourth edition of Halliday, Resnick, and Walker's *Fundamentals of Physics. eGrade Plus* was Wiley's first electronic product to combine teaching and learning tools with an e-book.

Bonnie E. Lieberman

*B*onnie E. Lieberman, senior vice president and general manager, Higher Education. Bonnie joined Wiley in 1990 as publisher of the Sciences, Foreign Language, and Psychology group in Higher Education, after having held various positions at other publishing houses, including editorial director at Macmillan and editorial, marketing, and sales positions at McGraw-Hill. Later the same year, she was promoted to vice president and editorial director for the College Division, where she was responsible for product acquisition and development. With Will Pesce, she led the turnaround of the division in the mid-1990s. In 1996, she was named senior vice president of Higher Education, with the responsibility for overseeing the company's Higher Education business, helping teachers to teach and students to learn, in media from print to the Web.

a set of multimedia modules for teaching chemistry. But it became substantially more expensive than anticipated, and the market did not respond enthusiastically to the concept," so it was not published.[52]

The next step was a big one. Early in 1999, David Sidman, who worked in Timothy King's Planning and Development group, set up a meeting between Higher Ed and an entrepreneur he knew named Nick Maris. Greek-born and a British citizen, Maris owned a company, Maris Technologies, which specialized in creating educational simulations and animations, tapping the expertise of a team of Russian programmers and designers based in the city of Korolev and formerly employed by the Soviet space program.

Maris showed the Higher Ed team one of their consumer products, called *RedShift*. It was a "mathematically accurate multimedia model of the universe, very impressive," recalled Frank Lyman, director of new media. "What struck us was that they weren't just good programmers; they really knew science, too." Wiley's first project with Maris was *CD-Physics* (1999), an interactive multimedia companion to the celebrated David Halliday, Robert Resnick, and Jearl Walker text.

It was soon followed by *GeoDiscoveries*, for the geography texts by Alan and Arthur Strahler and by Harm de Blij and Peter Muller, and the *Interactions* series, keyed to Gerard Tortora and Sandra Grabowski's *Principles of Anatomy and Physiology*.[53]

"We had acquired Tortora with the Pearson Education list in May of 1999," said Bonnie Lieberman. "We had two years during which we could sell it with its original software component. For the next edition we needed to develop our own. It was really quite an achievement to come out with a competing product in that time, a testament to our working relationship with Maris."[54]

As the Maris collaboration was blossoming, something else was germinating at the University of Nebraska–Lincoln. Plagued by a shortage of teaching assistants to grade exams, professors John Orr and William Lewis of the Department of Mathematics and Statistics began administering basic skills tests for their students through computers and the Internet with automatic grading. By 1999, their students were practicing homework problems on their own at their computers. Following an initial contact by Ruth Baruth, Wiley began to partner with Orr and Lewis to produce Wiley Web Tests, and in 2000 expanded the offering by adding homework assignment, delivery, and grading capability, tying it to specific Wiley texts, and rebranding it as *eGrade*.[55]

"We thought we had a new learning model when we created products that integrated text and multimedia," said Kaye Pace, "but what really got us traction in the use of technology for teaching and learning was becoming part of the homework assignment with *eGrade*. It allowed us to tap into students' motivation through the activities they needed to perform to get their grades."[56]

Higher Ed had an exciting new product, and with the dot.com frenzy peaking, Internet startup companies approached Wiley with proposals on a regular basis. "But we knew that it wasn't sustainable to keep doing 'one-off' projects," said Joe Heider, who managed Higher Ed's editorial and technology teams. "We needed a coherent, scalable approach" across all disciplines. Coordinating multiple vendors had become burdensome, their viability could be an issue, and there was always the concern that a technology developed for Wiley might be passed along to a competitor.

These considerations led to an intensive planning effort in the summer of 2000, in which management formulated a technology strategy that would protect the core print business while existing products migrated to digital formats. The idea of having an in-house development capability became increasingly attractive; Maris was the candidate of choice. Maris had developed its own teaching and learning platform, called Edugen, which allowed Maris to create products relatively economically, without the need to reprogram them for revisions or upgrades. "They were the first company we had found with reusable programming," recalled Heider, "and we knew that would benefit the scalable approach we had decided on. That, and the successes we had had with them, gave us the conviction that Maris was the right company for us to acquire."

Wiley acquired Maris in November 2002, incorporating it into the new Web Publishing Technology (WPT) group and renaming it Training and Educational Services (TES). The process of acquiring a company in Russia was no small achievement, requiring a concerted due-diligence effort by a team that included Deni Auclair, Deirdre Silver, and Gregory St. John, the head of WPT, with Frank Lyman as the Higher Ed representative.[57]

The Training and Educational Services (TES) staff

Marsha Gordon, director, Wiley Faculty Network, and Brad Franklin, consultant, Learning Technologies

Working with Maris between 2001 and 2003, the Physics team developed an online synthesis of *CD-Physics* and *eGrade*, based on a successful pilot at the Pennsylvania State University known as the Interactive Homework Edition (IHE). Cutnell and Johnson's *Physics* was also adapted to the new product model after research and publishing experience showed that students will generally read a text only when they become stuck on a homework problem. The IHE provided a direct link from each assigned problem to the relevant section of the electronic text or multimedia content.[58]

Another outcome of the summer 2000 strategic plan was the decision to create a series of stand-alone electronic learning courses. Known as Wiley eLearning, the initiative was headed by Jerry Weissberg, hired in May 2001 to assemble a team and work with Maris on building a dedicated electronic learning platform. It ultimately proved too costly to support two separate platforms, but the effort provided useful insight into online content delivery.

In the summer of 2002, Higher Ed management resolved to expand the IHE product model significantly, beginning with an in-depth examination of the instructional process. "We knew we had excellent content and technology resources for students and instructors alike," said Bruce Spatz, who managed Higher Ed's Digital Publishing Group, "but our offerings had become quite complex; there was no direct way to go from one resource to another." Higher Ed needed a more integrated product model and began by holding focus groups with instructors and students. "We didn't start by talking about technology," said Spatz, "but by asking about their teaching and learning challenges, and we continued to consult with them as we developed our prototype." The new product—*eGrade Plus*—launched in the fall of 2003 and was available for 35 titles by January 2004. Begun at the University of Nebraska, *eGrade Plus* was ultimately developed through the efforts of Higher Ed in collaboration with the Web Publishing Technology group and their Russian colleagues.[59]

By this time, *eGrade Plus* had evolved well beyond the function implicit in its name into a platform for all types of content, including a complete electronic version of the text, with unique views for instructors and students and in a broadening range of subject areas. To recognize this and to capitalize on Wiley's good name in the market, the product was relaunched as *WileyPLUS* in the fall of 2005.

While students who grew up with video games were, for the most part, comfortable in a digital environment, faculty responses ranged from enthusiasm to fear, even hostility. As Higher Ed gained insights from the NSF coalitions and the various projects that preceded the launch of *WileyPLUS*, it became clear that faculty would need support in the new technological environment. All through the 1990s, Wiley sales representatives and editors made connections with "Lone Rangers," who were using technology for the first time. They inspired Higher Ed to think about how to use the lessons learned from technophiles to deal with the problems of technophobes. Regional sales manager Howard Weiner, for example, recognized the need to encourage faculty by developing a peer-to-peer support system. In 2000, Dr. Marsha Butler (later Gordon), an educational and counseling psychologist teaching at the University of Tennessee and Roane State Community College, was hired to build the Faculty Resource Network (later renamed the Wiley Faculty Network). The WFN began by using four faculty mentors in accounting and biology to connect with customers online. One of the first mentors, Brad Franklin, was already informally consulting with faculty about how to use *EGrade Plus*. (In 2003, Franklin joined Wiley full time as a learning technologies consultant with the WFN.)

The WFN experienced immediate success with the academic community and soon expanded into additional disciplines. As *eGrade Plus* evolved into *WileyPLUS*, the WFN continued to grow and to support it. In 2007, the WFN network included 60 mentors supporting all Higher Ed disciplines, and the program, in addition to virtual presentations, included workshops, guest lecture series, and a Web site that provided access to teaching kits, faculty tutorials, and showcase courses. According to Gordon, "The network also provides a product feedback loop that goes back into editorial and product development, thus increasing our effectiveness. This way, we can build stronger products while partnering with faculty to help them be successful at using them."[60]

Higher Education Acquisitions and Partnerships

Throughout the 1990s, the acquisition of existing titles from competing publishers augmented the recovery of Higher Education. In 1994, for example, Wiley acquired a college engineering list from Houghton Mifflin. Buying lists, or even individual titles, was somewhat safer and less costly than developing books from scratch. Following some smaller acquisitions, Wiley paid Pearson $57 million in 1999 for 55 college textbooks and instructional packages in biology, engineering, mathematics, teacher education, economics, and general social sciences. It was an opportune move. The U.S. Department of Justice had forced the sale of these lists as a condition for Pearson's acquisition of Prentice Hall from Simon & Schuster's Higher Education business because the combination would give Pearson too much market power in these disciplines. As the negotiations drew to a close, the excitement at Wiley was so palpable that Pesce felt he had to remind the board to "remember the words of that esteemed philosopher, Yogi Berra: 'It ain't over till it's over.'" Wiley's stature as a middle-sized educational publisher assured the Justice Department's approval of the sale.[61]

The Pearson lists were a bargain. Among the Pearson titles were gems such as Jacquelyn Black's *Microbiology;* Abraham Silberschatz's *Operating System Concepts;* J. David Irwin's *Circuits;* Gary Musser and William Burger's *Mathematics for Elementary Teachers;* and a new list in teacher education. The biggest prize of all was *Principles of Anatomy and Physiology* by Gerard J. Tortora and Sandra Grabowski, a leading introductory textbook in its field and one that generated $10 million in revenue per annum.

The Pearson acquisition offered an opportunity to begin to address another Higher Ed challenge with a

INSIDE THE BOOKS

Tortora's *Anatomy and Physiology* Titles

Gerard Tortora

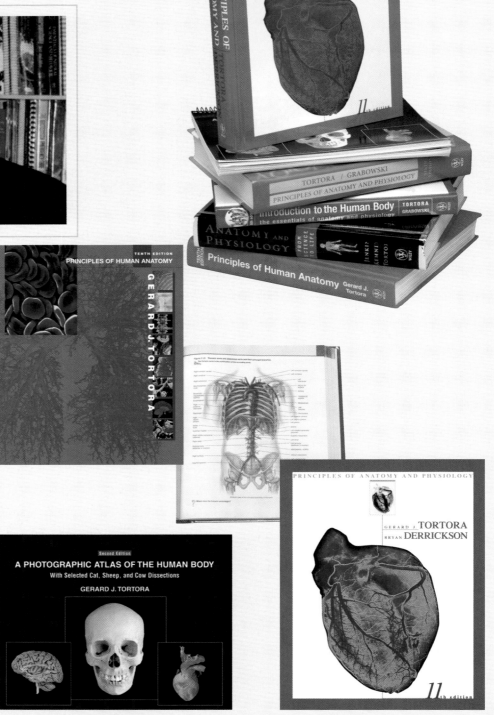

Since 1975, when the first edition of Gerard J. Tortora's *Principles of Anatomy and Physiology* exploded onto the scene, nearly 5 million nurses, nutritionists, and allied health and medical professionals have been introduced to the human body using a text written by this astonishingly successful author. The immediate success of *PAP* led to the development and publication of best-selling texts for related courses: for the one-semester anatomy course, *Principles of Human Anatomy*; an essentials version of *PAP, Introduction to the Human Body (IHB)*; and laboratory manuals for the co-requisite courses. In addition, Tortora and two co-authors produced the leading microbiology text on the market.

As a competitor once noted, Gerard Tortora is perhaps the most successful author in all of college publishing. His commitment to his students as well as to excellence in his texts ensures that he will continue on this road for a long time to come.

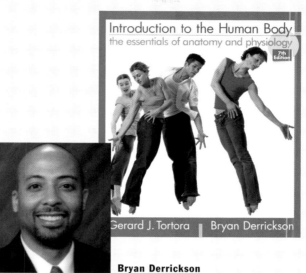

Sandra Grabowski

Bryan Derrickson

With the Pearson acquisition in the summer of 1999, Wiley acquired the rights to all of the Tortora anatomy and physiology texts, two of which were at the time co-authored with Sandra Grabowski of Purdue University. New co-authors have joined Tortora since that acquisition. Bryan Derrickson from Valencia College became co-author of both *PAP* and *IHB*, while Mark Nielsen of the University of Utah joined Tortora on the eleventh edition of *Principles of Human Anatomy*. The breadth of the franchise continued to grow as well. Gail Jenkins of Montgomery College in Maryland, and Christopher Kemnitz of the University of Wisconsin–Superior, teamed up with Tortora to produce a new first edition for the two-semester A&P course in the spring of 2006. *Anatomy and Physiology: From Science to Life* took a unique modular, case-driven approach, offering an alternative to the comprehensive and traditionally organized texts like *Principles*.

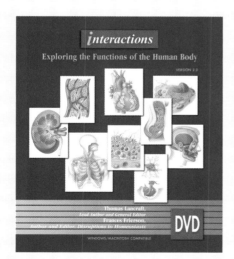

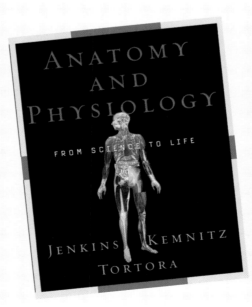

Gail W. Jenkins

Christopher P. Kemnitz

Interactions focused on the physiological processes within each system of the body using animations, interactivity, and clinical correlations to enhance student understanding.

small step toward diversifying into new disciplines and reducing the reliance on the limited number of disciplines in which it published. Pearson's education titles, for example, brought more than the beginning of a textbook presence in a new discipline. They also complemented Jossey-Bass's highly esteemed educational list for professionals. The result was more cross-business collaboration, one of Pesce's highest priorities. Pesce referred to "the incredible leverage that can be achieved by making product-line acquisitions in core publishing areas." Higher Ed continued to troll for properties, acquiring in 2001 nearly 50 titles that International Thomson was required to divest as a result of its acquisition of Harcourt. These titles added more power in key Wiley markets—environmental science, chemistry, business, math, psychology, and modern language. They included *Environment* by Peter Raven and Linda Berg; *Foundations of College Chemistry* by Morris Hein and Susan Arena; *The Earth Through Time* by Harold Levin; *Marketing Research Essentials* by Carl McDaniel and Roger Gates; *Financial Institutions, Markets, and Money* by David Kidwell et al.; *Analytic Trigonometry with Applications* by Raymond Barnett et al.; *Psychology and the Challenges of Life* by Jeffrey Nevid and Spencer Rathus; *Cognition* by Margaret Matlin; and *Horizontes* by Graciela Gilman and K. Josu Bijuesca. In the same year, Higher Ed also bought out Fitzgerald Publishing, a small publisher of life sciences textbooks.[62]

Higher Ed also partnered with companies that could provide complementary skills, capabilities, or content. For example, in 1996, Higher Ed formed an alliance with the Public Broadcasting System's Nightly Business Report, which at the time was the most-watched business news program in the United States. Wiley repackaged videos of the programs and sold them to supplement business texts. In 1997, Wiley formed an alliance with Dow Jones Interactive Publishing to develop the Wiley Business Extra program, featuring content from Dow Jones and *The Wall Street Journal Interactive Edition.*

The full text of selected Dow Jones stories was posted on the Business Extra electronic news folder hosted at Wiley's Web site, along with discussion questions for classroom assignments.

In 1997, Pesce became Wiley's chief operating officer and Bonnie Lieberman had been head of Higher Education for a year. The sum of their efforts was the restoration of Wiley's venerable higher education publishing business to profitability and growth. Higher Ed had outrun the industry average in revenue growth by annual multiples of two to four times consistently since 1992. The Group's operating income and cash flows had improved for the fourth straight year, reflecting consistent improvements in performance in all aspects of the business. In a mature, competitive market, Wiley was regularly taking market share. The formula for that success was a nice combination of returning to the fundamentals of collaborative publishing, systematic revision of established titles, aggressive cultivation of new authors, sensitivity to the market, and the judicious application of technology.

By 2003, Higher Ed's evolving relationship to the academic world was summed up in words that were heard frequently at Wiley: helping teachers to teach and students to learn. In a change of direction unlike any in its history as a textbook publisher, Wiley had moved ahead following its fiscal year 2000 strategic plan. It had become a partner in the educational process by working closely with faculty. It had worked with technology companies and content providers to explore alternative product development. To do this, selling and marketing had to change. Sales representatives and their marketing allies were moving into a consulting role, helping faculty make decisions about course materials and the ways in which Wiley's technology could enhance the learning

Joe Heider

Steve Kraham

Kaye Pace

Susan Elbe

Anne Smith, Jay O'Callaghan, and Bruce Spatz

experience. Higher Ed continued to publish traditional textbooks, but technology supplemented and improved the traditional approach. For students in particular, Higher Ed's new strategic direction laid the groundwork for additional changes that would improve the educational experience while reducing the price of texts.[63]

Higher Ed revenue by 2003 reached $176 million, having grown from $112 million in 1998. Lieberman had also built a highly collaborative team consisting of Joseph Heider, vice president of Product and e-Business Development; Steve Kraham, vice president of Marketing; Ann Berlin, vice president of Production; Patty Stark, vice president of Sales; Frank Lyman in New Media development; and publishers Kaye Pace, Susan Elbe, Anne Smith, and Bruce Spatz. Although Higher Ed remained a difficult and not entirely predictable business, Lieberman and her team continued to outperform the best in the industry.

Scientific, Technical, and Medical

The 1989 Liss acquisition, skillfully engineered by Charles Ellis, brought new talent and new energy to Wiley's scientific, technical, and medical publishing operations. The acquisition doubled the number of Wiley journals published in the United States and added to its book list. Over the next two years, Liss and InterScience, Wiley's existing STM business, were brought together into a new STM division under the leadership of Eric Swanson.

The STM market in the 1990s, both in the United States and abroad, was in flux as research funding patterns shifted. In the United States, federal research and development (R&D) spending declined from 1989 until 2001 when it picked up a bit in the first two years of George W. Bush's presidency. The most significant increases in federal R&D funding came from the doubling, at the expense of other programs, of the National Institutes of Health's budget between 1998 and 2003. Defense-related programs continued to consume a significant and growing share of the federal R&D budget. At colleges and universities, federal R&D funding doubled between 1989 and 2003, with the bulk of the increase coming again from the NIH. Funding from the National Science Foundation (NSF) also doubled. But while the NIH provided 63 percent of total academic R&D funding, the NSF was responsible for only 14 percent. In a continuation of a trend that began in the 1960s, more R&D funding came from the corporate sector than from the federal government; the growing gap between private and government research funding reflected a continuing shift away from basic to applied research. The R&D funding picture in the United Kingdom and Germany was unimpressive, showing annual increases of 1 and 3 percent of GDP, respectively, while countries such as China and Korea increased their R&D budgets to 10 percent and more of GDP.[64]

Despite sectoral and geographic shifts in research spending patterns, one thing was clear: research activity—knowledge development—grew dramatically in the 1990s. So did STM publishing, which provided essential research content in numerous formats, including databases, journals, handbooks, and major reference works. The accelerated pace of innovation in areas such as computing and biotechnology meant a growth in research materials. Wiley authors Simon M. Sze and Kwok K. Ng, for example, noted that 250,000 papers on semiconductor devices alone were published between 1981 and 2006. However, this research growth did not always translate into increased sales of content.[65]

While increases in certain aspects of R&D funding, such as increases in the NIH budget in the United States, looked impressive, they did not translate readily into expanding markets for STM publishers. STM publishing was still a difficult business. The continued underfunding of public higher education, combined with universities' reducing the percentage of

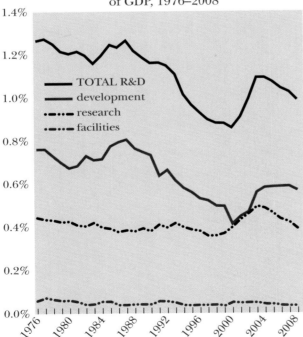

Trends in U.S. Federal R&D as Percentage of GDP, 1976–2008

Source: AAAS analysis of R&D in annual AAAS R&D reports. 2008 figures are President's request. R&D includes conduct of R&D and R&D facilities. Data to 1984 are obligations from the NSF Federal Fund survey. GDP figures are from OMB, Budget of the U.S. Government FY 2008. FEB/'07 PRELIMINARY © 2007 AAAS

funds allocated to libraries, meant that academic library budgets were constrained. With budgets growing slowly and costs mounting, librarians purchased fewer research monographs, one important component of the STM publishing program, while they and academic administrators complained that too many journals had become both redundant and expensive, not a good combination. Journal prices had always been higher than mass-market books or magazines because of the costs of bringing high-quality information to relatively few people. Nonetheless, the hard fact was that library budgets did not keep pace with the growth of scholarly output. As journal prices continued to rise in the early 1990s, more and more libraries turned to cutting subscriptions, while others formed buying consortia to increase their buying power.[66]

For publishers, then, the growth of journals revenue was slowing as research libraries had their budget growth trimmed. New journal titles had become difficult to launch successfully, while the continuing growth in content and price of existing journals constricted library spending on scholarly content. It was clear, moreover, that the online world would transform journal publishing—and STM's leadership had examined the possibilities through scenario planning—but no one knew exactly how or when.

Responding to these trends, STM publishing at Wiley changed dramatically in this era. Wiley began the decade with two journals publishing centers, New York and Chichester, from which the company served

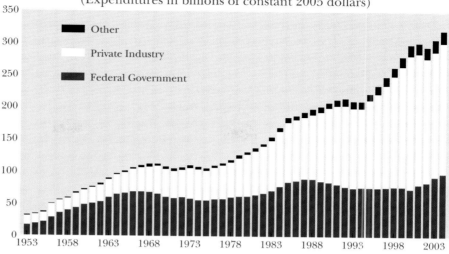

U.S. R&D Funding by Source, 1953–2004
(Expenditures in billions of constant 2005 dollars)

Source: NSF, Division of Science Resources Statistics. (Data for 2004 are preliminary.)
MAY '06 © 2006 AAAS

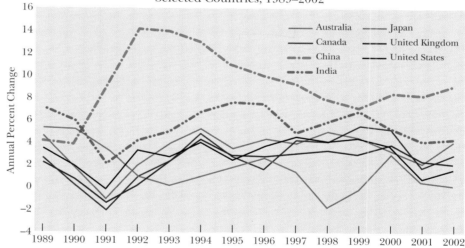

Annual Growth Rate for Gross Domestic Product, Selected Countries, 1989–2002

Source: Based on International Monetary Fund, World Economic Outlook Database, September 2006.

increasingly globalized research communities. The number of both overseas journal editors and contributors grew, while journal sales reached beyond the traditional centers of research in North America, Europe, and Japan. These changes were driven by the ways in which researchers and journal authors were using the computer and the World Wide Web to share research. Wiley's STM managers recognized both the opportunities and the challenges in these trends, and ultimately, none had a negative impact on Wiley's STM business.

Bert Sutherland, a Wiley board member with intimate knowledge of the research world, liked to say "Watch the physicists," because he saw them as the vanguard when it came to new uses of the Internet. Wiley staff paid particular attention, for example, in 1991 when Paul Ginsparg, a physicist at the Los Alamos National Laboratory, launched arXiv, a digital archive for preprints of journal articles in physics. This successful experiment suggested that the next logical step would be for scientists in the same discipline to create their own online journal—effectively bypassing peer review and both commercial and professional-society publishers. In the 1980s, Wiley had conducted its own experiments with the Internet, putting the *Harvard Business Review* online in 1984 and its own polymer journals online in cooperation with the American Chemical Society in 1986. Ginsparg's arXiv, experiments with open source content, and questions about peer review were part of the business terrain through which Wiley had to maneuver.

In 1992, Eric Swanson, head of STM publishing in the United States, and John Jarvis, his British counterpart, analyzed how Wiley's competitors in the journals business—Elsevier, Wolters Kluwer, Springer-Verlag, McGraw-Hill, Thomson, and Blackwell—were using technology and determined on a flexible response to the changes in the journals market. They partnered with the competition when it was opportune and found their own way when necessary. In one experiment, Wiley arranged to deliver individual journal articles to readers by using an automated order fulfillment system—an IBM 486 running OS/2, a fax machine, and a dial-up modem! Wiley quickly realized, though, that by leveraging the

Gregory St. John came to Wiley from Liss, where in the 1980s he led the effort to digitize journal subscription lists. At Wiley, he was charged with building STM's presence on the Internet, including, at first, the construction of an electronic delivery system for journals and then for all Wiley content when he became head of Web Publishing Technology in May 2002.

rapidly evolving technology of the Internet—which within a couple of years included graphical Web browsers, broadband connections, PDF files, and the like—it could deliver digital content directly to end users or their libraries. Wiley teamed up with TRW (a company with strength in information systems), Wide Area Information Servers (WAIS), Inc., Sun Microsystems, and a coalition of eight universities to create a digital library for engineers known as the "Colibratory." During the same period, Wiley, Springer, and AT&T took part in the Red Sage Project, a pilot program that delivered journals electronically on the campus of the University of California at San Francisco, one of the country's leading medical schools. After printing the journals, the publishers scanned them, then sent them to AT&T for storage and distribution. Wiley's contribution was some 15 of its biology journals. As part of the Red Sage Project, Wiley became a node on an intranet system.[67]

The expectation of Wiley's most sophisticated customers that journals would be made available online was very much on the minds of STM's managers when they embarked on Wiley's first scenario planning exercise in 1994. More than one of the scenarios posited just such a marketplace. Having gone through this anticipatory exercise, STM came to appreciate that the electronic dissemination of scholarship—far from being a threat— offered opportunities to serve customers better. After this planning exercise, both corporate Wiley and STM stepped up investment in the company's digital presence, while STM invested in the technology needed to move Wiley's journals online.[68]

In 1995, in an effort led by Rosemary Altoft and Gregory St. John, STM launched a path-breaking new publication. The *Journal of Image Guided Surgery* was

INSIDE THE JOURNALS

InterScience

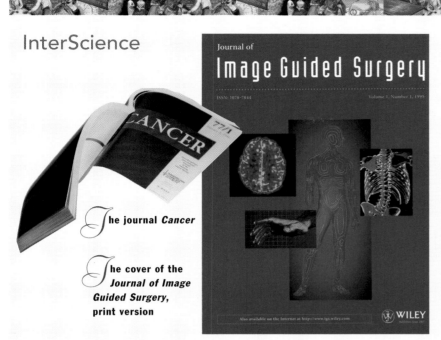

*T*he journal *Cancer*

*T*he cover of the *Journal of Image Guided Surgery*, print version

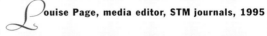

*L*ouise Page, media editor, STM journals, 1995

*T*he home pages of *Cancer Online* and *Wiley Neuroscience Website*

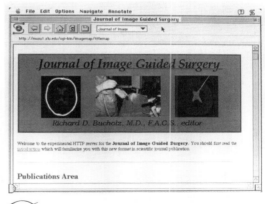

A page from the online *Journal of Image Guided Surgery*

The home page of Wiley InterScience

both interactive *and* available via the World Wide Web. A review in *JAMA*, the Journal of the American Medical Association, applauded Wiley and the editors for "conducting an innovative, scientific experiment in techno-publishing." A panel of more than 60 expert judges agreed, awarding the journal's development team with the Literary Market Place Award for Technical Achievement/Innovation.[69]

In February 1996, Eric Swanson and John Jarvis, the head of the U.K. business, began the initiative that moved Wiley's journals to the World Wide Web. By October, an analysis of the likely growth of Wiley's journal business with and without an investment in the Internet distribution of journal content was ready for top-level review. Initial investment was approved, and discussions of how to create such a service began. In late 1996, Wiley engaged Zuno Digital Publishers, a subsidiary of Mitsubishi Europe, to develop its electronic delivery platform, which was named Wiley InterScience.

> **Wiley InterScience was a huge step in the transformation of Wiley's journals**

While a prototype was up and running in beta testing by the fall of 1997, critical flaws still existed, and Zuno was faltering. When Zuno failed to find other clients, and Mitsubishi suffered huge losses in Japan and elsewhere, Mitsubishi withdrew its support for Zuno, leaving Wiley, in early 1998, in a precarious position. Pesce and Swanson flew to Europe to negotiate with Mitsubishi. Wiley gladly accepted $1 million from Mitsubishi for failure to fulfill its contract (in accordance with a stipulation originally inserted into the contract by Wiley attorney Marjorie Normand and tenaciously maintained in hard negotiations).[70]

Wiley then hired engineering director Andrew Townsend and eight software engineers from Zuno to continue the project. Wiley's team set up shop in Ealing, a suburb of London, and their colleagues began to speak of "the spirit of Ealing," heralding the company's aggressive drive in technological innovation. Gregory St. John moved to Ealing for a year, co-managing the nascent operation with Rosemary Altoft. Board member Bert Sutherland offered insights as the project unfolded. Meanwhile, the 1997 beta version of Wiley InterScience remained up and running. Wiley InterScience represented an effective alternative to the traditional annual subscriptions for paper journals with licenses that were based on use and could extend for a number of years. Reed Elfenbein of STM Marketing and attorney Normand worked with customers, including members of STM's Library Advisory Boards, to hammer out licensing terms that would be beneficial for both Wiley and its major customers. Wiley's Library and Advisory Boards had been set up in Europe and the United States in 1992.[71]

LIBRARY CONSORTIA AND DIGITAL CONTENT

The online licensing of journals content, begun by Academic Press in 1997, led to a movement among libraries to form consortia as a way to bargain with publishers over the amount and price of content to be delivered online. In the print world, libraries bought journal subscriptions on an annual basis. With the advent of electronic journal delivery, each academic library no longer had to buy its own set of print journals. Instead, libraries banded together to license the right to access journals, and later books, in digital format, based on the number of students, instructors, and researchers who would be using the content. The transactions were essentially as follows: The publisher would offer all the content subscribed to by each of the consortium members to the entire constituency of all the members, at a total price fractionally higher than the total sum already being spent by the consortium members on print subscriptions. Thus was born the so-called "Big Deal." The Big Deal was originally controversial, with some librarians protesting that it was an attempt to force their university to license more content than it wished to acquire. Publishers responded by building more flexibility into their initial offer, with the understanding that the more content an institution licensed the better the deal. Wiley's Big Deal has given millions of researchers worldwide instant access at their desktop computers to more content than was ever available in their institutions' libraries. Moreover, access is concurrent without limitation: 20 or 200 readers can read the same content online simultaneously and can print it out for themselves.

STM launched the commercial version of Wiley InterScience in early 1999. By April 30, over $8 million dollars in annual revenue were under license. "Customer uptake has been encouraging," Eric Swanson proclaimed in June 1999, adding that "more than 2,400 institutional customers" had signed up and that the platform's "customer base is increasing rapidly."[72]

On the basis of these strong results, Wiley InterScience's managers pushed for additional funding, largely to establish a new sales force, skilled in relationship building, that could convert customers from print subscriptions to electronic-access licensing and obtain customer feedback. The most important forums for customer feedback were Wiley's Library Advisory Boards. "Electronic publishing is far and away the primary thing we discuss," said Craig Van Dyck, vice president for Production and Manufacturing and the advisory boards' liaison. "We're talking about the same issues as before—product development, sales models, and distribution channels—but in a new environment. Everything needs to be revisited." Thanks to the librarians' input, Wiley InterScience permitted users to set up personalized home pages through which they could get quick access to their favorite functions and features, making Wiley the first commercial publisher to provide this service.[73]

Craig Van Dyck, former vice president for Production and Manufacturing and vice president, Global Content Management

Wiley InterScience was a huge step in the transformation of Wiley's journals business. Its impact was important not only for STM books as well, but also for the ways in which people in Higher Education and Professional/Trade thought about their businesses. According to Pesce, "we were really on our way when we realized that Wiley InterScience was not a project with a beginning, middle, and end. It was a way of life for our STM business." Thus STM grew while simultaneously finding its way in the evolving digital

CROSSREF

One of Wiley's most important industry contributions in the 1990s was its leadership in the development of CrossRef. This reference-linking service was initially developed by Wiley and Academic Press, who were joined at its launch by an alliance of 14 others. CrossRef allows a researcher who, for example, is reading a Wiley journal online to click on a reference citation in the article and then link directly to the cited content on another publisher's platform, subject to the target publisher's access control practices.[74]

CrossRef had its genesis in the Digital Object Identifier (DOI) technology (a kind of indelible electronic watermark that allows publishers to track the uses of their content) developed in 1996–1997 by the Association of American Publishers' Enabling Technologies Committee. Timothy King was the Committee's first chair, followed by Craig Van Dyck,

*C*rossRef board dinner, Budapest, 2006. Left to right: Pieter Bolman, receiving plaque of Service for CrossRef, Carol Bekar, Eric Swanson.

who at the time was working for Springer-Verlag in a partnership with the Corporation for National Research Initiatives (CNRI). Once the Committee was established, Charles Ellis, Wiley CEO and chairman of a joint committee of the International Publishers Association and the international STM organization, led efforts to rally publishers around the DOI as the industry standard. Subsequently, Wiley's Andrew Stevens and David Sidman worked with CNRI, using DOI to create the metadata database that became CrossRef's technological backbone. In a task they likened to "herding cats," Eric Swanson and Pieter Bolman of Academic Press (CrossRef's first two chairmen) recruited 14 other publishers to test the concept in a reference-linking pilot. Van Dyck, who subsequently joined Wiley, worked with Ed Pentz at Academic Press to bring CrossRef to life technically, and Wiley's Susan Spilka and Roy Kaufman contributed communications and legal expertise to the new alliance.

CrossRef was launched in June 2000. Since then, under the leadership of executive director Pentz, CrossRef has grown and evolved, extending services for online research to include forward linking, sophisticated searching tools, and other cutting edge technology. By 2007, over 2,400 publishers were members of CrossRef.

landscape. Between 1991 and 1995, the number of Wiley journals, both those published in New York and those published in Chichester, jumped from 223 to 307, and total pages increased from 164,868 to 255,084. By the end of 1995, all Wiley journals accepted electronic submission of manuscripts (up from just two in 1993). By the end of Charles Ellis's tenure in 1998, half of Wiley's some 400 journals were available online. Within two years, virtually all of the company's journals were available via its Wiley InterScience platform.[75]

To describe the company's response to the rapidly changing environment, Pesce likes to say, "Wiley has created more new business models in the past five years than in all previous years." Wiley InterScience was the first of these. People in STM emphasized that Wiley InterScience, once established, was a service provider as well as a content delivery system. To further their cause, Wiley InterScience's managers circulated a five-page memo called "The Secret Diary of Jörg Muller: A Day in the Life of An Academic." A hapless stereotype of a scientist, Jörg rose at 8 a.m., an hour and a half after his alarm went off, and began a long day of tussling with ill-conceived, haphazard computer systems, pining for the day when he would be able to read, write, submit, review, and edit journal articles painlessly, online. Actually, Jörg was a real person, a software engineer on the original Ealing team that built Wiley InterScience. His "diary" helped Wiley to understand the consumption and use of online information.

Working through Ealing, STM added enhanced features to Wiley InterScience, including EarlyView, which provided articles before the print issues became available, MobileEdition, which gave access to abstracts on handheld devices, and ArticleSelect and Pay-Per-View, which allowed users to purchase individual articles not covered by their subscriptions. Such functionality added significant value to the user experience, further differentiating what publishers like Wiley did from self-publishing online.[76]

By 2002, over six million scientists and other professionals accessed Wiley InterScience through academic and corporate libraries. Daily user sessions numbered over 31,000. By the end of 2003, InterScience generated 60 percent of the company's global journals subscription revenue. STM also strove to lower costs to users by speeding the process of publication. In 2000, its production team managed to cut the time between article acceptance and publication for the important *Journal of Polymer Science* from 26 to 10 weeks and later to 8. This compression attracted more and better articles from scientists and researchers eager to make their research available as quickly as possible, an important achievement in an increasingly author-driven business.[77]

STM Acquisitions

Acquisitions were another important aspect of STM's strategy. As it kept pace with technology, Wiley's corporate management constantly raised their expectations for STM. Acquisitions increased in frequency and scale, further enhancing STM's global status. In 1992, Wiley U.K. bought REDEL, a Paris-based publisher of "English Audio Reviews—The Biomedical Sciences," which provided a platform for broadening Wiley's list in professional language training. Belhaven Press was then acquired from Pinter Publishers in Great Britain, with its list of earth and environmental science titles. In the United States, in 1996 Wiley acquired Technical Insights, a New Jersey–based publisher of print and electronic newsletters in science and technology. Its titles, such as *Insider R&D* and *Genetic Technology News*, were targeted to very specific audiences, usually technology managers. Wiley paid $4 million for the company, which had an annual revenue of about $2.5 million. Wiley quickly built on its list by acquiring, a la carte, such titles as *Nutrition Research Newsletter* and *Science & Government Report*.[78]

These acquisitions, though they cost several millions, were small compared to what took place in June 1996, when Wiley acquired a 90 percent stake in a leading but financially strapped and poorly managed German journals and book publisher, VCH Publishing Group. The price after Wiley acquired the final 10 percent was a lofty $100 million, a huge commitment by Wiley's standards. (By comparison, Wiley bought Liss in 1989 for $38 million, the costliest acquisition to that time.)

The VCH acquisition was to be Charles Ellis's crowning achievement, but it took some scrambling. VCH began by running an auction on a confidential basis. Both Wiley and the Dutch publisher Elsevier were preparing to submit bids when Elsevier pre-empted the auction process and persuaded VCH to accept its bid on an exclusive basis. Elsevier was struggling through its

PROFILE

VCH

In 1921, three German chemical societies—Deutsche Chemische Gesellschaft (DChG: German Chemical Society), Verein Deutscher Chemiker (VDCh: Association of German Chemists), and the Verein zur Wahrung der Interessen der chemischen Industrie Deutschlands (Association for the Protection of the Interests of the German Chemical Industry)—founded Verlag Chemie to provide information for their members about the latest research in the sciences and the chemical industry. Verlag Chemie's first offices were in Berlin and Leipzig.

At first, Verlag Chemie published the journals of its founding societies, *Berichte der Deutschen Chemischen Gesellschaft, Zeitschrift für Angewandte Chemie, Die Chemische Industrie*, and *Chemisches Zentralblatt* (in those days the leading chemical abstracting service). In time, other societies arranged to have their journals published by Verlag Chemie, such as the Deutsche Bunsen-Gesellschaft für Physikalische Chemie (*Zeitschrift für Elektrochemie*, later renamed *Berichte der Bunsengesellschaft für Physikalische Chemie*), the Deutsche Vereinigung für gewerblichen Rechtsschutz und Urheberrecht (*GRUR*), the Deutsche Pharmazeutische Gesellschaft (*Archiv der Pharmazie*), the Deutsche Bodenkundliche Gesellschaft and Deutsche Gesellschaft für Pflanzenernährung (*Zeitschrift für Pflanzenernährung und Bodenkunde*). Biographies and well-known reference works and series were also published under the Verlag Chemie imprint, including DECHEMA's *ACHEMA* catalogs and the *Corrosion Handbook*, the *Gmelins Handbuch der anorganischen Chemie, Poggendorffs biographisch-literarisches Handwörterbuch für Mathematik, Astronomie, Physik mit Geophysik, Chemie, kristallographie, und verwandte Wissensgebiete*, and *Vom Wasser*. All publications were in German, the lingua franca of science in those days, and a significant share of Verlag Chemie's revenue came from the export of their publications.

The rise of the Nazi party in Germany in the 1930s affected German scientists and their publications. In 1936, the VDCh incorporated Nazi content into its statutes, but the DChG avoided such concessions for a time. By 1938, the chemical societies had been brought into the Nationalsozialistischer Bund Deutscher Technik. Limited availability of paper during World War II led to drastically reduced volumes of all journals as well as affecting the book program. During the war, Verlag Chemie's Berlin offices were destroyed in a bombing raid. After the war, the managing director, Eduard Kreuzhage, together with renowned chemists (functioning as trustees of the founding chemical

*P*eter Gölitz congratulating Haymo Ross, deputy editor of *Angewandte Chemie* on the tenth anniversary of the journal.

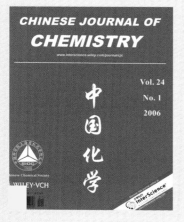

societies, which had not officially been refounded) restarted the publishing house in 1947 in Heidelberg. The offices were soon relocated to Weinheim, a small town north of Heidelberg where appropriate offices and housing were available.[79]

In 1956 and in 1967, the refounded societies took over the shares directly, and from 1967 onward, Verlag Chemie was 90 percent owned by the GDCh (Gesellschaft Deutscher Chemiker) and 8 percent owned by the DPhG (Deutsche Pharmazeutische Gesellschaft).

From the 1960s to the 1980s, Verlag Chemie broadened its publishing program to include physics (co-owning the Physik Verlag), biology, pharmacology, medicine (founding Edition Medizin), geology, and humanities (founding Acta Humaniora). Verlag Chemie became the official publisher of Deutsche Forschungsgemeinschaft (DFG, German Research Foundation) and acquired Ernst & Sohn (a Berlin-based traditional civil engineering and architectural publishing house, founded in 1827). Parallel to this, Verlag Chemie expanded its English-speaking program and established subsidiaries: the first one in 1976 in New York, later in Switzerland, England, and Japan. Becoming more and more international, and having grown beyond chemistry, Verlag Chemie changed its name and became known as VCH.

When the Berlin Wall fell in 1989, VCH had won the race to acquire and integrate East Germany's largest and most prominent science and humanities publishing house, Akademie Verlag. Its program embraced several hundred scientific journals, series, and many renowned special editions.[80]

375

merger with Reed, the British publisher, an integration that left VCH puzzled by the role of the different representatives of the new company with whom they met. Elsevier failed to deliver its offer by the time the exclusive ran out, and Wiley was back in the race. The Gesellschaft Deutscher Chemiker (GDCh), owner of VCH's most important chemistry journals, had apparently no interest in selling to Elsevier, something Elsevier did not find out until the final moment of the negotiation.[81]

"It was like the movies," recalled Ellis. "A James Bond film," according to U.K. managing director Jarvis. Wiley's team (Peter Clifford, James Dicks, Ernest Kirkwood, Robert Long, Jarvis, Timothy King, and Richard Rudick) was working out of the German Chemical Society's office one night, waiting for King to return from a 3 a.m. meeting with their lawyers. King had called to ask Jarvis to be ready to open the door, which Jarvis, by then exhausted, forgot to do. "About 15 minutes later, we all heard stones sporadically hitting the window . . . 'Could that be Elsevier spies?' was the general comment, but when I looked out the window," said Jarvis, "there was Tim standing in the shrubbery looking like a vagrant and clearly not happy with his forgetful colleagues."[82]

With Elsevier in the bidding, the price tag for VCH was higher than Wiley might otherwise have paid, but the acquisition made Wiley one of the largest chemistry publishers in the world, while bringing a wealth of journals, books, and major reference works. "What we have purchased is a jewel in the field of high-quality

Timothy King, a British citizen with a degree in natural sciences from Cambridge University, joined Wiley in 1987. His experience ranged from sales to editorial to general management, and from Europe to Mexico, where he ran McGraw-Hill's operations. Under Charles Ellis, he became senior vice president, Strategic Planning. King became interim managing director of Wiley-VCH for a year after the VCH acquisition.

STM publishing, as well as a partnership with a leading chemistry society in continental Europe," said Ellis. VCH's integration proceeded smoothly, exceeding the financial targets set in the acquisition model. The new business, now under the name Wiley-VCH, became profitable within a year, thanks in large part to the efforts of Timothy King, who spoke German and spent a year as interim managing director in Weinheim, where VCH was located. He was responsible for bringing *Helvetica Chimica Acta*, the Swiss Chemical Society's primary research journal, to Wiley-VCH. Wiley appointed Dr. Manfred Antoni managing director, reporting to Jarvis, who became the company's senior vice president, Europe.[83]

VCH brought a unique capability to Wiley in the form of an in-house editorial operation managed by Peter Gölitz, who also served as editor of *Angewandte Chemie*, which was now the global journals program's largest revenue producer. Wiley's journals were assembled by editorial boards—with the help of Wiley colleagues, of course—whose members were not Wiley employees. In VCH's case, Gölitz and his colleagues, assisted by editorial boards and advisors, published nearly 100 journals per year from their Weinheim offices.

In August 1997, Wiley-VCH sold Akademie Verlag, its humanities book and journals program, to Oldenbourg, allowing it to focus on the much larger STM and professional publishing areas, which expanded further with the creation of a pan-European journals program in February 1997. This was an important initiative in which Wiley-VCH joined forces with the chemical societies of five European countries to merge their national journals into two pan-European journals, *European Journal of Organic Chemistry* and *European Journal of Inorganic Chemistry*. Instrumental in this had been Professor Heindirk tom Dieck, the secretary general of the GDCh, and Dr. Eva E. Wille, a VCH veteran of

the pre-Wiley era; tom Dieck, the driver behind the plan to sell to Wiley, argued that an American partner would enhance Wiley-VCH's ability to develop European journals. Wiley augmented its Wiley-VCH list with the acquisition of Hüthig Publishing Group's scientific books and journals program (except its astronomy program) in 1998. Hüthig's list included the famous

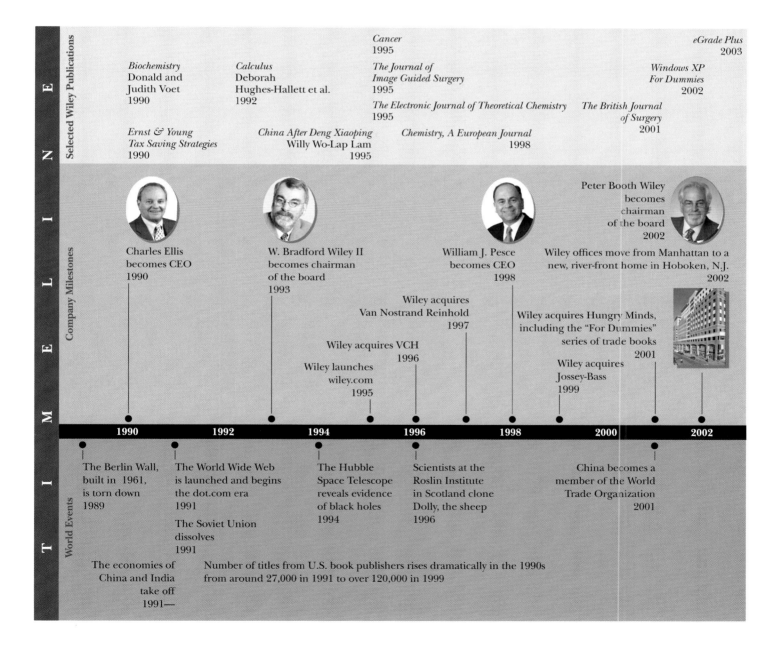

German polymer journals founded by the Nobel laureate Hermann Staudinger as well as the program of Johann Ambrosius Barth, a famous German (later East-German) publishing house founded at the end of the eighteenth century. Among Johann Ambrosius Barth's journals had been the *Annalen der Physik* (founded in 1799, and the publisher of all the important Einstein papers), *Astronomische Nachrichten* (the oldest astronomical journal, founded in 1821), as well as important chemistry journals like *Journal für praktische Chemie* and *Zeitschrift für anorganische und allgemeine Chemie* and leading textbooks like *Organikum*, by Heinz Becker. Wiley-VCH paid about $8 million for Hüthig, which had revenue of about $4 million, fighting off last-minute attempts by Elsevier and Wolters Kluwer to push Wiley aside. In 2001, Wiley-VCH acquired GIT Verlag, a controlled-circulation magazine business based in Darmstadt.[84]

The Societies Initiative

With three publishing centers, New York, Chichester, and Weinheim, STM was more global—and more expansive—than ever. STM seized every opportunity to grow its journals program, acquiring titles and occasionally publishers in the life sciences, material sciences, chemicals, agrochemicals, petrochemicals, biochemistry, engineering, health sciences, pharmaceuticals, and medical robotics. STM's next major initiative was really an intensification of efforts begun first in Chichester in the 1960s and later built on in New York. Professional society publishing originated in seventeenth-century England with the formation of the Royal Society and its first serial publication, *Philosophical Transactions* (1665). Society publishing expanded dramatically in Europe and the United States in the nineteenth century as part of the self-organization and definition of professional

Publishing with Scientific Societies

*E*rnest Kirkwood, formerly e-business development director, presently vice president and publishing director, Physical Sciences, in the United Kingdom.

THE COCHRANE COLLABORATION

Wiley's partnerships with nonprofit organizations have extended beyond societies to the famous Cochrane Collaboration, a network of research groups that maintains a database on evidence-based medicine. Recognizing that its STM business served "mature" markets that would not generate the degree of revenue growth that the company was seeking to achieve, Wiley set out to identify and develop tangentially related businesses and publishing programs. Some of these ventures were more successful than others. The extension of Wiley's growing life and medical sciences publishing program into the nascent field of evidence-based medicine (EBM) was among the most successful.

In April 2003, The Cochrane Collaboration named Wiley as its publishing partner, an important step into EBM. Cochrane is an international not-for-profit organization that enables well-informed decisions about healthcare by preparing, maintaining, and making accessible systematic reviews of the effects of healthcare interventions. It serves the information needs of physicians, clinical researchers, nurses, midwives, dentists, patients, and healthcare policymakers at medical institutions, universities, corporations, and healthcare organizations around the world.

THE COCHRANE COLLABORATION®

Michael Davis, vice president and publishing director, Life Sciences, and Deborah Dixon, vice president and journals publishing director, Medicine, Europe, were instrumental in forging the partnership. Wiley and Cochrane, according to Davis, wanted to "extend both the reach and the commercial potential of The Cochrane Collaboration's publications, such as *The Cochrane Database of Systematic Reviews*, by leveraging the *Wiley InterScience* online platform and Wiley's global marketing and sales capabilities."

Wiley built on the successful alliance with Cochrane to launch other EBM initiatives, including the acquisition in 2005 of InfoPOEM, Inc., a leading provider of EBM content and Web-based search tools, and in 2006 of the Health Economic Evaluations Database (HEED), an online source of health economic information and evaluations.[85]

---

life. Until 1961, when Wiley acquired Interscience Publishers, Wiley had avoided the journals business even though William Halsted Wiley, William O. Wiley, and Edward P. Hamilton were active members of engineering societies. Both New York and Chichester acquired journals with the purchase of Interscience Publishers in 1961. Chichester continued to build partnerships with societies, but on a limited basis.[86]

Prior to the acquisition of Interscience Publishers, Wiley showed almost no interest in journals publishing with one exception, the publication in 1955 of a journal for the Operations Research Society of America. Following the acquisition of Interscience in 1961 with its well-known journals program in polymer chemistry and the establishment of a publishing program in England during the 1960s, Wiley editors grew the journals list. The company acquired additional journals, including many with society relationships, when it bought Alan R. Liss in 1989. Liss's oldest journal, *The Anatomical Record*, was the product of a partnership with the American Association of Anatomists, the original agreement for which was signed in 1923 by a company Liss acquired.

In 1985, Liss had acquired the publishing contract for the *International Journal of Cancer*, the journal of the Union Internationale Contre le Cancer (UICC), the Geneva-based umbrella organization of national cancer societies. Then secretary-general of the UICC, Dr. Gerald Murphy, was a long-time "friend of the house," a relationship that continued through Swanson and Wiley medical publisher Thomas Mackey after Alan Liss's death in 1992. By the early nineties, Murphy was senior vice president, Medical Affairs, at the American Cancer Society, when the ACS decided it was unhappy with the publisher of its flagship journal *Cancer*. In 1995, when the *Cancer* contract was up for renewal, Murphy was able to ensure that Wiley got a chance to bid. Although Wiley's sale of its medical business in the late 1980s was a strike against it, Wiley's position as the publisher of the UICC journal helped. Publisher Brian

Crawford led an all-hands, no-efforts-spared presentation to the society, which included creation of an online version of *Cancer* by Gregory St. John and his team, based on *Image Guided Surgery,* their earlier online journal.[87]

Simultaneously, in the 1980s, Wiley U.K. was pursuing new society relationships. But it was the ACS contract that really marked the beginning of the rapid growth of Wiley's medical society publishing program and spurred the expansion of advertising sales operations to develop a rapidly growing revenue stream, as advertising contributes significant revenue to many medical journals. Meanwhile, the acquisition in 1996 of VCH, with its long-standing relationship with the German chemical and pharmaceutical societies, brought important new relationships in the sciences to Wiley. Among the journals acquired was *Angewandte Chemie,* one of the world's leading chemistry journals.

Part of the rationale for the acquisition of VCH was its status as a premier professional-society publisher. By 2001 Wiley had established journal publishing relationships with such important societies as the American Neurological Society, the American College of Rheumatology, the Movement Disorder Society, and the French chemical society. Strong society partnerships inevitably paid off for STM's book program as well. In 2001, for example, Wiley formed an alliance with the Institute of Electrical and Electronic Engineers (IEEE) for a book series.[88]

Managing a society relationship was a more intricate and financially less lucrative affair than managing journals for which Wiley owned the copyright. First, Wiley people had to invest considerable personal time in building and sustaining a society relationship. Like so much of publishing, society publishing was very much about people and relationships. In the competitive environment in which a handful of publishers were competing for contracts, societies, who owned the copyrights, had leverage to exact the best terms possible from publishers. Among those with whom Wiley was competing were Blackwell, Elsevier, Wolters Kluwers' Lippincott Williams & Wilkins brand, and the Nature group of publications owned by the

Von Holtzbrinck family. Societies, naturally enough, wanted the best royalties possible and a commitment from publishers to build and sustain society Web sites at the highest standards. For the publisher, margins were reduced by the need to pay royalties and provide other services to the society. On the positive side of the equation, societies themselves took responsibility for editorial work and for sustaining a high-quality editorial team. In the end, the resulting relationships with the greater world of researchers and scholars made this financial model not only palatable but desirable.

Further steps called for a more systematic campaign. In 2002, Ernest Kirkwood, the e-business development director in the United Kingdom, took on the task of building a vast database that would track all society journals, providing information on length and terms of contracts so that Wiley would be prepared to compete more aggressively for society journals when their contracts came up for renewal. Part of what Wiley had to offer societies was innovative Web services. Wiley was already building community practice sites for disciplines such as physics. These sites facilitated communication among researchers and professionals for discussion, resource sharing, and developing ways to address particular issues endemic to their work. Kirkwood's e-business group transformed these sites into society microsites and society networks. "The offer of such services," Kirkwood recalled, "proved a major differentiator from the competition in our proposals when we won over two major new pieces of society business." This new initiative led to more society business, including *The British Journal of Surgery* (agreement signed in 2001) and *Hepatology*, the journal of the American Association for the Study of Liver Diseases (agreement signed in 2002). Ultimately, STM's society initiative, its experience competing successfully for society contracts, and its emergence as important force in the global STM market, led to the most dramatic event in Wiley's 46-year history of acquisitions—the acquisition in Wiley's 200th year of Blackwell Publishers, the world's preeminent society publisher.[89]

STM Books

While STM's journals business flourished, its books were a thornier problem. Wiley's renown as a publisher of handbooks and series of books in science and technology stretched back to the nineteenth century. With the Interscience acquisition in 1961, Wiley became known worldwide as a leading publisher of such major reference works as the *Kirk-Othmer Encyclopedia of Chemical Technology*, first published in 1947, and the *Encyclopedia of Polymer Science and Technology*, which Wiley launched in 1964. Over the following decades, Wiley's STM book program was extended by the growth of Chichester as a major STM publishing center, the Liss acquisition in 1989, and the VCH acquisition in 1996. By the end of the 1980s, it was clear that two types of books—printed research monographs and conference proceedings, of which Wiley published quite a few—had an uncertain future. Pressures to deliver research outcomes in a timely manner favored dissemination by journal article via the Internet over the more deliberative book publishing and distribution systems. At the same time, library budgets were coming under increasing pressure, and so sales of short-run monographs and proceedings declined, and the economics of monograph publishing became less favorable—though still profitable, as Eric Swanson was quick to point out. Other book products—STM's venerable series, handbooks, upper level texts, and major reference works—were essential in the worlds of education and research, but they also faced market pressure. Swanson, Jarvis, and their colleagues planned for the eventuality that book content would join journal content on the Web. But with librarians putting the highest priority on sustaining their journals collections, the question became when. The challenge was finding the proper level of investment in the right kind of book development while funding the migration of all content to the web.[90]

Journal publishing is characteristically more profitable than STM book publishing, providing a steady flow of subscription revenue (with high renewal rates) and lacking the promotional expenses associated with each new book title. But STM book publishing has certain advantages over trade publishing. Sales are more stable, with fewer returns. The average price point is substantially higher, and production values need not be as high; royalties, too, are generally lower.

Through the mid-1990s, one successful editorial strategy was to focus on advanced textbooks, which were not only not dependent on library purchases, but could also in some cases command a dual audience of students and professionals. "A book like *March's Advanced Organic Chemistry* contains thousands of reactions," said Janet Bailey, publishing director for physical sciences books. "It's used as an advanced textbook, but it also serves as a reference to the field, something organic and synthetic chemists want to have on their shelves." Other books targeting narrow markets also did well, such as books for electrical engineers and statisticians, as well as a program of occupational health and safety titles acquired from Van Nostrand-Rinehold.[91]

Another fruitful endeavor was the publication of long-standing series, some in cooperation with societies, some published serially in numbered volumes,

383

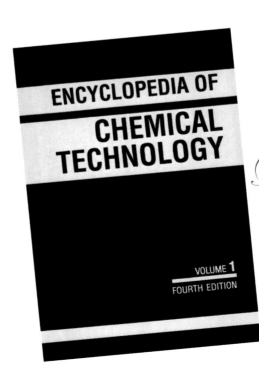

A mainstay for chemists, biochemists, and engineers at academic, industrial, and government institutions, *Kirk-Othmer Encyclopedia of Chemical Technology*, fourth edition, published in 27 volumes.

many of them continuing to this day with 50 to 100 volumes or more. Two of the long-standing encyclopedias are *Ullman's Encyclopedia of Industrial Chemistry* and *Patty's Industrial Hygiene and Toxicology*. These have been especially successful in the discipline of chemistry, meeting the scientist's need to know what reactions and transformations have been documented in the literature. While the number of standing library orders for these titles has diminished over time, a number continue to sell well to individuals who need an ongoing update in their fields.

Wiley's strategies toward the STM book market varied according to the time and location of publishing. As other publishers pulled back from this market, Swanson commented in a 1993 memo, "we are now increasing both our revenue and our profits from this core business." While librarians in the United States bought fewer books, European libraries continued to buy books, and European bookstores, which traditionally stocked substantially more STM books than their American counterparts, generated stronger individual sales. Asian libraries followed suit often because they lacked the electronic infrastructure for the delivery of digital content. In the United States, Swanson trimmed investment in the book business as he and his team steered the journals business into the digital era. VCH brought its own book titles to Wiley and after 1996, continued to publish significant numbers of books. In the United Kingdom, John Jarvis, later dubbed the "International Book Cheese" by Brad Wiley II, continued to invest in the STM book program.[92]

The big question was when non-journal content would become viable on the Web. The answer came with the new 24-volume *Wiley Encyclopedia of Electrical and Electronics Engineering*, launched in print in March 1999 and online in January 2000. By the end of 2001, it was joined by the electronic *Kirk-Othmer*, the fourth edition of which had been published in print over seven years through 1999, and *Ullmann's Encyclopedia of*

Industrial Chemistry, a landmark work first published in 1914 and acquired with VCH. The online *Kirk-Othmer* was Wiley's first major reference work to incorporate monthly updating. In late 2001, Wiley InterScience OnlineBooks launched with a search capability that integrated book, journal, and major reference work content, another Wiley first. By the end of 2002, more than 200 titles were available through this new service.[93]

Throughout the 1990s, the strategy for major reference works called for a mix of new multivolume sets, new editions of established works, CD (and, later, online) versions, and spin-off products such as concise versions of *Kirk-Othmer* and the *Encyclopedia Of Polymer Science and Technology*. Beginning in 1999, after Will Pesce called for a financial review for all book programs, there was a concerted effort to improve the organization of the STM book publishing operation. Janet Bailey was brought in to coordinate production, marketing, and editorial colleagues in Hoboken into a more effective team. At the same time, a decision was made to focus on chemistry, electrical engineering, statistics, and some of the life sciences, through handbooks, reference works, and advanced-level text references, and also by seeking to publish works of an applied and practical nature that would appeal to individual scientists, engineers, and researchers, such as the Wiley-IEEE Press book series described earlier.[94]

As Wiley's international sales force generated strong STM book sales, the results also began to reflect growing activity through Amazon.com, which had opened its virtual doors in 1995. Amazon endowed STM books with visibility traditionally denied them in the brick-and-mortar world—in this regard, the Amazon effect was more significant for STM titles than for trade—and gave equal billing to backlist and front-list titles.

At the time of Wiley's move to Hoboken in 2002, 20 percent of STM's total global revenue came from its book program. A further resurgence of the business still lay ahead. In the fall of 2003, an all-out campaign to revitalize STM book publishing was mounted when Steven Miron, Wiley's managing director in Asia, was appointed the new "International Book Cheese."[95]

After the VCH merger, STM was the largest line of business at Wiley, accounting for 47 percent of revenue and an even higher percentage of earnings in fiscal 1997. STM's leadership, which had reported to the head of professional reference and trade books, was elevated to coequal status in 1998 when Will Pesce, who became the company's chief executive that year, asked Eric Swanson to report directly to him because he thought the challenges and opportunities in STM warranted his close attention. Throughout the 1990s, STM led the way in the delivery of digital content and in the development of tools that facilitated researchers' use of content, learning lessons that would over time be transferred to Wiley's other businesses. STM, too, was Wiley's most global operation. Wiley U.K. had been building its journals and books program since the company first opened its doors in London. The VCH acquisition brought another important STM location into the fold. What followed was the development of global planning, an idea that Wiley had embraced as early as the 1980s.[96]

Professional/Trade

While Higher Education was recovering and STM was adapting to the digital world and growing as a global enterprise, Stephen Kippur and his team were, at first quietly, then dramatically, rebuilding Wiley's traditional professional and reference book business, moving it from relative obscurity into an industry powerhouse. In 20 years, beginning in 1985 when Kippur became head

of what was then known as the Business, Law, and General Books Division, this business grew from a mere $13 million in revenue and 22 employees to some $400 million and 800 employees. Wiley had been a trade publisher in the nineteenth century and in the intervening years had come out with an occasional trade title, but it focused primarily on educational, professional, scientific, and technical publishing—at least until the early 1960s, when it formed a joint venture with Basic Books to publish Science Editions. That experiment faltered, but trade publishing returned as a focus for Wiley in the 1980s under Kippur's leadership.

Charles Ellis, who had experience with trade publishing in England, made P/T's growth a corporate priority. There was no question in his mind that the company had to search for new sources of revenue following the Wilson divestiture. Professional and trade books fit Ellis's broader strategy of refocusing on core businesses and were closer to Wiley's traditional competencies than running training seminars, writing computer software, or any of the other diversification alleys it had explored in the 1980s. "We will publish serious nonfiction," Ellis explained, "as an extension of the other kinds of publishing we do," and sell trade books through bookstores and other wholesale and retail channels. The expansion of P/T coincided with the exit of Wiley's long-time rival McGraw-Hill from the trade business after 60 years. Another competitor, Addison-Wesley, also gave up trade publishing. Wiley took care to enter (or re-enter) the trade business on its own terms, however. "We won't allow ourselves to heed the siren call of trying to publish best sellers, with high advances and high [book] returns," Ellis explained.[97]

Kippur began the mid-1980s working with Jeffrey Brown, Ruth Greif, Gwenyth Jones, Margie

> Stephen Kippur and his team [turned] Wiley's professional and reference book business . . . into an industry powerhouse.

385

*S*tephen Kippur, executive vice president of Wiley and president, Professional/Trade, with some of his team members and their titles as of 2007.

*J*effrey Brown, vice president and general manager, Business and Psychology

*G*wenyth Jones, vice president, Publishing Information Systems and Technologies

*M*argie Schustack, vice president, Marketing Operations

*K*athleen Schowalter, senior vice president, Professional and Consumer Publishing

Schustack, and Katherine Schowalter. The team grew to include Kitt Allan, Robert Chiarelli, Jack Day, Elizabeth Doble, Dean Karrel, Joseph Marchetti, Larry Olson, Joan O'Neil, and George Stanley. Their ideas were not circumscribed by established trade practices, so they could build the business according to what made sense to them. In fact, they developed a highly unusual collaborative publishing approach unmatched in the industry. By convention, trade book publishing was editorially driven. All else involved in producing a book—marketing, sales, distribution, financial, production, and manufacturing—was subordinated to the judgments of the editorial staff, or the "editorial mandarins," as one former Wiley publisher described the editors at a competing trade house. Almost from the beginning, Kippur jettisoned that convention in favor of a process in which all the functional personnel required to produce a book were brought together in collegial synchronization. Running through the whole process was financial discipline. Known to his team as "Mr. Gross Margins," Kippur demanded that everyone involved in a book project understand the financial consequences of their publishing decisions and work together to achieve their financial goals. Forecasting and re-forecasting were facts of life for the group's editors and managers, as they constantly recalibrated the financial prospects of each publishing project. Jack Day, a vice president for retail sales, once remarked, tongue-in-cheek, "I've spent more time forecasting than I have with my kids!" Morale was high at P/T, and its collaborative model kept everyone it touched fully engaged.

All this, vice president and marketing director Larry Olson opined, was a "distinctive advantage for Wiley" over its trade book competitors, which subsequently adopted Wiley's model.[98]

Expansion of the Trade List

In its 1992 strategic plan, P/T set forth its vision to grow its lists to be a leader in selected categories, specifically management, marketing, real estate, investment, careers, small business, technology, travel, hospitality, math, psychology, architecture, and general interest. Some books, such as *Architectural Graphic Standards*, sold only to professionals. But the distinction between professional and trade titles was not always clear. "We recognized by the early 1990s that that line had blurred," said Kippur. "A finance book can go to a practitioner or to someone just interested in the field. On the other hand, a book like Christopher M. Byron's *Martha Inc.: The Incredible Story of Martha Stewart Living Omnimedia*, a bestselling trade title, may be used by business professionals as a case study." Over the next decade, P/T pursued both professional and trade markets through careful category management, alliance building, multi-channel sales, and acquisitions of small—and increasingly larger— publishers in complementary categories. Its trade list filled out nicely in terms of both the range and number of titles and the variety of media formats (hardcover, paperback, CD) it offered.[99]

The acquisition of a single title, the *Ernst & Young Tax Guide*, in 1990, enabled Wiley's unique type of trade publishing to take off. That best-seller, Kippur recalled, "totally changed our profile with bookstores," which previously had regarded Wiley's trade offerings as low-volume, niche, sci-tech, and professional products that did not merit much shelf space. Because every bookseller had to have the *Tax Guide*, it now became easier for Wiley's trade salespeople to get a hearing with buyers for bookstores and distributors, who gave them three minutes to show Wiley's other titles. The *Tax Guide* also helped Wiley get into "big-box" stores, such as Wal-Mart, and to expand its presence in the emerging bookstore chains, such as Barnes & Noble and Borders. "After that . . . we felt much more accomplished, much more prepared to take on visible projects" said Joan

O'Neil, vice president and publisher, Wiley Finance. P/T began to climb into the ranks of the *New York Times* bestseller lists with books like Robert Hagstrom's *The Warren Buffet Way* (1994) and Peter Bernstein's *Against the Gods: The Remarkable Story of Risk* (1996).[100]

The experience highlighted a trend that P/T could exploit as new and changing distribution channels reshaped trade book retailing. The expansion of efficient chain "superstores," such as Barnes & Noble and Borders, was good for his group, Kippur explained, as "they did not discriminate among publishers." The emergence of such "warehouse clubs" as Sam's and Costco boded well for Wiley, too. These big outlets enabled P/T to reach mass markets quickly with books that had potential for big sales, such as Byron's *Martha Inc.*, Adeline Yen Mah's *Falling Leaves: Memoir of an Unwanted Chinese Daughter,* and George Soros's *Soros on Soros: Staying Ahead of the Curve*. And no one benefited more than the P/T group from the impact that online booksellers would have on the book business. Amazon.com and its

The publication of the *Ernst & Young Tax Guide* in 1990 led to the signing of additional titles, such as the two above.

he Alchemy of Finance, The Warren Buffet Way, and *Why Should White Guys Have All the Fun?*

subsequent imitators empowered buyers by making it easy to search for and find books that were not readily available in most bookstores. That anyone with a snippet of a title or author's name could order a book and have it delivered to the door within a day proved to be a blessing to publishers and readers alike. By offering continuing access to Wiley's backlist, Amazon and other outlets, such as Books 24x7, brought in millions of dollars in sales on an annual basis by the end of the decade. In fact, online outlets were responsible for most of P/T's annual sales increases on a year-to-year basis.[101]

The growth of its trade publishing program brought Wiley into interesting new areas like children's nonfiction books. Among the most successful were those of juvenile science writer Janice VanCleave, who by 1995 had written 24 books of interactive science experiments and

projects that sold, in aggregate, 900,000 copies. Wiley was becoming a "need to know" company even for kids, especially those who loved VanCleave's "gooey, slippery, slimy" experiments. Other juvenile books, such as David Suzuki's popular Looking At series, also sold well. Many were done in black and white to keep prices low.[102]

*eter L. Bernstein and his book *Against the Gods: The Remarkable Story of Risk.* In this unique exploration of the role of risk in our society, Bernstein argues that the notion of bringing risk under control is one of the central ideas that distinguishes modern times from the distant past. *Against the Gods* chronicles the remarkable intellectual adventure that liberated humanity from oracles and soothsayers by means of the powerful tools of risk management that are available to us today.

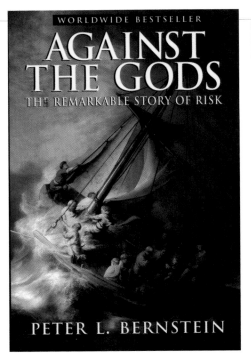

*Thera*Scribe, launched in January 1996, was a software product that provided mental health profession-als with a template for creating effective treatment plans rapidly and efficiently, using behavioral defini-tions, therapeutic interventions, and diagnostic suggestions that were provided on CD modules. Each mod-ule focused on a specific client population or treatment setting, with adult psychology, child psychology, adolescent psychology, and addiction treatment among the top sellers; print editions of the modules were offered as well. Wiley developed *Thera*Scribe jointly with Dr. Arthur E. Jongsma Jr., who as a consulting psy-chologist in the mid-1990s had identified a strong need for a tool that would assist practitioners in writing treatment plans that would meet the requirements of accrediting bodies, insurance companies, and third-party payors. *Thera*Scribe 5.0, released in 2007, was the first version to incorporate evidence-based treat-ment interventions, required by a growing number of funding sources and insurers. The first successful pro-ductivity-enhancing CD-ROM–based products in Professional/Trade, with annual revenue that by 2007 had topped $1 million, *Thera*Scribe also provided a model for subsequent products that delivered Wiley content directly into customer workflows, an increasingly important area of publishing activity across the company.

Practice *Planners*

TheraScribe®
ESSENTIAL 1.0
The Easy-to-Use Treatment Planning System
for Helping Professionals

Van Cleave was one of a number of franchise authors whose names acquired the force of a brand through multiple successes in a focused area. Within the business arena, Patrick Lencioni's 1998 *The Five Temptations of a CEO* launched a top-selling series of concise and engaging "leadership fables" that continued on with unabated strength nearly a decade later, includ-ing a training package released in late 2007 that was keyed to Lencioni's 2002 *The Five Dysfunctions of a Team.* James M. Kouzes and Barry Z. Posner's *The Leadership Challenge*, first published in 1987, advanced the then-novel proposition that leadership is a learnable skill embodying quantifiable behavior; it provided the cornerstone of a franchise that by late 2002 had migrated successfully to the Web with *LPI Online*, an electronic version of its *Leadership Practices Inventory* evaluation and feedback component. Additionally, P/T saw tremen-dous developments with Thera*Scribe*—the leading mental health treatment planning and clinical record management software system. This new branded product allowed one to easily maintain professional treatment plans and clin-ical records.

389

*C*hildren reading from the *200 Gooey, Slippery, Slimy, Weird & Fun Experiments* by Janice VanCleave. A former public school science teacher turned author and lecturer, VanCleave has sold two million books.

Jeff Bezos, CEO of Amazon.com, Dec. 1, 2000

Professional and Trade was able to handle any dip in the trade market better than most because of the company's "multiple channels of distribution." As channels grew or atrophied, P/T Sales, led by George Stanley, made constant adjustments in the way it deployed its sales force, working closely with customers to ensure the highest level of service. Even with the decline of the independent bookstore, P/T continued to field an independent-store sales force, which was deeply appreciated by independent bookstore owners. Simultaneously, Stanley and his colleagues built specialized sales teams to work with Amazon and Barnes & Noble, its largest customers. Using sophisticated point-of-sale data, sales people worked hand in hand with large retailers who were developing and refining the organization of their stores by category. P/T used other sophisticated means to sell its product. During the 1990s, P/T set up a telemarketing unit in Colorado Springs under the leadership of Thomas Conter, who also ran Wiley Law. When the Internet overtook telemarketing as a sales channel, Wiley scaled back and then reorganized this operation, taking advantage of individual customer calls to "upsell" product. Equipped with databases of product information, Wiley's customer service operators could find a book for a customer who called asking, for example, for a book about performance-based compensation. The customer service person would then also offer a related title at a discount.[103]

P/T tracked the trends in the bookselling world and responded with flexibility and precision. For example, Amazon required that publishers provide data feeds to populate features, such as author information and "Search Inside the Book," on its website. P/T not only complied quickly by creating systems that fed digital information seamlessly into Amazon's systems; it also set up an Amazon sales force under Charles Deane, who was also responsible for mass-market, online, and business-development channels. The result: Amazon rated Wiley as its most cooperative publisher and became responsible for significant increases in P/T sales while helping to reduce returns.

P/T Acquisitions

As with Wiley's other businesses, acquisitions were integral to P/T's strategy. They were aimed at building strength in categories where Wiley could lead. The push began modestly in 1991, when Wiley Law purchased the James Publishing Group, with its 15 subscription-based titles for paralegals, and the law assets of Professional Education Systems, Inc. (PESI) to bolster its presence in medical malpractice, trial practice, and bankruptcy law. Wiley purchased QED Information Sciences' book assets in 1993, including Robert Chapman's *OS/2 Presentation Manager Programming for COBOL Programmers* and Kenneth Pugh's *Learn C and Save Your Job*. This purchase significantly increased the size and weight of Wiley's already large computer book list. Wiley's purchase of QED made sense for both parties. QED had a good reputation but insufficient scale to make its publications highly profitable. Because of its larger presence in the market, Wiley was able to increase print runs and use its buying power with printers to reduce per-copy costs. By 1996, Wiley published over 90 Internet-related titles.[104]

Kippur and his team were unafraid to divest when the opportunity beckoned or threats surfaced. In 1997 Wiley sold off its Colorado Springs–based Wiley Law publishing program to Wolters Kluwer for $26.5 million, because P/T "could not be a leading contender without substantial further investments" in a field increasingly dominated by three major players. The proceeds from the sale were plowed into the purchase of key publishing assets from Van Nostrand Reinhold (VNR). Van Nostrand had been a major Wiley competitor since the 1840s. Having merged with Reinhold in 1969, it was later sold to Thomson, which put VNR up for sale in 1997.[105]

VNR's lists reinforced Wiley's position in architecture, the culinary arts, industrial science, and business technology. Among its best-selling titles were the Culinary Institute of America's *The Professional Chef*, a title that generated almost 40 percent of VNR's revenue, and Frank Ching's *Building Construction Illustrated*. *The Professional Chef* was a "must-have" book for every culinary student and professional chef. It fit well on the shelf with a growing list of educational and professional cooking titles, including those by bestseller Wayne Gisslen, which was moved to P/T when Wiley's Occupational Division was closed down in the 1980s. Ching's title, another "must have" book, complemented Wiley's venerable *Architectural Graphic Standards*.[106]

Both the culinary and architecture lists were good examples of the way in which P/T was able to drive growth through alliances with a broad range of corporations and organizations, combining content, services, and capabilities to reach new markets across its publishing categories. *Architectural Graphic Standards* was the fruit of a partnership with the American Institute of Architects that dated back to 1932. *The Professional Chef*, the flagship of a line of products created jointly with the Culinary Institute of America, was also complemented by offerings that derived from robust relationships with Weight Watchers International and General Mills. Other partners included the American Society of Interior Designers, for its ASID-branded professional books, and Morningstar, for a series of investment guides.[107]

By early 1997, P/T reported its revenue was up for the eleventh straight year, at a time when most other trade publishers had been suffering serious setbacks. Inside Wiley, excitement abounded. And then came a series of large and transformative acquisitions. The first was Jossey-Bass, a well-respected San Francisco–based publisher known for its series in leadership, social sciences, and higher education. P/T had offered $18 million for Jossey-Bass back in 1993. Then part of Macmillan, which was on the block due to the bankruptcy of its parent, Maxwell Communication Corporation, Jossey-Bass was acquired by Simon & Schuster when it offered to buy all of Macmillan in 1994. In 1999, after Simon & Schuster was sold to Pearson Education in 1998 and Pearson put Jossey-Bass on the block, Wiley was ready. With sales of about $34 million per year on approximately 200 new book titles and 35 periodicals, Jossey-Bass joined the Wiley family for $82 million in cash as part of the P/T group.[108]

What Wiley saw in Jossey-Bass was another knowledge publisher—one that took a long-term view of its markets and sold high-quality books in subject areas that fit with the existing P/T list through trade, library, direct sales, college, and international channels. The Jossey-Bass mission, "to develop healthy and responsible organizations, communities, and leaders" by publishing high-quality books, periodicals, training materials, and other media, had kept it prosperous. Nevertheless, integration of the company into Wiley posed a more formidable challenge than anticipated.[109]

PROFILE

JOSSEY-BASS

In San Francisco in 1967, the year of the Human Be-In, Jann Wenner launched *Rolling Stone,* with the iconic image of John Lennon on the cover. In the same year and place, Allen Jossey-Bass also launched his first publication, *Aging and Mental Disorder in San Francisco* by Marjorie Fiske Lowenthal, a professional title for psychologists and psychiatrists. Allen Jossey-Bass had traded on his twelve-year career at Prentice-Hall in New York to start a small house that published books written for "the thoughtful reader." The basic formula was to produce research-based books that moved their readers, mostly professionals, from theory to practice, often in partnership with a burgeoning number of new practitioner associations, such as the American Association for Higher Education. With contracts with a number of leading academics and social scientists, an initial investment of $40,000, and frugal living on borrowed money in a sublet flat in San Francisco's bohemian North Beach, Jossey-Bass turned a profit within a year.[110]

Emphasizing high-quality titles in the social sciences—higher education, business, healthcare, religion, human resources, psychology, parenting, and leadership—and high-quality staff, Jossey-Bass continued to grow. By the early 1970s, the publishing house had an established reputation in its chosen areas. Management, public administration, and health series were added in the 1980s. The company forged prestigious partnerships with many organizations, including the Peter F. Drucker Foundation for Nonprofit Management (now the Leader to Leader Institute), the Center for Creative Leadership, the

Allen Jossey-Bass

Carnegie Foundation for the Advancement of Teaching, and the American Hospital Association. In 1996, Jossey-Bass acquired Pfeiffer & Company, a leading publisher of human resource development training materials.[111]

After prolonged negotiations during which Jossey-Bass attempted to ensure that the reputation of his publishing house would not suffer, he sold the company in 1989 to Maxwell Communications. But when Robert Maxwell and his company got into financial trouble, they cut Jossey-Bass's budget and instituted a hiring freeze even though the company was profitable. CEO Steve Piersanti, who refused to follow Maxwell's dictates, was summarily fired. Under the guidance of Lynn Luckow, the new CEO, the company expanded its publishing agenda in the 1990s to include K–12 educational reform, leadership, and nonprofit management titles.[112]

To get the most synergy and to serve the broader vision of a collaborative company, the integration had to be accomplished quickly and completely, Stephen Kippur explained. In particular, Jossey-Bass's book acquisitions process had to conform to the P/T group's collaborative, bottom-line-oriented regimen. Wiley had long since learned that acquired assets had to be monitored carefully and be brought into reasonable operating conformity with the rest of the enterprise while protecting the company's publishing culture. Through a series

of careful deliberations about best practices—who employed them and whose to use—compromises were struck, and books continued to be signed and sold. Part of the solution was to assign key Jossey-Bass managers larger responsibilities in the rest of Wiley. Thus, Jossey Bass's head of journals, Susan Lewis, was made responsible for all P/T journals, while Lenny Friedman, Jossey-Bass's manager of direct marketing, took on a larger role in P/T and STM. In 2000, Jossey-Bass's Debra S. Hunter was appointed its president. According to Hunter, "Wiley understood who we were." P/T's ability to work all the potential sales channels, including overseas sales, for Jossey-Bass titles—text, trade and professional—worked wonders for her organization.[113]

With the new strengths brought by the Jossey-Bass acquisition, P/T continued to follow its plan to become a leading publisher in each of its chosen categories. It expanded its professional lists in accounting, environmental management, and human resources; it developed both software and print publications in business valuation; and it acquired titles in computing, manufacturing, architecture, and psychology. The 1999 acquisition of the J. K. Lasser tax guides built on P/T's already strong presence in the area of financial planning; through careful management, the brand became the market leader, regarded as the most trusted name in the tax preparation category. P/T's global revenue increased from about $131 million, or 28 percent of Wiley's total, in fiscal year 1998, to some $196 million, or 32 percent of Wiley's total, in fiscal 2001.[114]

Two niche acquisitions, of Frank J. Fabozzi Publishing (U.S.) and Wrightbooks Pty. Ltd. (Australia), contributed nicely to P/T's growth in fiscal year 2002. Fabozzi published professional finance titles, while Wrightbooks emphasized personal finance. The increasing publication of business and finance titles overseas pointed to the need for global editorial and marketing coordination.[115]

Then in September 2001, just ten days after the terrorist attacks on the Pentagon and World Trade Center, Wiley bought Hungry Minds (formerly IDG Books), an Indianapolis-based publisher known for its For Dummies and CliffsNotes series in addition to such other powerful brands as the Bible technology series, Frommer's travel guides, Betty Crocker cookbooks, Howell Book House pet books, and Webster's New World Dictionaries. At $184.7 million, Wiley paid a good price for an undervalued (read undermanaged)

*D*ebra S. Hunter, president of Jossey-Bass

company which in 2000 had earned only $12.1 million on $243.3 million in revenue. The move was particularly bold given that the dot.com bubble had burst and Hungry Minds was a major technology publisher that had invested heavily in putting its content online, with only limited success. But Kippur and his technology publishing team were not scared off. Some had experienced the mid-1980s shakeout in the computer industry and survived. They did not see the latest downturn, as dramatic as it was, as a reason not to invest in building an essential technology list.[116]

It was an acquisition by invitation, and negotiations went smoothly. Wiley's balance sheet was sufficiently robust to obtain financing for the deal quickly on good terms. Wiley's first tender offer ever included $90.2 million for all the common stock and $92.5 million to extinguish Hungry Minds' outstanding debt, plus acquisition fees. The negotiations were unique in the annals of American publishing: Kippur and King reached a final agreement on the price with Pesce, who was calling on a cell phone from a rental truck he was driving while helping his son move into a college dormitory. With the acquisition came some 2,500 active titles. When Stephen Kippur and his team showed up for their first meeting with the Hungry Minds staff at their headquarters in Indianapolis, they were overwhelmed by their greeting: a standing ovation. The integration of Hungry Minds, following the "best practices" approach developed with Jossey-Bass, proceeded quickly and smoothly. The integration of the companies proved to be a boon for Wiley, reinvigorating Wiley's new colleagues. Within a short time, for example, publisher Mike Spring and his colleagues moved Frommer's up to the top position on the travel book list, where Frommer's resided, with one or two slips, for the next six years.[117]

Hungry Minds brought a number of competitive strengths that complemented P/T's own and allowed Wiley to build on its already strong organization.

Hungry Minds' superior branding and marketing skills represented a quantum leap over Wiley's branding capabilities and were transferable to Wiley's other publishing businesses. A state-of-the-art production operation, with special talents in rapid turnaround and full color, came with the Indianapolis offices and was soon leveraged for a wide range of P/T titles and for some from Higher Education. Hungry Minds introduced Wiley to a proven teaching methodology which was embedded in every For Dummies title and to a sophisticated form of book "packaging." Each title was carefully organized with chapter outlines, step-by-step instruction, paragraphs

PROFILE

FOR DUMMIES

The brand that launched a thousand titles had its genesis in a chance remark. In 1987, John Kilcullen, then a national accounts manager for Bantam Doubleday Dell's new electronic publishing division, heard from a friend about a customer in a Software Etc. store who was looking for a basic book on the DOS operating system—"Something like DOS for dummies," as the friend put it. The words stuck. Opportunity followed later, when Kilcullen was invited to sign on as founding vice president of sales and marketing for IDG Books Worldwide, Inc., launched in early 1990 by IDG (International Data Group), a publisher of magazines such as *PC World* and *Macworld*. Promoted almost immediately to publisher, he began putting out a series of computer books, co-branded with the magazines and in niche topic areas, with mixed results.

Needing a hit to sustain the venture, Kilcullen retrieved the For Dummies idea, linking it to Microsoft's upcoming release of MS-DOS 5.0. "It took him some time to find the right author for *DOS For Dummies*," recalled Marc Mikulich, known as "original employee number nine" for his May 1991 start at IDG Books, and later vice president of brand management at Wiley. "Then he heard Dan Gookin speaking at a conference, talking about how he would write great material and editors would then 'wave a creative magnet over it.' Dan's irreverent humor clicked with John's own perspective, and what he wanted *DOS For Dummies* to be."[118]

But *DOS For Dummies* launched with two strikes against it. First, it violated conventional "day-and-date" wisdom that the release of a book on software should coincide with the release of the software itself. MS-DOS 5.0 had been out for five months by the time *DOS For Dummies* appeared in November 1991. Second, there was considerable resistance to the title, both within IDG and from bookstore chains, where it was feared customers would be embarrassed to walk up to the checkout counter with it. But Kilcullen stood by his conviction that the word "dummies" would be perceived as sympa-

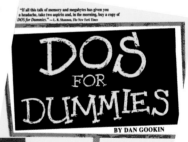

Steven Berkowitz (president) and John J. Kilcullen (CEO) of Dummies, 1998.

marked "Remember," "Technical Stuff," "Tip," etc. for easy use. Not only could For Dummies titles be sold to students; their template influenced the way in which some new Higher Education textbooks were shaped to be more effective teaching tools. Also new to Wiley was the way in which the For Dummies series was built around an editorial process that required close contact between editors, authors, and freelancers. For Dummies authors were commissioned, while Wiley retained all rights. For Dummies translations were carefully monitored to ensure that the books retained

thetic, a "term of endearment," even, as it has since been called.

"The board finally agreed to a print run of 7,500 copies," Mikulich said. "They were gone in a week. The same thing happened with the next 7,500. And then we got an order for 50,000 copies, from Costco." Success followed success with *Macs For Dummies*, and the brand was off and running. Soon other publishers were gunning for IDG with copycat series like Complete Idiot's Guides, but none gained traction. "We had two advantages," Mikulich explained. "We were first, and people bonded with For Dummies. But we also did what we did very well. The first book was the template for the entire series, with its eye-catching yellow and black cover, its icons, cartoons, trademark humor, and the 'Dummies Man' character. We delivered consistency."

Hungry Minds touted For Dummies as a "Reference for the Rest of Us," and its "need-to-know" orientation attracted Wiley. Millions of perfectly smart consumers flocked to the series for help, a timely response to a world chock full of problems that Dummies authors, following a carefully crafted pedagogical template, reduced to clear and simple instructions. As the editors explain, "For Dummies products give you the easiest and best way (or two) to get the job done, so that you can move on with more important things—like your life! . . . For Dummies gives you everything you *need* to know without making it seem like a big deal." That was a great way to pitch to the MTV generation and a society that has always valued "know-how" while simultaneously deprecating intellectuals as "nerds," "geeks," and "brainiacs."[119]

For Dummies even provided a guide to Wiley's home portal for Wiley colleagues.

The brand also moved with the market. Emerging just as the personal computer was making the transition from "geek gadget" to essential business productivity tool, it followed a run of technology titles with *Personal Finance For Dummies* in 1994, and caught the wave of the Internet with *The Internet For Dummies*. Dr. Ruth's 1995 bestseller, *Sex For Dummies*, was a prime example of the brand's successful extension into almost every area of human interest.

In fact, saying that the brand has launched a thousand titles is an understatement. A 2007 "For Dummies" search on the Wiley Web site, www.wiley.com, yielded 1,368 matches. More than 125 million For Dummies books were in print, in categories such as "At Home," "Health, Mind & Spirit," and "Travel," translated into 39 languages, and distributed in over 40 countries.[120]

Arthur Frommer, founder of the Frommer's travel guides, and Dr. Ruth Westheimer, both For Dummies authors, celebrate Wiley's anniversary.

CULINARY PUBLISHING

With the Hungry Minds acquisition in 2001, Wiley became a leading culinary publisher, with offerings that ranged from trade cookbooks for novices and dedicated foodies alike to professional and educational publications in areas such as food safety, beverages, and restaurant management. Much of Wiley's culinary publishing tapped the power of well-known consumer brands, several of which were managed through partnerships with leading corporations, educational institutions, and nonprofit organizations. Partners included General Mills (Betty Crocker and Pillsbury cookbooks), Weight Watchers International (*Weight Watchers New Complete Cookbook* and other titles), The Culinary Institute of America (*The Professional Chef* and other titles), Condé Nast (*The Bon Appétit Cookbook*), the National Restaurant Association Educational Foundation (*ServSafe* titles), and Barton Brands (*Mr. Boston Official Bartender's and Party Guide,* 2005). Wiley's culinary partnerships were part of a larger program that also included cookbook series like *1000 Recipes,* must-have basic cookbooks like Mark Bittman's *How to Cook Everything,* standard textbooks like Wayne Gisslen's *Professional Cooking* and *Professional Baking,* and standout individual titles like Marcus Samuelsson's *The Soul of a New Cuisine* (2006) and M.F.K. Fisher's classic *The Art of Eating* (2004).

General Mills, one of the world's largest packaged food companies, published the first edition of *Betty Crocker's Picture Cook Book* in 1950. Later renamed, the *Betty Crocker Cookbook* is generally acknowledged to be the best-selling cookbook ever published. The Wiley–General Mills partnership that originated with the Hungry

their framework and witty edge even in French, Spanish, or some 37 other languages. The transfer of expertise worked both ways. While Hungry Minds excelled at moving products to markets quickly, Wiley excelled at distribution, especially on the Web and outside the United States, areas where Hungry Minds was weak. The combination was a powerful tonic for the newly wed companies.[121]

Together, Wiley and Hungry Minds dealt with the softness in the technology market by emphasizing titles that appealed to consumers, such as *Digital Photography For Dummies,* which helped carry the list until corporate technology spending once again increased. In this market, the breadth and depth of Hungry Minds' technology list was a boon to Wiley's technology program, which had more titles geared to professionals.[122]

With its collection of some of the best-known brands in the country, the acquisition of the Hungry Minds list sent a clear message: Wiley was becoming a leading force in trade publishing, especially in its chosen

Minds acquisition represented a conjunction of strengths. "The food business and the cookbook business are both tough and highly competitive," said vice president and group executive publisher Robert Garber, "and each partner appreciates the expertise and experience that the other brings to the relationship. Teams meet regularly to exchange information and plan upcoming projects in a creative process that goes far beyond simply developing manuscripts and turning them into books."[123]

As a partner, Wiley was able to extend the reach of the General Mills books and the brands they represent through its experience in multi-channel marketing and distribution. For decades, a Betty Crocker cookbook was expected to sell into all channels at a single price and in one format. With the rapid diversification of sales channels, however, the publishing program came to include products in a variety of formats at appropriate price points. New titles included *Cocina Betty Crocker* (2005), a dual English/Spanish-language version of the *Betty Crocker Cookbook*. P/T's custom publishing team headed by Lisa Coleman put together special editions for companies such as Avon Products and USA Detergent, as well as a cluster of inexpensive topic-specific cookbooks targeting

*R*obert Garber, vice president and group executive publisher for Travel, Cooking, Architecture/Design, and Engineering.

customers in the grocery and discount club channels, while P/T's proprietary publishing team under Robert Ipsen worked with the cookbook publishing group to create *the Betty Crocker Sunday Dinner Cookbook* (2007), which appeared under the imprint of the Deseret Books chain.

With a partner of General Mills' size and reputation—boasting a portfolio of more than 100 leading food brands—there are potent opportunities for cross-promotion. When Wiley published *Betty Crocker Baking for Today* (2005), which used Gold Medal flour in all of the recipes, according to vice president and publisher Natalie Chapman, "General Mills featured it on 59 million packages of Gold Medal flour." Additionally, when General Mills redesigned their magazines to reach out to a younger audience, they shared the results of that effort with Wiley, which informed Wiley product designs as well.

An underlying rapport supports the collaboration. "Both organizations are disciplined, fiscally responsible, and focused on growth," said Garber. "Both sides understand each other's priorities. We value their brand equities, and they know they can depend on us to protect and promote them."[124]

categories. The acquisition soon increased both the P/T group's margins and its contribution to corporate profits. Hungry Minds also boosted P/T's U.S. revenue to $253.1 million for fiscal year 2002, or nearly double the group's U.S. revenue prior to the acquisition. P/T was now the largest of Wiley's businesses, accounting for 35 percent of global revenue (the European and Asian operations, broken out separately for reporting purposes, also benefited from revenue generated by Hungry Minds products). Higher Ed stood at $141.3 million and

STM at $164.9 million; these two businesses had grown nicely, too, if not quite as dramatically in financial terms. Wiley successfully published volume after volume and Web page after Web page of quality content and services while delivering impressive financial results. As the dot.com era unfolded, it was becoming clearer that Wiley needed to move incrementally, but quickly, to the post–dot.com world, in which those who controlled content and understood how to deliver it to their customers would play a leading role.[125]

Toward Global Publishing

By 2002, STM, with worldwide revenue of $277 million, was Wiley's closest thing to a global business. There were strong publishing centers in New York, Chichester, and Weinheim. The market for STM products in Asia, particularly China and India, was beginning to outpace the mature markets in Europe, Japan, and North America. Over the 1990s, the logic of every STM initiative—whether the launching of Wiley InterScience, the acquisition of VCH, or the society journals initiative—pointed to a need for greater global coordination that would eventually lead to truly global planning.

That STM moved faster toward global coordination than other parts of the company was understandable: despite national and regional research journals, and national competition, research was increasingly conducted across borders, with the results communicated through journals with international editorial boards. In the decade and a half after 1989, the growth of Higher Education and Professional/Trade also called for greater global coordination as overseas offices that started out as sales and marketing operations evolved into publishing centers in their own right. Building the foundation for a truly global Wiley was one of Ellis's and his team's most vital contributions. Pesce and his colleagues would take globalization to the next level.[126]

Wiley had experimented tentatively with global editorial coordination for almost a decade, and Brad Sr. had proclaimed the advent of global strategy formulation in 1988, the year of Ellis's arrival. Global meetings in the 1980s, however, produced little of substance. The leaders of Wiley's international companies would return to their bailiwicks and continue working as they had before. Ellis could not compel global coordination, but he eased the way. In 1989, he eliminated the International Division. He believed that senior managers should live and/or work for a time beyond their own backyards, and he supported the necessary increase in expenditures that permitted people to travel more frequently and to accept overseas assignments. Technology also played a major role in global coordination. With the World Wide Web and the construction of Wiley's global digital infrastructure known as the CORE system, publishers, editors, sales, and marketing could communicate directly, eliminating the need for international support staff in New York. The bifurcation of the globe into an American home office and a group of foreign subsidiaries had made sense in the time of Brad Sr., but technology and freer trade blurred the lines between "home" and "abroad" and dictated a more integrated cross-border approach. Global markets were becoming both more integrated and more complex, and the distinctions spelled out in the 1982 strategic plan between a developed and a developing world were too rigid to capture the nuances of change in both areas.[127]

The 1990s were also an era of intensifying globalization in the world economy. The European economy became more fully integrated as the European Economic Community, formed in 1958, evolved into the European Community, as set out in the Maastricht Treaty of 1992. The next year the euro, a new currency, was introduced and soon joined the dollar and the pound as an important global currency. As the economies of the Asian "Tigers" (Hong Kong, South Korea, Singapore, and Taiwan) took off, their governments invested more heavily in education and research. The Tigers were soon joined by a second group of tigers (Indonesia, Malaysia, Thailand, and the Philippines) and then, within a decade, both were overshadowed by the economies of China and India.[128]

For Wiley, global change was no small matter. In the mid-1990s, about 40 percent of Wiley's revenue came from outside the United States. After the VCH acquisition, for a time nearly half of Wiley's revenue derived from international markets. That percentage came down again with the acquisition of Hungry Minds, but increased again in 2007 with the acquisition of Blackwell Publishing. As Wiley's business globalized, so did its managers. The ability to "manage across cultures" began to appear as a desired competency in individual performance evaluations and development plans. As a cadre of global managers began to emerge, high-potential employees from various locations were temporarily assigned to positions in different locales to enhance this particular skill.[129]

Traditionally, like most multinationals, Wiley had given its foreign companies wide berth to operate their businesses as they saw fit. Brad Sr.'s philosophy was to find the best local manager and give him room to operate. Home rule by country worked well enough in a world that had not yet conquered time and distance, at least not cost-effectively, and where vast gaps in development existed between countries. At Wiley, home rule was for the most part profitable, though local conditions varied greatly. With its International Editions Wiley set prices that students, whether in Sweden or Indonesia, could afford. In the United Kingdom, professors taught from notes rather than textbooks, so rather than adopting a book, as was common in the United States, they merely listed books as "recommended" or "highly recommended," giving students more discretion regarding which books (if any!) to buy. Similarly, New York–centric editorial practices were doomed to fail, Peter Wiley argued in 1992, because they were based, for example, on "premises that may not apply in Asia and the less developed parts of the world." Big, four-color textbooks, the growing predominance of scientific journals over monographs, and the progress toward digital delivery systems preoccupied publishers in the developed economies (Western Europe, North America, and Japan) but not in the emerging ones, where books, especially inexpensive ones, still held sway during this period.[130]

STM led the way in the globalization of publishing decisions. In the early 1990s, there were two distinct

STM led the way in the globalization of publishing decisions.

centers of STM publishing, New York and Chichester, both with forceful leaders in Eric Swanson and John Jarvis. The acquisition of VCH in 1996 required a higher level of global coordination, particularly in chemistry where Eva Wille, the head of book publishing at VCH, joined the STM team representing both her own book program and her husband, Peter Gölitz's chemistry journals program. The development of Wiley InterScience also furthered global coordination. "Working globally on Wiley InterScience was a natural catalyst to spur global editorial coordination," recalled Jarvis. "From this period onward, the frequency and regularity of global STM meetings increased." They were face to face when possible, by video conference when not.[131]

In 1998, Pesce, when he became CEO, appointed Swanson and Jarvis as co-leaders of Wiley's global STM business, giving Swanson primary responsibility for journals and Jarvis primary responsibility for books. With Pesce's support, they formed a global STM management team that met regularly to discuss strategic issues. These were then translated into operational action plans, the majority of which were implemented locally. The arrangement affected not only editorial strategy but also production, fulfillment, and distribution, all of which became globally coordinated activities, with incentive structures realigned accordingly. Managers selected for the Global STM team in both editorial and non-editorial roles, in turn, had the major share of their performance-based compensation tied to global performance. "These individuals retained their local responsibilities," explained Jarvis, "but gradually their role transitioned into global strategic leadership around their subject area."[132]

In 1998, Pesce also announced the formation of leadership teams for Higher Education under

INFORMATION TECHNOLOGY: GOING GLOBAL

Information technology has helped Wiley overcome geographic and business boundaries, guided by a strategy that rests on two underlying components working together: a global platform that enables uniformity of operations, and a global network through which collaborative communication flows across the organization.

A Global Platform

By 1960, computers had begun to handle Wiley's billing and payroll operations and to provide detailed sales analyses. It would be nearly three decades, however, before a system was initiated that could integrate the operations of all Wiley locations worldwide. "Before then, our businesses around the world had disparate technologies," said Warren Fristensky, Wiley's chief information officer. "Every quarter, everyone would roll up their numbers, and we'd see where we were. But apart from Brad Wiley Sr.'s travels, there wasn't much connection between locations when it came to technology."[133]

A mid-1980s effort at modernization did not fare well. However, new, affordable hardware—specifically, IBM's AS/400 system, in 1988—brought hope of realizing Brad Sr.'s vision of globalization. By using common systems and databases for distribution, royalty, production, sales, and reporting operations, said Fristensky, Wiley "could share people, practices, and technology around the world seamlessly. We would reduce costs, and give ourselves the flexibility to expand the business."

Wiley's new global information system, launched in stages between 1989 and 1996, was called CORE—not, as one might assume, an acronym, but a true core at the center of things, as playfully acknowledged by the bushels of apples distributed to all participants in the U.S. launch. The first CORE implementation was in Singapore. "We decided to start with the smallest place," said Edward Russell, chief architect of CORE. "It proved to be the most complex, because of its multiple currencies and the nature of its markets."

Each iteration of CORE informed the next; the 1990 Australian version improved on Singapore's, and the

1991–1992 U.K. version improved on that. When Fristensky joined Wiley in May 1992, he spent his first month assembling a team, chaired by Robert Wilder and including Susan Kantrowitz, Anthony DiNinno, Debra Hill, and others, to visit and see the U.K. CORE in operation. With the team reassured that the system could handle the U.S. load, U.S. CORE was phased in between 1994 and 1995, with the Canadian version following about a year later.

In 1992, the Technology Steering Committee (TSC), a senior management team, under Stephen Kippur, was convened to help manage the company's change to the IBM AS/400 common platform worldwide. This platform was the foundation of unified information systems that permitted global fulfillment, inventory management, and sales processes. No longer did a sales representative in Australia have to wait a day to get an answer from someone in New York to a question about titles, pricing, or stock availability.

CORE is made up of modules—thousands of them, organized by functional area (sales, marketing, finance, etc.) and sharing a common set of databases. Order processing, for example, includes modules for pricing, discounting, and customer management. "The elegance of the architecture is that it's simple and integrated," said Fristensky. "When the Internet came along and we wanted to enable people to order online, we just took the appropriate existing order-processing pieces and wrapped them in some Web functionality, and that became the wiley.com shopping cart."

CORE provides the behind-the-scenes functionality for many of Wiley's customer-facing Web applications, including wiley.com, *WileyPLUS*, dummies.com, frommers.com, and Wiley InterScience. All tap into CORE's data and functionality to display and sell Wiley products, with Wiley's Coltrane system providing book cover images and marketing information, and OTIS (Online Title Information System) doing the same for online products. CORE also supports such internal systems as Camps.com (Contact Account Management Planning System), used by Higher Ed sales reps.

Warren Fristensky, chief information officer

Dominic Coppola, vice president of Electronic Support Services

After the global rollout of WileyNet in 1995, the next efforts focused on adding systems around CORE, such as Book Project Management, the Coltrane title and marketing information system, and the J. D. Edwards accounting system. "Upgrades enabled us to do things other publishers weren't doing, like provide authors with online statements and direct deposit for their royalties," Fristensky said. Customers could now track orders in real time regardless of whether they were placed online, by phone, or by fax. In 2004, *eCORE* was added to handle all online products and Wiley InterScience's complex subscription licenses database. Fristensky explained, "CORE can be extended without disrupting the business; it's like changing a tire while the car is rolling."[134]

A Global Network

Long before the "e-" prefix became ubiquitous, WileyNet, the company's internal data network, was designed and created. In the fall of 1986, mainframe systems engineers, working in Wiley's Eastern Distribution Center in New Jersey, planned the company's first network, which initially linked 200 employees in New York to systems in New Jersey. The first local area network (LAN) was deployed in New York in 1990, linking personal computers together. Soon after, network bridges were added to connect the New York and New Jersey systems. People could share information seamlessly, sending and receiving files and documents electronically within seconds. Voice and fax services were subsequently added over these new links.[135]

WileyNet officially evolved into a U.S. wide-area network (WAN) in late 1990. In 1991, it was extended to Canada and then to Chichester the next year, thanks to Wiley-leased circuits running beneath the Atlantic Ocean. "Beginning in the 1990s," explained Dominick Coppola, vice president of Electronic Support Services, "Wiley adopted a strategy to consolidate its distributed systems, networks, and services, such as e-mail and calendaring." The first e-mail services of WileyNet were created in 1993.[136]

By March 2000, the entire company was live, with Lotus Notes as its unified e-mail and calendaring system, supported by standard address conventions and support practices. WileyNet and its related local area networks were now enabling colleagues throughout Wiley—in 25 cities and 10 countries, in different time zones—to experience a level of collaboration that would have been inconceivable just a few years before.

Wiley's Web Site

For its first few years, the TSC focused on internal business systems. By 1994, with the growth of the Internet and other digital information technologies, technology was playing a greater role in product development. Moreover, boundaries—geographic and otherwise—were blurring as a more global marketplace began to emerge. The TSC formed the Internet Product Management Team (IPMT) in 1995 to oversee the delivery of products and services over the Internet. Convened by Timothy King, this cross-business task force included Gregory St. John (STM), Reed Elfenbein (STM Marketing), Dominick Coppola (Information Technology), Lee Northshield Thompson (P/T Marketing), Gwen Jones (P/T), Susan Spilka (Corporate Communications); Robert Ipsen (P/T Computer Books Editorial), Susan Saltrick (Higher Ed), and Stephen Kraham (Higher Ed Marketing), among others. The team focused on the creation of wiley.com, which launched in 1995, and provided information about the company and its products. Within a year, a Web catalogue of Wiley's U.S. titles was developed, a static brochure that relied on existing fulfillment procedures. It took five more years to launch a fully e-commerce–enabled site. The work of the IPMT formed the basis for later product development, cross-company collaboration, enabling e-commerce with a shopping-basket application programming interface and access-control systems, and Web-based production and content management systems.

Wiley's "solid systems foundation and infrastructure framework . . . allowed Wiley to meet and exceed the global challenges of customer-facing and content-delivery applications," said Coppola, and its standards, practices, and services have evolved, continuing to provide a firm basis for improvement and growth. Michael Silverstein, vice president, Technology Services, provided examples. "Wiley InterScience," he noted, "launched commercially in January 1999, marking the beginning of the Internet hosting era for Wiley." Frommers.com, dummies.com, and cliffsnotes.com followed. Higher Education's *eGrade Plus* was launched in 2003 and relaunched as *WileyPLUS* in 2005. With a broad range of business systems and a growing family of external Web sites meeting customer needs worldwide, Wiley had become a more global enterprise than ever before. In 1998, the TSC was disbanded after Will Pesce created leadership councils for each of the publishing groups and the company's approach to technology development moved deeper into each of the three businesses.[137]

Bonnie Lieberman and P/T under Stephen Kippur. "With each passing day," Pesce wrote, "geographical and organizational boundaries are blurring . . . As a result of the evolution of technology and the geographic expansion of wholesalers, distributors, and intermediaries [such as Amazon], many customer relationships are being transformed from local, regional, or national accounts to global ones." Pesce noted that while reorganization might appear to have negative consequences at a particular location, "it may actually generate long-term benefits for the Company globally. We must recognize that our customers do not care how we are organized internally. They want their needs satisfied with a high level of service at the best price." The new leadership teams were assigned responsibility for the financial performance of the core businesses on a global basis.[138]

In 2001, after Pesce, Swanson, and Jarvis moved the global STM organization to the next level, they announced that the leadership team would prepare "one global strategic plan" for STM. The objective was to facilitate "more effective allocation of human and financial resources and more customer-centric product development, sales, and marketing activities." While STM was leading the way toward greater global planning, Australia, Canada, Germany, and Singapore were adding more and more indigenous publishing to their operations. They would be followed by China, India, and Japan early in the new millennium. Over time, more local publishing would require greater global coordination in all of Wiley's businesses.[139]

United Kingdom

Beginning in 1989, the British operation developed in several related strategic directions, first under the continuing leadership of Michael Foyle and then under John Jarvis, who succeeded Foyle as managing director of the British company in May 1993. Jarvis, a cell biologist Ph.D., came to Wiley from Elsevier in 1979 as a medical editor with a brief to accelerate the development of the

British journals program, which Jamie Cameron had directed throughout the 1970s. Foyle and Jarvis focused first on expansion through organic growth in STM publishing, particularly journals, hiring new editors and increasing productivity targets for existing commissioning editors. The British STM business, composed almost exclusively of high-level research journals and books, had been nurtured for almost three decades and was highly profitable, but was feared to be approaching maturity as academic funding declined, revenue growth became harder to achieve, and the necessity of digitizing content became apparent. Much of the growth would have to come from taking market share from others and later from the society journals publishing initiative. Wiley U.K. was eager to publish more titles with industrial and commercial applications, as opposed to those for purely academic audiences, while the publication of conference proceedings and specialist monographs was curtailed.

By the mid-1990s, with the digital transition well under way, Jarvis introduced a new strategic theme—"Repositioning the Business"—that ran through all facets of the company for many years. It was intended to facilitate the launch of new business models and to change the way in which business processes and those who administered them were organized. Moving away from the traditional vertical organizational silos of editorial, marketing, and production, the editorial and marketing teams merged into cross-functional publishing teams in 1995. In 2001, Production was renamed "Content Management" and content management specialists were assigned to publishing teams.

The digital revolution was unfolding quickly. Academics, scientists, and librarians were calling for journal content to be available electronically as well as in print. As Wiley InterScience was being developed, U.K. editors were also experimenting with digitization of other products. Verity Waite, who had joined Wiley in 1978 as Foyle's personal assistant when he was marketing director, had progressed to medical editor and was responsible for Wiley U.K.'s first commercial software product, PatientWise, launched in 1995. Directed at the

At Wiley U.K.

*V*erity Waite, communications advisor

*J*ohn Jarvis, managing director (retired)

*S*ally Smith, associate editorial director

403

U.K. general practitioner market, it summarized common disorders, medical investigations, and surgical procedures for patients. It forced a reevaluation of many systems and processes and facilitated the transformation of many of them. Such CD-based products were already being surpassed, however, by the rapid development of the Web. In response, Chichester launched its first electronic journal, *Electronic Journal of Theoretical Chemistry,* in 1995.[140]

The e-journal's launch was written up in *Wiley Europe*, the first issue of the renamed house newsletter. The issue's theme was "Eurocentricity," reinforcing Charles Ellis's and then Will Pesce's push for Chichester to focus more on continental Europe. Small steps had already been taken with the opening in 1990 of offices in Strasbourg (publishing engineering), Berne (chemistry), and Chantilly (biomedicine). Little did anyone realize then that these European adventures would be dwarfed by the acquisition of VCH less than a year later. In June 1996, *Wiley Europe* announced—"We are really Wiley Europe now!"[141]

In addition to continuing the development of the STM business, the U.K. leadership team was keen to develop into adjacent publishing disciplines, investing in more textbook publishing and, in April 1992, acquiring Chancery Law from Bloomsbury Publishing, which comprised a list of journals, books, and looseleaf manuals for lawyers specializing in European Community law. In 1993, Chancery was folded into the newly established Professional Division, headed by Steven Mair. The new division was intentionally symbolic of the equal status of professional publishing in what had been fundamentally an STM company. Chancery Law was later sold, in 1999 when Wiley exited legal publishing.[142]

As P/T publishing expanded in the United States in the early 1990s, U.K. editors, such as Michael Coombs, Diane Taylor, and David Wilson, turned out a limited number of trade titles in popular science, psychology, and business as part of the Professional Division, building on the solid reputation of the journals list in these subjects. The importation of American trade titles added to Wiley U.K.'s offerings for trade outlets. In

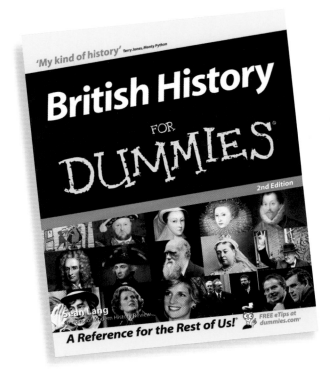

April 2000, Wiley U.K. set up its own trade publishing operation under the direction of Stephen Smith, paralleling more closely the directions being taken in the United States. Also in 2000, U.K. P/T bought Capstone, a small publisher with 40 titles in business and management founded by Mark Allin and Richard Burton. Allin and Burton then launched a digital series of management titles known as ExpressExec. The growing trade list was enhanced by new titles in current events and science edited by Sally Smith.[143]

As elsewhere, the Hungry Minds acquisition in 2001 forever changed Wiley's profile in the U.K. and European publishing scene. Generally viewed as an STM and text publisher, Wiley could now clearly claim shelf space in retail outlets, particularly with its For Dummies titles. Amazon U.K. and wholesalers such as Gardners began to take notice. Jarvis observed that Wiley U.K. had barely existed for some of these trade players, but suddenly he was invited to lunches to describe Chichester's latest consumer titles.[144]

The next step was for Wiley U.K. to publish its own Dummies titles, which it quickly did with *Rugby For Dummies* by Patrick Guthrie et al. (2004), *British History For Dummies* by Sean Lang (2004), *Arthritis For Dummies* by Barry Fox and Nadine Taylor (2004), *Formula One Racing For Dummies* by Jonathan Noble and Mark Hughes (2004), *Diabetes For Dummies* by Sara Jarvic and Alan L. Rubin (2003), and *Sudoku For Dummies* by Andrew Heron and Edmund James (2005). The last two titles made it clear: P/T in the United Kingdom was publishing for more than the domestic market, and its titles could be sold in any market where For Dummies titles were bought. *Sudoku For Dummies* brought in $6 million in revenue and spawned an entire line of *Sudoku For Dummies* titles. To expand the reach of the Frommer's brand, better known in the United States than overseas, P/T published titles such as *Frommer's Brazil* by Shawn Blore and Alexandra de Vries (2002), and *Frommer's British Columbia and the Canadian Rockies* by Bill McRae with Shawn Blore (2002).[145]

The establishment of a P/T publishing program in the United Kingdom complemented a similar program that was initiated in Germany in 2001 by managing director Manfred Antoni and publisher Jürgen Boos. Their business and finance list included titles such as the translations of Robert G. Eccles' *ValueReporting Revolution* and Laurence J. Brahm's *China's Century* and Barabara Bierach's *Das dämliche Geschlecht,** which made it to the top ten of German business bestsellers of 2002. Boos's team then turned to established German authorities, such as Professor Jürgen Weber, a German specialist in financial accounting at the Wissenschaftliche Hochschule für Unternehmensführung (Scientific University of Leadership and Management). The German P/T list expanded dramatically with the acquisition of the German For Dummies list in 2005. Publishing Director Hartmut Gante began to work closely with his global counterparts to build a global For Dummies list and coordinate editorial plans in other P/T subjects.

Several new faces arrived to steer Chichester from an STM print publisher to a European STM/P&T/

---

* The book is about women in business. This title is a pun that does not readily translate.

Higher Ed multimedia publisher. Paul Holmes came from Mercury Communications in 1993 to assist Robert Long in developing a marketing organization suitable for the new digital landscape, and Sally Morris came in 1995 to augment and professionalize the management of information assets in an increasingly complex world of digital rights and permissions. A further sign of growth was the arrival of Angela Poulter from Elsevier, also in 1995, to lead a local Human Resources team.

Wiley U.K. had produced undergraduate textbooks since the early days of its indigenous publishing program when New York and London were squabbling over the direction of the U.K. publishing program. A major problem was to sort out the appropriate educational levels for which U.S. and British texts could be sold. The United States published extensively for introductory-level courses, while some colleagues in the U.K. argued that British content was better suited for the advanced secondary level in the United Kingdom. Nevertheless, the U.S. texts, given their superior production values (e.g., illustration programs and uses of color), sold well to first-year undergraduates in the United Kingdom. In the 1960s and 1970s, Wiley's U.S. texts were used in many major scientific and technical first-year undergraduate courses in the United Kingdom, while the United Kingdom focused on the second- and third-year undergraduate and postgraduate texts. Subsequently, this trend continued, but with a much greater focus given to adaptations of U.S. titles for the U.K., Scandinavian, and other European markets. Strategic liaison between the U.S. and U.K. offices increased under the U.K. leadership first of Lynn Udall in the 1980s and then of Simon Plumtree in the 1990s.[146]

Chichester began publishing for the pharmaceutical industry in collaboration with the New York Medical Division in the 1980s, a program that was abandoned with the sale of Park Row in the late 1980s. Wiley U.K. returned to the business with the acquisition of A&M Publishing in 2002, but this time the interface with the pharmaceutical industry was built around co-development

and information management, although reprint sales and space advertising remained significant.[147]

In little more than a decade Chichester moved from a largely British publisher working in relative isolation from New York to a European publisher whose publishing programs were more closely aligned with those in New York and Weinheim. And because of its four-decade-long history as an STM publishing center, Chichester under Jarvis took a coequal role with Eric Swanson in moving STM toward a global planning regime. The U.K. operation had grown from a company with sales (in U.S. dollars) of $37.1 million and 277 people at the end of fiscal year 1989 to $106.6 million and 491 people at the end of fiscal year 2002.[148]

Australia

After Great Britain, Australia was Wiley's second outpost, having been founded soon after the company went public in 1962. Originally in the textbook import business, the Australian company broadened its publishing program with the acquisition of Jacaranda and its elementary and high school publishing in 1976. Jacaranda Wiley, the company's new name until 1999, when it became Wiley Australia, would follow a pattern similar to that in Great Britain, Canada, and Singapore. Through the 1990s and into the new century, Australia sustained and built its existing businesses—Jacaranda plus the import of American textbooks—while establishing a larger local publishing presence.

The early 1990s in Australia were difficult times for textbook publishers at all educational levels. The economy was in deep recession, particularly in the state of Victoria, which was Jacaranda's prime market because of its "booklist" system, which required that parents purchase texts for secondary school students. Financially, Jacaranda Wiley was also badly affected by its 1991 agreement to acquire the local subsidiary of Houghton Mifflin, a small and unprofitable operation in Melbourne, which the parent company in Boston wanted to be rid of.

Wiley Around the World

Asia

Australia

Canada

Indianapolis

Chichester

Cleveland

Germany

Hoboken

San Francisco

Moscow

The planned synergies with Wiley's new P/T division never developed as the dozen or so U.K. agencies with which Houghton Mifflin had marketing and distribution agreements (Andre Deutsch, Victor Gollancz, Element, Aurum, and others) led to overstocking and severe inventory write-offs, major turmoil, and cost blowouts in distribution plus internal strains between Houghton Mifflin's trade culture and Wiley's professional publishing orientation. Fiscal years 1992 and 1993 were therefore disastrous for Wiley Australia. Operating profit declined from 9.7 percent in 1991 to a substantial loss in 1993.[149]

In 1993, Peter Donoughue, who joined the company in 1982 from McGraw-Hill, was promoted to managing director of Jacaranda Wiley after heading Jacaranda. With guidance from Will Pesce, who assumed corporate responsibility for Australia at the same time, Donoughue's first task was to draw up a plan to bring the company back to substantial profitability as quickly as possible. This meant downsizing (21 staff members were let go in April 1993), the sale of Jacaranda's barely profitable primary school business to Heinemann (Reed), and the winding up or sale of a number of production operation profit centers (Jacaranda Software, Jacaranda Photographics, Jacaranda Cartographics). The process of terminating the multitude of small and very unprofitable trade agencies was also begun. As Donoughue described it, "1993 was the year of downsizing, restructure, market focus, and service improvement."[150]

John Draper, an experienced distribution logistics manager, was hired to transform the company's customer service and distribution operation. Major investments were made in a new warehouse and new technologies, such as barcoding/scanning, radio frequency terminals, and laser printing of invoices. By the end of 1994, the service turnaround was complete, and the company was acknowledged by the industry as a benchmark performer.

In the meantime, Donoughue had hired Peter Van Noorden to head Jacaranda and Lucy Russell to head the College operation. Van Noorden had worked previously for Jacaranda as an editor in the Melbourne office but had been poached by Heinemann to develop a new secondary school atlas to compete with the dominant Jacaranda Atlas. Donoughue attracted him back with the mandate to build Wiley's by now stagnant secondary school business where revenue growth had stalled and profitability was declining. Van Noorden brought talented teachers and authors into publishing for the first time and initiated new programs such as Science Quest, Society and Environment, and Maths Quest that would become established brands and propel the division into the high-growth decade to come. Revenue bounced back in fiscal year 1997 with 14% growth, reaching pinnacles of growth in fiscal years 2000 and 2001 of 32% and 29%, respectively. Jacaranda achieved number one market share status in the year 2000 and increased its dominance in the new decade.[151]

Lucy Russell faced challenges of a different, perhaps more complex, sort. In the late 1990s, the Australian dollar suffered a sharp decline during the Asian financial crisis, substantially eroding Higher Education's margins on imported product. Prices could only be increased so far without causing a severe backlash from students. Moreover, the indigenous list was heavily weighted to accounting around a few strong titles such as the adaptation of *Principles of Accounting*, by John Helmkamp, Leroy Imdieke, and Ralph Smith, an older U.S. title that U.S. Higher Ed no longer supported. Revenue, dependent on new edition cycles, fluctuated dramatically. Financial results in the late 1990s were poor.

Russell cut sales overhead by adopting a risky strategy of using mostly in-house sales representatives and cutting the number of representatives in the field. At the same time, the investment in local publishing was substantially increased. The business strongly recovered. Revenue growth in fiscal year 2002, the first full year of the new sales model, was 22 percent. The local publishing list was expanded beyond accounting to include management, marketing, and psychology.[152]

In the 1990s, Wiley Australia also built up its local trade program with titles in history, current events,

*A*ustralian prime minister John Howard (right) and Peter Donoughue attend the 2006 launch of *Cricket For Dummies* in Canberra.

and personal finance. To enhance its trade presence, the company in 2001 purchased Wrightbooks, a Melbourne-based publisher of 40 titles a year in the field of personal finance and investment, with revenue of $2.5 million. Lesley Beaumont, the daughter of owner/founder Geoff Wright, joined Wiley's P/T group as publisher. After Wiley acquired the For Dummies brand in 2001, the Australian P/T organization under Shawn Casey added local titles, such as *Weight Training For Dummies* by Kelly Baker, Liz Neporent, and Suzanne Schlosberg and *MYOB For Dummies* by Veechi Curtis, to a growing list of imports, further building the trade list. With these new titles, P/T's revenue represented 40 percent of the Australian operation's sales, making P/T the strongest growth driver in the division.[153]

By the end of 2002, a decade after Donoughue's appointment, Wiley Australia had become a high-performing, highly respected company with a reputation for excellent performance and service. At the end of fiscal year 1989, Australia had sales of U.S. $13.8 million and employed 118 people; at the end of fiscal year 2002, a staff of 142 produced U.S. $32.7 million in revenue. The School Group won the Australian Publishers Association's annual Excellence in Educational Publishing award six

times out of the award's seven-year history, which began in 1994. The Higher Education group won the Australian Campus Booksellers Association's Tertiary Publisher of the Year award. The company was recognized as a best practices organization because of its human relations policies and programs, specifically as they addressed the Australian government's agenda for the advancement of women in the workplace. By 2006, the company had been given Employer of Choice status for the previous five years, an accreditation granted by the Equal Opportunity in the Workplace agency to only 100 or so companies a year. No other publisher has ever been similarly recognized.[154]

Canada

Canada, with an office that opened in Toronto in 1968, was another early Wiley outpost. By the 1990s, efforts to build Canadian publishing programs for elementary and high school students and the trade were faltering. The Canadians, led by John Dill, continued to import U.S. college texts while adapting selected U.S. titles, such as Donald Kieso and Jerry Weygandt's *Intermediate Accounting* and John Schermerhorn's *Management: The*

Competitive Advantage, for the Canadian market. They also published a series of Canadian accounting casebooks and an outdoor recreation title. But the Higher Education editorial department lacked stability. Developmental editors who left were not replaced; freelancers were hired instead.

Like Australia, Canada was experiencing a serious recession, accompanied by new taxes on goods and services. Professors trimmed adoption lists, and students turned more frequently to used books and the all-too-popular photocopy machine. Dill moved quickly to rebuild the text publishing program, hiring Diane Wood in 1990 to manage Higher Education. In 1994, Dill sold the Canadian high school publishing program and used the funds to acquire twelve business and economics texts from Butterworth, including the respected *Managerial Finance in a Canadian Setting* by Peter A. Lusztig and Bernhard Schwab. At this time, Carolyn Wells joined Wiley Canada from Butterworth as a marketing manager and played a huge role in the success of the accounting program. By 1995, when John Horne was hired to head the editorial department, Wiley Canada had established its reputation as the leading publisher in intermediate accounting.[155]

Horne moved quickly to broaden the accounting list. He hired Maureen Fizzell, an instructor at Simon Fraser University, to adapt Robert E. Hoskin's *Financial Accounting*, recently published in the United States, and then signed Nicola Young of Saint Mary's University to join the Kieso author team. She worked with V. Bruce Irvine and W. Harold Silvester, the original Canadian authors, on the fifth Canadian edition of *Intermediate Accounting*. A few years later Irvine and Silvester retired, and Young was joined by Irene Wiecek, from the University of Toronto, for the next edition. To further build the list, Horne signed Barbara Trenholm from the University of New Brunswick to adapt and co-author a Canadian edition of

Jerry Weygandt's *Accounting Principles*. This text, with editorial direction from Karen Staudinger and marketing support from Carolyn Wells, was the most successful accounting text in Canadian history. With the publication of Trenholm's next adaptation, Weygandt, Kieso, and Paul Kimmel's *Financial Accounting: Tools for Business Decision-Making* (2001), Wiley Canada became the leading publisher in the accounting market. Horne pressed on into other business disciplines, including management, human resources, and finance. In 1996, Wiley was named Campus Publisher of the Year by the Canadian College Booksellers Association.[156]

Dill was adamant about the need to expand Wiley's indigenous list while protecting the company's position in its chosen fields. When Dill departed from Wiley, Pesce appointed Wood in 1993, who became the first woman to lead one of Wiley's international companies. Wood agreed with Dill's emphasis on indigenous publishing and sent the same message to her colleagues. "By the late 1990s," recalled Wood, "the publishing landscape had really changed in Canada. Our competitors were publishing adaptations in markets that had not previously required Canadian content, such as psychology, statistics, information technology, and others. They had also significantly ramped up their local programs . . . bringing out four-color titles whose main attraction was that they were home-grown."[157]

The decision was made to expand the publishing program beyond the business disciplines. So Higher

William Zerter, president, Wiley Canada

John Dill, past president, Wiley Canada

Diane Wood, past president, Wiley Canada

Success in Canadian Accounting Publishing

*W*orking with Barbara Trenholm of the University of New Brunswick to adapt Jerry Weygandt's *Accounting Principles*, Karen Staudinger, editorial manager, and Carolyn Wells, marketing manager, helped produce a best seller.

Carolyn Wells, marketing manager, Wiley Canada

Karen Staudinger, editorial manager, Wiley Canada

Barbara Trenholm

Education focused on adapting market-leading titles in Wiley's core disciplines, starting with Gerald C. Davison and John M. Neale's *Abnormal Psychology,* which was a success from the start. Adaptations of leading titles in geography and environmental science were also added to the list. Simultaneously, Wells, now head of marketing in Higher Education, worked closely with U.S. Professional/Trade to adapt Wayne Gisslen's *Professional Cooking*. When Wood was replaced by William Zerter in 2002, Higher Education's Canadian editorial program was responsible for 20 percent of the company's revenue.[158]

On the trade side, Dill hired Julia Woods in 1988 as vice president of Professional, Reference, and Trade. Dill and Woods charged Karen Milner, a young marketer turned editor, with building a new professional and trade list specifically for the Canadian market. The old trade list had disappeared from sight. "I walked into my new office on the first day of my new job to find a completely clean slate," Milner recalled. "Not a scrap of paper or a single lead." Following the model used in

Higher Education, Milner started by publishing Canadian adaptations of U.S. books and subscription products for professional accountants.[159]

With the recession in the early 1990s, Milner found it difficult to get accounting firms to support authors who would be giving up billable hours to work on book projects. She turned instead to trade publishing. Her first book, by Ranjit Kumar and Barbara Murck, *On Common Ground: Managing Human–Planet Relationships,* was about sustainable development. Published in 1992 in conjunction with the Foundation for International Training, it was just in time for the Earth Summit in Brazil. Milner spread her list over subjects such as technology, project management, finance, and personal finance. Personal finance produced a winner: Sandra Foster's *You Can't Take It With You: The Common Sense Guide to Estate Planning for Canadians* (1996), the first Canadian book on the subject. Foster became a franchise author for Wiley Canada, publishing other books and multiple editions of her initial bestseller, which by 2006 had sold 100,000 in five editions. With

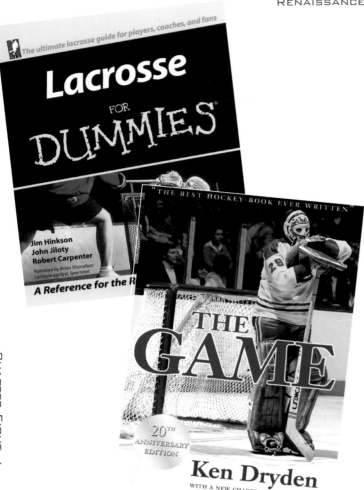

iley Canada launched sports titles in the fall of 2003 with hockey star Ken Dryden's classic, *The Game,* 20th Anniversary Edition and *Lacrosse For Dummies* by Jim Hinckson, John Jiloty, and Robert Carpenter.

this success, Wood and P/T vice president Beth Bruder encouraged Milner to grow her list in personal finance and business, subjects that aligned nicely with P/T publishing in the United States. The Canadians soon published titles that sold beyond their relatively small market, such as Stanley Brown's *Strategic Customer Care* (1999) and *Customer Relationship Management* (2000), Ian Gordon's *Relationship Marketing* (1998), and Judy Allen's *Event Planning* (2000). Milner's list was unique; a handful of authors returned repeatedly to Wiley to write successful books.[160]

As with the U.K., the 2001 purchase of Hungry Minds brought both titles and talent to the Toronto office. Robert Harris, the For Dummies publisher,

became P/T's general manager, and Jennifer Smith moved from head of sales to vice president and publisher. Under Harris and Smith, Canadian P/T added For Dummies and Frommer's titles to their list. The Canadian trade list grew accordingly, branching out to health, parenting, current affairs, and even true crime and sports. The sports titles were launched in the fall of 2003 with hockey star Ken Dryden's classic, *The Game, 20th Anniversary Edition* and Jim Hinckson, John Jiloty, and Robert Carpenter's *Lacrosse For Dummies.*

By the end of fiscal year 2002, Canadian textbook sales had increased from $8 million in 1989 to $17 million. The trade list brought in more than $9 million, up from less than $4 million in 1989. With 101 employees, Canada's total revenue was nearly $28 million in 2002. The strength of the Canadian operation was recognized by the Great Place to Work Institute Canada in 2005 when Wiley Canada was named to the Top 30 Employers to work for in British Columbia.[161]

Asia

Charles Ellis regarded Asia in the early 1990s as a weak operation, yet one with significant potential. Japan had become an economic powerhouse, while the Asian Tigers, plus Malaysia, Thailand, Indonesia, and the Philippines, were making their own contributions to growth despite the post–Gulf War recession, which continued to plague the region. Wiley's Singapore operation handled the printing, warehousing, and distribution of Wiley International Editions, textbooks priced to local markets that accounted for 60 percent of Asian sales. STM books and journals, including major reference works, made up an additional 30 percent of revenue, with P/T business and technology books the remaining 10 percent. Wiley's fiscal year 1993 operating plan for Asia captured some of the problems Wiley faced in the region. Growth rates for the Asian Tigers, particularly South Korea and Taiwan, had fallen; the size of the market in Bangladesh, China, India, Pakistan, and the Philippines was limited by their poverty; government spending on higher education and scientific research was declining; India, encouraged by the International Monetary Fund, was limiting imports; and piracy was rampant.[162]

Hoping to strengthen ties with their Asian colleagues, Ellis and Peter Wiley visited Tokyo, Hong Kong, and Singapore in early 1992. It was not an encouraging trip. Singapore's managing director had run things too informally for too long, resulting in botched agency relationships, excessive returns, and high levels of overstocking at Wiley distributors. To make matters worse, U.S. publishers were losing an estimated $300 million a year to Asian pirates, $100 million in China alone.[163]

Ellis believed that the key to renewal in Asia would be new management. In September 1992, he hired Stephen Smith, an experienced manager from Simon & Schuster who had spent much of his professional life outside of his native England, to head the Asian operation. Ellis charged him with devising and implementing a plan to accelerate Wiley's growth. Smith set about building a new sales and marketing team, forging closer links between Asian colleagues and the rest of the company, expanding the customer base, and developing new product and pricing strategies to capture market

growth opportunities. In fiscal 1993, revenue in Asia outside Japan was nearly (U.S.) $4.7 million, well below plan. By the end of fiscal year 2002, revenue had grown to (U.S.) $25 million, including Japanese revenue of (U.S.) $3.92 million. Most significantly, Smith and his colleagues had added new sources of revenue via journal and foreign rights sales. Asian journal sales outside of Japan grew from less than $5 million in fiscal year 1993 to $21 million in 2002. Smith recognized that Singapore's distribution and customer service operations were among the best in Asia, staffed by a team of long-serving and talented individuals headed by Khee How Foo, general manager of Finance and Organizations, and Manamshan Appesamy, warehouse manager, and that the old autocratic management had not come close to realizing its potential. In 1994, Smith relocated the company's Singapore headquarters from a dreary industrial estate to a more attractive setting, a move that helped improve operations and also symbolized a new approach to the business. In March 1993, Smith convened the first Asian regional sales meeting. Twelve people attended, only five of them dedicated to sales and marketing. The company clearly lacked the sales power to take advantage of its excellent infrastructure.[164]

Stephen M. Smith

Stephen M. Smith joined Wiley in September 1992, prior to which he was president of Simon & Schuster's U.K. Academic and Professional Group, with management responsibility for the European operations of Simon & Schuster and Prentice Hall. During his time with Simon & Schuster, he spent two years in the Middle East and six years as managing director of the Asian subsidiary in Singapore.

As vice president of Wiley Asia, Smith resided for four years in Singapore, where he was a significant contributor to the rapid growth of Wiley's revenue and profits in the Asian market. As senior vice president for international development, he was responsible for Wiley's operations in Asia and Australia, a post that he has held since September 1995. He has been a member of Wiley's leadership team since 1996. Smith was appointed a member of the management board of Wiley Europe with responsibility for professional and trade publishing in May 2000. Named Wiley Europe's chief operating officer in early 2006, Smith assumed responsibility for the overall direction and leadership of Wiley's businesses in Europe on May 1, 2007, upon the retirement of John Jarvis. Smith also retained corporate responsibility for Wiley Asia and Wiley Australia.

Smith received his B.S. from Oxford Brookes University. He has been an active participant in industry campaigns to combat copyright infringement around the world.

Wiley Asia's growth can be seen in the increasing number of people attending its sales meetings. At left, Steven Miron, who joined Wiley Asia as regional manager for South Korea and Taiwan and who was promoted in 1996 to head Wiley Asia.

First under Smith and then under Steven Miron, who succeeded Smith in 1996, Wiley Asia embarked on an ambitious program of organizational growth matched by correspondingly rapid revenue growth. Smith brought in P. C. Tham to head sales, Miron as regional sales manager for South Korea and Taiwan, Audrey Wee as promotions manager, and Derek Lee as Hong Kong sales manager. With Miron's advancement to Asian head, Hee-Jeong Ihn became Korea's country manager, adding new dynamism to that sales and marketing operation. Ihn was Wiley's second female country manager. The new energy and esprit were palpable as Wiley's Asian colleagues gained a reputation for working incredibly long hours and leading active social lives. At Wiley's

Asian sales meeting in Bangkok in 1998, fully 60 Wiley colleagues from 11 countries participated, the vast majority of whom were directly involved in sales and marketing.

Wiley's Asian revenue doubled from fiscal year 1993 to fiscal 1995 and then doubled again in the three years to fiscal 1998. "We turned on the tap," as Smith put it. With product from the United States, Great Britain, and Germany, the Asian organization was able to match Wiley content to the growing demand for texts, research materials, and professional, business, finance, and technology books in the English-language markets of the region.[165]

At the end of 1997, a run on the Malay and Thai currencies triggered a recession that spread to other Asian economies. Miron and his associates made some quick adjustments in Wiley's prices, betting that it was better to lose some revenue in the short run in order to maintain strong customer relationships for the long haul. They were right. By 1999, the regional economy was on the road to recovery, and sales picked up again.

As the Asian economy maintained its overall growth profile, Wiley's Asian managers recognized a need for content that was relevant to Asian readers. At the same time, academic and professional interest in all aspects of the Asian growth phenomenon was increasing. In response, Smith hired Henry Leung in 1994 to develop a line of trade books, which included Willy Wo-Lap Lam's *China after Deng Xiaoping*, published in 1995. Over time, the P/T list evolved under the editorial direction of Nick Wallwork, focusing on books in business and finance for both Asian and global markets.

*H*ee-Jeong Ihn, area manager, Territory Sales, Korea

Following the reinvigoration of the book-sales infrastructure, the Asian management team looked for other ways in which Wiley's presence in Asian markets could benefit the company more widely. Prior to 1995, the Asian sales force focused almost exclusively on books, while Wiley's Tokyo office actively promoted and sold journal subscriptions and STM books. Starting in fiscal 1996, Wiley instituted a new incentive plan aimed at rewarding the sales force for supporting both the journals and the translation and licensing businesses. From then on, journals revenue grew dramatically in the rapidly maturing Asian economies. Asia continued to emerge as a vital source of STM content as well as a dynamic market for it; from 2000 to 2004, the number of Wiley journal articles authored by Asian researchers increased dramatically.

India

Smith also assumed responsibility for Wiley's Indian operation known as Wiley Eastern, in which corporate Wiley held a minority interest. The Indian company was poorly managed, while all foreign publishers were plagued by the incredible bureaucratic inefficiencies of India's infamous "License-permit Raj." Most vexing, according to Ellis, was the government's "self-imposed embargo" that required a punitive deposit in the central bank before importing published material. "Unusual accounting procedures," extreme slowness in settling accounts, and "ambivalence about copyright"—that is, piracy—were other big problems. In early 1993 Wiley decided to sell the company it had established in 1965 and set up a new operation. In March 1995, Wiley sold its share of Wiley Eastern to its majority joint venture partners, by which time Wiley had set up a liaison office in New Delhi to facilitate the distribution of its imported titles into the Indian market.[166]

India's ruling Congress Party had already recognized that the limitations imposed by its state-directed economy caused the country's growth rate to lag. In 1980, Prime Minister Rajiv Ghandi introduced the first economic reforms, followed in the early 1990s by Prime Minister P. V. Narasimha Rao's economic liberalization program. These spelled the end of the License-permit Raj, and the Indian economy began to take off.

In 1994, Arun Bharti was appointed general manager of the new Wiley India, and it began to prosper. Bharti expanded the sales force with dramatic results. In line with the rest of the Asian organization, the sale of journals and, once Wiley InterScience was established, the licensing of journal and book content added to the impressive results. India sales grew from $1.8 million in fiscal year 1989 to $5.1 million at the end of fiscal year 2002. Bharti was promoted to vice president in 2005.[167]

*A*run Bharti, director, Sales and Marketing, Wiley India   *V*ikas Gupta, managing director, Wiley India

With the purchase of Hungry Minds in 2001, Wiley acquired partial, and later in 2006, full ownership of Dreamtech, which was run by Vikas Gupta. Dreamtech reprinted For Dummies titles and also published its own computer books, 16 of which were authored or coauthored by Gupta himself. India was added to the growing list of international publishing centers. With its editorial capabilities, Dreamtech began to play a role in global Wiley—reviewing and editing content for computer books published in the United States while exploring ways to adapt educational materials, particularly with engineering content, for the Indian market. Upon completion of the Blackwell acquisition in 2007, Gupta was appointed managing director while Bharti became director of sales and marketing for Wiley-Blackwell.[168]

China

The world's and Wiley's interest in China, Asia's other great population center, surged after Deng Xiaoping's and later Jiang Zemin's economic reforms (starting in the late 1970s) turned the country into an economic powerhouse. But it would take sustained attention to this

market—and a radical shift in the government's attitude toward some aspects of piracy—before Wiley saw significant levels of sales and reliable profits.[169]

Between the late 1970s and the early 2000s, the Chinese market imported small quantities of research-level STM books, with all imports passing through a handful of government-owned entities, most notably the China National Publications Import Export Corporation. Some years were better than others, but overall the business was not enticing. The scholarly journals market was virtually nonexistent, as rampant piracy meant that Wiley sold but few subscriptions to most of its journal titles. The government had barred joint ventures, Wiley's first ambition in China, and though co-publishing arrangements were important, they produced limited results. The first book co-published by Wiley and its local partner, Higher Education Press, the publishing arm of the Ministry of Education, was Zhilun Xu's *Applied Elasticity*, appearing in early 1992. Within a year, Wiley added more co-publishing deals for titles in accounting, engineering, and computers. Miron's fluency in Mandarin and support from his Chinese-speaking colleagues in Hong Kong, Singapore, and Taiwan were key in building these new relationships.[170]

Under international pressure, the Chinese government's response to piracy was a contradictory one. Starting in 1979, various Wiley colleagues discussed the importance of an international copyright regime with Chinese officials and their publishing counterparts. In 2000, after a concerted campaign by the Publishers' Association in the United Kingdom, the Association of American Publishers, the International Publishers Association, Wiley, and other publishing companies, the Chinese government signed the Berne Convention for the Protection of Literary and Artistic Works. It quickly became apparent that the government was ready—no official explanation was ever offered—to limit journals piracy, probably because China was on the threshold of World Trade Organization membership. The change was a boon for Wiley's journals business, leading to a rapid increase in licensing to major consortia, such as the China Academic Library Information System (CALIS), and in article submissions from Chinese scholars. Simultaneously, Wiley extended its co-publishing program and opened a Beijing office in early 2001 under the direction of Wendy Ding, who, a few years later, became country manager. On the P/T front, Wiley launched a Chinese For Dummies translation program in 2003, licensing rights to China Machine Press, one of its largest Asian partners. By 2004, about 20 business and lifestyle titles had been published and new titles on China-specific subjects were being developed, establishing a solid Asian beachhead for the global brand. The Chinese government also announced preliminary steps to open up the textbook market, mandating that 10 percent of Chinese texts be published in English. Illegal copying of texts remained a serious problem, however, encouraging Wiley to be cautious about entering the textbook market outside its relationship with Higher Education Press. China, now a sizeable scientific, technical, and medical journal and translation rights market, still demanded great patience.[171]

Japan

Japan presented another set of challenges. As early as Wiley's 1982 strategic plan, Japan was grouped with the industrialized economies of the world as an important Wiley market. During the decade, as Japanese per capita income surpassed that of the United States, trade tensions rose, together with a growing and often exaggerated fear, in the United States, of Japan's global economic hegemony. With its sophisticated economy, Japan produced a steady demand for research materials, while Japanese researchers, both corporate and academic, also contributed their content to Wiley journals. As a market for books and journals, Japan usually accounted for about 10 percent of Asian sales. But then, in 1992–1993, the so-called Bubble Economy burst, and Japan entered a period of economic stagnation. Starting in 1992, research and development funding began to decline, bottoming out two years later. After that, R&D expenditures increased slowly (2 to 5 percent) during the rest of the decade. Government funding in the 1990s focused on medical technology (human genomes, cloning, transplants) and on nanotechnology, particularly after the invention of the carbon nanotube by Sumio Iijima in 1991.[172]

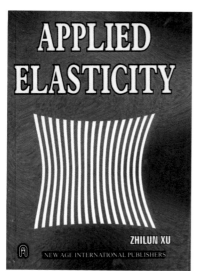

Wiley's publications ranged from Xhilun Xu's *Applied Elasticity*, the first book Wiley published with Higher Education Press, its local partner in China, to Chinese memoirs published for Western markets, such as Harry Wu's *Bitter Winds*, a 1995 memoir covering Wu's 19-year imprisonment in the Chinese labor camp system.

Starting as a sales representative in Taiwan in 1993, Theresa Liu became the general manager for China and Taiwan in 2005, making her Wiley's third female country manager.

In 1991, long-time managing director Hiroshi Tsukabe retired and was replaced by Tadashi Hase, who had begun working for Wiley as a sales representative in 1984. Hase, assisted by Setsuko Saito, stepped up direct-marketing efforts for Wiley journals, including greater attendance at society exhibitions. When Wiley InterScience was launched in 1999, Hase hired two new colleagues to work on securing new licensing agreements. For a number of years, Wiley in Japan hired freelancers to help Japanese researchers prepare their journal articles in English. In 1998, Antoine Bocquet was hired as a permanent staff member with the same responsibility. In 2001, Wiley Japan launched its first journal, *The Chemical Record*, in a partnership with seven Japanese chemical societies. By the end of fiscal year 2002, there were seven employees in the Tokyo office overseeing a $25.8 million business, 85 per cent of which was journal sales.[173]

By 2002, Wiley's Asia business was, in Stephen Smith's estimation, "unrecognizable" compared to the collection of underperforming fiefdoms it had been a decade earlier. Thirty Wiley colleagues in Singapore became 100, and revenue grew to $33 million. Wiley weathered the regional financial crisis of 1997–1998 by working closely with its customers to sustain their journal subscriptions, even as book sales faltered, returns increased, and booksellers defaulted. Bear Stearns analysts praised the company for keeping its eye on profits rather than "simply stuffing its pipeline with deeply discounted products to gain market share." As a bonus, sales of George Soros's *The Alchemy of Finance* (1994) and *Soros on Soros* (1995) jumped every time Malaysian Prime Minister Mahathir accused the famous financial specula-

*T*adashi Hase, director of Sales & Marketing, Wiley-Blackwell, Japan

*R*yoji Noyori, one of Wiley Japan's authors, won the Nobel Prize in Chemistry in 2001.

tor of causing the crisis. Despite tough times for a few years after the crisis, Brad II's prediction proved correct that "the morale and self-confidence" of the Wiley Asia team was "strong enough . . . to withstand several years of flat sales and unstable business conditions." Smith and Miron had prepared the ground for greater growth in the twenty-first century.[174]

Latin America, The Middle East, and Africa

Patient nurturing of markets was a Wiley hallmark, and Wiley had long been committed to its customers in Latin America, the Middle East, and Africa. In 1996, Stephen Smith assumed responsibility for these areas, too.

In Latin America, Smith continued to support the company's long relationship with the Noriega family and their company, Limusa, the largest distributor in Latin America. Fully 90 percent of Limusa's list was composed of Wiley titles. From New York and later Hoboken, Laurie Rubin oversaw the sale of P/T titles south of the U.S. border. The company continued to look for ways to expand its presence in Latin America, though persistent illegal copying, the elitist nature of higher education, and an underdeveloped R&D infrastructure were stubborn constraints.[175]

In the Middle East, Wiley sold its International Editions, especially in the sciences, technology, and engineering, in markets that included Saudi Arabia, Jordan, Egypt, Lebanon, and Turkey. In 2001, Wiley opened an office in Tehran, run by Mehdi Omranloo, to meet strong demand for scholarly and academic books and journals from Iranian universities and professionals.[176]

In South Africa, Nelson Mandela's election as president in 1994 marked the end of apartheid and the beginning of a new era in which the country's institutions of higher education were open to all. The next year, Charles Ellis, Peter Wiley, and Robert Long, Sales and Marketing director, visited Johannesburg, Pretoria, and Capetown, meeting with wholesalers, academic bookstore owners, local publishers, officials in the Ministry of Education, and various academics. Ellis and Long were eager to increase Wiley's sales in the continent's leading economy, while exploring the possibility of an acquisition or at least a co-publishing arrangement. Wiley was represented by May Bowden, a sales representative whose life on the road was a dangerous one given the number of killings and carjackings at the time. Peter found it moving to visit Mamelodi, a segregated township outside Pretoria known as a center of African National Congress support, where he discovered Deborah Hughes-Hallett and Andrew Gleason's *Calculus* being taught in a brand new community college. In the long run, Ellis and Long decided that Wiley was best represented by increasing its sales efforts. Publishing opportunities at the post-secondary level remained modest, but opportunity existed to develop sales of market-priced college textbooks as well as professional and trade books for business readers. Wiley long ago had learned the lesson that a patient presence in a less-developed country could eventually lead to larger sales.

The Move to Hoboken

While Wiley became a global publishing company, its headquarters moved across the Hudson River to Hoboken. New York had long been one of the United States' two capital cities. Washington (where Brad Sr. once thought about moving Wiley) ruled in politics; New York in finance, fashion, the performing arts, and publishing. Because Manhattan, in particular, symbolized publishing as powerfully as Wall Street symbolized finance, it was hard for some to think of publishing happening anywhere else. But Wiley, by the end of the millennium, had long since become more than a New York publishing company; its publishing offices and markets extended around the world. As Wiley outgrew its offices at 605 Third Avenue in New York, its senior managers looked elsewhere, reviewing sites inside and outside the city. Hoboken, across the Hudson River to the west, beckoned, and in the summer of 2002, after 195 years in Manhattan, the company began moving its headquarters to a new building on Hoboken's waterfront.

The move across the river cut lease costs dramatically. Wiley's lease for eight floors in the Waterfront Corporate Center began with an initial rental rate that was a little more than half the rental rate for the New York offices. Wiley also benefited from a package of tax and other incentives worth $17 million over the 15 years of the lease. "There are lots of different ways to spend money," Pesce noted. "I wanted to take it from the landlord and give it back to stockholders and invest in technology." Yet the move was animated by far more than cost savings. The new building had significantly more community space (conference rooms, cafeteria, pantries) than the cramped New York building, where board meetings, Peter Wiley recalled, were "enhanced by the noise of the nearby elevator bank, which made it sound like we were meeting in a bowling alley." From Pesce's standpoint, the new facility would be "more supportive of Wiley's culture"—more collegial, more technology-friendly. "What we hoped to accomplish,"

The 2002 ribbon-cutting ceremony in Hoboken, with, from left, Deborah Wiley, Stephen Kippur, Bonnie Lieberman, John Jarvis, Stephen Smith, Richard Rudick, Hoboken Mayor David Roberts, Will Pesce, SJP Properties CEO Steven J. Pozycki, Peter Wiley, Clifford Kline, Eric Swanson, William Arlington, Timothy King, and Ellis Cousens.

he said, "was to have more collaborative meeting space, to have the technology more seamlessly integrated into the facility, to have it be a more open environment."[177]

Since the unsettled days of the late 1980s, Wiley had become not only "the place to be" but a place where talented people came to stay, and the company did not want to lose personnel because of the move. As a consequence, under Timothy King's supervision, the move was undertaken only after much deliberation and with a strategic and tactical precision that was typical of how the *new* Wiley executed its plans. Committees were organized to discuss and plan the move, and delegations of colleagues visited the new space. The process was as collaborative as possible, with colleagues helping to design their own new work spaces and define the relationships among them. Steps were taken, such as the establishment of a bus service from Grand Central Station in New York to Wiley's new office and commuting subsidies, to ease the transition. Quality-of-life surveys conducted before and after the move indicated a strong consensus that work life was better in New Jersey. In turn, Wiley made life better for Hoboken, where the presence of its relatively well paid employees attracted better retailers and restaurateurs as well as other solid businesses. Wiley's efforts to be a good corporate citizen, evidenced by working with the public school system, became more effective in Hoboken, where the company could have a bigger impact in a smaller community.[178]

The relocation of Wiley's headquarters was accompanied by significant investments in new offices elsewhere in the world. Having grown too large for the converted Corn Exchange in Chichester, the British office was moved to the Atrium, a new building in the center of town. In Germany, VCH added a new wing to its Weinheim offices. Canada moved its warehouse to a new facility in 2004, while the Australian headquarters in Brisbane moved to a new building in 2005. The days of foreign subsidiaries were over. Wiley was no longer an American company with overseas markets and operations. Now there were publishing programs in nine countries outside the United States—Australia, Canada, China, England, India, Singapore, Japan, Korea, and Germany. Out of necessity, global planning, which Brad Sr. had evoked in 1982, was finally becoming a reality.[179]

Computers and Worklife at Wiley

The pace of change at Wiley accelerated in the 1990s with the advent of voice mail, e-mail, video conferencing, and especially the Internet as a vehicle of content delivery. "If there ever was a leisurely pace to publishing, that changed dramatically in the '90s," said Jeff Brown, who managed Professional/Trade's business and psychology programs. "Communication became more direct. Where once you'd send a letter to an author through the U.S. mail, or leave a message with an assistant, now there was e-mail, which compressed the whole manuscript development process."[180]

Computers and e-mail dramatically increased expectations of "how much you could accomplish in a day," Brown continued. Authors' ability to prepare their manuscripts on computers, and the capacity for subsequent electronic editing, saved a great deal of time and paper. "But some fundamentals don't change," he cautioned. "You still have to take time to read a 400-page manuscript, and editorial recommendations and choices are still human judgments." Nor did computers, even with their word-counting functions, make estimating book length easier. In the old days, "typewriters had only two sizes of type," said George Telecki, associate publisher of electrical and computer engineering books—"pica and elite. An experienced editor could look over a typewritten manuscript and quickly estimate a proposed book's final page count quite accurately." Moreover, the computer's capacity for formatting and for inserting illustrations sometimes led authors to "think they've done everything necessary short of actually printing the book," said Telecki, but "considerations of layout, design, and typography . . . often preclude our accommodating their ideas."[181]

Nevertheless, computerization and the Internet had a powerful effect on how Wiley did business. "From my perspective, the Web has changed everything," said Gregory St. John, vice president of web publishing technology. Wiley's host of technology solutions "have utterly changed our dialogue with customers, sales channel partners, and suppliers. With our authors and typesetters, we think 'online first' now for a sizable portion of our content." Online sales, either directly through wiley.com or through channel partners like amazon.com and barnesandnoble.com, became increasingly important. In addition, "Wiley InterScience and *WileyPLUS* have brought us a whole new relationship with our customers by allowing us to see how they are using our information, which then helps us design better products for them . . . As our products evolve, so do our business models, as well as our approaches to marketing and sales." In short, concluded St. John, "The Web has fundamentally changed customer expectations . . . It really is a different world, and it's only just beginning."[182]

Susan Elbe, vice president and publisher for business disciplines, elaborated on how this new dialogue with customers played out in Higher Education. "*WileyPLUS* combines electronic texts with resources for online study and administration of homework, tests, and other course elements," she said. "We can monitor overall

activity in it, and learn how students interact with the content. In the future, we'll be communicating much more directly with them through blogs, podcasts, and e-mail, and we'll be able to give them more choices about how they access our products—online, e-book, or print, offered in a range of price points to fit their budgets."[183]

"In essence, our customers are becoming virtual focus groups," said Margie Schustack, head of Professional/Trade marketing operations. "We can listen to constituencies and communities on the Internet, and have direct access to what they think and feel in ways we never could before. It's less and less about us coming up with a catchy slogan and advertising it to everyone, and more and more about giving people the information they want, when and how they want it." But as with the fundamentals of editing, some things don't change. "Brands have taken on a new importance," concluded Schustack. "People like to know that the information they're getting is coming from a source they can trust."[184]

Protective Engagement

As distinctions diminished between home and abroad, and as Wiley committed itself to growth as a global entity composed of a diversified and balanced portfolio of businesses, the firm's governance also demanded renewal. On January 1, 1993, Brad II replaced his father as Wiley's chairman. Form followed fact here; with Brad Sr. aging in the late 1980s, Brad II had stepped in already as a de facto leader of the board. He participated in the decisions about the transitions in leadership from Neilly to McMullin and on to Ellis. During the troubled 1980s, Brad and his siblings, drawing a clear line between oversight and management, spelled out their commitment to active participation in governance and support for professional management. The board with Brad II in the chair resembled in some ways the board his father had chaired. The tasks were the same: critical oversight, including an annual review of management's strategic plan, review of quarterly financial

THE *Publishing craft*

DIGITAL PRODUCTION COMES OF AGE

In the 1990s, faster computers with greater capacities for graphics and new typesetting technologies transformed the printing craft. Instead of standing at drafting tables and working with pens, pencils, T-squares, waxers, and loupes, creative artists began doing it all on computer screens. The change was a little slow in coming. "We had to write a long proposal to justify the [1993] purchase of our first computer used for design, a little Mac," said Jean Morley, head of the team that created book covers as well as advertising and promotional materials for Professional/Trade and STM. "Within a month, it had proven its worth."[185]

But some new issues have arisen. "You can't make an oil painting look like a watercolor; it's a different medium," said Morley. "The same is true of an image as it appears on screen, compared to a [digital] printout . . . or its final printed version. Designers have to know what the end result is going to look like, and our challenge is not just to educate ourselves, but the publishing teams, too." As elsewhere, the fundamentals of line, shape, color, form, and texture still apply, said Morley. "It's important when I'm hiring that I find people who still have intuition and a sensibility for those things, and not just the technical skill."[186]

At the same time, cultural reverberations from the media—television, and, increasingly, the Internet—began to inform product design and development, particularly in Higher Education. "MTV and electronic devices, with their intense color and visual fragmentation, have affected the way students learn," said Madelyn Lesure, who designs textbooks and the packaging for their supplementary media. "Our designs had to reflect that, while keeping the integrity of our content."[187]

Typesetting, too, changed dramatically. Digital typesetting allowed for data transfer, enabling publishers to outsource manuscripts to keyboarders, typesetters, illustrators, and media producers worldwide. Offshore outsourcing of composition was a cost-saving measure that often improved quality while allowing resources to be allocated toward additional services.

*J*ean Morley, vice president, Creative Services

The development of Portable Document Format (PDF) by Adobe Systems in the early 1990s, and its subsequent refinements, allowed for the transfer of exact duplicates of pages, including fonts and artwork, between different computer platforms (Macs and PCs). Files could be saved at different resolutions, allowing for screen or print views. Plating technology soon allowed printers to plot plates directly from PDF files and eventually to develop direct-to-press printing technology that bypassed plates completely. Proofing, too, began to be computerized: Authors, designers, and production people began to proofread PDFs, marking them up electronically in Adobe Acrobat and avoiding the mail delay and the sometimes illegible handwriting of traditional proofing. "Electronically, everything is trackable," said Morley. It also saved time and rendered geographical boundaries irrelevant.[188]

The development of PDF also created a boom in short-run digital printing, and print on demand (POD), which made it economically possible to print one book at a time, allowed publishers to keep low-selling books in print. POD was also used for custom printing and for personalizing mailing pieces, while

*M*adelyn Lesure, senior designer and manager, Media Design

*A*nn Berlin, vice president,
Production and
Manufacturing, Higher Education

PDF was used in the production of electronic books.

The launch of the World Wide Web in the early 1990s had a profound impact on distribution. Online publications could be sold individually or by subscription, and interactivity made products more useful and entertaining. Expanding beyond print products, publishers produced and sold content in myriad formats. To do so, they had to move beyond QuarkXPress page layout and PDF to HTML, Java, Flash, and an ever-expanding array of other tools.[189]

Content management systems and digital archives became important tools for the management and storage of content for easy retrieval and reuse, and coding systems were developed to allow file sharing and the generation of both electronic and print products. SGML (Standard Generalized Markup Language) was originally developed so that the government and large industries could share documents that had to be available over decades. The idea was to code elements within documents by element function, not appearance. The coded document could be used to generate myriad products. A successor, XML (Extensible Markup Language), was developed by the World Wide Web Committee and released in 1997. Similar to SGML but simpler to use, it gained much wider usage. XML also allowed the production of alternative versions of texts, for example, for physically impaired readers.[190]

Electronic books combined text content with the ability to search inside the book, and online books allowed for links outside the book, to other Web sites and to content such as simulations, online quizzes, audio, and video. Although slow to gain in popularity, hundreds of thousands of electronic books were available for sale by 2007.

*E*lizabeth Doble, vice
president, Production
and Manufacturing, P/T

423

*F*ull speed on web
printing press

*A*nna Melhorn, senior illustration editor, Higher
Education, working with Adobe Acrobat files
for this book, *Knowledge for Generations*

*T*he Quark file for the cover of *Psychology in
Action* by Karen Huffman

results, evaluation of the CEO's performance, planning for CEO succession, and reviewing and setting compensation levels for the CEO and his leadership team. Essential to maintaining best governance practices was diligent and supportive monitoring of the relationships among the family, the board, and management. Rigorous board recruitment procedures were initiated in the 1980s and improved on in the 1990s. The board began to evaluate its own performance starting in 1995, well before the Sarbanes-Oxley law of 2002 mandated it.[191]

Under Brad II, the board continued to reflect a diverse range of professional experiences. Andrew H. Neilly Jr. and Charles B. Stoll, respectively vice chairman and a Wiley retiree, represented continuity with the company's publishing past, as did H. Allen Fernald, president and CEO of Down East Enterprises, a family publishing firm based in Maine. Gary J. Fernandes, senior vice president of Electronic Data Systems, and William R. Sutherland, director of Sun Microsystems Laboratories, came from companies that were both

Chichester

Indianapolis

Toronto

Somerset

Brisbane

San Francisco

Weinheim

Hoboken

customers and companions in the effort to master the intricacies of technological change. Marketing was represented, as were banking and the chemical industry, another large Wiley R&D-driven customer. What was missing since the retirement of Dr. Robert Sproull, a Wiley author and president of the University of Rochester, was an eminent academic. That seat was filled in 1993 by Dr. Warren Baker, president of California Polytechnic State University San Luis Obispo. The three Wileys brought the board's size to 15. The emerging board was characterized by fewer long-standing interpersonal relationships, more careful selection of board candidates, and a greater geographical diversity than before.[192]

*B*rad Wiley II, past chairman of the board and current board member

Brad's first challenge came almost immediately, when the Bass Management Trust bought 8.4 percent of Wiley's A shares in 1994. The Bass fortune came from Texas oilman Sid Richardson and was managed by Thomas Taylor. Taylor contacted Wiley, proposing that he, as the purported representative of Wiley's A shareholders, should name five members to Wiley's board. Taylor appeared to have the support of the largest nonfamily owner of A shares. To outsiders, it must have looked like Wiley was still struggling to survive despite two new CEOs and the transition from Brad Sr. to the sixth generation. From the inside, it was apparent that under Ellis's leadership, Wiley was well on its way to a dramatic turnaround. There had been a number of buyout offers in the 1980s, all of which were rejected by the family. At the same time as the Bass purchase, Wiley B shares were also being acquired by Theodore L. Cross, a publisher with experience in start-ups and mergers. No one at Wiley had ever encountered the kind of blustery Texas hardball favored by Taylor. After a series of negotiations between Ellis, Peter Wiley, who chaired the Committee on Directors, and Taylor, it was agreed, under threat of a proxy fight, that Taylor would join two other candidates of his choice on the board slate for the annual election in September 1993.[193]

Taylor's contributions as a board member were mixed. The presence of a large outside investor encouraged Ellis and CFO Robert Wilder to increase their communication with the investing community, which meant more opportunities to explain just how well Wiley had done since the 1993 turnaround. Taylor called for a business unit analysis. He was particularly interested in the underperforming Higher Education business, leading the Wileys and Ellis to suspect that the analysis might be the first step in an attempt to break up the company. In fact, the analysis demonstrated that despite Higher Education's lagging performance, which was improving, Wiley's three core businesses fit well together, linking students to postgraduates and ultimately to professionals in Wiley's selected disciplines.[194]

Taylor's presence changed the tone and substance of board meetings. Discussions were guarded, while Taylor showed little interest in the underlying issues facing a publishing business, focusing instead on the ownership structure and quarterly financial performance. At times, he seemed consumed with following stock prices on a small hand-held device. As a consequence, discussions of financial issues increased at the expense of strategic analysis. During the board debate prior to the VCH acquisition in 1996, one Bass board member complained that the purchase would have a negative impact on the quarter's earnings per share.

426

"Five weeks is a long time in this business," he announced, to the astonishment of other board members. ("I assume," Peter remarked, "he was discussing the investment, not the publishing business." To those familiar with publishing, "the five-week [earnings per share] impact of an acquisition with the strategic importance of VCH is totally inconsequential.")[195]

When Will Pesce was elected CEO in 1998, he, Brad, and Henry McKinnell Jr., the chairman and CEO of Pfizer, who had joined the board in 1996, agreed that a smaller board would enhance discussions of both financial and strategic issues. The slate of board candidates presented to shareholders in the summer of 1999 contained ten directors. One of the Bass directors had left earlier due to lack of interest and nonparticipation. A second was dropped from the slate. Deborah Wiley also withdrew from the slate: With only ten board members, the Wileys preferred to give up one seat on the board so as to increase the proportion of outside directors and make clear their commitment to board independence. The next year, the Bass family replaced Taylor with John L. Marion Jr., and Marion was added to Wiley's board with the strong support of board members and management. Board discussions improved dramatically, with Marion, a thoughtful student of publishing and publishing technology, making important contributions.[196]

As performance improved and it became clear that the sixth generation of Wileys was fulfilling their governance responsibilities, Wiley was no longer considered a takeover target. When Harcourt General made a cautious inquiry in 1997, the Wileys discussed with the board why, as the majority shareholders, they were declining Harcourt's offer. Speaking on behalf of the family, Peter explained that the family believed the value of the company could best be maximized by realizing the company's strategic planning under the existing management and ownership structure, and that discussions with Harcourt would have a destabilizing effect on the company, its staff, and its authors, which could undermine its value. Harcourt General's owners, it

turned out, did not have a long-term interest in publishing. They sold Harcourt General's publishing operations to Elsevier shortly thereafter.[197]

There had been differences of opinion on the board about the impact of family control on share price and valuation. Taylor raised the issue soon after his election to the board, pointing to a study that argued that shares in companies with a control group traded at a discount— meaning that Wiley was undervalued because of the family's presence. But, insofar as the public equity market provides one form of valuation for publicly traded firms with a family control group, the steady appreciation of Wiley shares during the 1990s appeared to refute Taylor's argument. A 2003 study in the *Journal of Law and Economics* based on more recent research on family firms argued that "in large publicly traded companies, firms with founding family presence outperform those with more dispersed ownership structures [and] that the salient element in limiting family opportunism in U.S. firms is the relative influence of independent and family directors." The consensus at Wiley was that family control protected the corporation—its financial health, its ability to plan for the long term, and its necessarily creative culture—while a board with a majority that was independent encouraged the critical oversight necessary to stay the course.[198]

In 2002, Brad II passed the baton to his younger brother Peter who felt strongly that he had to continue to preside over an active board of directors. Brad II, with board input and support, had insisted on best governance practices. Peter would do the same. The "professionalization" of the Wiley board, which paralleled Brad Sr.'s earlier insistence on the professionalization of management, would continue.

In all matters pertaining to the company, the family spoke less in shouts than in whispers. After he left the board, McKinnell described the Wileys less as supervisors than facilitators among equals on the board. The Wileys used their influence prudently, their veto never. "You would think," McKinnell continued, "in a two-tier board structure like Wiley's that it would matter who was elected by the family and who was elected by the shareholders. Nobody ever knew. If you ask me was I an A director or a B director, I didn't know."[199]

Family involvement was also based on the idea that presence was an important aspect of protective engagement. Each sibling brought a different background to this presence, Brad as a magazine, newspaper, and Higher Education editor; Peter as an editor, journalist, and author; and Deborah as a long-time Wiley editor with a long history of industry involvement. Presence meant attending events such as sales meetings, where family members could interact with large numbers of

Selected Publishing Mergers and Acquisitions, 1990–2002

Acquirer	Acquisitions / Events (by year)
General Cinema	• Harcourt, Brace Jovanovich 1991 • General Cinema's name changed to Harcourt General 1993
Thomson	• Maxwell Macmillan Professional and Business Reference 1991 • Course Technology 1992 • West 1996 • Harcourt Higher Education 2001
Paramount Communications	• Macmillan Computer Publishing 1991 • Macmillan Publishing USA, (including Jossey-Bass) 1994
Reed Elsevier	• Reed and Elsevier merge 1992 • Harcourt General (including Academic, W. B. Saunders, Mosby) 2001
CBS (as Viacom)	• Paramount (including Simon & Schuster, Macmillan, Jossey-Bass, and Prentice Hall) 1994 • Jossey-Bass acquires Pfeiffer 1996
Von Holtzbrinck	• Farrar, Straus & Giroux 1994 • Macmillan Ltd 1999
Pearson	• HarperCollins 1996 • Scott, Foresman 1996 • Simon & Schuster Educational, Professional, and Reference; Macmillan; Jossey-Bass; Allyn & Bacon; and Prentice Hall 1998
McGraw-Hill	• Times Mirror Higher Education (including Irwin, Mosby College, and Wm. C. Brown) 1996 • Appleton-Lange 1999 • Tribune Education 2000
Wiley	• VCH 1996 • Van Nostrand Reinhold 1997 • 55 higher education Pearson titles 1999 • Jossey-Bass 1999 • Hungry Minds 2001
Bertelsmann	• Random House 1998 • Springer-Verlag 1999
Vivendi	• Houghton Mifflin 2001

1990   1995   2000   2005

Sources: *The Encyclopedia of New York City* edited by Jenneth T. Jackson, "Book Publishing," Yale University Press, 1995
The Columbia Electronic Encyclopedia 6th edition, 2006 Columbia University Press (website)
Mergers, Acquisitions and Access STM Publishing Today, by Kathleen Robertson. Library and Information Services in Astronomy IV July 2-5, 2002
Company websites.
The Academic Publishing Industry, A Story of Merger and Acquisition, by Mary H. Monroe. Prepared for the Association of Research Libraries (website)

*D*eborah Wiley with, from left, Barry Z. Posner and James M. Kouzes, authors of *The Leadership Challenge.*

their colleagues, or visiting Wiley's increasingly far-flung offices. It meant meeting with individuals or small groups of colleagues, whether editors or warehouse staff, to find out more about their work lives and their publishing insights, and with authors and customers whenever called upon to do so. Peter liked to describe Wiley as having "a listening culture" where each colleague was respected and plumbed for his or her special knowledge. Presence also meant continuing their father's involvement in industry affairs. Deborah Wiley raised funds for the New York Public Library, sat on the boards of the Association of American Publishers and the Book Industry Study Group, and chaired both the AAP's International Committee and its International Copyright Protection Committee. She also chaired the National Book Foundation from 1996 to 2007. "They are very interested in people's thoughts and perceptions of the market," Bonnie Lieberman observed, adding that the Wileys often met with author prospects to speak about Wiley and the Wiley family commitment.[200]

One concern tempered the advantages of family control: the fear of lassitude. Brad II once observed that family ownership "can generate an atmosphere internally of unwarranted security, complacency, and uncritical loyalty to an enterprise whose ownership structure is relatively independent of market influences." The Wiley family was patient, but patience had limits. "Management requires a degree of autonomy to run the business," the Wileys wrote, *"as long as performance is satisfactory"* (emphasis added). On the positive side, Brad II said, family ownership could engender a "corporate environment conducive to creativity and integrity in product and staff." From the mailroom to the boardroom, Wiley employees knew they need not fear a takeover as long as the Wiley family controlled the company, and thus they could focus confidently on the long term, not the next quarter. Veteran Wiley editor Wayne Anderson said that though he frequently heard the mantra that the company was too small and would soon be gobbled up by one of the big players, he took solace in family control, adding that Brad made it a point "to assure the staff that we were not going to be sold. We were encouraged by what he said." Eric Swanson explained that "the influence of family . . . is one of the powerful plusses here" and makes Wiley decidedly different from other companies.[201]

Small publishers tend to be nimble, with low overhead, lean staffs, and close ties to niche markets, but they also must play it safe or risk swift annihilation. Large publishers face fewer financial constraints and can better weather market turbulence, but they can also be difficult to manage and can lose touch with authors and customers. Wiley consciously strove for a middle position that, according to the 1997 Annual Report, "allows us to be highly focused and agile, with short lines of communication, and to identify opportunity and move quickly to capitalize on it." The best validation of this approach was that the company, using scenario planning, was able to write *and* execute its strategic plans. It produced reliable organic growth, and after earlier disappointments, such as Wilson Learning, all of Wiley's large acquisitions under Ellis and Pesce proved wise decisions.[202]

The Wileys' engagement, the family argued, was designed to protect Wiley's independence. The Wileys were often heard to say that they would worry about independence and the resulting stability of the company so that their colleagues could focus on quality publishing without concerns about who might be their next owner, as the employees of so many other publishing companies had over the years. Independence was a strategic asset: it was beneficial to Wiley's staff and to its authors, customers, and shareholders. The family could point to the continuation of Wiley's long history of quality publishing and the company's financial results as proof of their argument.

The Wiley family's continuing and carefully institutionalized relationship with the firm infused the organization with a mood of steadfastness plus excitement. It communicated to employees, and not just employees near the top, that work life could be both stable and mobile and that time spent on the job for Wiley was time spent for themselves and for larger communities too.

The years between 1989 and 2002 bore witness to the most radical transformations in Wiley's 200-year history. Wiley was still deeply committed to publishing, but publishing itself had changed. And Wiley, having mastered judicious and controlled experimentation, had sometimes kept pace with those changes, at other times had forged ahead. Charles Ellis brought Wiley back from the brink of disaster by focusing on publishing fundamentals and Wiley's three core businesses. He and his colleagues introduced Wiley to scenario planning, which brought both rigor and flexibility to Wiley's strategic planning process. Scenario planning, among other things, guided a dramatic step-up in investment in technology, supporting not only the creation of an internal global communications system replete with new publishing tools, but also—in the most profound shift in modern publishing—the transformation of Wiley content to a digital format and from there its delivery to customers via the World Wide Web. In another breakthrough, Ellis and company moved Wiley away from the traditional organization of an American company with foreign subsidiaries toward global coordination and then planning.

With Ellis's departure, Will Pesce took up the leadership reins, emphasizing as he had in his successful turnaround of the Higher Education business that Wiley needed to continue to build on positive changes in the company's work culture in a highly self-conscious way. Wiley was to become "the place to be." Pesce urged his colleagues to challenge themselves to follow through with their ideas about change in the workplace by measuring the results *and* making additional changes in areas where the company had fallen short. Collaboration became a Pesce watchword: collaboration among colleagues in Wiley's three businesses and greater collaboration across geographical boundaries. Collaboration would eventually lead to global planning, another radical departure, in STM, and to the beginnings of global planning in P/T and Higher Education. Both the Ellis and Pesce leadership teams added to Wiley's underlying growth by making larger and larger acquisitions, the most important of which were Alan R. Liss, VCH, Jossey-Bass, and Hungry Minds. They chose companies that complemented and built on Wiley's core businesses and then, with great skill, carefully integrated these new enterprises into global Wiley. The company's mastery of the strategic planning process meant that when Ellis and Pesce told Wiley's board of directors on an annual basis that they would deliver certain financial results, they did at least that and often much better. In the ten years between 1992 and 2002, Wiley's revenue grew from $255 million to $734 million, more than tripling in size, while earnings per share rose from $.05 to $1.03, and the stock price, after stock splits were taken into account, grew by a factor of ten from $2.52 to $26.60. Over these years, Wiley had changed from a venerable publisher struggling to sustain its traditions to a recognized leader in the global publishing industry.[203]

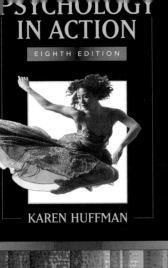

PSYCHOLOGY IN ACTION

EIGHTH EDITION

KAREN HUFFMAN

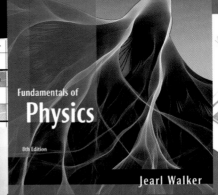

Su Do Ku
FOR DUMMIES

Andrew Heron

James

Fundamentals of

Physics

8th Edition

Jearl Walker

The

Profess

ch

The Culinary Ins

int™ fo
plicatio

AIChE

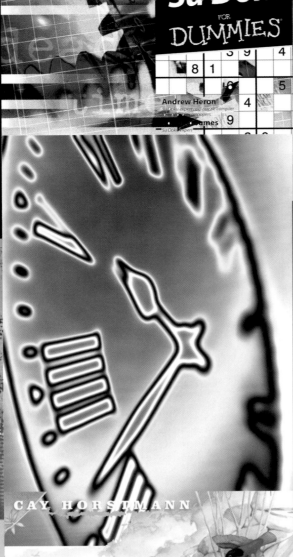

CAY HORSTMANN

THE

MERCK MANUAL

EIGHTEENTH EDITION

New York Times Bestseller

New for 2004
30-page Update!

CONQUER
THE CRASH

You Can SURVIVE and PROSPER
in a Deflationary Depression

Expanded and Updated

Robert R Prechter Jr

er

assSpectrometryReviews

The #1 Journal in
Spectroscopy
Impact Factor
13.2731

WILEY

InterScience

ULLMANN'S
Sixth Edition

ENCYCLOPEDIA
OF
INDUSTRIAL
CHEMISTRY

WILEY-VCH

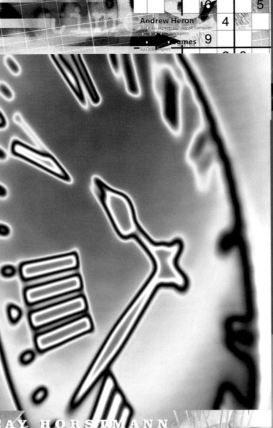

BIG
JAVA

2ND EDITION

MTV
EUROPE

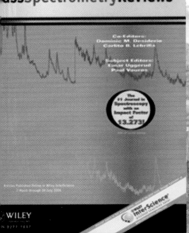

JAN

Caption

JOURNAL OF ADVANCED NURS

Betty Crocker

COOKB

Everything You
Need to Know to
Cook Today

Ushering In Wiley's Third Century

Chapter Nine

✦

Publishing Without Boundaries

In early 2002, as Wiley prepared to move its global headquarters across the Hudson after 195 years in New York City, a question about title pages arose. Like other publishers, Wiley traditionally listed the cities where it had locations on its title pages. By replacing "New York" with "Hoboken," would Wiley lose the prestige of publishing from one of the world's historic publishing centers?

Deborah Wiley's response sent a message about Wiley in the 21st century: she eliminated the list of cities altogether! With Wiley publishing from more than 20 locations, the development and proliferation of the World Wide Web, and the emergence of a truly global marketplace, the physicality of the book and its publishing location were less and less important.

Wiley was redefining what it meant by "publishing." Communication around the world among Wiley colleagues, authors, editors, partners, and customers became far more rapid, often taking place in real-time. In addition to delivering content printed on paper between the covers of a book or journal, Wiley was now able to interact with customers in entirely new ways. The company began to deliver content directly into their workflows and educational processes—customized tools to help them achieve their objectives. Through these new ways of publishing, the author could engage customers in a continuous dialogue—akin to Norbert Wiener's famous feedback mechanism—about what they wanted to read plus how they wanted to use the content. These new possibilities for content creation, enhancement, and distribution were creating new markets and opening up new sales channels.

Embracing Risk

The Chinese expressions for "crisis," *wei ji* 危機; "transition," *zhuan ji* 轉機; and "opportunity," *ji hui* 機會, all share the character for "risk," *ji* 機.[1] So Wiley colleagues read in the in-house publication *Wiley World* in 1998, when interest in China was heating up. *Ji* is an appropriate notion with which to close this history of Wiley. History never stands still. Events surge ahead ceaselessly, moving at a faster pace than ever. How well the company manages the continuing risk of crisis, transition, and opportunity will determine the direction of the next chapters of Wiley history. Success will strengthen the company's culture, business, and financial performance. Failure will inhibit the company's ability to respond to accelerating marketplace challenges.[1]

The first notable act of Wiley's third century illustrated the company's appetite for calculated risk when the opportunity is great and its promise is achievable. On Friday morning, November 17, 2006, the eve of its bicentennial, Wiley announced that it had entered into a definitive agreement to acquire the outstanding shares of Blackwell Publishing (Holdings) Ltd. The acquisition was completed on February 5, 2007.

Based in Oxford, England, Blackwell Publishing is one of the world's foremost academic and professional publishers. Known as the world's preeminent society publisher because of its partnerships with 665 academic, medical, and professional societies, Blackwell published 825 journals and had more than 6,000 books in print. Its revenue in 2006 was approximately £224 million, roughly equivalent to that of Wiley's global STM business. Blackwell's publishing programs included journals, books, and online content in the sciences, technology, medicine, the social

*R*ené Olivieri, chief operating officer, Wiley-Blackwell

*R*obert Campbell, senior publisher, Wiley-Blackwell

sciences, and the humanities. Besides Oxford, Blackwell has offices in Edinburgh; Berlin; Copenhagen; Malden, Massachussetts; Ames, Iowa; Melbourne; Singapore; Tokyo; and Shanghai. Blackwell Ltd., the library services and retailing business, was not part of the acquisition. The purchase price of £572 million, or approximately U.S. $1.2 billion, was financed with a combination of debt and cash.

At the time of publication of *Knowledge for Generations*, the integration of the two businesses was moving ahead on schedule. There are risks involved in any transaction of this magnitude, but Wiley's successful track record with acquisitions, as well as the high degree of compatibility between the two companies' publishing programs, markets, missions, values, and cultures, has substantially reduced the risks. Managing change will no doubt present challenges, but Wiley's and Blackwell's leaders are confident that the constituencies they serve are benefiting from the combined companies' enhanced capabilities.

Before announcing the agreement, Wiley secured commitments from Blackwell's five major shareholders (Nigel Blackwell, Julian Blackwell, Philip Blackwell, René Olivieri, and Robert Campbell), as well as the support of its board. The Blackwells and the board let it be known that they would only support a sale to a company like Wiley, another venerable publisher with a founding family still involved and a culture deeply rooted in similar values. When a major competitor provided a financially attractive offer to acquire Blackwell in the days preceding Wiley's announcement of the transaction, it was rejected by Blackwell's board of directors, who remained firmly committed to Wiley. "People sometimes ask me to quantify the value of Wiley being *the place to be*. Based on this experience, I can now tell them," explained Pesce.[2]

A Long Courtship

The Blackwell announcement, which came on the 96th anniversary of W. Bradford Wiley's birth and nearly eight years after his death, marked the consummation of a half-century-long courtship. Brad Sr. had pursued Richard Blackwell about acquiring Blackwell decades before at the Frankfurt Book Fair. The mutual regard and respect between Wiley's and Blackwell's leaders never waned, even after they passed the reins to their successors: Throughout the 1990s and into the new millennium, Will Pesce, Tim King, John Jarvis, Eric Swanson, René Olivieri (Blackwell's CEO), Robert Campbell (Blackwell's president), and Nigel Blackwell (Blackwell's chairman) carefully cultivated a continuing relationship by leading industry initiatives together while competing for the same authors and society partnerships in a way that elicited mutual admiration.[3]

The competitive sparring between the two companies took an ironic twist with one medical journal. During the mid-1980s, the British Diabetic Association (BDA) decided it wanted to lend its name to a new journal, to be called *Diabetic Medicine,* and sought a publishing partner. At the BDA's annual meeting at the University of Norwich, Peter Saugman, son of Per Saugman (managing director of Blackwell Scientific in the 1960s) bid for the opportunity, almost as a formality, assuming it was a done deal. There was, however, late and unexpected competition from Wiley's U.K. medical publisher, John Jarvis, and managing director, Charles Stoll, whose "soft, yet authoritative, American voice was perfect on the day." Wiley won the contract and began a fifteen-year-long publishing relationship with the BDA. Publishing is all about ebb and flow, and in the late 1990s, Blackwell finally took *Diabetic Medicine* away from Wiley. There was a lot of good-humored banter when Wiley realized that it would regain the journal through the Blackwell acquisition.[4]

A meeting between Pesce and Nigel Blackwell in London in March 2002 strengthened the relationship between the two companies and their leadership. At the time, a major competitor was aggressively pursuing Blackwell. Nigel's uncle Julian supported the bid, and their disagreement became public. Pesce made it clear that Wiley was interested in joining forces with Blackwell, however long it took, but he promised he would not pursue the matter until Nigel and his leadership team were ready to do so. Swanson and Jarvis served as Wiley ambassadors for the next couple of years, staying in touch with Campbell, Olivieri, and others on industry matters, but there was no further serious discussion until 2005, when Peter Wiley and Jarvis approached Nigel Blackwell and Olivieri. In 2006, Pesce, King, Swanson, Jarvis, and Ellis Cousens, Wiley's chief financial and operations officer, met Olivieri, Campbell, and CFO Chris Hall. The meeting began as an exploration of the benefits of a joint venture or partnership, such as combining technology platforms. As the discussions progressed, it became clear to all that the two companies shared many values and placed similar importance on their excellent relationships with society partners, customers, and colleagues. It was also unmistakable that their publishing programs and organizational strengths were uniquely complementary. The meeting resulted in a growing mutual respect and a continuing dialogue.[5]

In the following months, Pesce and Olivieri spoke frequently, evaluating a range of strategic possibilities. They concluded that together Wiley and Blackwell could deliver even greater value to customers, authors, society partners, and shareholders than they could as separate entities. As a result, the Blackwell board granted Wiley the opportunity to make a purchase offer on an exclusive basis. After careful reviews of the financial and strategic possibilities, including a scenario planning analysis, Wiley's board of directors voted to support Pesce's proposal, and Blackwell's board and principal shareholders accepted Wiley's offer

PROFILE

BLACKWELL PUBLISHING

Blackwell Publishing, like Wiley, was a company with a long and honorable tradition dating from 1845, when Benjamin Harris Blackwell, the son of a tailor from London's East End, opened a second-hand bookstore just outside the Oxford city limits. When Benjamin died in 1854, his widow had to shutter the shop.[6]

In 1879, Benjamin Henry ("Harry") Blackwell, the son of Benjamin Harris, opened B.H. Blackwell, a shop selling "Second-Hand Books in Ancient and Modern Literature" near the Oxford University colleges. Harry was a self-taught man from a modest background. His widowed mother supported her three children by doing needlework. At the age of 13, Harry left school—to his everlasting regret—to be apprenticed to a bookseller. In his own firm, Harry moved quickly into the new book business, starting with an education catalogue in the shop's first year. In 1895, he published his first catalogue of European titles, noting the presence of Blackwell agents "in the leading Continental Cities." The expansion of the British Empire and its institutionalization, including the construction of numerous universities at home and abroad, provided Blackwell with an important outlet for its books and historical documents. By 1913, India had become its largest overseas market, but American academic libraries also became important customers.[7]

Harry's amicable relations with Oxford dons and their students led to the publication in 1879 of Blackwell's first book, *Mensae Secundae: Verses Written in Balliol College*, and then the publication of a poetry magazine called *Waifs and Strays*. Blackwell soon became known in Oxford circles as "the literary man's house-of-call." Harry continued to publish manuscripts—everything from a lecture titled *On an Evolutionist Theory of Axioms* to *Manual of Cyclist Drill for the Use of the Cyclist Section of the Oxford University Rifle Volunteer Corps (O.U.R.V.C.)* to *Economic Aspects of State Socialism* by Sir Howard Llewellyn Smith *(1887)*— brought to him by his Oxford neighbors. The bookstore remained at the center of his business until his son, Basil, entered the business in 1913.[8]

Unable to devote sufficient energy to building a successful publishing program, Harry placed his son,

Benjamin Henry Blackwell, known as the Founder of the Blackwell empire, opened a bookstore in Oxford in 1879, 34 years after his father's death led to the closing of the first Blackwell store in the Oxford area. Henry focused on book retailing, then on distribution, while venturing into publishing. He was also the librarian at Oxford City's first public library and a founder and the first librarian of the Temperance Society Library. His son, Basil H. Blackwell, known as the Gaffer, was born in his parents' flat above the Blackwell bookstore. The first member of the family to receive a formal education (at Oxford, of course), Basil grew the bookselling side of Blackwell while moving into many types of publishing, laying the foundation for global Blackwell. Sir Basil was the first member of the British book trade to be knighted.

Benjamin Henry Blackwell (1849–1924)

Sir Basil H. Blackwell (1889–1984)

Basil, known as the Gaffer, at the Oxford University Press for a year so that he could learn all aspects of the publishing business before joining his father in 1913. Basil, doing business as a publisher after 1922 as Blackwell & Mott, turned out to be a creative and energetic publisher with a wide range of interests including poetry, fiction, children's books, educational texts, and the Shakespeare Head Press, which he took over from its founder when it almost went out of business in 1927. Inspired by William Morris's Kelmscott Press, the

With a growing presence in school publishing, Basil turned his attention to scientific publishing in 1939 with the establishment of Blackwell Scientific Publications (BSP). Basil was inspired by the establishment of a handsome endowment for the Oxford Medical School by Lord Nuffield. The year before, Basil had suggested to the Blackwell board of directors that "the Company might be very well advised to consider the development of a medical publishing and bookselling side in conjunction with Blackwell & Mott." BSP's first title, *Essentials of General Anaesthesia* by R. R. Macintosh, appeared in 1940 and quickly sold out. BSP also distributed books on behalf of North American medical publishers.[10]

In 1946, Basil's son Richard joined B. H. Blackwell. Three years later, the year that Brad and Esther Wiley visited Europe for the first time, Richard was given "a roving commission to familiarize himself with every part of the firm's operations." In a paper titled "Specialization," he noted a number of trends that Blackwell would take advantage of, including the importance of exports, and the worldwide expansion in education.

In the postwar period, Blackwell & Mott (later called Blackwell Publishers) grew its educational publishing programs accordingly, urged on by Richard. In 1966, Richard became managing director and in 1969

CHAPTER NINE

435

.H. Blackwell, 50 Broad St., Oxford, the bookstore founded by Benjamin Henry Blackwell in 1879. Henry Blackwell and his family lived for a time above the store. One neighbor, an Oxford history professor, described the store as "the literary man's house-of-call." The bookstore was also a place with the "freedom and good fellowship of the tavern, with perhaps the same likelihood of rebuke for wasting time and money on returning home."

founder and then Basil published fine editions of classic works starting with a new edition of Shakespeare. With little capital and a small sales force, it was a challenge for Basil to compete with the established London houses, such as Macmillan and Longmans, or with the newcomers, such as Jonathan Cape, Faber & Faber, and Victor Gollancz. Basil did publish such renowned authors as W. H. Auden, Robert Graves, Graham Greene, D. H. Lawrence, A. A. Milne, Vita Sackville-West, Stephen Spender, J.R.R. Tolkien, and Evelyn Waugh.[9]

mong the famous authors published by Basil Blackwell were the poet W. H. Auden and Graham Greene. Greene took his first book, a volume of poetry titled *Babbling April*, to Blackwell in 1925.

PROFILE

BLACKWELL PUBLISHING (CONTINUED)

Three generations of Blackwells: (from left to right) Miles, Sir Basil, Nigel, Richard, and Julian. Richard and Julian are Sir Basil's sons; Miles was Julian's son; and Nigel is Richard's. All five Blackwells served as heads of various Blackwell companies. Nigel was chairman of Blackwell Publishers when it was sold to Wiley in 2007.

he replaced his father as chairman. In 1975, David Ellis was appointed managing director, the first nonfamily manager to assume this senior position.[11]

Meanwhile, BSP was also growing rapidly under Per Saugman, a Dane who joined the firm as sales manager in 1952. The company broke new ground in medical publishing by visiting medical schools to identify and sign young textbook authors, who later became eminent professors. In 1955, Saugman, who by now was managing director, started BSP's journals list by launching the *British Journal of Haematology*. From the mid-1960s, BSP gained international status, expanding into biology under the direction of editor Robert Campbell starting in 1968, and building its expertise in journal publishing. BSP opened an office in Edinburgh in 1966, initially to support book publishing, but ultimately it became solely devoted to journals production. In 1963, the company purchased Munksgaard of Copenhagen,

which developed a strong journals list in dentistry, dermatology, immunology, and transplantation. And in 1971, BSP started a venture in Melbourne, Australia, which later became a wholly owned subsidiary.[12]

In the late 1970s, a new managing director, David Martin, transformed Blackwell Publishers into a world-recognized publisher of outstanding academic books. René Olivieri took over as managing director in 1987. With the financial demands of building up the scholarly book publishing program and the introduction of the National Curriculum in the United Kingdom, Blackwell Publishers sold its education list and concentrated on its own journals program, which paralleled but was distinct from BSP's. By the early 1990s, Blackwell Publishers had became the leading international publisher of journals for societies in social sciences and humanities. Its first North American office was opened in New York in 1984 and moved to Malden, Massachusetts, in 1989.

The transformation into a truly transatlantic company was complete by the end of the twentieth century, with more than half the company's sales and new copyrights coming from the American market.

By the mid-1980s, under the leadership of Mark Robertson, BSP had developed an extensive program of journals with societies in Australia, then in Japan, and more recently in other parts of Asia. By the 1980s, the journals list was contributing two-thirds of BSP's total sales. In 1987, when Robert Campbell took over from Per Saugman as managing director, the company expanded in Europe and launched a Professional Division. In the mid-1990s, BSP invested heavily to make all its journals available online. To reflect the wider range of services BSP now offered, the company changed its name to Blackwell Science in 1993. The company's European offices started Blackwell Healthcare Communication Ltd. (BHCL), a medical communication company working primarily with the pharmaceutical industry, which merged in 1999 with Bullet Communications (acquired in 1997) to form Avenue HKM (Healthcare Knowledge Management). The company also acquired the Iowa State Press, a publisher of veterinary books and journals, and launched Blackwell Synergy in 1999, a new online journals service offering full text with reference and citation linking.

In 2001, Blackwell Publishing Ltd. (BPL) was established by merging Blackwell Publishers and Blackwell Science. The new company was the world's largest independent society publisher. Richard's son, Nigel Blackwell, who had been chairman of Munksgaard, BSP, and Blackwell Publishers, became chairman of BPL with René Olivieri as CEO. Over the course of its history, Blackwell Publishing grew into a leading global publishing company with an international reputation for providing the best in publishing services, and the world's leading society publisher, with a list of 825 journals, 6,000 books in print, and 650 new books published each year.

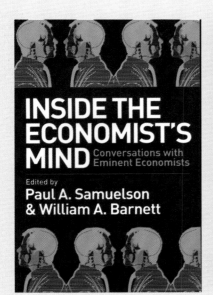

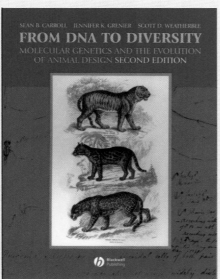

Inside the Economist's Mind edited by Paul A. Samuelson & William A. Barnett

From DNA to Diversity, ed. 2, by Sean B. Carroll, Jennifer K. Grenier, and Scott D. Weatherbee

Journal of Advanced Nursing

*W*iley CEO Will Pesce visited Blackwell to speak to new colleagues soon after the Blackwell acquisition was announced in November 2006. (From left to right) Robert Campbell, Andrew Robinson, John Jarvis, William Arlington, Nigel Blackwell, Steve Hall, Sue Corbett, René Olivieri, Will Pesce, Eric Swanson, Jon Walmsley, Steve Smith, Mike Fenton, and Philip Carpenter.

with enthusiasm. The two companies began the long process of due diligence and ironing out details, working together in a way that laid a solid foundation for the future. Pesce, King, Cousens, and Wiley's general counsel, Gary Rinck engaged in protracted negotiations, primarily with Olivieri and Blackwell's advisors. In the end, all Blackwell shares were sold to Wiley.[13]

Wiley and Blackwell were already two of the world's most respected publishers. With their merger, Wiley's Scientific, Technical, and Medical publishing business combined with Blackwell to become Wiley-Blackwell, a formidable global enterprise. The combined portfolio had approximately 1,250 scholarly, peer-reviewed journals at the time of the acquisition (the count reached 1,400 by September 2007) and an

*G*ary Rinck, senior vice president and general counsel

extensive collection of books with global appeal in the sciences, technical fields, medicine, the social sciences, and the humanities. The corporation, with its Higher Education and Professional/Trade businesses, continues to be known as John Wiley & Sons, Inc., and all three businesses continue to work on ways to collaborate.

Swanson was chosen to lead Wiley-Blackwell, and Olivieri was named as its chief operating officer and the co-leader, along with Wiley Europe's new managing director, Stephen Smith, of the critically important transition team. Soon after the acquisition was completed, Wiley-Blackwell's new global organization was announced; the structure is similar to one that Wiley employed in 2003 to revive its STM Global Books program. Publishing operations are arranged by subject area rather than by location, so that global collaboration is ensured within each of the five Wiley-Blackwell business units for all product—books, journals, and other formats. Both Wiley and Blackwell colleagues hold leadership positions: Philip Carpenter became general manager, Social Sciences and Humanities; Susan Corbett, general manager, Medicine; Michael Davis, general manager, Life Sciences; Stephen Miron, general manager, Physical Sciences and Engineering; and Jon Walmsley, general manager, Professional business units. The general managers all report directly to Swanson and Olivieri. (In October 2007, Olivieri announced his resignation from Wiley-Blackwell, effective January 1, 2008.) Other members of the Wiley-Blackwell leadership team include Reed Elfenbein, director of Sales and Marketing; Chris Hall, finance director; Michael Fenton, director of Operations; and Robert Campbell, senior publisher.[14]

The Blackwell acquisition plan was driven by the revenue growth potential of the merged business and the resulting cost savings for the two companies. Significant synergies are being achieved by combining global sales, marketing, and content management capabilities; capitalizing on Blackwell's successful off-shoring and outsourcing of various content-management, manufacturing, and shared support services; implementing a single Web platform; integrating technology resources; and transitioning to a common financial reporting, distribution, and customer service infrastructure.[15]

Wiley-Blackwell's increased capabilities come from the expertise drawn from all parts of two global organizations. For example, both Blackwell and Wiley separately had substantial and well-known journals programs. Together, Wiley-Blackwell is a force that cannot

Together, Wiley-Blackwell is a force that cannot be ignored.

be ignored. Blackwell's preeminence in developing and managing publishing relationships with societies; Wiley's innovative brand management skills; the depth and breadth of Wiley's publishing programs across its three core businesses; Wiley's multichannel marketing and sales; and both companies' reputation for quality and collaborative, customer- and partner-friendly cultures are all sources of competitive advantage. The balance between Wiley's and Blackwell's publisher-owned and society-owned journals is almost perfect. Of Wiley's 425 journals, about one-third were society-owned. With Blackwell, about two-thirds of its 825 journals were society-owned. Thus, together, about half of Wiley-Blackwell journals are society-owned and half are publisher-owned. Both companies share strengths in medicine and life sciences. Wiley's strength in the physical sciences is matched by Blackwell's in the social sciences and humanities. The combined companies are now able to invest more in online products and services than they could as separate entities, which is a benefit for the scholarly and scientific community. Greater investment in Wiley-Blackwell's online products and services is sure to benefit Wiley's customers in other markets, such as Higher Education, as synergies between Wiley InterScience and *WileyPLUS* have done in recent years. Global market reach is strengthened and extended, and Wiley-Blackwell is committed to finding an effective balance between a global perspective and strong local identity. Wiley-Blackwell aims to be the most responsive, innovative, financially competitive, and professional publishing partner in the industry, providing partners and authors with exceptional service that is focused on their unique needs.[16]

"In Dreams Begins Responsibility"

Pesce quoted the poet William Butler Yeats in his communications with colleagues about the Blackwell acquisition. The passage he cited, "In dreams begins responsibility" captures both companies' deeply ingrained ethos that privilege begets obligation—that the merger was about more than the bottom line. It was not a new idea at Wiley. It was the genesis, for example, for the annual Wiley Prize in Biomedical

THE WILEY PRIZE

In 2001, Deborah Wiley pulled together the people and resources to create the Wiley Foundation and *The Wiley Prize in Biomedical Sciences* to acknowledge the contributions of the scholarly community to our corporate success. *The Wiley Prize in Biomedical Sciences* recognizes contributions that have opened new fields of research or have advanced novel concepts or their applications in a particular biomedical discipline. It honors a specific contribution or a series of contributions that demonstrate significant leadership and innovation. The award, which is given by the Wiley Foundation, includes a $25,000 grant and the opportunity to present a public lecture at The Rockefeller University, the venue for the awards ceremony.

Among the many distinguished recipients of *The Wiley Prize in Biomedical Sciences*, three have also been awarded the Nobel Prize in Physiology or Medicine. Dr. Andrew Z. Fire and Dr. Craig C. Mello, co-recipients of the *Wiley Prize* in 2003, received the 2006 Nobel Prize in Physiology or Medicine for their discovery of RNA interference—gene silencing by double-stranded RNA. Dr. H. Robert Horvitz, a co-recipient of the *Wiley Prize* in 2002, shared the 2002 Nobel Prize in Physiology or Medicine for his work on how genes regulate organ development and cell death. Dr. Elizabeth H. Blackburn, Morris Herzstein Professor of Biology and Physiology in the Department of Biochemistry and Biophysics at the University, of California, San Francisco, and Dr. Carol Greider, Daniel Nathans Professor and Director of Molecular Biology & Genetics at Johns Hopkins University, were awarded the 2006 *Wiley Prize;* both also received the 2006 Lasker Award for Basic Medical Research, along with Dr. Jack W. Szostak, Harvard Medical School.[17]

*T*he sixth annual *Wiley Prize in Biomedical Sciences* was awarded jointly in April 2007 to Dr. F. Ulrich Hartl, director of the Max Planck Institute in Munich, Germany, and Dr. Arthur L. Horwich, Eugene Higgins Professor of Genetics and Pediatrics at Yale University School of Medicine and Investigator, Howard Hughes Medical Institute. Both were recognized for their elucidation of the molecular machinery involved in protein folding. Shown here, from left, are D. Qais Al-Awqati, jury member; Deborah E. Wiley, senior vice president, Corporate Communications; Dr. Gunter Blobel, jury chairman; Colette Bean, associate publisher; Patrick Kelly, vice president and director, Journal Publishing; Elizabeth Cox, editor; Dr. F. Ulrich Hartl; Dr. Arthur L. Horwich.[18]

Sciences, initiated in 2001 by Deborah Wiley in her role as chairperson of the Wiley Foundation to recognize groundbreaking research discoveries.[19]

For both Wiley and Blackwell, increased stature meant increased responsibility to the world's scholarly and scientific community. Nigel Blackwell articulated his sense of obligation to these, saying, "At heart, Blackwell and Wiley share a common publishing ethic and consistently high standards and values. Combining them makes overwhelming sense for the global academic and professional community." Pesce elaborated on their vision for the acquisition: "For our authors and society partners, we intend to provide best of class service through our extensive network of editorial, production, marketing, and sales talent. For our customers, we intend to provide more access to more content by more people than ever before in the history of the two companies. For our colleagues, we intend to provide intellectually stimulating and financially rewarding opportunities." The belief that a company's responsibilities toward its diverse stakeholders (authors, society partners, customers, shareholders, and colleagues) are not mutually exclusive, but are intrinsically connected and drive growth, had been a key element in both companies' continuing success. This belief provides Wiley-Blackwell colleagues with a standard to follow in the years ahead.[20]

Zhuan Ji Transition

Much is made by the media of the risk for publishers in an era of rapid technological change, but Wiley, informed by its continuing use of scenario planning as a way to analyze the implications of technological change, has seen this change as more opportunity than risk. While new forms of media have enhanced and broadened the distribution of the written word, new and old forms of publishing both compete with and complement each other. Tim King predicted 15 years beforehand that "in the year 2006, not only will there be extraordinary electronic networks out there doing extraordinary things, but the print medium will continue to exist, just as newspapers, radios, and televisions all coexist. What will change is the role of each. We are facing evolution, not revolution."[21]

King was on target, and right not to be alarmist, yet wise to be alert and to prepare for many different scenarios. Managing the risk of the Internet requires innovation, but it does not pose a threat to the core of what publishers do. This is well understood at Wiley, as demonstrated by the ongoing development of Wiley InterScience (which is poised to evolve further as it merges with Synergy, Blackwell's online platform), *WileyPLUS*, and frommers.com, to name but a few examples.

As the digital migration continues, the marketplace presents daily and long-term challenges. Wiley prepares to remain successful under possible future scenarios and much in between. Broadly speaking, it plans to do so by growing revenue and earnings faster than the industry average while remaining prudent in its acquisitions and by enhancing the company's position as the "place to be" for all of its stakeholders. The company is laying plans to both protect itself from the threats inherent in each scenario and to capitalize on emerging opportunities. Keeping pace with the speed of change and continuing to provide customers around the world with what they want and need, when they want and need it, has compelled colleagues across Wiley to change.[22]

The Internet's increasingly pervasive influence is compelling companies like Wiley to rethink the way that they do business. Some prognosticate that in the end technology will render publishing obsolete. Others, including Wiley's leadership, see opportunities to generate growth and deliver more value to customers by responding to the changing marketplace by being innovative, reducing costs whenever possible, increasing interaction with customers, investing in technology, and advancing global collaboration. The continuing evolution of the journal and textbook business models is a good example.[23]

Adding Value

The daily work of researchers has been profoundly changed by their institutions' and publishers' investments in Web technologies over the last 10 or 12 years. Despite the migration to the Web, the role of publishers has not diminished; they still perform a vital function in the assessment and dissemination of scientific knowledge. They also build and develop the journals, books, and major reference works (MRWs) that provide the registration and certification system that gives researchers confidence in the knowledge that they are reading peer-reviewed and publisher-processed and -authenticated material—something that they would not get from an unmediated, open network. Many scientists also write and read Web logs ("blogs") and collaborative Web sites ("wikis") and post articles on their professional Web sites, but these do not replace the authoritative "version of record," which needs to be stable and trusted in order to be cited by other researchers.

Some people argue that the Internet ought to end authors' dependence on publishers by enabling them to communicate directly with referees, reviewers, and readers. Publishers have traditionally coordinated the development, production, distribution, and gate-keeping of books and journals and minimized the costs through economies of scale.[24]

Publishers take significant risks and make major investments to launch and maintain journals in print and online, investments that are essential to the publication of quality content and its broad dissemination. Peer-reviewed research journals are essential to the establishment of "the minutes of science," as Jan Velterop, director of Open Access at Springer, so eloquently puts it, where research is validated,

> **Publishers take significant risks and make major investments to launch and maintain journals.**

authenticated, and protected and can become part of the permanent body of knowledge. Researchers want to have their articles published in highly regarded journals as measured by their "impact factor," a citation metric established by the Institute for Scientific Information (now Thomson Scientific).[25]

"Open access" is actually a catchphrase that refers to several business models in which the user does not pay for access.[26] A number of organizations, notably the Public Library of Science (PLoS), have launched open access, "author-pays" journals that are supported by philanthropic grants in order to challenge subscription-based, "user-pays" journals. The National Library of Medicine (NLM) of the National Institutes of Health (NIH) has created PubMed Central, a free digital repository of journal articles, with ambitions to establish an institution with greater capabilities than a simple repository. In 2005, the NIH instituted a policy to encourage its grant recipients to deposit their published journal articles in PubMed Central within 12 months of publication. The policy results in the depositing of articles after the peer-review process has been completed and considerable value has been added by publishers. NIH funding pays for the research, but publishers pay for the editorial and peer-review processes, production, marketing, sales, and the considerable investment in Web platforms, such as Wiley InterScience, which distribute content and provide customers with tools like search and navigation capabilities, online manuscript submission and management, cross-product searching, reference and citation linking, and personalization options for accessing and using content.[27]

"What is problematic is an unfunded mandate from a government funding agency [the NIH] that sets up the government as a publisher in competition with both commercial and nonprofit publishers while failing to recognize the value added by publishers," said Eric Swanson, senior vice president of Wiley-Blackwell. "Mandates like this will have serious and unintended consequences for the research community and publishers," he explains. Meanwhile, compliance with the NIH policy has been low, in part because many authors seem to find the process cumbersome.[28]

Ultimately, it is a matter of who pays for the publishing process, which is not free. If the government decides to go the route of mandating free user access, they will likely have to contend with fees imposed by the copyright owners to cover their costs.

Wiley-Blackwell believes that open market competition can and should ultimately settle this debate. Any viable, sustainable, and scalable business model will

> Researchers want to have their articles published in highly regarded journals as measured by their "impact factor."

have to deliver sufficient financial returns to provide ongoing investment in technology, without relying on the support of charitable foundations. That may be a continuation of the demand-side subscription model (in which the library pays on behalf of the reader); it may shift over time to a supply-side Open Access model (in which the author uses research funds to pay for publication); or it may be some mix of the two, such as the agreement Wiley reached with the Howard Hughes Medical Institute (HHMI), a major private contributor of biomedical research, to deposit into PubMed Central, the NIH digital archive, peer-reviewed articles that are based on HHMI-funded research. Wiley will be paid directly by the HHMI.

In response to changing customer needs, Wiley has proffered the licensing model—the renting of electronic access—for its online journals. Licensing benefits both the customer and the publisher, especially when libraries negotiate together as consortia, a movement that quickly caught on during the 1990s. (While publishers gain from revenue growth, more libraries increase their purchasing power and gain more access to more content.) Another example of a new business model is Wiley's agreement in early 2007 with the New York Public Library (NYPL) to provide free online access to over 300 peer-reviewed journals that until now have principally been available through academic or corporate collections. NYPL patrons will be able to access the full

Expanding the Business

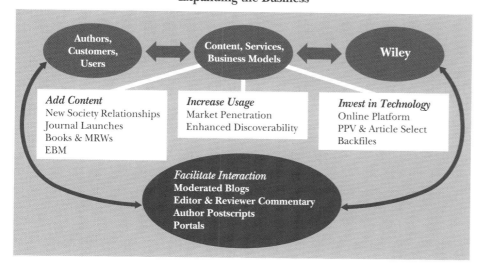

Wiley is connected to authors, customers, and users through the content and services it creates and the business models it introduces. The company is expanding its scientific, technical, medical, and scholarly business by adding more content, increasing usage, investing in enabling technology, and facilitating interaction.

text of journal articles online via Wiley InterScience. In addition, Wiley offers its customers many journal article purchase options, including Pay-Per-View and Article Select individual article access. Using another business model, STM grew its portfolio of controlled-circulation (advertising-driven) journals significantly in the year before the Blackwell acquisition through acquisition and new launches. In addition, every issue of every Wiley journal ever printed will be available on Wiley InterScience by the end of 2007. The journals collection dates from 1799 when *Annalen der Physik* was first published and comprises over 1.5 million articles of scientific and scholarly research. A vigorous book and major reference work backfile initiative is under way as well.

Technology is affecting not only how customers purchase content but also how they interact with it. Clinicians and reviewers, for example, can make comments on the evidence-based medicine content in the Cochrane Library through the use of the "Cochrane Correspondence," a moderated site that allows the medical community to incorporate findings from the latest clinical trials, offer opinions and commentary on recommended treatments, and improve the knowledge base of proven clinical treatment.

In 2005, Wiley was selected by the Society of Hospital Medicine to assume publication of The Hospitalist. This controlled-circulation newsletter is published monthly in print and online for medical doctors who specialize in hospital practice throughout the United States.

PIRATES OF THE PRINTED PAGE AND MORE

The battle against outright piracy and more subtle forms of copyright violation is a never-ending one. As technology enhances the communication of knowledge, it also facilitates the unauthorized replication of intellectual content. Validating the authenticity of content, protecting the integrity of authors' works, and warding off pirates have all become more complex endeavors in the Internet age.

Copyright protection has been of major concern to Wiley since well back in the nineteenth century. John Wiley was a leading advocate for international copyright reform, and the failure of the U.S. copyright movement was a prime factor in his 1848 decision to leave fiction and focus on knowledge publishing. As long as English authors could be pirated with impunity in the United States, he perceived, it would be difficult to develop American literature, since American authors, who by U.S. law had to be properly compensated, were considerably more expensive to publish. Congress did not pass an international copyright law until 1891.

In recent years, Wiley executives have played important roles in the campaign. Former CEO Charles Ellis served as chairman of the Copyright Committee of the Association of American Publishers (AAP) from 1983 to 1985, and championed the industry position in the successful suit against Texaco for unlawful photocopying of journal content. Richard Rudick, Wiley's former general counsel, was active on the AAP Copyright Committee for many years, and served as chairman of the International Publishers Association (IPA) Copyright Committee. In 1994, Tim King, current head of Planning and Development, was the founding chair of the AAP's Enabling Technologies Committee, responsible for identifying the requirements for successful publishing on the Internet. A key outcome of the committee's work was the creation and implementation of the Digital Object Identifier (DOI) program, now an essential element of digital copyright management. And since 1994, Deborah Wiley has served as chair of the AAP's International Copyright Protection Committee, which combats illegal photocopying, book piracy, and trademark infringement worldwide. Roy Kaufman, legal director, serves on the board of directors of the Copyright Clearance Center (CCC). Many other Wiley colleagues, too numerous to mention, have played equally important roles as part of industry efforts.

Wiley has taken the lead in other efforts to protect its intellectual property. In 2001, the legal department became aware of a document delivery company that was pocketing copyright fees it charged its customers. "We brought suit, along with Elsevier," said legal director Roy Kaufman. "In addition to achieving our primary objective—to stop someone from profiting by the theft of our intellectual property—we won a healthy settlement that more than paid for our efforts. We decided the best thing to do would be to reinvest the settlement in additional anti-piracy efforts." Over time, Wiley's collaboration with other publishers resulted in an informal task force, with Wiley playing a primary role in such things as ferreting out violators. "We do this in various ways," said Kaufman, "through search algorithms, public databases, and leads provided by authors and colleagues; we also subscribe to alert services." In the overwhelming majority of cases, a "cease and desist" letter produces the desired result. Litigation is pursued as a last resort, and only in clear-cut cases, with the settlements serving to fund the ongoing initiative.

More recently, digital piracy has been on the rise, and illegal copies of Wiley e-books have shown up regularly on file-sharing peer-to-peer Web sites and on e-commerce sites. In 2004, Kaufman and Gary Rinck, Wiley's general counsel, decided to do more to combat

Wiley's copyright protection team includes, from left, Ray DeSouza, Kathleen Robbins, both enforcement associates, Roy Kaufman, legal director, and Patrick Murphy, paralegal and head of the antipiracy initiative.

this activity. In October 2004, paralegal Patrick Murphy was promoted to lead the effort and was soon joined by representatives of two other publishing companies. In addition to searching eBay and other Web sites, the group works with the U.S. Customs and Border Protection Agency to seize pirated goods and block the importation of lower-cost textbooks from parts of the world where Wiley sells at prices more appropriate to local market conditions. The group has also stopped unscrupulous subscription agents who have purchased journal subscriptions at individual rates and then resold them to institutions.

Wiley protects its trademarks as vigilantly as its content, policing the Web to find unauthorized uses of Wiley trademarks; the most common violations involve the For Dummies brand. However, trademark violation is less cut-and-dried than is copyright infringement, because some uses have First Amendment protection, such as parody, and Wiley balances these issues when deciding whether to pursue a trademark infringement case. Policing Wiley trademarks enforces the value of its brands, preserving their identities and preventing brand dilution.

The effectiveness of these campaigns has drawn media attention, and they continue to attract the participation of other publishers as well. "No one else has the level of resources dedicated to it that we do," said Kaufman. "We find the violations, we arrange for lawyers to represent the co-litigants in the instances when we proceed to litigation, and we queue up the cases. But we're always looking for other publishers to join us. It doesn't just benefit Wiley; it benefits the whole publishing community, ensuring that our interests and those of all our authors are well protected."[29]

446

The Price and Value Proposition

In the higher education textbook market, *ji* 機, the character for risk, stands out boldly. Since the late 1970s, publishers like Wiley have had to respond to serious competition from the used-book business, the increasing costs of higher education, buyer resistance (including students who do not always buy the assigned textbook), the increasing sophistication of online education (both public and private), and the changing demographics of the student population. As with its other businesses, Wiley has turned these challenges into opportunities.

Textbooks and learning materials, thoughtfully orchestrated by authors, editors, and instructional designers, all of whom are brought together by the publisher, provide structure for academic courses. Effective textbooks and learning tools and resources are expensive to produce. The basic economics of college textbook publishing require the presence of a broad audience to minimize the financial risk of publication. Most of the costs associated with creating a textbook come from the input of authors assisted by knowledge workers—the researchers, reviewers, photographers, illustrators, designers, editors, production managers, marketers, and sales representatives, among others, who create and distribute them.

Textbooks are not mass-market products. Sales of a top-selling textbook are a fraction of the sales of a blockbuster novel, but the publishing process is vastly more labor-intensive and costly. Product development costs are "spread" over the revenues generated by the sale of that product. Most, if not all, publishers still develop both traditional print and digital content, along with their associated costs, in response to customer preferences, and will do so for the immediate future.

> As with its other businesses, Wiley has turned these challenges into opportunities.

At the same time, the cost of higher education in both private and public institutions has continued to increase with more of the cost of education allocated back to the student. Increased teaching loads are putting more demands on professors. To accommodate the projected increases in student enrollments and fewer resources available, greater numbers of institutions of higher learning are compelled to engage adjunct and part-time instructors to meet student demand. Students and professors are finding that content closely aligned with what is taught in classes, accompanied by digital tools, enhances the educational experience and helps prepare the student for employment.

Ironically, one "solution" that is widely promoted to lower the cost of textbooks actually makes the problem worse. The aggressive and successful used-book market in the United States cannibalizes legitimate sales and shrinks the textbook market so that new book development costs have to be spread over fewer sales. The result is higher book prices.

Wiley has recognized that no matter what the cost of a textbook is—$10 or $100—it is too expensive if it is not read by the student. Students perceive a gap between the price and the value of the textbooks they are assigned if they don't use all of the book's content in the course. Wiley's response has been to develop and promote products, services, tools, and business models that deliver value to customers and to offer products in a variety of formats, both print and electronic, to appeal to different customers.

To maximize learning and to ensure that students receive a return on their college education investment, today's offerings include not only texts but also many value-added resources such as e-books, workbooks, software, Web-based content, online assessment, self-study features, tutoring, and other direct

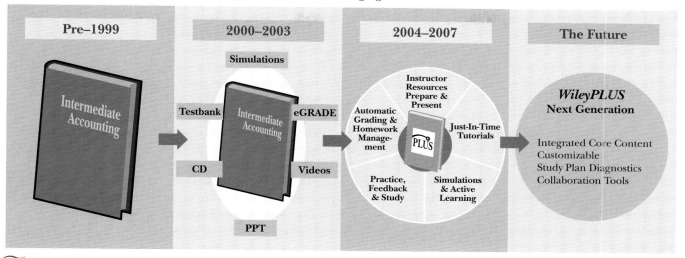

Higher Education's Changing Product Models

The Wiley textbook is evolving from a purely print product to a digital product that includes customizable content with learning tools for both teachers and students.

support services for both students and professors. These tools can deliver different types of content, accommodate diverse student learning styles, and stimulate different ways of thinking. The demand for them is reinforced year after year in market research with both students and faculty.

WileyPLUS has been at the center of Wiley's strategy. This powerful online tool effectively integrates print, online, CD-ROM, and classroom resources, using an activities-based interface that accommodates course planning, presentations, study, homework, testing, and assessment. Homework can be assigned and automatically graded by the *WileyPLUS* testing engine, bringing students immediate feedback as well as access to a variety of context-sensitive support resources that build confidence and understanding— hints and explanations, direct links to text content, interactive problem-solving, and practice quizzes. The flexibility of *WileyPLUS* enhances the instructor's ability both to motivate students and to shape their learning experience. Students have responded to survey questions with comments like, "*WileyPLUS* revolutionized

how I study," "It made my learning much easier," and "I believe it has helped me to achieve a better grade." The Wiley Faculty Network (WFN) through its peer-to-peer network helps other faculty integrate Wiley technology into their curricula and tailor its use to their needs, thereby encouraging student use and facilitating learning.

The demand for texts that fit tightly with specific curricula and tools that will assist teachers and students has moved Higher Education to become more deeply involved in the educational process; hence Higher Education's mission of "helping teachers to teach and students to learn." Investment in technology is also allowing the company to tailor content from across its businesses for specific global markets in a timely and cost-efficient manner. The Precise Custom Textbook Series, jointly developed by Wiley India, U.S. Higher Education, and Wiley software engineers in Russia, is one example. This initiative is allowing sales representatives and editorial staff to create print books precisely tailored to the needs of Indian curricula.[30]

Some of Higher Education's newest projects include all Microsoft Official Academic Course (MOAC) materials and the Wiley Visualizing series, published in partnership with the National Geographic Society. Shown here are the cover and an interior from *Visualizing Geology*, by Barbara W. Murck, Brian J. Skinner, and Dana Mackenzie, illustrating the way that the series combines text and images to reach students more effectively.

Technology is not the only thing that's changing rapidly. Higher Education is also capitalizing on growth fields, demographic shifts, and advances in the understanding of the learning process itself. Wiley has joined with Microsoft to serve college students preparing for certification in Microsoft technologies, as Microsoft's sole publishing partner worldwide for all Microsoft Official Academic Course (MOAC) materials. The company has also partnered with the National Geographic Society to incorporate its visual content into the new Wiley Visualizing textbook series, which combines text and images in a unique way that incorporates the latest research findings on learning styles. The new Wiley Pathways is geared to the growing number of older community and career college students, often employed and with families, who are pursuing post-secondary education with a strong career focus in such growth areas as business, healthcare management, and emergency management.

How frommers.com engages travelers

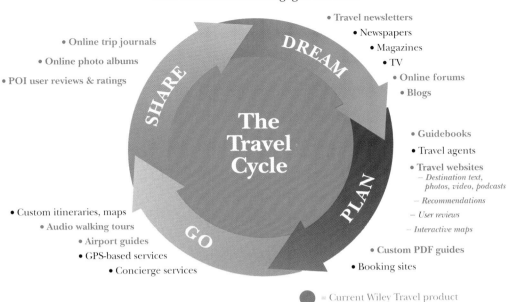

The Travel Cycle

- Travel newsletters
- Newspapers
- Magazines
- TV
- Online forums
- Blogs

- Guidebooks
- Travel agents
- Travel websites
  - *Destination text, photos, video, podcasts*
  - *Recommendations*
  - *User reviews*
  - *Interactive maps*
- Custom PDF guides
- Booking sites

- Online trip journals
- Online photo albums
- POI user reviews & ratings

- Custom itineraries, maps
- Audio walking tours
- Airport guides
- GPS-based services
- Concierge services

DREAM · PLAN · GO · SHARE

= Current Wiley Travel product

The Travel Cycle describes how travelers imagine, plan, travel, and reflect on their experience. The products and information provided for the traveler by Wiley appear in blue type as an example of Wiley's continuous dialogue with its customers.

Print *and* Electronic Delivery

A familiar mantra within Wiley is Pesce's "print *and* electronic, not print *or* electronic." Wiley's travel program is an excellent example. When Wiley acquired the Frommer's travel guide business with Hungry Minds in 2001, it was primarily a print on paper business. Today, Wiley's travel program has evolved so that it actively engages with customers throughout the travel cycle.

Most people begin their travel experience with a dream for a trip, followed by a planning phase, the trip itself, and sharing the experience with family, friends, and colleagues. With frommers.com, Wiley interacts with customers throughout this travel cycle. Frommer's offers travel newsletters, online forums, and blogs that help shape the dream; photos, videos, interactive maps, podcasts, and recommendations, as well as a link to purchase guidebooks to help plan trips; walking tours and airport guides to take along; and online journals, photo albums, and user reviews and ratings for sharing the experience with others. These capabilities were enhanced with the acquisition in 2006 of WhatsonWhen, a travel content, marketing, and Web site building services company.

*F*rommer's Web site

By engaging with customers in this way, Wiley is enhancing the value of the Frommer's brand and is also creating new revenue streams to fuel future growth. New streams of revenue from the consumer programs, including Web site advertising, digital licensing, downloadable products, and custom or private-label Web services, all simultaneously serve to promote physical book sales and reinforce brands. Frommers.com, dummies.com, and cliffsnotes.com have produced double-digit growth in revenue for several years from advertising, sponsored links, and content licensing. Internet advertising is often more appealing than print ads because the number of impressions can be measured and they are triggered by keywords that target the correct customers. Digital licensing has also grown rapidly, with branded content in demand by major public Web sites, portals, and other Web operations. Wiley optimizes its sites to facilitate natural search, delivers site-specific newsletters, and manages relationships with related Web sites. Google Adwords and other search-based advertising programs are also utilized to connect interested parties to our offerings.[31]

Wiley is taking advantage of a wide variety of online marketing approaches. Amazon.com's "e-mail blasts" enable authors to send bulk e-mailings to their own established customer lists, amassed through speaking engagements and professional associations. Wiley has found this program to be especially useful in promoting its business books, generating sales of as many as 4,000 books in a single day. Professional/Trade is also an active participant in Amazon's Search Inside the Book, Amazon Upgrade, and AmazonConnect initiatives. Upgrade gives purchasers the option to also buy online access to a title when they purchase the book; there are currently about 2,000 Wiley titles available in this program, with more being added all the time. AmazonConnect encourages authors to post title- and author-specific blogs—a great way for authors to interact with readers and a good way to sell more books. Amazon and Wiley's partnership continues to grow and evolve.

The Global Marketplace

For a global company like Wiley, the story would not be complete without consideration of the interplay of global, regional, and local markets. Wiley colleagues have mastered the ability to publish for each or for all three, from a journal with a global audience, a text, or a journal with particular emphasis on Asian markets to *Curling For Dummies,* which has not yet posted significant sales outside of Canada.

Since Stephen Smith and Steven Miron turned around Wiley's Asian business in the 1990s, Wiley's Asian colleagues, now under the direction of Mark Allin, have posted impressive sales figures. Asia has experienced rapid growth in the professions, research and development, and university enrollments. For example, while the number of doctoral degrees in natural science and engineering conferred in the United States, the United Kingdom, and Germany have either not increased or have declined, they have risen in China, South Korea, and Japan. "With rapidly changing market situations and commitment comes risk and error," Brad Wiley reported after a three-week trip to Asia in 2007. "The terrain going forward will be riddled with opportunity. Unlike in the 'mature' markets of Europe and the U.S., Asia presents difficult choices about which opportunity is golden and is relevant, misleading or a fool's errand."

Editors in Singapore's P/T program, started in 1994 and now focused on business and finance titles, continues to sign local authors while publishing titles that travel outside the region. Wiley opened its first Beijing office in 2001 with a team of five sales and support staff under the guidance of Theresa Liu, who previously led Wiley's sales team in Taiwan. Over the next few years, China became a beehive of activity. By fiscal 2007, the number of colleagues in Beijing had increased nearly fivefold, and an office was opened in Shanghai. In early 2006, Wiley established a fourth STM publishing program, to acquire more content from Asia-Pacific authors, under the direction of Ann-Marie Halligan (based in Singapore) to complement its programs in the United States, the United Kingdom, and Germany. New STM editors were also hired in Beijing, Taipei, Tokyo, and Sydney. The Blackwell acquisition brought a strong editorial presence in Shanghai and more editorial staff in Tokyo, where Wiley's staff went from 8 to 36 people. Colleagues in the Shanghai office are responsible for ten journals published in partnerships with the Chinese Academy of Sciences and the Chinese Academy of Social Sciences. The Tokyo staff, servicing Wiley's largest scientific, technical, and medical market outside the United States, is responsible for 41 journals in these areas. There have also been steady advances in Chinese translation licensing and co-publishing of key P/T titles.[32]

In February 2006, Wiley acquired the outstanding shares of its Indian joint-venture company, Wiley Dreamtech, to form Wiley India Private Ltd. The new venture adds a strong distribution network and a market-leading position in the publication of professional, technology, and computer books to the company's established presence in the Indian higher education and STM markets. The Precise Custom Textbooks Series, mentioned previously, illustrates an important point about global Wiley in its third century. Editorial development is taking place in India with close collaboration with U.S. colleagues, while content customization capabilities and related educational tools are being developed by colleagues in Russia, among other places. Wiley's future success will be driven by collaboration across businesses and borders.

Wiley has invested heavily in Asia over the last decade and a half, but the Blackwell acquisition has highlighted the fact that the United States, despite its challenges, remains the world's leader in research and development and an important growth market. "Blackwell realized, as Columbus thought he had 500 years earlier, that it could reach the East by sailing West," said Olivieri. "We started commissioning American authors even before we had any offices there.

For more than a decade, the 'conquest of America,' both in terms of commissioning and sales, became the central mission of the entire organization." And indeed Wiley-Blackwell colleagues in Hoboken and Malden, Massachusetts, continue to sustain existing journals while searching for new prospects, particularly among American academic and professional societies.[33]

Asia offers attractive economies for production services, and Wiley has taken advantage of these services for years. Many books and journals from across the company are typeset and printed in China, India, and Singapore. This trend will accelerate as a consequence of the union with Blackwell, which already prints a significant portion of its journals in Singapore and Malaysia.

In other parts of the world, Wiley continues to grow. The Middle East has produced impressive results. Wiley's exhibition stand at the Tehran Book Fair in May 2007 was staffed by 40 people who sold $1.57 million of Wiley materials in a ten-day period. Africa and Latin America remain relatively small markets (although South Africa is a U.S. $2.6 million market for Wiley), but with Wiley's historic presence, established relationships, and cumulative experience in both these regions, Wiley is poised to increase its commitment when conditions dictate.[34]

*D*elhi Bookfair (2004). Steve Miron, Vikas Gupta, Peter Wiley, Mark Allin, Arun Bharti.

452

Sustaining Value and Ramping Up Investor Relations

The challenge of continued successful management unites firm and family. Wiley has evolved from being a sole proprietorship to a family partnership to a family-managed private corporation to a publicly traded multinational with professional management, independent governance, and sufficient family ownership to protect and sustain the company's culture, mission, and values. With Jesse Wiley, a member of the seventh generation, working at Jossey-Bass, a Wiley imprint, the family continues to plan for another generation who will be actively engaged in the evolution of Wiley with management, the board of directors, and colleagues.

*J*esse Wiley, associate editor, Jossey-Bass

Focusing on governance, board chairman Peter Wiley and his brother Brad continue their work with Will Pesce and the board's governance committee to ensure that Wiley's board remains independent and rigorous in its oversight role through thoughtful recruitment and regular self-evaluations.

As a publicly traded company, Wiley has benefited from management's efforts to increase the number of shareholders by enhancing Wiley's profile in the investor community. Wiley began to reach out to investors during Charles Ellis's tenure. The turnaround that Ellis and his team achieved made the company more attractive to outside investors. The Bass family's acquisition of a significant stake in the company also served as a catalyst for change. Bass representatives on the board pushed for greater exposure of the company in the investor community as a means to increase liquidity (in other words, high daily trading volume of Wiley shares).

A significant milestone was reached in July 1995, when Wiley shares were listed on the New York Stock Exchange. Ellis viewed the move to the Big Board as a means of "providing greater visibility for the company which would result in greater liquidity for shareholders," as well as an affirmation of the company's rising fortunes, as reflected in the growth in earnings per share, which doubled between fiscal year 1990 and fiscal year 1995.[35]

Ellis was by nature a cautious communicator, holding his cards close to his chest unless there was a good reason to do otherwise. Robert Wilder, then chief financial and operations officer, and Peter Clifford, Wiley's comptroller and chief accounting officer, were wary of Wall Street's focus on short-term gains. But Ellis and they recognized the need to develop a rapport with investors and the investment community to convey the company's strengths and attract the kind of investors who appreciated Wiley's way of building value. Each year in early September, Ellis and Wilder sponsored an investor breakfast at the company's headquarters for a dozen or so of the company's largest institutional owners. Later, other members of the management team were asked to join the breakfast.

Throughout the nineties, Wiley provided an increasingly comprehensive view of the company's operations. Deborah Wiley took responsibility for corporate communications under Charles Ellis, and hired Susan Spilka in 1993. Spilka steadily cranked out announcements of acquisitions, large and small, and of publishing partnerships during this period of rapid growth, thereby raising the company's profile in the media and familiarizing more investors, authors, and other stakeholders with the fundamental changes that were taking place.[36]

Wiley's relationship with the investor community expanded and improved significantly under Pesce's leadership. Spilka served as an initial investor relations contact, providing information to potential investors and analysts. Working with Pesce, she further developed the annual report to shareholders as a vehicle to convey the company's strategies, accomplishments, and objectives, as well as showcasing the expanding scope of its publishing programs. Board member John Marion, who served from 1999 to 2005, brought to the board his

*S*usan Spilka, corporate communications director

deep understanding of the investment community, his considerable knowledge of publishing and related industries, and his appreciation for Wiley. He developed an excellent rapport with Pesce, as he took the time to learn about Wiley and the publishing business.

In June 2000, Wiley hired Kekst & Company, an investor relations consulting firm, to help develop an integrated financial communications and investor relations program to achieve greater recognition and support for the company within the investment community. At fiscal 2000 year end, Wiley began hosting quarterly conference calls with investors and reaching out proactively to investors through participation in media conferences.

These efforts accelerated with Pesce's recruitment of Ellis Cousens as executive vice president and chief financial and operations officer to succeed Wilder when he retired in March 2001. Cousens, who was described by Pesce as a "strategic thinker with strong financial, analytical, and communications skills," developed his finance career at both publishing and consumer marketing companies. He joined Wiley from Bertelsmann, where he had structured and

implemented an $800 million partnership with Time Warner.

Cousens set out with Pesce, Spilka, and Kekst to strengthen relationships with the investment community. He reached out to existing and potential investors and analysts, seeking to expand Wiley's institutional investor base. One of his initial steps was to open up the annual breakfast to a wider range of investors and analysts, although the first of such expanded meetings had to be postponed due to the September 11 attacks. Cousens and Pesce began to present sell-side conferences and the amount of quarterly information and disclosure was expanded to increase investor confidence and understanding of the key drivers of Wiley's performance. The focus both internally and externally was shifted to a balanced view of strategy and financial results, including free cash flow as a critical measure of long-term value and of current performance.

The next few years saw a marked improvement in Wiley's investor relations profile. Several sell-side analysts initiated coverage and the ranks of new institutional investors grew significantly, as did the average daily trading volume of the company's Class A shares. Consistent performance and a record of meeting or

453

*E*llis Cousens and Will Pesce

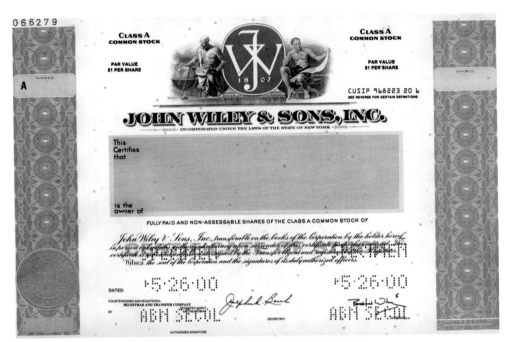

A stock certificate for Wiley's Class A shares, JW.A.

about 700 registered shareholders. By the end of fiscal year 2007, Wiley stock was owned by approximately 1,500 registered shareholders and an estimated 5,000 beneficial shareholders (who own their shares through mutual funds and retirement funds), and the trading volume averaged more than 110,000 each day. One hundred dollars invested in John Wiley & Sons Class A shares on April 30, 2002 yielded $148 on April 30, 2007.[37]

From 2002, the company has brought in more new investors than at any other time since it went public in the 1960s. This outcome

exceeding expectations certainly helped the outreach efforts. During the late 1980s, trading volume averaged 300 to 500 shares a day. In fiscal year 1992, there were

is a direct result of Wiley's efforts to provide comprehensive information to investors and its ability to deliver strong results.

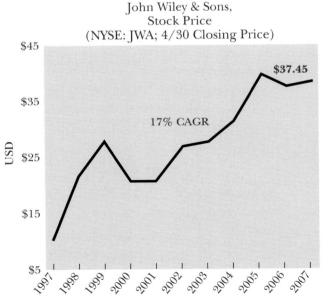

CAGR stands for Compound Annual Growth Rates.

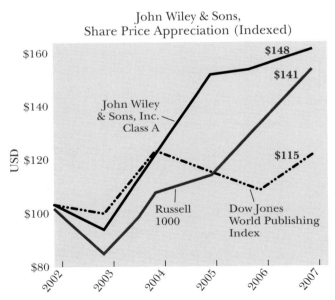

Source: John Wiley & Sons 2007 Annual Report.

The above graph provides an indicator of the cumulative total return to shareholders of the company's Class A Common Stock as compared with the cumulative total return on the Russell 1000 and The Dow Jones Word Publishing Index, for the period from April 30, 2002, to April 30, 2007. The Company has elected to use the Russell 1000 Index as its broad equity market index because it is currently included in the index. Cumulative total return assumes $100 invested on April 30, 2002, and reinvestment of dividends throughout the period.

The strength of Wiley's performance over the past decade, clearly evident in these key measures, has helped raise the company's profile and attract new investors.

John Wiley & Sons, 2007 Revenue

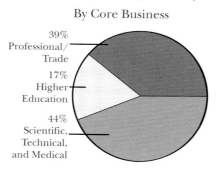

By Core Business

39% Professional/Trade

17% Higher Education

44% Scientific, Technical, and Medical

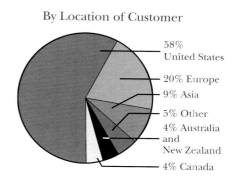

By Location of Customer

58% United States

20% Europe

9% Asia

5% Other

4% Australia and New Zealand

4% Canada

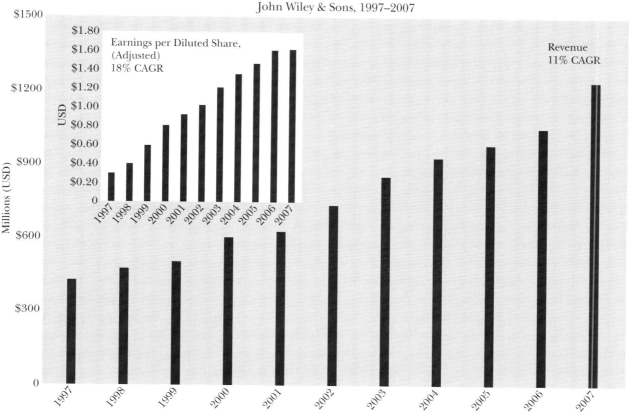

John Wiley & Sons, 1997–2007

Earnings per Diluted Share, (Adjusted) 18% CAGR

Revenue 11% CAGR

Source: John Wiley & Sons Annual Reports.   CAGR stands for Compound Annual Growth Rate.   Adjusted for stock splits, for illustrative purposes.

There has been more coverage in leading business publications, such as the 2005 article in *Barron's* in which an investor described Wiley as ". . . a stock for all seasons, a company that delivers when the economy is headed up or down." Recognition of the company's strong performance increased as Wiley was named to *Fortune's* "Best Companies" lists in 2005 and 2006; *Forbes's* Best Big Companies in 2006, and S&P's MidCap 400 in 2006. What JP Morgan Chase had to say about Wiley when initiating coverage early in 2007 captures the dramatic improvement in the company's reputation in the investment community:

We believe John Wiley is a well managed, core publishing holding suitable for long-term investors . . . Wiley's management team . . . has an especially strong track record over the past decade in the broader media space. The company has consistently outperformed peers. It is an experienced team with all but one of the top six executives with more than 15 years experience. Culture is also a strength at the company. One reason could be that management not only preaches ethics but historically has backed it up.[38]

456

All Wiley, All the Time

Wiley begins its third century with yet another transformation in its underlying business. In the early nineteenth century, Charles Wiley morphed from a printer into a retailer and publisher. His son John added an important partnership with George Palmer Putnam, a London office, and an import and export business. Both father and son published a wide range of subjects from *belles lettres* to engineering. In the second half of the century, John and his sons reinvented their business, dropping fiction and many nonfiction subjects, while focusing on texts and professional titles in science and technology. The fourth generation followed in their predecessors' path, adding more texts, professional titles, and a modicum of nonfiction trade books. In the three decades after World War II, Wiley became an international business, expanded its textbook offerings, and added more scientific, technical, and professional publishing, starting with the acquisition of Interscience Publishers in 1961. The 1980s saw Wiley move beyond the confines of its traditional publishing program by adding a training company and occupational publishing to Wiley's portfolio. In the 1980s, Wiley also began its first serious experimentation with technology. Wiley in the 1990s went back to building the three core businesses—Higher Education, Professional/Trade, and STM (now STMS or Wiley-Blackwell)—for which Wiley is known today. The development and proliferation of the World Wide Web inspired the company to make an aggressive effort, moving content online and building digital tools to enhance the customers' experience. In the twenty-first century, Wiley is building on the cumulative experience of the past 200 years to adapt and change yet again, this time into a "content, tools, services, and solutions provider."[39]

The company's current strategic plan calls for its three main businesses to strengthen its 200-year legacy of quality publishing. To support its businesses and enable colleagues to respond rapidly and flexibly to customers' needs as the Web continues to evolve and expectations

DISCOVER **WILEY**

continue to change, Wiley has undertaken the *Discover Wiley* and *Content Technology* initiatives. *Discover Wiley* is set to launch in 2007. Its mission is to "organize all of Wiley's information and make it easy to access and use . . . to make all of Wiley—products, people, competencies, and capabilities—discoverable." The *Content Technology* initiative is designed to make all Wiley content available to customers in immediately usable form, allowing the company to acquire, create, and manage all of its content without respect to location, business, or product boundaries; to search and browse all of its content; to assemble and reuse rich content in customizable ways; and to publish for multiple sales channels. Text-mining tools and semantic tagging will enable Wiley to offer customers a richer, more "intelligent," dynamic, and useful content. Ultimately, customers will be able to search across all the company's content on a given topic and download the results in a common format with rights and pricing information. In short, customers will be able to get the content they need when they need it in whatever format they choose—all Wiley, all the time.[40]

Persevering in the Middle

Over the long haul, publishing processes and global markets will undoubtedly shift and shift again. Even a firm as old as Wiley, a firm whose sense of the future has been well informed by scenario planning, must accept the limits of its predictive capabilities. Wiley has survived and prospered through many epic events in part because it "perseveres in the middle," an idea that originated with Rosabeth Moss Kanter, the Ernest L. Arbuckle Professor of Business Administration at Harvard Business School, and is often quoted by Pesce. Kanter's explanation of the concept highlights a capability and competitive strength that Wiley fine-tuned over the past 15 years, "One of the mistakes leaders make in change processes is to launch them and leave them," Kanter wrote. "So many things can go wrong in the middle, you can estimate wrong, run into obstacles, and the critics will surface in the middle. Constant monitoring is important to keep ideas on track or to redirect them if circumstances change—and they change constantly. In the middle then, the persistence and perseverance of the change leader makes the difference between success and failure. Leaders need to have the stamina and resilience to stick with it and turn difficult middles into successful achievements."[41]

Pesce aptly described Wiley's ability to persist, persevere, and succeed in his remarks to the board of directors as it approved moving forward with the Blackwell acquisition:

In the late 80s, Wiley was in serious trouble. We had revenue of about $200 million, essentially no profits, and a market cap of less than $300 million. There was an "us against them" mentality separating the leadership of the company from the people who were leading the publishing business. Morale was pretty low. Fortunately, with the support of the Wiley family and the board of directors, we began a successful journey to revitalize Wiley. Highlights of that revitalization include fixing our Higher Education business; selling the training business; investing in enabling technology; launching Wiley InterScience, WileyPLUS, *and* frommers.com; *building partnerships with companies like Amazon and, more recently, Microsoft; acquiring VCH, Jossey-Bass, J. K. Lasser, the Tortora franchise, and Hungry Minds; moving across the river to free up cash to reinvest in our business. With the Blackwell acquisition, today Wiley is well on its way to becoming a company*

*I*n 2006, Wiley was recognized for the second consecutive year on the *Fortune* list of "100 Best Companies to Work For."

with revenue of $2 billion, healthy operating margins, free cash flow of $150 million, and a market cap of $2.5 billion. Today, we are a company recognized by our colleagues as the place to be. *Today . . . on the eve of our bicentennial, we've made a decision to transform Wiley by consummating a marriage made in publishing heaven. We all know it hasn't been easy and we all know that it will not be easy, but lasting accomplishments rarely are.*[42]

Wiley's ability to navigate through the transitions of the next few years will depend on the very capabilities that have helped it survive over two centuries. If Wiley succeeds and is able to take advantage of the opportunities that lie ahead, there is potential for transformative growth. If it is stymied in too many areas, there will probably be a period of regrouping, but its history has shown that it does not mean the end of the road. In the modern world, however, nothing sits still for long.

Assessing and managing risk has always been the publisher's day-in, day-out companion, and over the past decade Wiley has developed effective tools for this purpose. At least since its revivification in the early 1990s, Wiley has exhibited entrepreneurial instincts. It has completed over 60 acquisitions since 1989. It has adapted and changed in so many ways.[43]

Wiley's planning prudently anticipates several different futures. The good news is that none of these scenarios supplant the vital role of publishers that Charles Schuchert of Yale University's Peabody Museum of Natural History alluded to when he wrote to William O. Wiley in 1932: "Godspeed to Wiley & Sons, and may they ever continue to be the helpful intermediary between authors and the studious public!" Fifty years later Brad Sr. remained anxious about the "proper

457

458

refereeing of information:" It was hard to overstate the danger "if misinformation gets out." Whether the (mis)information was sold in printed form, in multimedia formats, or digitally alone, the threat was the same. Only true publishers could ensure quality, and quality he believed was not a technology issue. Brad frequently advised the industry to embrace technology because he believed it could never supplant publishers' main function of intermediating between author and reader. "The discovery and identification of men of ideas by publishers who take professional responsibility for maximum distribution of these ideas," he argued, "will remain virtually unchanged."[44]

Publishers ensure that readers are not inundated with works that are poorly conceived and written or simply incorrect. Here, successful publishers excel and add considerable value. Were publishers not adept at separating the marketable wheat from the valueless chaff, their businesses would suffer, as it is they who bear the financial risk of publication.[45]

A central fact about publishing, as Dan Lacy of McGraw-Hill put it in 1963, is that it is "pure entrepreneurship." Technology may render it easier/cheaper for authors to print and distribute books themselves, but few authors will ever publish enough books to build a profitable business by efficiently diversifying their risks. Publishers will always be able to offer authors some safe harbor by investing in a wide portfolio of titles, some of which will succeed, some of which will not. The theory of portfolio

One of Wiley's core strengths remains its people. The belief that colleagues should be respected as human beings first, professionals second, informs managerial practices and human resources programs and helps enhance Wiley as "the place to be" for all its stakeholders. This philosophy, articulated by Pesce and reflective of the Wiley family's long-held beliefs, is stated explicitly in the company's official vision statement. Proof of its effectiveness can be found in the large number of colleagues who have been with Wiley for 25 years or more. Members of the 25 Year Club, active and retiree alike, are honored at an annual luncheon; as of 2007, the U.S.-based club numbered some 200 people.

choice, which Wiley helped to spawn in 1959 by publishing *Portfolio Selection: Efficient Diversification of Investments,* an improved version of Harry Markowitz's doctoral dissertation, is applicable. Books can be likened to equities (shares in corporations) with uncertain returns. Publishers' catalogs or backlists are therefore like financial portfolios because the average performance, not the variability of returns from individual books, is paramount.[46]

As one editor notes, "this business is not like doing market research for soft drinks." In knowledge publishing, intuitive feel for the market can be as important as the most intricate understanding of statistical sampling techniques and focus groups. The relationship between book quality and book sales is complex, and setting the optimal price will ever remain a challenge.[47]

Publishing has proven to be a durable business. In his oft-quoted criticism of John Kenneth Galbraith's ideas, Friedrich Hayek asserted that mankind's only natural wants are food, shelter, and sex, and that everything else we learn from our environment (or, as he believed, are persuaded to want through advertising). It was a list at least one item short. Alongside the need to eat, be fruitful, and stay out of the rain, the need to know deserves an equal place. Publishing is chief among the ways we humans satisfy the need to know, and the nature of publishing has been changing since time immemorial. The difference now is the rate of change and the proliferation of options, which is what strategic plans attempt to wrestle to the ground. Latent in them all is the ultimate question: what is or will be a book (or a journal)? If content written, edited, polished, and marketed is to survive the onslaught of alternative forms of media, then it must create superior value for its producers and consumers alike.

In 1996, Wiley entitled its annual report "Publishing Without Boundaries." Like most slogans, this one is partly real and partly wishful. Customers do "not care how we are organized internally," Pesce pointed out. "They want their needs satisfied with a high level of service at the best price." He also knows that too many boundaries within the organization hinder service to customers and stymie value creation. The company works hard to breach the silos, to collaborate across boundaries.

When Charles Wiley founded the company in 1807, Napoleon was emperor of France; Alexander I was the Russian czar; George III was king of the United Kingdom; and Thomas Jefferson was America's third president. In 1807, Robert E. Lee, the Confederate general, and Henry Wadsworth Longfellow, the American poet, were born. Beethoven was composing and Washington Irving was writing.

In financial terms, Wiley's revenue reached $1 million in 1929, 122 years after the Wiley story began. It took 12 more years to reach $2 million in 1941. The company has reached many financial milestones since, and it has done so at an accelerated pace—revenue of $100 million in 1980, $500 million in 1999, and $1 billion in 2006. Wiley is well on its way to reaching another milestone, $2 billion in revenue.

While the company has adapted and changed in so many ways, there has been one constant over the course of two centuries—the Wiley family. Members of the family are already planning for the next generation's engagement in the global enterprise that bears their name.

As it embarks on its third century, Wiley will continue to be guided by a mission and values statement it calls The Wiley Vision:

John Wiley & Sons, Inc., aspires to be a valued and respected provider of products and services that make important contributions to advances in knowledge and understanding, a role that is essential to progress in a healthy and prosperous society. While fulfilling that role, we strive to build lasting, collaborative relationships with all of our stakeholders. We are dedicated to sustaining Wiley's performance-driven culture, which requires our unwavering commitment to the highest standard of ethical behavior and integrity in everything we do.

The company is investing in a future that extends well beyond its bicentennial year. Will there be a next edition of *Knowledge for Generations*, perhaps in 2032 on the occasion of the 225th anniversary? If so, in what format will it be published? If history provides any insight, there will indeed be a story worth writing, a compelling story about adapting and changing while sustaining a truly distinctive and distinguished culture.

Wiley Celebrates 200 Years of Publishing

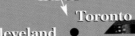

San Francisco

Ames
Indianapolis

Cleveland

Toronto

Malden
Hoboken

Copenhagen

Oxford
Ealing
Chichester

Berlin
Weinheim

Moscow

Beijing

Seoul

Tokyo

Delhi

Taiwan

Singapore

Brisbane

Melbourne

Notes

ARRANGEMENT OF NOTES

Explanatory note numbers are with the sentences they refer to; citations to sources have been consolidated at the paragraph level. Outside (non-Wiley) secondary or tertiary source materials come first, separated by a semicolon and concluded with a period, conventions used throughout. Next listed are non-Wiley primary source materials, after which are materials published by Wiley. Listed last are materials from Wiley's archives; in most cases, to save space, the abbreviation JWSA is implied.

Within each chapter's sources, full titles of secondary works and certain primary sources are given in full at first mention and in short form (author's or editor's last name, short title) thereafter. Other abbreviations are given below.

Archives

AAS, American Antiquarian Society, 185 Salisbury Street, Worcester, Mass.

EPO, Edison Papers Online, http://edison.rutgers.edu/.

HSP, Historical Society of Pennsylvania, 1300 Locust St., Philadelphia, Pa.

ISUA, Iowa State University Archives, Iowa State University, Ames, Iowa.

JWSA, John Wiley & Sons Archives, 111 River Road, Hoboken, N.J.

LCP, Library Company of Philadelphia, 1314 Locust St., Philadelphia, Pa.

NYCMA, New York City Municipal Archives, 31 Chambers Street, New York, N.Y.

NYCSC, New York City Surrogates Court, 31 Chambers Street, New York, N.Y.

NYHS, New York Historical Society, 170 Central Park West, New York, N.Y.

NYPL, New York Public Library, Fifth Avenue and 42nd Street, New York, N.Y.

UVA, University of Virginia, Albert and Shirley Small Special Collections Library, P.O. Box 400110, Charlottesville, Va.

Databases

ANBO, American National Biography Online

APS, American Periodical Series

LOC. Library of Congress American Memory Collection

OCLC, OCLC (Online Computer Library Center)/First Search

OEDO, Oxford English Dictionary Online

U.S. Census, http://fisher.lib.virginia.edu/collections/stats/histcensus/

CHAPTER ONE

[1]John Wiley & Sons, Inc., has gone by numerous names during its 200-year existence: Van Winkle & Wiley; Van Winkle, Wiley & Co.; Charles Wiley & Co.; Wiley & Halsted; Goodrich & Wiley; Wiley & Long; Wiley & Putnam; John Wiley; John Wiley & Son; John Wiley & Sons; and, finally, John Wiley & Sons, Inc. Herein we usually call the company simply Wiley. "JWS History: Wiley Names & Locations, 1807–1963."

[2]Lewis Coser, Charles Kadushin, and Walter Powell, *Books: The Culture and Commerce of Publishing* (Chicago: University of Chicago Press, 1982), 13–15.

[3]John Wiley & Sons, Inc., Strategic Plan, FY07–09.

[4]John Franklin Brown, "Textbooks and Publishers," *The Elementary School Journal* 19 (1919): 382–88. Robert B. Downs, *Books That Changed the World* (New York: Penguin, 2004). [Kendall B. Taft, ed.] *The First One Hundred and Fifty Years: A History of John Wiley and Sons, Incorporated, 1807–1957* (New York: John Wiley & Sons, Inc., 1957), 78, 89, 179; John Hammond Moore, *Wiley: One Hundred and*

Seventy-Five Years of Publishing (New York: John Wiley & Sons, 1982), 116–17. Joel Mokyr, *Gifts of Athena: Historical Origins of the Knowledge Economy* (Princeton, N.J.: Princeton University Press, 2002).

[5]For a truer picture of the competitive environment, one must sort out the businesses inside a media conglomerate such as Bertelsmann with which Wiley competes.

[6]Ronald C. Anderson and David M. Reeb, "Who Monitors the Family?" *Journal of Law and Economics* (3 Mar. 2003), 46.

CHAPTER TWO

[1]Mathew Carey, "An Oration Delivered Before the Booksellers Convened in New York, at Their First Literary Fair, June 4th, 1802," Mathew Carey Papers, Edward C. Gardiner Collection, HSP.

[2]*New Jersey Journal*, 26 May, 1 Sept., 24 Nov. 1790. Gelston & Saltonstall to Thomas Mumford, 20 May 1791, to Joseph Howland, 7 Apr. 1792, and to Samuel Parkman, 15 Apr. 1792, Gelston &

Saltonstall Letterbook; Charles Tillinghast to John Lamb, 9 May 1780, 29 Nov. 1783, Box III, #9, Box IV, #140, John Wiley to John Lamb, 26 Nov. 1777, Box I, #234, Lamb Papers, NYHS. John Hammond Moore, Wiley: *One Hundred and Seventy Five Years of Publishing* (New York: John Wiley & Sons, 1982), 3. John Wiley to Charles [Tillinghast?], 7 Apr. 1781. De Forest, *Ballard*, 50.

3James W. Morley, *The Wiley Family: A Brief History of the Ancestry of Pauline, Barbara and Henry Wiley* (Privately published, 2002), 5, 7, 16, 18–21; Louis Effingham De Forest, *Ballard and Allied Familes* (New York: Privately published, 1924), 48–50. Includes Charles Wiley Ballard's memoir about his grandfather, Jack Wiley. *Gaine's Universal Register, or, American and British Kalendar for the Year 1776* (New York: H. Gaine, 1775), 161; *Journal of the House of Representatives of the United States* (New York: Francis Childs and John Swaine, 1790), 84; De Forest, *Ballard*, 49. John Wiley to John Lamb, 12 Apr., 26 Nov. 1777, Box I, #108, #234, Lamb Papers, NYHS; "In Camp," 20 Dec. 1777, George Washington Papers, LOC. Moore, *Wiley*, 2, 4. "Military Record of Major John Wiley"; J. L. Davenport to William H. Wiley, 22 May 1913, Major John Wiley: Military Record, JWS History; J. H. Moore Notes, Wiley History, 1720–1925; William H. Wiley memo, 16 June 1914; "Wiley Family Genealogy," Wiley Family Histories, Genealogy.

4*New Jersey Journal*, 14 Oct. 1795; *American Minerva*, 19 Oct. 1795; John L. Blake, ed., *A Biographical Dictionary: Comprising a Summary Account of the Lives of the Most Distinguished Persons of All Ages, Nations, and Professions*, 13th ed. (Philadelphia: H. Cowperthwait & Co., 1859), 1,321; William O. Wheeler, *Descendants of Rebecca Ogden, 1729–1806, and Caleb Halsted, 1721–1784* (Morristown, N.J., 1909), 2, 87; De Forest, *Ballard*, 49–51. Alexander Hamilton to Joseph Howell, Jr., 22 Apr. 1790, Harold Syrett et al., eds., *Papers of Alexander Hamilton* (New York: Columbia University Press, 1961–1987), 6:371. Moore, *Wiley*, 9. Extract of a Letter from Doctor Charles Wiley Ballard, 21 July 1896, Wiley's [*sic*] before WBW: Letter re Major John Wiley.

5William Breitenbach, "Sons of the Fathers: Temperance Reformers and the Legacy of the American Revolution," *Journal of the Early Republic* 3 (1983): 69–82.

6*New Jersey Journal*, 1 Sept. 1790; Charles S. Griffin, "The Taxation of Sugar in the United States, 1789–1861," *Quarterly Journal of Economics* 11 (1897): 296–309; Roy F. Nichols, "Trade Relations and the Establishment of the United States Consulates in Spanish America, 1779–1809," *Hispanic American Historical Review* 13 (1933): 298–313; Gilman Ostrander, "The Making of the Triangular Trade Myth," *William and Mary Quarterly* 30 (1973): 635–44; Selwyn H. H. Carrington, "The American Revolution and the British West Indies' Economy," *Journal of Interdisciplinary History* 17 (1987): 823–50; Farley Grubb, "The End of European Servitude in the United States: An Economic Analysis of Market Collapse, 1772–1835," *Journal of Economic History* 54 (Dec. 1994): 794–824.

7David Gilchrist, ed., *The Growth of the Seaport Cities, 1790–1825: Proceedings of a Conference Sponsored by the Eleutherian Mills–Hagley Foundation, March 17–19, 1966* (Charlottesville: University Press of Virginia, 1967); Robert C. Alberts, *The Golden Voyage: The Life and Times of William Bingham, 1752–1804* (Boston: Houghton Mifflin Co., 1969); Thomas Doerflinger,

A Vigorous Spirit of Enterprise: Merchants and Economic Development in Revolutionary Philadelphia (Chapel Hill: University of North Carolina Press, 1986), 335–44.

8Moses Waddel to William W. Woodward, 23 Feb. 1808, Gratz—University and College Presidents, HSP.

9Tench Coxe, *A View of the United States of America* (Philadelphia: William Hall and Wrigley & Berriman, 1794), 160–62. Carey, "Oration," 1802, Mathew Carey Papers, Edward C. Gardiner Collection, HSP; Charles C. Savage, "George Bruce and His Connection with the Art of Printing," A Paper Read Before the New York Historical Society, 2 Oct. 1866, NYHS, 6.

10By definition, the quantity demanded of a luxury good, price and quality constant, increases with wealth. All figures adjusted in 1996 U.S. dollars. Frederick Hill, *The Story of a Street: A Narrative History of Wall Street from 1644 to 1908* (New York: Harper & Brothers Publishers, 1908), 153. U.S. Census.

11Farley W. Grubb, "Growth of Literacy in Colonial America: Longitudinal Patterns, Economic Models, and the Direction of Future Research," *Social Science History* 14 (1990): 451–82; John E. Murray, "Generation(s) of Human Capital Literacy: Literacy in American Families, 1830–1875," *Journal of Interdisciplinary History* (Winter 1997), 413–35; Paul Starr, *The Creation of the Media: Political Origins of Modern Communications* (New York: Basic Books, 2004), 48.

12Interestingly, most of those with no books listed in their estate inventories owned at least one bookcase. Did they use them as general pieces of furniture or did their books take flight in their final days or, more ominously, right after their demise? Economic historians note that many estate inventories are devoid of portable, high-value bearer items like money and clothes. This suggests that 75 percent represents the minimum percentile of descendants in the sample who owned books. Starr, *Creation*, 48. Gunston Hall Plantation Probate Inventory Database, http://www.gunstonhall.org/probate/inventory.htm; Catalog of Books in the Library of Charles Riche, Burlington, New Jersey, 13 Aug. 1814, Society Collection, under Charles Riche; Henry W. Pearce, 8 Dec. 1820, Dreer Collection, under J. Reed, HSP; David Bruce, "Autobiography," n.d., NYHS. Henry W. Boynton, *Annals of American Bookselling, 1638–1850* (New York: John Wiley & Sons, 1932), 154–55.

13*New York Evening Post*, 13 Aug. 1821; Peter B. Wiley, *A Free Library in This City* (San Francisco: Weldon Owen, 1996), 22–87. "Copy of the Minutes of the Permanent Committee of the Philada. Prison, March 30th 1812," Bradford Collection, HSP.

14Commonplace book, no author, no date, reverse of Minutes of Meetings of the Book Sellers Company of Philadelphia, 1802–1805, Am. 31175; Robert Vaux to Jonah Thompson, 10 Aug. 1805, Vaux Collection, HSP; Book Club Minutes, 1825–1836, NYHS.

15Jeffrey D. Groves, "The Book Trade Transformed," in Scott E. Casper, Joanne D. Chaison, and Jeffrey D. Groves, eds., *Perspectives on American Book History: Artifacts and Commentary* (Boston: University of Massachusetts Press, 2002), 128. Mathew Carey, *Address to the Printers and Booksellers Throughout the United States* (Philadelphia: Mathew Carey, 1801); James Fenimore Cooper to Carey & Lea, 6 Nov. 1831, in James Franklin Beard, ed., *The*

Letters and Journals of James Fenimore Cooper (Cambridge: Harvard University Press, 1960–1968), 2:150. Boynton, *Annals*, 151.

[16]Aubert J. Clark, *The Movement for International Copyright in Nineteenth Century America* (Washington, D.C.: Catholic University of America Press, 1960), 24–25. Carey, "Oration," 1802, Mathew Carey Papers, Edward C. Gardiner Collection, HSP.

[17]New York City Directories, 1795 and 1807; Clark, *Movement for Copyright*, 36; Allan Pred, *Urban Growth and the Circulation of Information: The United States System of Cities, 1790–1840* (Cambridge, Mass.: Harvard University Press, 1973); Cheryl Denise Bohde, "Evert A. Duyckinck and the American Literary Renaissance: The New York City Literary Marketplace and Poe, Hawthorne, Fuller, and Melville," (Ph.D. Diss., Texas A&M University, 1992), 7; Edwin G. Burroughs and Mike Wallace, *Gotham: A History of New York City to 1898* (New York: Oxford University Press, 1999), 441; Starr, *Creation*, 143; Robert E. Wright, *The First Wall Street: Chestnut Street, Philadelphia, and the Birth of American Finance* (Chicago: University of Chicago Press, 2005).

[18]Clark, *Movement for Copyright*, 28; Matthew J. Bruccoli, ed., *The Profession of Authorship in America: 1800–1870: The Papers of William Charvat* (n.p.: Ohio State University Press, 1968), 302. Richard H. Dana to Charles Wiley, 22 Aug. 1821, Wiley's [*sic*] before WBW: Ch. Wiley–R. H. Dana Corr., 1821–1825.

[19]For an overview of early printing processes and people, see Rollo G. Silver, *The American Printer* 1787–1825 (Charlottesville: University Press of Virginia, 1967).

[20]A dearth of sources has stymied other scholars of early New York printing, including famous book scholar and founder of the AAS Isaiah Thomas, who wrote in 1810: "I have not been so fortunate in collecting materials respecting printing in New York, as to give me entire satisfaction." Isaiah Thomas to James Swords, 14 May 1810, Box 7, folder 14, Pintard Papers, NYHS. The history of American publishing has also suffered because publishers regularly rid themselves of old documents. For a general discussion as well as one specific to Wiley, see Carl Randall Cluff, "Salvaged Cargo: Herman Melville, John Wiley, and the Revised Edition of *Typee*," (Ph.D. Diss., University of Tennessee, Knoxville, 1997), 7–10. Silver, *American Printer*, 1, 2, 6, 30–34. Isaac Riley, "Invoices of Boxes of Lawbooks," Nov. 1811–Feb. 1812, Misc. Riley; Savage, "George Bruce," 2 Oct. 1866, NYHS. Boynton, *Annals*, 156–57; Moore, *Wiley*, 4.

[21]Luke White, Jr., *Henry William Herbert & the American Publishing Scene, 1831–1858* (Newark, N.J.: Carteret Book Club, 1943), 10; Chandler Grannis, ed., *What Happens in Book Publishing*, 2nd ed. (New York: Columbia University Press, 1967), 443. Charles Wiley to Richard H. Dana, 28 Apr., 26 May 1821, Wiley's [*sic*] before WBW: Ch. Wiley–R. H. Dana Corr., 1821–1825.

[22]*New York Commercial Advertiser*, 5 Feb. 1811, 19 Aug. 1812; *New York Evening Post*, 29 Apr. 1811; *New York Times*, 22 Feb. 1891. U.S. Census; OCLC.

[23]Incidentally, the *Analectic Magazine* was the first to reprint Francis Scott Key's ditty about the courageous defense of Fort McHenry near Baltimore the night of 13–14 Sept. 1814. In 1931 that song, rechristened "The Star-Spangled Banner," became the U.S. national anthem.

[24]Algernon Tassin, "American Authors and Their Publishers," *The Bookman: A Review of Books and Life* (Apr. 1914), 178–89. James Kirke Paulding to Mathew Carey and Son, 5 July 1815, in Ralph M. Aderman, ed., *The Letters of James Kirke Paulding* (Madison, Wisc.: University of Wisconsin Press, 1962), 41.

[25]The fee was 56¼ cents per 1,000 ems for brevier (a type size about halfway between pica and agate), 1,000 ems being equal to a typeset line of brevier about seven feet long. Silver, *American Printer*, 17.

[26]New York City Directory, 1814. Manhattan Tax Records, First Ward, 1816–1818, NYCMA.

[27]In 1817, for example, Van Winkle & Wiley received subscriptions in New York for Boston publisher Wells & Lilly's uniform edition of the Latin Classics. Presumably some sort of commission or *quid pro quo* was involved. *American Monthly Magazine and Critical Review* (June 1817), 129. *New York Evening Post*, 23 Nov. 1816; *The National Register, a Weekly Paper* (28 June 1817), 410; Hill, *Story of a Street*, 152–53; "Recollections of Washington Irving," *The Continental Monthly* (1862), 1:693. Manhattan Tax Records, First Ward, 1808.

[28]Georg Friedrich de Martens and William Cobbett, *Summary of the Law of Nations, Founded on the Treatise and Customs of the Modern Nations of Europe* (Philadelphia: T. Bradford, 1795); Rosalind Remer, *Printers and Men of Capital: Philadelphia Book Publishers in the New Republic* (Philadelphia: University of Pennsylvania Press, 1996), 4, 18–19, 46–48. List of Subscribers to Martans [*sic*] Law of Nations, 1795, Bradford Collection, HSP.

[29]Mason Locke Weems to Mathew Carey (1809) in Jeffrey D. Groves, "The Book Trade Transformed," in Casper et al., *Perspectives*, 112–13.

[30]"Domestic Literary Intelligence," *Analectic Magazine* (Aug. 1814), 172; Richard Brookhiser, *Gentleman Revolutionary: Gouverneur Morris—The Rake Who Wrote the Constitution* (New York: Free Press, 2003).

[31]*New York Evening Post*, 29 Nov. 1814.

[32]Joseph Coppinger, "Preface," and "Brewing Company," 15 Aug. 1814; Joseph Coppinger to Thomas Jefferson, 6 Apr. 1815; Thomas Jefferson to Joseph Coppinger, 25 Apr. 1815, Thomas Jefferson Papers, Series 1, General Correspondence, LOC.

[33]*Centinel of Freedom*, 27 May 1817; *Poulson's Daily American Advertiser*, 31 May 1817; *American Monthly Magazine and Critical Review* (Aug. 1817), 313.

[34]*New York Commercial Advertiser*, 8 Aug., 19, 27 Sept. 1817, 3 Nov. 1818. *New York City Directory*, 1810, 1813–1815; W. A. Thompson to John McKesson, 23 Dec. 1816, Box I, #130, John McKesson Papers, NYHS.

[35]*New York Evening Post*, 21 Apr. 1820. Moore, *Wiley*, 11.

[36]A lease could have resale value if it locked in a low rental rate over a long period. A long-term lease was a good way for middling sorts like Charles to speculate on rising real estate prices. "Henry Brevoort," in James G. Wilson and John Fiske, eds., *Appleton's Cyclopedia of American Biography* (New York: D. Appleton and Co., 1888), 1:368. A. H. Inkseep, *Catalogue of Books, For Sale at Public Auction* (New York: Van Winkle & Wiley, 1815). Charles Wiley to Henry Brevoort, 23, 26 Feb., 24 June 1819.

[37] Hugh Maxwell, Day Book, 1803–1806, Am. 9350; Thomas Clark Account Book, 1812–1820, Amb. 208, HSP.

[38] Samuel G. Goodrich, *Recollections of a Lifetime* (New York: Miller, Orton and Mulligan, 1857), 2:111.

[39] Only the name of Charles's erstwhile partner, printer C. S. Van Winkle, appears on the cover page, but Halleck clearly stated in one of his letters that "the bookseller who brought out Irving's *Sketch-Book*" had also agreed to publish *Fanny*. Moore, *Wiley*, 11. Washington Irving to Henry Brevoort, 3 Mar. 1819, in Pierre M. Irving, ed. *The Life and Letters of Washington Irving* (New York: G. P. Putnam, 1864), 1:414–16. Evert A. Duyckinck, *Portrait Gallery of Eminent Men and Women of Europe and America*, 2 vols. (New York: Johnson, Wilson and Company, 1873), 2:155; Frank L. Mott, *Golden Multitudes: The Story of Best Sellers in the United States* (New York: R. R. Bowker Co., 1947), 305; William Charvat, *The Profession of Authorship in America, 1800–1870* (New York: Columbia University Press, 1992), 33. Boynton, *Annals*, 157–59.

[40] S. Austin Allibone, ed., *A Critical Dictionary of English Literature* (Philadelphia: Childes & Peterson, 1859), 936; *A Memorial of Washington Irving* (New York: Charles B. Richardson, 1860), x; Evert A. Duyckinck and George L. Duyckinck, eds., *Cyclopaedia of American Literature* (Philadelphia: Baxter Publishing Co., 1881), 1:738–39; "The House of Murray," *Harper's New Monthly Magazine* 71 (June–Nov. 1885), 515–16.

[41] *New York Evening Post*, 21 June 1819; *New York Commercial Advertiser*, 24 June 1819.

[42] "The House of Murray," *Harper's New Monthly Magazine* 71 (June–Nov. 1885), 515–16; "Washington Irving," *ANBO*.

[43] *New York Commercial Advertiser*, 19 Apr., 2 Aug. 1820; *New York Evening Post*, 22 Apr. 1820; Sidney F. Huttner and Elizabeth S. Huttner, *A Register of Artists, Engravers, Booksellers, Bookbinders, Printers & Publishers in New York City, 1821–1842* (New York: Bibliographic Society of America, 1993), 245.

[44] Anon., "Introductory Remarks to the Constitution of The Typographical Association of New York" (1833), as printed in Jeffrey D. Groves, "The Book Trade Transformed," in Casper et al., *Perspectives*, 124–25. See also Ronald J. Zboray, "A Fictive People: Antebellum Economic Development and the Reading Public for American Novels, 1837–1857" (Ph.D. Diss., New York University, 1984), 27–34.

[45] Alexander C. Wylly to James Fenimore Cooper, 20 May 1823, James Fenimore Cooper Collection, AAS.

[46] Helen Maria Williams, *Letters Written in France in the Summer 1790 to a Friend in England: Containing Various Anecdotes Relative to the French Revolution*, 4th ed., 4 vols. (London: T. Cadell, 1794); Peter Pindar, *Peter Pindar's Works, Complete: Elegantly Printed in Octavo, and Hot-Pressed* (London: J. Walker, 1794); Dominique de St. Quentin, *A New Grammar of the French Language* (London: W. Baynes, 1794); Royall Tyler, *The Algerine Captive, or, The Life and Adventures of Doctor Updike Underhill* (Walpole, N.H.: D. Carlisle, 1797); "Booksellers' Trade Sale," *American Publishers' Circular and Literary Gazette* (19 Sept. 1857), 594; "Damon and Pythias," *New England Magazine: An Illustrated Monthly* (Mar.–Aug. 1896),

672–73; Robert Battistini, "Complexity and the Eighteenth-Century Literary Imagination: Royall Tyler's *Algerine Captive*," http://novel.stanford.edu/pdf/battistini.pdf. Thomas Allen to Thomas Bradford, 14 Oct. 1794, Bradford Collection; Hugh Maxwell, Day Book, 1803–1806, Am. 9350; Carey, "Oration," 1802, Mathew Carey Papers, Edward C. Gardiner Collection; Wiley & Halsted to M. Carey, 11 Feb. 1822, Mathew Carey Correspondence, Edward Carey Gardiner Collection, Vol. 1, no. 783, HSP.

[47] William D. Robinson to Mathew Carey, 8 Dec. 1820, Mathew Carey Papers, Edward C. Gardiner Collection, HSP.

[48] James Rivington to Thomas Bradford, 11 Aug. 1795, Bradford Collection, HSP.

[49] *Baltimore Patriot*, 12 Jan. 1816. Charles Wiley to Richard H. Dana, 22 June 1821, Wiley's [*sic*] before WBW: Ch. Wiley–R. H. Dana Corr., 1821–1825.

[50] Stuart Banner, *Anglo-American Securities Regulation: Cultural and Political Roots, 1690–1860* (New York: Cambridge University Press, 1998), 15–20, 122–25. Carey, "Oration," 1802, Mathew Carey Papers, Edward C. Gardiner Collection; Minutes of Meetings of the Book Sellers Company of Philadelphia, 1802–1805, Am. 31175, HSP.

[51] Edward Bulwer Lytton, *Rienzi, the Last of the Tribunes* (Philadelphia: E. L. Carey & A. Hart, 1836); White, *Henry William Herbert*, 12; Janet Belknap Randel, "The Role of Nineteenth Century American Authors in Securing International Copyright," (M.A. Thesis, Florida State University, 1961), 17.

[52] Tassin, "American Authors," 178–89; White, *Henry William Herbert*, 9; Randel, "Role of American Authors," 67; Burroughs and Wallace, *Gotham*, 441; B. Zorina Khan, "Do Property Rights Matter? Evidence from U.S. International Copyright Law, 1790–1910," (Working Paper), 10. John Miller to James Fenimore Cooper, 28 June 1823, Beard Collection, AAS.

[53] David Bruce, "Autobiography," n.d., NYHS.

[54] Beard, *Letters*, 1:95. Emporium of Arts and Sciences Circular, Joseph Delaplaine, 1814, Bradford Collection, HSP; Entry of 11 Mar. 1824, Records of the Meetings, Literary and Philosophical Society of New York, 1814–1834, NYHS. *APS*; OCLC.

[55] In addition to exchanging books, Charles and Carey engaged in a sort of book arbitrage between their two cities. In February 1820, Charles told Carey that he "must supply this market with all speed with *Ivanhoe*" because two printers were preparing a new run, indicating current demand but a delayed supply. Charles Wiley to Mathew Carey, 21 Feb. 1820, Mathew Carey Correspondence, 1:452, HSP. Charles Wiley to Mathew Carey, 11 Feb. 1820, Wiley's [*sic*] before WBW: Charles Wiley to Matthew [*sic*] Carey, 1820. Mathew Carey, *An Appeal to Common Sense and Common Justice, or, Irrefragable Facts Opposed to Plausible Theories* (Philadelphia: H.C. Carey & Lea, 1822). Wiley & Halsted to M. Carey, 1 Mar. 1822, Mathew Carey Correspondence, Edward Carey Gardiner Collection, Vol. 1, no. 784, HSP.

[56] *North American Review* (Apr. 1821), 261–63; *Niles' Weekly Register*, 8 June 1822, 22 Mar. 1823; Susan S. Williams, "Publishing an Emergent 'American' Literature," in Casper et al., *Perspectives*, 165; Starr, *Creation*, 113.

[57]Henry C. Carey, *Letters on International Copyright* (New York: Hurd and Houghton, 1868), 68; Clarence Gohdes, *American Literature in Nineteenth-Century England* (New York: Columbia University Press, 1944), 15.

[58]Tassin, "American Authors," 178–89; Ali Lang-Smith, "James Lawson," *ANBO*. John Mennons to James Lawson, 12 Feb., 14 July 1821, Papers of James Lawson, UVA.

[59]Mennons seems, though, to have conflated Wiley's short-lived magazine, *Analectic*, with a more successful periodical of the same title published in Philadelphia. Tassin, "American Authors," 178–89. John Mennons to James Lawson, 12 Feb. 1821, 18 Aug. 1821, 2 Mar., 27 Apr., 1 Aug. 1822, 19 Nov. 1823, Papers of James Lawson, UVA. OCLC.

[60]*New York Evening Post*, 31 May 1821; "The Idle Man," *The Literary Companion* (23 June 1821): 23; Anon., "Richard Henry Dana," *Scribner's Monthly* (May 1879), 105–110. Charles Wiley to Richard H. Dana, 26, 29 May, 22 June, 22 Aug., 25 Sept. 1821, Wiley's [sic] before WBW: Ch. Wiley–R. H. Dana Corr., 1821–1825.

[61]*Baltimore Patriot*, 7 Nov. 1821; James Fenimore Cooper to John Murray, 29 Nov. 1822, in Beard, *Letters*, 1:85; Anon., "Dana," 105–10; Duyckinck and Duyckinck, *Cyclopaedia*, 1:786. Charles Wiley to Richard H. Dana, 29 Aug., 25 Sept., 29 Nov. 1821, 12 Feb., 17 Mar. 1822, Wiley's [sic] before WBW: Ch. Wiley–R. H. Dana Corr., 1821–1825.

[62]Soon after Dana died in 1879, *Scribner's Monthly* recalled *The Idle Man* as "a work handsomely issued in well printed octavo numbers, somewhat in the style of Irving's 'Sketch Book,' but displaying much more vigor of thought and strength of style." Anon., "Dana," 105–10.

[63]Anon., "Dana," 105–10. Moore, *Wiley*, 24, 27. Charles Wiley to Richard Dana, 13 Dec. 1822, Wiley's [sic] before WBW: Ch. Wiley–R. H. Dana Corr., 1821–1825.

[64]"James G. Percival," *The New-York Mirror: A Weekly Gazette of Literature and Fine Arts* (26 Jan. 1828), 228; Goodrich, *Recollections*, 2:138; Tassin, "American Authors," 178–89; Charles T. Hazelrigg, *American Literary Pioneer: A Biographical Study of James A. Hillhouse* (New York: Bookman Associates, 1953), 106–7. John Mennons to James Lawson, 1 Aug. 1822, Papers of James Lawson, UVA; Samuel Griswold Goodrich to James G. Percival, 27 Nov. 1822, Letters of Samuel Griswold Goodrich, UVA.

[65]Joseph Doddridge, *Logan, the Last of the Race of Shikellemus, Chief of the Cayuga Nation* (Buffaloe Creek, Va.: Solomon Sala, 1823) and reprinted by A. K. Newman of London; John Neal, *Seventy-Six* (Baltimore: J. Robinson, 1823) and reprinted by G. and W. B. Whittaker of London; James McHenry, *The Wilderness* (New York: Bliss and White, 1823), published in London by A. K. Newman; Susan Linn De Witt, *Justina, or, The Will: A Domestic Story* (New York: Charles Wiley, 1823) and reprinted in London by A. K. Newman. John Mennons to James Lawson, 29 July 1822, John Mennons to James G. Brooks, 1 Aug. 1822, Papers of James Lawson, UVA; John Miller to James Fenimore Cooper, 25 Aug. 1823, James Fenimore Cooper Collection, AAS.

[66]Beard, *Letters*, 1:24; Alan Taylor, *William Cooper's Town: Power and Persuasion on the Frontier of the Early American Republic* (New York: Knopf, 1995); James Fenimore Cooper to Paul Hamilton, 28 Apr. 1811, in Beard, *Letters*, 1:25.

[67]The root of this story appears to be Tassin, "American Authors," which says: "Charles Wiley was the first [sic] publisher of Cooper. They had fallen in with each other while travelling." Tebbel and Boynton may have misconstrued this. Further complicating matters, Boynton says the year the pair met was 1820. John Tebbel, *Between Covers: The Rise and Transformation of Book Publishing in America* (New York: Oxford University Press, 1987), 22. Boynton, *Annals*, 160. *The Minerva*, Vol. 1, no. 44, 348–49; Charles Hemstreet, *Literary New York* (New York: G. P. Putnam's Sons, 1903), 126; Beard, *Letters*, 1:24, 83. James Fenimore Cooper to Rufus W. Griswold, 27 May 1844, James Fenimore Cooper Collection, AAS. Moore, *Wiley*, 15.

[68]Alexander Cowie, *The Rise of the American Novel* (New York: American Book Co., 1948), 123; Alan Taylor, "Fenimore Cooper's America," *History Today* (Feb. 1996), 23. Charles Wiley to James Fenimore Cooper, 7 Jan. 1822, James Fenimore Cooper Collection, AAS. Moore, *Wiley*, 15. Charles Wiley to Richard Dana, 13 Dec. 1822, Wiley's [sic] before WBW: Ch. Wiley–R. H. Dana Corr., 1821–1825.

[69]Blake, *Biographical Dictionary*, 1,321; Firmin Dredd, "Some Pioneer New York Publishers," *The Bookman: A Review of Books and Life* (Feb. 1900), 556–62; "The Great Newspapers of the United States," *The Bookman: A Review of Books and Life* (Apr. 1902), 149–64; Tassin, "American Authors," 178–89; Nelson F. Adkins, "James Fenimore Cooper and the Bread and Cheese Club," *Modern Language Notes* 47 (1932): 71–79; Hazelrigg, *Hillhouse*, 104, 106. "Biographical Sketches," Aeronaut, Literary Confederacy, 1816–1832; Box 10, Folder 1, #34, Box 11, Folder 3, #44, Gulian C. Verplanck Papers; Entry for 3 Feb. 1814, "Bill to Incorporate," Records of the Meetings, Literary and Philosophical Society of New York, 1814–1834, NYHS; Receipt, 28 June 1824, Beard Collection, AAS. Hand copy of *Publishers Weekly*, 28 Feb. 1891, JWS History: Various Histories 19th–20th Century.

[70]Taylor, "Fenimore Cooper's America," 24. James Fenimore Cooper to John Murray, 29 Nov. 1822, in Beard, *Letters*, 1:85–86.

[71]*National Gazette and Literary Register*, 14 Jan. 1823; *New York Spectator*, 17, 28 Jan. 1823; *Niles' Weekly Register*, 8 Feb. 1823; *The Minerva*, Vol. 1, no. 44, 348–49.

[72]*The Port Folio* (15 Mar. 1823), 230; *New York Mirror, and Ladies' Literary Gazette* (2 Aug. 1823), 4–5.

[73]Richard H. Dana to James Fenimore Cooper, 2 Apr. 1823, James Fenimore Cooper Collection, AAS; James Fenimore Cooper to Richard Henry Dana, 14 Apr. 1823, in Beard, *Letters*, 1:85. James K. Paulding, *Koningsmarke: The Long Finne* (New York: Charles Wiley, 1823), Vol. 2, Book 6, Chap. 1, 67–74.

[74]*National Gazette and Literary Register*, 14 Jan. 1823; *The British Critic*, Series 3, Vol. 2 (July 1826), 406–38; Beard, *Letters*, 1:76. Washington Irving to Charles Wiley, 6 Mar. 1822, James Fenimore Cooper Collection, AAS; James Fenimore Cooper to Washington Irving, 30 July 1822, in Beard, *Letters*, 1:75; John Miller to James

Fenimore Cooper, 28 June 1823; James de Peyster Ogden to James Fenimore Cooper, 13 Sept. 1823, Beard Collection, AAS.

[75]Gohdes, *American Literature*, 40. John Miller to James Fenimore Cooper, 5 Feb., 4 Dec. 1824, AAS; James Fenimore Cooper to William Branford Shubrick, 25–30? Jan., 5 Feb. 1824, in Beard, *Letters*, 1:110; James Fenimore Cooper to Rufus W. Griswold, 27 May 1844, James Fenimore Cooper Collection, AAS.

[76]*Carolina Centinel*, 1 Nov. 1823; Blake, *Biographical Dictionary*, 1,321; Hazelrigg, *Hillhouse*, 104; Bruccoli, *Profession of Authorship*, 77; Tebbel, *Between Covers*, 22; James Fieser, ed., *The Life of George Tucker* (London: Thoemmes Continuum, 2004), 65. Boynton, *Annals*, 163.

[77]Mary E. Phillips, *James Fenimore Cooper* (New York: John Lane Company, 1912), 45–46; Beard, *Letters*, 1:24; Hazelrigg, *Hillhouse*, 107; Fieser, *George Tucker*, 65–66. James Fenimore Cooper to George Roberts, 1840, as quoted in Hugh C. MacDougall, "Transcriber's Preface," *Tales for Fifteen: or, Imagination and Heart*, James Fenimore Cooper Society Website, http://www.oneonta.edu/external/cooper/texts/tales.html; James Fenimore Cooper to Rufus W. Griswold, 27 May 1844, James Fenimore Cooper Collection, AAS.

[78]White, *Henry William Herbert*, 25; Beard, *Letters*, 1:84. James Fenimore Cooper contract with Charles Wiley, Nov. 1824, Beard Collection; James Fenimore Cooper to Rufus W. Griswold, 27 May 1844, James Fenimore Cooper Collection, AAS.

[79]*North American Review* (July 1825), 254, (Apr. 1826), 253–74; *New York Literary Gazette and Phi Beta Kappa Repository* (10 Dec. 1825), 222; *New York Review and Atheneum Magazine* (Jan. 1826), 106–25.

[80]*The United States Literary Gazette* (1 Sept. 1825), 440. John Miller to James Fenimore Cooper, 6 May 1825; Charles Wiley and John Wiley to James Fenimore Cooper, ?Oct. 1825, Beard Collection, AAS.

[81]The *New York Evening Post*, 10 Jan. 1826, and the *New York Mercantile Advertiser*, 10 Jan. 1826, published precisely the same obituary. The only other obituaries found read simply: "DIED. Charles Wiley, aged 45." *New York Telescope*, 14 Jan. 1826; *The Farmer's Cabinet*, 4 Feb. 1826.

[82]Henry C. Carey & Lea to James Fenimore Cooper, 15 Nov. 1825, 18 Feb. 1826, Beard Collection, AAS. James Fenimore Cooper to Carey & Lea, 6 Nov. 1831, in Beard, *Letters*, 2:150.

[83]*The New York Review and Atheneum Magazine* (Mar. 1826), 286.

[84]*National Gazette and Literary Register*, 9 May 1823; Beard, *Letters*, 1:84; Remer, *Printers*, 149–52?. Baudy to James Fenimore Cooper, 7 Oct. 1826, R. Riker to James Fenimore Cooper, 31 May 1826, Beard Collection, AAS.

[85]DeWitt Clinton, *An Introductory Discourse* (New York: Van Winkle and Wiley, 1815), 60.

[86]The Major may have lived in N.J., near Hackensack, for some time. By 1820 or so, however, he appears to have lived near Charles, at 40 Reade Street. *Centinel of Freedom*, 17 Jan. 1815. De Forest, *Ballard*, 49. *New York Evening Post*, 26 Apr. 1821; *New York Mercantile Advertiser*, 30 Jan., 13, 31 Mar. 1826; *The New-Yorker*

(4 July 1840), 255; *New York Times*, 22 Feb. 1891; Wheeler, *Descendants of Rebecca Ogden*, 6; Robert E. Wright and George D. Smith, *Mutually Beneficial: The Guardian and Life Insurance in America* (New York: New York University Press, 2004). Moore, *Wiley*, 4, 27. "A Short History of John Wiley & Sons, Inc.," JWS History: Various Histories 19th–20th Century; William H. Wiley memo, 16 June 1914, Wiley Family Histories, Genealogy.

Chapter Three

[1]Charles Dickens, *American Notes for General Circulation*. (London: Penguin Classics, 2000), chapter 6.

[2]Charles Dickens, Letter to John Forster, February 17, 1842.

[3]Peter Ackroyd, *Dickens: Private Life and Public Passions* (New York: Harper Perennial. Reprint edition, 1992). Charles Dickens, Letter to John Forster, February 17, 1842.

[4]Ackroyd, *Dickens*.

[5]Paul Schlicke, ed. *Oxford Reader's Companion to Dickens* (Oxford University Press, 1999).

[6]John Miller to James Fenimore Cooper, 30 Jan. 1826, Beard Collection; H. C. Carey to James Fenimore Cooper, 4 Apr. 1826, James Fenimore Cooper Collection, AAS.

[7]John was born on 4 Oct. 1808; Charles died on 9 Jan. 1826, almost a full 10 months before John's eighteenth birthday.

[8]*New York Mercantile Advertiser*, 30 Jan., 13, 31 Mar. 1826; New York Evening Post, *The Bookmakers: Reminiscences and Contemporary Sketches of American Publishers* (New York: New York Evening Post, 1875), 77; Sidney F. Huttner and Elizabeth S. Huttner, *A Register of Artists, Engravers, Booksellers, Bookbinders, Printers & Publishers in New York City, 1821–1842* (New York: Bibliographic Society of America, 1993), 245. Carey & Lea to James Fenimore Cooper, 15 Feb. 1826, James Fenimore Cooper Collection, AAS. John Hammond Moore, *Wiley: One Hundred and Seventy Five Years of Publishing* (New York: John Wiley & Sons, 1982), 4. J. C. Derby, *Fifty Years Among Authors, Books and Publishers* (New York: G. W. Carleton & Co., 1884), 292–93. David Bruce, "Autobiography," n.d., NYHS.

[9]*Miller's New York As It Is* (New York: James Miller, 1866), 79; "John Wiley," *New York Times*, 22 Feb. 1891; Carl Randall Cluff, "Salvaged Cargo: Herman Melville, John Wiley, and the Revised Edition of *Typee*," (Ph.D. Diss., University of Tennessee, Knoxville, 1997), 120; Ezra Greenspan, *George Palmer Putnam: Representative American Publisher* (University Park: Pennsylvania State University Press, 2000), 186 nn.26, 31; "George Barrell Cheever," *ANBO*. Henry W. Boynton, *Annals of American Bookselling, 1638–1850* (New York: John Wiley & Sons, 1932), 166, 174.

[10]"List of New Books," *The American Monthly Review* (Aug. 1832), 175; Post, *Bookmakers*, 77; Derby, *Fifty Years*, 267. James Kirke Paulding to Henry D. Gilpin, 4 Mar. 1829, in Ralph M. Aderman, ed., *The Letters of James Kirke Paulding* (Madison, Wisc.: University of Wisconsin Press, 1962), 99; Samuel Whelpley, *The Triangle: A Series of Numbers Upon Three Theological Points*,

Enforced from Various Pulpits in the City of New York (New York: Van Winkle & Wiley, 1816).

[11] Derby, *Fifty Years*, 292, 294.

[12] "Manly Piety, In Its Principles," *American Monthly Magazine* (1 Mar. 1834), 20; "John Wiley," *New York Times*, 22 Feb. 1891. J. H. Moore's Notes.

[13] *The Western Monthly Magazine, and Literary Journal* (Apr. 1833), 192; Henry C. Carey, *Letters on International Copyright* (New York: Hurd and Houghton, 1868), 62; Luke White, Jr., *Henry William Herbert & the American Publishing Scene, 1831–1858* (Newark, N.J.: The Carteret Book Club, 1943), 22–23; Matthew J. Bruccoli, ed., *The Profession of Authorship in America, 1800–1870; The Papers of William Charvat* (n.p.: Ohio State University Press, 1968), 307–310; James J. Barnes, *Authors, Publishers, and Politicians: The Quest for an Anglo-American Copyright Agreement, 1815–1854* (Columbus: Ohio State University Press, 1974), 4, 30–48; Cheryl Denise Bohde, "Evert A. Duyckinck and the American Literary Renaissance: The New York City Literary Marketplace and Poe, Hawthorne, Fuller, and Melville," (Ph.D. Diss., Texas A&M University, 1992), 2–6.

[14] James Fenimore Cooper, *The Monikins* (Philadelphia: Carey, Lea, & Blanchard, 1835); "Cooper Coopered," *The New World* (18 July 1840), 97–101; Derby, *Fifty Years*, 295. James Fenimore Cooper to Carey, Lea, & Blanchard, 9 Feb. 1834, 8 Sept. 1837, 13 Apr., 23 May 1838, 13 Oct. 1841, to Richard Bentley, 6 July, Dec. 1837, 22 Sept. 1842, to James De Peyster Ogden, 5 Feb. 1839, to George Roberts, 22 Jan. 1841, to Rufus Wilmot Griswold, 11 July 1842, to Wiley & Putnam, 29 Sept. 1844, to John Wiley, 20 Nov. 1844 in James Franklin Beard, ed., *The Letters and Journals of James Fenimore Cooper* (Cambridge: Harvard University Press, 1964), 3:30, 268, 289, 302, 325, 367, 4:110, 177, 301, 315, 322, 480, 491, 6:10, 326; Wiley & Putnam to James Fenimore Cooper, 19 Apr., 8 May 1839, 1 July 1844, 8 Dec. 1846, 4 Oct. 1847, Beard Collection, AAS. Boynton, *Annals*, 165.

[15] *Fishkill Standard*, 18 Sept. 1876; James G. Wilson and John Fiske, eds., *Appleton's Cyclopaedia of American Biography* (New York: D. Appleton & Co., 1888), 90.

[16] Stephen E. Ambrose, *Duty, Honor, Country: A History of West Point* (Baltimore: Johns Hopkins University Press, 1999), 94, 97, 99. James Gregory McGivern, *First Hundred Years of Engineering Education in the United States (1807–1907).* (Spokane, Washington: Gonzaga University Press, 1960), 37–38.

[17] Post, *Bookmakers*, 77; Hellmut Lehmann-Haupt, Lawrence C. Wroth, and Rollo G. Silver, *The Book In America: A History of the Making and Selling of Books in the United States,* 2nd ed. (New York: R. R. Bowker Co., 1951), 200; John Tebbel, *A History of Book Publishing in the United States: Vol. I, The Creation of an Industry, 1630–1865* (New York: R. R. Bowker Co., 1972), 263; Greenspan, *Putnam*, 52; Leona Rostenberg and Madeleine B. Stern, *From Revolution to Revolution: Perspectives on Publishing & Bookselling, 1501–2001* (New Castle, Del.: Oak Knoll Press, 2002), 125–49.

[18] George P. Putnam, *Chronology; or, An Introduction and Index to Universal History, Biography, and Useful Knowledge* (New York: D. Appleton & Co., 1833); Post, *Bookmakers*, 11–12; Greenspan, *Putnam*, 53–54, 59–65. *ANBO.*

[19] William Cullen Bryant, *An Address to the People of the United States in Behalf of the American Copyright Club* (New York: American Copyright Club, 1843), 8; George Palmer Putnam, "Introductory Statistical Sketch," (1855) as printed in Jeffrey D. Groves, "The Book Trade Transformed," in Scott E. Casper, Joanne D. Chaison, and Jeffrey D. Groves, eds., *Perspectives on American Book History: Artifacts and Commentary* (Boston: University of Massachusetts Press, 2002), 114–15; Carey, *International Copyright*, 65; Barnes, *Authors*, 6; Ronald J. Zboray, "A Fictive People: Antebellum Economic Development and the Reading Public for American Novels, 1837–1857" (Ph.D. Diss., New York University, 1984), 191. U.S. Census.

[20] Early GDP estimates vary somewhat, but the upward trend is clear in all series. All figures adjusted in 1996 U.S. dollars. See Louis D. Johnston and Samuel H. Williamson, "The Annual Real and Nominal GDP for the United States, 1790 – Present," Economic History Services, Apr. 1, 2006, http://eh.net/hmit/gdp/ and Thomas S. Berry, *Estimated Annual Variations in Gross National Product, 1789 to 1909* (Richmond: Bostwick Press, 1968).

[21] Carey, *International Copyright*, 61; O. H. Cheney, *Economic Survey of the Book Industry, 1930–1931* (New York: National Association of Book Publishers, 1931), 17; White, *Herbert*, 17, 19, 40; Barnes, *Authors*, 4–8. Zboray, "Fictive People," 306–9, 313; Bohde, "Duyckinck," 2; Paul Starr, *The Creation of the Media: Political Origins of Modern Communications* (New York: Basic Books, 2004), 102.

[22] Lydia Maria Child, *The Mother's Book* (1831), as printed in Scott E. Caspar, "Antebellum Reading Prescribed and Described," in Casper et al., *Perspectives*, 139–40. Wiley & Putnam, *American Book Circular* (Apr. 1843).

[23] Zboray, "Fictive People," 324–27.

[24] Zboray, "Fictive People," 246; Peter B. Wiley, *A Free Library in This City: The Illustrated History of the San Francisco Public Library* (San Francisco: Weldon Owen, 1996), 70–72. Sandown, New Hampshire Social Library, Miscell. Ms., Sandown Social Library, Librarian's Record Book, 1825–1863, 2 vols., NYHS. U.S. Census. Edward Edwards, *Free Town Libraries, Their Formation, Management, and History; In Britain, France, Germany, & America* (New York: John Wiley and Son, 1869), 269–343.

[25] Francis Wayland, *Thoughts on the Present Collegiate System in the United States* (Boston: Gould, Kendall, and Lincoln, 1842), 43; Thomas Adamson, *A Reply to "Considerations and Arguments, Proving the Inexpediency of an International Copyright Law, by John Campbell,"* (New York: Bartlett & Welford, 1844), 10–11; Carey, *International Copyright*, 58–60; Diane Ravitch, *The Great School Wars: A History of New York City's Public Schools* (Baltimore: Johns Hopkins University Press, 1974); Zboray, "Fictive People," 192, 293–306; Starr, *Creation of the Media*, 86. Edwards, *Free Town Libraries*, 276–77.

[26] Wayland, *Collegiate System*, 8; Carey, *International Copyright*, 59–60; Donald Tewksbury, *The Founding of American Colleges and Universities Before the Civil War* (New York: Columbia University Press, 1932); David B. Potts, "Curriculum and Enrollment: Assessing the Popularity of Antebellum Colleges," in Roger Geiger, ed., *The*

American College in the Nineteenth Century (Nashville: Vanderbilt University Press, 2000), 37–45. Moses Waddel to William W. Woodward, sundry dates, Gratz—University and College Presidents, HSP. Wiley & Putnam, *American Book Circular* (Apr. 1843).

[27]Philip Milledoler, "Account of Books &c. Given to My Children," 1841–49, NYHS. Anon., Diary Kept at Female Academy, Misc. Microfilm, Reel 14, 1831–32; Anon., Book Reviews, 1838, NYHS, 420–22.

[28]Zboray, "Fictive People," 3, 5–6, 61, 331.

[29]Lehmann-Haupt et al., *Book In America*, 145–77; Zboray, "Fictive People," 11.

[30]Lehmann-Haupt et al., *Book In America*, 175–77; Zboray, "Fictive People," 23.

[31]Jacob Abbott, *The Harper Establishment* (New Castle, Delaware: Oak Knoll Press, 2001).

[32]Bruccoli, *Authorship in America*, 299-303; Zboray, "Fictive People," 67–114, 130–39.

[33]"Stereotyping," *The Manufacturer and Builder* (1869), 99–102; Zboray, "Fictive People," 44–45; Starr, *Creation of the Media*, 128. Charles C. Savage, "George Bruce and His Connection with the Art of Printing," A Paper Read Before the New York Historical Society, 2 Oct. 1866, 2–3, NYHS.

[34]Zboray, "Fictive People," 11, 24; Edward Byrn, *The Progress of Invention in the Nineteenth Century* (New York: Russell & Russell, 1900), 154–70. Savage, "George Bruce," 18.

[35]Aubert J. Clark, *The Movement for International Copyright in Nineteenth Century America* (Washington, D.C.: Catholic University of America Press, 1960), 29; Lehmann-Haupt et al., *Book In America*, 166–70; Byrn, *Progress*, 154–70. Zboray, "Fictive People," 46. "Rags, Cotton and Paper," Eric Holzenberg to SHARP-L Listserv, 29 Aug. 2005.

[36]Lehmann-Haupt et al., *Book In America*, 148–53; Zboray, "Fictive People," 41–42, 46.

[37]Robert Burton, *The Anatomy of Melancholy* (Oxford: Henry Cripps, 1621); *The New-Yorker* (12 Jan. 1839), 269; Bryant, *American Copyright Club*, 10; *Monthly Trade Gazette* (Apr. 1855), 4; Zboray, "Fictive People," 56. Savage, "George Bruce," 7.

[38]*The New-York Mirror: A Weekly Gazette of Literature and Fine Arts* (29 July 1837), 39; Barnes, *Authors*, 1–29.

[39]Co-publishing or correspondent publishing was common in this period. See Zboray, "Fictive People," 121.

[40]William Jay, *War and Peace: The Evils of the First, and a Plan for Preserving the Last* (New York: Wiley & Putnam, 1842).

[41]Moore, *Wiley*, 37–38. Putnam, *Chronology*; Post, *Bookmakers*, 11–12; Greenspan, *Putnam*, 53–54, 59–65. *ANBO*.

[42]Edwin G. Burroughs and Mike Wallace, *Gotham: A History of New York City to 1898* (New York: Oxford University Press, 1999), 718, 790.

[43]*The New-Yorker* (20 Apr. 1839), 77; *American Monthly Magazine* (June 1838), 592; "American Publishing House in London," *The New-Yorker* (13 Jan. 1839), 269; *Arcturus, A Journal of Books and*

Opinion (Nov. 1841), 377; *Southern Quarterly Review* (Oct. 1842), 539; *Dial Essays* (1842); William Allen Butler, *Evert Augustus Duyckinck: A Memorial Sketch* (New York: Trow's, 1879), 7; Bohde, "Duyckinck," 23.

[44]Greenspan, *Putnam*, 68–69. Wiley & Putnam to James Fenimore Cooper, 19 Apr. 1839, 4 Oct. 1847, Beard Collection, AAS.

[45]*London Times* (15 March 1847), 5; Derby, *Fifty Years*, 507; Clarence Gohdes, *American Literature in Nineteenth-Century England* (New York: Columbia University Press, 1944), 37, 40; Greenspan, *Putnam*, 70–73.

[46]Epes Sargent, *Velasco: A Tragedy, In Five Acts* (Boston: Eastburn's Press, 1837; New York: Harper & Brothers, 1839); Eugene Exman, *The Brothers Harper: A Unique Publishing Partnership and Its Impact Upon the Cultural Life of America from 1817 to 1853* (New York: Harper & Row, 1965), 358; Greenspan, *Putnam*, 74, 159. Sir Thomas W. Talfourd to Wiley & Putnam, 24 Jan. 1839, Papers of Epes Sargent, UVA.

[47]John Jay, *Letters to Godfrey: Originally Contributed to Blackwood's Magazine, by an American Citizen* (New York: William Van Norden, 1847), 8, 13; Barnes, *Authors*, 33–39; Greenspan, *Putnam*, 115–16. Wiley & Putnam to P. R. Fendall, 8 July 1845, Correspondence of Philip Fendall and W. W. Seaton, UVA.

[48]"The Home Library," *The Orion, A Monthly Magazine of Literature and Art* (May 1844), 149–50; Butler, *Duyckinck*; "Evert A. Duyckinck," in Wilson and Fiske, *Appleton's Cyclopaedia*, 2:278; Burroughs and Wallace, *Gotham*, 686.

[49]Richard Newman, *The Transformation of American Abolitionism: Fighting Slavery in the Early Republic* (Chapel Hill, N.C.: University of North Carolina Press, 2001); James L. Huston, *Calculating the Value of the Union: Slavery, Property Rights, and the Economic Origins of the Civil War* (Chapel Hill, N.C.: University of North Carolina Press, 2003).

[50]"Interesting Document," *African Repository and Colonial Journal* (March 1834), 22; William E. Channing, *The Works of William E. Channing, D.D.* (Boston: James Munroe and Co., 1843), 2:8; Bruccoli, *Authorship in America*, 310–13; Candy G. Brown, *The Word in the World: Evangelical Writing, Publishing, and Reading in America, 1789–1880* (Chapel Hill: University of North Carolina Press, 2004).

[51]*Harper's New Monthly Magazine,* (Jan. 1876) 52:228; *Atlanta Constitution*, 28 Apr. 1895; Edward H. Kraus, "A Notable Centennial in American Mineralogy," *American Mineralogist* (1938), 23:145–48; Julian C. Gray, "Finding the Right Mineralogy Text: Dana's System of Mineralogy," *Tips and Trips* (Apr. 1999), 28:7.

[52]"Fownes' Prize Essay," *Littell's Living Age* (Sept. 1844) 2:418.

[53]Greenspan, *Putnam*, 159; Wiley & Putnam, *American Book Circular* (Apr. 1843).

[54]Edward Widmer, *Young America: The Flowering of Democracy in New York City* (New York: Oxford University Press, 1999), 53.

[55]William Cullen Bryant, *The Fountain and Other Poems* (New York: Wiley & Putnam, 1842); "Home Library," *Orion*; *Southern Literary Messenger* (May 1844), 326–27; Widmer, *Young America*, 99–100; Greenspan, *Putnam*, 163–64. Cornelius Mathews to Edward Moxon, 27 Feb. 1844, Papers of Cornelius Mathews, UVA.

[56]"Comment," *The New Yorker*, 14 Feb. 1948. Polly Morrice to John H. Moore, 1 June 1981. George Haven Putnam, *George Palmer Putnam: A Memoir* (New York: G. P. Putnam's Sons, 1912), 104–6; Ellen Ballou, *The Building of the House: Houghton Mifflin's Formative Years* (Boston: Houghton Mifflin Co., 1970), 118; Greenspan, *Putnam*, 80, 122–28, 160, 165, 172.

[57]Herman Melville, "Hawthorne and His Mosses," *Literary World* (1850), as printed in Susan S. Williams, "Publishing an Emergent 'American' Literature," in Casper et al., *Perspectives*, 170; Ezra Greenspan, "Evert Duyckinck and the History of Wiley and Putnam's Library of American Books, 1845–1847," *American Literature* 64 (1992): 677–93; Bohde, "Duyckinck"; Williams, "Publishing," in Casper et al., *Perspectives*, 185. [Kendall B. Taft, ed.], *The First One Hundred and Fifty Years: A History of John Wiley and Sons, Incorporated, 1807–1957* (New York: John Wiley & Sons, Inc., 1957), 14–21.

[58]Butler, *Duyckinck*, 8; Widmer, *Young America*, 103–111. Nathaniel Hawthorne to Horatio Bridge, 17 Apr. 1845, in "Personal Recollections of Nathaniel Hawthorne," *Harper's New Monthly Magazine* (Feb. 1892), 367; Evert A. Duyckinck to Nathaniel Hawthorne, 2 Oct. 1845, in *Personal Recollections of Nathaniel Hawthorne* (New York: Harper & Brothers, 1893).

[59]Cluff, "Salvaged Cargo," 28–29.

[60]*New York Evangelist* (9 Apr. 1846); *Brooklyn Eagle* (15 Apr. 1846), 2; *New York Courier and Enquirer* (17 Apr. 1846); *Knickerbocker* (May 1846); "Typee," *The American Review: A Whig Journal* (1846), 415–16. *Salem Advertiser*, 25 March 1846; "Nathaniel Hawthorne," in Wilson and Fiske, *Appleton's Cyclopaedia*, 3:127; Bohde, "Duyckinck," 24, 37; Michael Winship, *American Literary Publishing in the Mid-Nineteenth Century: The Business of Ticknor and Fields* (New York: Cambridge University Press, 1995), 189; Williams, "Publishing," in Casper et al., *Perspectives*, 173–75, 187–88; Rostenberg and Stern, *Revolution*, 127; "Herman Melville," *ANBO*. Melville biographer Hershel Parker tells the *Typee* publication and expurgation story in *Herman Melville, A Biography, Vol. 1, 1819–1851* (Baltimore: Johns Hopkins University Press, 1996), 393–406.

[61]Bruccoli, *Authorship in America*, 211–15; Cluff, "Salvaged Cargo," 93, 102–142.

[62]Exman, *Brothers Harper*, 285; Bohde, "Duyckinck," 218–38; Cluff, "Salvaged Cargo," vii, 17, 143, 145–51, 170–83; Widmer, *Young America*, 111–20; "Herman Melville," *ANBO*.

[63]Bohde, "Duyckinck," 171–72. Robert N. Hudspeth, ed., *The Letters of Margaret Fuller*, Vol. IV (Ithaca, NY: Cornell University Press, 1987), 1845–47.

[64]*Brooklyn Eagle* (9 Aug. 1845), 2; Frank L. Mott, *Golden Multitudes: The Story of Best Sellers in the United States* (New York: R. R. Bowker Co., 1947), 109, 307; Bohde, "Duyckinck," 35; "Edgar Allan Poe," *ANBO*. Poe to Cooke, 9 Aug. 1846, as printed in *The Century Illustrated Monthly Magazine* (1894), 862. "Edgar Allen [*sic*] Poe Argued with Us Too," *Wiley Footnotes* (1949), 4.

[65]Kevin MacDonnell, "Henry David Thoreau," *Firsts: The Book Collector's Magazine* (1998); Widmer, *Young America*, 106; Greenspan, *Putnam*, 175–76. Ralph Waldo Emerson to Evert A. Duyckinck, 14 Oct. 1845, Correspondence Files, Duyckinck Collection, NYPL. Charles Ellis to Brad Wiley II et al., 31 Oct. 1995.

[66]*Brooklyn Eagle* (8 Aug. 1845), 2; Greenspan, *Putnam*, 166. Ralph Waldo Emerson to Wiley & Putnam, 8 May 1846, Gratz—American Poets; Charles Lyell to Messrs Wiley & Putnam, 25 May 1846, Gratz—European Scientists, HSP. Wiley & Putnam to James Fenimore Cooper, 8 Dec. 1846, Beard Collection, AAS.

[67]"The American Library," *Blackwood's Magazine* (Nov. 1847), 574–92; *Littell's Living Age* (20 May 1848), 383; Greenspan, *Putnam* 207–8.

[68]Clark, *International Copyright*, 64–67, 73; Bohde, "Duyckinck," 40–41, 48–52; Widmer, *Young America*, 10, 14, 95, 110–11; Greenspan, *Putnam*, 182–84; Meredith McGill, *American Literature and the Culture of Reprinting, 1834–1853* (Philadelphia: University of Pennsylvania Press, 2003), 200–204; "Evert A. Duyckinck," *ANBO*. Cornelius Mathews to Geo. Frederick Holmes, 19 July 1844, to Edward Moxon, 27 Feb. 1844, Papers of Cornelius Mathews, UVA. Boynton, *Annals*, 177.

[69]"Wiley and Putnam's Catalogue," *Brother Jonathan: A Weekly Compend of Belles Lettres and the Fine Arts*. (25 Nov. 1843), 360.

[70]Greenspan, *Putnam*, 78–79, 114–15, 136. Clinton G. Gilroy, *The Art of Weaving* (London: Wiley & Putnam, 1845); *Wiley & Putnam's Literary News-Letter and Monthly Report of New Books, Foreign and American* (Dec. 1845), Vol. 4, No. 49; Daniel P. Kidder, *Sketches of Residences and Travels in Brazil, Embracing Historical and Geographical Notices of the Empire and Its Several Provinces*, 2 vols. (London: Wiley & Putnam, 1845); *List of New and Valuable Works Published by Wiley and Putnam* (London and New York: 1845), 4, 6; Moore, *Wiley*, 54.

[71]*Brooklyn Eagle* (8 March 1843), 2; London Times, 7, 19 May 1847. Cornelius Mathews, *An Appeal to American Authors and the American Press, in Behalf of International Copyright* (New York: Wiley & Putnam, 1842); Cornelius Mathews, *The Better Interests of the Country, in Connexion with International Copy-right* (New York: Wiley & Putnam, 1843); Boynton, *Annals*, 170.

[72]Francis Lieber and E. Wigglesworth, eds., *Encyclopaedia Americana: A Popular Dictionary of Arts, Sciences, Literature, History, Politics and Biography,* 13 vols. (Philadelphia: Carey, Lea, & Carey, 1829–1833); Clark, *International Copyright*, 56–57; G. Edward White, *The Marshall Court and Cultural Change, 1815–1835* (New York: Oxford University Press, 1991), 888–921; "Joseph Story," "John Marshall," *ANBO*.

[73]Clark, *International Copyright*, 51–63; Barnes, *Authors*, 74–77. Sidney P. Moss, *Charles Dickens' Quarrel with America* (Troy, N.Y.: Whitston Publishing Co., 1984), 61. Francis Lieber, *On International Copyright in a Letter to the Hon. William C. Preston, Senator of the United States* (New York and London: Wiley & Putnam, 1840).

[74]Clark, *International Copyright*, 24–25; Lyman Ray Patterson, *Copyright in Historical Perspective* (Nashville: Vanderbilt University Press, 1968), 180–221; Barnes, *Authors*, 49–50.

[75]Clark, *International Copyright*, 25–27; Barnes, *Authors*, 50.

[76]*London Times*, 7, 19 May 1847; Brander Matthews, *American Authors and British Pirates* (New York: American Copyright League, 1889); White, *Herbert*, 16; Clark, *International Copyright*, 40, 50.

[77]Clark, *International Copyright*, 34–37; Zboray, "Fictive People," 119; Starr, *Creation of the Media*, 116, 122.

78Adamson, *Reply*; Clark, *International Copyright*, 40.

79Clark, *International Copyright*, 43–44; Patterson, *Copyright*, 227; Barnes, *Authors*, 60–65; Mark Rose, *Authors and Owners: The Invention of Copyright* (Cambridge, Mass.: Harvard University Press, 1993), 131–33.

80Grenville A. Sackett, *A Plea for Authors, and the Rights of Literary Property* (New York: Adlard and Saunders, 1838); Clark, *International Copyright*, 46–51; Augustine Birrell, *Seven Lectures on the Law and History of Copyright in Books* (New York: Augustus M. Kelley, 1971), 10–11.

81Bryant, *American Copyright Club*, 10–11.

82Carey, *International Copyright*, 21, 23, 36.

83Carey, *International Copyright*, 6, 26–27, 56. Circular of Booksellers, Employing Printers, Bookbinders, and others, Philadelphia, 30 Dec. 1837, AAS.

84Anon., *Considerations on International Copyright* (Philadelphia: T. K. and P. G. Collins, Printers, 1853). Circular of Booksellers.

85Adamson, *Reply; London Times*, 7, 19 May 1847; Carey, *International Copyright*; Anon., *A Memorial of American Authors* (New York, 1885); American Copyright League, *What American Authors Think About International Copyright* (New York: American Copyright League, 1888); Clark, *International Copyright*, 44–46, 54–55, 76–78; Barnes, *Authors*, 63–94; McGill, *American Literature*, 76–108. Cornelius Mathews to Geo. Frederick Holmes, 19 July 1844, Papers of Cornelius Mathews, UVA.

86Anon., *Considerations on International Copyright*; Carey, *International Copyright*, 4; Lehmann-Haupt et al., Book In America, 203; Clark, *International Copyright*, 81–181; Birrell, *Copyright in Books*, 30–37; Barnes, *Authors*, 241–62; B. Zorina Khan, "Do Property Rights Matter? Evidence from U.S. International Copyright Law, 1790–1910," (Working Paper, 2003), 5; E. Peshire Smith to Henry C. Carey, 27 Dec. 1856, 31 Oct., 12 Dec. 1869, Henry C. Cary Papers, HSP.

87Samuel G. Goodrich, *Recollections of a Lifetime* (New York: Miller, Orton and Mulligan, 1857), 2:379–93; Carey, *International Copyright*, 63; Algernon Tassin, "American Authors and Their Publishers," *The Bookman: A Review of Books and Life* (Apr. 1914), 178–89; Clark, *International Copyright*, 38–39; Bruccoli, *Authorship in America*, 286–87; Zboray, "Fictive People," 3.

88Adamson, *Reply*, 15; Clark, *International Copyright*, 24–25; Birrell, *Copyright in Books*, 37; Barnes, *Authors*, 49, 70; Khan, "U.S. International Copyright Law," 8. Minutes of Meetings of the Book Sellers Company of Philadelphia, 14 Jan. 1803, 1802–1805, Am. 31175, HSP; Nicklin and Johnson to P. R. Fendall, 20 Dec. 1838, Correspondence of Philip Fendall and W. W. Seaton, UVA. Lieber, *International Copyright*, 62–63.

89Adamson, *Reply*, 13–14; American Copyright League, *International Copyright*, 7.

90Joseph H. Davis, "A Quantity-Based Annual Index of U.S. Industrial Production, 1790–1915: An Empirical Appraisal of Historical Business-Cycle Fluctuations," (Ph.D. Diss., Duke University, 2002); Lawrence A. Peskin, *Manufacturing Revolution: The Intellectual Origins of Early American Industry* (Baltimore: Johns Hopkins University Press, 2003); Sean Patrick Adams, *Old Dominion, Industrial Commonwealth: Coal, Politics, and Economy in Antebellum America* (Baltimore: Johns Hopkins University Press, 2004); Doron S. Ben-Atar, *Trade Secrets: Intellectual Piracy and the Origins of American Industrial Power* (New Haven: Yale University Press, 2004).

91Putnam, *Putnam*, 99–101; Greenspan, *Putnam*, 147, 191–231.

92George Palmer Putnam, "Advice to a Young Publisher," *American Publishers' Circular and Literary Gazette*, 15 Aug. 1863.

93*Scientific American* (26 Jan. 1850), 149; "John Wiley," *New York Times*, 22 Feb. 1891. James Fenimore Cooper to Mrs. Cooper, 9 March 1850, in Beard, *Letters and Journals*, 6:155.

94*The American Review* (Sept. 1849), 327; Post, *Bookmakers*, 11; Derby, *Fifty Years*, 296; Stephen Jenkins, *The Greatest Street in the World: The Story of Broadway* (New York: G.P. Putnam's Sons, 1911), 75; Putnam, *Putnam*, 46–47; Edward Crane, *A Century of Book Publishing, 1848–1948* (New York: D. Van Nostrand Company, 1948), 5; Birrell, *Copyright in Books*, 23; Greenspan, *Putnam*, 216–486; Nancy Cook, "Reshaping Publishing and Authorship in the Gilded Age," in Casper et al., *Perspectives*, 223; Starr, *Creation of the Media*, 123. George P. Putnam to James Fenimore Cooper, 3 March, ? Apr., 27 July 1849, Beard Collection, AAS.

95*The Cultivator* (July 1849), 230; *Scientific American* (17 March 1855), 215; *American Publishers' Circular and Literary Gazette*, 1 Sept. 1855. *Wiley & Putnam* catalog, n.d.; Wiley & Putnam, *Supplement No. 1 to the Catalogue of English Books & Prints*, n.d.; Wiley & Putnam, *List of English Books . . . Recently Imported For Sale by Wiley and Putnam* (Sept. 1847).

96*New York Times*, 26 Dec. 1851; *Monthly Trade Gazette* (Apr. 1855), 1. John Wiley to Henry C. Carey, 19, 20, 25 Jan., 7 Nov. 1855, Henry C. Carey Papers, Edward Cary Gardiner Collection; John Wiley, Circular Letter and American Book Fair Proposals, Oct.1855, HSP. John Wiley, *Catalogue of Books Published by John Wiley, With a List of Miscellaneous Works Offered for Sale by Him* (1853); *Wiley & Halsted's Monthly List of New Books, American and English* (Jan. 1856, Sept. 1856); Moore, *Wiley*, 55–57.

97*Horticulturalist and Journal of Rural Art and Rural Taste* (Oct. 1859), 474; Robert Peter, "Remarks on Liebig's 'Letters on Modern Agriculture,' &c." *Southern Planter* (Aug. 1860), 486.

98"The City Book-Stalls," *Arcturus, A Journal of Books and Opinion* (Nov. 1841), 345; *American Publishers' Circular and Literary Gazette*, 7 June 1856; *New York Times*, 19 March 1863; Tebbel, *Book Publishing*, 263; Winship, *American Literary Publishing*, 156, 171–72, 196, 202.

99*Brooklyn Eagle* (16 Jan. 1860), 3. *Wiley & Halsted's Monthly List* (Jan. 1856, Sept. 1856). J. H. Moore's Notes.

100David Stevenson, *Sketch of the Civil Engineering of North America* (London: J. Weale, 1838); *New York Times*, 24 March 1859; *American Publishers' Circular and Literary Gazette*, 2, 9, 16, 23, 30 Apr., 7, 14, 21, 28 May, 4, 11, 18, 25 June, etc. weekly throughout 1859. Anon., Book Reviews, 1838, NYHS, 389.

101Floyd Tifft, "The House of Wiley," *Rensselaer Polytechnic Institute Alumni News* (Sept. 1948), 10; Winship, *American Literary Publishing*, 186–87.

CHAPTER FOUR

[1]New York Evening Post, *The Bookmakers: Reminiscences and Contemporary Sketches of American Publishers* (New York: New York Evening Post, 1875), 77–78. "A Short History of John Wiley & Sons, Inc.," JWS History: Various Histories 19th–20th Century; "John Wiley and Charles Wiley hereby continue," Wiley's [*sic*] before WBW: John/Charles Wiley Partnership, 1869; Wiley's [*sic*] before WBW: Charles Wiley (Photo incl. [*sic*]), 1835–1916.

[2]*American Publisher & Bookseller: A Record of American and Foreign Literature* (Aug. 1869), 14; *Publishers Weekly* (17 Aug. 1946), 715; Edward Crane, *A Century of Book Publishing, 1848–1948* (New York: D. Van Nostrand Co., 1948), 40–41; Hellmut Lehmann-Haupt, Lawrence C. Wroth, and Rollo G. Silver, *The Book In America: A History of the Making and Selling of Books in the United States*, 2nd ed. (New York: R. R. Bowker Co., 1951), 215–17; F. N. Doubleday, *The Memoirs of a Publisher* (Garden City, N.Y.: Doubleday, 1972), 178–79. "Booksellers and bookselling," 1869–1870, Am. 99801, HSP; John Wiley's Sons to Thomas Edison, 4 Nov. 1882, EPO. John Hammond Moore, *Wiley: One Hundred and Seventy-Five Years of Publishing* (New York: John Wiley & Sons, 1982), 74. "Wiley's History in the '80s and '90s and Early in the 20th Century," JWS History: Various Histories 19th–20th Century.

[3]*New York Times* (7 Aug. 1893), 3; Calvin Rice, *Memoirs of Deceased Members*, "William Halsted Wiley," (New York: American Society of Civil Engineers, n.d.), 2. W. Bradford Wiley, "My First 50 Years," Chap. 3, 1.

[4]*Proceedings of the Semi-Centennial Celebration of the Rensselaer Polytechnic Institute* (Troy, N.Y.: Wm. H. Young, 1875), 29; Philip James Mosenthal and Charles F. Horne, *The City College: Memories of Sixty Years* (New York: G. P. Putnam's Sons, 1907), 401; "Maj. William H. Wiley, 83, Dies in East Orange," *New York Times Herald Tribune* (3 May 1925), 23; "Major Wiley Dies of Heart Attack," *New York Times*, 3 May 1925. Rice, *Deceased Members*. "In Memoriam, Samuel E. Norris," *Footnotes* (1949), 5; [Kendall B. Taft, ed.], *The First One Hundred and Fifty Years: A History of John Wiley and Sons, Incorporated, 1807–1957* (New York: John Wiley & Sons, Inc., 1957), 224; Moore, *Wiley*, 75. JWS History: J. H. Moore Notes, Wiley History, 1720–1925; "Very Rouph [*sic*] Draft of Suggested Introduction," "A Short History of John Wiley & Sons, Inc.," "Wiley, William Halsted," JWS History: Various Histories 19th–20th Century.

[5]Post, *Bookmakers*, 77–78. "List of Books Published During 1906," 1906, JWS Operations: Wiley Books Catalogs, 1906–1910.

[6]*New York Times*, 21 Dec. 1874, 11 Feb. 1889; W. G. Collingwood, *The Life of John Ruskin* (London: Methuen, 1911); Lehmann-Haupt et al., *Book In America*, 196; Candy G. Brown, *The Word in the World: Evangelical Writing, Publishing and Reading in America, 1789–1880* (Chapel Hill: University of North Carolina Press, 2004).

[7]Edward Byrn, *The Progress of Invention in the Nineteenth Century* (New York: Russell & Russell, 1970), 118–32; David Billington, *The Innovators: The Engineering Pioneers Who Made America Modern* (New York: John Wiley & Sons, 1996), 139–58.

[8]Alfred D. Chandler, Jr., *The Visible Hand: The Managerial Revolution in American Business* (Cambridge: Harvard University Press, 1977), 79–206; Billington, *Innovators*, 159–77.

[9]Byrn, *Invention*, 76–87; Joseph and Frances Gies, *The Ingenious Yankees* (New York: Thomas Y. Crowell, 1976), 312–29; Paul Israel, *From Machine Shop to Industrial Laboratory: Telegraphy and the Changing Context of American Invention, 1830–1920* (Baltimore: Johns Hopkins University Press, 1992); Billington, *Innovators*, 119–38; Stephen Van Dulken, *Inventing the 19th Century: 100 Inventions That Shaped the Victorian Age, from Aspirin to the Zeppelin* (New York: New York University Press, 2001).

[10]Elting E. Morison, *From Know-How to Nowhere* (New York: Basic Books, 1974); Gies and Gies, *Ingenious Yankees*; Israel, *From Machine Shop to Industrial Laboratory*; Marvin Perry, *An Intellectual History of Modern Europe* (Boston: Houghton Mifflin, 1993); Charles Flowers, *A Science Odyssey: 100 Years of Discovery* (New York: William Morrow & Co., 1998), 17–33, 135–36; Jacques Barzun, "Curing Provincialism: Why We Educate the Way We Do," *American Educator* (Fall 2002); Michael Windelspecht, *Groundbreaking Scientific Experiments, Inventions and Discoveries of the 19th Century* (Westport, Conn.: Greenwood Press, 2003). "Scientist," OEDO.

[11]William H. Wiley to Alfred Tate, 19 Nov. 1888, EPO.

[12]Laurence Veysey, *The Emergence of the American University* (Chicago: University of Chicago Press, 1965). Frederick Rudolph, *The American College and University: A History* (Athens: University of Georgia Press, 1962), 241–63. Quotation on 246.

[13]John H. Thelin, *A History of American Higher Education* (Baltimore and London: The Johns Hopkins University Press, 2004), 90. Frederick Rudolph, *The American College and University: A History* (Athens: University of Georgia Press, 1962), 243–46; Laurence Veysey, *The Emergence of the American University* (Chicago: University of Chicago Press, 1965); John Tebbel, *A History of Book Publishing in the United States, Vol. II: The Expansion of an Industry, 1865–1919* (New York: R. R. Bowker, 1975), 571; David O. Levine, *The American College and the Culture of Aspiration, 1915–1940* (Ithaca: Cornell University Press, 1986), 49.

[14]The categorizations of titles were chosen by the authors. Others would undoubtedly categorize some books differently, as arbitrary decisions were made regarding titles that spanned categories; e.g., books about electrochemistry, forestry, architecture and engineering, and so forth. Nevertheless, all observers would agree that Wiley's strengths were in chemistry, engineering, mathematics, and allied applied fields.

[15]*Directory of Booksellers, Stationers, Newsdealers and Music Dealers and List of Libraries in the United States and Canada Complete to November 1st, 1870* (New York: John H. Dingman c/o Charles Scribner & Co., 1870), 256–57; *Publishers Weekly*, 30 Jan. 1904; *Publishers Weekly* (27 Jan. 1917), 249; "William Halsted Wiley," *Publishers Weekly* (9 May 1925), 1,578–79; Rice, *Deceased Members*, 2; Lehmann-Haupt et al., *Book In America*, 321.

[16]Crane, *A Century*; Tebbel, *A History, Vol. II*, 185–246.

[17]Lehmann-Haupt et al., *Book In America*, 356–57; Roger Burlingame, *Endless Frontiers: The Story of McGraw-Hill* (New

York: McGraw-Hill, 1959), 170–253. Moore, *Wiley*, 103–7. S. E. Norris? Remembrances, n.d.

[18]*The Chautauquan: A Weekly Newsmagazine* (Jan. 1892), 511–12; Thomas Lawler, *Seventy Years of Textbook Publishing: A History of Ginn and Company, 1867–1937* (Boston: Ginn & Co., 1937); Lehmann-Haupt et al., *Book In America*, 328; Tebbel, *A History, Vol. II*, 535–39; Paul Starr, *The Creation of the Media: Political Origins of Modern Communications* (New York: Basic Books, 2004), 141. "Extracts from Mr. Hayden's Notes on Texas A & M College, College Station, Texas," covered by John Wiley & Sons to J. B. Davidson, 26 Mar. 1923; "Washington State College, Pullman, Wash., visited by F. D. Hayden, Dec. 6, 1923," covered by John Wiley & Sons to J. B. Davidson, 10 Jan. 1924, J. Brownlee Davidson Papers, ISUA.

[19]"Three Recent Books on Industrial Management," *Harvard Business Review* (July 1924), 507–8; Levine, *American College*, 53–60. J. B. Davidson to C. O. Reed, 5 Dec. 1923, John Wiley & Sons to J. B. Davidson, 22 July 1924, J. Brownlee Davidson Papers, ISUA.

[20]Emily Fogg-Meade, "The Place of Advertising in Modern Business," *Journal of Political Economy* (Mar. 1901), 218–42.

[21]*New York Times*, 30 Aug. 1873; *Brooklyn Eagle* (11 June 1890), 6; Tebbel, *A History, Vol. II*, 559–78. Moore, *Wiley*, 72–75, 110.

[22]Rudolph, *American College*, 486; Veysey, *American University*, 175–77; Roger Geiger, "The Era of Multipurpose Colleges in American Higher Education, 1850–1890," in Roger Geiger, ed., *The American College in the Nineteenth Century* (Nashville: Vanderbilt University Press, 2000), 130. Moore, *Wiley*, 68.

[23]American Library Association, *A Survey of Libraries in the United States,* 4 vols. (Chicago, American Library Association, 1926), 1:213–57.

[24]Edward Edwards, *Free Town Libraries: Their Formation, Management, and History in Britain, France, Germany, & America* (New York: John Wiley and Son, 1869), 275–77; *Publishers Weekly* (30 Jan. 1904), 149; Lehmann-Haupt et al., *Book In America*, 142; Starr, *Creation of the Media*, 86. Wayne A. Wiegand and Donald G. Davis Jr., eds., *Encyclopedia of Library History* (New York: Garland Publishing, Inc., 1994), 9, 10.

[25]Edwards, *Free Town Libraries;* American Library Association, *Survey of Libraries*, 1:31–36, 53–57; Herbert Hungerford, *How Publishers Win: A Case Record Commentary on Personal Experiences and Interviews with Prominent Publishers Showing How Books and Periodicals Are Made and Marketed* (Washington, D.C.: Ransdell Inc., 1931), 287–91; Tebbel, *A History, Vol. II*, 99; Bennett Cerf, *At Random: The Reminiscences of Bennett Cerf* (New York: Random House, 1977), 75; Ann Fabian, "Laboring Classes," in Scott E. Casper, Joanne D. Chaison, and Jeffrey D. Groves, eds., *Perspectives on American Book History: Artifacts and Commentary* (Boston: University of Massachusetts Press, 2002), 285; Roque J. Calvo, "Professional Societies . . . Where the Scientific Tale Unfolded," in National Academies (U.S.), *Facilitating Interdisciplinary Research* (Washington, D.C.: National Academies Press, 2004).

[26]Lawrence P. Grayson, *The Making of an Engineer* (New York: John Wiley & Sons, 1993), 16–33, 43.

[27]*The Manufacturer and Builder* (Mar. 1883), 70, (Jan. 1890), 22; Levine, *American College*, 47; Yehouda Shenhav, "From Chaos to Systems: The Engineering Foundations of Organization Theory, 1879–1932," *Administrative Science Quarterly* (Dec. 1995), 557–585. OCLC.

[28]"Mansfield Merriman," in James G. Wilson and John Fiske, eds., *Appleton's Cyclopaedia of American Biography* (New York: D. Appleton & Co., 1888). Lazarus White, *The Catskill Water Supply of New York City* (New York: John Wiley & Sons, 1913); Taft, *Wiley*, 84–85, 125, 212; Moore, *Wiley*, 102.

[29]*Brooklyn Eagle* (16 Oct. 1898), 33; *Trenton Times* (19 June 1903), 1; *New York Times*, 30 Nov. 1903; "Major Wiley Dies of Heart Attack," *New York Times*, 3 May 1925; "William Halsted Wiley," *Publishers Weekly* (9 May 1925), 1,578–79. Taft, *Wiley*, 225. "Wiley, William Halsted," JWS History: Various Histories 19th–20th Century; W. H. Wiley Scrapbook, 1902–1909; W. H. Wiley Scrapbook, 1906.

[30]WBW: William Halsted Wiley (Photo), 1842–1925, JWSA.

[31]*Brooklyn Eagle* (15 Jan. 1888), 14; "Earnest Apostle of Cleanliness," *New York Times* (9 Jan. 1909), 17; Lionel S. Marks, *Mechanical Engineers' Handbook* (New York: McGraw-Hill, 1916). William Kent, *The Mechanical Engineers' Pocket-Book* (New York: John Wiley & Sons, 1916); Moore, *Wiley*, 82. S. E. Norris? Remembrances, n.d.

[32]*Publishers Weekly* (26 Jan. 1901), 95; Crane, *A Century*, 36; Tebbel, *A History, Vol. II*, 652. John Wiley & Sons to W. A. Foster, 15 Apr. 1924, J. Brownlee Davidson Papers, ISUA. Moore, *Wiley*, 100. S.E. Norris? Remembrances, n.d.; "Wiley's History in the '80s and '90s and Early in the 20th Century," JWS History: Various Histories 19th–20th Century; Memo to Matheson re: F. W. Classon, 1 Oct. 1954.

[33]William W. Ellsworth, *A Golden Age of Authors: A Publisher's Recollection* (Boston: Houghton Mifflin Co., 1919), 105–9; Raymond Shove, *Cheap Book Production in the United States, 1870 to 1891* (Urbana: University of Illinois Library, 1937), 51; Tebbel, *A History, Vol. II*, 383, 471, 513. Moore, *Wiley*, 93.

[34]Byrn, *Invention*, 154–70; Lehmann-Haupt et al., *Book In America*, 145–77; Windelspecht, *Groundbreaking Scientific Experiments*, 189–92.

[35]Lehmann-Haupt et al., *Book In America*, 147–53.

[36]Lehmann-Haupt et al., *Book In America*, 168–75; Nancy Cook, "Reshaping Publishing and Authorship in the Gilded Age," in Casper et al., *Perspectives*, 224.

[37]William D. Robinson to Mathew Carey, 17 Dec. 1820, Mathew Carey Papers, Edward C. Gardiner Collection, HSP; John Wiley & Sons to J. B. Davidson, 30 Jan. 1922, J. B. Davidson to John Wiley & Sons, 6 Feb. 1922, J. Brownlee Davidson Papers, ISUA. S. E. Norris? Remembrances, n.d.; "Notes on John Wiley & Sons, Inc., and F. H. Gilson Company," 9 Apr. 1951, S. E. Norris to E. P. Hamilton, 28 Mar. 1946, JWS History: Various Histories 19th–20th Century.

[38]John Wiley & Sons to J. B. Davidson, 21 Mar. 1924, J. Brownlee Davidson Papers, ISUA.

[39]John Wiley & Sons to J. B. Davidson, 14 Aug. 1924, J. Brownlee Davidson Papers, ISUA. "In Memoriam, Samuel E. Norris,"

Footnotes (1949), 5; Moore, *Wiley*, 99, 127. "Wiley Staff in 1914"; "Wiley's History in the '80s and '90s and Early in the 20th Century," JWS History: Various Histories 19th–20th Century; Wiley, "My First 50 Years," Chap. 3, 10.

[40]"University of Idaho, visited by F. D. Hayden, May 5, 6, 1922," covered by John Wiley & Sons to J. B. Davidson, 15 May 1922, J. Brownlee Davidson Papers, ISUA. Moore, *Wiley*, 98–99, 111. JWS History: Various Histories 19th–20th Century.

[41]Aubert J. Clark, *The Movement for International Copyright in Nineteenth Century America* (Washington, D.C.: Catholic University of America Press, 1960), 183. Taft, *Wiley*, 210. John Wiley [Jr.] to William O. Wiley, 21, 22 July 1890; William H. Wiley to William O. Wiley, 20 June 1892; "First Section," "Wiley's History in the '80s and '90s and Early in the 20th Century," JWS History: Various Histories 19th–20th Century.

[42]William H. Wiley to William O. Wiley, 20 June 1892, JWSA.

[43]John Wiley & Sons to J. B. Davidson, 8 Mar. 1922; "Extracts from Mr. Hayden's Notes on the University of California (University Farm) Davis, Cal., 4/10/22"; "Extracts from Notes for Prof. J. B. Davidson," covered by John Wiley & Sons to J. B. Davidson, 22 Apr. 1922, "University of Idaho, visited by F. D. Hayden, May 5, 6, 1922," covered by John Wiley & Sons to J. B. Davidson, 15 May 1922, "Extracts from F. E. Mee's Notes on Ohio State University Visited March 8th (P.M.) 9th and 10th," covered by John Wiley & Sons to J. B. Davidson, 26 Mar. 1923, J. Brownlee Davidson Papers, ISUA.

[44]*New York Times*, 4 Feb. 1873; *Brooklyn Eagle* (20 Dec. 1896), 13, (25 Apr. 1897), 19; Rice, *Deceased Members*, 3. John Wiley & Sons to J. B. Davidson, 1 Mar. 1922; J. B. Davidson to John Wiley & Sons, 15 Mar. 1922; "Extracts from Notes for Prof. J. B. Davidson," covered by John Wiley & Sons to J. B. Davidson, 22 Apr. 1922; John Wiley & Sons to J. B. Davidson, 3 Apr., 11 Oct. 1923, 11 Feb. 1924, J. Brownlee Davidson Papers, ISUA.

[45]John Wiley & Sons to J. B. Davidson, 11 Oct. 1923, 20 Aug. 1924, J. Brownlee Davidson Papers, ISUA.

[46]*Scientific American* (17 Oct. 1874), 248, (18 Aug. 1877), 105. J. B. Davidson to John Wiley & Sons, 10 Mar. 1922, J. Brownlee Davidson Papers, ISUA.

[47]Moore, *Wiley*.

[48]*Scientific American* (4 Nov. 1871), 297; *Quarterly Journal of Economics* (Mar. 1927), 67.

[49]J. B. Davidson to John Wiley & Sons, 17, 20 Apr. 1922; "University of Idaho, visited by F. D. Hayden, May 5, 6, 1922," covered by John Wiley & Sons to J. B. Davidson, 15 May 1922, J. Brownlee Davidson Papers, ISUA.

[50]Moore, *Wiley*.

[51]Taft, *Wiley*, 59–60, 212; Moore, *Wiley*, 81–82, 102. "A Short History of John Wiley & Sons, Inc.," JWS History: Various Histories 19th–20th Century.

[52]"The Literature of Scientific Management," *Quarterly Journal of Economics* (May 1914), 521; G. W. Carleton, *Publishers Weekly* (17 Aug. 1946), 712; Leland Jenks, "Early Phases of the

Management Movement," *Administrative Science Quarterly* (Dec. 1960), 421–47. OCLC. Taft, *Wiley*, 134–36. Wiley, "My First 50 Years," Chap. 4, 5.

[53]R. C. Archibald, "Methods of German Publishers," *Science* (14 July 1922), 45; Julie Ann Miller, "Special Book Section: Why a Book? Changes in Biology-Book Publishing," *BioScience* 39 (1989): 180–83; John J. McCusker, "Comparing the Purchasing Power of Money in the United States (or Colonies) from 1665 to 2003," Economic History Services, 2004, http://www.eh.net/hmit/ppowerusd/. John Wiley & Sons to J. B. Davidson, 22 July 1924, J. Brownlee Davidson Papers, ISUA. S.E. Norris? Remembrances, n.d.

[54]Hungerford, *How Publishers Win*, 288; Lehmann-Haupt et al., *Book In America*, 195; Tebbel, *A History, Vol. II*, 112–15; Cerf, *At Random*, 281.

[55]Hungerford, *How Publishers Win*, 282; Shove, *Cheap Book Production*, ix–x, 25; Lehmann-Haupt et al., *Book In America*, 196, 214–15, 250–54; Tebbel, *A History, Vol. II*, 481–88, 641.

[56]Hungerford, *How Publishers Win*, 283; Tebbel, *A History, Vol. II*, 112, 426; Cerf, *At Random*, 72–283. Booklovers Library, Oct. 1903, Society Miscellaneous, Libraries, HSP.

[57]*Mail & Express Souvenir Edition of the Centennial Celebration of Washington's Inauguration*, 29–30 Apr. 1889; *New York Times*, 25 Jan 1891; Augustine Birrell, *Seven Lectures on the Law and History of Copyright in Books* (New York: G. P. Putnam's Sons, 1899), 179; Hungerford, *How Publishers Win*, 313; Tebbel, *A History, Vol. II*, 151–52, 156. Hugh Agnew, "Can Standardization Reduce Advertising Costs?" *Annals of the American Academy of Political and Social Science* (May 1928), 253–58; Lehmann-Haupt et al., *Book In America*, 143; Tebbel, *A History, Vol. II*, 145–46.

[58]*New York Times*, 30 Aug. 1873; *Journal of Home Economics* (Oct. 1924), 608; Crane, *A Century*, 39–40; Tebbel, *A History, Vol. II*, 496. Moore, *Wiley*, 75.

[59]Tebbel, *A History, Vol. II*, 152. Henry Keller, Jr., to John Wiley & Sons, 16 Feb. 1922, J. B. Davidson to John Wiley & Sons, 21 Feb. 1922, John Wiley & Sons to Henry Keller, Jr., 22 Feb. 1922, John Wiley & Sons to J. B. Davidson, 2 Mar. 1922, J. B. Davidson to John Wiley & Sons, 7 Mar. 1922, J. Brownlee Davidson Papers, ISUA.

[60]Hungerford, *How Publishers Win*, 284; Starr, *Creation of the Media*, 148. Wiley Family Oral History: Interview WBW w/ PBW, 1991, 33; Wiley, "My First 50 Years," Chap. 3, 83.

[61]John Wiley & Sons to J. B. Davidson, 27 Dec. 1921, 7 Jan. 1922, 13 Aug. 1924, J. B. Davidson to John Wiley & Sons, 10 Jan. 1922, J. Brownlee Davidson Papers, ISUA.

[62]Tebbel, *A History, Vol. II*, 150, 160–66. Taft, *Wiley*, 41.

[63]*Directory of Booksellers, 1870*, 256–57.

[64]Birrell, *Copyright in Books*, 36; Arthur Waugh, *A Hundred Years of Publishing, Being the Story of Chapman & Hall, Ltd.* (London: Chapman & Hall, 1930), 251–53, 273; Lehmann-Haupt et al., *Book In America*, 203; Tebbel, *A History, Vol. II*, 640–41. Moore, *Wiley*, 97.

[65]Waugh, *Chapman & Hall*, 273–75, 287; Lehmann-Haupt et al., *Book In America*, 205; Simon Nowell-Smith, *International Copyright*

Law and the Publisher in the Reign of Queen Victoria (Oxford: Clarendon Press, 1968), 64–84.

[66]Taft, *Wiley*, 73; Moore, *Wiley*, 97. William B. Wiley, "Emergence of John Wiley & Sons as an International Publisher," n.d; "WBW Letters: UK, 1957–1960."

[67]Taft, *Wiley*, 73. John Wiley & Sons to J. B. Davidson, 5 June 1922, J. B. Davidson to John Wiley & Sons, 2 June 1922, J. Brownlee Davidson Papers, ISUA.

[68]Levine, *American College*, 47, 52–53.

[69]John Wiley & Sons to J. B. Davidson, 14 June, 22 Dec. 1921, J. Brownlee Davidson Papers, ISUA.

[70]John Wiley & Sons to J. B. Davidson, 8 July 1920, 23 June, 27 Dec. 1921, 27 Feb. 1922; J. B. Davidson to John Wiley & Sons, 29 Mar. 1923, J. Brownlee Davidson Papers, ISUA.

[71]John Wiley & Sons to J. B. Davidson, 13 July 1920, 7, 8 Jan. 1922, 3 Apr, 20 Nov. 1923; "Extracts from F. E. Mee's Notes on Ohio State University Visited March 8th (P.M.) 9th and 10th," covered by John Wiley & Sons to J. B. Davidson, 26 Mar. 1923, J. Brownlee Davidson Papers, ISUA.

[72]OCLC. http://www.rofflehaus.com/wiki/J._Brownlee_Davidson; http://www.eng.iastate.edu/coe/profile/2004/kanwar.asp; http://www.eng.iastate.edu/tour/davidson.asp; http://www.asabe.org/awards/historic2/images_05.html.

[73]John Wiley & Sons to J. B. Davidson, 14 June 1915, 14 June, 22 Dec. 1921; J. B. Davidson to John Wiley & Sons, 17 June 1915, 20 Jan. 1923, J. Brownlee Davidson Papers, ISUA.

[74]John Wiley & Sons to J. B. Davidson, 4 Aug. 1920, 3 Apr. 1923; F. A. Wirt to J. B. Davidson, 6 May 1922, J. B. Davidson to John Wiley & Sons, 8 May 1922; "Extracts from F. E. Mee's Notes on Ohio State University Visited March 8th (P.M.) 9th and 10th," covered by John Wiley & Sons to J. B. Davidson, 26 Mar. 1923, J. Brownlee Davidson Papers, ISUA.

[75]John T. Bowen to J. B. Davidson, 20 Mar. 1922, 17 Mar. 1923, J. B. Davidson to John T. Bowen, 13, 20, 23 Mar. 1923; John Wiley & Sons to J. B. Davidson, 15 Sept., 6 Nov. 1920, 8 Mar. 1922, 30 Jan., 3 Apr., 19 July, 25 Oct. 1923, 2, 8 Feb., 7, 21 Mar., 21 Aug., 23 Sept. 1924; J. B. Davidson to John Wiley & Sons, 13 Mar., 5 May 1922, 24 Jan., 5, 12 Feb., 3, 15 Mar. 1924; J. A. Gamble to John Wiley & Sons, 22 Aug. 1924, J. B. Davidson to J. A. Gamble, 9 Sept. 1924, J. Brownlee Davidson Papers, ISUA.

[76]John Wiley & Sons to J. B. Davidson, 15 Oct. 1920, 20 Mar. 1922, 22 July 1924; J. B. Davidson to John Wiley & Sons, 14 June 1921, 5 Aug. 1924, J. Brownlee Davidson Papers, ISUA.

[77]John Wiley & Sons to J. B. Davidson, 8 July 1920, 7 Jan., 14 Nov., 22 Dec. 1921; J. B. Davidson to John Wiley & Sons, 16 Nov. 1921, J. Brownlee Davidson Papers, ISUA.

[78]John Wiley & Sons to J. B. Davidson, 26 Oct. 1920, 16, 28 Aug. 1922, J. B. Davidson to John Wiley & Sons, 22 Aug. 1922, J. Brownlee Davidson Papers, ISUA.

[79]John Wiley & Sons to J. B. Davidson, 15 Sept. 1920, 7 Oct. 1922, 20 Feb. 1924, J. Brownlee Davidson Papers, ISUA.

[80]John Wiley & Sons to J. B. Davidson, 13 July 1920, 7 Jan. 1922, 12 June 1924; J. B. Davidson to John Wiley & Sons, 20 Aug., 19 Sept. 1920, 19 Sept. 1921, 26 Jan., 8 May 1922, 10 June 1924, J. Brownlee Davidson Papers, ISUA.

[81]John Wiley & Sons to J. B. Davidson, 14, 23 June 1921, 7 January 1922, 14 April 1922, 15, 26 March 1923; J. B. Davidson to John Wiley & Sons, 19 September 1920, 8 May 1922, 12 March 1923; John Wiley & Sons to Oscar M. Broin, 14 April 1923; Extracts from F. E. Mee's Notes on Ohio State University Visited March 8th (P.M.) 9th and 10th," covered by John Wiley & Sons to J. B. Davidson, 26 March 1923.

[82]J. B. Davidson to John Wiley & Sons, 27 June 1921, 29 Mar., 29 Oct. 1923, 23 Oct. 1924; John Wiley & Sons to J. B. Davidson, 12, 20 Nov. 1923, J. Brownlee Davidson Papers, ISUA. Allen Kimball and Clinton Cowgill, "A Handbook on Architectural Design," [1921?].

[83]Frank Kranich, *Farm Equipment for Mechanical Power* (New York: Macmillan, 1923). J. B. Davidson to John Wiley & Sons, 22 Oct. 1923, John Wiley & Sons to J. B. Davidson, 12 Nov. 1923, J. Brownlee Davidson Papers, ISUA.

[84]J. B. Davidson to John Wiley & Sons, 8 Jan., 13, 16, 27 Mar., 19 June 1922, 20 Jan. 1923, 15 Mar. 1924; John Wiley & Sons to J. B. Davidson, 19 Mar., 11 May, 15 June 1922, J. Brownlee Davidson Papers, ISUA.

[85]John Wiley & Sons to J. B. Davidson, 1, 6 Nov. 1920, 8 Feb., 14 June 1921, 20 Jan., 18 Feb., 16, 29 Mar., 26 Apr., 4 May, 5 June, 7 Oct. 1922, 20 Jan., 13 Feb., 4 June 1923; J. B. Davidson to John Wiley & Sons, 6 May, 2, 3 June 1924; A. E. Jennings to John Wiley & Sons, 27 Mar. 1922, J. B. Davidson to W. L. Powers, 7 Apr. 1922, J. Brownlee Davidson Papers, ISUA.

[86]John Wiley & Sons to J. B. Davidson, 27 Sept., 3 Nov. 1922; E. W. Lehmann to J. B. Davidson, 10 Mar. 1924; J. B. Davidson to John Wiley & Sons, 30 Sept. 1922, 18 Mar. 1924, J. Brownlee Davidson Papers, ISUA.

[87]Taft, *Wiley*, 224; Moore, *Wiley*, 93. Certificate of Incorporation of John Wiley and Sons, 14 Jan. 1904.

[88]Taft, *Wiley*, 45–47, 73, 98; Moore, *Wiley*, 97–98, 105–7.

[89]"William Halsted Wiley," *Publishers Weekly* (9 May 1925), 1,578–79; Rice, *Deceased Members*, 2. Moore, Wiley, 106. Martin Matheson's Big Black Book.

[90]*Publishers Weekly* (23 Jan. 1926), 240.

CHAPTER FIVE

[1]F. Scott Fitzgerald, "My Lost City" in *The Crack-Up*. (New York: New Directions, 1945), 25.

[2]Ben Yagoda, *About Town*: The New Yorker *and the World It Made* (New York: Scribner, 2000), 27, 28.

[3]David Stravitz, *The Chrysler Building: Creating a New York Icon, Day by Day* (New York: Princeton Architectural Press, 2002), xiv; "The Chrysler Building," http://xroads.Virginia.edu/~1930s/DISPLAY/chrysler/front.html.

[4]Charles Madison, *Book Publishing in America* (New York: McGraw-Hill Book Company, 1966), 67. Samuel E. Norris, *The Manuscript: A Guide for Its Preparation* (New York: John Wiley & Sons, 1927), 2. American Institute of Architects Press Release, 5 May 1989, "JWS Records: AIA Honors JWS 4 'Standard' Book, 1989"; Wiley Family Oral History: Interview WBW w/ PBW, 1991, 14–15; Memorandum on Group Interview, 2 Oct. 1992, "JWS Oral Interview, 1992"; W. Bradford Wiley, "My First 50 Years," Chap. 3, 7, Chap. 4, 27.

[5]O. H. Cheney, *Economic Survey of the Book Industry, 1930–1931* (New York: National Association of Book Publishers, 1931), 11, 156, 161.

[6]Arthur K. Getman to Edward Hamilton, 17 Nov. 1948, "JWS Records: Advertising, 1926–1950"; Edward Hamilton to M. Frank Redding, 8 Oct. 1962, "Wiley's [*sic*] before WBW: E. P. Hamilton History, 1962."

[7]Edward Hamilton to M. Frank Redding, 8 Oct. 1962, "Wiley's [*sic*] before WBW: E. P. Hamilton History, 1962."

[8]As in Chapter 4, we here track the first time Wiley published a book and substantial revisions, not each new edition and certainly not mere reprinting activity. As Hamilton himself noted, "in the earlier days of publishing, the term 'new edition' seems to have been used carelessly," often applied to "little more than a new printing, perhaps with minor corrections." "Today," he wrote in 1952, "we insist that a new edition mean a really substantial revision." We have been even more stringent here, counting a new edition as a new title only if it was rewritten, greatly enlarged, or so thoroughly changed that a new title was assigned or new authors were added. A certain amount of discretion was involved, so other observers would undoubtedly come up with slightly different figures, but our counts concur closely with the internal records available. For example, by our count Wiley published 97 books in 1953, which is very close to the 104 titles listed in "Wiley Books Published in 1953," *Footnotes* (May 1954), 6. Our figures are consistently lower than those given in *Publishers Weekly* because we count only substantive editions. Edward Hamilton, "Engineering Literature," *Library Journal* (15 Nov. 1952), 1,939–41. Edward Hamilton, "Present State of Engineering Literature," 26 June 1952, "Wiley's [*sic*] before WBW: Hamilton Speeches, 1952–1955."

[9]Cheney, *Economic Survey*, 163. John Hammond Moore, *Wiley: One Hundred and Seventy Five Years of Publishing* (New York: John Wiley & Sons, 1982), 116. Mary Lispenard Ward, "John Wiley & Sons, Inc.: A Very Brief History," (Baltimore: Enoch Pratt Free Library, 1931).

[10]*New York Social Register* (1930), 879. Moore, *Wiley*, 121. Wiley Family Oral History: Interview WBW w/ PBW, 1991, 18.

[11]"An Important Event in Technical Publishing!" *Journal of Engineering Education* (Oct. 1932); John Tebbel, *A History of Book Publishing in the United States, Volume III, The Golden Age Between Two Wars, 1920–1940* (New York: R. R. Bowker Company, 1978), 5, 254–55, 377–78. [Kendall B. Taft, ed.], *The First One Hundred and Fifty Years: A History of John Wiley and Sons, Incorporated, 1807–1957* (New York: John Wiley & Sons, Inc., 1957), 93. A Short History of John Wiley & Sons, Inc., "JWS History: Various Histories 19th–20th Century"; "JWS Records: Advertising, 1926–1950"; Wiley, "My First 50 Years," Chap. 4, 17.

[12]"Radio Book Review," *New York Times* (30 June 1929), 16; Cheney, *Economic Survey*, 112; Hollister Noble, "The Problems of Broadcast Advertising," *New York Times Book Review* (14 Feb. 1932), 9.

[13]"A History of John Wiley & Sons, Inc.," *New York Journal of Commerce* (29 Sept. 1927). Moore, *Wiley*, 112, 127. "JWS History: WBW Research (Annual Reports), 1932–1961"; Edward Hamilton to Arthur K. Getman, 1 Dec. 1948, "JWS 150th Anniversary: Planning, 1955–1957"; "Wiley Family Oral History: Interview WBW w/ PBW," 1991, 18.

[14]"Marketing's MM: Martin Matheson and the Marketing Division," *Wiley Bulletin* (Fall 1959), 2.

[15]"Extracts from Mr. Mee's Notes on Ohio State University, December 15–16, 1922," covered by John Wiley & Sons to J. B. Davidson, 27 Dec. 1922; J. B. Davidson to John Wiley & Sons, 11 Feb. 1924; John Wiley & Sons to J. B. Davidson, 16, 20 Feb., 24 Mar. 1924, J. Brownlee Davidson Papers, ISUA. Norris, *Manuscript*, v.

[16]Moore, *Wiley*, 113–14.

[17]Peter Adams, "Technology in Publishing: A Century of Progress," in Richard Abel and Lyman Newlin, eds., *Scholarly Publishing: Books, Journals, Publishers, and Libraries in the Twentieth Century* (New York: John Wiley & Sons, 2002), 29. Norris, *Manuscript*.

[18]Norris, *Manuscript*, 9–10, 12, 32–33.

[19]Norris, *Manuscript*, 6–7. Edward P. Hamilton, "Author! Author! Some Random Thoughts on Ideal Technical Books and Their Authors," n.d., "Wiley's [*sic*] before WBW: Hamilton Speeches, 1944–1952."

[20]Norris, *Manuscript*, 11. Martin Matheson, "In Praise of the Preface," n.d., "JWS Employees: Martin Matheson, 1953–1972."

[21]Hamilton, "Engineering Literature," 1,939–41. "Notes on Indexing," n.d., "JWS History: Publicity, 1927–1957."

[22]Norris, *Manuscript*, 16, 40.

[23]GDP given in year 2000 dollars. Thorstein Veblen, *The Theory of the Leisure Class* (New York: Macmillan, 1899); R. L. Duffus, *Books: Their Place in a Democracy* (Boston: Houghton Mifflin Company, 1930), 208–25; Cheney, *Economic Survey*, 44; Roy Rosenzweig, *Eight Hours For What We Will: Workers and Leisure in an Industrial City, 1870–1920* (New York: Cambridge University Press, 1985); Kathy Peiss, *Cheap Amusements: Working Women and Leisure in Turn-of-the-Century New York* (Philadelphia: Temple University Press, 1987); Richard E. Abel, "The Change of Book and Journal Infrastructure: Two Publishers, Consolidation, and Niche Publishers," in Abel and Newlin, eds., *Scholarly Publishing*, 25; Mary Beth Norton et al., *A People and a Nation* (Boston: Houghton Mifflin, 2005), 659.

[24]Per capita income given in year 2000 dollars. Cheney, *Economic Survey*, 12, 19; "Successful A.I.B. Man: The Career of O. H. Cheney an Encouragement to All Institute Members," *Bankers' Magazine* (Sept. 1908), 427; Roger Burlingame, *Endless Frontiers: The Story of McGraw-Hill* (New York: McGraw-Hill, 1959), 254; Tebbel, *History of Book Publishing III*, 69. Wiley, "My First 50 Years," Chap. 3, 10.

[25]Cheney, *Economic Survey*, 20–37.

[26] Cheney, *Economic Survey*, 56.

[27] Duffus, *Books*, 224; Cheney, *Economic Survey*, 43; Richard Lykes, *Higher Education and the United States Office of Education* (Washington, D.C.: Government Printing Office, 1975), 106.

[28] "Let Them Know the Prices," *Publishers Weekly* (6 Dec. 1930), 2,544; Madison, *Book Publishing*, 547–56; Adams, "Technology in Publishing," 32.

[29] "Familiar Forces Drive Prepress," *Graphic Arts Monthly* (May 2003), 30–31.

[30] "An Industry Time Line," *Printing Impressions* (May 2002), 34–36.

[31] Michael Wallace and Arne Kalleberg, "Industrial Transformation and the Decline of Craft: The Decomposition of Skill in the Printing Industry, 1931–1978," *American Sociological Review* (June 1982), 307–24.

[32] Wallace and Kalleberg, "Industrial Transformation," 307–24; Walker Rumble, *The Swifts: Printers in the Age of Typesetting Races* (Charlottesville: University of Virginia Press, 2003); Caroline Archer, "Printer's Tramps," *Printweek* (July 29, 2004), 46.

[33] Cheney, *Economic Survey*, 73; Roland Marchand, *Advertising the American Dream: Making Way for Modernity, 1920–1940* (Los Angeles: University of California Press, 1985); David Goldfield et al., *The American Journey* (Upper Saddle River, N.J.: Prentice Hall, 1998), 797; Norton et al., *A People and a Nation*, 658.

[34] Cheney, *Economic Survey*, 82–89.

[35] Cheney, *Economic Survey*, 157; Mahala Saville, "Publishing Houses and Their Birthdays," *Wilson Bulletin* (Feb. 1941).

[36] "Long Service with John Wiley & Sons," *Publishers Weekly* (6 Dec. 1930), 2,543; William Miller, *The Book Industry* (New York: Columbia University Press, 1949), 142; Alice Smith, *A Peril and a Hope: The Scientists' Movement in America: 1945–47* (Chicago: University of Chicago Press, 1965), 532.

[37] Moore, *Wiley*, 118. Wiley Family Oral History: Interview WBW w/ PBW, 1991, 10; Wiley, "My First 50 Years," Chap. 3, 9.

[38] George Soule, "Toward Mitigating the Evils of Overproduction," *New York Times* (11 Jan. 1931), 64; J. L. Snider, Accounting Review (Sept. 1931), 234; Frederick C. Mills, "Money, Prices, Credit, and Banking," *American Economic Review* (Dec. 1933), 747; E. A. Kincaid, *Accounting Review* (Dec. 1933), 365–66; "Best Sellers Here and Elsewhere," *New York Times* (15 Jan. 1934), 13.

[39] "Does America Lack Foreign Consciousness?" *The World Tomorrow* (Nov. 1931); Cheney, *Economic Survey*, 187–88.

[40] "You'll Find It in Peele," (June 1941), "JWS Records: Advertising, 1926–1950."

[41] "Sixth Printing," *New Outlook* (Apr. 1934); "Answers Thousands of Questions In Your Field of Work," 1938, "JWS Records: Advertising, 1926–1950."

[42] Malcolm M. Willey, *Depression, Recovery and Higher Education: A Report by Committee Y of the American Association of University Professors* (New York: McGraw-Hill Book Company, 1937), 221–67; Louis R. Wilson, *The Geography of Reading: A Study of the Distribution and Status of Libraries in the United States* (Chicago: University of Chicago Press, 1938), 199; Frederick Rudolph, *The American College and University: A History* (Athens, Ga.: University of Georgia Press, 1962), 469; David Henry, *Challenges Past, Challenges Present: An Analysis of American Higher Education Since 1930* (San Francisco: Jossey-Bass Publishers, 1975), 12–16; David Levine, *The American College and the Culture of Aspiration, 1915–1940* (Ithaca: Cornell University Press, 1986), 191. Wiley, "My First 50 Years," Chap. 3, 11.

[43] Willey, *Depression*, 17–63; Rudolph, *American College*, 442.

[44] *Publishers Weekly* (6 Dec. 1930), 2,580; Miller, *Book Industry*, 65. "History of Braunworth & Co.," n.d., Becker Brothers Engraving Co. to Leroy Jordan, 3 Apr. 1951, "Notes on John Wiley & Sons, Inc., and F. H. Gilson Company," 9 Apr. 1951, W. F. Etherington & Co., Inc. to Leroy Jordan, 10, 16 Apr. 1951, "JWS Alliances: Historical Business Associates, 1951."

[45] "A Few Months Ago," *Footnotes* (Apr. 1949), 5. Goodwin Dillen to Martin Matheson, 29 Nov., 30 Dec. 1948, "JWS 150th Anniversary: Planning, 1955–1957."

[46] "The House of Wiley Observes Its 125th Anniversary," *Publishers Weekly* (10 Dec. 1932), 2,186–87; "Technical Publishing House Celebrates 125th Anniversary," *Engineering News Record* (15 Dec. 1932); "John Wiley & Sons Celebrate 125th Anniversary," *Industrial & Engineering Chemistry* (20 Dec. 1932); "More Than a Century," *Engineering News Record* (22 Dec. 1932); "The House of Wiley," *N.A.C.S. Bulletin* (Jan. 1933), 15; "To Commemorate," *Wilson Bulletin* (Jan. 1933); "Representatives," *Electric Journal* (Jan. 1933); "John Wiley & Sons Celebrate 125th Anniversary," *Bookbinding Magazine* (Jan. 1933); "Announcing! Annals of American Bookselling," *Library Journal* (Jan. 1933). W. H. Timbie to William O. Wiley, 30 Nov. 1932, Vladimir Karapetoff to William O. Wiley, 29 Nov. 1932, Robert Peele to William O. Wiley, 10 Dec. 1932, "JWS 125th Anniversary Correspondence, 1932."

[47] Tebbel, *History of Book Publishing III*, 30, 254, 615. *The House of Wiley* (New York: John Wiley & Sons, 1948), 30. Clarence Linder to W. Bradford Wiley, 13 Apr. 1959, Seawright memo, 3 June 1959, J. Kenneth Maddock to Charles F. Savage, 5 Apr. 1966, "Wiley Books Written by Members of General Electric Staff," 21 Aug. 1961, "JWS Alliances: General Electric, 1951–1956"; Wiley Family Oral History: Interview WBW w/ PBW, 1991, 14–15, 65; Wiley, "My First 50 Years," Chap. 3, 7, Chap. 4, 19–20, 27.

[48] "JWS Records: Annual Bestsellers, 1929–1963"; American Institute of Architects Press Release, 5 May 1989, "JWS Records: AIA Honors JWS 4 'Standard' Book, 1989"; Group Interview, 22 Oct. 1992, "JWS Oral Interview, 1992"; Wiley, "My First 50 Years," Chap. 3, 38.

[49] "Wiley Hosts Celebration of M.I.T. Press' Independence," *Publishers Weekly* (5 Nov. 1962), 24–25; Tebbel, *History of Book Publishing III*, 606; M. Mitchell Waldrop, *The Dream Machine: J. C. R. Licklider and the Revolution That Made Computing Personal* (New York: Penguin, 2001), 95. *House of Wiley*, 27, 29. "Sales—By Year—On M.I.T. Books," 1950, "JWS Records: Sales by Title, 1912–1959."

[50] Harry Lydenberg, *Some Presses You Will be Glad to Know About* (New York: University Books, Inc., 1937); Miller, *Book Industry*, 10;

Marsh Jeanneret, *God and Mammon: Universities as Publishers* (Urbana, Ill.: University of Illinois Press, 1989), 1–142; Peter Givler, "University Press Publishing in the United States," in Abel and Newlin, eds., *Scholarly Publishing*, 107–120.

[51]Miller, *Book Industry*, 122–25; Hendrik Edelman, "The Growth of Scholarly and Scientific Libraries," in Abel and Newlin, eds., *Scholarly Publishing*, 193–208.

[52]Wilson, *Geography of Reading*, 117–55, 159.

[53]William O.'s daughter Elizabeth Darby aspired to work for Wiley but found limitations placed on her work by her father and Hamilton. Wiley, "My First 50 Years," Chap. 3, 1.

[54]Floyd Tifft, "The House of Wiley," *Rensselaer Polytechnic Institute Alumni News* (Sept. 1948), 6–11; "William Ogden Wiley Dies; Of Book Publishing Firm," *New York Herald Tribune* (16 Jan. 1958), 10.

[55]"Warns Colgate Men to Develop Culture," *New York Times* (14 June 1932), 19; Charles Scribner Jr., *In the Web of Ideas: The Education of a Publisher* (New York: Charles Scribner's Sons, 1993), 3–4; "W. Bradford Wiley," *New York Times* (12 Feb. 1998), E12. Moore, *Wiley*, 128. "Wiley Family Genealogy," 2–3; Wiley Family Oral History: Interview WBW w/ PBW, 1991, 10; Wiley, "My First 50 Years," Chap. 3, 2.

[56]"Miss Esther Booth to Wed W. B. Wiley," *New York Times* (5 Jan. 1936), N6. Wiley Family Oral History: Interview WBW w/ PBW, 1991, 22–23.

[57]"Announcements," *Modern Language Journal* (Mar. 1949), 243; Edmond L. Volpe, "Let's Be Fair: Comment on A. Poulin," *College English* (Mar. 1972), 727–28; Ann Orlov, "Demythologizing Scholarly Publishing," *Annals of the American Academy of Political and Social Science* (Sept. 1975), 53; Frank Freidel, "American Historians: A Bicentennial Approach," *Journal of American History* (June 1976), 17; "William H. Y. Hackett, Jr.," *Proceedings and Address of the American Philosophical Association* (June 1986), 726.

[58]C. David Mead et al., "The Textbook Industry and Profession," *Bulletin of the Midwest Modern Language Association* (Spring 1970), 1–26; Orlov, "Demythologizing," 53; Lewis Coser, "Publishers as Gatekeepers of Ideas," *Annals of the American Academy of Political and Social Science* (Sept. 1975), 20.

[59]"Marketing a Wiley Book," 1951, "JWS Operations: Marketing a Wiley Book, 1951."

[60]Levine, *American College*, 163–69, 191–93. Moore, *Wiley*, 113. Wiley Family Oral History: Interview WBW w/ PBW, 1991, 41, 51–52; Wiley, "My First 50 Years," Chap. 3, 4, Chap. 4, 5, 8.

[61]"Meet Wiley's President," *Footnotes* (Dec. 1949), 1; Moore, *Wiley*, 112, 142.

[62]Edward P. Hamilton, "Author! Author! Some Random Thoughts on Ideal Technical Books and Their Authors," n.d., "Wiley's [sic] before WBW: Hamilton Speeches, 1944–1952."

[63]Miller, *Book Industry*, 143.

[64]Robert van Gelder, "Technical Books as Valued Wartime Tools," *New York Times Book Review* (22 Feb. 1942), 2; Austin Stevens, "War Reinstates Technical Books," *New York Times* (3 Jan. 1943), A50;

Burlingame, *McGraw-Hill*, 324, 329–30. Moore, *Wiley*, 102, 142–46. "Wiley Family Genealogy," "Wiley Family Histories, Genealogy."

[65]Stevens, "War Reinstates Technical Books," A50; Burlingame, *McGraw-Hill*, 324, 326; M. Frank Redding and Roger H. Smith, *Revolution in the Textbook Publishing Industry* (Washington, D.C., Occasional Paper No. 9, Technological Development Project, National Education Assocation, 1963), 4; Lykes, *Higher Education*, 122–40.

[66]"JWS Records: Sales by Title, 1912–1959"; "JWS Records: 100,000 Copies Sales Record, 1917–1965"; "Imagine," (1942), "A Book Shows How . . . And a Clock Proves It," (1940?), "JWS Records: Advertising, 1926–1950."

[67]Austin Stevens, "War Reinstates Technical Books," A50.

[68]Austin Stevens, "War Reinstates Technical Books," A50.

[69]George Barrett, "In the Technical Book Rack," *New York Times Book Review* (19 Mar. 1944), 26. Robert Higgy, *Fundamental Radio Experiments* (New York: John Wiley & Sons, 1943).

[70]*Publishers Weekly*, (22 Jan. 1944), 292–95; "Books and Authors," *New York Times Book Review* (20 Feb. 1944), 10. Wiley Family Oral History: Interview WBW w/ PBW, 1991, 48.

[71]*Publishers Weekly*, (22 Jan. 1944), 283. Wiley Family Oral History: Interview WBW w/ PBW, 1991, 44; Wiley, "My First 50 Years," Chap. 4, 8.

[72]Smith, *Peril and a Hope*; Jessica Wang, *American Science in an Age of Anxiety: Scientists, Anticommunism, and the Cold War* (Chapel Hill: University of North Carolina Press, 1999).

[73]Edward Crane, *A Century of Book Publishing, 1848–1948* (New York: D. Van Nostrand Co., 1948), 52–67; Miller, *Book Industry*, 22. *Publishers Weekly* data as compiled in Martin Matheson's Big Black Book.

[74]Tifft, "House of Wiley," 6–11. *House of Wiley*; "Recent Changes in Wiley Personnel," *Footnotes* (Apr. 1949), 4. Wiley, "My First 50 Years," Chap. 4, 20.

[75]"Modern Décor for New Quarters at Wiley Building," *Footnotes* (Apr. 1949), 2; "Lifted Face, Same Facade," *Footnotes* (May 1954), 2; Moore, *Wiley*, 167. Edward Hamilton to E. A. Smith, 20 Apr. 1949, "WBW Letters: Europe, 1949–1951"; Edward Hamilton to W. Bradford Wiley, 7 Mar. 1956, "Wiley's [sic] before WBW: E. P. Hamilton Letters to WBW, 1954–1961."

[76]Lewis Gannett, "Books and Things," 1946, "JWS History: Clippings, 1941–1946"; Edward P. Hamilton, "Author! Author! Some Random Thoughts on Ideal Technical Books and Their Authors," n.d., Edward Hamilton, "Present State of Engineering Literature," 26 June 1952; "Wiley's [sic] before WBW: Hamilton Speeches, 1944–1952."

[77]James T. Farrell, *Will the Commercialization of Publishing Destroy Good Writing? Some Observations on the Future of Books* (n.p., 1946), 2, 8; Tifft, "House of Wiley," 6–11; Miller, *Book Industry*, 50; Scribner, *Web of Ideas*, 52. Edward Hamilton, "Engineering Literature and Its Role in Pan American Development," 20 July 1949, "Wiley's [sic] before WBW: Hamilton Speeches, 1944–1953."

[78]"Author Tells Story of Writing Book," *Footnotes* (Apr. 1949), 2.

[79]Tifft, "House of Wiley," 6–11. "Bethe's New Book Starts Nuclear Studies Program," *Wiley Bulletin* (Dec. 1947), 2; *House of Wiley*, 17–18; Taft, *Wiley*, 54. Wiley Family Oral History: Interview WBW w/ PBW, 1991, 58.

[80]Wiley, "My First 50 Years," Chap. 4, 18–19.

[81]Maxim Mikulak, "Cybernetics and Marxist-Leninism," *Slavic Review* (Sept. 1965), 450–65. J. H. Milsum, "Cybernetics Simplified," *Quarterly Review of Biology* (Dec. 1969), 455; Bruce Jackson, "'The Greatest Mathematician in the World': Norbert Wiener Stories," *Western Folklore* (Jan. 1972), 1–22; David Halloway, "Innovation in Science: The Case of Cybernetics in the Soviet Union," *Science Studies* (Oct. 1974), 299–337; Peter Galison, "The Ontology of the Enemy: Norbert Wiener and the Cybernetic Vision," *Critical Inquiry* (Autumn 1994), 228–66; Edmund O. Wilson, *Consilience: The Unity of Knowledge* (New York: Vintage, 1998); Susan Williamson, "Norbert Wiener," *ANBO*.

[82]Henry Pratt Fairchild to William O. Wiley, 19 Nov. 1932, "JWS 125th Anniversary Correspondence, 1932"; Arthur K. Getman to Edward Hamilton, 17 Nov. 1948, "JWS Records: Advertising, 1926–1950."

[83]Martin Matheson, "Selling Books to Scientists," *Science* (17 Apr. 1953): 406–9. *House of Wiley*, 13. "P&I Mailing Lists," "Frequency of Use of General Mailing Lists," Martin Matheson's Little Black Book.

[84]"How the 'Class System' of Democracy Affects America's Youth," *Publishers Weekly* (30 Apr. 1949); "Ready in August—A Modern Treatment," *Professional Geographer* (June 1950); "Just Published!" *Journal of Chemical Education* (Aug. 1950); Lawrence P. Grayson, *The Making of an Engineer: The Illustrated History of Engineering Education in the United States and Canada* (New York: John Wiley & Sons, 1993), 75. "New Twist in Advertising," *Footnotes* (May 1954), 5. "JWS Records: Advertising, 1926–1950"; PTL to ID, 14 Mar. 1957, "JWS 150th Anniversary History, Distribution List, 1957."

[85]Miller, *Book Industry*, 89–101. "Three-Dimensional Sales Promotion," *Footnotes* (Dec. 1949), 3; "International Boom in Sales," *Footnotes* (May 1954), 3. "Domestic Trade Accounts," 1954–1956, "JWS 150th Anniversary: Correspondence, 1955–1956."

[86]" 'With Our Compliments'," *Wiley Bulletin*, (Spring 1952), 2. "Sales and Advertising Division Budget—1955," "Free Distribution of Books," Martin Matheson's Little Black Book; Wiley, "My First 50 Years," Chap. 4, 27.

[87]"New Radio Team—Sleeper and Sleeper," *Footnotes* (Apr. 1949), 3; "In The Times," *Footnotes* (Dec. 1949), 7; "Photosynthetic Shmoo," *Footnotes* (Dec. 1949), 8; Taft, *Wiley*, 40, 42, 102; Moore, *Wiley*, 148–49.

[88]E. P. Hamilton, "The Textbook from the Publisher's Point of View," *Journal of Engineering Education* (June 1951), 589–93; Tifft, "House of Wiley," 6–11. Moore, *Wiley*, 181. Edward P. Hamilton, "Author! Author! Some Random Thoughts on Ideal Technical Books and Their Authors," n.d., "Wiley's [*sic*] before WBW: Hamilton Speeches, 1944–1952"; Wiley Family Oral History: Interview WBW w/ PBW, 1991, 60.

[89]"The Story of John Wiley," *Book Production Magazine* (Apr. 1963), 54–57. "Meet Wiley's Educational Department," *Wiley Bulletin* (Dec. 1947), 7; *House of Wiley*, 28; "What We Are Doing About Visual Aids," *Footnotes* (Dec. 1949), 7.

[90]Miller, *Book Industry*, 72.

[91]Crane, *Century of Book Publishing*, 69; Tifft, "House of Wiley," 11; Miller, *Book Industry*, 69, 72, 75; Hamilton, "Textbook," 592; Hamilton, "Engineering Literature," 1,939–41. Edward Hamilton, "Draft of a Paper Tentatively Entitled 'International Aspects of Technical Literature'," 21–25 June 1948, "Wiley's [*sic*] before WBW: Hamilton Speeches, 1944–1953".

[92]Moore, *Wiley*, 151–54, 157. Martin Matheson to W. B. Wiley, 4 Jan. 1951, "JWS Records: Sales by Title, 1912–1959"; Wiley, "My First 50 Years," Chap. 4, 15.

[93]"Editors at Large!," *Footnotes* (May 1954), 4; Moore, *Wiley*, 132, 152–53, 157. "JWS History: WBW Research (Annual Reports), 1932–1961"; "JWS History: Organization, 1946–1970"; "JWS Employees: Keith Hogan, 1st Sales Job, 1953"; Wiley Family Oral History: Interview WBW w/ PBW, 1991, 68–69.

[94]Hamilton, "Engineering Literature," 1,940. "What is 'Footnotes'?," *Footnotes* (Apr. 1949), 1; "News of Interest to Wiley Authors," *Footnotes* (Apr. 1949), 2; Moore, *Wiley*, 154–55. "College Index Numbers," 1951, "College Textbook Catalog Price and Production Cost vs. General Wholesale Prices," 1952, Martin Matheson's Little Black Book.

[95]Miller, *Book Industry*, 28. "Export Sales Figures," Martin Matheson's Little Black Book; William B. Wiley, "Emergence of John Wiley & Sons as an International Publisher," "WBW Letters: UK, 1957–1960."

[96]"Cooperating with CARE," *Footnotes* (Dec. 1949), 2; "In the Mail," *Footnotes* (Dec. 1949), 2.

[97]"Williams & Wilkins Company v. The United States," http://fairuse.stanford.edu/primary_materials/cases/c487F2d1345.html. Whitney Darrow to Melville Minton, 19 Sept. 1945, Edward P. Hamilton and Whitney Darrow, "A Report on Publishing and Bookselling in Australia and New Zealand," (Oct. 1945) in "Wiley's [*sic*] before WBW: E. P. Hamilton Report/Austral & NZ, 1945"; Edward Hamilton to M. Frank Redding, 8 Oct. 1962, "Wiley's [*sic*] before WBW: E. P. Hamilton History, 1962."

[98]Tifft, "House of Wiley," 6–11; Edward Hamilton, "Outposts of U.S. Books," *The Record* (May-June 1951), 24–28; Burlingame, *McGraw-Hill*, 379–81. "Meet Wiley's President," *Footnotes* (Dec. 1949), 5. Edward Hamilton, "Draft of a Paper Tentatively Entitled 'International Aspects of Technical Literature'," 21–25 June 1948, Edward Hamilton, "Engineering Literature and Its Role in Pan American Development," 20 July 1949, "Wiley's [*sic*] before WBW: Hamilton Speeches, 1944–1953."

[99]Edward Hamilton, "Draft of a Paper Tentatively Entitled 'International Aspects of Technical Literature'," 21–25 June 1948, "Wiley's [*sic*] before WBW: Hamilton Speeches, 1944–1953."

[100]Edward Hamilton, "Outposts of U.S. Books," *The Record* (May-June 1951), 24–28.

[101]Tifft, "House of Wiley," 6–11; Hamilton, "Textbook," 592. "Three-Dimensional Sales Promotion," *Footnotes* (Dec. 1949), 3. "Foreign Lists," Martin Matheson's Little Black Book.

[102]*Thirty Years in Chichester, a Celebration* (Chichester: John Wiley & Sons, 1997), 3–8. Moore, *Wiley*, 151. Edward Hamilton to W. Bradford Wiley, 14 Apr. 1949, Edward Hamilton to E. A. Smith, 20

Apr. 1949, W. Bradford Wiley to Edward Hamilton, 8, 13 a.m., 13 p.m., 27 Apr. 1949, to Jack Snyder, 26 Apr., 9 May 1949, "WBW Letters: Europe, 1949–1951"; W. B. Wiley to John Moore, "The Beginnings of Wiley's Efforts to Establish a Base for Distribution and Publishing in England," 22 Sept. 1981, "WBW Letters: UK, 1957–1960."

[103]*Chichester.* 3–8.

[104]*Chichester.* 14–15.

[105]"International Boom in Sales," *Footnotes* (May 1954), 1; "European Book Marts Under Close Wiley Scrutiny," *Footnotes* (May 1954), 1; "Translations, Translations, and More Translations," *Footnotes* (May 1954), 3; " 'Asia Bulletin' Highlights Wiley Growth," *Wiley Bulletin* (Fall 1957), 8; "Asia Publishing President in New York," *Wiley Bulletin* (Fall 1959), 6; Moore, *Wiley*, 114. W. Bradford Wiley to Jack Snyder, 9 May 1949, "WBW Letters: Europe, 1949–1951"; Edward Hamilton to W. Bradford Wiley, 1 Mar. 1956, "Wiley's [*sic*] before WBW: E. P. Hamilton Letters to WBW, 1954–1961."

[106]"Export Sales Figures," "Comparison of Foreign Sales, 1950"; "Export Sales—3," Martin Matheson's Little Black Book.

[107]Miller, *Book Industry*, 86, 93. "Soft, Pleasing Voices," *Footnotes* (May 1954), 5. Edward Hamilton to W. Bradford Wiley, 6 Apr. 1954, 24 June 1955, and other letters of Edward Hamilton to W. Bradford Wiley in "Wiley's [*sic*] before WBW: E. P. Hamilton Letters to WBW, 1954–1961."

[108]*Publishers Weekly* (16 Jan. 1954), 196; "Rudolf Triest, 63, Publisher, Is Dead," *New York Times*, 29 Dec. 1954, "Rudolf M. Triest, Book Publisher," *New York Herald Tribune*, 29 Dec. 1954. "E. A. Smith, Treasurer," *Footnotes* (May 1954), 1; "Wiley Officers Step Up," *Footnotes* (May 1954), 2. Memo, 29 Dec. 1954, Rudolf M. Triest to Edward Hamilton, 15, 17 Mar. 1951, to William B. Wiley, 12 July 1951, "JWS Employment: Rudolf M. Triest, 1951–1955"; "JWS Employees: Samuel E. Norris, 1943–1948"; A. H. Neilly to the Staff, 23 Aug. 1971, "JWS Employees: J. Stetson Barnes, 1970–1971."

[109]Tifft, "House of Wiley," 6–11. Edward Hamilton to Arthur K. Getman, 1 Dec. 1948, "JWS 150th Anniversary: Planning, 1955–1957"; "JWS 150th Anniversary: E. P. Hamilton's London Speech, 1957."

[110]Hamilton, "Textbook," 589–93.

[111]Miller, *Book Industry*, 34. "Educational Attainment," "Survey of Scientists," "Number of Engineers," "Industrial Employment, 1953–1954," Martin Matheson's Little Black Book; Edward Hamilton to W. Bradford Wiley, 14 Apr. 1949, Edward Hamilton to E. A. Smith, 20 Apr. 1949, "WBW Letters: Europe, 1949–1951"; Martin Matheson to W. B. Wiley, 4 Jan. 1951, 11 Oct. 1955, "JWS Records: Sales by Title, 1912–1959"; Edward Hamilton to W. Bradford Wiley, 8 Mar., 27 Aug. 1954, 23, 27 Aug., 4 Sept. 1956, 17 July, 1, 21 Oct. 1957, 4, 16 Aug. 1958, "Wiley's [*sic*] before WBW: E. P. Hamilton Letters to WBW, 1954–1961."

[112]"Vice-President Warren Sullivan Attends Harvard Business School," *Wiley Bulletin: Science and Industry Edition* (Spring 1958), 2. Edward Hamilton to W. Bradford Wiley, 25 Feb. 1954, "Wiley's [*sic*] before WBW, E. P. Hamilton Letters to WBW, 1954–1961"; Wiley Family Oral History: Interview WBW w/ PBW, 1991, 62–63, 95; Wiley, "My First 50 Years," Chap. 3, 32–33, Chap. 4, 24–25.

CHAPTER SIX

[1]Proxy Statements, John Wiley & Sons, 1966.

[2]"John Wiley Names President," *New York Times* (26 June 1956), 57; "William Ogden Wiley Dies; Of Book Publishing Firm," *New York Herald Tribune* (16 Jan. 1958), 10. http://www.wiley.com/WileyCDA/Section/id-146.html; "Wiley Family Genealogy," Wiley Family Histories, Genealogy; "Addendum to Board of Directors minutes, March 23, 1978," Wiley's [*sic*] before WBW: E. P. Hamilton Documents, 1949–1977.

[3]W. Bradford Wiley, "My First 50 Years."

[4]"Gordon S. Ierardi of Book Company," *New York Times* (18 Feb. 1966), 33. Peter Wiley interview with Charles Stoll, 31 Sept. 1993, "JWS Oral History: Interview C. B. Stoll w/ PBW, 1993."

[5]John Hammond Moore, *Wiley: One Hundred and Seventy Five Years of Publishing* (New York: John Wiley & Sons, 1982), 157. Proxy Statements, John Wiley & Sons, 1982, 1983; Bradford Wiley II to All Wiley Employees, 28 Mar. 1994, "JWS Employees: Charles B. Stoll, 1961–1989."

[6]Mauck Brammer, "Textbook Publishing," in Chandler Grannis, ed., *What Happens in Book Publishing*, 2nd ed. (New York: Columbia University Press, 1967), 347; Abe Goldman, "The Prospective New Copyright Law," in Kathryn Henderson, ed., *Trends in American Publishing* (Champaign, Ill.: Allerton Park Institute, 1967), 39–48; Dan Lacy, "Major Trends in American Book Publishing," in Henderson, ed., *Trends in American Publishing*, 12; "Myrdals Named for Peace Prize," *New York Times* (16 Aug. 1970), 76; Henry Raymont, "War Foes to Sell 2 Russell Essays," *New York Times* (23 Aug.1970), 25; "Associations: Wiley Heads AAP," *Publishers Weekly* (8 Feb. 1971), 45; John Dessauer, *Book Publishing: What It Is, What It Does* (New York: R. R. Bowker Co., 1974), 14–16; Andrew H. Neilly, *Ex Libris* (Jan. 1975), 9; Ralph Shoffner, "Appearance and Growth of Computer and Electronic Products in Libraries," in Richard Abel and Lyman Newlin, eds., *Scholarly Publishing: Books, Journals, Publishers, and Libraries in the Twentieth Century* (New York: John Wiley & Sons, 2002), 231. John Wiley & Sons Annual Report, 1966, 1975, 1977 "JWS Records: Annual Reports, 1963–1970"; "JWS Records: Annual Reports, 1971–1977"; W. Bradford Wiley, "An International Publisher's View of Trends and Developments in the Flow of Materials," 18 July 1976, "WBW Talks: American Library Assoc. Address, 1976"; "Presentation of the Curtis G. Benjamin Award," 14 Mar. 1983, "WBW in Public: Curtis Benjamin Award, 1975–1983."

[7]Marjorie Hunter, "Newsmen at House Hearing Accuse U.S. of Attempting Censorship," *New York Times* (26 June 1971); Henry Raymont, "Publishers Told of Censor Peril," *New York Times* (2 May 1972); Henry Raymont, "Publisher Calls Beacon Press Case Threat to Freedom," *New York Times* (18 July 1972), 13; Neilly, *Ex Libris*, 10–11. W. Bradford Wiley, "Constitutional and Statutory Rights and Privileges and the Obligations of Publishers," 27 Apr. 1972, "WBW Talks; Publishers—Obligations, Rights, 1972."

[8]Moore, *Wiley*, 114, 161–62, 217.

[9]"Publisher Promotes Aide," *New York Times* (15 Feb. 1961), 51; "You Meet Such Interesting People," *Publishers Weekly* (20 Feb. 1961), 50; (24 Apr. 1961), 54; Charles Madison, "Current Trends in

American Publishing," in Henderson, ed., *Trends in American Publishing*, 2. Warren Sullivan résumé, 1971, "JWS Employees: Warren Sullivan, 1958"; Peter Wiley interview with Warren Sullivan, 29 Mar. 1993, "JWS Oral History: Interview W. Sullivan w/ PBW, 1993"; Peter Wiley interview with Charles Stoll, 31 Sept. 1993, "JWS Oral History: Interview C. B. Stoll w/ PBW, 1993"; Interview with Liz Ann Stoll, Nov. 2004.

[10]Dessauer, *Book Publishing*, 54. Richard Cook to Martin Matheson, 25 Mar. 1957, "JWS Operations: Staff Memos, 1955–1957"; Gall Report on AAP Seminar, 23–28 Sept. 1976, "JWS International: USSR Book Publishing, 1976 (2)"; Wiley, "My First 50 Years," Chap. 5b, 4.

[11]Walter Wingo, *Pattern for Success: Presenting the Harvard Business School Advanced Management Program* (Garden City, N.Y.: Doubleday & Co., 1967), 110; Thomas McCraw, ed., *The Essential Alfred Chandler: Essays Toward a History Theory of Big Business* (Boston: Harvard Business School Press, 1988), 13, 156; Alfred Chandler, "Introduction to *Strategy and Structure*," in McCraw, ed., *Essential Alfred Chandler*, 172, 174; Kenneth R. Andrews, *The Concept of Corporate Strategy* (Homewood, Ill.: Irwin, 1971), 28. Andrews equates his definition with that of Chandler on page 29. In a 1985 discussion with a Wiley executive, Andrews defined strategy as "the goals and objectives of the entire business that distinguishes it from its competitors." Richard Johnson to EMG, 25 Nov. 1985, JWSA.

[12]Moore, *Wiley*, 156–57, 180. Board Minutes, John Wiley & Sons; Wiley, "My First 50 Years," Chap. 4, 28, Chap. 6.

[13]1950 and 1970 per capita income given in year 2000 USD. Lacy, "Major Trends," 1; Dan Lacy, "The Changing Face of Publishing," 423–37; John J. McCusker, "Comparing the Purchasing Power of Money in the United States (or Colonies) from 1665 to 2003." Economic History Services, 2004, http://www.eh.net/hmit/ppowerusd/.

[14]Robert Follett, "Current Trends in Educational Publishing—A Personal View," in Henderson, ed., *Trends in American Publishing*, 60–74; Lacy, "Major Trends," 1, 2, 6, 11; Lloyd Averill, "Viability of Liberal Arts," in G. Kerry Smith, ed., *Twenty-Five Years, 1945–1970* (San Francisco: Jossey-Bass, 1970), 160–70; Richard McKeon, "Future of Liberal Arts," in Smith, ed., *Twenty-Five Years*, 171–83; Seymour Harris, *A Statistical Portrait of Higher Education* (New York: McGraw-Hill, 1972), 454, 456–60, 464; *Digest of Education Statistics*, 1980, 94–95, 1987, Table 111; John R. Thelin, *A History of American Higher Education* (Baltimore: Johns Hopkins University Press, 2004), 299–300.

[15]A. H. Raskin, "Industrial Gain Noted in Soviet," *New York Times* (20 Jan. 1957), 15.

[16]Lacy, "Major Trends," 1, 2; Harris, *Statistical Portrait*, 619. Neil Reynolds, "Corporate Aid to Education: A Philosophy and Some Methods," *Wiley Bulletin: Science and Industry Edition* (Spring 1958), 5, 8; "American Educators List Ideas Needing Public Support," *Wiley Bulletin: Science and Industry Edition* (Spring 1958), 8; "Sarnoff Proposes Industry Provide Science Teachers," *Wiley Bulletin: Science and Industry Edition* (Spring 1958), 1, 10.

[17]Emerson Greenaway, "The American Public Library: The People's Reading Center and University," in Roger H. Smith, ed., *The*

American Reading Public: What It Reads, Why It Reads (New York: R. R. Bowker Co., 1963), 167–71; Leonard Shatzkin, "The Book in Search of a Reader," in Smith, ed., *The American Reading Public*, 130; Robert Frase, "The Economics of Publishing," in Henderson, ed., *Trends in American Publishing*, 36; Lacy, "Major Trends," 15; Madison, "Current Trends," 26; Patrick Williams, *The American Public Library and the Problem of Purpose* (New York: Greenwood Press, 1988), 85–98.

[18]The URL of Montgomery County's online public access catalog, or OPAC, is currently http://spica.mclinc.org/polaris/Search/default.aspx?ctx=1.1033.0.0.1.

[19]Maurice Tauber, "The Library," *Journal of Higher Education* (Dec. 1965), 517–18; Rolland E. Stevens, "The Library," *Journal of Higher Education* (Apr. 1968), 233–34; Warren Haas, "America's Libraries: Distinguished Past, Difficult Future," *Proceedings of the American Philosophical Society* (June 1996), 125–34.

[20]*New York Times* (6 Nov. 1955), F18; Joseph Dunn, "Industry Turns to the Librarian," *New York Times* (19 May 1957), F7; "Special Libraries Assn. Will Mark Anniversary," *Los Angeles Times* (8 Mar. 1959), 14; Susan Billingsley, "Industrial Libraries—Some Personnel Problems Not in the Books," *Personnel Journal* (Sept. 1961), 170–73; "Electronic Literature Keeps Librarian Busy," *Los Angeles Times* (21 Apr. 1963), OC10; Eugene Jackson and Ruth Jackson, "The Industrial Special Library Universe: A 'Base Line' Study of Its Extent and Characteristics," *Journal of the American Society for Information Science* (May 1977), 135–52.

[21]Paul Berry, "Development of Library Resources," *Annals of the American Academy of Political and Social Science* (Nov. 1964), 126–32; Stevens, "The Library"; Ann Mozley, "Change in Argonne National Laboratory: A Case Study," *Science* (1 Oct. 1971), 30–38; S. David Freeman, "Argonne's Role," *Science* (7 Apr. 1972), 7; Bernard Spinrad, "Argonne: Hope for Revitalization," *Science* (3 Dec. 1982), 946.

[22]M. Frank Redding and Roger H. Smith, *Revolution in the Textbook Industry* (National Education Association, Occasional Paper No. 9, 1963), iv–v; Charles Madison, *Book Publishing in America* (New York: McGraw-Hill, 1966), 403–6.

[23]Dan Lacy, "The Economics of Publishing, Or Adam Smith and Literature," in Smith, ed., *American Reading Public*, 54; Roger H. Smith, "Introduction," in Smith, ed., *American Reading Public*, ix–x; Eric Proskauer, "Scientific Books: Doomed . . . or Rejuvenated?" *Scientific Research* (15 Apr. 1968); John Tebbel, *Between Covers: The Rise and Transformation of Book Publishing in America* (New York: Oxford University Press, 1987), 440; Moore, *Wiley*, 172.

[24] "Index of Book Prices by Category, Selected Years," *Publishers Weekly* (28 Jan. 1963), 223.

[25]Michael Harris to G. V. Novotny and R. B. Polhemus, 10 June 1970, Michael Harris to Beatrice Shube, 4 Oct. 1972, Beatrice Shube to Albert Simon, 24 May 1979, "JWS College Division: Simon/Thompson Series, 1966–1979."

[26]Dessauer, *Book Publishing*, 52; Neilly, *Ex Libris*, 5; Ron Robin, *Scandals and Scoundrels: Seven Cases That Shook the Academy* (Berkeley: University of California Press, 2004), 5. Eric Proskauer, "Journals and Serials as Selective Information Filters," 2 Sept. 1969, "JWS Employees: Dr. Eric S. Proskauer, 1969–1971."

27"Wiley, Publisher, 150 Years Old," *Publishers Weekly* (10 June 1957), 36.

28"Wiley, Publisher, 150 Years Old," *Publishers Weekly* (10 June 1957), 36; Neilly, *Ex Libris*, 5. Anon., *You Are Invited to Join the Illustrious Company of Wiley Authors* (New York: John Wiley & Sons, 1978). John Wiley & Sons Annual Report, 1969, "JWS Records: Annual Reports, 1963–1970"; John Wiley & Sons Annual Report, 1974, 1975; "JWS Records: Annual Reports, 1971–1977."

29We again track only substantial revisions as "new" titles. "In a house such as Wiley," *Publishers Weekly* reminded readers in 1957, "the word *edition* is never synonymous with the word *printing*." Nevertheless, tracking all new editions does not give readers as good an idea about the condition of the company as the number of new titles plus only substantially revised books.

30 "Wiley, Publisher, 150 Years Old," *Publishers Weekly* (10 June 1957), 36; Lacy, "Major Trends," 5. W. Bradford Wiley, "Something about Books," n.d., WBW Talks: Books in the US."

31"The Textbook and Industry . . . ," *Wiley Bulletin: Science and Industry Edition* (Spring 1958), 2, 7; "Four New Books for Management Are Sponsored by ORSA," *Wiley Bulletin: Science and Industry Edition* (Spring 1958), 4; "Wiley Space Technology Program Keeps Pace with U.S. Space Effort," *Wiley Bulletin: Science and Industry Edition* (Fall 1958), 1, 3. Edward Hamilton to W. Bradford Wiley, 17 July 1957, "Wiley's [*sic*] before WBW: E. P. Hamilton Letters to WBW, 1954–1961"; Warren Sullivan to Travelers, 18 Mar. 1959, "JWS Board: Absecon Strategy Meeting, 1960."

32Redding and Smith, *Revolution in the Textbook Industry*, 16.

33Brammer, "Textbook Publishing," 326. ? to W. Bradford Wiley, 17 Oct. 1957, "WBW Letters: UK, 1957–1960"; Lauren Fransen to Vladimir Nazarov, 1 Nov. 1978, "JWS International: USSR General Reports, 1974–1978"; Wiley, "My First 50 Years," Chap. 5b, 2–3.

34Roger Burlingame, *Endless Frontiers: The Story of McGraw-Hill* (New York: McGraw-Hill, 1959), 403; Stanley Unwin and Philip Unwin, *The Truth about Publishing*, 8th ed. (London: George Allen & Unwin, 1976), 30; Carnegie Council on Policy Studies in Higher Education, *Three Thousand Futures: The Next Twenty Years for Higher Education* (San Francisco: Jossey-Bass, 1981), 11. Moore, *Wiley*, 180–81. Wiley, "My First 50 Years," Chap. 5b, 3.

35A. H. Neilly to C. B. Stoll and Francis Lobdell, 18 June 1970.

36*Publishers Weekly* (19 Jan. 1959), 42, 46.

37Brammer, "Textbook Publishing," 326, 336.

38James T. Farrell, *Will the Commercialization of Publishing Destroy Good Writing? Some Observations on the Future of Books* (n.p., 1946), 4; "The Story of John Wiley," *Book Production Magazine* (Apr. 1963), 54–57; Curtis Benjamin, "Technical, Scientific and Medical Publishing," in Chandler Grannis, ed., *What Happens in Book Publishing*, 2nd ed. (New York: Columbia University Press, 1967), 353–55; Richard E. Abel, "The Change of Book and Journal Infrastructure: Two Publishers, Consolidation, and Niche Publishers," in Abel and Newlin, eds., *Scholarly Publishing*, 26.

39Gerald Gross, ed., *Publishers on Publishing* (London: Secker & Warburg, 1962), 171–76; Brammer, "Textbook Publishing," 348; Madison, "Current Trends," 21; F. N. Doubleday, *The Memoirs of a Publisher* (Garden City, N.Y.: Doubleday & Co., 1972), 113; Lewis Coser, Charles Kadushin, and Walter Powell, *Books: The Culture and Commerce of Publishing* (Chicago: University of Chicago Press, 1982), 22–25.

40Lacy, "Major Trends," 4.

41"New Stock Issues: Corporation Shares to Be Offered to the Public for Investment," *New York Times* (3 Jan. 1929), 39; Redding and Smith, *Revolution in the Textbook Industry*, 11; Madison, "Current Trends," 21; Bennett Cerf, *At Random: The Reminiscences of Bennett Cerf* (New York: Random House, 1977), 195.

42"The Scholarly Dollar," *Time* (10 Oct. 1960); Redding and Smith, *Revolution in the Textbook Industry*, 10; Lacy, "Changing Face," 425; Madison, "Current Trends," 20.

43Gay Talese, "Fenimore Cooper's Publisher Acquires Textbook Company," *New York Times* (28 June 1961), 32; "John Wiley & Co. Stock Will 'Go Public' in May," *Publishers Weekly* (12 Mar. 1962); "Maurits Dekker, 95, Retired Publisher," *New York Times* (20 Jan. 1995), B7. "Report by WS of Luncheon Meeting of WBW and WS with Dr. Maurits Dekker, Interscience Publishers," 21 Dec. 1960; Special Meeting, Board of Directors, 12–15 Mar. 1961; John Wiley & Sons, "Prospectus," 21 Feb. 1962, John Wiley & Sons, "Tombstone," Apr. 1962, Reynolds Research, "A Report for Account Executives," 13 Aug. 1962, "JWS Stock: Public Stock Offering, 1962–1967"; "A Directory of American Book Publishing," 1973, "JWS History: Various Histories 19th to mid 20th Cent.,"; "Group Interview," 22 Oct. 1992; Wiley, "My First 50 Years," Chap. 5b, 10, 12, 12a, 13, Chap. 6; Tim King interview, 22 June 2005.

44"Random House Will Buy Knopf in Merger," *New York Times* (17 Apr. 1960), 1; Redding and Smith, *Revolution in the Textbook Industry*, 11–13; Roger Shugg, "The Professors and Their Publishers," in Smith, ed., *American Reading Public*, 113; "Science Publishing Pioneer Retires," *Publishers Weekly* (7 May 1973), 32. "Eric Proskauer Memorial Service," 16 Dec. 1991, "JWS Employees: Dr. Eric Proskauer Memorial, 1991"; "Group Interview," 22 Oct. 1992; Wiley, "My First 50 Years," Chap. 5b, 9.

45"Wiley and Interscience Plan to Merge," *Publishers Weekly* (3 July 1961), 158; Thomas Wilson, "American Book Publishing: Hazards and Opportunities," in Smith, ed., *American Reading Public*, 113; Brian Cox, "The Pergamon Phenomenon, 1951–1991: Robert Maxwell and Scientific Publishing," *Learned Publishing* 15 (2002): 273–78. "Report by WS of Luncheon Meeting of WBW and WS with Dr. Maurits Dekker, Interscience Publishers," 21 Dec. 1960; "A Directory of American Book Publishing," 1973, "JWS History: Various Histories 19th to mid 20th Cent."; Wiley, "My First 50 Years," Chap. 5b, 9; Tim King interview, 22 June 2005.

46"Wiley and Interscience Plan to Merge," *Publishers Weekly* (3 July 1961), 158. "Report by WS of Luncheon Meeting of WBW and WS with Dr. Maurits Dekker, Interscience Publishers," 21 Dec. 1960; Wiley, "My First 50 Years," Chap. 5b, 6–10.

47Neilly, *Ex Libris*, 9; Ezra Greenspan, "Evert Duyckinck and the History of Wiley and Putnam's Library of American Books,

1845–1847," *American Literature* 64 (1992): 677–93. Moore, *Wiley*, 11. "Report by WS of Luncheon Meeting of WBW and WS with Dr. Maurits Dekker, Interscience Publishers," 21 Dec. 1960; Corporate Management Group, Planning Meeting, 26–29 Oct. 1976; Wiley Family Oral History: Interview WBW w/ PBW, 1991, 101–2; Wiley, "My First 50 Years," Chap. 5b, 17; Tim King interview, 22 June 2005; Eric Swanson interview, 22 June 2005.

[48]Ken McKenna, "Outsiders Fill Board Seats," *New York Herald Tribune*, (19 Jan. 1966), 38. Rudolf M. Triest to Edward Hamilton, 15, 17 Mar. 1951, "JWS Employment: Rudolf M. Triest, 1951–1955"; Board Minutes, John Wiley & Sons, 1955–1963; Proxies, John Wiley & Sons, 1964–1968; A. H. Neilly to W. Bradford Wiley, 14 Nov. 1972; "JWS Employees: Board + Managers [*sic*] Bios, 1980"; Peter Wiley interview with Charles Stoll, 21 Jan. 1993, "JWS Oral History: Interview C. B. Stoll w/PBW, 1993"; Wiley, "My First 50 Years," Chap. 6, first draft; Richard Blodgett interview of Andrew Neilly, 31 Mar. 2004.

[49]Lacy, "Major Trends," 4; "John Wiley & Sons Expects 7 1/2% Sales Gain in Fiscal '74," *Wall Street Journal* (22 June 1973), 7. W. Bradford Wiley to the Staff, 8 Mar. 1968, "JWS Operations: Financial Results, 1964–1969."

[50]"Wiley and Interscience Plan to Merge," *Publishers Weekly* (3 July 1961), 158. Reynolds Research, "A Report for Account Executives," 13 Aug. 1962, "JWS Stock: Public Stock Offering, 1962–1967."

[51]Talese, "Fenimore Cooper's Publisher," 32. "Report by WS of Luncheon Meeting of WBW and WS with Dr. Maurits Dekker, Interscience Publishers," 21 Dec. 1960; GTC to Andrew Neilly, 10 Dec. 1963, "JWS Employees: Martin Matheson, 1953–1972."

[52]"Union's Arbitration Demand Upheld in Merger Situation," *Publishers Weekly* (13 Apr. 1964); Anon., "The Successor Employer's Duty to Arbitrate: A Reconsideration of John Wiley & Sons, Inc. v. Livingston," *Harvard Law Review* (1968): 418–34. "JWS Interscience: Lawsuits, 1961–1962"; Wiley Family Oral History: Interview WBW w/ PBW, 1991, 95–96; "Group Interview," 22 Oct. 1992; Peter Wiley interview with Charles Stoll, 21 Jan. 1993, "JWS Oral History: Interview C. B. Stoll w/PBW, 1993"; Wiley, "My First 50 Years," Chap. 4, 25, Chap. 5b, 17–18, Chap. 6, first draft.

[53]"Scholarly Dollar"; "John Wiley & Co. Stock Will 'Go Public' in May," *Publishers Weekly* (12 Mar. 1962); "Story of John Wiley," 54–57; Harry Gilroy, "Book Sales Soar at Science House," *New York Times* (23 June 1963), 69.

[54]Doubleday was a notable exception but so much so that when Doubleday merged with George H. Doran & Co., Doran insisted on keeping his Manhattan office. "I simply could not conceive of a huge business attempting to operate at a considerable distance from its most important contacts," he recalled. Gross, *Publishers on Publishing*, 174.

[55]"Book Publishers Like Manhattan," *New York Times* (24 Aug. 1958), R1; "American Book Publication—1962," *Publishers Weekly* (21 Jan. 1963), 45; "Story of John Wiley," 54–57; Gilroy, "Book Sales Soar," 69. Special Meeting, Board of Directors, 12–15 Mar. 1961; W. Bradford Wiley to the Staff, 20 Nov. 1962, "JWS Operations: Memo re 605 Third Avenue, 1962."

[56]Moore, *Wiley*, 195. "JWS History: Organization, 1946–1970"; John Wiley & Sons Annual Report, 1972, "JWS Records: Annual Reports, 1971–1977"; Wiley, "My First 50 Years," Chap. 5b, 29.

[57]"Ierardi," 33. "Wiley Prestige in Social Sciences Grows Through Efforts of Editor Gordon Ierardi," *Wiley Bulletin: Educational Edition* (Spring 1959), 2, 6. Andrew H. Neilly to Laura Ierardi, 20 June 1985, Laura Ierardi to Ed Burke, 9 June 1985, "JWS Employees: Gordon S. Ierardi, 1966–1985."

[58]"Engineering Editor Stoll Tells of Professional Hazards in 'Author Hunting' and 'List Building'," *Wiley Bulletin: Educational Edition* (Fall 1958), 2. Ruth McMullin to Charles Ellis, 30 Oct. 1989, Bradford Wiley II to All Wiley Employees, 28 Mar. 1994, "JWS Employees: Charles B. Stoll, 1961–1989."

[59]"JWS STM Division: Records, Data, 1948–1978."

[60]"Story of John Wiley," 54–57.

[61]*A Guide for Wiley-Interscience and Ronald Press Authors*, 2nd ed. (New York: John Wiley & Sons, 1979), ix. "JWS College Division: Records, 1945–1980"; W. Bradford Wiley to the Staff, 15 Apr. 1968; Charles Stoll to Board of Directors, 15 June 1976; Corporate Management Group, Planning Meeting, 26–29 Oct. 1976.

[62]"Story of John Wiley," 54–57; "Portal Press, New Wiley Subsidiary," *Publishers Weekly* (28 Feb. 1966), 69. "Expansions," "JWS Subsidiaries: Expansion History, 1959–1980"; John Wiley & Sons Annual Report, 1963, 1965, 1966, "JWS Records: Annual Reports, 1963–1970"; A. H. Neilly to C. B. Stoll and Francis Lobdell, 18 June 1970; "Group Interview," 22 Oct. 1992; Peter Wiley interview with Charles Stoll, 21 Jan. 1993, "JWS Oral History: Interview C. B. Stoll w/PBW, 1993"; Wiley, "My First 50 Years," Chap. 5b, 31.

[63]John Wiley & Sons Annual Report, 1965, "JWS Records: Annual Reports, 1963–1970"; Conference on Corporate Objectives, 22–24 Aug. 1967.

[64]Brammer, "Textbook Publishing," 323, 326; "Big Stock Offering Is Placed for Wiley," *New York Times* (12 Apr. 1967), 67. John Wiley & Sons, "Prospectus," 17 Mar. 1967, "JWS Stock: Public Stock Offering, 1962–1967"; John Wiley & Sons Annual Report, 1969, "JWS Records: Annual Reports, 1963–1970"; A. H. Neilly's Talk to Security Analysts, 25 Nov. 1969, "JWS Operations: Financial Results, 1964–1969"; A. H. Neilly to C. B. Stoll and Francis Lobdell, 18 June 1970; A. H. Neilly to W. Bradford Wiley, 14 Nov. 1972; Corporate Management Group, Planning Meeting, 26–29 Oct. 1976; "Group Interview," 22 Oct. 1992.

[65]John Wiley & Sons Annual Report, 1973, 1975, "JWS Records: Annual Reports, 1971–1977"; Charles Stoll to Board of Directors, 15 June 1976.

[66]"New Data Processing Subsidiary of Wiley," *Publishers Weekly* (6 Oct. 1969); "Wiley Acquires Firms in Technology Fields," *Publishers Weekly* (15 Dec. 1969), 21. Moore, *Wiley*, 214. "Expansions," "JWS Subsidiaries: Expansion History, 1959–1980"; John Wiley & Sons Press Release, 12 Sept. 1969, "JWS Subsidiaries: Contemporary Systems, 1969"; "A Directory of American Book Publishing," 1973, "JWS History: Various Histories 19th to mid 20th Cent."; John Wiley & Sons Annual Report, 1974,

"JWS Records: Annual Reports, 1971–1977"; Charles Stoll to Board of Directors, 15 June 1976; Peter Wiley interview with Charles Stoll, 21 Jan. 1993, "JWS Oral History: Interview C. B. Stoll w/PBW, 1993."

67Henry Raymont, "Book Publishers Feel Economy Pinch," *New York Times* (3 Feb. 1971), 30. A. H. Neilly to C. B. Stoll and Francis Lobdell, 18 June 1970; John Wiley & Sons Annual Report, 1972, "JWS Records: Annual Reports, 1971–1977"; John Wiley & Sons memorandum, 23 Apr. 1972, "JWS Subsidiaries: Becker-Heyes [*sic*], 1969–1972"; A. H. Neilly to W. Bradford Wiley, 14 Nov. 1972; Joseph Becker to Alex Zakharov, 9 Dec. 1974, "JWS International: USSR General Reports, 1974–1978"; Peter Wiley interview with Charles Stoll, 21 Jan. 1993, "JWS Oral History: Interview C. B. Stoll w/PBW, 1993."

68Burlingame, *Endless Frontiers*, 395–400; David Henry, *Challenges Past, Challenges Present: An Analysis of American Higher Education Since 1930* (San Francisco: Jossey-Bass, 1975), 110; Coser et al., *Books*, 47. "Expansions," "JWS Subsidiaries: Expansion History, 1959–1980"; John Wiley & Sons Annual Report, 1971, 1972, 1974, "JWS Records: Annual Reports, 1971–1977"; "Summary of Five Year Plans, Fiscal 1976–1980," 10 Dec. 1974; Peter Wiley interview with Charles Stoll, 21 Jan. 1993, "JWS Oral History: Interview C. B. Stoll w/PBW, 1993."

69Alan Lesure to Peter Booth Wiley, Dec. 18, 2006.

70Alan Lesure to Peter Booth Wiley, Dec. 18, 2006.

71Moore, *Wiley*, 218. A. H. Neilly Jr. to the Board of Directors, 21 Apr. 1972, "JWS Subsidiaries: Becker-Heyes [*sic*], 1969–1972"; Wiley, "My First 50 Years," Chap. 5b, 35–37.

72A. H. Neilly to W. Bradford Wiley, 14 Nov. 1972; "Summary of Five Year Plans, Fiscal 1976–1980," 10 Dec. 1974; Corporate Management Group, Planning Meeting, 26–29 Oct.1976.

73*New York Times* (18 Jan. 1948, 30 Mar. 1958, 1 Feb., 16 Aug., 13 Dec. 1959, 13 Mar. 1966); *Los Angeles Times* (28 Oct. 1962); Cerf, *At Random*, 78. Special Meeting, Board of Directors, 12–15 Mar. 1961; "Summary of Five Year Plans, Fiscal 1976–1980," 10 Dec. 1974; Bradford Wiley and Townsend Hoopes, "Moscow Seminar on American Publishing Practices," 18 Oct. 1976, "JWS International: AAP Moscow Seminar, 1976"; Corporate Management Group, Planning Meeting, 26–29 Oct. 1976; Richard Blodgett interview of Andrew Neilly, 31 Mar. 2004.

74"Wiley-Basic Books to Publish Science Paperbacks," *Publishers Weekly* (3 July 1961), 158; Raymond Walters Jr., "Paperbacks Continue Advance in New Titles and Publishers," *New York Times* (20 Feb. 1963), 7; Irston Barnes, "A Mixed Bag of Books, Scientific and Simple," *Washington Post* (14 July 1963), C11; Shatzkin, "The Book in Search of a Reader," 134; Madison, *Book Publishing*, 376–77. "JWS Alliances: Science Editions, 1961–1968."

75*New York Times* (1 May 1960), BR28; Elizabeth Fowler, "Books: Housing," *New York Times* (20 June 1971), F14. "JWS Oral History: Interview W. Sullivan w/ PBW, 1993," Peter Wiley conversation with Simon Michael Bessie, July 1989.

76Martin Matheson to A. H. Neilly Jr., 15 June 1966, "JWS Employees: Martin Matheson, 1953–1972."

77Benjamin, "Technical, Scientific and Medical Publishing," in Grannis, ed., *What Happens in Book Publishing*, 356. Conference on Corporate Objectives, 22–24 Aug. 1967; W. Bradford Wiley, "Something about Books," n.d., "WBW Talks: Books in the US."

78Benjamin, "Technical, Scientific and Medical Publishing," in Grannis, ed., *What Happens in Book Publishing*, 364–65; Eric Ashby, *Any Person, Any Study: An Essay on Higher Education in the United States* (New York: McGraw-Hill, 1971), 24. A. H. Neilly to M. Matheson and W. G. Suter, 9 Dec. 1965, "JWS Employees: Martin Matheson, 1953–1972"; Conference on Corporate Objectives, 22–24 Aug. 1967; John Wiley & Sons Annual Report, 1973, "JWS Records: Annual Reports, 1971–1977"; Corporate Management Group, Planning Meeting, 26–29 Oct. 1976; "JWS Oral History: Interview A. H. Neilly w/ PBW, 1992."; John Wiley & Sons Annual Report, 1980.

79"Robert G. St. Clair," *Chicago Tribune* (14 Jan. 1979), B23. *A Guide for . . . Authors*, ix; Moore, *Wiley*, 228–29, 239. "Expansions," "JWS Subsidiaries: Expansion History, 1959–1980"; Charles Stoll to the Board of Directors, 15 June 1976; A. H. Neilly to the Staff, 10 Jan. 1979, "JWS Subsidiaries: Patient Care, 1979."

80"Executive Changes," *New York Times* (28 Sept. 1971), 64; "Who's News," *Wall Street Journal* (29 Sept. 1971), 18.

81Gillespie Associates, *An Assessment of Present Corporate Environment: An Analysis Prepared for John Wiley and Sons, Inc.* (Westport, Conn.: May 1972); "Participative Management," 1 Feb. 1977, "JWS Employees: Andrew H. Neilly, Reports, 1977–1993"; Peter Wiley interview with Charles Stoll, 21 Jan. 1993, "JWS Oral History: Interview C. B. Stoll w/PBW, 1993."

82"Management Guide," 14 Nov. 1974; "Summary of Five Year Plans, Fiscal 1976–1980," 10 Dec. 1974; John Wiley & Sons Annual Report, 1976, "JWS Records: Annual Reports, 1971–1977"; Corporate Management Group, Planning Meeting, 26–29 Oct. 1976.

83Andrew H. Neilly to the Staff, 14 Sept. 1970, "JWS Employee Programs: Miscellaneous, 1970–1986"; Interview with A. H. Neilly Jr., 1 Nov. 1992.

84W. Bradford Wiley, "Something About Books," n.d., "WBW Talks: Books in the US"; Ronald A. Watson, "John Wiley & Sons Ltd., 1962–1976: A Personal Memoir," n.d.; W. Bradford Wiley to the Staff, 15 Apr. 1968; John Wiley & Sons Annual Report, 1974, 1975, 1976, "JWS Records: Annual Reports, 1971–1977"; Interview with A. H. Neilly Jr., 1 Nov. 1992, "JWS Oral History: Interview A. H. Neilly w/ PBW, 1992"; Interview with Liz Ann Stoll, Nov. 2004.

85"Story of John Wiley," 54–57; Harris, *Statistical Portrait*, 426, 433, 435; Michael Sissons, "British Agent Finds Indigenous Publishing, Not American Competition, the Factor to Watch in the World Book Market," *Publishers Weekly* (21 Feb. 1977). W. Bradford Wiley, "The American Book Abroad," 11 Nov. 1969, "WBW Talks: [The] American Book Abroad"; W. Bradford Wiley to V. I. Najdenov, 28 Mar. 1978, "JWS International: USSR 1973"; Wiley, "My First 50 Years," Chap. 5a, 1–3.

86Wilson, "American Book Publishing," 118; Harry Gilroy, "Publishers Seek to Aid New Lands," *New York Times* (2 June 1965), 42; Lacy, "Major Trends," 13. "Frank Forkert Bound for Mid-East, Asian Sales and Reprint Sessions," *Wiley Bulletin: Science and Industry Edition* (Fall 1958), 2. "Overseas Department," 1961; Peter

Wiley interview with Warren Sullivan, 29 Mar. 1993, "JWS Oral History: Interview W. Sullivan w/ PBW, 1993"; Wiley, "My First 50 Years," Chap. 8, with Collins Edit.

[87]W. Bradford Wiley to Edward Hamilton, 8 Apr. 1949, Edward Hamilton to W. Bradford Wiley, 14 Apr. 1949, "WBW Letters: Europe, 1949–1951"; "A Report on England," 1958, "JWS Employees: Warren Sullivan, 1958."

[88]"Scholarly Dollar"; "A Report on England," 1958, "JWS Employees: Warren Sullivan, 1958."

[89]Edward Shils, "The Bookshop in America," in Smith, ed., *American Reading Public*, 142; "A Report on England," 1958, "JWS Employees: Warren Sullivan, 1958."

[90]"RC's Guest List for the Cocktail Party," 14 March 1957, Martin Matheson to J. S. Barnes, 29 Jan. 1957, "JWS 150th Anniversary History, Distribution List, 1957"; "A Report on England," 1958, "JWS Employees: Warren Sullivan, 1958"; Warren Sullivan and Martin Matheson to the Board of Directors, 17 Dec. 1958, William B. Wiley, "Emergence of John Wiley & Sons as an International Publisher," Warren Sullivan, "W.S. Report of Visit to London," 6–19 Feb. 1960, "WBW Letters: UK, 1957–1960"; Ronald A. Watson, "John Wiley & Sons Ltd., 1962–1976: A Personal Memoir," n.d.

[91]"John Wiley & Sons Opens Branch in London," *Publishers Weekly* (10 Oct. 1960), 26–27. "Wiley Ltd. Marks New Era in International Publishing," *Wiley Bulletin: Science and Industry Edition* (Fall 1960), 1, 3. "A Report on England," 1958, "JWS Employees: Warren Sullivan, 1958"; Warren Sullivan and Martin Matheson to the Board of Directors, 17 Dec. 1958, "WBW Letters: UK, 1957–1960"; Brad Wiley and Warren Sullivan, "John Wiley & Sons, Ltd., Report," Oct. 1959, "JWS Subsidiaries: Wiley Ltd., 1959–1969"; "W. B. Wiley's Comments to Ronald Watson's Memoir: John Wiley & Sons, Inc. 1962–1976," 14 June 1993.

[92]*Thirty Years in Chichester: A Celebration*, 87–88

[93]Daniel Melcher, "The Role of Computers," in Henderson, ed., *Trends in American Publishing*, 50. Warren Sullivan, "W.S. Report of Visit to London," 6–19 Feb. 1960, "WBW Letters: UK, 1957–1960"; "JWS Employees: J. Burgess Whiteside, 1965"; "Wiley Ltd.," 13 Aug. 1965, "London 1965"; W. Bradford Wiley to Peter Wiley, 7 Oct. 1976, "WBW Letters: PBW, 1976"; Andrew Neilly to Brad Wiley, 23 Aug. 1965; Burgess Whiteside to Brad Wiley, 21 Oct. 1965; Ronald A. Watson, "John Wiley & Sons Ltd., 1962–1976: A Personal Memoir," n.d.

[94]W. B. Wiley to John Moore, "The Beginnings of Wiley's Efforts to Establish a Base for Distribution and Publishing in England," 22 Sept. 1981, "WBW Letters: UK, 1957–1960"; Wiley Family Oral History: Interview WBW w/ PBW, 1991, 89–94; Wiley, "My First 50 Years," Chap. 5b, 19–25; Ronald A. Watson, "John Wiley & Sons Ltd., 1962–1976: A Personal Memoir," n.d.

[95]John Jarvis conversation with Peter Wiley; A. H. Neilly, "Report of Meetings at John Wiley & Sons Ltd.," 4, 5, 6, Oct. 1967, "JWS Subsidiaries: Wiley Ltd., 1959–1969"; John Wiley & Sons Annual Report, 1968, "JWS Records: Annual Reports, 1963–1970"; W. B. Wiley to John Moore, "The Beginnings of Wiley's Efforts to Establish a Base for Distribution and Publishing in England," 22 Sept. 1981, "WBW Letters: UK, 1957–1960."

[96]*Thirty Years in Chichester*, 65, 93–94

[97]Peter Wiley conversation with Andrew H. Neilly, Jr., November 1, 2006.

[98]J. H. Moore, *Wiley: One Hundred Seventy Five Years of Publishing*, 194.

[99]"Wiley and 5 Mexican Firms Form Editorial Limusa-Wiley," *Publishers Weekly* (13 Aug.1962), 35; "Story of John Wiley," 54–57. William B. Wiley, "Emergence of John Wiley & Sons as an International Publisher," n.d. "WBW Letters: UK, 1957–1960"; Warren Sullivan to an author, Feb. 1957, "JWS Operations: Author Letter, re Translations, 1957"; "JWS Subsidiaries: E. P. Hamilton Letter Limusa, 1961"; Andrew H. Neilly, "Report," 6 Dec. 1964, "JWS Subsidiaries: Limusa-Wiley, Agreements, 1971–1985"; John Wiley & Sons Annual Report, 1965, 1967, "JWS Records: Annual Reports, 1963–1970"; Wiley, "My First 50 Years," Chap. 8, with Collins Edit, 1993.

[100]"Story of John Wiley," 54–57; Gilroy, "Book Sales Soar," 69. Moore, *Wiley*, 192–94. "A Directory of American Book Publishing," 1973, "JWS History: Various Histories 19th to mid 20th Cent."; Charles Stoll to the Board of Directors, 15 June 1976; Peter Wiley interview with Charles Stoll, 21 Jan. 1993, "JWS Oral History: Interview C. B. Stoll w/PBW, 1993"; Wiley, "My First 50 Years," Chap. 8, with Collins Edit.

[101]William B. Wiley, "Emergence of John Wiley & Sons as an International Publisher," n.d. "WBW Letters: UK, 1957–1960"; Wiley's International Publishing Programs, 31 Jan. 1977, "JWS Subsidiaries: Expansion History, 1959–1980"; John Wiley & Sons Annual Report, 1966, 1967, 1968, "JWS Records: Annual Reports, 1963–1970"; "JWS Subsidiaries: Wiley Eastern Ltd., History, 1966–1980"; Peter Wiley interview with Warren Sullivan, 29 March 1993, "JWS Oral History: Interview W. Sullivan w/ PBW, 1993"; Wiley, "My First Fifty Years," Chap. 8, with Collins Edit.

[102]"Wiley & Sons in Joint Brazilian Venture," *Publishers Weekly* (29 Apr. 1968); "U.S. Publisher Arrives in Brazil for Two-Week Visit," *Brazil Herald* (28 Feb. 1971). "JWS International: Brazil, 1971"; "A Directory of American Book Publishing," 1973, "JWS History: Various Histories 19th to mid 20th Cent."; "Summary of Five Year Plans, Fiscal 1976–1980"; Andrew Neilly and Charles Stoll, "Notes on Visit to Limusa," 12 Mar. 1979, "JWS Subsidiaries: Limusa-Wiley, Agreements, 1971–1985"; Wiley's International Publishing Programs, 31 Jan. 1977, "JWS Subsidiaries: Expansion History, 1959–1980."

[103]"Tuttle-Wiley to Publish New Modern Asia Editions," *Asahi Evening News* (13 Apr. 1957); "Wiley, Publisher, 150 Years Old," *Publishers Weekly* (10 June 1957), 35–36; Gilroy, "Book Sales Soar," 69; "Japan Seizes Pirated Books," *New York Times* (25 Sept. 1960), 3. Martin Matheson to Charles E. Tuttle, 7 Mar. 1957, Charles E. Tuttle to Warren Sullivan, 1 Mar. 1957, "JWS 150th Anniversary: Tokyo, 1957"; Peter Wiley interview with Warren Sullivan, 29 Mar. 1993, "JWS Oral History: Interview W. Sullivan w/ PBW, 1993"; Wiley, "My First 50 Years," Chap. 8, with Collins Edit.

[104]"Expansions," "JWS Subsidiaries: Expansion History, 1959–1980"; "ESP Memo Re The Continental Study, Discussion with R. A. Watson on January 30, 1970," 3 Feb. 1970, "JWS

Subsidiaries: Wiley Ltd., 1970–1997"; John Wiley & Sons Annual Report, 1971, "JWS Records: Annual Reports, 1971–1977"; Eric Proskauer, "European Trip," May 1971, "JWS Employees: Dr. Eric S. Proskauer, 1969-1971"; Peter Wiley interview with Charles Stoll, 21 Jan. 1993, "JWS Oral History: Interview C. B. Stoll w/PBW, 1993."

[105]William Zerter, "Notes from meeting with Geoff Dean," Sept. 2006.

[106]Moore, *Wiley*, 237. William B. Wiley, "Emergence of John Wiley & Sons as an International Publisher," n.d. "WBW Letters: UK, 1957–1960"; Hassan El Aroussy, Mohammed Najim, Mahmud El Amin to Brad Wiley, 1 June 1965, "WBW Letters: Travels, 1957-1992"; John Wiley & Sons Annual Report, 1975, "JWS Records: Annual Reports, 1971–1977"; W. Bradford Wiley, "The Free Flow of Information," Feb. 1978, "WBW Talks: Franklin in Cairo, 1978"; Stephen Smith to Peter Wiley, June 2006; Gabi Garbain to Steve Smith, e-mail, June 6, 2006.

[107]Warren Sullivan to an author, Feb. 1957, "JWS Operations: Author Letter, re Translations, 1957"; John Wiley & Sons Annual Report, 1965, "JWS Records: Annual Reports, 1963–1970"; W. Bradford Wiley, "The American Book Abroad," 11 Nov. 1969, "WBW Talks: [The] American Book Abroad."

[108]Irving Spiegel, "Exchange of Publishing Groups Is Arranged by U.S. and Soviet," *New York Times* (21 July 1962), 36; "A Report on Book Distribution," *Publishers Weekly*, (14 Jan. 1963), 40; Curtis Benjamin et al., *Book Publishing in the U.S.S.R.: Report of the Delegation of U.S. Book Publishers Visiting the U.S.S.R., August 20–September 17 1962* (New York: American Book Publishers Council; American Textbook Publishers Institute, 1962); Robert L. Bernstein et al., *Book Publishing in the U.S.S.R.: Report of the Delegation of U.S. Book Publishers Visiting the U.S.S.R., October 21– November 4 1962* (New York: American Book Publishers Council; American Textbook Publishers Institute, 1970); W. Bradford Wiley, ed., *Book Publishing in the U.S.S.R.: Reports of the Delegations of U.S. Book Publishers Visiting the U.S.S.R.* 2nd ed. (Cambridge, Mass.: Harvard University Press, [1971]); "Publishers Hail Soviet Move Despite Problems," *New York Times* (27 Feb. 1973); "The U.S.S.R. and International Copyright," *Publishers Weekly*, 12 Mar. 1973; "Some Implications of the Soviet Union's Becoming Party to the Universal Copyright Convention," *Current Contents* (11 Apr. 1973), 5–7; Neilly, Ex Libris, 9; Herbert Lottman, "The Soviet Way of Publishing," *Publishers Weekly* (18 Sept. 1978), 101–118. Warren Sullivan to an author, Feb. 1957, "JWS Operations: Author Letter, re Translations, 1957"; Warren Sullivan, "W.S. Editorial Report," 6 Nov. 1959, "WBW Letters: UK, 1957–1960"; Edward Hamilton to M. Frank Redding, 8 Oct. 1962, "Wiley's [*sic*] before WBW: E. P. Hamilton History, 1962"; W. Bradford Wiley, "The American Book Abroad," 11 Nov. 1969, "WBW Talks: [The] American Book Abroad"; "WBW Oral History: Delegation to Moscow, 1970"; Bradford Wiley and Townsend Hoopes, "Moscow Seminar on American Publishing Practices," 18 Oct.1976, "JWS International: AAP Moscow Seminar, 1976"; "American Literature in the Soviet Union: Facts and Figures," (1976?) "JWS International: USSR Book Publishing, 1976 (2)"; Lauren Fransen to Allen J. Rose, 11 Nov. 1977, "JWS International: USSR Delegation to US, 1977"; Wiley, "My First 50 Years," Chap. 6.

[109]Herbert Lottman, "The Soviet Way of Publishing," 101–18; Robert Bernstein, "Soviet Publishing From Other Perspectives," *Publishers Weekly* (18 Sept. 1978), 119–21; Martin Levin, "How to Start Doing Business with the Russians," *Publishers Weekly* (18 Sept. 1978), 122–25; "The Soviet-American Press," *National Review* (28 Sept. 1979), 1198. Theodore Waller, "Random Comments on the Current Copyright Situation in the U.S.S.R.," 8 June 1973, International: USSR, 1973"; Mr. and Mrs. W. B. Wiley and M. Foyle, "Report on Visit to Moscow/Leningrad," 17–29 Sept. 1974, "JWS Call Report on AAP Seminar, 23–28 Sept. 1976, "JWS International: USSR Book Publishing, 1976 (2)"; W. Bradford Wiley to V. I. Najdenov, 28 Mar. 1978, W. Bradford Wiley to V. Najdenov, 14 June 1978, W. Bradford Wiley to V. Moldavan, 26 July 1978, W. Bradford Wiley, "Report of a meeting with Vasilij Antonovich Slastenenko," 21 Oct. 1978, and others "JWS International: USSR State Committee Letters, 1973–1978"; M. Orlando to W. B. Wiley, 21 Oct. 1977; W. B. Wiley to Michael Foyle, 1 Nov. 1977, "JWS International: USSR Delegation to US, 1977"; Wiley, "My First 50 Years," Chap. 6.

[110]W. Bradford Wiley et al., *Book Publishing and Distribution in Rumania: Report of the Delegation of U.S. Book Publishers Visiting Rumania, October 1–10, 1965* (New York: American Book Publishers Council; American Textbook Publishers Institute, 1965). "JWS International: Romania, 1965"; "JWS International: Hungary, 1972–1990"; James Cameron to A. I . Petrenko, 30 Dec. 1977, James Cameron to L. O. Chua, 30 Dec. 1977, James Cameron to W. B. Wiley, 19 Jan. 1978, "JWS International: USSR State Committee Letters, 1973–1978"; Lauren Fransen to Vladimir Nazarov, 1 Nov. 1978, "JWS International: USSR General Reports, 1974–1978"; Wiley, "My First 50 Years," Chap. 6.

[111]J. L. Dusseau and J. W. Gramling, "London and Moscow: Impressions and People," 26 Aug.–1 Sept. 1973, "JWS International: USSR 1973"; Townsend Hoopes to Robert Bernstein, 1, 23 Apr. 1976, Robert Bernstein to Townsend Hoopes, 13 Apr. 1976, "JWS International: USSR Book Publishing, 1976 (2)."

[112]Wilson, "American Book Publishing," 118; Lacy, "Major Trends," 13; Madalynne Reuter, "Final Judgment Ends U.S. Case Against 21 Firms," *Publishers Weekly* (13 Dec. 1976), 23; Sissons, "British Agent Finds Indigenous Publishing"; Peter Standish, "After the Consent Decree: The Effect of the Traditional Market Agreement," *Publishers Weekly* (25 Apr. 1977), 44–8. William B. Wiley, "Emergence of John Wiley & Sons as an International Publisher," n.d. "WBW Letters: UK, 1957–1960"; R. A. Watson to R. E. Barker, 5 Feb. 1970, R. E. Barker to R. A. Watson, 9 Feb. 1970, W. B. Wiley to Charles Leib, 20 Dec. 1974, "JWS Records: Anti-Trust Suit, Documents, 1966–1974"; W. B. Wiley to the Staff, 2 Dec. 1974, "JWS Records: Anti-Trust Suit, WBW Statement, 1974"; "Summary of Five Year Plans, Fiscal 1976–1980," 10 Dec. 1974; Ronald Watson to R. E. Barker, 26 Mar. 1975, "JWS Records: Anti-Trust Suit, Documents, 1975"; "JWS Records: Anti-Trust Consent Decree, 1976"; Wiley, "My First 50 Years," Chap. 8, with Collins Edit.

[113]"Franklin Project Elects New Chief," *New York Times* (7 Oct. 1964), 42; "Franklin Book Programs: Global Publishing Aid Is Varied and Expanded," *Publishers Weekly* (15 Mar. 1965), 28–32; Harry Gilroy, "Group Hailed for Supporting Publishers Abroad,"

New York Times (27 Oct. 1966), 56; "Five New Directors Elected by Franklin Book Programs," *New York Times* (28 Oct. 1965), 40. Edward Hamilton to M. Frank Redding, 8 Oct. 1962, "Wiley's [*sic*] before WBW: E. P. Hamilton History, 1962"; "JWS International: Franklin Book Program Tour, 1964 (1) (2) (3)"; Wiley, "My First 50 Years," Chap. 6, Chap. 7, with WBW/PBW Edits.

[114]"Marketing's MM: Martin Matheson and the Marketing Division," *Wiley Bulletin* (Fall 1959), 2. "Summary of Five Year Plans, Fiscal 1976–1980," 10 Dec. 1974.

[115]William Murray, *Adventures in the People Business: The Story of World Book* (Chicago: Field Enterprises Educational Corporation, 1966), 239; Melcher, "The Role of Computers," 50. "New IBM Machines Expedite Work in All Depts," *Wiley Bulletin: Science and Industry Edition* (Spring 1958), 2.

[116]Wiley Family Oral History: Interview WBW w/ PBW, 1991, 67; Wiley, "My First 50 Years," chap. 4, 23.

[117]A. H. Neilly to C. B. Stoll and Francis Lobdell, 18 June 1970; Martin Matheson to International Sales Department, 22 Jan. 1964, "Data Study," memo, 28 Dec. 1964, "JWS Employees: Martin Matheson, 1953–1972"; McKinsey & Company, "Integrated Performance Planning," March 1965, "JWS Operations: McKinsey Report, 1965"; W. S. Diefenbach to A. H. Neilly, 15 Jan. 1968, "JWS Strategy: Strategic Planning, Methodology, 1968"; Interview with A. H. Neilly, Jr., 1 Nov. 1992, "JWS Oral History: Interview A. H. Neilly w/ PBW, 1992"; Peter Wiley interview with Andrew Neilly, 14 Nov. 1992; Peter Wiley interview with Charles Stoll, 21 Jan. 1993, "JWS Oral History: Interview C. B. Stoll w/PBW, 1993"; Wiley, "My First 50 Years," chap. 5b, 4–5, 30.

[118]Wiley's 100 Bestsellers," 1957–1963, "JWS Records: Annual Bestsellers, 1929–1963"; John Wiley & Sons Annual Report, 1971, "JWS Records: Annual Reports, 1971–1977."

[119]Shugg, "Professors and Their Publishers," 104; Unwin and Unwin, *The Truth about Publishing*, 28–37, 46. "MM to AHN," 24 Feb. 1965, Martin Matheson's Big Black Book.

[120]For a more extended discussion of the economics of book publishing, see Unwin and Unwin, *The Truth about Publishing*, 38–42 and Herbert Bailey, *The Art and Science of Book Publishing,* 3rd ed. (Columbus: Ohio University Press, 1990).

[121]"Cinema of 'Cholesterol' Suggested by Kritchevsky as Added Attraction," *Wiley Bulletin: Science and Industry Edition* (Fall 1958), 7.

[122]Martin Matheson to Andrew H. Neilly, 4 Nov. 1965, "JWS Employees: Martin Matheson, 1953–1972"; Interview with A. H. Neilly, Jr., 1 Nov. 1992, "JWS Oral History: Interview A. H. Neilly w/ PBW, 1992."

[123]Murray, *Adventures in the People Business,* 237–38; Benjamin, "Technical, Scientific and Medical Publishing," 361–62; Dessauer, *Book Publishing,* 93, 196; Neilly, *Ex Libris,* 7; Cerf, *At Random,* 36. Interview with A. H. Neilly Jr., 1 Nov. 1992, "JWS Oral History: Interview A. H. Neilly w/ PBW, 1992"; Peter Wiley interview with Charles Stoll, 21 Jan. 1993, "JWS Oral History: Interview C. B. Stoll w/PBW, 1993"; W. B. Wiley, "The Publisher and the Computer: New

Roles and New Responsibilities," n.d., "WBW Talks: Publisher and the Computer, no date."

[124]Benjamin, "Technical, Scientific and Medical Publishing," 362; Neilly, *Ex Libris,* 5; Unwin and Unwin, *The Truth about Publishing,* 168. Ronald A. Howard to Beatrice Shube, 5 Oct. 1972, 1 Mar. 1973, "JWS College Division: Howard Series, 1963–1973."

[125]Shatzkin, "The Book in Search of a Reader," 128; Shils, "The Bookshop in America," 139; Theodore Wilentz, "American Bookselling in the 1960s," in Smith, ed., *The American Reading Public,* 151–52; Louis Epstein, "Bookstores: A Main Distribution Agency for Books," in Henderson, ed., *Trends in American Publishing* 91–93. Moore, *Wiley,* 194. Andrew Neilly to Wiley Authors, 11 Sept. 1962, "JWS Operations: Agency Plan, 1962"; Robert Dundas to W. B. Wiley, 18 Feb. 1983, R. McCullough to W. B. Wiley, 23 Feb. 1983, "WBW Letters: PBW, 1976"; Peter Wiley interview with Warren Sullivan, 29 March 1993, "JWS Oral History: Interview W. Sullivan w/ PBW, 1993."

[126]Shils, "The Bookshop in America," 144; Epstein, "Bookstores," 91; Sam Weller, "Technical Books in the General Bookstore," in Charles B. Anderson and G. Roysce Smith, eds., *A Manual on Bookselling: How to Open and Run Your Own Bookstore,* 2nd ed. (New York: Harmony Books, 1974), 176–84.

[127]Paul Horvitz, "A Note on Textbook Pricing," *American Economic Review* (Sept. 1965), 844–48.

[128]Unwin and Unwin, *The Truth about Publishing,* 152–55. "MM's Assignments as Consultant in 1960," Martin Matheson's Big Black Book; "Marketing's 'MM': A Profile of Martin Matheson and the Development of the Marketing Division," n.d., "JWS Employees: Martin Matheson, 1953–1972."

[129]Lacy, "Economics of Publishing," 62; Marshall Best, "In Books, They Call It Revolution," in Smith, ed., *The American Reading Public,* 70.

[130]Doubleday, *Memoirs of a Publisher,* 278; Unwin and Unwin, *The Truth about Publishing,* 166. "Selling Books to Scientists and Engineers," *Wiley Bulletin: Science and Industry Edition* (Fall 1958), 2, 4, 8.

[131]Lacy, "Economics of Publishing," 63. "Wiley Books, Bookmen to Be on Display at Major Conventions," *Wiley Bulletin: Science and Industry Edition* (Fall 1959), 10. "MM's Assignments as Consultant in 1960," Martin Matheson's Big Black Book; Martin Matheson to Andrew Neilly, ?1963, "JWS Employees: Martin Matheson, 1953–1972"; W. Bradford Wiley, "An International Publisher's View of Trends and Developments in the Flow of Materials," 18 July 1976, "WBW Talks: American Library Assoc. Address, 1976,"

[132]"The Wiley Bulletin," *Wiley Bulletin: Science and Industry Edition* (Spring 1958), 1.

[133]Lacy, "Economics of Publishing," 51.

[134]"Story of John Wiley," 54–57; Unwin and Unwin, *The Truth about Publishing,* 232. Lauren Fransen to Vladimir Nazarov, 1 Nov. 1978, "JWS International: USSR General Reports, 1974–1978."

[135]William Miller, *The Book Industry* (New York: Columbia University Press, 1949), 102; "Wiley Plans Far Western Distribution

Center," *Publishers Weekly* (1 Jan. 1962), 43. "24 Hour Customer Service Maintained by Order Staff," *Wiley Bulletin: Educational Edition* (Spring 1959), 4; Moore, *Wiley*, 209. "A Report on England," 1958, "JWS Employees: Warren Sullivan, 1958"; McKinsey & Company to Francis Lobdell, "Survey of the Physical Distribution System," Jan. 1965; John Wiley & Sons Annual Report, 1967, "JWS Records: Annual Reports, 1963–1970."

[136]*Distribution Dialogue* (1971), 1. McKinsey & Company to Francis Lobdell, "Survey of the Physical Distribution System," Jan. 1965.

[137]Lacy, "Economics of Publishing," 56; Shatzkin, "The Book in Search of a Reader," 131; Coser et al., *Books*, 7; "Returns," Martin Matheson's Big Black Book; "JWS Subsidiaries: Wiley Eastern Ltd., History, 1966–1980."

[138]"Wiley Art Department Masters of Quality, Quantity; Over 14,000 Illustrations Processed in 57," *Wiley Bulletin: Science and Industry Edition* (Fall 1958), 5.

[139]Brammer, "Textbook Publishing," 347; Lacy, "Major Trends," 12; Peter Adams, "Technology in Publishing: A Century of Progress," in Abel and Newlin, eds., *Scholarly Publishing*, 31–35.

[140]"Story of John Wiley," 54–57. Wiley, "My First 50 Years," Chap. 4, 23.

[141]"Complex Photon Machine Composes Entire Books Photographically," *Wiley Bulletin: Science and Industry Edition* (Spring 1958), 7. Daniel Melcher and Nancy Larrick, *Printing and Promotion Handbook: How to Plan, Produce, and Use Printing, Advertising, and Direct Mail*, 3rd ed. (New York: McGraw-Hill, 1966), 246–48; Coser et al., *Books*, 6; Richard Southall, *Printer's Type in the Twentieth Century* (London: British Library; New Castle, DE: Oak Knoll Press, 2005).

[142]Shatzkin, "The Book in Search of a Reader," 136; Lacy, "Major Trends," 12; Dessauer, *Book Publishing*, 80; Theresa Hilbert to Barbara Russiello, July 10, 2007.

[143]Unwin and Unwin, *The Truth about Publishing*, 111. A. H. Neilly to C. B. Stoll and Francis Lobdell, 18 June 1970; W. B. Wiley, "The Publisher and the Computer: New Roles and New Responsibilities," n.d., "WBW Talks: Publisher and the Computer, no date."

[144]John Wiley & Sons Annual Report, 1967, 1969, "JWS Records: Annual Reports, 1963–1970"; John Wiley & Sons Annual Report, 1974, "JWS Records: Annual Reports, 1971–1977"; W. Bradford Wiley, "Something about Books," n.d., "WBW Talks: Books in the US."

[145]Unwin and Unwin, *The Truth about Publishing*, 78. *Author's Guide for Preparing Manuscript and Handling Proof* (New York: John Wiley & Sons, 1950); *A Guide for Wiley Authors in Preparation of Manuscript and Illustrations* (New York: John Wiley & Sons, 1960); *Be Your Own Compositor* (New York: John Wiley & Sons, 1975).

[146]Madison, "Current Trends," 23. Moore, *Wiley*, 204–6, 228. A. H. Neilly to C. B. Stoll and Francis Lobdell, 18 June 1970.

[147]Moore, *Wiley*, 206. Richard Blodgett interview of Andrew Neilly, 31 Mar. 2004.

[148]Wiley, "My First 50 Years," Chap. 2, 10, Chap. 3, 7, Chap. 4, 6–7.

CHAPTER SEVEN

[1]Carolyn T. Anthony, "John Wiley at 175," *Publishers Weekly* (24 Sept. 1982), 42, 45–46; Lizanne Adams to Jane Borko, 17 Nov. 1981, Deborah Wiley to the Corporate Manager Group, 17 Feb. 1982, "Schedule of 175th Anniversary Events (Worldwide)," 8 Mar. 1982, "175th Anniversary"; W. Bradford Wiley, "International Book Publishing," 3 Apr. 1982, "WBW Talks: International Book Publishing, 1982"; John Wiley & Sons, Inc. Invitations Accepted, 175th Anniversary Dinner, 2 Nov. 1982, "JWS 175th Anniversary: General, 1982"; Richard Johnson to EMG, 19 Nov. 1985, "JWS Operations: Executive Management Group, 1985–1986."

[2]R. Gordon Douglas and Thomas O. Gay, *Wiley: Two Thousand and Seven* (New York: John Wiley & Sons, 1982), 14.

[3]John J. McCusker, "What Was the Inflation Rate Then?" Economic History Services, 2001, http://www.eh.net/hmit/inflation. W. Bradford Wiley, Remarks, 29 Mar. 1979, "WBW Talks: JWS Managers, 1979."

[4]Stanley Unwin and Philip Unwin, *The Truth about Publishing*, 8th ed. (London: Allen & Unwin, 1976), 230; Carter Henderson, "The Decline of Industrialism," *Quarterly Journal of Business and Economics* (Summer 1979), 19; John J. McCusker, "Comparing the Purchasing Power of Money in the United States (or Colonies) from 1665 to 2003." Economic History Services, 2004, http://www.eh.net/hmit/ppowerusd/.

[5]Heinz Goetze, *Springer-Verlag: History of a Scientific Publishing House*, Part 2 (New York: Springer-Verlag, 1996), 74–94.

[6]"John Wiley: 175 Years of Publishing," *The Bookseller* (9 Oct. 1982), 1413. Brad Wiley II to Ruth McMullin, 9 Jan. 1988, "Wiley Family: WBW II Family, Business, 1987–1991."

[7]Major competitors are listed in Long Range Business Plan, FY 1982–1986, 23 Apr. 1981.

[8]"John Wiley: 175 Years of Publishing," 1413; W. Bradford Wiley, "My First 50 Years," Chap. 3, 7–8.

[9]Caroline Persell, "Scholars and Book Publishing," in Mary Frank Fox, ed., *Scholarly Writing & Publishing: Issues, Problems, and Solutions* (Boulder, Colo.: Westview Press, 1985), 46; Barbara Dean, "Development of Public Libraries," in Richard Abel and Lyman Newlin, eds., *Scholarly Publishing: Books, Journals, Publishers, and Libraries in the Twentieth Century* (New York: John Wiley & Sons, 2001), 181.

[10]James Wallace and Jim Erickson, *Hard Drive: Bill Gates and the Making of the Microsoft Empire* (New York: John Wiley & Sons, 1992), 204, 208; *Time* (3 Jan. 1983).

[11]Allan F. Hussey, "Aggressive Marketing Helps John Wiley Book Steady Gains," *Barron's* (May 1978), 40, 44; "Neilly Named IPA Vice President," *Inside Wiley* (Nov./Dec. 1984), 3; John Wiley & Sons Press Release, 23 Aug. 1978; "Teamsters Strike at EDC: EDC Operations, 1967–1978"; W. B. Wiley, "Remarks on the Ocassion [*sic*] of Andrew H. Neilly's Retirement Dinner," 16 Sept. 1992, "WBW Talks: Oper-Met Anniversary, 1992."

[12]"JWS Employees Programs: Insurance & Retirement"; "An UnEmployee" to Joseph Kelly, 1 Nov. 1978, "Teamsters Strike at EDC: EDC Operations, 1978."

[13]"A Year for Union Collisions with the Guidelines," *BusinessWeek* (8 Jan. 1979), 70–72. "Court Order 3/26," Andrew Neilly to All Employees, 25 Apr. 1979, Andrew Neilly to the Staff, 8 May, 16 July 1979, Bryan Broderick to All Those on Strike, 8 May 1979, J. B. Storjev to W. J. Maytham, R. B. Polhemus, R. P. Zeldin, 5 June 1979, Russell Ackoff to Gerald Papke, 7 June 1979, Andrew Neilly to Michael Harris, 16 July 1979, "JWS Operations: Teamster Strike, 1979;" "Teamsters Strike at EDC: EDC Operations, 1967–1978"; "Teamsters Strike at EDC: Union Materials, 1977–1979"; "Teamsters Strike at EDC: EDC Operations, 1978"; "Teamsters Strike at EDC: Strike Related Documents, 1979–1980."

[14]John Wiley & Sons, Inc., Annual Report, 1979. Revenue figures broken down by line of business not available until the 1990s.

[15]Long Range Business Plan, FY 1982–1986, 23 Apr. 1981.

[16]Edward Hamilton to W. Bradford Wiley, 24 Aug. 1956, "Wiley's [*sic*] before WBW: E. P. Hamilton Letters to WBW, 1954–1961."

[17]"Executive Changes," 64; "Who's News," 18, JWSA.

[18]Long Range Business Plan, FY1982–1986.

[19]Long Range Business Plan, FY1982–1986.

[20]Daniel Machalaba, "John Wiley & Sons, in a Bid to Speed Up Its Publishing, Tests Electronic Systems," *Wall Street Journal* (31 Oct. 1980), 14; Andrew Pollack, "Computers Let a Thousand Publishers Bloom," *New York Times* (8 Oct. 1987), A1; Peter Adams, "Technology in Publishing: A Century of Progress," in Abel and Newlin, eds., *Scholarly Publishing*, 35–36; "Wiley Ltd. Adopts High-Tech Composition," 3. W. Bradford Wiley, *Communications Revolution in Book Publishing*, 9 Feb. 1983; Richard Johnson, Report to the Board of Directors, 28 Nov. 1984, 6 Mar. 1985, "Reports to the Board, August 1983–May 1985;" Andrew Neilly to George Smith, 5 Dec. 2006.

[21]Report to the Board of Directors, 29 Sept. 1983.

[22]John Hammond Moore, *Wiley: One Hundred and Seventy-five Years of Publishing* (New York: John Wiley & Sons, 1982), 246.

[23]Dan Lacy, "Major Trends in American Book Publishing," in Kathryn Henderson, ed., *Trends in American Publishing* (Champaign, Ill.: University of Illinois Graduate School of Library Science [14th Allerton Park Institute, 1967]), 7; Andrew H. Neilly, *Ex Libris* (Jan. 1975), 13; Carnegie Council on Policy Studies in Higher Education, *Three Thousand Futures: The Next Twenty Years for Higher Education* (San Francisco: Jossey-Bass, 1981), 36–37; Summary of Five-Year Plans, Fiscal 1976–1980, 10 Dec. 1974; "JWS Strategy: Strategic Plan FY 76–80, 1974"; W. Bradford Wiley, "The Outlook for the College Market: 1981–1982," "WBW Talks: College Market, 1981"; Charles Stoll to EMG Members, 7 Aug. 1984, "JWS Employees: Charles B. Stoll, 1961–1989"; Donald Ford to Richard Blodgett, 8 Dec. 2004.

[24]Paul Horvitz, "A Note on Textbook Pricing," *American Economic Review* (Sept. 1965), 844–48; Persell, "Scholars and Book Publishing," 46–47; George Ritzer, "Problems, Scandals, and the Possibility of 'TextbookGate': An Author's View," *Teaching Sociology* (Oct. 1988), 373–80; Richard McKenzie, "Kickbacks in University Textbook Adoptions," *BioScience* (May 1989), 326–27; Julie Ann Miller, "The Price of Previously Owned Texts," *BioScience* (Mar. 1992), 192–95; John Mutter, Jim Milliot, and Karen Holt, "What Price Used Books?" *Publishers Weekly* (27 Sept. 2004), http://www.publishersweekly.com/article/CA455643.html; Hal Varian, "Reading Between the Lines of Used Book Sales," *New York Times* (28 July 2005). Andrew Neilly, Report to the Board of Directors, 4 Dec. 1986, "Reports to the Board, September 1985–June 1987."

[25]Dale Bremmer and Michael Mazur, "Monopolists That Advertise with Recyclable Free Samples: Beware of Professors Selling Gifts?" *Southern Economic Journal* (Apr. 1993), 803–07; Duane Monette, "Sixteen Textbook Authors Respond," *Teaching Sociology* (Oct. 1988), 413–15; Ritzer, "Problems, Scandals," 378–80; Miller, "Price of Previously Owned Texts," 192–95.

[26]Claire Poole, "Stubborn Patriarch," *Forbes* (6 Feb. 1989), 99; Miller, "Price of Previously Owned Texts," 192–95. Andrew Neilly to Peter Wiley, 1 May 2007.

[27]Andrew Neilly to Peter Wiley, 11 Jan. 2007.

[28]Laura Landro, "Book Industry Faces More Consolidation," *Wall Street Journal* (13 Mar. 1987), 7; Pollack, "Computers Let a Thousand Publishers Bloom," A1.

[29]Martin Matheson to GTC, 16 Dec. 1963, Martin Matheson to Andrew H. Neilly, 4 Nov. 1965, "JWS Employees: Martin Matheson, 1953–1972"; Wayne Anderson to Serje Seminoff, 25 Mar. 1987, "JWS College Division: Correspondence, 1985–1988."

[30]Max Horkheimer and Theodor Adorno, *Dialectic of Enlightenment* (New York: Social Studies Association, 1944); Neilly, *Ex Libris*, 4; Ron Robin, *Scandals and Scoundrels: Seven Cases That Shook the Academy* (Berkeley: University of California Press, 2004), 5; Corporate Management Group, Planning Meeting, 26–29 Oct. 1976.

[31]Dan Lacy, "Major Trends in American Book Publishing," in Henderson, ed., *Trends in American Publishing*, 7. Charles Stoll to EMG Members, 7 Aug. 1984, "JWS Employees: Charles B. Stoll, 1961–1989"; Donald Ford to Richard Blodgett, 8 Dec. 2004; W. Bradford Wiley, "The Outlook for the College Market: 1981–1982," "WBW Talks: College Market, 1981."

[32]William L. Stephens, *Accounting Review* (Jan. 1978), 286–287. Donald Ford to Richard Blodgett, 8 Dec. 2004.

[33]"Wiley Fetes Accounting Authors," *To Our Authors* (Summer 1978), 1.

[34]"Acquisition Analysis: CPA Examination Review," 1986, "JWS Operations: Acquisition Analysis, 1986"; Dick Lynch to Peter Wiley, 29 Nov. 2006.

[35]Madalynne Reuter, "Scott, Foresman Acquires Wiley's College English List," *Publishers Weekly* (13 Nov. 1981), 12; James Atlas, *Battle of the Books: The Curriculum Debate in America* (New York: W. W. Norton, 1992); Ronald Strickland, "Curriculum Mortis: A Manifesto for Structural Change," in Henry Giroux and Kosta Mysiades, eds., *Beyond the Corporate University: Culture and Pedagogy in the New Millennium* (New York: Rowman & Littlefield, 2001), 73–87; Jeffrey Williams, "Franchising the University," in

Giroux and Mysiades, eds., *Beyond the Corporate University*, 17; "John Wiley: 175 Years of Publishing," 1413; Rick Leyh memo, 5 July 2006. Brad Wiley II to Peter Wiley, 29 May 2007.

[36]John Wiley & Sons Annual Report, 1975.

[37]Peter Wiley interview with Alan Lesure, 23 Jan. 2007.

[38]John P. Dessauer, *Library Acquisitions: A Look into the Future* (New York: Book Industry Study Group, 1976), 89. Andrew H. Neilly, Report to the Board of Directors, 20 June 1985. McGraw-Hill Annual Report, 1985.

[39]John Wiley & Sons Annual Report, 1975. JWS Annual Catalogues, 1979, 1981.

[40]Walter Mayham, Tom Conter, Memo, 26 Nov. 1984.

[41]"McClellan's Analysis of Computer Industry Hits Bestseller Lists Across the Country," *Inside Wiley* (Nov./Dec. 1984); AHN Jr. Report to the Board of Directors, Sept. 20, 1984. Robert Douglas Memo, Oct. 22, 1984.

[42]JWS Annual Catalogues, 1979, 1981.

[43]Lewis I. Gidez, "Editorial Operations," in Council of Biology Editors, *Economics of Scientific Journals* (Bethesda, Md.: Council of Biology Editors, 1982), 36–50; Margaret Broadbent, "Copy Editing," in *Economics of Scientific Journals*, 51–56; Joanne Fetzner, "Purchasing Typesetting Separate from Printing," in *Economics of Scientific Journals*, 57–62; Robert V. Ormes, "Presswork, Binding, and Paper," in *Economics of Scientific Journals*, 63–67; George B. Roscoe, "Distribution and Postage," in *Economics of Scientific Journals*, 68–73; Milton Paige, "Subscription Fulfillment," in *Economics of Scientific Journals*, 74–80.

[44]Roger L. Geiger, *Research and Relevant Knowledge: American Research Universities Since World War II* (New York: Oxford University Press, 1993), 310–11, 315, 319, 320, 322.

[45]Rush Welter, *Problems of Scholarly Publication in the Humanities and Social Sciences* (New York: American Council of Learned Societies, 1959), 68; A. H. Neilly's Remarks for Stockholders' Meeting, 6 Sept. 1984, "JWS Employees: Andrew H. Neilly, Documents, 1986–1988"; Robert Douglas, Report to the Board of Directors, 22 Oct. 1984, Wiley Press Release, 14 Nov. 1984, "Reports to the Board, August 1983–May 1985"; Charles Stoll to Maggie Irwin, 24 Apr. 1985, "JWS Employees: Charles B. Stoll, 1961–1989"; A. H. Neilly's Remarks to the Shareholders of John Wiley & Sons, 19 Sept. 1985, "JWS Stock: Report to Stockholders, 1969–1987." Peter Wiley interview with Mary Curtis, 28 Sept. 2006.

[46]Peter Wiley interview with Mary Curtis, 28 Sept. 2006.

[47]Peter Wiley interview with Mary Curtis, 28 Sept. 2006. Andrew H. Neilly Report to Board of Directors, 20 June 2006.

[48]John Wiley & Sons Annual Report, 1979.

[49]Long Range Business Plan, FY1982–1986.

[50]John Collins to Charles Ellis, 28 Mar. 1989, "JWS Subsidiaries: Wiley Eastern Ltd., 1989 [1]."

[51]Wilson successfully hedged its withdrawal from South Africa in 1985. W. Mathew Juechter, Report to the Board of Directors, 3 Sept.

1985, "Reports to the Board, September 1985–June 1987." Wiley also considered hedging its peso risks, but "all agreed that hedging was outrageous" due to the price. As it turned out, however, the futures market knew the future value of the peso better than Wiley and Limusa did. A. H. Neilly's Report of a Visit to Editorial Limusa, 13–15 May 1985, "JWS Subsidiaries: LIMUSA-Wiley, 1984–1988."

[52]Anthony, "John Wiley at 175," 46; "International Division Profile," *To Our Authors* (Summer 1981), 2; A. Higham, Report to the Board of Directors, 20 June, 4 Sept. 1985, "Reports to the Board, August 1983–May 1985"; John Collins to Carol Brodyn, 9 Mar. 1989, "JWS Subsidiaries: Wiley Eastern Ltd., 1989 [1]."

[53]Anthony, "John Wiley at 175," 46; John Wiley & Sons Press Release, 6 May 1982, "JWS Subsidiaries: Heyden & Sons Ltd., London, 1982"; C. B. Stoll to Board of Directors, 2 Aug. 1983; Andrew Neilly, Report to the Board of Directors, 7 June 1985, "Reports to the Board, August 1983–May 1985"; John Wiley & Sons Press Release, 11 Feb. 1986, "Reports to the Board, September 1985–June 1987"; "JWS Finance Committee: Budget Review, 1990"; Peter Wiley interview with Charles Stoll, 21 Jan. 1993, "JWS Oral History: Interview C. B. Stoll w/ PBW, 1993." John Wiley & Sons Annual Report, 1988.

[54]*Thirty Years in Chichester: A Celebration*, 131–134.

[55]*Thirty Years in Chichester*, 76.

[56]Timothy Jacobson interview with Michael Foyle, 10 Aug. 2006.

[57]Anthony, "John Wiley at 175," 46. "International Division Profile," *To Our Authors* (Summer 1981), 2. A. Higham, Report to the Board of Directors, 20 June, 4 Sept. 1985, "Reports to the Board, August 1983–May 1985"; John Collins to Carol Brodyn, 9 Mar. 1989, "JWS Subsidiaries: Wiley Eastern Ltd., 1989 [1]."

[58]Peter Wiley interview with Geoff Dean, 15 Sept. 2006.

[59]Peter Wiley interview with Geoff Dean, 15 Sept. 2006.

[60]Moore, *Wiley*, 192–94. John Wiley & Sons Annual Report, 1968, "JWS Records: Annual Reports, 1963–1970"; "Expansions," Wiley's International Publishing Programs, 31 Jan. 1977, "JWS Subsidiaries: Expansion History, 1959–1980"; Andrew Neilly, Report to the Board of Directors, 7 June 1985, "Reports to the Board, August 1983–May 1985"; C. B. Stoll to A. Higham, 27 June 1986, "JWS Employees: Charles B. Stoll Reports, 1976–1994"; "The Strategic Fit of Current Investments in Canada and Australia," 1 May 1987, "JWS Subsidiaries: Investments in Canada & Australia, 1987"; Peter Wiley interview with Charles Stoll, 21 Jan. 1993, "JWS Oral History: Interview C. B. Stoll w/ PBW, 1993"; Peter Wiley interview with Geoff Dean, 15 Sept 2006; Geoff Dean to Peter Wiley, 25 Feb. 2007; William Zerter interview with Geoff Dean, Sept. 2006.

[61]Peter Wiley interview with Geoff Dean, 15 Sept. 2006.

[62]Andrew H. Neilly and C. H. Lieb, "Report," 12–16 Apr. 1966, "JWS Subsidiaries: Limusa-Wiley, Agreements, 1971–1985"; W. B. Wiley and A. H. Neilly, "Notes on Meetings with Editorial Limusa," 5–8 Feb. 1974, Andrew Neilly and Charles Stoll, "Notes on Visit to Limusa," 12 Mar. 1979, "JWS Subsidiaries: Limusa-Wiley, Agreements, 1971–1985"; Report to the Board of Directors, 20 June 1984, A. Higham, Report to the Board of Directors, 20 June 1985, Andrew Neilly, Report to the Board of Directors, 7 June 1985,

"Reports to the Board, August 1983–May 1985"; D. E. Wiley to W. B. Wiley, A. H. Neilly, and J. A. E. Higham, 18 Mar. 1985, A. H. Neilly's Report of a Visit to Editorial Limusa, 13–15 May 1985, Richard Rudick to Luis Barona Mariscal, 25 July 1985, Luis Barona Mariscal to Andrew H. Neilly, 7 Oct. 1985, Richard D. Roberts to Andrew H. Neilly, 22 Oct., 13 Nov. 1985, Andrew H. Neilly to Richard D. Roberts, 10 Dec. 1985, Adrian Higham to W. B. Wiley et al., 30 Jan. 1986, Andrew H. Neilly to All Staff, 4 Mar. 1986, John Wiley & Sons Press Release, 4 Mar. 1986, Lauren Fransen's Trip Report, 12–19 Mar. 1988, "JWS Subsidiaries: LIMUSA-Wiley, 1984–1988"; A. Higham, Report to the Board of Directors, 4 Sept., 12 Dec. 1985, A. Higham to Carlos Noriega Milera, 22 Nov. 1985, Andrew Neilly, Report to the Board of Directors, 12 Mar. 1986, "Reports to the Board, September 1985–June 1987"; John Wiley & Sons Press Release, 3 Mar. 1986, 16 June 1986, "JWS Operations: Financial Results, 1977–1988"; Peter Wiley interview with Charles Stoll, 21 Jan. 1993, "JWS Oral History: Interview C. B. Stoll w/ PBW, 1993"; Wiley, "My First 50 Years," Chap. 8; Tim King interview, 22 June 2005; Carlos Noriega Arias to Peter Wiley, 29 Aug. 2006.

63A. Higham, Report to the Board of Directors, 20 June 1985, "Reports to the Board, August 1983–May 1985"; A. Higham, Report to the Board of Directors, 4 Sept. 1985, "Reports to the Board, September 1985–June 1987"; Gabi Sharbain to Steve Smith, 22 June 2006.

64E. B. Desai to Andrew Neilly, 7 Mar. 1984, 23 Mar. 1985, W. B. Wiley's Comments on Desai's Letter, 7 Mar. 1984, "JWS Subsidiaries: Wiley Eastern Ltd., 1984–1984 [sic]"; "Notes on Adrian Higham's Visit to Bombay, India," 6–9 Oct. 1986, "JWS Subsidiaries: Wiley Eastern Ltd., 1966–1986"; A. Machwe to J. A. E. Higham, 7 Dec. 1987, "JWS Internat. Publ. Developm. Progr.: WEL Letters, 1986–1988"; John Collins to Charles Lieb, 1 Sept. 1988, "Wiley Eastern Ltd.," 1988, "JWS Subsidiaries: Wiley Eastern Ltd., 1988 [4]"; Quentin Smith, "Report on a Visit to Wiley Eastern Ltd.—October 1988," 9 Nov. 1988, "JWS Subsidiaries: Wiley Eastern Ltd., 1988 [5]"; John Collins to Charles Ellis, 28 Mar. 1989, "JWS Subsidiaries: Wiley Eastern Ltd., 1989 [1]"; E. B Desai to W. Bradford Wiley, 11 May 1989, Charles Ellis to W. Bradford Wiley et al., 1 June 1989, "JWS Subsidiaries: Wiley Eastern Ltd., 1989 [2]," Wiley, "My First 50 Years," Chap. 8.

65"US Book Firm May Go into Publishing," Straits Times (15 Feb. 1982); "John Wiley: 175 Years of Publishing," 1412; A. Higham, Report to the Board of Directors, 3 June 1986, "Reports to the Board, September 1985–June 1987"; Brad Wiley to Eruch Desai, 18 Apr. 1989, Tina Papatsos to John Collins, 18 Apr. 1989, A. Machwe to E. B. Desai, 26 Apr. 1989, A. Machwe to John Collins, 28 Apr. 1989, "JWS Subsidiaries: Wiley Eastern Ltd., 1989 [1]"; John Collins to Lauren Fransen, 16 June 1989, "JWS Subsidiaries: Wiley Eastern Ltd., 1989 [2]."

66"JWS Subsidiaries: Wiley Singapore, 1982–1993"; "JWS Internat. Publ. Developm. Progr.: New Delhi Meetings, 1986–1987"; John Collins to Charles Ellis, 25 Mar. 1988, "JWS Internat. Publ. Developm. Progr.: Jacaranda, 1988"; "JWS Internat. Publ. Developm. Progr.: WEL Letters, 1986–1988," "JWS Internat. Publ. Developm. Progr.: Singapore, 1988–1990."

67"How Distribution Works: Japanese Distributors and Importers Are Fast, Efficient, and Perform a Multitude of Tasks for Their Money," Publishers Weekly (12 Jan. 1990); Charles Stoll to Maggie Irwin, 24

Apr. 1985, "JWS Employees: Charles B. Stoll, 1961–1989"; Tony Llewellyn to John Wilde et al., 27 Nov. 1987, "JWS Internat. Publ. Developm. Progr.: Japan, 1987"; Bob Long to Adrian Higham et al., 27 Nov. 1987, "JWS International: Japan Correspondence, 1987–1993"; Wiley, "My First 50 Years," Chap. 8; Tadashi Hase to Peter Wiley, 8 Mar. 2007.

68Status Report U.S.S.R., 1 Oct. 1980, M. Foyle to W. B. Wiley, 14 Jan. 1983, Martin Levin to All Participants in the U.S. Book Store in Moscow, 19 Sept. 1988, "JWS International: USSR General Reports, 1979–1989."

69Lynette Owen, "Moscow—A Conditional Promise of Future Reward," The Bookseller (27 Sept. 1991), 841–43; W. Bradford Wiley to G. D. Komkov, 23 May 1979, "JWS International: USSR State Committee Letters, 1979"; Brad Wiley to Morton Moskin, 18 Apr. 1988, A. H. Neilly's Notes on a Visit to Moscow and Leningrad, 12–21 Sept. 1989, "JWS International: USSR General Reports, 1979–1989"; Michael Foyle and Mark Bide, "USSR Visit September, 1991"; Wiley, "My First 50 Years," Chap. 6.

70Peter Wiley, Memorandum, 20 June 2006; Curtis Benjamin, "U.S. Book Sales Overseas: An Ebbing Tide," Publishers Weekly (29 Apr. 1983), 22–24; Edwin McDowell, "Lack of Copyright in China Disturbs U.S. Authors," New York Times (10 Jan. 1984), C11; Gordon Graham, "The Shrinking World Market," Publishers Weekly (4 May 1984), 20–21; Shirley Horner, "About Books," New York Times (16 Nov. 1986), 36. Copyright Treaty with China, "Copyright: Chinese Copyright, 1979–1986"; Richard Rudick to Subcommittee on Patents, Copyrights, and Trademarks, 29 Apr. 1988, "Bern [sic] Copyright Convention: JWS & Hearings, 1988"; Wiley, "My First 50 Years," Chap. 6.

71"John Wiley: 175 Years of Publishing," 1412; "Wiley Hosts Chinese Interns," Inside Wiley (Nov. 1982), 2; William B. Wiley, "Emergence of John Wiley & Sons as an International Publisher," n.d. "WBW Letters: UK, 1957–1960"; W. Bradford Wiley's Speech at the China Institute in America, 19 Mar. 1985, "Copyright: Chinese Copyright, 1979–1986"; Peter Wiley interview with Charles Stoll, 21 Jan. 1993, "JWS Oral History: Interview C. B. Stoll w/ PBW, 1993"; Wiley, "My First 50 Years," Chap. 9. PBW speech, Beijing, Nov. 2005.

72McDowell, "Lack of Copyright in China," C11. Charles Stoll to Publishers and Editors, 8 Jan. 1981, "Copyright: Chinese Copyright, 1979–1986"; John Wiley & Sons and Shanghai Scientific and Technical Publishers, Supplement to Agreement of 22 Mar. 1985, "CHINA GENERAL—CURRENT"; Charles Stoll to EMG, 18 Nov. 1983, Charles Stoll to Maggie Irwin, 24 Apr. 1985, "JWS Employees: Charles B. Stoll, 1961–1989"; Richard Rudick to Subcommittee on Patents, Copyrights, and Trademarks, 29 Apr. 1988, "Bern [sic] Copyright Convention: JWS & Hearings, 1988"; Peter Wiley interview with Charles Stoll, 21 Jan. 1993, "JWS Oral History: Interview C. B. Stoll w/ PBW, 1993"; Wiley, "My First 50 Years," Chap. 9.

73"John Wiley: 175 Years of Publishing," 1412–13. Adrian Higham's Notes on Visit to Seoul, Korea, 16–20 Nov. 1987, "JWS Internat. Publ. Developm. Progr.: Korea, 1987"; Brad Wiley to Stephen Smith, 21 Apr. 1993, "JWS Subsidiaries: Wiley Singapore, 1982–1993."

74Brad Wiley, Notes for a Talk at the Breakfast Meeting, 5 Jan. 1987, "WBW Talks: Global Strategy, 1987"; R. S. Rudick to Ruth

McMullin, 25 Apr. 1989, "JWS Subsidiaries: Outside Directors in Subsidiaries, 1989."

[75]Adams, "Technology in Publishing," in Abel and Newlin, eds., *Scholarly Publishing,* 36.

[76]Copyright Clearance Center 2006 Annual Report. Doug Black of Copyright Clearance Center e-mail 22 Dec. 2006 to Jennifer MacMillan, JWS.

[77]W. Bradford Wiley to Charles Ellis et al., 10 Dec. 1990, "Publishing Outside JWS: Copyright Clearance Center, 1984–1992"; Brad Wiley to Peter Urbach, 6 Oct. 1992, Peter Urbach to Brad Wiley, 23 Oct. 1992, Peter Urbach to CCC Board of Directors, 13 Mar. 1992, "History of the CCC," n.d., "Publishing Outside JWS: Copyright Clearance Center, 1984–1992."

[78]Richard Rudick to Board of Directors, 7 Sept. 1984, "Publishing Outside JWS: Copyright Clearance Center, 1984–1992".

[79]Edwin McDowell, "6 Publishers of Journals Sue Texaco over Photocopying," *New York Times* (7 May 1985), C16; Edwin McDowell, "Royalties from Photocopying Grow: A $1 Million Payment to Publishers 'Is Just the Tip of the Iceberg'," *New York Times* (13 June 1988), D9; "'Textbook' Anthologies on Campuses Are Curbed by Ruling on Copyrights," *New York Times* (16 Apr. 1991), A14; Copyright Clearance Center, *Annual Review,* 1990, Charles Ellis to Peter Urbach, 9 Apr. 1992, Peter Urbach to CCC Board of Directors, 21 Apr. 1992, "Publishing Outside JWS: Copyright Clearance Center, 1984–1992," Peter Wiley interview with Richard Rudick, June 2004; Richard Rudick interview, Jan. 2006.

[80]Charles Stoll to Lewis Flacks, 21 Nov. 1983, W. Bradford Wiley to Myer Kutz, 29 May 1985, Meeting with Copyright Delegation of People's Republic of China, 27 May 1986, "Copyright: Chinese Copyright, 1979–1986"; W. Bradford Wiley, "China and Copyright: A Layman's Report," 19 Mar. 1985, W. Bradford Wiley China Lecture, Oct. 1985, W. Bradford Wiley, China Lecture, Pine Manor College, Nov. 1985, "WBW Talks: China and Copyright, 1985"; Andrew Neilly to Nicholas Veliotes, 22 May 1987, Richard Rudick to Larry Levinson et al., 9 Sept. 1987, Richard Rudick to Alvin Abbott et al., 14 Sept. 1987, Richard Rudick to James Fox, 21 Sept. 1987, "Bern [*sic*] Copyright Convention: JWS Position, 1987"; Richard Rudick to Subcommittee on Patents, Copyrights, and Trademarks, 29 Apr. 1988, "Bern [*sic*] Copyright Convention: JWS & Hearings, 1988"; Wiley, "My First 50 Years," Chap. 9.

[81]Andrew Neilly to Charles Ellis, 26 July 1990, "JWS Subsidiaries: Wilson Learning Corporation, 1990 (1)."

[82]Peter Wardley, "The Emergence of Big Business: The Largest Corporate Employers of Labour in the United Kingdom, Germany and the United States c. 1907," *Business History* (1999), 88–116; Robert E. Wright, *The Wealth of Nations Rediscovered: Integration and Expansion in American Financial Markets* (New York: Cambridge University Press, 2002); Robert E. Wright, *The First Wall Street: Chestnut Street, Philadelphia, and the Birth of American Finance* (Chicago: University of Chicago Press, 2005); Robert E. Wright and David J. Cowen, *Financial Founding Fathers: The Men Who Made America Rich* (Chicago: University of Chicago Press, 2006); Thomas Weiss, "Services," in Susan B. Carter et al., *Historical Statistics of the United States* (New York: Cambridge University Press, 2006), 4:1061–68. James F. Gillespie to Robert

Badger, 12 Sept. 1980, "JWS Subsidiaries: Wilson Learning Corporation, 1980–1982."

[83]Poole, "Stubborn Patriarch," 99; *Wilson Learning Bulletin* (Summer 1980). Richard Berman to Robert Hauck, 5 Mar. 1982, in Bankers Trust Company, *John Wiley & Sons, Inc. Proposed Acquisition of Wilson Learning Corporation,* "JWS Subsidiaries: Wilson Learning Acqu Eval, 1980–1981"; Charles Ellis to Ad Hoc "Sequel" Committee, 28 Aug. 1990, "JWS Subsidiaries: Wilson Learning Corporation, 1990 (2)." R. C. Badger's Report on Second Visit to Wilson Learning, 25–26 Aug. 1980, Hauck Telephone Conversation with Mat Juechter, 5 Nov. 1980, Andrew Neilly to the Staff, 8 Feb. 1982, John Wiley & Sons Press Release, 4 May 1982, "JWS Subsidiaries: Wilson Learning Corporation, 1980–1982"; John Wiley & Sons Press Release, 8 Feb. 1982, June 1984, "JWS Newsletters: News from Wiley, 1982–1990"; "Wilson Learning Mission Statement, 1983–1986," n.d., "JWS Strategy: Missions Statements, 1964–1986"; Robert Hauck to Andrew H. Neilly, 18 July 1990. Peter Wiley, Memorandum, June 2006.

[84]John Kostouros, "Is Mickey Mouse Leaving Disneyland?" *Minneapolis/St. Paul CityBusiness* (30 Apr. 1986), 14; Poole, "Stubborn Patriarch," 99; Piper Jaffray & Hopwood, Wilson Learning Corporation, 1981, "JWS Subsidiaries: Wilson Learning Acqu Eval, 1980–1981"; Andrew Neilly to the Staff, 3 May 1982, "JWS Subsidiaries: Wilson Learning Corporation, 1980–1982."

[85]Anthony, "John Wiley at 175," 44–46; Alan Fernald interview, 24 Jan. 2006.

[86]Report to the Board of Directors, 29 Sept. 1983, 20 June 1984, Deborah Wiley, Report to the Board of Directors, 20 June 1985, "Reports to the Board, August 1983–May 1985"; Alpha-Omega Business Plan, Nov. 1983, "JWS Strategy: Wiley's Learning Technologies, 1983–1987"; Wiley Learning Technologies, "Managing Software Development," 1985, "Reports to the Board, September 1985–June 1987."

[87]W. Mathew Juechter, Report to the Board of Directors, 3 Sept. 1985, "Reports to the Board, September 1985–June 1987."

[88]Richard W. Stevenson, "Pretoria Divestment Quickens," *New York Times* (26 May 1986), 27; John Wiley & Sons Press Release, June 1984, "JWS Newsletters: News from Wiley, 1982–1990"; Report to the Board of Directors, 20 June 1984, Andrew Neilly, Report to the Board of Directors, 8 Mar., 7 June 1985, "Reports to the Board, August 1983–May 1985"; A. H. Neilly's Remarks for Stockholders' Meeting, 6 Sept. 1984, "JWS Employees: Andrew H. Neilly, Documents, 1986–1988"; A. H. Neilly's Remarks to the Shareholders of John Wiley & Sons, 19 Sept. 1985, "JWS Stock: Report to Stockholders, 1969–1987"; *Training Group Strategic Business Plans Summary, 1986–1991,* 8 Jan. 1986, "JWS Strategy: WLC Strategic Business Plan, 1986."

[89]"Wiley Launches Software Programs," *Inside Wiley* (Summer 1982), 1–2, 4; W. Bradford Wiley, *Communications Revolution in Book Publishing,* 9 Feb. 1983; A. H. Neilly's Report to the Stockholders of John Wiley & Sons, 9 Sept. 1982, A. H. Neilly's Remarks to the Shareholders of John Wiley & Sons, 19 Sept. 1985, "JWS Stock: Report to Stockholders, 1969–1987"; Robert Douglas to the Board of Directors, 30 May 1984, "JWS College Division: Software Strategies, 1984"; R. O. Johnson to A. H. Neilly, 10 Nov.

1986, "JWS Operations: Wiley Research and Development, 1985–1987"; Richard Johnson, Report to the Board of Directors, 26 Feb. 1987, "Reports to the Board, September 1985–June 1987."

[90]Edwin McDowell, "Audio Cassettes a Hit at Booksellers' Meeting," *New York Times* (28 May 1986), C15; Tom Spain, "Wiley Introduces New Audio Line," *Publishers Weekly* (13 June 1986), 39; "Some Big Thoughts in Short Form," *New York Times* (31 Aug. 1986), F2; Jack Egan, "Publishing for the Future," *New York* (16 Aug. 1982), 10; Anthony, "John Wiley at 175," 45. Richard Johnson, Report to the Board of Directors, 28 Nov. 1984, 5 June 1985, "Reports to the Board, August 1983–May 1985"; R. O. Johnson to A. H. Neilly, 10 Nov. 1986, "JWS Operations: Wiley Research and Development, 1985–1987;" Richard Johnson, Report to the Board of Directors, 12 Dec. 1986, "Reports to the Board, September 1985–June 1987."

[91]C. B. Stoll to A. H. Neilly, 2 July 1985, Andrew Neilly to Charles Stoll, 8 Aug. 1985, "JWS College Division: Correspondence, 1985–1988"; Andrew Neilly, Report to the Board of Directors, 19 Sept. 1985, "Reports to the Board, September 1985–June 1987"; Andrew Neilly to Charles Ellis, 26 July 1990, "JWS Subsidiaries: Wilson Learning Corporation, 1990 (1)." Robert Wilder to Peter Wiley, 10 Aug. 2006.

[92]Gladys Topkis, "Book Publishing: An Editor's-Eye View," in Fox, ed., *Scholarly Writing & Publishing*, 74; Andrew Neilly, Report to the Board of Directors, 13 Dec. 1984, 8 Mar. 1985, "Reports to the Board, August 1983–May 1985"; Andrew Neilly, "Notes on a Meeting with Harold Miller, Houghton Mifflin," 23 Oct. 1985, "JWS Operations: Executive Management Group, 1985–1986"; "Group Interview," 22 Oct. 1992. Rick Leyh memo, 5 July 2006.

[93]Alan Lesure to Peter Wiley, 18 Dec. 2006.

[94]Gary Quinlan, Report to the Board of Directors, 3 June 1986, Andrew Neilly, Report to the Board of Directors, 4 Sept. 1986, 12 June 1987, "Reports to the Board, September 1985–June 1987"; Wiley Organizational Survey Results, Training, Dec. 1987, "JWS Operations: Organizational Survey, Publishing, 1987"; Harry Woodward to EPIC, SBS, Sales Force, Management Committee, 14 Jan. 1988, "JWS Subsidiaries: Wilson Learning Corporation, 1988–1989"; Andrew Neilly to Charles Ellis, 26 July 1990, "JWS Subsidiaries: Wilson Learning Corporation, 1990 (1)"; Charles Ellis to Ad Hoc "Sequel" Committee, 28 Aug. 1990, "JWS Subsidiaries: Wilson Learning Corporation, 1990 (2)."

[95]Harry Woodward to EPIC, SBS, Sales Force, Management Committee, 14 Jan. 1988, Peter Wiley to Brad Wiley, Brad Wiley II, Deborah Wiley, 6 June 1989, "JWS Subsidiaries: Wilson Learning Corporation, 1988–1989"; Tim King, "Overview of the Training Industry and Wilson's Position in It," 23 Aug. 1990, "JWS Subsidiaries: Wilson Learning Corporation, 1990 (2)."

[96]John Kostouros, "Welcome to the Marriage, Dear," *Minneapolis/St. Paul CityBusiness*, (30 Apr. 1986); Andrew Neilly to the Staff, 27 Mar. 1986, "JWS Subsidiaries: Wilson Learning Corporation, 1984–1987"; R. O. Johnson to A. H. Neilly, 24 Jan. 1987, "JWS Employees: Cabot Jaffee, 1987"; Wiley Organizational Survey Results, Training, Dec. 1987, "JWS Operations: Organizational Survey, Publishing, 1987"; Robert Sproull to Brad Wiley II, 17 Feb. 1988, "JWS Subsidiaries: Wilson Learning Corporation, 1988–1989"; Charles Ellis to Ad Hoc "Sequel" Committee, 28 Aug. 1990, "JWS Subsidiaries: Wilson Learning Corporation, 1990 (2)."

[97]Peter Wiley to Brad Wiley, Brad Wiley II, and Deborah Wiley, 17 Mar. 1987, "Wiley Family: Family Meetings, 1986–1988"; Wiley Organizational Survey Results, Training, Dec. 1987, "JWS Operations: Organizational Survey, Publishing, 1987"; A. W. Molnar to the Staff, 15 Jan. 1988, Robert Sproull to Brad Wiley II, 17 Feb. 1988, A. H. Neilly's Report on a Telephone Conversation, 2 Dec. 1988, Peter Wiley to Brad Wiley, Brad Wiley II, Deborah Wiley, 6 June 1989, Charles Ellis, Notes on 7/2/90 Meetings in Minneapolis, 5 July 1990, "JWS Subsidiaries: Wilson Learning Corporation, 1988–1989."

[98]Peter Wiley interview with Nancy Wolfberg, 7 May 2007.

[99]Philip Boroff, "Book on Wiley: Low Profits, Mergers Talk," *Crain's New York Business* (10 July 1989), 7. John Wiley & Sons Press Release, 7 June 1984, 3 Mar. 1986, "JWS Operations: Financial Results, 1977–1988"; Andrew Neilly, Report to the Board of Directors, 8 Mar., 7 June 1985, "Reports to the Board, August 1983–May 1985"; Andrew Neilly, Report to the Board of Directors, 12 Mar., 19 June 1986, "Reports to the Board, September 1985–June 1987"; Peter Wiley to Brad Wiley, Brad Wiley II, and Deborah Wiley, 17 Mar. 1987, "Wiley Family: Family Meetings, 1986–1988"; Peter Wiley to the Wileys, 23 Jan. 1989, "Wiley Family: Family Memorandum, 1989."

[100]Albert Henderson, "The Growth of Printed Literature in the Twentieth Century," in Abel and Newlin, eds., *Scholarly Publishing*, 4; "McClellan's Analysis of Computer Industry Hits Bestseller Lists Across the Country," *Inside Wiley* (Nov./Dec. 1984), 2; A. H. Neilly's Remarks for Stockholders' Meeting, 6 Sept. 1984, "JWS Stock: Report to Stockholders, 1969–1987"; Andrew Neilly to the Staff, 8 July 1986, "JWS Operations: Financial Results, 1977-1988"; Robert Douglas, Report to the Board of Directors, 18 Dec. 1986, "Reports to the Board, September 1985–June 1987."

[101]Richard O. Johnson to EMG, 19 Nov. 1985, "JWS Operations: Executive Management Group, 1985–1986," JWSA.

[102]"Heirs and Races," *The Economist* (9 Mar. 1991), 69; A. H. Neilly's Notes from a Meeting with Kenneth Andrews and Deborah Wiley, 5 June 1985, "JWS Employees: Andrew H. Neilly, Documents, 1986–1988"; Richard O. Johnson to EMG, 19 Nov. 1985, "JWS Operations: Executive Management Group, 1985–1986"; "JWS Personnel Committee: PBW Notes, 1986–1987"; John Wiley & Sons Press Release, 8 Dec. 1988, "JWS Newsletters: News from Wiley, 1982–1990"; Tim King interview, 22 June 2005.

[103]"Personal and Confidential (AHN File)," 8 Aug. 1985, "JWS Employees: Andrew H. Neilly, 1971–1988"; Andrew Neilly to Wayne Smith, 23 Aug. 1986, Background Material on K. Wayne Smith, "JWS Operations: Candidates for COO, 1986"; Peter Wiley to Brad Wiley, Brad Wiley II, and Deborah Wiley, 19 Sept. 1986, 16 Dec. 1986, "Wiley Family: Family Meetings, 1986–1988"; Andrew Neilly, Report to the Board of Directors, 4 Dec. 1986, 2 Mar. 1987, "Reports to the Board, September 1985–June 1987"; "JWS Operations: Wayne Smith for COO, 1986;" Peter Wiley interview of Rita Irons, 10 Nov. 2006.

[104]Andrew Neilly to George Smith, 5 December 2006.

[105]Lewis Coser, Charles Kadushin, and Walter Powell, *Books: The Culture and Commerce of Publishing* (Chicago: University of Chicago Press, 1982), 34. W. Bradford Wiley to the Staff, 9 Apr.

1987, "JWS Employees: R. McMullin Letters, 1987–1990"; Ruth R. McMullin, "Statement to Wiley Board," 22 May 1990, "JWS Employees: RMM [sic] Files [2]"; John Wiley & Sons Press Release, 20 June 1990, "JWS Newsletters: News from Wiley, 1982–1990"; Tim King interview, 22 June 2005; Eric Swanson interview, 22 June 2005; Andrew Neilly to George Smith, 5 Dec. 2006.

106Brad Wiley to Peter Wiley, 12 Sept. 2006; Peter Wiley interview of Rita Irons, 10 Nov. 2006.

107Employment Agreement, Ruth R. McMullin, 13 Apr. 1987, "JWS Employees: RMM [sic] Files [1]"

108A. H. Neilly and W. Bradford Wiley to the Staff, 9 Apr. 1987, "JWS Employees: R. McMullin Letters, 1987–1990"; Employment Agreement, Ruth R. McMullin, 13 Apr. 1987, "JWS Employees: RMM [sic] Files [1]"; John Wiley & Sons Press Release, 20 Apr. 1987, 20 Dec. 1988, "JWS Newsletters: News from Wiley, 1982–1990"; Andrew Neilly, Report to the Board of Directors, 12 June 1987, "Reports to the Board, September 1985–June 1987"; Brad Wiley II to D. Wiley, P. Wiley, W. B. Wiley, 27 Aug. 1987, "Wiley Family: WBW II Family, Business, 1987–1991"; W. Bradford Wiley to the Staff, 8 Dec. 1988, "JWS Employees: RMM's Exec. Employment Agreement."

109A. H. Neilly to Ruth McMullin, 7 Apr. 1987, Brad Wiley II to Ruth McMullin, 30 Apr. 1987, "JWS Employees: R. McMullin Letters, 1987–1990."

110Andrew Neilly, Report to the Board of Directors, 19 Mar., 25 June 1987; Robert Wilder to Peter Wiley, 5 July 2006.

111Poole, "Stubborn Patriarch," 99; Boroff, "Book on Wiley," 7; "John Wiley & Sons Inc. Reports Earnings for Qtr to April 30," New York Times (23 June 1989), D7; "Wiley Acquires Park Row Publishers," Inside Wiley (Nov./Dec. 1984), 1; James Gillespie to Andrew Neilly, 17 Apr. 1981, "JWS Strategy: Gillespie Consulting JWS, 1972–1981"; Kenneth Collins and Andrew Ford to Board of Directors, 18 June 1984, Warren Tourtellot to Kenneth Collins, 16 May 1984, "JWS Subsidiaries: Current Series, 1984"; Kenneth Collins and Andrew Ford to the Executive Management Group, 19 June 1984, John Wiley & Sons Press Release, 2 Oct. 1984, "JWS Subsidiaries: Park Row Press, 1984"; Report to the Board of Directors, 20 Sept. 1984, Andrew Neilly, Report to the Board of Directors, 8 Mar. 1985, "Reports to the Board, August 1983–May 1985"; Robert Douglas, Report to the Board of Directors, 19 June, 18 Dec. 1986, Ruth McMullin, Report to the Board of Directors, 11 June 1987, Gary Quinlan, Report to the Board of Directors, 2 Sept. 1986, "Reports to the Board, September 1985–June 1987"; Technology Marketing Group, Inc., "Discussion Notes on the Business and Market Evaluation of the Medical Division," 1 May 1987, "JWS Operations: Evaluation of Medical Division, 1985–1987"; Peter Wiley to Brad Wiley, Brad Wiley II, Deborah Wiley, 24 July 1987, "Wiley Family: PBW Family, Board, 1987–1991"; Ruth McMullin to W. Bradford Wiley, 16 Feb. 1988, "JWS Operations: Financial Results, 1987–1988"; John Wiley & Sons Press Release, 1 Dec. 1988, "JWS Operations: Financial Results, 1977–1988"; John Wiley & Sons Press Release, 22 Aug. 1990, "JWS Newsletters: News from Wiley, 1982–1990"; Training Group Strategic Business Plans Summary, 1986–1991, 8 Jan. 1986, "JWS Strategy: WLC Strategic Business Plan, 1986"; Harry Woodward to EPIC, SBS, Sales Force, Management Committee, 14

Jan. 1988, "JWS Subsidiaries: Wilson Learning Corporation, 1988–1989." Brad Wiley II to PBW, 12 Sept. 2006.

112Ruth McMullin to the Finance Committee, 10 June 1987, "Reports to the Board, September 1985–June 1987"; Report to the Board of Directors, 20 Sept. 1984, Andrew Neilly, Report to the Board of Directors, 7 June 1985, "Reports to the Board, August 1983–May 1985"; John Wiley & Sons Press Release, 3 Jan., 8, 21 Sept. 1989, "JWS Newsletters: News from Wiley, 1982–1990"; Ruth McMullin to Wiley Management, 30 Jan. 1990, "JWS Employees: PBW Discussion w/ CE re RMM [sic], 1990." Ruth McMullin interview, 11 Jan. 2006; Robert Wilder to Peter Wiley, 5 July 2006.

113Ruth McMullin to the Finance Committee, 10 June 1987, "Reports to the Board, September 1985–June 1987"; Andrew Neilly to the Staff, 16 July 1987, "JWS Operations: Distribution Center, 1985–1987."

114James Gleick, "All Alone by the Astrophone," New York Times (28 Dec. 1986), BR9; "Publisher Agrees to Acquire Harper & Row's Text List," Wall Street Journal (10 Sept. 1987), 55; "Upbeat College Sales Conference Cites New Opportunities," Wiley World (Sept. 1987), 2; William Smith to Andrew Neilly and Brad Wiley, 12 June 1984, John Wiley & Sons Press Release, 6 Jan., 3 Mar. 1986, "JWS Operations: Financial Results, 1977–1988"; Serje Seminoff to Board of Directors, 14 Mar. 1985, "JWS College Division: Correspondence, 1985–1988"; Robert Douglas, Report to the Board of Directors, 20 Mar., 18 Dec. 1986, "Reports to the Board, September 1985–June 1987"; John Wiley & Sons Press Release, 4 Sept. 1987, "JWS College Division: Harper College List Acquisition"; A. H. Neilly's Report to Stockholders, 17 Sept. 1987, "JWS Stock: Report to Stockholders, 1969–1987."

115A. H. Neilly and W. Bradford Wiley to the Staff, 9 Apr. 1987, "JWS Employees: R. McMullin Letters, 1987–1990"; Employment Agreement, Ruth R. McMullin, 13 Apr. 1987, "JWS Employees: RMM [sic] Files [1]"; John Wiley & Sons Press Release, 20 Apr. 1987, 20 Dec. 1988, "JWS Newsletters: News from Wiley, 1982–1990"; Andrew Neilly, Report to the Board of Directors, 12 June 1987, "Reports to the Board, September 1985–June 1987"; Brad Wiley II to D. Wiley, P. Wiley, W. B. Wiley, 27 Aug. 1988, "Wiley Family: WBW II Family, Business, 1987-1991"; W. Bradford Wiley to the Staff, 8 Dec. 1988, "JWS Employees: RMM's [sic] Exec. Employment Agreement."

116Peter Wiley to Brad Wiley, Brad Wiley II, and Deborah Wiley, 18 July 1988, "Wiley Family: Family Meetings, 1986–1988"; William Sutherland to Ruth McMullin, 13 Nov. 1989, Ruth R. McMullin to Wiley Corporate and Publishing Officers, 11 May 1990, "JWS Employees: R. McMullin Letters, 1987–1990."

117Steven Kippur interview, 29 Sept. 2006; Michael Allen Co. Report, 15 Sept. 1987, Ruth McMullin to the Board, 26 Mar. 1989, "McMullin Papers."

118Poole, "Stubborn Patriarch," 101; Ruth McMullin, Report to the Board of Directors, 11 June 1987, "Reports to the Board, September 1985–June 1987"; Michael Allen Company, Expense Trends and Budget Review Program: Domestic Publishing Group, John Wiley & Sons, 15 Sept. 1987, "JWS Operations: Expense Trends & Budget Review, 1987"; A. H. Neilly's Report to Stockholders, 17 Sept. 1987, "JWS Stock: Report to Stockholders, 1969–1987"; Ruth McMullin to Department Managers, 3 June 1988, "JWS Employees: R.

McMullin Letters, 1987–1990"; Brad Wiley II to D. Wiley, P. Wiley, W. B. Wiley, 27 Aug. 1988, "Wiley Family: WBW II Family, Business, 1987–1991"; Deborah Wiley, Peter Wiley, Brad Wiley II to Ruth McMullin, 17 Apr. 1989, "Wiley Family: Family Memorandum, 1989"; Rick Leyh memo, 5 July 2006.

[119]Wiley Organizational Survey Results, Publishing, Dec. 1987, "JWS Operations: Organizational Survey, Publishing, 1987."

[120]"The feelings of isolation and discouragement that employees can experience are an unfortunate side effect of the changes we have been going through." Ruth McMullin to Wiley Management, 30 Jan. 1990, "JWS Employees: PBW Discussion w/ CE re RMM [sic], 1990."

[121]Wiley Organizational Survey Results, Publishing, Dec. 1987, "JWS Operations: Organizational Survey, Publishing, 1987"; "JWS Employees: R McMullin Employee Assessments, 1990"; Fleishman-Hillard, Inc., "Report to John Wiley & Sons, Inc. on Aspects of Communications," Jan. 1990, "JWS Operations: Aspects of Communications, 1990"; "Discussion w/ Charles Ellis re Ruth McMullin," 15 Jan. 1990, "JWS Employees: PBW Discussion w/ CE re RMM [sic], 1990"; Brad Wiley II, Outline of Conversation Today, 13 Apr. 1990, "Wiley Family: WBW II Family, Business, 1987–1991."

[122]A. H. Neilly to Executive Management Group, 20 Sept. 1985, "JWS Operations: Executive Management Group, 1985"; Wiley Family Oral History: Interview WBW w/ PBW, 1991, 58, 64, 103; Wiley, "My First 50 Years," Chap. 4, 17–18; Tim King interview, 22 June 2005.

[123]"McMullin Discusses New Corporate Direction," *Wiley World* (Sept. 1987), 1; Wayne Anderson to Serje Seminoff, 25 Mar. 1987, "JWS College Division: Correspondence, 1985–1988"; Velma Lashbrook, Wiley Organizational Survey: Corporate Overview (Dec. 1987), "JWS Operations: Organizational Survey, Overview, 1987"; Wiley Organizational Survey Results, Publishing, Dec. 1987, "JWS Operations: Organizational Survey, Publishing, 1987"; "JWS Operations: Exit Interviews, 1988"; Fleishman-Hillard, Inc., "Report to John Wiley & Sons, Inc. on Aspects of Communications," Jan. 1990, "JWS Operations: Aspects of Communications, 1990".

[124]All stock data are from the Center for Research in Security Prices (CRSP), which adjusts prices for stock splits, mergers, and other events, providing an unbroken series. All Wiley stock prices in this chapter predate four stock splits in the 1990s.

[125]The official letter, which came from vice chairperson Deborah Wiley, was dated 24 May 1990 and became effective 31 May. "JWS Employees: RMM [sic] Files [2]."

[126]"John Wiley's Ellis Is Appointed Chief," *Wall Street Journal* (29 May 1990); Wiley Organizational Survey Results, Publishing, Dec. 1987, "JWS Operations: Organizational Survey, Publishing, 1987"; Brad Wiley II to Nils Kindwall, 9 Mar. 1990, Brad Wiley II telephone conversation with Bill Eiseman, 14 Mar. 1990, "Reflections upon Conversation," 15 Mar. 1990, "Synopsis of Conversation," 15 Mar. 1990, "JWS Employees: PBW Discussion w/ CE re RMM [sic], 1990"; Brad Wiley II to the Wiley Family, n.d., 10 May 1990, "Wiley Family: WBW II Family, Business, 1987–1991"; Ad Hoc Committee to W. B. Wiley, 18 May 1990, Ruth McMullin to W. Bradford Wiley, 21 Oct. 1991, Richard Rudick to Ruth McMullin, 8 Nov. 1991, "JWS Employees: R. McMullin Letters, 1987–1990"; W. Bradford Wiley

to Gary Fernandes, Nils Kindwall, Charles Stoll, 11 June 1990, "Questions and Answers," 22 May 1990, Ruth McMullin to Richard Rudick, 15 June, 2, 10, 14 Aug., 11, 17 Sept. 1990, Carmen Moret to Ruth McMullin, 6 Nov. 1990, W. Bradford Wiley to Ruth McMullin, 8 June 1990, Ruth McMullin to W. Bradford Wiley, 1, 10 June, 24 Oct. 1990, Ruth McMullin to Paul Roblesky, 11 Nov. 1990, Anthony Brisbin to Ruth McMullin, 12 Nov. 1990, Richard Rudick to Ruth McMullin, 6, 8, 23 Aug., 19 Nov., 27 Dec. 1990, Ruth McMullin to W. Bradford Wiley, 24 Oct. 1990, Ruth McMullin to Board of Directors, 24 Oct. 1990, "JWS Employees: RMM [sic] Files [2]"; John Wiley & Sons Press Release, 25 May 1990, "JWS Newsletters: News from Wiley, 1982–1990"; Peter Wiley interview with Jo Bacchi, July 2004.

[127]"Charles R. Ellis Named Wiley Chief Executive Officer; Ruth R. McMullin Resigns," *PR Newswire*, 25 May 1990; "John Wiley's Ellis Is Appointed Chief," *Wall Street Journal* (29 May 1990); Deborah Wiley, Corporate, 22 Nov. 1988, "Wiley Family: DEW re JWS, 1988"; Brad Wiley II to the Wiley Family, 10 May 1990, "Wiley Family: WBW II Family, Business, 1987–1991"; W. Bradford Wiley to the Staff, 25 May 1990, "JWS Employees: RMM [sic] Files [2]."

[128]Boroff, "Book on Wiley," 7; W. Bradford Wiley to the Staff, 16 Feb. 1989, John Wiley & Sons Press Release, 16 Feb. 1989, "JWS Subsidiaries: Allan R. Liss, 1989"; Ruth McMullin to Wiley Management, 30 Jan. 1990, "JWS Employees: PBW Discussion w/ CE re RMM [sic], 1990"; John Wiley & Sons Press Release, 1 June 1989, "JWS Newsletters: News from Wiley, 1982–1990"; Eric Swanson interview, 22 June 2005.

[129]"Wiley Will Sell Unit, Wilson Learning Corp., to Japanese Investors," *Wall Street Journal* (1 Feb. 1991); "Wiley to Sell Wilson Learning to Japanese Investment Group," *Publishers Weekly* (15 Feb. 1991), 8; *Training Group Strategic Business Plans Summary, 1986–1991*, 8 Jan. 1986, "JWS Strategy: WLC Strategic Business Plan, 1986"; Wilson Learning Corporation Strategic Review: 1990–1995, "JWS Subsidiaries: WLC Strategic Review, 1980–1995"; Timothy King, "Overview of the Training Industry and Wilson's Position in It," 23 Aug. 1990, "JWS Subsidiaries: Wilson Learning Corporation, 1990 (2)"; J. P. Morgan, "Project Sequel: Analysis of Options to Maximize Shareholder Value," 29 Aug. 1990, "JWS Strategy: Maximize Shareholder Value, 1990 (1)"; Gary Fernandes to the Board of Directors, 31 Aug. 1990, Charles Ellis to Shozo Mori, 11, 18 Sept., 5, 22 Oct. 1990, Shozo Mori to Charles Ellis, 2 Oct., 27 Nov. 1990, "JWS Subsidiaries: Wilson Learning Corporation, 1988–1989"; Michael Lobdell to Board of Directors, 31 Jan. 1991, P. Clifford to C. Ellis, D. Rudick, R. Wilder, 7 July 1992, "JWS Subsidiaries: Nippon Wilson Learning Corp., 1991–1992"; "Dunham Special Incentive Board Discussion," 21 Mar. 1991, "JWS Subsidiaries: WLC + A. Dunham, 1990"; Peter Wiley interview with Richard Rudick, June 2004.

[130]Interviews with Stephen Kippur, 21 Sept. 2006, Oct. 2006.

[131]John Lehmann-Haupt interview with Jeffrey Brown, 22 Sept. 2006.

[132]John Lehmann-Haupt interview with Susan Elbe, 25 Sept. 2006.

[133]John Lehmann-Haupt interview with Madelyn Lesure, 25 Sept. 2006.

[134]John Lehmann-Haupt interview with Jean Morley, 28 Sept. 2006.

[135]Joyce Kachergis, "Workshop: The New Reprographic Technologies as a Solution to the Problems of Scholars and Publishers," in Weldon Kefauver, ed., *Scholars and Their Publishers* (New York: Modern Language Association of America, 1977), 51–58; Topkis, "Book Publishing," 88; R. O. Johnson to A. H. Neilly, 9 Aug. 1985, "JWS Operations: Wiley Research and Development, 1985–1987."

[136]Anthony, "John Wiley at 175," 46; Mark Bide, "A Publisher's View," in William A. Forster, *Getting in Print, Staying in Print* (Hatfield, Herts., U.K.: 1990); "Wiley Ltd. Adopts High-Tech Composition," 3; W. Bradford Wiley, *Communications Revolution in Book Publishing*, 9 Feb. 1983; Richard Johnson, Report to the Board of Directors, 5 June 1985, "Reports to the Board, August 1983–May 1985"; R. O. Johnson to A. H. Neilly, 9 Aug. 1985, "JWS Operations: Wiley Research and Development, 1985–1987"; Andrew Neilly, Report to the Board of Directors, 19 June 1986, Richard Johnson, Report to the Board of Directors, 20 Sept. 1986, 12 Dec. 1986, "Reports to the Board, September 1985–June 1987"; Ruth R. McMullin to the Board of Directors, 2 Mar. 1988, "JWS Employees: R. McMullin Letters, 1987–1990."

[137]John Lehmann-Haupt interview with George Telecki, 26 Sept. 2006.

[138]John Lehmann-Haupt interview with Jean Morley, 28 Sept. 2006.

[139]George Kurian, *Directory of American Book Publishing: From Founding Fathers to Today's Conglomerates* (New York: Simon & Schuster, 1975), 279–80; Coser et al., *Books*, 23–29, 56; "John Wiley: 175 Years of Publishing," 1411; Kenneth Davis, *Two-Bit Culture: The Paperbacking of America* (Boston: Houghton Mifflin, 1984), 371; John Tebbel, *Between Covers: The Rise and Transformation of Book Publishing in America* (New York: Oxford University Press, 1987), 44–49; Landro, "Book Industry Faces More Consolidation," 7; First Boston Research, "Acquisitions and Leveraged Buyouts in the Book Publishing Industry: A Perspective on Valuation," 9 Nov. 1984.

[140]"John Wiley & Sons Gets Shareholder Approval for Stock-Trade Plan," *Wall Street Journal* (10 Sept. 1982), 6; "John Wiley: 175 Years of Publishing," 1411; "John Wiley & Sons Inc.," *Wall Street Journal* (24 June 1983), 28; "Wiley Class A Stock Listed on NASDAQ NMS," *Publishers Weekly* (2 Aug. 1985), 18; James Gillespie to Andrew Neilly, 17 Apr. 1981, "JWS Strategy: Gillespie Consulting JWS, 1972–1981"; John Wiley & Sons Press Release, 9 Sept. 1982, 16 July 1985, "JWS Newsletters: News from Wiley, 1982–1990"; Minutes of Meeting of the Executive Committee of Board of Directors of John Wiley & Sons, Inc., 22 Dec. 1982, "JWS First Boston Plan: Wiley's Board, Committee Notes, 1981–82"; Report to the Board of Directors, 29 Sept. 1983, "Reports to the Board, August 1983–May 1985"; First Boston Research, "Acquisitions and Leveraged Buyouts in the Book Publishing Industry: A Perspective on Valuation," 9 Nov. 1984; "WBW Talks: Address to Management, 1987"; Richard Rudick to the Executive and Policy Committee of the Board of Directors, 17 Jan. 1994, "JWS Stock: Shareholder Rights vs. Directors Resp, 94"; Peter Wiley interview with Richard Rudick, June 2004; Peter Wiley interview with Jo Bacchi, July 2004.

[141]"Report of a Meeting with Robert Maxwell," 4 Oct. 1986, Tim Rix to W. Bradford Wiley, 18 Mar. 1987, Robert G. Knechtel to W. Bradford Wiley, 13 Apr. 1988, "WBW Letters: Proposals, 1987–1993"; "A. H. Neilly's Report of a Meeting with Harold Miller," 29 Mar. 1988, "JWS Operations: Buy-Out Offers, 1988–1989."

[142]Coser et al., *Books*, 31–33, 44–45; Poole, "Stubborn Patriarch," 99–101.

[143]Robert J. Cole, "Bids for Harper & Row Spur Publishing Stocks," *New York Times* (13 Mar. 1987), D2; "Holding in Book Publisher Is Increased by Cross Group," *Wall Street Journal* (11 March 1988), 26; Poole, "Stubborn Patriarch," 101; Boroff, "Book on Wiley," 7; "Family Ownership Proves Effective Takeover Deterrent," *BP Report on the Business of Book Publishing* (28 Aug. 1989), 2–3; Peter Wiley to Brad Wiley, Brad Wiley II, Deborah Wiley, 24 July 1987, "Wiley Family: PBW Family, Board, 1987–1991"; Brad Wiley II, Aide Memorandum, 27 Aug. 1987, "Wiley Family: WBW II Family, Business, 1987–1991"; Brad Wiley to Brad Wiley II, Peter Wiley, and Deborah Wiley, 20 Oct. 1987, Peter Wiley to Brad Wiley, Brad Wiley II, and Deborah Wiley, 26 Sept. 1988, "Wiley Family: Family Meetings, 1986–1988"; Ruth McMullin to the Executive Compensation and Development Committee of the Wiley Board, 13 Jan., 6 Dec. 1988, "JWS ECDC Committee: Records, PBW Notes, 1988." A. H. Neilly's Remarks for Stockholders' Meeting, 6 Sept. 1984, "JWS Employees: Andrew H. Neilly, Documents, 1986–1988"; Brean Murray, Foster Securities Inc., Report, 5 Aug. 1985, "JWS Operations: Executive Management Group, 1985-1986"; Deborah Wiley, Corporate, 22 Nov. 1988, "Wiley Family: DEW re JWS, 1988"; Kevin McCabe to W. Bradford Wiley and Peter Wiley, 11 Oct. 1989, "JWS Stock: Ownership, Notes, Letters, 1989–1991"; PaineWebber, "John Wiley & Sons," *Media Stock Developments* (9 Feb. 1990), 25, "JWS Operations: Aspects of Communication, 1990"; Charles Ellis to W. Bradford Wiley and Richard Rudick, 19 Dec. 1990, "JWS Records: Holtzbrinck's Interest in JWS, 1990–1991."

[144]Coser et al., *Books*, 2, 23, 26; Tebbel, *Between Covers*, 463–64.

[145]Anthony, "John Wiley at 175," 45; Poole, "Stubborn Patriarch," 101; "Publishers' Title Output: 1990–91," *Publishers Weekly* (9 Mar. 1992); *Inside 605* (Nov./Dec. 1986); "Wiley's Race to the Finish," "Wiley-New York Loosens Collar, Rolls Up Sleeves, Clubs McGraw-Hill," "E.D.C. Women's Softball Team Vies for League Championship," *Inside Wiley* (Nov./Dec. 1983), 2–3. Wiley Organizational Survey Results, Publishing, Dec. 1987, "JWS Operations: Organizational Survey, Publishing, 1987"; "JWS Operations: Exit Interviews, 1988"; "JWS Operations: Human Resources Indicators, 1992."

[146]NDS Steering Committee to Staff, 26 Feb. 1986, "JWS College Division: Correspondence, 1985–1988"; *Report to Shareholders*, 31 July 1986, "JWS Stock: Report to Stockholders, 1969–1987"; Andrew Neilly, Report to the Board of Directors, 4 Sept. 1986, "Reports to the Board, September 1985–June 1987"; W. Bradford Wiley to the Staff, 9 Apr. 1987, "JWS Employees: R. McMullin Letters, 1987–1990"; Kevin McCabe to Members of the Audit Committee, 1 Mar. 1990, "JWS Employees: PBW Discussion w/ CE re RMM [*sic*], 1990."

[147]Topkis, "Book Publishing," 78–83; W. Bradford Wiley, *Communications Revolution in Book Publishing*, 9 Feb. 1983; "Notes from International Strategic Action Team Meeting," Tarrytown, New York, 18–20 Aug. 1986, "JWS Subsidiaries: Wiley's Global Strategy,

1986"; Richard Johnson, Report to the Board of Directors, 20 Sept. 1986, Robert Douglas, Report to the Board of Directors, 18 Dec. 1986, "Reports to the Board, September 1985–June 1987."

[148]Richard Johnson, Report to the Board of Directors, 20 Sept. 1986, "Reports to the Board, September 1985–June 1987."

[149]Coser et al., *Books*, 56, 70–93; Topkis, "Book Publishing," 97 n23. Stephen Kippur to the Staff, 7 Feb. 1985, "JWS Operations: Senior Editors @ Professional and Reference Division, 1985"; Peter Wiley to Brad Wiley, Brad Wiley II, Deborah Wiley et al., 2 Dec. 1986, "Wiley Family: PBW Family, Board, 1987–1991."

[150]Unwin and Unwin, *The Truth about Publishing*, 169, 204; Michiko Kakutani, "Millions of Books Endangered as Result of Tax Ruling," *New York Times* (5 Oct. 1980), 1; Coser et al., *Books*, 7; Persell, "Scholars and Book Publishing," 47; Poole, "Stubborn Patriarch," 101; Burt Helm and Hardy Green, "Google This: 'Copyright Law'," *Business Week* (6 June 2005): 42; [Kendall B. Taft, ed.], *The First One Hundred and Fifty Years: A History of John Wiley and Sons, Incorporated, 1807–1957* (New York: John Wiley & Sons, 1957), 61, 63–64; Lynne Ames, "A Down-to-Earth Writer," *New York Times* (22 July 1979), WC2; Edwin McDowell, "Publishing: A Gold Mine for Technical Writers," *New York Times* (6 May 1983), C29; Carolyn Anthony, "The Volatile World of Computer Books," *Publishers Weekly* (24 Nov. 1989), 26; OCLC/First Search; "Wiley Fetes Accounting Authors," *To Our Authors* (Summer 1978), 1; "Wiley Celebrates 3 Best-Sellers," *To Our Authors* (Summer 1981), 1; Pat Russo, "Author Begins Fourth Decade," *To Our Authors* (Summer 1981), 2; "Awards to Wiley Authors," *To Our Authors* (Summer 1981), 4; Moore, *Wiley*, 113, 232–33; "A Short History of John Wiley & Sons, Inc.," n.d., "JWS History: Various Histories 19th–20th Century"; Andrew Neilly, Report to the Board of Directors, 7 June 1985, "Reports to the Board, August 1983–May 1985"; Robert Douglas, Report to the Board of Directors, 18 Dec. 1986, "Reports to the Board, September 1985–June 1987"; Peter Wiley to Brad Wiley, Brad Wiley II, Deborah Wiley et al., 2 Dec. 1986, Peter Wiley to Brad Wiley, Brad Wiley II, Deborah Wiley, 5 June 1987, "Wiley Family: PBW Family, Board, 1987–1991"; Wiley Family Oral History: Interview WBW w/ PBW, 1991, p. 19; Wiley, "My First 50 Years," Chap. 5b: 3–4.

[151]Brad Wiley II, Memo, 30 June 2006.

[152]Brad Wiley II, Memo, 30 June 2006.

CHAPTER EIGHT

[1]Nicholas F. R. Crafts, "The world economy in the 1990s: A long-run perspective," in Paul W. Rhode and Gianni Toniolo, eds., *The Global Economy in the 1990s: A Long-Run Perspective.* (Cambridge: Cambridge University Press, 2006), 21–24.

[2]John Wiley & Sons Annual Reports; John Wiley & Sons, Inc. Annual Meeting of Shareholders, Sept. 18, 2003.

[3]"William Pesce Will Follow Ellis at Wiley," *Publishers Weekly* (19 Jan. 1998), 233. Timothy Jacobson interview of Jo Bacchi, 21 Dec. 2005; Charles Ellis to Zu Zhenquan, 30 Nov. 1990, "CHINA GENERAL—CURRENT"; W. Bradford Wiley, "Board of Directors," 20 June 1991, "WBW Talks: JWS Board of Directors, 1991."

[4]Peter Wiley interview of Charles Ellis 15 Mar. 2001, 13 June 2003; "JWS Employees: PBW Notes on Charles Ellis, 1991." John Wiley & Sons Press Release, 25 May 1990, "JWS Newsletters: News From Wiley, 1982–1990".

[5]Richard Blodgett interview of Eric Swanson, Aug. 2004; W. Bradford Wiley to the Staff, 25 May 1990, "JWS Employees: RMM [*sic*] Files [2]."

[6]"William Pesce Will Follow Ellis at Wiley," *Publishers Weekly* (19 Jan. 1998), 233. Peter Urbach to CCC Board of Directors, 21 Apr. 1992, "Publishing Outside JWS: Copyright Clearance Center, 1984–1992."

[7]Peter Wiley interview of Charles Ellis, 13 June 2003.

[8]Richard Blodgett interview of Charles Ellis, 20 Feb. 2004; Timothy Jacobson interview of William Arlington, 12 Jan. 2006; Timothy Jacobson interview of Richard Rudick, 24 Jan. 2006.

[9]Peter Wiley interview of Eric Swanson, Dec. 11, 2006.

[10]At the end of fiscal year 1992 (Apr. 30, 1992), Professional and Trade provided 68 percent of Wiley's revenues, while educational publishing accounted for the rest. Breakdown of revenue by business sector before this date is at best confusing.

[11]Richard Blodgett interview of Charles Ellis, 20 Feb. 2004; William Pesce, Wiley shareholder's meeting presentation, Sept. 2006. Fiscal 1992 Results, Board of Directors Meeting, 18 June 1992.

[12]Vista Computer Services, *Publishing Perspectives: The Organizational Impact of Publishing in New Media* (1995), 46. Eric Herr to Ruth McMullin, 13 July 1988; Charles Ellis to Ruth McMullin, 26 July 1988, "JWS Employees: Eric Herr, 1988."

[13]John Wiley & Sons Annual Report, 1995, 4.

[14]For background, see Ralph Shoffner, "Appearance and Growth of Computer and Electronic Products in Libraries," in Richard Abel and Lyman Newlin, eds., *Scholarly Publishing: Books, Journals, Publishers, and Libraries in the Twentieth Century* (New York: John Wiley & Sons, 2002), 209–55.

[15]Ira Fuchs, "Networked Information Is Not Free," in Robin Peek and Gregory Newby, eds., *Scholarly Publishing: The Electronic Frontier* (Cambridge: M.I.T. Press, 1996), 166. George Smith interview of Timothy King, 9 Nov. 2006. L. Conley to C. Ellis et al., 20 Sept. 1991, "Multi-Division: Electronic Publishing, 1980–1994." Boston Consulting Group, "Digital Document Discovery," 10 Aug. 1992, "JWS Operations: Digital Document Discovery, 1992."

[16]Peter Wiley interview of Charles Ellis, 13 June 2003; Richard Blodgett interview of Brad Wiley II, Sept. 2004. Charles Ellis to John Collins, 11 Nov. 1991, "JWS Subsidiaries: Jacaranda-Wiley, 1991–1994."

[17]Charles Ellis to Peter Wiley, 2 Feb. 2007. Timothy Jacobson interview of Timothy King, 22 June 2005. William Pesce to Wiley Employees, 27 July 1998. Bob Long to Peter Wiley and Charles Ellis, 2 June 1995, "JWS International: PBW South Africa Report, Letters, 1995." "Human Resources Leading Indicators," 17 Mar. 1992, "JWS Operations: Human Resources Indicators, 1992." "JWS ECDC Committee: Records, PBW Notes, 1990."

[18]Eric Swanson, "Opening Remarks/Journal Conference," 8 Sept. 1994, "JWS Records: Wiley Journals Conference, 1994." See also

Pierre Wack, "Scenarios: The Gentle Art of Re-Perceiving," *Harvard Business School Working Paper* (Dec. 1984).

[19]This particular example was provided to the authors from proprietary documents.

[20]John Wiley & Sons, 2004–2005 Scenario Planning Report.

[21]Timothy Jacobson interview of Tim King, 22 June 2005.

[22]Timothy Jacobson interview of Tim King, 22 June 2005. "Acquisition Program," 5 Mar. 1991, "JWS Subsidiaries: Acquisitions Program, 1991."

[23]John A. Jones, "John Wiley & Sons Ready for Surge in College Textbooks," *Investor's Business Daily* (19 Nov. 1992), 32. Timothy Jacobson interview of Jo Bacchi, 21 Dec. 2005.

[24]See annual reports. The 1998 operating and net income figures reflect downward adjustments for extraordinary gains from divestiture activity.

[25]"World's Most Respected Companies," *Financial Times* (30 Nov. 1998), 1; John Wiley & Sons Annual Report, 1998, 1999; "Wiley Online Service Goes Live," *Publishers Weekly* (8 Mar. 1999), 17. Charles Ellis, President's Report to the Board of Directors, Fourth Quarter, FY 1995. John Wiley & Sons, Annual Reports 1991, 1998. President's Report, FY 1997.

[26]Peter Wiley memorandum, Aug. 2006.

[27]Timothy Jacobson et al. interview of William Pesce, 7 Feb. 2006. Peter Wiley memorandum, Aug. 2006. Speaker's notes, Annual Meeting of Shareholders, Sept. 21, 2006.

[28]William Pesce, communication with authors, 16 Nov., 2006.

[29]Timothy Jacobson et al. interview of William Pesce, 7 Feb. 2006.

[30]Peter Wiley notes Sept. 2006.

[31]Wm Smith Special Opportunities Research Company, "John Wiley & Sons, Inc.," 11 Mar. 2002, "Contacts & Analysts Reports."

[32]Richard Blodgett interview of Charles Ellis, 20 Feb. 2004. William Pesce communication with authors, 2 Nov. 2006.

[33]Tamar Lewin, "When Books Break the Bank: College Students Venture Beyond the Campus Store," *New York Times* (16 Sept. 2003), B1, B4.

[34]Karen De Witt, "Colleges Are Seeing More Students But Less Money," *New York Times* (5 Aug. 1992), B8. "College Division FY2000 Operating and Strategic Plan," (Jan. 1999), "JWS Board: Evaluation of Pearson College Titles, 1999."

[35]"College Publishing Strategic Plan FY94–FY98" [24 Nov. 1992]; FY 1998 Strategic Plan [Mar. 1997]; William Pesce, communication with authors, 16 Nov. 2006.

[36]William Pesce, communication with authors, 2 Nov. 2006.

[37]William Pesce to Peter Wiley, Jan. 11, 2007.

[38]Timothy Jacobson interview of Bonnie Lieberman, 22 June 2005.

[39]Steve Kraham to Barbara Heaney, 12 July 2007.

[40]Susan Elbe to Barbara Heaney, 10 Aug. 2007.

[41]William Pesce, Sales Meeting Speeches, Jan., 1993, Aug., 1994.

[42]Warren Baker to Peter Wiley, 30 Nov., 2006.

[43]"Industry Briefing Materials for Synthesis: A National Engineering Education Coalition," 25 Apr. 1991, "JWS College Division Records, 1985–1992." Wayne Anderson to John Lehmann-Haupt, 6 Feb., 2007.

[44]Wayne Anderson to John Lehmann-Haupt, 14 Feb., 2007.

[45]Peter Wiley interview of Ruth Baruth, 28 Dec. 2006. "JWS College Division: Calculus by Harvard University, 1992."

[46]Peter Wiley interview of Ruth Baruth, 28 Dec. 2006.

[47]E-mails from Bonnie Lieberman, 22 Feb. 2007, 6 Mar. 2007, and Kaye Pace, 23 Feb. 2007, to John Lehmann-Haupt.

[48]Ellis explained, too, that the agreement was made "to capitalize on the added value of electronic formats to complement what Wiley publishes."

[49]E-mails from Wayne Anderson, 6 Feb. 2007, Bonnie Lieberman, 22 Feb 2007, 6 Mar. 2007, and Kaye Pace, 23 Feb. 2007, to John Lehmann-Haupt. John Wiley & Sons Press Release, 26 Apr. 1994, "JWS Multi-Division: New Media, 1989–1993."

[50]Digital Information Group, "John Wiley & Sons: The Impact of New Technologies on Wiley's Business" (Mar. 1995).

[51]Peter Wiley interview of Wayne Anderson, 3 Apr. 2003; "Custom Publishing," *Wiley World* (Nov.–Dec. 1994), 6; "Wiley Custom Services Program," *Wiley World* (Feb.–Mar. 1999), 3. E-mails from Charity Robey, 5 Feb. 2007, and Jay Beck, 20 Feb. 2007, to John Lehmann-Haupt.

[52]John Lehmann-Haupt interview of Kaye Pace, 1 Feb. 2007.

[53]John Lehmann-Haupt interview of Frank Lyman, 1 Feb. 2007.

[54]John Lehmann-Haupt interview of Bonnie Lieberman, 29 Jan. 2007.

[55]"The History of *WileyPLUS*," Internal *WileyPLUS* Certification Course, Chap. 2.

[56]John Lehmann-Haupt interview of Kaye Pace, 1 Feb. 2007.

[57]John Lehmann-Haupt interviews with Bonnie Lieberman, 29 Jan. 2007, Kaye Pace, 1 Feb. 2007, Frank Lyman, 1 Feb. 2007, and Joe Heider, 27 Feb. 2007.

[58]John Lehmann-Haupt interviews with Bonnie Lieberman, 29 Jan. 2007, Kaye Pace, 1 Feb. 2007, Frank Lyman, 1 Feb. 2007, and Joe Heider, 27 Feb. 2007.

[59]"*eGrade Plus*: a Giant Step for Higher Ed," *Wiley World* (May–June 2004), 4.

[60]John Lehmann-Haupt interview with Dr. Marsha Gordon, 11 Feb. 2007.

[61]Jim Milliot, "Acquisitions Push Wiley Sales, Earnings," *Publishers Weekly* (13 Mar. 2000), 20. William Pesce to the Board of Directors, 19 Feb. 1999, 23 Mar. 1999, Acquisition Proposal: Pearson Higher Education Titles, n.d., "JWS Educational Publishing Group: Pearson College List, 1999." Wm Smith Special Opportunities Research Company, "John Wiley & Sons, Inc.," 11 Mar. 2002, "Contacts & Analysts Reports"; "College Division FY2000 Operating and

Strategic Plan," (Jan. 1999), "JWS BOard [*sic*]: Eval of Pearson College Titles, 1999."

[62]Jim Milliot, "Wiley Has Solid Start," *Publishers Weekly* (9 Sept. 2002), 10. John Wiley & Sons, President's Report, Second Quarter FY 2000, "JWS Board: Agenda for Directors, 1999."

[63]Operating and Strategic Plan, FY 2000–2002.

[64]Roger L. Geiger, *Knowledge and Money: Research Universities and the Paradox of the Marketplace* (Stanford: Stanford University Press, 2004), 134–135. Organisation for Economic Co-operation and Development, http://www.oecd.org; Worldbank database http://web.worldbank.org/WBSITE/EXTERNAL/DATASTATISTICS/0,,menuPK:232599~pagePK:64133170~piPK:64133498~theSitePK:239419,00.html. NSF, Division of Science Resources Statistics, Trends in Industry R&D, 1991–2004, chart compiled by AAAS, http://www.aaas.org/spp/rd/guihist.htm May 2006; AAAS analysis of R&D in AAAS Reports VIII–XXXII, Trends in Federal R&D, FY 1995–2008, April 2007; NSF, Federal Funds for Research and Development; Trends in Federal Research by Discipline, FY 1970–2006, chart compiled by AAAS, http://www.aaas.org/spp/rd/guihist.htm Feb 2007; AAAS, based on OMB Historical Tables in Budget of the United States Government FY 2008, Federal Spending on Defence and Nondefence R&D, Outlays for the conduct of R&D, FY 1949–2008, billions of constant FY 2007 dollars, chart compiled by AAAS; AAAS, based on NSF, Federal Science and Engineering Support to Universities, Colleges, and Nonprofit Institutions, http://www.aaas.org/spp/rd/guihist.htm Nov. 2006; Table 1D, Federal obligations for total research by detailed field of science and engineering: Department of Defence, fiscal 1970–2003, www.nsf.gov/statistics/nsf04335/pdf/tab1d.pdf; NSF, Division of Science Resources Statistics, U.S. R&D Funding by Source, 1953–2004, chart compiled by AAAS, http://www.aaas.org/spp/rd/guihist.htm May 2006; AAAS, based on NSF, National Patterns of R&D Resources Trends in U.S. Industry R&D. 1991–2004, chart compiled by AAAS, http://www.aaas.org/spp/rd/guihist.htm May 2006.

[65]Albert Henderson, "Diversity and the Growth of Serious/Scholarly/Scientific Journals," in Abel and Newlin, eds., *Scholarly Publishing*, 138. "Every new venture," writes Henderson, erstwhile editor of *Publishing Research Quarterly*, "represents a failure of someone to satisfy the needs of authors and readers." See also Andrew Odlyzko, "Tragic Loss or Good Riddance? The Impending Demise of Traditional Scholarly Journals," in Peek and Newby, eds., *Scholarly Publishing*, 92. Simon M. Sze and Kwok K. Ng, Physics of Semiconductor Devices, 3rd ed. (Hoboken, N.J.: John Wiley & Sons, 2006), v.

[66]Ira Fuchs, "Networked Information Is Not Free," in Peek and Newby, eds., *Scholarly Publishing*, 172; Timothy B. King, "Journal Publishers, Librarians and Scholarly Information: Contemplating a Future Scenario," *Logos* (1990), 24-29; Jack Goellner, "The Impact of the Library Budget Crisis on Scholarly Publishing," in Abel and Newlin, eds., *Scholarly Publishing*, 273; Brian Hayes, "The Economic Quandary of the Network Publisher," in Peek and Newby, eds., *Scholarly Publishing*, 131; Henderson, "Diversity," 155; Michael Gorman, "The Economic Crisis in Libraries: Causes and Effects," in Abel and Newlin, eds., *Scholarly Publishing*, 257–71;

Ann Okerson, "University Libraries and Scholarly Communication," in Peek and Newby, eds., *Scholarly Publishing*, 183, 186, 188.

[67]Gerry Grenier, "Document Delivery Overview," *Publishing Technologies Update* (Fall 1993), 1; Ken Rawson, "Document Delivery Pilot Project," *Publishing Technologies*, 1–2; Sally Taylor, "AT&T, Springer, Wiley in Document Delivery Project," *Publishers Weekly* (18 Oct. 1993), 7. Tim King to Charles Ellis et al., 10 Apr. 1992, Tom Conter to Tim King, 6 Aug. 1992, "JOURNAL STRATEGY"; John Wiley & Sons Press Release, 1 Apr. 1993, "JWS Multi-Division: New Media, 1989–1993"; "Document Delivery Pilot Project Status Report," 15 Feb. 1993, "Document Delivery Pilot Project"; "JWS Strategy: ARPA Proposal—Digital Library, 1993"; Charles Ellis, President's Report to the Board of Directors, First Half, FY1994, n.d.; John Wiley & Sons Annual Report, 1994.

[68]Peter Wiley interview of Charles Ellis, 13 June 2003.

[69]The journal was later retitled *Computer Aided Surgery*. Barbara Carlson and Paul Baron, *JAMA* (2 July 1997), 79–81. Brian Crawford, "New Information Technologies and the Future of Wiley's Journal Business," 14 Dec. 1995; John Wiley & Sons Press Release, 27 Feb. 1996, "JWS Newsletters: News @ Wiley, 1996–1997."

[70]"Wiley Collaborates with Zuno to Launch Wiley InterScience," *Information Today* (Nov. 1997), 48.

[71]Richard Baggaley to Rosemary Altoft, 21 Nov. 1997, "JWS InterScience Division: Library Advisory Board, 1997"; John Wiley & Sons Press Release, 9 Sept. 1997, "JWS InterScience Division: www.access to 400 STM Journals, 1997."

[72]Catherine Graham, "InterScience Launched Commercially," *Information World Review* (May 1999), 10; "Wiley Online Service Goes Live," *Publishers Weekly* (8 Mar. 1999), 17. John Wiley & Sons Press Release, 24 June 1999, "JWS InterScience Division: Online Journal Service, 1999."

[73]Kathy Miller, "Wiley on the Web," *Information World Review* (Dec. 1997), 18. John Wiley & Sons Press Release, 22 Feb. 1999, "JWS InterScience Division: Online Journal Service, 1999"; John Lehmann-Haupt, "A Sounding Board for Wiley," *Wiley World* (Feb.–Mar. 2002), 10.

[74]"Scholarly Publishers Agree Terms [*sic*]," *Information World Review* (Jan. 2000), 1. Wm Smith Special Opportunities Research Company, "John Wiley & Sons, Inc.," 11 Mar. 2002, "Contacts & Analysts Reports"; William Pesce, President's Report, FY 2002.

[75]Brian Crawford, "New Information Technologies and the Future of Wiley's Journals Business," 7 Sept. 1995; John Wiley & Sons Annual Report, 1998.

[76]Susan Mendelsohn, "Wiley Finds Mobile Take-Up Strong and Adds Ejournal Titles," *Information World Review* (Mar. 2002), 6. John Wiley & Sons Annual Report, 2000.

[77]Jim Milliot, "Wiley Posts Double-Digit Gains in Sales, Earnings," *Publishers Weekly* (23 June 2003), 9. Wm Smith Special Opportunities Research Company, "John Wiley & Sons, Inc.," 11 Mar. 2002, "Contacts & Analysts Reports"; John Wiley & Sons, President's Report, Second Quarter FY 2000, "JWS Board: Agenda for Directors, 1999"; Brian Crawford, "New Information Technologies and the Future of Wiley's Journal Business," 14 Dec.

1995; Brian Crawford, "Journals Publishing Operational Review," 21 Nov. 2003.

[78]Peter Wiley interview of Charles Ellis, 13 June 2003. John Wiley & Sons Press Release, 24 July 1992, "Corporate Announcements"; Charles Ellis, President's Report to the Board of Directors, First Half, FY1994, n.d.; John Wiley & Sons Press Release, 14 Oct. 1998; Charles Ellis, President's Report to the Board of Directors, First Quarter, FY 1997, n.d.; John Wiley & Sons Annual Report, 1997; John Wiley & Sons Press Release, 24 Sept. 1996.

[79]For a discussion of the confiscation and sale of German patents, see Roger Burlingame, *Endless Frontier: The Story of McGraw-Hill* (New York: McGraw-Hill, 1959), 231–232.

[80]Charles Ellis to the Board of Directors, 16 Apr. 1996, "JWS Subsidiaries: Wiley-VCH Acquisition Documents, 1996"; e-mail, Eva Wille to Peter Wiley, 3 July 2007.

[81]Peter Wiley to Bert Sutherland, 26 June 1996, "JWS Subsidiaries: Wiley-VCH Acquisition Documents, 1996"; Timothy Jacobson interview of Jo Bacchi, 21 Dec. 2005; Peter Wiley interview of Richard Rudick, June 2004; Richard Blodgett interview of Charles Ellis, 20 Feb. 2004. Tim King to Peter Wiley, Mar. 26, 2007.

[82]John Jarvis to Peter Wiley, Nov. 16, 2006; e-mails, Robert Long and James Dicks to John Lehmann-Haupt, 6 Feb. 2007.

[83]John Wiley & Sons, President's Report, FY 1997; Richard Blodgett interview of Charles Ellis, 20 Feb. 2004; John Wiley & Sons Press Release, 5 Feb. 1997.

[84]John Wiley & Sons Press Release, 17 Feb. 1998, 10 June 1998, "JWS Newsletters: News @ Wiley, 1998-1999;" John Wiley & Sons Annual Report, 1998, 1999; President's Report to the Board of Directors, First Quarter, FY 1998, "JWS Board Presentation: President's Report, 1998"; William Pesce, President's Report to the Board of Directors, First Quarter, FY 1999, n.d.

[85]JohnWiley & Sons Press Release, "Wiley and The Cochrane Collaboration Form Publishing Partnership," 9 April 2003.

[86]Susan Mendelsohn, "Wiley Buys in UK and Germany," *Information World Review* (Jun 2002), 4; "John Wiley & Sons Launches 'Current Protocols in Microbiology,'" *Computers in Libraries* (Oct. 2005), 41; "John Wiley & Sons Acquires Journals, Announces Upcoming Journal Launch," *Computers in Libraries* (Nov.-Dec. 2005), 43; "Wiley Adds Two to Int'l Unit," *Publishers Weekly* (20 May 2002), 20; William Pesce, President's Report, FY 2002; William Pesce, President's Report, Third Quarter, FY 2001; John Wiley & Sons Annual Report, 1999; John Wiley & Sons Press Release, 14 July, 14 Oct. 1998; Carol Bacchus-Wermke, Patrick Kelly, Peter Wiley, and Eric Swanson, e-mails to Susan Spilka, 30 June–2 July 2007.

[87]Eric Swanson to Peter Wiley, 12 Aug. 2007.

[88]John Wiley & Sons Press Release, 28 Feb. 2001.

[89]Ernest Kirkwood to Peter Wiley, 7 Dec. 2006.

[90]FY 1997 Strategic Plan Corporate Narrative, Mar. 1996.

[91]John Lehmann-Haupt email and telephone interviews with Janet Bailey, 4 June, 6 June 2007.

[92]Eric Swanson to InterScience and Liss Staff, 17 May 1993, "JWS STM Division: Records, 1986–1993"; Eric Swanson to Peter Wiley, 12 Aug. 2007.

[93]Conversation between Susan Spilka and Andy Phillips, June 2007; Draft of Oct. 10, 2001 press release announcing launch of *Wiley InterScience Books Online*, as the service was originally called.

[94]John Lehmann-Haupt email and telephone interviews with Janet Bailey, 4 June, 6 June 2007.

[95]Conversation between Susan Spilka and Andy Phillips, June 2007.

[96]John Wiley & Sons Annual Report, 1997; William Pesce to Wiley Employees, 27 July 1998.

[97]Edwin McDowell, "Wiley Expands Its Range of Books," *New York Times* (11 Mar. 1991). Peter Wiley to Brad Wiley, Brad Wiley II, and Deborah Wiley, 3 Nov. 1987, "Wiley Family: Family Meetings, 1986–1988."

[98]"Wiley Professional and Trade 20th Anniversary," DVD.

[99]Timothy Jacobson and George Smith interview of Steven Kippur, 29 Sept. 2006.

[100]Timothy Jacobson and George Smith interview of Steven Kippur, 29 Sept. 2006; John Lehmann-Haupt e-mail from Joan O'Neil, 1 Oct. 2007. "Wiley Professional and Trade 20th Anniversary," DVD.

[101]Richard Abel, "The Change of Book and Journal Infrastructure: Two Publishers, Consolidation, and Niche Publishers," in Abel and Newlin, eds., *Scholarly Publishing*, 25–27; Michael Shatzkin, "Fasten Your High-Tech Seatbelts," *Publishers Weekly* (24 May 1999), 28–31. Timothy Jacobson and George Smith interview of Steven Kippur, 29 Sept. 2006; Professional Reference & Trade Strategic Plan FY94–FY98; FY 1998 Strategic Plan, Mar. 1997; President's Report to the Board of Directors, First Quarter, FY 1998, "JWS Board Presentation: President's Report, 1998"; John Wiley & Sons Annual Report, 1999.

[102]Bill Smith, "Gooey, Slippery, Slimy . . . Science; Janice VanCleave's Experiments Capture Kids' Curiosity," *St. Louis Post-Dispatch* (18 Oct. 1993), D1. Strategic Plan, FY 1996–2000, General Interest and Children's Books, "JWS P+T Division: Development of 'Trade,' 1988–1997"; John Wiley & Sons Annual Reports, 1997, 1998, 1999; Kate Bradford to Peter Wiley, 21 Sept. 1999, "PBW Correspondence: Authors, 1999."

[103]President's Report to the Board of Directors, First Quarter, FY 1998, "JWS Board Presentation: President's Report, 1998."

[104]Jim Milliot, "Wiley's New Look: A Niche Purchase, Two Divestitures," *Publishers Weekly* (20 Sept. 1993), 8; Kate Maddox, "Readers Sold on the Web—Publishers Booked Solid," *Communications Week* (22 July 1996), IA01. John Wiley & Sons Press Release, 19 Nov. 1991, "Corporate Announcements"; Charles Ellis to Executive and Policy Committee, 13 Aug. 1997, "JWS Divestitures: Wiley Law Publications, 1997"; John Wiley & Sons Press Release, 4 Apr. 1991, "JWS Newsletters: News @ Wiley, 1991–1993"; Charles Ellis to Board of Directors, 3 Aug. 1993, "JWS Divestiture: Divisions in Australia & Canada, 1993"; Charles Ellis, President's Report to the Board of Directors, First Half, FY1994, n.d.; John Wiley & Sons Press Release, 15 Sept. 1993, "JWS Subsidiaries: QED Information Systems, 1993."

[105]"Wiley to Sell Legal Unit to Dutch Publisher," *New York Times* (6 Sept. 1997), 51; "Wiley Reports Strong '98 Gains," *Publishers Weekly* (6 July 1998), 17. Peter Wiley interview of Charles Ellis, 13 June 2003; John Wiley & Sons Press Release, 3 Sept. 1997, "JWS Divestiture: Wiley Law Publication, 1997"; "Acquisition Proposal: Van Nostrand Reinhold," 21 Aug. 1997, Charles Ellis to Board of Directors, 28 Aug. 1997, "JWS Acquisition Strategy: Van Nostrand Reinhold, 1997."

[106]"Acquisition Proposal: Van Nostrand Reinhold," 21 Aug. 1997, "JWS Acquisition Strategy: Van Nostrand Reinhold, 1997."

[107]David Chen, "John Wiley Acquires a Trade Book Unit," *New York Times* (10 Oct. 1997), B6. John Wiley & Sons Annual Report, 1998.

[108]Craig Lundberg, "Creating and Managing a Vanguard Organization: Design and Human Resource Lessons from Jossey-Bass," *Human Resource Management* (Spring 1991), 89–112; William Sievert, "Jossey-Bass: Academic Publishing's 'Gadfly'" *Chronicle of Higher Education* (11 Sept. 1978). "JWS Acquisitions Strategy: Macmillan, 1993."

[109]Acquisition Opportunity: Jossey-Bass, n.d., "JWS Subsidiaries: Jossey-Bass Acquisition, 1999;" William Pesce, President's Report, First Quarter, FY 2000.

[110]"Milestones in the Growth of Jossey-Bass, Inc.: From the 615 Montgomery Era to the 350 Sansome Era," n.d. "Jossey-Bass Inc., Publishers—A Timeline," 14 July 1992, "Jossey-Bass Timeline," n.d.

[111]Acquisition Opportunity: Jossey-Bass, n.d., "JWS Subsidiaries: Jossey-Bass Acquisition, 1999;" Jossey-Bass Press Release, 25 Apr. 1996.

[112]Acquisition Opportunity: Jossey-Bass, n.d., "JWS Subsidiaries: Jossey-Bass Acquisition, 1999;" Jossey-Bass Press Release, 25 Apr. 1996.

[113]Patricia Holt, "Practicing What It Publishes," *San Francisco Chronicle* (3 May 1992). George Smith, Timothy Jacobson, and Robert Wright interview of Steven Kippur, 21 June 2005; "Wiley Professional & Trade 20th Anniversary," DVD.

[114]"Wiley Has Strong Second Quarter; Inks More Deals," *Publishers Weekly* (8 Dec. 1997), 16. "Acquisitions, Alliances, and Partnerships," *Wiley World* (Mar.–Apr. 1995), 1. John Wiley & Sons Press Release, 23 May 1994, "JWS Subsidiaries: Executive Enterprises, 1994"; John Wiley & Sons Press Release, 9 May 1994, "JWS Subsidiaries: ValuSource, 1994"; John Wiley & Sons Press Release, 6 Feb., 14 Feb., 23 May 1995, "JWS Newsletters: News @ Wiley, 1994–1995"; Charles Ellis, President's Report to the Board of Directors, Fourth Quarter, FY 1995, n.d.; John Wiley & Sons Press Release, 5 Mar. 1996, "JWS Subsidiaries: CPPC, 1996"; John Lehmann-Haupt e-mail from Joan O'Neil, 1 Oct. 2007.

[115]John Wiley & Sons Annual Report, 2002.

[116]"John Wiley & Sons to Acquire Hungry Minds for .37 Times Revenue," *Weekly Corporate Growth Report* (20 Aug. 2001), 11,491; Calvin Reid, "Wiley Buys Hungry Minds," *Publishers Weekly* (20 Aug. 2001), 16. John Wiley & Sons Annual Report, 2002. George Smith, Timothy Jacobson, and Robert Wright interview of Steve Kippur, 21 June 2005; Timothy Jacobson interview of Tim King, 22 June 2005.

[117]*Mergent Industrial Manual* (Apr. 2006). Wm Smith Special Opportunities Research Company, "John Wiley & Sons, Inc.," 11 Mar. 2002, "Contacts & Analysts Reports"; Richard Blodgett interview of Gary Rinck, Mar. 2004.

[118]John Lehmann-Haupt interview of Marc Mikulich, 1 Mar 2007; e-mails, John Kilcullen to John Lehmann-Haupt, 16 Mar 2007, Marc Mikulich to John Lehmann-Haupt, 19 Mar 2007.

[119]Anon. *A Global Phenomenon For Dummies* (New York: Hungry Minds, 2002), 10, 12.

[120]John Wiley & Sons Annual Reports.

[121]Robert Levine, "Dummies for Dummies," *Business 2.0* (Dec. 2004), 76; Joan Morris, "Endearing Titles Turn 'For Dummies' Series Into Booming Book Industry," *Knight Ridder Tribune Business News* (10 June 2004), 1. Timothy Jacobson interview of Nils Kindwall, 6 Feb. 2006.

[122]Henry Gilgoff, "Publisher Repeats Recall for 'For Dummies' Book Containing Burn Hazard," *Knight Ridder Tribune Business News* (16 Oct. 2003), 1.

[123]All quotes in this and the next two paragraphs from John Lehmann-Haupt interviews of Robert Garber and Natalie Chapman, 19-20 Feb. 2007; e-mails, Robert Garber to John Lehmann-Haupt, 12 Mar. 2007; Natalie Chapman to John Lehmann-Haupt, 12 Mar. 2007; Peter Wiley interview of Robert Garber, Jan. 2007.

[124]John Lehmann-Haupt interviews of Robert Garber and Natalie Chapman, 19-20 Feb. 2007; e-mails, Robert Garber to John Lehmann-Haupt, 12 Mar. 2007; Natalie Chapman to John Lehmann-Haupt, 12 Mar. 2007.

[125]For a discussion of Web 1.0 and 2.0, see Tim O'Reilly, "What is Web 2.0," at www.oreillynet.com/pub/a/oreilly/tim/news/2005/09/30/what-is-web-20.html. John Wiley & Sons Annual Report, 2002, 2003.

[126]Peter Wiley interview of Charles Ellis, 13 June 2003.

[127]Charles Ellis to John Collins, 16 Mar. 1992, "JWS Subsidiaries: Jacaranda-Wiley, 1990–1994."

[128]W. Bradford Wiley, "My First 50 Years," Chap. 5b, 26; Peter Wiley interview of Charles Ellis, 13 June 2003.

[129]Emily DeNitto, "Writing a Success Story: Publisher Wiley Revives Core Areas," *Crain's New York Business* (7 Aug. 1995), 3; Jim Milliot, "Wiley Stresses Global Growth," *Publishers Weekly* (2 Sept. 1996), 11. John Wiley & Sons Annual Reports, 1997–2005; David Nadel and Kimberly Laidlaw, "John Wiley & Sons, Inc.: Punching Above Its Weight," (New York: Bear Stearns, 13 Apr. 2000).

[130]Peter Wiley to William Pesce, 23 May 1996, "JWS Subsidiaries: Wiley Ltd. & PBW Letters, 1996"; Peter Wiley to Charles Ellis, 28 Sept. 1992, "CHINA GENERAL—CURRENT."

[131]John Jarvis to Peter Wiley, 11 Dec. 2006.

[132]William Pesce to Wiley Employees, 27 July 1998; John Jarvis to Peter Wiley, 11 Dec. 2006.

[133]E-mail from Warren Fristensky to John Lehmann-Haupt, 13 Mar. 2007; All quotes in this section are from John Lehmann-Haupt interview of Warren Fristensky (with Eddie Russell teleconferenced in), 27 Feb. 2007.

134E-mail from Warren Fristensky to John Lehmann-Haupt, 9 Mar. 2007.

135"Welcome to WileyNet," *Wiley World* (Apr.–May 2000), 2.

136Teleconference with Dominick Coppola and Mike Silverstein, 23 Mar. 2007; e-mails from Mike Silverstein to John Lehmann-Haupt, 23, 26 Mar. 2007.

137"What's New @ wiley.com," *Wiley World* (Jan.–Mar. 1996), 6; *Wiley World* (Oct.–Nov. 1997); Teleconference with Dominick Coppola and Mike Silverstein, 23 Mar. 2007; e-mails from Mike Silverstein to John Lehmann-Haupt, 23, 26 Mar. 2007.

138William Pesce to Wiley Employees, 27 July 1998.

139William Pesce to Wiley Employees, 24 Jan. 2001.

140Verity Waite to Peter Wiley, 16 June 2007.

141*Wiley Europe*, June 1996.

142John Wiley & Sons Press Release, 24 Apr. 1992, "JWS Newsletters: News @ Wiley, 1991–1993."

143John Jarvis to Peter Wiley, 11 Dec. 2006.

144John Jarvis to Peter Wiley, 11 Dec. 2006.

145Joseph Marchetti to Peter Wiley, 15 July 2007.

146Charles Ellis to John Collins, 16 Mar. 1992, "JWS Subsidiaries: Jacaranda-Wiley, 1990–1994."

147John Wiley & Sons Annual Report, 2002.

148Jim Dicks to Susan Spilka, 20 Sept. 2007.

149FY 1992 Result, 27 April 1992, "JWS Subsidiaries: Jacaranda-Wiley, 1992;" "FY1993-1997 Strategic Plan," 19 Dec. 1991, "JWS Subsidiaries: J-W Strategic Plan FY 1993–1997, 1991"; Jacaranda-Wiley Press Release, 3 Sept. 1991, "JWS Alliance: Jacaranda Wiley/Houghton Mifflin, 1991"; John Collins to Charles Ellis, 5 Mar. 1992, Quentin Smith to John Collins, 27 Apr. 1992; Quentin Smith to Peter Wiley, 4 June 1992; Charles Ellis to John Collins, 24 Sept. 1992; John Collins to Peter Wiley, 19 Feb. 1993; "JWS Subsidiaries: Jacaranda-Wiley, 1991–1994."

150Jim Milliot, "Wiley's New Look: A Niche Purchase, Two Divestitures," *Publishers Weekly* (20 Sept. 1993), 8; Charles Ellis to Board of Directors, 3 Aug. 1993, "JWS Divestiture: Divisions in Australia & Canada, 1993"; Peter Wiley interview of Charles Ellis, 13 June 2003; Charles Ellis, President's Report to the Board of Directors, Fourth Quarter, FY 1994, n.d.; "Quality Down Under," Wiley World (May–June 1995), 3; Peter Donoughue appointed Deputy Managing Director of Jacaranda-Wiley, *Wiley World* (Sept.–Oct. 1992), 1.

151John Wiley & Sons Annual Report, 1997.

152John Wiley & Sons Annual Report, 2002.

153William Pesce, President's Report, FY 2002.

154Peter Donoghue to Peter Wiley, 23 Oct. 2007; Charles Ellis, President's Report to the Board of Directors, First Nine Months, FY 1997, Second Quarter, FY 1998, n.d.; William Pesce, President's Report, FY 2002.

155Jim Milliot, "Wiley's New Look: A Niche Purchase, Two Divestitures," *Publishers Weekly* (20 Sept. 1993), 8; "Butterworths Titles Acquired," *Wiley World* (Feb.–Mar. 1993), 5. Charles Ellis to Board of Directors, 3 Aug. 1993, "JWS Divestiture: Divisions in Australia & Canada, 1993."

156"Wiley Canada Named *Campus Publisher of the Year*," *Wiley World* (July–Aug. 1995), 4.

157Diane Wood to William Zerter, 9 Feb. 2007.

158Karen Staudinger to William Zerter, 12 Feb. 2007; Diane Wood to William Zerter, 9 Feb. 2007.

159Karen Milner to Peter Wiley, 22 Feb. 2006.

160Karen Milner to Peter Wiley, 22 Feb. 2006.

161William Zerter to Peter Wiley, 15 Sept. 2007.

162Michael Foyle et al., Presentation to Board of Directors, 17 Mar. 1993, "JWS Board Presentation: European and Asian Markets, 1993"; John Wiley & Sons SEA PTE., LTD., FY1993 Budget, Executive Summary; Financial Review for FY1992.

163Valerie Barth to Stephen Smith, 22 Feb. 1993, Stephen Smith to Valerie Barth, 12 Mar. 1993, Stephen Smith to Peter Clifford, 30 Mar. 1993, "JWS Subsidiaries: PBW Singapore Letters, 1992–1994"; Michael Foyle et al., Presentation to Board of Directors, 17 Mar. 1993, "JWS Board Presentation: European and Asian Markets, 1993."

164Ian Garrard to Barbara Heaney, 24 Aug. 2007. Stephen Smith to Barbara Heaney, 13 July 2007.

165Stephen Smith to Barbara Heaney, 13 July 2007.

166"Representative Offices in Asia," *Asia Round-Up* (May 1994), 1. Stephen Smith to Richard Rudick, 20 Apr. 1993, Stephen Smith to Charles Ellis, 27 Jan. 1993, A.G. MacKintosh to Stephen Smith, 23 Apr. 1993, Stephen Smith to Asang Machwe, 7 May 1993, Charles Ellis to Jo Bacchi et al., 2 Mar. 1995, "JWS Subsidiaries: Wiley-Eastern Ltd., 1993–1995"; Asange Machwe to Brad Wiley, 9 June 1993, Charles Ellis to Richard Rudick et al., 29 June 1993, Charles Ellis to Asanga Machwe, 30 Aug. 1993, Charles Ellis to W. Bradford Wiley et al., 27 Nov. 1991, "Publishing Outside JWS: IPA and International STM, 1988–1993"; Brad Wiley II to Stephen Smith, 30 Mar. 1993, Stephen Smith to Brad Wiley, 21 July 1994, Peter Wiley to Brad Wiley II and Charles Ellis, 26 July 1994, "JWS Subsidiaries: PBW Singapore Letters, 1992–1994."

167Arum Bharti to Barbara Heaney, 27 Aug. 2007.

168John Wiley & Sons Press Release, Feb. 3, 2007, "Wiley Acquires the Minority Shares of Its Dreamtech Joint Venture, Expanding Its Stake in India's High-Growth Markets."

169Peter Wiley to Charles Ellis, 28 Sept. 1992, John Collins to W. Bradford Wiley, 27 Apr. 1990, "CHINA GENERAL—CURRENT."

170"Business Ventures," *Asia Round-Up* (July 1993), 1. Though it sold no copies of them in China and few in Asia outside China, Wiley's U.S. P/T organization published three books by dissident Chinese authors for the U.S. market: *Falling Leaves,* by Adeline Yen Mah, *Daughter of China,* by Meihong Xu and Larry Engelmann, and Harry Wu and Carolyn Wakeman's *Bitter Winds*, a memoir covering Wu's 19-year imprisonment in the Chinese labor camp system. Yang Lingkang to Brodford [*sic*] Wiley, 7 Mar. 1992, "CHINA GENERAL—CURRENT"; "Wiley Opens Beijing Office," *Wiley World* (Mar.–Apr. 2001), 22. E-mail from Kris Kliemann, 15 Mar. 2007.

[171]Steven Miron to Peter Wiley, 27 July 2007; Theresa Liu to Peter Wiley, 3 Sept. 2007.

[172]"U.S. Book Exports Hit by Recession," *Publishers Weekly* (9 Mar. 1992), 7.

[173]Tadashi Hase to Peter Wiley, Mar. 13, 2007. U.S. National Science Board, U.S. and International Research and Development: Funds and Technology, 1981–2001.

[174]"Wiley in Asia: Crisis, Transition, and Opportunity," *Wiley World* (May–June 1998), 1–3, 12. John Wiley & Sons Annual Report, 1999; David Nadel and Kimberly Laidlaw, "John Wiley & Sons, Inc.: Punching Above Its Weight," (New York: Bear Stearns, 13 Apr. 2000); Brad Wiley II to William Pesce and Stephen Smith, 18, 22 Sept. 1998, "JWS Subsidiaries: WBW II Asia Report, 1998."

[175]Peter Wiley, "Conversation with Lauren Fransen Re Limusa," 9 Apr. 1999, "PBW Correspondence: JWS/Guadalajara, 1999"; Gustavo R. de Menezes to Robert E. Wright, 13 Feb. 2006.

[176]Mehdi Omranloo to Peter Wiley, 19 Sept. 2007.

[177]Tony Zadravec, "New York, New York!" *Bits & Pieces* (Oct.–Nov. 1996), 6. Memo from Timothy King to William Pesce, Dec. 1999; Peter Wiley, memorandum to authors, 6 July 2006; William Pesce, President's Report, Second Quarter, FY 2001.

[178]"NJBIA Salutes New Jersey's Finest Awards For Excellence: Enterprise Award," *New Jersey Business* (1 Oct. 2003), 22.

[179]John Wiley & Sons Annual Reports. It is interesting to note that Wiley continued to segment the reporting of its revenues geographically, so that investors could see only domestic sales by lines of business.

[180]John Lehmann-Haupt interview of Jeff Brown, 22 Sept. 2006.

[181]John Lehmann-Haupt interview of Jeff Brown, 22 Sept. 2006; John Lehmann-Haupt interview of George Telecki, 26 Sept. 2006.

[182]John Lehmann-Haupt interview of Gregory St. John, 25 Sept. 2006.

[183]John Lehmann-Haupt interview of Susan Elbe, 25 Sept. 2006.

[184]E-mail, Margie Schustack to John Lehmann-Haupt, 29 Sept. 2006.

[185]John Lehmann-Haupt interview of Jean Morley, 28 Sept. 2006.

[186]John Lehmann-Haupt interview of Jean Morley, 28 Sept. 2006.

[187]John Lehmann-Haupt interview of Madelyn Lesure, 25 Sept. 2006.

[188]John Lehmann-Haupt interview of Jean Morley, 28 Sept. 2006.

[189]Barbara Heaney interview of Ann Berlin, August 2006.

[190]Barbara Heaney interview of Ann Berlin, August 2006.

[191]"John Wiley & Sons, Inc.," *Wall Street Journal* (18 Dec. 1992), B4.

[192]John Wiley and Sons Annual Report, 1994.

[193]"JWS Stock: Bass Brothers, 1994"; Peter Wiley interview of Charles Ellis, 13 June 2003.

[194]Matthew Greco, "Bass Talks Tough to Wiley," *Mergers & Corporate Policy* (7 Mar. 1994), 1, 12. Charles Ellis to File, 28 July 1994, "JWS Board: Bass Proposed Directors, 1994 (1)."

[195]Peter Wiley interview of Charles Ellis, 13 June 2003; Peter Wiley to Bert Sutherland, 26 June 1996, "JWS Subsidiaries: Wiley-VCH Acquisition Documents, 1996."

[196]In 2005 John Marion resigned from the board as the Bass family reduced its Wiley holdings. The Trust sold its last share in 2007, having realized a substantial gain on its investment in Wiley.

[197]Brian J. Knez to Charles R. Ellis, 13 Mar. 1997; JWS Board Minutes, 25 Apr. 1997.

[198]Thomas M. Taylor & Co., "Insider, Family, and Public Ownership at Public Companies: Resolving the Problem of the Control Discount," n.d.; Ronald C. Anderson and David M. Reeb, "Who Monitors the Family?" (5 Mar. 2003) Available at SSRN: http://ssrn.com/abstract=369620 or DOI: 10.2139/ssrn.369620.

[199]George Smith and Timothy Jacobson interview of Henry McKinnell, 1 Mar. 2006.

[200]Peter Booth Wiley to Blackwell colleagues in Oxford, 28 Feb. 2007; Timothy Jacobson interview of Bonnie Lieberman, 22 June 2005.

[201]To this day, the New York publishing scene is very chummy. It was even more so in the past, when "most of the people [in the industry] knew one another." (Wiley, "My First 50 Years," Chap. 3, 8). Timothy Jacobson interview of Nils Kindwall, 6 Feb. 2006; Timothy Jacobson interview of Allen Fernald, 24 Jan. 2006; Peter Wiley interview of Wayne Anderson, 3 Apr. 2003; Timothy Jacobson interview of Eric Swanson, 22 June 2005. Brad Wiley, Brad Wiley II, Peter Wiley, and Deborah Wiley to the Board of Directors, 7 Dec. 1987; Brad Wiley II, Notes on Family-Company Relationship, Oct. 1987, "Wiley Family: WBW II Family, Business, 1987–1991."

[202]Lewis Coser, Charles Kadushin, and Walter Powell, *Books: The Culture and Commerce of Publishing* (Chicago: University of Chicago Press, 1982), 46. Richard Blodgett interview of Charles Ellis, 20 Feb. 2004. John Wiley & Sons Annual Report, 1997.

[203]John Wiley & Sons Annual Report, 2002.

CHAPTER NINE

[1]"Wiley in Asia: Crisis, Transition, and Opportunity," *Wiley World* (May–June 1998), 12.

[2]William J. Pesce, conversation with Susan Spilka, Jan. 2007.

[3]Peter Wiley, conversation with Susan Spilka, Dec. 2006.

[4]John Jarvis e-mail to Susan Spilka, 18 Sept. 2007; John Jarvis e-mail to Peter Wiley, 2 Oct. 2006.

[5]William J. Pesce, conversation with Susan Spilka, Jan. 2007.

[6]A.L.P. Norrington, *Blackwell's 1879–1979: The History of a Family Firm.* (Oxford: Blackwell, 1983), 1-3; *A Guide to the Merton Blackwell Collection*, compiled and edited by Julian Reid, Rita Ricketts, and Julia Walworth, Merton College Oxford, in association with Blackwell's, 2004; see also www.blackwellpublishing.com.

[7]Norrington, *Blackwell's*, 5, 40.

[8]Norrington, *Blackwell's*, 23, 25.

[9]Norrington, *Blackwell's*, 49, 64, 86.

[10]Norrington, *Blackwell's*, 86–87, 134–135.

[11] Norrington, *Blackwell's*, 140, 172.

[12] Norrington, *Blackwell's*, 164–167.

[13] William J. Pesce, conversation with Susan Spilka, Jan. 2007.

[14] Eric Swanson and René Olivieri, Global Leadership Announcement to Wiley colleagues, 21 Dec. 2006.

[15] John Wiley & Sons Annual Report 2007, 4.

[16] M. Niazi-Sai, first quarter 2008 Conference Call briefing memo to William Pesce and Ellis Cousens, 11 Sept. 2007.

[17] "The Wiley Foundation Announces Recipients of Sixth Annual Wiley Prize in Biomedical Sciences," John Wiley & Sons Press Release, 29 Jan. 2007.

[18] "Wiley Prize Is Awarded," *Wiley World* (July–Aug. 2007), 35.

[19] William J. Pesce e-mail to all Wiley colleagues, 16 Nov. 2006.

[20] "Wiley Acquires Blackwell Publishing," *Wiley World* (Jan.–Feb. 2007), 7.

[21] Timothy B. King, "The Impact of Electronic and Networking Technologies on the Delivery of Scholarly Information," 1991, "Multi-Division: Electronic Publishing, 1980–1994."

[22] John Wiley & Sons Scenario Planning Report, 2004–2005.

[23] Lewis Coser, Charles Kadushin, and Walter Powell, *Books: The Culture and Commerce of Publishing* (Chicago, University of Chicago Press, 1982), 373.

[24] Brian Hayes, "The Economic Quandary of the Network Publisher," in Robin Peek and Gregory Newby, eds., *Scholarly Publishing: The Electronic Frontier* (Cambridge: M.I.T. Press, 1996), 123. See also Fytton Rowland, "The Need for Management of Electronic Journals," in Peek and Newby, eds., *Scholarly Publishing*, 243.

[25] Thomson Scientific (then the Institute for Scientific Information) began publishing Journal Citation Reports in 1975 as part of the Science Citation Index and the Social Sciences Citation Index. The impact factor indicates a journal's importance in its field by measuring how often an "average article" in the journal is cited in a particular year or period. It is calculated by dividing the number of current year citations by the source items published in that journal during the previous two years. http://scientific.thomson.com/free/essays/journal citationreports/impactfactor/. Jan Velterop, "Keeping the minutes of science," in *Proceedings of Electronic Libraries and Visual Information Research (ELVIRA) Conference* (Aslib, London, No. 2–14 May 1995).

[26] Though how "open" is open to question. Even Wikipedia "has a clear power structure that gives volunteer administrators the authority to exercise editorial control, delete unsuitable articles, and protest those that are vulnerable to vandalism." Katie Hafner, "Growing Wikipedia Refines Its 'Anyone Can Edit' Policy," *New York Times*, 17 June 2006, 1.

[27] William Pesce, President's Report to the Board of Directors, Second Quarter, FY 1999, n.d.

[28] Susan Spilka interview with Eric Swanson, 20 June 2007.

[29] John Lehmann-Haupt interview with Roy Kaufman 15 Mar. 2007, e-mail 20 Mar. 2007; Timothy King e-mail to John Lehmann-Haupt 20 Mar. 2007; Richard Rudick, "Wiley and Copyright," 8 Feb. 1997; Nader F. Darehshori (Houghton Mifflin) Curtis Benjamin Award nomination form for Charles Ellis 3 Feb. 1998.

[30] Richard Blodgett interview with Bonnie Lieberman, 8 Mar. 2004.

[31] Jeffrey A. Trachtenberg, "Publishers Embrace Web as Travel Agent," *Wall Street Journal*, 3 July 2007.

[32] John Wiley & Sons Annual Report, 1999. "Experience: A Viewpoint on Asia," *Wiley Yam Seng* (June 2007), 10.

[33] René Olivieri e-mail to Peter Wiley 16 Sept. 2007.

[34] Geoffrey Naylor e-mail to Susan Spilka, 17 Sept. 2007.

[35] John Wiley & Sons Annual Reports, 1990, 1995.

[36] Timothy Jacobson interview with Jo Bacchi, 21 Dec. 2005.

[37] William Pesce e-mail to Ellis Cousens and Susan Spilka 19 July 2007. Jo Bacchi and "Historical Prices," http://finance.yahoo.com. John Wiley & Sons Annual Reports, 1992, 30; 2007, 1.

[38] Jay Palmer, "Publishing for Dummies," *Barron'sOnline*, 28 May 2005; *Fortune*, January 25, 2005, January 23, 2006; http://money.cnn.com/magazines/fortune/fortune_archive/2005/01/24/8234059/index.htm; http://money.cnn.com/magazines/fortune/bestcompanies/2006/full_list/; The 400 Best Big Companies, John Wiley & Sons, http://www.forbes.com/lists/2007/88/biz_07platinum_John-Wiley-Sons_23OS.html; http://www.marketvolume.com/indexes_exchanges/sp400_components.asp; David Lewis, "John Wiley: Expect Stable Long-Term Growth but Valuation Full; Initiating at Neutral," *North America Equity Research* (JP Morgan, 23 Jan. 2007), 1, 11.

[39] John Wiley & Sons 2004–2005 Scenario Planning Report.

[40] "Discover Wiley: System Characteristics" memo from Andy Townsend, 15 Dec. 2006.

[41] "Succeeding in the World of Tomorrow," OHM Newsletter Aug. 2001 http://www.hseland.ie/ohmarchive/newsletter/20010829190510.html.

[42] "A Moment in Time," William J. Pesce speaking with Wiley board of directors, 26 June 2006.

[43] Richard Morgan, "The Wiley Way," http://www.thedeal.com, 4 Oct. 2004.

[44] "John Wiley: 175 Years of Publishing," *The Bookseller* (9 Oct. 1982), 1413. Timothy Jacobson et al. interview of William Pesce, 7 Feb. 2006. Charles Schuchert to William O. Wiley, 29 Nov. 1932, "JWS 125th Anniversary Correspondence, 1932"; W. Bradford Wiley, "An International Publisher's View of Trends and Developments in the Flow of Materials," 18 July 1976, "WBW Talks: American Library Assoc. Address, 1976"; W. Bradford Wiley, "Address," 18 Sept. 1968, "WBW Talks: Franklin Internat Book Fair, 1968."

[45] Lisa Freeman, "The University Press in the Electronic Future," in Peek and Newby, eds., *Scholarly Publishing*, 153.

[46] Dan Lacy, "Commercial Publishing: The Economics of Publishing, Or Adam Smith and Literature," in Roger H. Smith, ed., *The American Reading Public: What It Reads, Why It Reads* (New York: R. R. Bowker, 1963), 51; Harry Markowitz, *Portfolio Selection: Efficient Diversification of Investments* (New York: Wiley, 1959);

Lewis A. Coser, "Publishers as Gatekeepers of Ideas," *Annals of the American Academy of Political and Social Science* (Sept. 1975): 14–22; Barbara Levitt and Clifford Nass, "The Lid on the Garbage Can: Institutional Constraints on Decision Making in the Technical Core of College-Text Publishers," *Administrative Science Quarterly* (June 1989), 190-207; Carroll G. Bowen, "When Universities Become Publishers," *Science* (10 May 1963), 599–605.

[47]Levitt and Nass, "Lid on the Garbage Can," 194.

Photo Credits

Chapter 1

Page 1: John Bachmann, Humanities & Social Sciences Library/Print collection, Miriam and Ira D. Wallach Division of Art, Prints & Photographs, The New York Public Library. **Pages 2 & 3:** The Granger Collection. **Page 5:** Wiley Archives, photo by Andy Washnik. **Page 8** *(left):* Bo Zaunders/© Corbis. **Page 9** *(top):* University of California, Berkeley. **Page 9** *(inset):* Keith Ferris, The Culinary Institute of America. **Page 13** *(left):* The Granger Collection. **Page 13** *(center):* The Canal Museum. **Page 14:** The Granger Collection. **Page 15:** Sovfoto.

Chapter 2

Pages 16 & 17: Museum of the City of New York/© Corbis. **Page 18** *(top):* Collection of the New York Historical Society, Ascen#52.100.6. **Page 18** *(bottom):* Francis Guy, Tontine Coffee House, c.1797. Collection of The New York Historical Society, Ascen#1907.32. **Page 19** *(right):* Five Points by George Catlin, 1827. Courtesy Alice W. Lorillard. **Page 20:** Emmet Collection, Miriam and Ira D. Wallach Division of Art, Prints and Photographs, The New York Public Library, Astor, Lenox, and Tilden Foundations. **Page 21** *(top):* Wiley Archives, Photo by Andy Washnik. **Page 23** *(top):* No. 54469: William D. Smith. View of the Bay and Harbour of New-York, from the Battery. Courtesy of The New York Public Library. **Page 23** *(bottom left):* Courtesy United States Naval Academy Museum. **Page 23** *(bottom right):* Collection of the New York Historical Society, Ascen#1924.6. **Page 24:** Courtesy Scoville Memorial Library. **Page 26:** Emmet Collection, Miriam and Ira D. Wallach Division of Art, Prints and Photographs, The New York Public Library, Astor, Lenox and Tilden Foundations. **Page 28:** The Granger Collection. **Page 30:** P. Maverick. 29.100.2286—The J. Clarence Davies Collection. Courtesy

of the Museum of the City of New York. **Page 32** *(top):* Wiley Archives, Photo by Andy Washnik. **Page 32** *(bottom left):* The Granger Collection. **Page 32** *(bottom center):* Courtesy United States Naval Academy Museum. **Page 32** *(bottom right):* The Granger Collection. **Page 33:** The Canal Museum. **Page 39** *(top):* Time Life Pictures/Mansell/Getty Images. **Page 39** *(bottom):* The Granger Collection. **Page 42:** Emmet Collection, Miriam and Ira D. Wallach Division of Art, Prints and Photographs, The New York Public Library, Astor, Lenox and Tilden Foundations. **Page 47:** Stephen Kovacik/Massachusetts Historical Society. **Page 48** *(top):* The Granger Collection. **Page 48** *(bottom):* Wiley Archives, Photo by Andy Washnik. **Page 53** *(top):* The Canal Museum. **Page 53** *(right):* The Granger Collection.

Chapter 3

Pages 54 & 55: The New York Public Library, Astor, Lenox and Tilden Foundations. **Page 56:** Rischgitz/Getty Images, Inc. **Page 57:** The New York Public Library, Berg Collection. **Page 58:** Phelps Stokes Collection of American Historical Prints, New York Public Library. **Page 60** *(bottom):* Andy Washnik. **Page 61:** The Granger Collection. **Page 64** *(top):* West Point Museum Art Collection, United States Military Academy, West Point, NY #6954. **Page 64** *(bottom):* Wiley Archives, Photo by Andy Washnik. **Page 66:** The New York Public Library, Astor, Lenox and Tilden Foundations. **Page 67:** The Granger Collection. **Page 68:** Book courtesy of Don Embler, Photo by Andy Washnik. **Pages 70 & 71:** *The Harper Establishment* by Jacob Abbott; NY: Harper & Brother, 1855. **Page 72:** Humanities and Social Sciences Library/Print Collection, Miriam and Ira D. Wallach, New York Public Library Division of Art, Prints and Photographs. **Pages 74–76:** Wiley Archives, Photo by Andy Washnik. **Page 79:** Humanities and Social Sciences Library/Print

508

Collection, Miriam and Ira D. Wallach Division of Art, Prints & Photographs, New York Public Library. *Page 80:* Wiley Archives, Photo by Andy Washnik. *Page 81:* Humanities and Social Sciences Library/Henry W. and Albert A. Berg Collection of English and American Literature/New York Public Library. *Page 82:* The Granger Collection. *Page 83:* Humanities and Social Sciences Library/Henry W. and Albert A. Berg Collection of English and American Literature, New York Public Library. *Page 84 (top left):* Wiley Archives, Photo by Andy Washnik. *Page 84 (top right):* Photo by Rodney Dewey (1861) The Berkshire Athenaeum. *Page 84 (bottom left):* Wiley Archives, Photo by Andy Washnik. *Page 84 (bottom right):* Houghton Library, Harvard University. *Page 85:* Bettmann/© Corbis Images. *Page 86 (left):* Wiley Archives, Photo by Andy Washnik. *Page 86 (right):* Photo by Rischgitz/Getty Images. *Pages 87 & 89:* Wiley Archives, Photo by Andy Washnik. *Page 90 (top left):* The Granger Collection. *Page 90 (top center):* Humanities and Social Sciences Library/Print Collection, Miriam and Ira D. Wallach Division of Art, Prints and Photographs, The New York Public Library, Astor Lennox and Tilden Foundations. *Page 90 (top right):* Hulton Archive/Getty Images. *Page 90 (center right):* Library of Congress. *Page 90 (bottom left):* Emmett Collection, Miriam and Ira D. Wallach Division of Art, Prints and Photographs, The New York Public Library, Astor, Lennox and Tilden Foundations. *Page 90 (bottom right):* Hulton Archive/Getty Images. *Page 96 (left):* Wiley Archives, Photo by Andy Washnik. *Page 97 (right):* Historical Society of Pennsylvania, Edward Carey Gardiner Collection, Henry C. Carey Section, Box 80. *Page 98:* Bettmann/© Corbis.

Chapter 4

Pages 100 & 101: Smithsonian Institution. *Page 102:* Bettmann/© Corbis. *Page 105:* Wiley Archives, Photo by Andy Washnik. *Page 106 (top):* London Stereoscopic Company/Getty Images. *Page 107:* Wiley Archives, Photo by Andy Washnik. *Page 109:* Bettmann/© Corbis. *Pages 110 (bottom) & 111:* Courtesy of Rensselaer Polytechnic Institute. *Page 113 (right):* Roger Burlingame, *Endless Frontiers: The Story of McGraw-Hill* © 1959 McGraw-Hill. *Page 114:* National Museum of American History, Smithsonian Institution. *Page 116:* Courtesy Ohio State University Photo Archives. *Page 117:* The MIT Museum. *Page 118:* Library of Congress Prints and Photographs

Division, Washington, D.C. *Page 119 (top right):* Picture History. *Page 119 (bottom):* Wiley Archives, Photo by Andy Washnik. *Page 121 (top):* Wiley Archives, Photo by Andy Washnik. *Page 123 (top):* Kean Collection/Hulton Archive/Getty Images. *Page 123 (bottom):* The Granger Collection. *Page 125 (background photo):* Humanities and Social Sciences Library / Photography Collection, Miriam and Ira D. Wallach Division of Art, Prints and Photographs, New York Public Library. *Pages 127–129 & 132:* Wiley Archives, Photo by Andy Washnik. *Page 136 (top):* Pennsylvania State University Archives. *Page 136 (bottom):* Iowa State University. *Pages 140 (bottom) & 141 (bottom):* The Granger Collection.

Chapter 5

Pages 142 & 143: Hulton Archive/Getty Images. *Page 144:* Boeing Photo. *Page 145:* Underwood & Underwood/© Corbis. *Page 150 (top left):* *Rocks and Rock Minerals* by Louis V. Pirsson © 1915 by John Wiley & Sons, Inc. Courtesy of Yale University. *Page 150 (top right and bottom left):* Book courtesy of Joan Kalkut, photo by Andy Washnik. *Page 153 (bottom):* Wiley Archives, Photo by Andy Washnik. *Page 154:* Hulton Archive/Getty Images. *Page 155:* Redmond/© Corbis. *Page 157 (top):* The Granger Collection. *Page 157 (inset):* Bettmann/© Corbis. *Page 162:* Book courtesy of Steve Schultz, photo by Andy Washnik. *Page 163:* Iowa State University. *Page 164:* Courtesy of the Quinn & Boden Company. *Page 173:* Library of Congress Prints and Photographs Division. *Page 174 (bottom left):* University of Cincinnati Archives. *Page 176:* Minnesota Historical Society/© Corbis. *Page 177:* Eric Schaal/Time Life Pictures/Getty Images. *Page 178 (left):* Alfred Eisenstaedt/Pix Inc./Time & Life Pictures/Getty Images. *Page 183 (right):* Margaret Bourke-White/Time Life Pictures/Getty Images. *Page 189:* Harrison/Getty Images.

Chapter 6

Pages 196 & 197: Sovfoto. *Page 199 (left) and (bottom right):* The MIT Museum. *Page 201:* Hulton Archive/Getty Images. *Page 204 (left):* Jack Gould Photography, courtesy of the Fogg Art Museum, Harvard University Art Museums on deposit from the Carpenter Center for Visual Arts. Photo by Allan Macintyre, © 2004 President and Fellows of Harvard College. *Pages 204 & 205 (bottom):* Robert Altman Photography. *Page 205 (top left):* Lambert/The Image

Bank/Getty Images. *Page 205 (top right):* POPPERFOTO/ Alamy Images. *Page 206 (top):* Walter Sanders/Life Magazine/Time & Life Pictures/Getty Images. *Page 206 (bottom):* Lawrence Berkeley Laboratory. *Page 207:* SUPERSTOCK. *Page 208:* Courtesy of Indiana University. *Page 210:* Time Life Pictures/Getty Images. *Page 211:* AP/Wide World Photos. *Page 233 (top):* Courtesy of Jo Bacchi. *Page 234 (left):* Bachrach photographers. *Page 248* (top): The MIT Museum. *Page 251 (bottom):* Courtesy of Jearl Walker. *Page 252 (bottom left):* Dan Cutrona Photography. *Page 252 (right):* Courtesy of Peter Muller. *Page 253 (bottom):* Courtesy of Alan Strahler. *Page 260 (left):* Courtesy of Harris Printers. *Page 261 (top right):* Courtesy of RR Donnelley at Jefferson City, MO. *Page 261 (bottom):* Courtesy of Quad/Graphics.

Chapter 7

Pages 266 & 267: John Chiasson/Getty Images News and Sport Services. *Page 266 (top):* Ferdinando Scianna/ Magnum Photos, Inc. *Page 266 (center):* Burt Glinn/ Masterfile. *Page 266 (bottom):* Kaveh Kazemi/© Corbis. *Page 268:* Time Life Pictures/Getty Images. *Page 270:* Wiley Archives, photos by Kathy Bendo. *Page 274:* Time Life Pictures/Getty Images News and Sport Services. *Page 278:* Barbara Stitzer/PhotoEdit. *Page 279 (left):* Nebraska Books Company, Lincoln, Nebraska. *Page 283 (top right):* Courtesy of Donald Kieso. *Page 284:* Courtesy of John Schermerhorn. *Page 286 (top left):* Wiley Archives, photo by Andy Washnik. *Page 290 (top left):* Colin Cuthbert/Photo Researchers, Inc. *Page 290 (top right):* SSPL/The Image Works. *Page 290 (bottom center):* D. VoTrung/LookatSciences/ Phototake. *Page 290 (bottom right):* Jack Dykinga/USDA. *Page 291 (top left):* NASA/Goddard Space Flight Center Scientific Visualization Studio. *Page 291 (top right):* NASA. *Page 291:* (bottom left) Henry Groskinsky/Time Life Pictures/Getty Images. *Page 291 (bottom right):* JSC/NASA. *Page 302 (left) & Page 307:* Courtesy of Charity Robey. *Page 322:* Courtesy of Lee Goldstein. Photo by Andy Washnik. *Page 323:* John Harding//Time Life Pictures/ Getty Images. *Page 324 (bottom right):* Courtesy of Charity Robey. *Page 327:* Don Hogan Charles/New York Times Pictures. *Page 328 (left):* Courtesy of Beatrice Shube. *Page 328 (right):* Courtesy of Ted Hoffman. *Page 329:* Courtesy of Celia Kupferberg. *Page 331:* Courtesy of Susan Elbe, Joyce Krieger, Elizabeth Doble, and George Stanley.

Chapter 8

Pages 332 & 333: AP/Wide World Photos. *Page 334* (top): NASA. *Page 334 (bottom):* Chris Hondros/Getty Images News and Sport Services. *Page 335 (top right):* CERN. *Page 335* (bottom right): AP/Wide World Photos. *Page 338 (top):* Courtesy of Jo Bacchi. *Page 340:* Courtesy of Michelle Bigata. *Page 343 (top):* Financial Times. *Page 354 (bottom):* Courtesy of Frank Lyman. *Page 357:* Julian Clayton. *Page 363 (center right & bottom):* Ryan Flahive. *Pages 364 & 365:* Courtesy of Alida Setford, George Stanley, Ryan Flahive, Gene Aiello. *Page 368:* Courtesy of Janice Blount. *Pages 378 & 379:* Courtesy of George Stanley, Gene Aiello, Reed Elfenbein, Inez Pettis, Camille Carter, Helen Russo, Elizabeth Doble. *Page 381:* Courtesy of The Cochrane Collaboration. *Page 386:* Courtesy of Katherine Schowalter. *Page 388 (top):* Dan Lamont/© Corbis. *Page 409* (left): AAP Image. *Page 417:* Courtesy of Theresa Liu. *Page 418 (top):* AP/Wide World Photos. *Page 423 (bottom right):* SUPERSTOCK.

Chapter 9

Pages 434 & 435: From: *A Guide to the Merton Blackwell Collection,* Compiled and edited by Julian Reid, Rita Ricketts, and Julia Walworth © 2004 by Merton College Oxford. *Page 435 (bottom left):* Paul Dorsey/Time Magazine/Time & Life Pictures/Getty Images. *Page 435 (bottom right):* Time Life Pictures/Getty Images. *Page 436:* From: *BLACKWELL'S 1879–1979: The History of a Family Firm* by A.L.P. Norrington © 1983 B. H. Blackwell Ltd. *Pages 437 & 438:* The Blackwell Collection. *Pages 461 & 462:* Jakubaszek/Getty Images.

Name Index

A

Abel, Richard, 209
Abrams, Harry, 244
Ackerman, Frederick L., 166
Ackoff, Russell, 309
Ackroyd, Peter, 56
Adams, Isaac, 72
Adams, Roger, 184
Adorno, Theodor, 213
Al-Awqati, D. Qais, 440
Albert, Leo, 244
Albrecht, Robert, 287
Aldrich, Thomas Bailey, 66
Alexander, George W., 122
Allan, Kitt, 386
Allen, Judy, 412
Allen, Thomas, 42
Allin, Mark, 404, 450, 451
Alsop, Richard, 33
Altman, Edward, 213
Altoft, Rosemary, 368, 370
Andersen, Hans Christian, 107
Anderson, Wayne, 324, 351
Andrews, Kenneth, 202, 203, 220
Anton, Howard, 348, 349
Antoni, Manfred, 376, 404
Appleton, Daniel, 65, 124
Arbuckle, Ernest L., 456
Archibald, R. C., 129
Arena, Susan, 362
Arlington, William, 336, 338, 340, 344, 420, 438
Armstrong, Louis, 143
Armstrong, Neil, 211, 227
Arnold, Frank, 151
Astor, John Jacob, 39
Auclair, Deni, 354, 357
Auden, W. H., 435
Austen, Peter, 126
Avery, Martha, 302

B

Bacchi, Josephine, 233, 337, 338
Bailey, Janet, 383, 384
Bailey, Thomas Haines, 96
Baker, Kelly, 409
Baker, Nicholas, 177
Baker, Warren, 351, 425
Balbalis, John, 233, 258, 259
Ballantine, William, 30
Baltimore, David, 213
Bancroft, M., 61
Bandura, Albert, 213
Barlow, John Perry, 105
Barnard, William, 174
Barnes, J. Stetson, 193, 194, 195, 200, 202, 224
Barnes, Ralph, 14, 148, 172
Barnett, Raymond, 362
Barnett, William A., 437
Barth, Johann Ambrosius, 380
Barton, Bruce, 159
Baruth, Ruth, 352, 356
Bean, Colette, 440
Beasley, Carol L., 324
Beaumont, Leslie, 409
Becker, Heinz, 380
Becker, Joseph, 231
Beckett, S. H., 126
Beckman, William, 287
Bekar, Carol, 372
Bell, Alexander Graham, 102, 108
Belton, H. L., 126
Benjamin, Curtis, 201, 212, 254
Berg, Linda, 362
Berkeley, Edmund, 177
Berkowitz, Steven, 394
Berlin, Ann, 363, 423
Berners-Lee, Timothy, 334, 335
Bernstein, Peter L., 387, 388
Bernstein, Robert, 244
Berra, Yogi, 359
Bessie, Simon Michael, 231
Bethe, Hans, 177
Bezos, Jeff, 390
Bharti, Arun, 415, 416, 451
Bierach, Barbara, 404
Bijuesca, K. Josu, 362
Bikales, Norbert, 15, 226
Bin Laden, Osama, 268

Black, Jacquelyn, 359
Blackburn, Elizabeth H., 440
Blackwell, Basil H., 434, 435, 436
Blackwell, Benjamin Harris, 434
Blackwell, Benjamin Henry, 434, 435
Blackwell, Julian, 432, 433, 436
Blackwell, Miles, 436
Blackwell, Nigel, 433, 436, 437, 438, 441
Blackwell, Philip, 432
Blackwell, Richard, 239, 435, 436
Bleeker, George, 76
Bleich, Nettie, 229
Blore, Shawn, 404
Blyth, John, 98
Bocquet, Antoine, 418
Bodansky, Meyer, 150, 174
Bogoliubov, N. N., 299
Bohr, Niels, 109, 177, 192
Bolman, Pieter, 372
Bonaparte, Napoleon, 34, 76, 459
Boolootian, Richard, 249
Boos, Jürgen, 404
Boring, Edwin, 165
Bowden, May, 419
Bowen, John T., 137
Boynton, Henry Walcott, 164
Bradford, Thomas, 33, 42
Bradford, William, 25
Brady, James, 242, 285, 293, 329
Brahm, Laurence J., 404
Brett, George, 202
Brevoort, Henry, 36, 38
Bridges, Horatio, 82
Brink, Victor Z., 283
Brown, James, 350
Brown, Jeffrey, 320, 321, 385, 386, 420
Brown, Jerald, 287
Brown, Stanley, 412
Browning, Elizabeth Barrett, 76, 81, 82
Browning, Robert, 75
Bruce, David, 72
Bruce, George, 72
Bruder, Beth, 412
Bryant, William Cullen, 32, 66, 73, 75, 81
Buessem, Niels, 232, 292
Burger, William, 359

Burke, William, 77
Burlingame, Roger, 113
Burton, Richard, 404
Burton, Robert, 73
Bush, George W., 366
Butler (Gordon), Marsha, 359
Byron, Christopher M., 387

C

Calvin, Melvin, 182
Cambreleng, Churchill, 92
Cameron, Jamie, 238, 239, 295, 402
Campbell, Angus, 230
Campbell, Robert, 432, 433, 436, 437, 438, 439
Campbell, Thomas, 75
Campbell, Thomas C., 309
Cardell, William, 51
Carey, Henry C., 51, 52, 61, 66, 93
Carey, Mathew, 26, 31, 33, 41, 42, 43, 44
Carlyle, Thomas, 81, 82, 90, 92
Carnegie, Andrew, 108, 115
Carpenter, Philip, 438, 439
Carpenter, Robert, 412
Carpinteiro, Antonio, 235
Carroll, Sean B., 437
Carson, Rachel, 6
Carter, Deane G., 138
Carter, Jimmy, 268, 271
Carvill, H., 61
Casey, Shawn, 409
Cassidy, Thomas, 295
Cerf, Bennett, 229, 328
Cervantes, Miguel, 34
Chandler, Alfred D., 202
Chandler, Asa C., 133, 141
Channing, William, 77, 79
Chapman, Natalie, 397
Chapman, Robert, 390
Chase, L. W., 135, 136
Chatburn, George R., 138
Chateaubriand, Vicomte, 34
Cheever, George Barrell, 59
Cheney, O. H., 156, 157, 159, 184, 195, 254
Chernosvitova, Tatiana, 354
Chiarelli, Robert, 386
Child, Lydia Maria, 67, 85
Ching, Frank, 391
Chitty, Joseph, 30
Cholmondeley, Mary, 121
Churchill, Winston, 113, 121
Clark, D. K., 99
Clark, Joanna K., 7
Clark, Thomas, 37

Clarke, Arthur C., 288
Clarke, Edward, 34
Clay, Henry, 92
Clayton, Julian, 354
Clemm, Virginia, 86
Clifford, Peter, 340, 376, 452
Clinton, Bill, 231
Clinton, DeWitt, 13, 33, 49
Clurman, David, 230
Clymer, George, 72
Cobbett, William, 34, 42
Coffin, Joseph G., 140
Colbert, Edwin, 258
Colburn, Zerah, 99
Coleman, William, 46
Colenso, Michael, 238
Coleridge, Samuel Taylor, 35
Collins, John, 294, 295, 296, 336
Collins, Kenneth, 277, 278, 287, 289, 310
Columbus, Christopher, 39
Commons, John R., 161
Conner, William F. P., 139
Constant, Anita, 170
Conter, Thomas, 321, 390
Converse, Philip E., 230
Coombs, Michael, 238, 403
Cooper, James Fenimore, 13, 25, 33, 41, 47, 48, 50, 51, 53, 60, 66, 87, 88, 95, 164
Coppinger, Joseph, 33, 34, 35
Coppola, Dominic, 400, 401
Corbett, Sue, 438, 439
Cotton, Albert, 328
Cousens, Ellis, 344, 420, 433, 453
Cowper, William, 34
Cox, Elizabeth, 440
Crafts, Nicholas F. R., 335
Cranch, William, 30
Crane, Hart, 105
Crawford, Brian, 320, 381–382
Creager, William, 129
Creswell, Philip, 235
Cross, Theodore L., 327, 425
Cudlipp, Eileen, 320
Culhane, Lisa, 324
Curie, Marie, 109
Curie, Pierre, 109
Curtis, Mary, 289, 292, 310, 315
Curtis, Veechi, 409
Cutnell, John, 312, 329, 349, 350, 358

D

Dana, J. D., 13, 62, 80, 329
Dana, Richard Henry, 25, 27, 33, 46, 47, 50
Darby, Cynthia, 169

Darby, Elizabeth Wiley, 192
Darrow, Whitney, 190
Davidson, Jay Brownlee, 135, 136, 137, 139
Davies, Charles, 62, 63
Davis, James, 161
Davis, Michael, 381, 439
Davison, Gerald, 329, 411
Davy, Humphrey, 102
Day, Jack, 386
de Blij, Harm, 227, 251, 252, 285, 329, 348, 349, 350, 356
de Vries, Alexandra, 404
Dean, Geoff, 242, 296
Deane, Charles, 390
Defoe, Daniel, 25
Dekker, Maurits, 217, 222
Delaplaine, Joseph, 44
Deming, Horace, 151
Derby, J. C., 61
Derrickson, Bryan, 361
DeSouza, Ray, 445
Deutch, Carole, 7
Deutsch, Karl W., 165
Dewey, Melvil, 115
Dickens, Charles, 12, 55–57, 58, 75, 81, 90, 91, 93, 133
Dicks, James, 376
Diefenbach, William, 249, 254
Dill, John, 297, 409, 410, 411
Ding, Wendy, 417
DiNinno, Anthony, 400
Dirac, Paul, 213, 227, 328
Disraeli, Benjamin, 90, 92
Dixon, Deborah, 381
Doble, Elizabeth, 386, 423
Dobzhansky, Theodosius, 148, 182
Donoughue, Peter, 338, 344, 408, 409
Douglas, Robert, 228, 277, 278, 310, 315
Downing, Andrew Jackson, 62, 75, 96, 99, 166
Draper, John, 408
Drew, Charles, 151
Drozdov, Eugeny, 354
Drucker, Peter F., 392
Dryden, Ken, 412
Duffie, John, 287
Duncan, Rudolph, 151
Durand, Asher, 32
Durrant, James, 191–192, 237
Duyckinck, Evert A., 77, 79, 81, 82, 86, 87, 126
Dwight, Theodore, 62
Dwight, William, 112
Dyckman, Jacob, 32
Dyson, Freeman, 179

E

Eccles, Robert G., 404
Edison, Thomas, 102, 103, 108, 169
Eggleston, DeWitt, 127
Einstein, Albert, 109
Eiseman, William, 220
Eisman, William, 314
Elbe, Susan, 321, 324, 349, 352, 363, 421
Elfenbein, Reed, 320, 370, 401, 439
Ellenwood, Frank, 174
Elliot, Steve, 324
Ellis, Charles, 15, 314, 315, 319, 327, 336,
    337, 338, 339, 340, 341, 342, 344,
    345, 366, 372, 373, 376, 377, 385,
    403, 412, 414, 419, 421, 425, 429,
    444, 452
Ellis, David, 436
Emerson, Ralph Waldo, 82, 87
Ensign, Newton E., 14, 150
Eyring, Henry, 213
Ezekiel, Mordecai, 165

F

Fabozzi, Frank J., 393
Fairchild, Henry Pratt, 179
Faraday, Michael, 102
Fay, T. C., 34
Feller, William, 213
Fenton, Mike, 438, 439
Fernald, Allen, 275, 424
Fernandes, Gary J., 424
Ferris, Peter, 296
Feshbach, Herman, 268
Fielding, Henry, 34
Finkel, LeRoy, 287
Fire, Andrew Z., 440
Fiske, Richard, 176
Fitzgerald, F. Scott, 143, 297
Fizzell, Maureen, 410
Flahive, Ryan, 355
Fleisher, Pamela, 348
Fletcher, L. J., 126
Fletcher, Robert, 324
Flohn, George, 258
Flory, Paul, 213
Foo, Khee How, 413
Ford, Andrew E. Jr., 278, 293, 310
Ford, Donald, 282
Ford, Henry, 102, 103
Ford, Henry II, 271
Forkert, Frank, 235
Foster, Sandra, 411
Foster, W. A., 138
Fowler, Rosamund, 221
Fownes, George, 80

Fox, Barry, 404
Foyle, Michael, 238, 243, 244, 295, 296,
    336, 402
Francis, John W., 34
Franklin, Benjamin, 25
Franklin, Brad, 358, 359
Fraser, Russell, 185
Fraser, Simon, 410
Freel, James E., 228
French, Thomas, 113
Freud, Sigmund, 230
Freymann, M., 178
Friedman, Lenny, 392
Fristensky, Warren, 400, 401
Frommer, Arthur, 395
Fuller, Margaret, 62, 82, 85
Fuller, Robert G., 309
Fulton, Robert, 23

G

Galbraith, John Kenneth, 459
Gallatin, Albert, 73
Gante, Hartmut, 404
Garber, Robert, 397
Gardner, Charles K., 45
Gardner, Eldon J., 259
Gates, Roger, 362
Gaylord, Norman, 15, 226
Geiger, Roger L., 290
Geschke, Chuck, 322
Getman, Arthur K., 135, 139
Getman, Kendall, 185
Ghandi, Rajiv, 415
Gifford, William, 50
Gilbert, Julia Wiley, 192
Gillespie, James F., 234, 305, 313
Gillette, Paul, 309
Gilley, William B., 31, 34
Gillis, Diane, 233
Gilman, Graciela, 362
Gilpin, Thomas, 72
Ginsparg, Paul, 368
Gisslen, Wayne, 286, 312, 391, 396, 411
Glass, Mary Lou, 182
Gleason, Andrew M., 352, 419
Godwin, William, 36
Goeppert-Mayer, Maria, 213
Golant, Viktor, 299
Goldstein, Lee, 322
Gölitz, Peter, 374, 376, 399
Goodrich, Andrew T., 62
Goodrich, Samuel, 37, 47, 75
Gookin, Dan, 394
Gorbachev, Mikhail, 299
Gordon, Ian, 412

Gordon (Butler), Marsha, 358
Gottlob, Henry, 120
Gould, Jay, 103
Goulding, Ossian, 238
Grabowski, Sandra, 356, 359, 360
Granville, William, 129
Graves, Robert, 435
Gray, Christopher, 144
Greeley, Horace, 85
Greene, Graham, 435
Greene, Toby, 83
Greider, Carol, 440
Greif, Ruth, 324, 385
Grenier, Jennifer K., 437
Griffen, Augustus, 35
Grimshaw, William, 185
Gupta, Vikas, 416, 451
Gurley, Ralph, 79
Guthrie, Patrick, 404

H

Haas, Warren, 209
Hackett, Bill, 170
Hagstrom, Robert, 387
Hall, Calvin, 226, 249
Hall, Steve, 438
Halleck, Fitz-Greene, 36, 46
Halliday, David, 206, 250, 251, 285, 329,
    354, 356
Halligan, Ann-Marie, 451
Halsted, George Bruce, 134
Halsted, Julia, 7
Halsted, Oliver, 25, 33, 38
Halsted, Phoebe, 7, 20, 21, 232
Halsted, Robert, 99
Hamilton, Edward Parmalee, 7, 14, 111,
    124, 127, 141, 143–195, 197, 198,
    200, 202, 214, 220, 265, 381
Harkins, William E., 244
Harper, J., 43
Harris, James, 293
Harris, Michael, 225, 287, 304
Harris, Robert, 412
Hart, F. Ulrich, 440
Harwood, Carolyn, 176
Hase, Tadashi, 418
Hatfield, R. G., 62, 96, 127
Hauck, Robert, 277, 278, 295
Haven, John P., 112
Hawkins, R. R., 200
Hawthorne, Nathaniel, 59, 62, 75, 82, 83
Hayek, Friedrich, 459
Hayes, Robert, 231
Hazen, Robert, 350
Hazlitt, William, 81

Headley, J. T., 81
Heald, Henry T., 197, 198
Hebard, Edna, 230
Heider, Joe, 357, 363
Hein, Morris, 362
Heisenberg, Werner, 109
Helming, James, 185, 223
Helmkamp, John, 408
Hemingway, Ernest, 242, 297
Henney, Keith, 153
Henry, Richard, 46–47
Herbert, Deborah, 233, 262
Herbert, Henry William, 61
Heron, Andrew, 404
Herztein, Morris, 440
Higgins, Eugene, 440
Higgins, Raymond L., 309
Higgs, Robert, 213
Higgy, Robert, 173
Higham, Adrian, 239, 278, 295, 296
Hill, Debra, 400
Hill, Peter, 61
Hille, Einar, 242
Hillhouse, James, 47
Hinckson, Jim, 412
Hirshfeld, Clarence, 138, 174
Hittell, John S., 99
Hodges, Charles, 161
Hoe, Robert, 72
Hoffman, Ted, 328
Holleman, A. E., 14, 141
Hollingshead, A. B., 181
Holmes, Paul, 405
Holt, Michael, 213
Holum, John, 329
Hopkins, John, 110
Horne, John, 410
Horvitz, H. Robert, 440
Horvitz, Paul, 255
Horwich, Arthur L., 440
Hosack, David, 34, 49
Hoskin, Robert E., 410
Howard, John, 34
Hudson, Dennis, 295
Huffman, Karen, 312, 349, 423
Hughes, Lawrence, 244
Hughes, Mark, 404
Hughes-Hallett, Deborah, 352, 377, 419
Hugo, Victor, 81
Hume, David, 24
Humiston, Gerard, 242
Hunt, James G., 284
Hunter, Debra S., 392, 393
Huntington, David, 34
Huntington, Ellsworth, 151
Hussein, Saddam, 268

Ierardi, Gordon, 185, 200, 218, 222, 223
Ihn, Hee-Jeong, 414
Iijima, Sumio, 417
Imdieke, Leroy, 408
Ingrim, R. C., 126
Inskeep, A. H., 34, 36
Ipsen, Robert, 401
Ireland, Thomas R., 309
Irons, Rita, 234, 313
Irvine, V. Bruce, 410
Irving, Washington, 13, 33, 38, 39, 46, 50,
    57, 60, 76, 87, 459
Irving, William, 39
Irwin, J. David, 359
Ives, F. W., 126
Ives, Howard, 129

James, Edmund, 404
Jameson, Anna Brownell, 60, 62
Jandt, Fred, 309
Jarvic, Sara, 404
Jarvis, John, 295, 296, 344, 368, 370, 382,
    384, 399, 402, 403, 420, 433, 438
Jefferson, Thomas, 13, 22, 24, 32, 35, 73,
    459
Jenkins, Gail W., 361
Jensen, Peter, 277
Jiloty, John, 412
Jobs, Steve, 273
Johnson, Andrew, 76
Johnson, Kenneth W., 312, 329, 349, 350,
    358
Johnson, Lyndon B., 201, 208, 226, 231,
    245
Johnson, Philip, 167
Johnson, Richard O., 308, 309
Jones, Charles P., 329
Jones, Don, 244
Jones, Gwenyth, 320, 385, 386, 401
Jongsma, Arthur E. Jr., 389
Jordan, Anne, 8
Josephson, Matthew, 101
Jossey-Bass, Allen, 392
Judd, Charles, 157
Juechter, Mathew, 278, 306, 311
Justin, Joel, 129

Kagan, Jerome, 213
Kahn, Anita, 233

Kamm, Oliver, 150
Kanter, Rosabeth Moss, 456
Kantrowitz, Susan, 400
Karapetoff, Vladimir, 164
Karpov, Vadim, 354
Karrel, Dean, 386
Kaufman, Roy, 304, 372, 445
Keaton, Buster, 157
Keenan, Joseph Henry, 166
Keil, John M., 309
Kell, Walter G., 349
Keller, Henry, 131
Kellogg, Bill, 233
Kelly, Patrick, 440
Kemeny, John G., 226
Kemnitz, Christopher P., 361
Kennedy, John F., 15, 208, 226, 231
Kent, William, 14, 120, 126, 141, 174
Kerr, Chester Brooks, 244
Keyes, Frederick G., 166
Kidder, Daniel, 89
Kidder, Frank, 120
Kidwell, David, 362
Kieso, Donald E., 15, 227, 282, 283, 297,
    329, 348, 349, 409, 410
Kilcullen, John, 394
Kimball, Dexter, 129
Kimmel, Paul, 282, 410
Kindleberger, Charles P., 165
Kindwall, Nils, 275, 314
King, Timothy, 315, 336, 340, 341, 342,
    344, 356, 372, 376, 393, 398, 401,
    420, 433, 441, 444
Kippur, Stephen, 310, 315, 320, 321, 336,
    344, 345, 385, 387, 391, 392, 393,
    400, 402, 420
Kirkland, Caroline, 85
Kirkwood, Ernest, 376, 382
Klein, Sanford, 287
Kline, Clifford, 420
Knickerbocker, Diedrich, 39
Knopf, Alfred A., 217
Knoppers, Antonie, 220
Kouzes, James M., 389, 428
Kraham, Stephen, 348, 363, 401
Kraige, L. G., 186
Krane, Kenneth S., 250
Kranich, F. N., 139
Kritchevsky, David, 253
Kruk, Len, 233
Kuethe, Arnold, 148
Kugler, Francis, 96
Kulesa, Tom, 355
Kumar, Ranjit, 411
Kupferberg, Stella, 329
Kutz, Meyer, 310

L

Lacy, Dan, 221, 458
Ladd, Carl E., 135, 139
Lam, Willy Wo-Lap, 377, 415
Lane, Janet, 182
Lang, Sean, 404
Langfeld, Herbert, 165
Lansburgh, Richard, 114
Lautens, Gary, 297
Lawrence, D. H., 435
Lawrence, Ernest O., 206
Lawson, James, 45, 46
Leacock, Stephen, 297
Leavitt, Jonathan, 65
LeCato, Isabel, 169
Lee, Derek, 414
Lee, Robert E., 459
Lee, Tsai-Hwa, 249
Lencioni, Patrick, 389
Lennon, John, 266, 392
Lesley, Hubert, 172
Lesure, Alan B., 228, 278, 285, 310, 322
Lesure, Madelyn, 233, 422
Leung, Henry, 415
Levin, Harold, 362
Levin, Martin, 244
Lewis, Evelyn C., 157
Lewis, Nina, 233
Lewis, Susan, 392
Lewis, William, 356, 357
Leyh, Rick, 284, 310, 318
Licklider, J. C. R., 199, 277
Lieb, Charles, 220
Lieber, Francis, 89–90, 91, 98, 99
Lieberman, Bonnie, 344, 352, 353, 356, 362, 402, 420, 428
Lincoln, Abraham, 89
Lindzey, Gardner, 226, 249
Lipman, J. G., 139
Liss, Alan, 320, 381
Little, W. C., 96
Liu, Theresa, 417, 450
Lobdell, Francis, 193, 194, 195, 202, 224, 238
Locke, John, 6
London, Jack, 113
Long, George W., 63, 64
Long, Robert, 296, 340, 376, 405, 419
Longfellow, Henry Wadsworth, 59, 459
Lorrain, Claude, 107
Lorrain, Ghirlandaio, 107
Lovitt, George, 188
Low, John, 24
Lowell, Clotilda, 234
Lowell, James Russell, 88
Lowenthal, Marjorie Fiske, 392

Luckow, Lynn, 392
Luria, S. E., 15, 148, 213
Lusztig, Peter A., 410
Lyell, Charles, 88
Lyman, Frank, 354, 356, 357, 363
Lynch, Richard, 283
Lytton, Edward Bulwer, 43

M

Macaulay, Thomas Babington, 56
McClellan, Stephen, 288, 312, 313
McCracken, Daniel, 226, 248, 249, 330
McDaniel, Carl, 362
McDougal, Jack, 191
Macintosh, R. R., 435
McKenna, Jennifer, 324
Mackey, Thomas, 381
McKinnell, Henry, Jr., 426
McLean, Ephraim, 350
McMullin, Ruth, 15, 312, 314, 315, 316, 317, 318, 319, 325, 330, 336, 337, 342, 421
McNamara, Robert, 201
MacNeven, William, 34
MacPherson, Donald, 177
McRae, Bill, 404
Maddock, J. Kenneth, 177, 185, 200, 223
Madison, James, 32, 73
Mahan, Dennis H., 62, 63, 65, 99, 119, 128, 140
Mair, Steven, 403
Mandela, Nelson, 419
March, Jerry, 328
Marchetti, Joseph, 386
Marion, John, 426, 453
Maris, Nick, 356
Mark, Herman, 15, 226
Markowitz, Harry, 458
Marks, Elias, 34
Marshall, John, 90
Martin, David, 436
Martineau, Harriet, 90, 92
Marx, Karl, 6
Mason, William P., 141
Mast, S. O., 141
Matheson, Martin, 152, 153, 154, 179, 184, 190, 192, 202, 213, 231, 234, 251, 256
Mathews, Cornelius, 77, 88, 89, 90
Mathewson, C. H., 140
Matlin, Margaret, 362
Maxwell, Hugh, 37
Maxwell, Robert, 316, 325, 392
Mayer, Maria, 177

Mazzini, Giuseppe, 85
Meador, Rob, 352
Mee, F. E., 137, 152
Melhorn, Anna, 423
Mello, Craig C., 440
Melville, Herman, 13, 62, 82, 84, 85
Mennons, John, 45
Meriam, J. L., 186, 329
Merrill, William F., 170
Merriman, Mansfield, 14, 118, 134, 140
Mikulich, Marc, 394, 395
Milledoler, Philip, 69
Miller, John, 50, 58
Miller, Warren E., 230
Mills, Cliff, 308
Milne, A. A., 435
Milner, Karen, 411
Miron, Steven, 385, 414, 416, 418, 439, 450, 451
Mitchell, William E., 309
Moché, Dinah, 330
Montgomery, Robert, 282
Monypenny, John, 151
Moore, Thomas, 35, 90, 92
Moran, Michael J., 353
Morecroft, John, 151
Morgan, J. Pierpont, 103
Mori, Shozo, 320
Morley, Jean, 323, 324, 422
Morris, Christopher, 37
Morris, William, 106
Morse, Samuel F. B., 32
Morton, G. A., 151
Muller, Jörg, 373
Muller, Peter, 251, 252, 329, 348, 349, 350, 356
Murck, Barbara, 411
Murdoch, Rupert, 271, 316
Murphy, Gerald, 381
Murphy, Patrick, 445
Murray, John, 38, 78, 83
Musgnug, Charles, 124
Musser, Gary, 359

N

Nason, Alvin, 259
Nathans, Daniel, 440
Neale, John, 329, 411
Neilly, Andrew, 15, 167, 200, 221, 224, 233, 234, 239, 249, 251, 265, 266, 271–318, 336, 421, 424
Nelson, Frank, 216
Nelson, Gideon, 249
Neporent, Liz, 409

Neumann, Peter, 244
Neustadt, Richard, 230
Nevid, Jeffrey, 362
Nevins, Allan, 101
Newman, Harry, 295
Ng, Kwok K., 366
Nicdao, Fred, 235
Nielsen, Mark, 361
Niles, Hezekiah, 44, 45, 49
Nixon, Richard, 227
Noah, Mordecai Manuel, 32
Noble, Jonathan, 404
Normand, Marjorie, 370
Norris, Samuel E., 124, 152, 153, 193
Noyes, Henry, 300, 302
Noyori, Ryoji, 418
Nye, James, 348

O

O'Callaghan, Jay, 363
Ogilvy, David, 297
O'Grady, Eileen, 233
Olivieri, René, 432, 433, 436, 437, 438,
    439, 451
Olson, Larry, 386
Oman, William, 170
Omranloo, Mehdi, 419
O'Neil, Joan, 386, 387
O'Neill, Ellen, 233
Orlando, Marianne, 235, 278, 293, 295
Orr, John, 356, 357
Osborn, Richard N., 284
Osborne, Lydia, 53
Osgood, Elizabeth B., 7
O'Sullivan, John, 88

P

Pace, Kaye, 350, 353, 357, 363
Page, Louise, 369
Paley, Bill, 345
Parmelee, Maurice, 161
Paterson, William, 345
Patty, Frank Arthur, 287
Paulding, Hiram, 62
Paulding, James Kirke, 31, 32, 39, 51, 60
Pearce, Henry W., 24
Pearson, Frank A., 161
Peele, Robert, 162
Pender, Harold, 182
Penny, Scott, 354
Pentz, Ed, 372
Percival, James G., 47
Pershing, John "Black Jack," 147
Persons, Warren, 161

Pesce, William, 15, 330, 336, 338, 342,
    344, 345, 348, 350, 352, 353, 356,
    370, 371, 372, 377, 384, 385, 399,
    401, 403, 408, 419, 420, 426, 429,
    432, 433, 449, 452, 457, 459
Philip, Robert, 61
Pindar, Peter, 42
Pirsson, Louis, 129, 150
Platt, Isaac, 81
Pletscher, Tim, 229
Plutarch, 24
Poe, Edgar Allen, 62, 65, 75, 82, 86
Polhemus, Robert, 185, 278, 289, 324
Pope, Alexander, 24
Posner, Barry Z., 389, 428
Poulter, Angela, 405
Powers, W. L., 138
Pozycki, Steven J., 420
Pred, Allan, 213
Preston, Robert, 90
Prigogine, Ilya, 213
Prinz, Nancy, 352
Proskauer, Eric, 217, 218, 219, 222, 223,
    224, 225, 292
Przeworski, Adam, 213
Pugh, Kenneth, 390
Pulitzer, Joseph, 262
Putnam, George Palmer, 11–12, 13, 56,
    65–95, 113, 125, 133, 232, 456

Q

Quinlan, Gary, 310–311

R

Rafferty, Gertrude Genevieve, 7
Ramo, Simon, 226
Ramsey, Charles J., 14, 148, 166, 329
Ramsower, Harry C., 135
Rao, P. V. Narasimha, 415
Rathus, Spencer, 362
Raven, Peter, 362
Reagan, Ronald, 287, 288, 290
Redwood, Marjorie, 238
Reglein, Ned, 184
Resbane, Paul, 238
Resnick, Robert, 206, 250, 251, 285, 329,
    356
Reynolds, Edward, 277
Rice, Francis O., 177
Richards, Al, 223
Richards, Ellen H., 120
Richards, Thomas Addison, 79
Richards, William Cary, 79
Richardson, Sid, 425

Riche, Charles, 24
Riley, Isaac, 29, 31, 33, 34
Rinck, Gary, 344, 438, 445
Rivington, James, 42
Robbins, Kathleen, 445
Roberts, David, 420
Robertson, Mark, 437
Robey, Charity, 324
Robichaud, Cliff, 324
Robinson, Andrew, 438
Robinson, Gerald, 249
Robinson, M. R., 243
Robinson, William, 41
Rodman, John, 34
Roebling, John Augustus, 105, 116, 117
Roebling, Washington Augustus, 105, 112,
    116
Rogerson, James, 242, 296
Ross, Harold, 285
Ross, Haymo, 374
Rostow, W. W., 165
Rubin, Alan L., 404
Rubin, Dan, 295
Rubin, Laurie, 418
Rudick, Richard, 304, 305, 314, 320, 337,
    338, 344, 376, 420, 444
Runyon, Randolph, 192
Ruskin, John, 62, 106, 107
Russell, Bertrand, 337
Russell, Edward, 400
Russell, Lucy, 408
Ruth, Babe, 143

S

Sackville-West, Vita, 435
St. John, Gregory, 354, 357, 368, 370, 382,
    401, 421
Salas, Saturnino, 242
Saltrick, Susan, 353, 401
Sampson, Marmaduke, 79
Samuelson, Paul A., 437
Samuelsson, Marcus, 396
Sargent, Epes, 77
Saugman, Per, 433, 436, 437
Sawicki, Dennis, 233
Scalsky, William, 192
Schacher, Laurie, 233
Schermerhorn, John, 284, 409
Schetinnikov, Alexander, 354
Schetzer, Julius, 148
Schifferes, Justus J., 215, 226
Schlosberg, Suzanne, 409
Schoolcraft, Henry R., 37
Schowalter, Katherine, 320, 386
Schrödinger, Erwin, 109

Schuchert, Charles, 129, 457
Schultz, George P., 165
Schustack, Margie, 385–386, 421
Schwab, Bernhard, 410
Scott, Walter, 34, 48, 49, 56, 58
Scovill, H. T., 150
Scribner, Charles, 132
Scribner, Charles Jr., 169, 326
Scudder, John, 34
Seaborg, Glenn, 213
Searles, William H., 118, 129
Seely, Fred B., 14, 150
Seelye, Elwyn E., 194
Seminoff, Serje, 278, 310
Seybert, Adam, 44
Shakespeare, William, 24
Shapiro, Howard N., 353
Shaw, A. W., 217
Sheppard, Sheri D., 351
Sheridan, Philip, 112
Sherman, William Tecumseh, 112
Shewhart, Walter A., 150
Shirkov, D. V., 299
Shockley, William, 213
Shriner, Ralph L., 150
Shube, Beatrice, 235, 254, 328
Sidman, David, 372
Sigourney, Lydia, 85
Silberschatz, Abraham, 359
Silver, David, 309
Silver, Deirdre, 354, 357
Silverstein, Michael, 401
Silvester, W. Harold, 410
Simon, Herbert, 213
Skinner, B. F., 226
Skinner, Brian, 285
Sleeper, Catharine, 182, 183
Sleeper, Harold R., 14, 145, 148, 166, 182, 183, 329
Smith, Adam, 25, 43
Smith, Anne, 363
Smith, Bessie, 143
Smith, Elmer A., 193, 194
Smith, Guy H., 181
Smith, Howard Llewellyn, 434
Smith, John Jay, 78
Smith, Ralph, 408
Smith, Sally, 403, 404
Smith, Sidney, 44
Smith, Stephen, 344, 404, 413, 414, 415, 418, 420, 438, 450
Snyder, C. R., 309
Snyder, John, 185, 193, 195, 200
Sobel, David, 321
Solomons, T. W. Graham, 285, 348
Songqiao, Zhao, 302
Soros, George, 387, 418

Southey, Robert, 34
Spatz, Bruce, 358, 363
Spencer, John Canfield, 78
Spender, Stephen, 435
Spilka, Susan, 372, 401, 452, 453
Spring, Mike, 393
Sproull, Robert, 199, 220, 308, 425
Stacey, J. W., 182, 257
Stanley, George, 386, 390
Stark, Patty, 363
Staudinger, Hermann, 380
Staudinger, Karen, 410
Steentoft, Ove, 238
Stephens, William, 282
Stevens, Andrew, 372
Stevenson, David, 99
Stewart, Nathaniel, 287
Stilman, Galina, 244
Stilman, Leon, 244
Stokely, Frank E., 236
Stokes, Donald E., 230
Stoll, Charles, 185, 200, 202, 223, 277, 278, 295, 296, 302, 305, 309, 310, 316, 424, 433
Stoll, Lizanne, 235
Stone, Mead, 244
Stone, Walker, 200, 222, 223, 225
Stone, Walter G., 185
Story, Joseph, 90
Stowe, Harriet Beecher, 6
Strafella, Ronnie, 233
Strahler, Alan, 251, 253, 356
Strahler, Arthur, 148, 251, 253, 356
Stucky, Rita J., 309
Stukalin, Boris I., 243
Sullivan, Warren, 190, 192, 195, 200, 202, 232, 236, 239, 254
Suter, William, 223
Sutherland, Ivan, 248
Sutherland, William R. (Bert), 277, 307, 308, 314, 368, 370, 424
Sutter, William, 226
Suzuki, David, 388
Swanson, Eric, 320, 336, 337, 338, 340, 344, 346, 368, 370, 371, 381, 383, 384, 399, 405, 420, 433, 438, 439, 443
Swift, Jonathan, 24
Sze, Simon, 15, 366
Szostak, Jack W., 440
Szuprowicz, Bohdan, 287
Szuprowicz, Maria, 287

Talfourd, Thomas W., 77
Tan, Jaslyn, 11

Taylor, Diane, 403
Taylor, Frederick Winslow, 129
Taylor, Nadine, 404
Taylor, Thomas, 425
Teeter, T. A., 138
Telecki, George, 324, 421
Teller, Edward, 177, 230
Terlov, Fedor, 354
Thackeray, William Makepeace, 81
Tham, P. C., 414
Theil, Henri, 213
Thomas, Moses, 31
Thompson, Lee Northshield, 401
Thompson, W. A., 33, 35
Thoreau, Henry David, 87
Thurston, Robert H., 119, 140
Thye, Lenore Slater, 182
Tichy, H. J., 328
Tillinghast, Mary, 7, 20
Timbie, William Henry, 119, 127, 128, 129, 164, 183
Tinbergen, Nikolaas, 213
Tolkien, J. R. R., 435
Tolstoy, Leo, 75
tom Dieck, Heindirk, 377
Tongue, Benson H., 351
Tortora, Gerard, 356, 359, 360–361
Townsend, Andrew, 354, 370
Tracey, Ellie, 233
Trautwine, John, 117, 118, 119, 140
Trefil, James, 350
Trenholm, Barbara, 410
Triest, Rudolph, 169, 171, 193, 194
Trumbull, Jonathan, 73
Trundle, George T. Jr., 177
Tse-Tung, Mao, 300
Tsukabe, Hiroshi, 299, 418
Tucker, George, 51
Turban, Efraim, 350
Turner, J. M. W., 107
Twain, Mark, 48, 101, 330
Tyler, Royall, 41

Udall, Lynn, 405
Ulbricht, Tomlinson, 138
Unwin, Stanley, 159

V

Van Duzer, Theodore, 226
Van Dyck, Craig, 371, 372
Van Noorden, Peter, 408
Van Nostrand, David, 95, 99, 112, 113, 121, 151

Van Winkle, Cornelius, 30, 31, 34, 35, 36, 38
VanCleave, Janice, 388, 389
Vandenbempt, Ted, 244
Velterop, Jan, 442
Vernon, Thomas, 317
Vernoy, Mark, 312, 349
Verplanck, Gulian, 32, 51, 91
Volcker, Paul, 271
Voet, Donald, 15, 377
Voet, Judith, 15, 377
Volpe, Edmond L., 170
von Liebig, Julius, 62
Vsanova, Irina, 354

W

Waite, Verity, 402, 403
Waksman, Selman, 213
Walker, Jearl, 251, 354, 356
Wallwork, Nick, 415
Walmsley, Jon, 438, 439
Wanamaker, John, 254
Wang, Patricia, 300
Wardle, Thomas, 59
Warfield, Terry D., 282
Warnock, John, 322
Warren, Edward, 13
Warren, George F., 161
Warren, S. Edward, 119, 127, 140
Washington, George, 20
Watson, Ronald, 237, 238
Waugh, Evelyn, 435
Weatherbee, Scott D., 437
Weber, Jürgen, 404
Wee, Audrey, 414
Weed, Thurlow, 77
Weems, Mason, 33
Weiner, Howard, 359
Weiss, Harold, 249
Weiss, Rudi, 299
Weissberg, Jerry, 358
Welch, Jack, 317, 318
Weld, Harry, 165
Wellesley, Arthur, 34
Wells, Carolyn, 410
Wenner, Jann, 392
Westcott, Edward Noyes, 121
Westheimer, Ruth, 395
Weston, Abijah, 51
Wetherbe, James, 350
Weygandt, Jerry, 15, 227, 282, 283, 297,
        329, 348, 349, 409, 410
Wheeler, John, 177
Whelpley, Samuel, 31, 32, 33

Whinnery, John R., 226
White, Lazarus, 114
Whiteside, Burgess, 192, 235, 237, 238
Whitman, Walt, 83
Whitman, Walter G., 131
Whittelsey, Abigail, 62
Whittelsey, Samuel, 62
Whittier, John Greenleaf, 82
Wiecek, Irene, 410
Wiener, Norbert, 14, 148, 165, 177, 178,
        199, 431
Wiggins, Edward, 138
Wightwick, George, 96
Wilder, Robert, 309, 316, 336, 338, 340,
        344, 400, 425, 452
Wiley, Alice, 7, 124
Wiley, Charles (1782-1826), 1, 4, 7, 11, 13,
        17–53, 58, 63, 87, 122, 140, 257, 456
Wiley, Charles (1835-1916), 7, 60, 62, 102,
        104, 116, 124, 139, 140
Wiley, Deborah, 7, 170, 233, 234, 235, 263,
        274, 278, 306, 314, 324, 326, 420,
        426, 427, 428, 431, 440, 441, 444
Wiley, Elizabeth Osgood, 60
Wiley, Esther, 7, 169, 191, 192, 198, 199,
        227, 233, 235, 239, 240, 243, 244,
        247, 301, 302, 319
Wiley, Jesse, 7, 452
Wiley, John (1808-1891), 7, 11, 13, 26, 32,
        54–99, 125, 133, 444
Wiley, John "Jack" (1748-1829), 7, 20, 21
Wiley, John (1720-1760), 7, 20
Wiley, Lydia Osborn, 53, 59
Wiley, Osgood, 7, 60, 103, 106, 140, 146
Wiley, Peter Booth, 7, 233, 377, 399, 413,
        419, 420, 425, 426, 427, 428, 433,
        451, 452
Wiley, Sarah King, 7, 60, 104
Wiley, W. Bradford, 7, 15, 146, 165, 167,
        169, 170, 171, 190, 191, 192, 193,
        194, 195, 197, 198, 236–265, 267,
        268, 271, 273, 274, 275, 278, 283,
        284, 285, 294, 300, 301, 302, 303,
        304, 305, 306, 310, 312, 313, 314,
        315, 319, 322, 325, 326, 327, 328,
        336, 337, 344, 398, 399, 400, 420,
        421, 425, 426, 433, 435, 450, 457,
        458
Wiley, W. Bradford II, 7, 233, 314, 315,
        316, 317, 319, 324, 325, 327, 330,
        338, 377, 384, 418, 427, 428, 421,
        424, 425, 426, 450, 452
Wiley, William Carroll, 7, 169
Wiley, William Halsted (The Major), 7, 14,
        60, 102, 103, 104, 105, 106, 110,

111, 116, 118, 119, 120, 121, 124,
        126, 135, 137, 140-141, 381
Wiley, William O., 7, 14, 124, 126, 128,
        139, 140, 141, 144–171, 188, 192,
        197, 200, 381, 457
Wilkinson, Geoffrey, 213, 328
Wilkinson, Lawrence, 340
Wille, Eva, 377, 399
Williams, Barbara, 312, 349
Williams, Kenneth, 151
Williams, S. Wells, 74
Williamson, Hugh, 49
Wilson, David, 403
Wilson, E. D., 151
Wilson, Edmund O., 179
Wilson, Edwin, 151
Wilson, Larry, 306–307, 311, 313
Wilson, Robert E., 223
Wilson, Thomas, 247
Wilson, Woodrow, 120
Wirt, Frederick, 137
Wittman, Alan, 289
Wood, De Volson, 126, 127
Wood, Diane, 410
Woods, Julia, 411
Woods, Samuel, 24
Woodward, Robert, 134
Wright, Geoff, 409
Wright, J. C., 132, 161
Wu, Harry, 417
Wylly, Alexander, 41

X

Xiaoping, Deng, 416
Xu, Zhilun, 416, 417

Y

Yeats, William Butler, 440
Yen Mah, Adeline, 387
Young, Nicola, 410

Z

Zak, Theresa, 321
Zemin, Jiang, 416
Zerter, William, 410, 411
Zollman, Dean A., 309
Zworykin, Vladimir, 151

NAME INDEX

Subject Index

A

Abnormal Psychology (Davison and Neale), 411
academic conferences, marketing at, 181–182
academic libraries, 115
Academic Press
  in CrossRef development, 372
  online journal licensing, 371
Accounting Principles (Weygandt, Kieso, Kell), 349
The Accounting Review, 282
acquisitions (book). *See also* mergers and acquisitions
  in 1980s, 327
  Houghton Mifflin list (1994), 359
  International Thompson list, 362
  Pearson textbook list (1999), 359
  postwar years, 176–177
  STM, 373–380
Actions of Poisons, 35
Addison-Wesley
  Pearson acquisition, 273
  profitability (1976), 247
  as Wiley competitor (1980s), 281
An Address on Primary Education, 73
Advanced Inorganic Chemistry (Cotton and Wilkinson), 328
Advanced Organic Chemistry (March), 328
Advanced Research Projects Agency (ARPA), 199
Advances in Plasma Physics, 212
The Adventures of Captain Bonneville (Irving), 39
advertising. *See also* promotion
  in books, 114
  books (1958), 256
  during Great Depression, 161–162
  in-house, 181
  Wiley (1870), 114
  Wiley (1913), 114
  Wiley, in mass-media publications, 130, 179
  Wiley selected titles (1924), 131
  word-of-mouth, 256
Aeronautics (Wilson), 151
Against the Gods: The Remarkable Story of Risk (Bernstein), 387, 388
Agricultural Engineering (Davidson), 136
agricultural science series, 134–139
Airplane Maintenance (Lesley), 172

AITRC (Applied Information Technologies Research Consortium), 328
Alan R. Liss, 319–320, 324, 332
The Alchemy of Finance (Soros), 418
The Algerine Captive (Tyler), 41
Allyn & Bacon, 247
Alpha-Omega, 306
Amazon.com
  AmazonConnect, 450
  detailed information from, 5
  e-mail blasts, 450
  publisher data feeds, 390
  sales force, 390
  Search Inside the Book, 450
  STM book visibility, 384
  Wiley backlist access, 388
  Wiley support, 450
America, Russia, and the Cold War (LaFeber), 208
American Almanac, 78
American Book Circular (Wiley & Putnam), 80
American Book Council, 243
American Civil Engineers' Pocket Book (Merriman), 118
American Facts, 89
American Geophysical Union v. Texaco Inc., 304
American Heritage Publishing, 217
American House Carpenter (Hatfield), 96
American Institute of Architects (AIA), 167
American International Copyright Association (AICA), 92
American Library Association, 208
American literature
  in 1820s, 45
  Charles Wiley publication of, 45–47
  emergence, 44–47
  hindered by U.S. copyright law, 91
  Putnam publishing built on, 95
  status (1838), 45
  status (1868), 45
American Machinists' Handbook, 113
American Monthly Magazine, 61–62
American Notes, 57
The American Practical Brewer and Tanner (Coppinger), 34
American Review, 81
American Revolution, 20, 21, 22

American Textbook Publishers Institute, 185, 243
The American Voter (Campbell), 230
Analectic Magazine, 31
Analytic Trigonometry with Applications (Barnett), 362
Analytical Mechanics for Engineers (Seely and Ensign), 14, 141, 150
The Anatomical Record, 381
Anatomy and Physiology: From Science to Life (Jenkins, Kemnitz, and Tortora), 361
Anatomy of Melancholy (Burton), 73
Angewandte Chemie, 382
Angus Robertson, 236
Animal Parasites and Human Diseases (Chandler), 141
Ann Arbor Science, 239
Annalen der Physik, 380
Annals of American Bookselling (Boynton), 164
antebellum America, 65–73
Appeal to Common Sense and Common Justice (Carey), 44
Appleton-Century-Crofts, 271
Applied Calculus (Hughes-Hallett et al.)*,* 352
Applied Elasticity (Xu), 416
Applied Information Technologies Research Consortium (AITRC), 328
Architects' and Builders' Handbook (Kidder), 120
Architectural Graphic Standards (Ramsey and Sleeper), 166–167, 387, 391
  copies sold, 145
  as landmark, 145, 167
  longevity, 165
  seventy-fifth anniversary, 329–330
  as Wiley success, 166
  in Wiley timeline, 14, 148
Arcturus (Duyckinck), 81
Argonne National Laboratory, 209–210
Armstrong Cork Company, 209
ARPA (Advanced Research Projects Agency), 199
art department
  evolution, 258–259
  formation, 258
  in-house, 257
  type stamping, 259
The Art of Weaving, 89
Arthritis For Dummies (Fox and Taylor), 404
arXiv, 368
Ascent to Orbit (Clarke), 288
Asia. *See also* Jacaranda Wiley; Japan
  economies for production services, 451
  journal sales, 413
  management team, 415
  market, 450–451
  operating plan (1993), 412
  potential (early 1990s), 412
  renewal, 413
  revenue growth, 414
  Shanghai office, 450
  Singapore operation, 412, 450
  strengthening ties (1992), 414
  Tokyo office, 415
  trade books, 415
Asia Publishing Company, 192
Association of American Publishers, 304, 428
Astoria (Irving), 39
Astronomische Nachrichten, 380
Astronomy (Moché), 330
Atheneum Press, 231
atheneums, 25
Atomic Physics and Human Knowledge (Bohr), 177
The Atrium, 11
audio market, 309
Auditing Procedure (Eggleston), 127–128
Australia. *See also* Jacaranda Wiley; Wiley Australia
  Australian dollar decline (late 1990s), 408
  for exports (postwar years), 189, 190
  in global publishing, 405–409
  market (early 1960s), 240
  textbook publishing (1990s), 405
  as Wiley's second outpost, 405
authors
  American, 44
  American, British reprinting of books and, 91–92
  book promotion, 254
  during Brad Wiley years, 213
  editor relationships, 128–129
  electronic manuscripts (1986), 323–324
  Footnotes newsletter for, 176, 188
  foreign, U.S. copyright law and, 91
  guidelines (1979), 262
  in Higher Education turnaround, 349
  indexes, 137, 155
  loyalty, Great Depression, 164–165
  mistakes (1950s), 155
  New York publisher attraction (early 1800s), 27
  remuneration for, 253
  royalties, capping, 137
  style guidelines (1920s), 154
  textbook (early 1900s), 126–127
  typewriter use (1920s), 154
  Wiley & Putnam, 82–88
Automotive Repair (Wright), 132

B

Babbling April (Greene), 435
baby boom, 204
The Background of International Relations (Hodges), 161
backlists
  as backbone, 328–329
  Ronald Press, 232
  strength (1980s), 282, 329

Wiley sales (1962), 222
Wiley trade, 388
Ballinger, 239
Bantam, 271
Barnes & Noble, 387, 390
Basic Books, 230
Basic Books, Inc. v. Kinko's Graphics Corp., 304
Basic Programming (Kemeny and Kurtz), 226
Basic Radio Principles, 173
BASIC for Home Computers (Albrecht, Finkel, and Brown), 287
Bass Management Trust, 425
Becker & Hayes, 231, 265
Becker Brothers Engraving, 164
Behavior Therapy, 208
Belhaven Press acquisition, 373
Bell Telephone Laboratories, 209
Bell Telephone System, 108
belles lettres, 80–81
Benjamin Cummings, as Wiley competitor (1980s), 281
Berlin Wall, 332, 333
Berne Convention, 305
Berne office, 403
Berners-Lee browser, 334
Bertelsmann, 271, 273
Betty Crocker Baking for Today, 397
Betty Crocker Cookbook, 396, 397
Betty Crocker Sunday Dinner Cookbook, 397
Bibles, 37
bibliographies, guidelines (1979), 262
Bibliotheca Sacra, 79
Big Deal, 371
"big-box" stores, 387
bindings, perfect, 157
Biochemical Preparations (Carter), 148
Biochemical Preparations Series, 177–179
Biochemistry (Voet and Voet), 15, 377
Biographia Literaria (Coleridge), 35
biography titles, Charles Wiley & Co., 36
Biology of Cells, 208
biology publications (1926–1956), 149
Biomedical-Health Division (1971–1976), 232
birth rates, baby boom, 203
Black Monday stock market collapse, 335
Blackwell Publishing, 239. *See also* Wiley-Blackwell
    acquisition announcement, 432
    beginnings, 434
    Broad St., Oxford bookstore, 435
    BSP merger, 437
    courtship, 433–439
    exclusive purchase offer, 433
    as foremost academic and professional publisher, 432
    journals publication (1990s), 436–437
    medical publishing, 435
    offices, 432
    postwar period, 435–436
    profile, 434–437
    publications, 432
    publishing program, 432
    school publishing, 435
    shareholder commitments, 432
    Synergy, 441
    tradition, 434
    Wiley acquisition of, 382, 398, 432–441
Blackwell Scientific Publications (BSP), 435, 436, 437
Blackwood's Magazine, 78
Blanchard & Lea, 97
board of directors
    during 1985 challenges, 315
    Bass Management Trust share purchase, 425
    under Brad II, 424
    family control opinions, 426
    first-class and second-class directors, 220
    governance committee, 452
    makeup (1990s), 424–425
    outside, 220
    recruitment (1980s and 1990s), 424
    Taylor as member, 425–426
    Wiley family election, 12
    Wiley family influence (2000s), 426–427
Bohr-Wheeler project file, 177
The Bon Appétit Cookbook, 396
book agents, John Wiley as, 60
book clubs
    New Yorker suggestion, 25
    post-Civil War, 130
book exchanges, 41
book fairs, 97–98
Book Industry International Trade Committee, 246
Book Industry Study Group, 286, 428
book prices
    computer program determination, 254
    early 1900s, 129–130
    postwar years, 184
    publisher comparison, 253
    setting (1960s), 251–252
Book Project Management, 401
Book Publishing in the U.S.S.R., 243
book trade. *See also* publishing industry
    competition (1820s), 42–43
    cooperation (1820s), 41, 42
    as cutthroat, 43
    in early 1800s, 26–28
    networks of friends and advisors, 41
    New York as center, 26–27
bookbinding (1820s to 1850s), 72
books
    between the wars, 155–159
    as business, 6
    changes in, 4
    demand (1820), 24–25

books *(continued)*
  demand, literacy rates and, 68
  in early 1800s, 24
  as early republic medium, 25
  equities comparison, 458
  formats of today, 4
  as gifts (1840s), 69
  marketing (early 1900s), 129–133
  parts of, 4
  physical changes, 4
  price decline (1840s), 66
  quality, 4
  quality and sales relationship, 459
  in securing debts, 41
  specialized, 132
  by subscription, 33
BookScan, 5
booksellers
  in early 1800s, 33
  publisher relationship (postwar years), 193
  retailer discounts, 254, 255
  Wiley titles on the shelves, 255
bookselling
  in 1950s and 1960s, 254
  changes in, 4–5
  instant statistics, 5
  printing and publishing combination (early 1800s), 32
bookstore, Charles Wiley (Wall Street)
  in 1814, 31
  in 1819, 37
  advertisements, 35
  reaching customers with, 33
  reason for starting, 32
bookstore, John Wiley
  Broadway, 63, 65, 95
  first book published, 60
  map sales, 62
  Nassau Street, 60
bookstores
  chains, 387
  college, 255
  independent, decline of, 390
  as "natural resorts for the intellectual class" (1834), 61
The Book Without a Name, 77
Borders, 387
Boston Atheneum, 67
Boyd & Fraser, 273
Braunworth, 163
Bread and Cheese Club, 50
Brief Remarks on the Proposed New Tariff, 35
Britain
  50–50 company partnerships, 236
  book market in U.S. (1830–1853), 94, 95
  book pirating, 22
  financial panic, 58

reciprocity treaty with, 93
  Wiley book marketing (post-Civil War), 133–134
British Diabetic Association (BDA), 433
British History For Dummies (Lang), 404
The British Journal of Surgery, 377, 382
Broadcast Advertising (Arnold), 151
Brooklyn Bridge, 105
budgets, first (1951), 195
Building Construction Illustrated (Ching), 391
Business, Law, and General Books
  growth (late 1980s), 320
  in mid-1980s, 315
  revenue, 385
business publications (1926–1956), 149

C

Calculus (Hughes-Hallett and Gleason), 352, 377, 419
Calculus (Salas and Hille), 242
Calculus Consortium, 352
Call of the Wild (London), 113
Canada. *See also* Wiley Canada
  in global publishing, 409–412
  recession, 410
Cancer, 377
capital
  market successes, 265
  outside sources, 203
captains of industry, 101, 103
Carey & Lea
  1826 communication, 58–59
  Cooper and, 51, 52
  John Wiley as agent (1829), 60
Cases of Morbid Anatomy (Francis), 34
Catskill Water Supply of New York (White), 114
CD-Physics, 354, 356, 358
CERN (European Organization for Nuclear Research), 334, 335
Chantilly office, 403
Chapman & Hall, 191, 235
  discount and exchange rates, 236
  management consultant, 134
  relationship end, 237
  resistance, 236
  Wiley book supply, 192
  Wiley partnership, 133–134, 191
Characteristics of Women: Moral, Poetical, and Historical (Jameson), 60
Charles E. Merrill & Co., 108
Charles E. Tuttle Company, 241
Charles Scribner's Sons, 297
Charles Wiley & Co.
  formation, 35
  liquidity problems, 36
  printing and publishing program, 36

title pages, 36
titles published by, 36
Charles Wiley print shop. *See also* print shops
  apprenticeship, 29
  beginning, 29–31
  division of labor, 30
  Hudson Street, 30
  partners, 29
  Provost Street, 30
  Reade Street, 30
Chemical Examination of the Mineral Water of Schooley's Mountain (MacNeven), 34
The Chemical Journal, 418
Chemistry, A European Journal, 377
Chemistry, As Exemplifying the Wisdom and Beneficence of God (Fownes), 80
chemistry field, 12
chemistry publications
  Wiley (1926–1956), 149
  Wiley (1980s), 285
Chichester offices, 239, 246. *See also* John Wiley & Sons Ltd.; United Kingdom
Chilton and Litton, 271
Chilton Tractor Journal, 138
China
  book pirating, 303
  Brad Wiley approach, 300–302
  changing face of (1970s), 300–302
  Chinese For Dummies translation program, 417
  Chinese-language editions, 300
  co-publishing program, 417
  copyright laws, 305
  government response to piracy, 416
  Science Press co-publishing, 302
  SSTP co-publishing agreement, 303
  STM books, 416
  STM editors, 451
  textbook market, 417
  U.S. relations, 268
  Wiley business in, 302–303
  World Trade Organization membership, 416–417
China Academic Library Information System (CALIS), 417
China Academic Publishers, 302
China After Deng Xiaoping (Lam), 377, 415
China's Century (Brahm), 404
Chinese For Dummies translation program, 417
Cholesterol (Kritchevsky), 253
Christian Experience, or, A Guide to the Perplexed (Philip), 61
chromolithography, 122
Chronology, or, An Introduction and Index to Universal History, Biography, and Useful Knowledge (Putnam), 65
Chrysler Building, 144, 145
Church of the Puritans, 59
Circuits (Irwin), 359
circulating libraries, 25

City Tavern (New York), 49
Civil Engineer's Pocket-Book (Trautwine), 118, 119, 140
Civil War
  public library trend and, 67–68
  Putnam and, 76
Clinton's Ditch, 53
Cochrane Collaboration, 381
Cochrane Library, 444
Cognition (Matlin), 362
cold type
  defined, 260
  revolution, 260–261
Cold War
  arms race, 207
  fears, 206
  libraries during, 207–208
collaboration, 346, 429
A Collection of Prayers, 34
College Algebra and Trigonometry (Durbin), 258
College Division
  in 1967, 224
  in 1984, 286
  health, physical education, and recreation list sale, 316
  layoffs (mid-1980s), 313
college enrollment
  by age 18–24, in the United States (1963–1979), 205
  in 1840s and 1850s, 69
  in 1939, 171
  in 1946–1978, 204
  in 1960s and 1970s, 204
  in 1980–1990, 271
  in 1990–2004, 347
  in 1990s, 342
college libraries. *See also* libraries
  construction (1960s and 1970s), 208–209
  government subsidies, 209
  number of (1990), 273
college travelers, 170, 185
colleges
  bookstores, 255
  curricula changes (1960s through 1980s), 281
  foreign, technical books, 191
  graduate students (1950s to 1970s), 204
  landscape (1992), 347
  nontraditional students (1980s), 278
  science and (post-Civil War), 109–110
  student focus groups, 353
colophons, 132
The Coming Computer Industry Shakeout (McClellan), 288, 312, 313
Common Stocks for Common Sense Investors (Mitchell and Ireland), 309
communication
  company strategies, 453
  with investor community, 452–453
  technology, 108

Communist Manifesto (Marx), 6
competition
    in 1820s book trade, 42–43
    cutthroat, 43
    during Great Depression, 160
    educational publishing (1980s), 281
competition *(continued)*
    global, threat, 273
    open-market, 443
    publisher (1980s), 271
    World War II, 173–175
A Complete Treatise on Field Fortification (Mahan), 64, 65
complimentary books, 280
computers
    in 1990s, 420–421
    billing and payroll (1960), 203, 249
    book sales downturn, 313
    e-mail, 420–421
    Hewlett-Packard 3000, 323
    IBM 360-30, 257
    IBM 650, 249
    IBM 4341 mainframe, 322
    impact on education (early 1960s), 199
    NeXT, 335
    PCs, 321
    positive feedback cycle, 249
    in production (early 1980s), 322–323
    program for price determination, 254
    Wang VS80, 323
    Wiley and, 248
    Wiley WAN, 401
Concrete, Plain and Reinforced (Taylor), 129
Condominiums and Cooperatives (Clurman and Hebard), 230–231
Conjectural Inquiry into the Relative Influence of the Mind and Stomach (Marks), 34
Conservation of Our Natural Resources (Smith), 181
consumer price index (1969–2005), 262
Contemporary Systems Corporation, 228, 265
Content Technology initiative, 456
continuity products, 339
Continuous Frames of Reinforced Concrete (Cross and Morgan), 150
cookbooks
    Hungry Minds titles, 396, 397
    Van Winkle & Wiley, 33
copyright
    challenge (late 1970s and 1980s), 304–305
    protection, 12, 444–445
    Wiley executives in campaign, 444–445
Copyright Act of 1831, 92
Copyright Act of 1976, 201
Copyright Amendment Act, 56
Copyright Clearance Center (CCC), 304
copyright laws
    of 1790, 26
    of 1802, 26
    of 1891, 1893, 1895, 133
    of 1909, 133
    China (1980s), 305
    early, 11
    international, 60, 89–93
    nineteenth century, 43
    U.S., 91
CORE information system, 400–401
corporate libraries, 209
Corporate Management Group (CMG), 234
corporate training, 278, 306
corporation
    dividends, 140
    first structure as, 139–140
    joint-stock, transition to, 200
    performance (early 1900s), 140–141
The Cost of Cleanness, 119
Cottage Residences (Downing), 75–77, 166
Council for the Advancement of Technical Writing, 246
Council of Islamic Revolution, 268
cousin years. *See* fourth generation
The Creative Mystique (Silver), 309
Cricket For Dummies (Knight), 409
cross-divisional teams, 346
CrossRef, 372
The Culinary Institute of America, 9, 391, 396
culinary publishing, 396, 397
Curling For Dummies (Weeks), 450
curriculum reform movement, 351–352
Curtis G. Benjamin Award, 201
Customer Relationship Management (Brown), 412
Cybernetics (Wiener), 14, 148, 165, 177, 178
Cyclotron, 206, 207

D

D. Appleton, 97
D.C. Heath, 337
Dairy Engineering (1925), 6
dairy engineering, 137
Das dämliche Geschlecht (Bierach), 404
David Harum: A Story of American Life (Westcott), 121
debts, book security, 41
delivery formats, 9–10
Dellen, 273
Deltak, 306
Democratic Review, 89
Demographics. *See also* college enrollment
    after 1990–1991 recession, 342
    publishing environment and, 203
    shifts, Higher Education capitalizing on, 448
    U.S. population (1950–1980), 204
The Den, 32

designers
　　in digital production, 422
　　textbook, 184
　　yesterday and today, 5
Devotional Somnium, 34
DeVry, 347
Diabetes For Dummies (Javic and Rubin), 404
Diabetic Medicine, 433
The Dial, 85
Dictionary of Architecture, 208
Digital Computer Programming (McCracken), 226, 249
Digital Object Identifier (DOI) technology, 372
Digital Photography For Dummies, 396
digital production
　　content management, 423
　　design, 422
　　distribution, 423
　　electronic books, 423
　　file sharing, 423
　　PDF format, 422
　　print on demand (POD), 422–423
　　typesetting, 422
Dillon's University Bookshop, 236
direct mailings
　　effectiveness measurement, 256
　　McGraw-Hill, 236
　　post-Civil War, 131–132
　　postwar, 179
　　for specialized books, 132
Directory of Medical Research, 296
Discover Wiley initiative, 456
Diseases of Old Age (Scudder), 34
Disquisition on Imprisonment for Debt and Prohibiting Slavery
　　　　in . . . Missouri, 36
distillery (John "Jack" Wiley), 21
distilling, 21–22
distribution centers (Wiley)
　　Somerset, 257, 274
　　Utah, 275, 316
distribution systems
　　in 1920s, 156
　　in 1990s, 340
　　in-house, 257
　　of today, 5
　　World Wide Web impact, 423
The Diverting History of John Bull and Brother Jonathan
　　　　(Paulding), 31
doctorates
　　awarded by major field in the United States (1920–1999), 291
　　in the United States (1900–1999), 290
Doing Business with the People's Republic of China (Szuprowicz),
　　　　287
Don Quixote (Cervantes), 34
DOS For Dummies (Gookin), 394
Doubleday, 175, 216, 271

Down East Publications, 275
Dreamtech acquisition, 416
Dryden Press, 271
The Durability of Prepared Roll Roofings (Davidson), 136
Dynamics of the Airplane (Williams), 151

E

earnings. *See also* revenue
　　Wiley (1956), 211
　　Wiley (1957–1969), 212
　　Wiley (1957), 211
　　Wiley (1971–1979), 265
　　Wiley (1978), 274
　　Wiley (1979–1983), 268
　　Wiley (1980–1990), 311
　　Wiley (1991–1998), 342
　　Wiley (1992–2002), 429
earnings per diluted share
Wiley (1989–2007), 346
Wiley (1997–2007), 455
The Earth Through Time (Levin), 362
Eastern Distribution Center (EDC). *See also* distribution centers
　　capacity increase, 316–317
　　worker cost-of-living increase demand, 274
　　worker strike, 275
e-books. *See also eGrade Plus* and *WileyPLUS*
　　characteristics, 423
　　legal protection, 445
Economic Aspects of State Socialism (Smith), 434
economic policy titles, Wiley & Putnam, 73–74
The Economist Bookshop, 236
economy
　　in 1979, 268
　　industrialized, 108–110
　　world (1990s), 398
eCORE, 401
Edinburgh Review, 78
editorial operation
　　Canada, 411
　　For Dummies process, 395
　　head (1954), 185
　　in-house (Wiley-VCH), 376
　　internalizing, 257
　　in reorganization (1964), 222–223
　　strategy (Wiley fourth generation), 149
　　United Kingdom, 295
editors
　　author relationships, 128–129
　　craft, 5
　　data on books, 254
　　high-quality products and, 232
　　Interscience, 221
　　Random House, 254

editors *(continued)*
  reviewers and (1922), 128
  series, 128, 134, 137, 139
  STM, 451
education
  college (1840s and 1850s), 69
  late 1920s, 156–157
  public and private (1850), 68
  shifts in (1946–1978), 203–204
Education Reform, 73
Educational Division
  in 1979, 275
  in 1982, 278
  in 1989, 347
educational publishing. *See also* textbooks
  competition (1980s), 281
  decision point, 279
  demand elasticity, 280
  faculty word processing training, 286
  market (1980s), 279–286
  nontraditional students, 285–286
  profits (1980s), 281
  titles (Wiley & Putnam), 73
Effective Writing for Engineers (Tichy), 328
The Effective Woman Manager (Stewart), 287
eGrade Plus, 355, 357, 358, 359, 377, 401
Electrical Engineers' Handbook (Pender), 182
electrical publications (1926–1956), 149
Electron Optics and the Electron Microscope (Zworykin), 151
Electronic Journal of Theoretical Chemistry, 403
electronic manuscripts, 324
electronic technology products (1991), 339
Elementary Nuclear Theory (Bethe), 177
Elements of Calculus (Granville), 129
Elements of Descriptive Geometry (Warren), 13, 127, 140
Elements of Electricity (Timbie), 128, 174
Ellis, Charles
  acquisitions war chest, 342
  as CEO, 337
  fiscal 1993 as turning point, 339–340
  focus and renewal, 336–338
  leadership, 429
  in McMullin's tenure, 337
  management styles, 336
  as new leader, 336
  Professional/Trade beginnings, 385–386
  profile, 337
  as Publishing Division president, 336
  reasonable goals, 340
  renewal plan, 338–343
  team, 336–337, 338
  VCH acquisition, 373
Elmtown's Youth: The Impact of Social Classes on Adolescents (Hollingshead), 181

Elsevier
  Ellis work at, 337
  Reed merger, 376
  in VCH bidding, 373
e-mail, 420–421
Empire of Brazil (Kidder), 89
employees
  in 1914, 124
  in 1945, 175
  during turnaround period, 318
  layoffs (mid-1980s), 313
  in mid 1960s, 222
  number of (2007), 12
  stock options, 234
  Training and Educational Services (TES), 357
  in turnaround, 318, 327
  turnover, drop (1990s), 340
  Wiley hiring effort (1950s), 185
employer reputation, 200
The Emporium of Arts & Sciences, 44
Encouragement of Domestic Manufacturers, 35
Encyclopedia Americana, 90
Encyclopedia of Chemical Technology (Kirk-Othmer), 219, 288, 308, 383, 384
Encyclopedia of Polymer Science and Technology (Mark, Gaylord, and Bikales), 15, 226, 383, 384
engineering
  classroom (early 2000s), 351
  education (post-Civil War), 116
  field, 12
  knowledge growth, 117–118
  list downturn (1980s), 281
  need (post-Civil War), 117–118
  in post-Civil War period, 116–121
Engineering, Science, and Management War Training (ESMWT) program, 172
Engineering for Dams (Creager and Justin), 129
Engineering Mechanics (Meriam), 329
engineering titles
  John Wiley, 65
  Wiley (post-Civil War), 118–119
  Wiley (1926–1956), 149
Environment (Raven and Berg), 362
Equipment for the Farm and the Farmstead (Ramsower), 135
Erie Canal, 52
Ernst & Young Tax Guide, 387
Essay on Language, As Connected with the Faculties of Mind (Cardell), 51
An Essay on the Botanical, Chemical, and Medical Properties of the Fucus Edulis of Linnaeus (Griffen), 35
Essay on the Doctrine of Contracts (Verplanck), 51
Essentials of Electricity (Timbie), 128
Essentials of General Anaesthesia (Macintosh), 435
Essentials of Healthier Living (Schifferes), 215, 226

Essentials of Modern Biology (Nason), 259
Essentials of Modern Investments (Jones), 329
Europe
    journals (Wiley-VCH), 377–380
    library restocking (postwar), 189
    Wiley strategy (postwar years), 191
European Journal of Inorganic Chemistry, 377
European Journal of Organic Chemistry, 377
European Organization for Nuclear Research (CERN), 334, 335
Event Planning (Allen), 412
Evolution, Genetics, and Man (Dobzhansky), 148, 182
Examination of Water (Mason), 141
Excuses (Snyder and Higgins), 309
Experimental Electrical Engineering (Karapetoff), 164
Export Division, 190, 192
exports. *See also* overseas markets
    beginnings, 134
    development (postwar years), 189–192
    statistics (1950), 192
Extensible Markup Language (XML), 423
An Extract of a Translation of the History of New Sweed Land, 34

F

F. H. Gilson Company, 123, 164
Faculty Resource Network. *See* Wiley Faculty Network.
fairs, literary, 26
Falling Leaves: Memoir of an Unwanted Chinese Daughter
    (Yen Mah), 387
family companies, 20
family control
    basis, 427
    board of directors' opinions, 426
    concern, 428
    as disadvantage, 12
    independence, 429
    institutionalized relationship, 429
    patience, 428
    Wiley, 12
family trusts, 264
Fanny (Halleck), 36, 46
Farewell to Poverty (Parmelee), 161
Farm Buildings (Foster and Carter), 138
Farm Machinery and Farm Motors (Davison), 136
Farm Poultry Houses (Davidson), 136
FASB (Financial Accounting Standards Board), 282
Father's Magazine, 62
fiction
    post-Civil War, 130
    Wiley & Putnam, 75
Field Engineering: A Hand-Book of the Theory and Practice of
    Railway Surveying, Location and Construction (Searles), 118
Field Engineering (Searles), 129
Field Fortifications (Mahan), 140

Field Practice of Laying Out Circular Curves for Railroads
    (Trautwine), 117
Fields and Waves in Communication Electronics (Ramo, Whinnery,
    and Van Duzer), 226
The Field of Waterloo: A Poem (Scott), 34
Financial Accounting: Tools for Business Decision-Making
    (Weygandt, Kieso, and Kimmel), 410
Financial Accounting (Hoskin), 410
Financial Accounting (Kieso and Weygandt), 282
Financial Accounting Standards Board (FASB), 282
Financial Institutions, Markets, and Money (Kidwell), 362
Financial Times company ranking, 342, 343
financing, postwar, 217
The Five Dysfunctions of a Team (Kouzes and Posner), 389
Five Points district (New York), 19, 57
The Five Temptations of a CEO (Lencioni), 389
Follett College Book Company, 279, 280
footnotes
    guidelines (1979), 262
    in manuscript guidelines, 152
Footnotes newsletter, 176, 188
For Dummies. *See also* Hungry Minds
    acquisition, 336, 394–395
    editorial process, 395
    history, 394–395
    start of, 394
    success, 395
    template, 395
    translations, 395–396
    as Wiley publications, 6
    Wiley U.K. titles, 404
Forecasting Business Cycles (Persons), 161
foreign sales. *See also* sales
    nontariff barriers, 242
    tariffs, 242
    Wiley (1960–1962), 222
foreign subsidiary establishment, 235–236
foreign-sales hedge, 189
Formula One Racing For Dummies (Noble and Hughes), 404
Foundations: Design and Practice (Seelye), 194
Foundations of Aerodynamics (Kuethe and Schetzer), 148
Foundations of College Chemistry (Hein and Arena), 362
Fourth Avenue offices
    changes, 176
    interior (1950), 180
    PBX system, 176
    photograph (1950), 180
    Wiley fourth generation, 147
fourth generation
    author loyalty, 164–165
    editorial strategy, 149
    in Great Depression, 160–164
    knowledge publishing, 150–151
    number of first editions (1926–1956), 149
    publication by category, 149

fourth generation *(continued)*
    systemization and standardized procedures, 152
    takeover of, 146
    tradition and innovation, 147
    Wiley spirit, 148
frames, 28–29
Frank J Fabozzi acquisition, 393
Franklin Book Program, 247
Franklin Company, 30
Freeman, as Wiley competitor (1980s), 281
French Revolution, 22
From DNA to Diversity (Carroll, Grenier, and Weatherbee), 437
Frommer's Brazil (Blore and de Vries), 404
Frommer's British Columbia and the Canadian Rockies (McRae and Blore), 404
The Fruits and Fruit Trees of America (Downing), 99
Functions Modeling Change: A Preparation for Calculus (Connally et al.), 352
Fundamental Concepts of Biology (Nelson and Robinson), 249
Fundamental Radio Experiments (Higgy), 173
Fundamentals of Engineering Thermodynamics (Moran and Shapiro), 353
Fundamentals of Physics (Halliday, Resnick, and Walker), 251
Fundamentals of Plasma Physics (Golant), 299

G

G. J. Peters, 123
G. P. Putnam & Sons, 76
GAAP (Generally Accepted Accounting Principles), 282
The Game, 20th Anniversary Edition (Dryden), 412
Gas Engines for the Farm (Hirshfeld and Ulbricht), 138
General Chemistry (Brady and Humiston), 242
General Chemistry (Deming), 151
General Electric, 165, 209
General Theory of Relativity (Dirac), 227
General Virology (Luria), 148
Generally Accepted Accounting Principles (GAAP), 282
GeoDiscoveries, 355, 356
Geography: Realms, Regions, and Concepts (de Blij and Muller), 227, 350, 355
geography titles
    franchise teams, 251
    Wiley (1980s), 285
    Wiley publication of, 252–253
Germany
    John Wiley & Sons GmbH, 241–242
    Professional/Trade publishing, 404
Gesellschaft Deutscher Chemiker (GDCh), 376
Giant Brains or Machines That Think (Berkeley), 177
gift books, 68, 69
Gilded Age, 103
Ginn and Company
    agricultural science publication, 135
    calculus market, 129

going public, 217
    as Wiley competitor, 113–114
    Wiley purchase of textbook list, 229
    Xerox purchase, 263
Global Business Network (GBN), 340–341
global context, 10, 11
global marketplace, 450–451
global planning, 429
global publishing
    1950s through 1970s, 235–242
    Australia, 240, 405–409
    blurred boundaries, 402
    Book Project Management, 401
    Canada, 409–412
    Chapman & Hall and, 236–237
    CORE information system, 400–401
    digital infrastructure, 398
    economic consequences, 334
    editorial coordination, 398
    foreign subsidiaries, 235–236
    Germany, 241–242
    India, 240–241
    international contact (late 1950s), 235
    Jacaranda Wiley, 240
    Japan, 241
    John Wiley & Sons Australasia PTY., Ltd., 240
    John Wiley & Sons GmbH, 241–242
    John Wiley & Sons Ltd., 237–239
    Latin America, 241
    Limusa-Wiley, 240
    Mexico, 240
    network, 401
    new offices, 242
    path under Ellis, 344
    platform, 400–401
    presence (late 1970s), 242
    revenue outside United States, 398
    Soviet Union, 243–245
    Steentoft sales representative, 238
    STM lead, 399
    toward, 398–402
    translation rights, 242
    United Kingdom, 237–239, 402–405
    Wiley Arabooks, 242
    Wiley Eastern Ltd., 241
    Wiley's Web site, 401
    world economy (1990s) and, 398
glyphs, 28–29
governance, 452
Government Advisory Committee (GAC), 246
Government Printing Office, 113
Great Depression
    advertising in, 161–162
    author loyalty, 164–165
    books published during, 161

bookstores during, 163
college enrollments during, 163
unemployment, 156
Wiley good will during, 162–163
Wiley supplier relationships, 163–164
Wiley weathering of, 160–164
Great Inflation (1968–1981)
government tight money policies, 273
price jumps, 262
Great Society
background, 226
as loss, 227
problems, 227
self-teaching guides, 227
Wiley acquisition, 226–228
Grid Publishing, 284
Grolier, 273
Gross domestic product (GDP)
of selected countries, 366
U.S. federal R&D as a percentage of, 367
U.S. GDP (1900–1929), 155
group promotion of titles, 256
growth
Business, Law, and General Books (late 1980s), 320
Higher Education, 448
libraries (1830–1875), 67
libraries (1960s and 1970s), 209
Medical Division (1976–1981), 292
publishing industry (1800–1865), 70–73
publishing industry (1830–1860), 66
by publishing sector (1954–1959), 213
technology product market, 342
Wiley (1961–1966), 249
Wiley (1970s), 239
Wiley (1980s), 295–296
A Guide for Wiley-Interscience and Ronald Press Authors: In the Preparation and Production of Manuscript and Illustrations, 262, 263
Gulf & Western, 271

H

H. C. Baird, 97
H. K. Lewis bookstore, 236
Hachette, 273
Halsted Press
client list, 232
setup, 232
Sullivan as head, 202
Hamilton, Edward P.
as company owner, 148
as company president, 171
evolution as progressive, 194
increase in book titles, 141
in overseas markets (postwar years), 189–190

as philosopher, 171
profile, 143–144, 147
taking over of company, 143
Hamilton Publishing, 228, 285
Hand Book of the History of Painting (Kugler), 96
A Handbook for Farmers and Dairymen, 135
The Happy Sequel and Ellen, 34
Harcourt, Brace
going public, 217
profitability (1976), 247
school revenue (1959), 222
Harcourt Brace Jovanovich, 271
Harper, 175, 216
Harper and Brothers, 69, 70, 97
Harper and Row
list sales to Wiley (1987), 317
News Corporation acquisition, 271–273
profitability (1976), 247
as Wiley competitor (1980s), 281
Wiley territory invasion (mid-1980s), 310
Harvard Business Review, 289, 308, 368
Harvard Business School, Advanced Management Program, 195
Harvard University Press, Wiley relationship, 165–168
Harwal Publishing, 293
Health Economic Evaluations Database (HEED), 381
Heat-Power Engineering (Barnard, Ellenwood, and Hirshfeld), 174
Hepatology, 382
Hermann et Cie, 178
Hewlett-Packard (HP), 292
Heyden & Son, 295
HHMI (Howard Hughes Medical Institute), 443
Higher Education Group, 338
in 1989, 347
acquisitions and partnerships, 359–363
author ties, 348
business, 10
Canadian editorial program, 411
chemistry multimedia modules, 355–356
coherent, scalable approach, 357
collaborative team, 363
in curriculum reform movement, 351–352
demographic shifts, 448
digital technology in products, 353
employees, 350
evolving technology, 354–355
first editions, 350
growth fields, 448
Houghton Mifflin college engineering list, 359
IHE product model (2002), 358
in illegal copying activities, 354
leadership team, 348
Maris collaboration, 356
mission, 447
operating income and cash flows, 362
PBS alliance, 362

Higher Education Group *(continued)*
    revenue (1998–2003), 363
    revitalization deadline, 348
    sales representatives, 362
    scenario planning, 341
    student focus groups, 353
    in Synthesis Coalition, 351
    technology strategy (2000), 357, 358
    Wiley Custom Publishing System, 355
    Wiley Faculty Network (WFN), 359
    Wiley Lab Tests, 356–357
    WileyPLUS, 355, 358, 359
Highway Engineering, Rural Roads and Pavements, 138
Hints on Husband Catching, 96
Hints to Young Architects (Wightwick), 96
History of an Officer's Widow and Her Young Family (Hofland), 34
history titles
    Charles Wiley & Co., 36
    Van Winkle & Wiley, 34
A History of New-York (Knickerbocker), 39
Hoboken
    of 1866, 3
    of 1876, 2
    company artifacts, 6
    legal group, 11
    ribbon-cutting ceremony, 420
    Waterfront Corporate Center, 419
    Wiley move (2002), 384, 419–420
Holt, Rinehart & Winston, 170, 271, 281
The Home Library series, 81
Horizontes (Gilman and Bijuesca), 362
The Hospitalist, 444
Houghton, Mifflin Co.
    profitability (1976), 247
    Riverside Science Series, 113–114
    Wiley college engineering list acquisition, 359
    Wiley territory invasion (mid-1980s), 310
House for You (Sleeper and Sleeper), 182
Household Equipment (Thye), 182
Household Physics (Whitman), 131
The House of Wiley, 164, 165
Howard Hughes Medical Institute (HHMI), 443
Hubble Space Telescope, 335
human resources department, modernization, 234
Hungry Minds
    acquisition, 336, 393–397
    acquisition as conjunction of strengths, 397
    Bible technology series, 393
    brands, 336
    CliffsNotes series, 393
    competitive strengths, 393–394
    For Dummies, 393, 394–395
    Frommer's travel guides, 393
    General Mills Books, 396, 397
    integration, 393
    negotiations, 393
    soft technology market, 396
    teaching methodology, 394–395
Hurd & Houghton, 76, 81
hypermedia, 285

I

The Idle Man (Dana), 33, 46, 47, 50
IEEE (Institute of Electrical and Electronic Engineers), 382
imprint books
    Wiley (1958–1968), 212
    Wiley (1978), 212
A Inaugural Dissertation on the Pathology of the Human Fluids (Dyckman), 32, 33
independence, as strategic asset, 429
indexes
    author-prepared, 137, 155
    as essential, 137
    as great value, 154
    "Notes on Indexing" guide, 155
    poor, 154
India. *See also* Wiley Eastern Ltd.; Wiley India
    Congress Party, 415
    economic reforms, 415
    Wiley entrance, 240–241
Indo-American Textbook Program, 240–241
Industrial Drawing (Mahan), 99
Industrial Hygiene and Toxicology (Patty), 287
industrial libraries, 209
Industrial Management (Lansburgh), 114
industrialized economy, 108–110
inflation
    consumer price index (1969–2005), 262
    19698–1981, 262
    1979, 271
InfoPOEM, 381
Information Technology for Management: Improving Quality and Productivity (Turban, McLean, Wetherbe), 350
in-house printing, 255
initial public offerings, 217
Inside the Economist's Mind (Samuelson and Barnett), 437
Institute of Electrical and Electronics Engineers (IEEE), 382
intellectual property protection, 445
IntelliPro, 353
Interactive Homework Edition (IHE), 358
interactive science experiments (VanCleave), 388
Interactive Science Laboratory, 296
Interactive Technologies, 312, 313
interactive videodiscs, 309, 313
Intermediate Accounting (Kieso and Weygandt), 15, 227, 282, 297, 329, 409
Intermediate Principles of Accounting (Kieso and Weygandt), 282
international copyright. *See also* copyright; copyright law

fight for, 89–93
first serious movement, 92
Lieber on, 90–91
as "literary monopoly," 93
movement failure, 60, 94
opponents of, 92–93
reform advocacy, 89
supporters, 92
On International Copyright (Lieber), 90
International Dictionary of Medicine and Biology, 316
International Division
in 1982, 278, 293
challenges (mid 1980s), 294
Ellis elimination of, 338
International Journal for Numerical Methods in Engineering, 227
International Journal of Cancer, 381
International Journal of Circuit Theory and Applications, 244
International Science and Technology, 231
international strategy
in 1970s, 245–246
in 1980s, 293–305
global reach map (1976), 246
International Thompson
acquisition of South-Western Publishing, 271
Wiley list acquisition, 362
Internet. *See also* World Wide Web
pervasive influence, 441
risk management, 441
Internet Navigator, 351
Internet Product Management Team (IPMT), 401
The Interpretation of Dreams (Freud), 230
Interscience. *See also* Wiley-Interscience merger
editors, 221
European list, 237–238
homosexuality studies, 235
revenue (1960), 217
scientific journals, 220
technical encyclopedias, 219–220
titles, 219
Wiley distribution network access, 220
InterScience. See Wiley InterScience
Introduction to Inclusive Education (Jordan), 8
Introduction to Physiological Chemistry (Bodansky), 148, 150, 174
Introduction to the Human Body (IHB) (Tortora), 360
Introductory Russian Grammar (Stilman and Harkins), 244
investment risk (1980s), 278
Investments: Analysis and Management (Jones), 329
investor community
communication with, 452–453
relations profile, 453–454
relations program, 453
Iowa State College, 136, 138
Irrigation Principles and Practices (Israelsen), 139

J

J. & J. Harper, 43
J. K. Lasser tax guides, 393
Jacaranda Press, 240
Jacaranda Wiley. *See also* Asia, and Wiley Australia
in 1980s, 296
in 1993, 408
beginning of, 240
success, 296
Wiley Southeast Asia transfer, 298–299
Jacksonian Young Americans, 81, 82
Jai Press, 239
James E. Freel Associates, 228
James Publishing Group acquisition, 390
Japan. *See also* Wiley Japan
challenges (1982), 417
economic stagnation (1992), 417
Modern Asia Editions, 241
STM editors, 451
Wiley sales in, 189
jaundice (of Charles Wiley), 51
John Day, 144
John Wiley & Sons, Inc.
175th anniversary, 268, 269, 270
1985 as pivotal year, 309–313
backward-and-forward quality, 147
on "best company" lists (2005 and 2006), 455
as "best value" in publishing industry (1984), 325
book prices (early 1900s), 130
businesses, 10
colophon, 132
communications, 452–453
company respect ranking (1998), 342, 343
connections abroad (post-Civil War), 133–134
corporation restructuring (1904), 139–140
early publications, 6
employer reputation, 200
as family controlled business, 12
family ownership trusts, 264
first budget (1951), 195
first women employees, 124
Fourth Ave offices, 147, 176
fourth generation, 143–195
global publishing, 235–242, 398–419
going public, 217
Great Depression and, 160–164
Hoboken offices, 419–420
as joint-stock corporation, 200
as minor player (1903), 110
naming of, 104–106
orientation to Second Industrial Revolution, 108–110
ownership (postwar years), 192
as "persevering in the middle," 456–459

John Wiley & Sons, Inc. *(continued)*
  reorganization, 222–225
  as science and technology specialty, 110–115
  in takeover speculation, 325, 426
  traditionalists and progressives (postwar years), 193
  undervalue (1990s), 426
  as very old company, 1
  as victim of own success, 201
  West 26th Street mailing and shipping, 176
  workforce cutbacks (1933), 160
  worklife (1980s), 321–325
  worklife (1990s), 340
  worklife (post-Civil War), 124–126
  world wide offices, 2
John Wiley & Sons, Inc. v. Livingston, 221
John Wiley & Sons Australasia PTY., Ltd., 240
John Wiley & Sons GmbH, 241–242
John Wiley & Sons Ltd.
  acquisitions, 295
  beginning of, 237
  book program, 295
  Chancery Law acquisition, 403
  Chichester location, 239, 246
  computer book club, 295
  computerized composition system, 295–296
  Content Management, 402
  editorial, 295
  Electronic Journal of Theoretical Chemistry, 403
  as European publisher, 405
  For Dummies titles, 404
  growth (1970s), 239
  growth (1980s), 295–296
  Hungry Minds acquisition and, 404
  journals publishing, 295
  leadership team, 403
  new leadership, 404–405
  PatientWise, 402
  personal attention, 238
  pharmaceutical publishing, 405
  P/T publishing program, 404
  publishing program, 238
  "Repositioning the Business" theme, 402
  rocky start, 237–238
  sales (1989), 296
  Stag Place, 238
  STM business, 402
  trade titles (1990s), 403–404
  as viable business, 238–239
  Wilson Learning acquisition and, 296
joint ventures
  Editorial Limusa-Wiley, 240
  Latin America, 241
  Livros Tecnicos e Cientificos Editora, 241
  Wiley and Basic Books, 230
  Wiley and China's Science Press, 302

Jossey-Bass
  acquisition, 336, 391–393
  acquisition strengths, 393
  educational list, 362
  history, 392
  integration into Wiley, 391–392
  as knowledge publisher, 391
  manager assignment, 392
  mission, 391
  revenue (1998–2001), 393
Journal für praktishce Chemie, 380
Journal of Advanced Nursing, 437
Journal of an African Cruiser (Bridges), 82
Journal of Futures Markets, 289
Journal of Home Economics, 131
Journal of Image Guided Surgery, 368–370, 377
  Literary Market Place Award, 370
  online, 368–370
  print version, 369
Journal of Law and Economics, 426
Journal of Policy Analysis, 289
Journal of Polymer Science, 220, 373
journals publishing
  competitors (1992), 368
  growth (1980s), 292
  growth (1990s), 367
  John Wiley & sons Ltd., 295
  new (early 1980s), 289
  online, 368
  online availability, 268–270
  online licensing, 371
  reliability, 289
  risk, 289, 442
  sales in Asia (1993–2002), 413
  subscription renewal rates, 289
  Wiley (early 1980s), 289
  Wiley Japan, 418
  Wiley position on, 220
  Wiley-Blackwell, 439
The Journal of Image-Guided Surgery, 15
JP Morgan Chase, view of Wiley (2007), 455
juvenile titles (Van Winkle & Wiley), 34

K

Kekst & Company, 453
Kelmscott Press, 434
Kirk-Othmer Encyclopedia of Chemical Technology
  concise version, 384
  editors, 223
  in Interscience backlist, 219
  online (1984), 288, 308
  Wiley reputation with, 383
Knickerbocker, 88

knowledge
  advancement, 8–9
  defined, 8
  delivery formats, 9–10
  engineering, growth of, 117–118
  explosion (1980s), 290–291
  need for, 9
  revolution, 109
  in Second Industrial Revolution, 102
Koningsmarke; The Long Finne (Paulding), 50
Korean War, 185
Kumi Trading Company, 303

L

Laboratory Manual in Farm Machinery (Wirt), 137
Lacrosse For Dummies (Hinckson, Jiloty, and Carpenter), 412
Lalla Rookh (Moore), 35
Land Drainage (Powers and Teeter), 138
The Last of the Mohicans (Cooper), 48, 51, 52
Latin America. *See also* Limusa-Wiley
  joint ventures (1960s and 1970s), 241
  market (2007), 451
  market in postwar years, 190–191
  Noriega family relationship, 418
  Wiley expansion, 418–419
  Wiley subsidiaries, selling of, 297–298
Lawrence Berkeley National Laboratory, 206
layoffs, 313, 316
The Leadership Challenge (Posner and Kouzes), 428
Learn C and Save Your Job (Pugh), 390
Learning Experience Guides (LEGS), 232
Learning Group, 278, 306
Leather-Stocking Tales, 49
legal titles (Van Winkle & Wiley), 34
Leggat Brothers, 98
Letter to Henry Clay . . . on the Colonization and Civilization of Africa (Gurley), 79
A Letter to His Countrymen (Cooper), 63
Letters from Italy (Headley), 81
Letters on Modern Agriculture (Liebig), 98, 99
Letters on the Late War Between the United States and Great Britain (Cobbett), 34
libraries
  academic (1875–1925), 115
  circulating, 25
  Cold War era, 207–208
  college, 208–209, 273
  corporate, 209
  early 1800s, 24
  Europe (postwar), 189
  federal government funding, 208
  growth (1960s and 1970s), 209
  high school, 168
  industrial, 209
  nonacademic, modernization, 115
  political activities, 208
  professionalization, 115
  public, 67–68, 208, 273
  research, 208–209
  Sailor's Floating Library, 25
  secondary-school, 168
  social, 24–25, 67
  specialized, 115
  technical, 168
  U.S. (1790–1825), 25
  U.S. growth (1830–1875), 67
  U.S. per capita (1790–1830), 25
  volumes (1934), 168
  Wiley & Putnam distribution to, 78
Library and Advisory Boards, 370
Library Company of Philadelphia, 25, 67, 78
The Library of American Books, 82–83
The Library of Choice Reading, 81–82
Library of Congress, 67, 168
Library Services Act, 208
Life, Service, and Cost of Service of Farm Machinery (Davidson), 136
Light and Behavior of Organisms (Mast), 141
Limusa-Wiley
  in 1980s, 297–298
  deterioration, 241
  joint venture, 240
  shareholders, 240
  Wiley book pirating, 240
  Wiley sale, 298
Linotype
  1950s through 1970s, 261
  introduction, 122
  machine illustration, 123
  operators, 159
Lionel Lincoln (Cooper), 25, 41, 48, 50, 51
Lippincott, Ticknor, Derby & Miller, 97
literacy rates, 68
The Literary and Philosophical Society of New York, 49
The Literary and Scientific Repository, 44, 45, 47
The Literary Companion, 46
A Literary Fair, 26
Literary World, 88
literature
  American, emergence of, 44–47
  Charles Wiley & Co., 36
  Van Winkle & Wiley, 34
Little, Brown, 216
Livros Tecnicos e Cientificos Editora, 241, 298
Locomotive Engineering (Clark), 99
Logical Design of Digital Computers, 208
London office (Wiley & Putnam), 77

London Quarterly Review, 78
London Tract Society, 133
Long and Short Span Railway Bridges (Roebling), 112
Longmans, Green, 236
Looking At series (Suzuki), 388
LPI Online, 389

M

McCarthyism, 207
McGraw-Hill
    American Express failed bid, 271
    book pricing (1965), 253
    Grade B books, 165
    industrial management texts, 114
    market share (World War II), 173
    New York offices (1911), 113
    profitability (1974), 247
    publishing volume (1914), 121
    technical author publication, 113
    textbook series, 214
    as Wiley competitor, 112, 175, 281
Machine Composition Company of Boston, 259
Machinery for Growing Corn (Davison), 136
McKinsey, 249
Macmillan
    industrial management texts, 114
    profitability (1976), 247
    Scribner merger, 326
    as top-tier publisher (1958), 216
    warehouses, 257
    Wiley college lists purchase, 316
    as Wiley competitor, 113, 175, 281
    Wiley health, physical education, and recreation list purchase, 316
    Wiley territory invasion (mid-1980s), 310
McMullin, Ruth
    on board of directors, 314
    as CEO, 317–319
    company ascension, 318
    as COO, 315
    during turnaround, 316–319
    as executive vice president, 315
    first communication to board, 316
    golden parachute, 319
    interview, 314
    management history, 314
    management style, 318–319
    memo, 315
    mood, 318
    problems, 318–319
    in search for new leadership, 313–314
Macquarie Dictionary, 296
Macs For Dummies, 395

magazines (Wiley & Putnam), 78
Magnetic Circuits (MIT series), 165
The Man Nobody Knows (Barton), 159
Management: The Competitive Advantage (Schermerhorn), 409–410
Management for Productivity (Schermerhorn), 284, 312
Management in Small Doses (Ackoff), 309
Managerial Accounting (Kieso and Weygandt), 282
Managerial Control of Business (Trundle), 177
Managerial Finance in a Canadian Setting (Lusztig and Schwab), 410
Managing Organizational Behavior (Schermerhorn, Hunt, and Osborn), 284
Managing Software Development: Solving the Productivity Puzzle, 307, 308
Mandeville (Godwin), 36
Manfred (Byron), 35
Manhattan. *See also* New York City
    of 1807, 1, 17
    of 1842, 57
    of 1866, 3
    shops (1814), 18
Manly Piety in Its Principles (Philip), 61
A Manual for Marriageable Misses, 96
Manual of Cattle Feeding, 135
Manual of Engineering Drawing (French), 113
Manual of the Steam Engine (Thurston), 140
The Manuscript: A Guide for Its Preparation, 152, 153, 154
manuscripts
    electronic (mid-1980s), 324
    guidelines (1920s), 152
    nonprinted, series books, 138–139
March's Advanced Organic Chemistry, 383
margins, in manuscript guidelines, 152
Maris Technologies. *See also* TES
    CD-Physics for Windows (1999), 354
    acquisition, 357
    collaboration, 356
    working with, 358
marketing
    at academic conferences, 181–182
    department, internalizing, 257
    direct mail, 132–133, 180
    early 1900s, 129–133
    forthcoming books (1920s), 132
    in Higher Education turnaround (1990s), 349–350
    options (post-Civil War), 132–133
    return policy and, 131
    yesterday and today, 5–6
Marketing Research Essentials (McDaniel and Gates), 362
markets
    Africa, 451
    Asia, 450–451
    Europe, 402–405

global, 450–451
high education (1980s), 279–286
Latin America, 451
Middle East, 451
overseas (postwar years), 189–192
used-textbook, 446
Marshall Plan, 189
Martha Inc.: The Incredible Story of Martha Stewart Living Omnimedia (Byron), 387
Mass Spectrometry Reviews, 289
Mathematics for Elementary Teachers (Musser and Burger), 359
mathematics titles
calculus reform, 352
math series, 134
1926–1956, 149
Wiley & Putnam, 74
MBS Textbook Exchange, 255, 280
The Mechanical Engineer's Pocket-Book (Kent), 14, 120, 126, 141, 174
Mechanics (Meriam), 186
Mechanics of Materials (Merriman), 14, 140
Media Medica, 295
Medical Division
in 1979, 275
in 1982, 278
Current Series, 293
growth (1976–1981), 292
Houghton Mifflin medical program acquisition, 292–293
medical publishing
in 1980s, 292–293
Blackwell Publishers, 435
Van Winkle & Wiley, 33, 34
Wiley & Putnam, 74–75
Wiley exit, 316
Medical Ultrasound, 289
Medicinal Research Reviews, 289
MediVisuals, 345
Melville Publishing, 231
The Menace of Overproduction (Hamlin), 161
Menlo Park, 102, 103
mercantile trade, 22
mergers and acquisitions
1959–1962, 217–219
1959–1979, 218
1979–1989, 271–273
1990–2002, 427
Elsevier and Reed, 376
expansion through, 226–229
Farrar, Straus and Company and Noonday Press, 217
foreign publishers, 273
McGraw-Hill and F. W. Dodge Corporation, 217
McGraw-Hill and Tratec, 305
Macmillan and Free Press, 218
Prentice Hall and Deltak, 305–306
profit growth and, 229

Random House and Alfred A. Knopf, 217
timeline of, 15
Wiley, most important, 429
Wiley and Alan R. Liss, 319–320, 324
Wiley and Belhaven Press, 373
Wiley and Blackwell Publishing, 382, 432–441
Wiley and Chancery Law, 403
Wiley and Contemporary Systems Corporation, 228
Wiley and Dreamtech, 416, 451
Wiley and Frank J. Fabozzi, 393
Wiley and Ginn & Company, 229
Wiley and Great Society Press, 226–228
Wiley and Grid Publishing, 284
Wiley and Harwal Publishing, 293
Wiley and Health Economic Evaluations Database (HEED), 381
Wiley and Heyden & Son, 295
Wiley and Hungry Minds, 336, 393–397
Wiley and InfoPOEM, 381
Wiley and IntelliPro, 353
Wiley and Interscience, 217, 219–220
Wiley and J. K. Lasser tax guides, 393
Wiley and Jacaranda Press, 240
Wiley and James E. Freel Associates, 228
Wiley and James Publishing Group, 390
Wiley and Jossey-Bass, 336, 391–393
Wiley and Maris, 357
Wiley and Media Medica, 295
Wiley and Milady, 286
Wiley and QED Information Sciences, 390
Wiley and REDEL, 373
Wiley and Ronald Press, 232
Wiley and St. Clair Press, 229
Wiley and Scripta Technica, 292
Wiley and Technical Insights, 373
Wiley and Van Nostrand Reinhold (VNR), 391
Wiley and VCH Publishing, 99, 336, 373–380
Wiley and Wilson Learning Company, 278
Wiley and Wrightbooks, 393
Wiley strategy, 229
World Publishing and Meridian Books, 217–218
metal plates, 29
Method of Calculating Cubic Contents of Excavations and Embankments (Trautwine), 117
Methods of Correlation Analysis (Ezekiel), 165
Mexico, exports to, 189
Microbiology (Black), 359
Microsoft Office Academic Course (MOAC) materials, 448
Middle East, Wiley in, 419, 451
The Middle Kingdom (Williams), 74, 75
Milady, 286
military forms, 34
military titles
war-related, 34
Wiley & Putnam, 75

Mineral Springs of Western Virginia (Burke), 77
Mining Engineers' Handbook (Peele), 162
Mining in the Pacific States (Hittell), 99
Minutes of the New-York Baptist Association, 35
Missouri Books, 279, 280
MIT Press, Wiley relationship, 165
MOAC (Microsoft Official Academic Course) materials, 448
Moby Dick (Melville), 85
Modern Asia Editions, 241
Modern Internal Auditing (Brink), 283
Modern Painters (Ruskin), 106, 107
Modern Physics: A Textbook for Engineers (Sproull), 199
The Monikins (Cooper), 63
Monotype, 260, 261
Montgomery's Auditing, 232, 282, 283
Morgan Guaranty Trust, 236
Morrill Land Grant Act of 1862, 109, 117
Moscow Book Fair, 243, 300
Mosses from an Old Manse (Hawthorne), 71, 83
Mother's Magazine, 63
Motion and Time Study (Barnes), 14, 148, 172
Mr. Boston Official Bartender's and Party Guide, 396
multimedia, 285
multiple scenario planning, 340–341
Multivariable Calculus (McCallum et al.), 352
MYOB For Dummies (Curtis), 409

N

Narrative of Arthur Gordon Pym (Poe), 86
National Association of Book Publishers (NABP) publishing
    industry economic study, 156
National Defense Education Act of 1958, 207
National Distribution System (NDS), 313, 328
National Education Improvement Act, 208
National Institutes of Health (NIH), 442, 443
The National Library of Medicine (NLM), 442
National Medical Series, 293
National Science Foundation (NSF)
    coalition funding, 351
    funding, 175, 366
Nauka, 299, 300
Nebraska Book Company, 279, 280
Neilly, Andrew
    as CEO, 271, 274
    departure, 317
    as first nonfamily member to head firm, 274
    fiscal year 1982 fiscal plan, 275–278
    imprint, 275–278
    leadership team (1982), 277
    new leadership search, 313–315
    profile, 276
    turnaround and, 316–321

New York
    per capita annual income (1790–1820), 24
    population (1790–1820), 24
New York City
    in 1776, 20
    in 1807, 1
    in 1920s, 143–145
    booksellers (1795–1807), 27
    as center for publishing, 26–27
    Chrysler Building, 144, 145
    City Hall (1811), 19
    The Collect (1811), 19
    Dickens and, 57
    Five Points district, 19, 57
    in late 1970s and early 1980s, 266–268
    literary fair (1802), 19
    Medical Repository (1797), 19
    print shops (1795–1807), 27
    view (1810), 23
New York Mercantile Library, 67
New York Public Library, 208, 428, 443–444
New York Society Library, 67
New York State Library, 78
New York Typographical Society, 28
New Zealand exports (postwar years), 90, 189
NeXT computer, 335
Niles' Weekly Register, 44
1982 plan, 275–278
nonprofessional technical writers, 232
The Northern Traveller (Dwight), 62
The North American Review, 88
Norton, 144
Notes for Chemical Students (Austen), 126
"Notes on Indexing" guide, 155
Numerical Methods in Engineering, 239

O

*Observations on the Laws Governing the Communication of
    Contagious Diseases and Remarks on the Treatment
    of the Typhoid State of Fever* (Hosack), 34
occupational division, 228
Occupational Group (1980s), 285–286
occupational market
    domination, 228
    World War II, 174
Office of War Information (OWI), 173
Ogilvy on Advertising (Ogilvy), 297
Omoo: A Narrative of Adventures in the South Seas (Melville), 85
On Common Ground: Managing Human-Planet Relationships
    (Kumar and Murck), 411
175th anniversary, 268, 269, 270
online sales, 421

Online Title Information System (OTIS), 400
"open access," 442
open-market competition, 443
Operating System Concepts (Silberschatz), 359
Operations Research Society of America journal, 381
order-taking methods (1960s), 257
Ordnance and Gunnery (Mahan), 128
Organic Chemistry (Solomons), 350
Organic Reactions (Adams), 184, 195
Organikum (Becker), 380
Origin of Species (Darwin), 6
The Orion, A Monthly Magazine of Literature and Art, 79
*OS/2 Presentation Manager Programming for COBOL
        Programmers* (Chapman), 390
OTIS (Online Title Information System), 400
outsourcing, production, 262
overseas companies, 12
overseas markets
    Africa, 451
    Asia, 450–451
    book shipments, 191
    Europe, 402–405
    Latin America, 190–191, 451
    Middle East, 451
    postwar years, 189–192
    sales promotion, 191
    South Pacific, 190
    travel undertaken to, 190
Oxford, 175, 216
Oxford University Press, 170

P

Panic of 1819, 36, 37
papermaking, technology advances (1810s to 1850s), 72
Papers on Literature and Art (Fuller), 85
Park Avenue South offices, 222
Partial Differential Equations, 208
Patient Care, 232
Patient Care Publications (PCP), 232
Patty's Industrial Hygiene and Toxicology, 384
PCs. *See also* computers
    beginning use, 321
    HP, 292
    lowered pricing, 321
    wireless tablet, 321
PDF (Portable Document Format), 422
Pearson, 273, 359
Pennsylvania State College, 136
perfect binding, 157
Pergamon Press, 325, 337
Personal Computing, 292

Pesce, William J.
    CEO appointment, 344
    collaboration priority, 346, 429
    cross-divisional teams, 346
    goals, 344–345
    Higher Education revitalization deadline, 348
    insight, 345
    intertwinded interests view, 345–346
    leadership, 429
    "print and electronic," 449–450
    profile, 345
    reorganization, 346
    strategies, 344–345
    transition to CEO, 344
Philippine Education Co., 134
Philosophical Transactions, 380
philosophy titles (Wiley & Putnam), 75
Photo Department, 329
Photocells and Their Applications (Wilson), 151
photocomposition
    benefits, 260–261
    defined, 260
    machine use, 259–262
    machines (1970s), 260
    revolution, 260–261
Photon, 259
*Physical Geography: Science and Systems of the Human
        Environment* (Strahler), 148, 355
Physical Geography of China (Songqiao), 302
Physics (Cutnell and Johnson), 350
Physics (Halliday and Resnick), 6, 206, 250, 251, 329
Physics for Students of Science and Engineering (Resnick and
        Halliday), 226
Physics of Semiconductor Devices (Sze), 15
physics publications
    Wiley (1926–1956), 149
    Wiley (1980s), 285
The Pilot (Cooper), 48, 49, 50
The Pioneers (Cooper), 33, 45, 48
    Charles Wiley publication, 49
    critic response, 49–50
    profits, 50
piracy. *See also* copyright laws
    in 1800s, 43
    in 1830s and 1840s, 92
    battle against, 444–445
    China, 416
    problems, 43
pirates, 22, 78
Planning and Adorning the Farmstead (Davison), 136
plates, stereotyping, 71
pocket books, 118, 119

Pocket Books, 216, 217
POD (print on demand), 422–423
The Poetry and History of Wyoming, 75
poetry titles (Charles Wiley & Co.), 36
Poet's Pilgrimage to Waterloo (Southey), 34
political economy titles
    Charles Wiley & Co., 36
    Van Winkle & Wiley, 35
    Wiley & Halsted, 44
Popular Songs of Ireland (Croker), 96
population. *See* demographics
Portable Document Format (PDF), 422
Portfolio Selection: Efficient Diversification of Investments
        (Markowitz), 458
portfolio selection, 458
postal rates, 131–132
post-Civil War period
    book clubs, 130
    connections abroad, 133–134
    marketing, 129–133
    reference, 101
    steel production, 108
    Wiley as house divided, 107
postwar years. *See also* World War II
    acquisitions process, 176–177
    advertising, 180–181
    advertising production, 176
    book prices, 184
    changes and challenges, 179–188
    European strategy, 191
    growth, 175–176
    headquarter changes, 176
    low-price conundrum, 184
    manufacturing costs, 184
    marketing, 180–182
    professional books, 182–183
    profits, 184
    publications, 182
    revenue, 176
    search for overseas markets, 189–192
    series books, 177–179
    staff (1945), 175
    textbooks, 182–185
Poultry Breeding (1932), 6
Practical Farm Drainage, 135
Practical Hints for Draftsmen (MacCord), 128
A Practical Treatise on Pleading (Chitty), 30
Precise Custom Textbook Series, 447, 451
prefaces, in manuscript guidelines, 154
Prentice Hall
    Appleton-Century-Crofts purchase, 271
    in England (1959), 236
    profitability (1976), 247
    as top-tier publisher (1958), 216
    as Wiley competition (1980s), 281

prepublication subscriptions, 5
Presidential Power (Neustadt), 230
Prices (Warren and Pearson), 161
The Principles and Practice of Bookkeeping, 73
Principles of Accounting (Helmkamp, Imdieke, and Smith), 408
Principles of Anatomy and Physiology (Tortora and Grabowski),
        356, 359, 360
Principles of Genetics (Gardner), 259
Principles of Human Anatomy (Tortora), 360
Principles of Human Geography (Huntington), 151
Principles of Industrial Management (Kimball), 129
Principles of Radio (Henney), 153
Principles of Radio Communication (Morecroft), 151
Principles of Refrigeration, 208
print and electronic delivery, 449–450
print shops
    Charles Wiley, 20, 29–31
    New York (1795–1807), 27
    work subdivision, 28
printing
    abandonment by Charles Wiley, 40
    bookselling and publishing combination (early 1800s), 32
    changes (1950s), 155
    costs (1912), 129
    in-house, 255
    as low-status occupation (1813), 31
    out-of-house, 257
    payment for, 34
    post-American Revolution, 22
    runs (1850s), 69
    small-scale profitability, 22
    volume (mid-1960s), 257
    Web-offset, 158
printing presses
    cold type, 260–261
    in cousins' era, 158–159
    eighteenth-century, 29
    hand operation (early 1800s), 29
    Linotype, 122–123, 159, 261
    Monotype, 260, 261
Problems in Direct Fire, 130
production
    in 1807, 4
    digital, 422–423
    outsourcing, 262
    technology (1855), 69
productivity decline (1980s), 305
Professional and Reference Book Division, 223, 232
Professional Baking (Gisslen), 396
Professional Cooking (Gisslen), 286, 312, 411
Professional Division
    in 1979, 275, 287
    in 1982, 278
    Interscience journals, 287
    titles (1979), 287

Professional Education Systems, Inc. (PESI), 390
professional management, 233–235
professional publishing. *See also* Professional Division;
      Professional/Trade Group
  in 1980s, 287–288
  marketing in 1950s, 182–183
  opportunity exploration, 229–232
  Wiley distinction, 183
Professional/Reference business, 10
The Professional Chef, 391, 396
Professional/Trade Group
  acquisitions, 390–397
  bestsellers, 387
  in culinary publishing, 396
  distribution channels, 387
  editorial drive, 386
  Ellis growth, 385–386
  expansion, 385–386
  German, 404
  Hungry Minds acquisition, 393–397
  investments, 391
  leadership team, 385–386
  market dips, 390
  morale, 386
  in reorganization, 338
  revenue (1997), 391
  revenue (1998–2001), 393
  revenue (2002), 397
  scenario planning, 341
  telemarketing unit, 390
  trade list expansion, 387–390
  trend tracking, 390
  U.K., 404
  Van Nostrand Reinhold (VNR) acquisition, 391
profitable niches, 44
profits
  educational publishing (1980s), 281
  growth with mergers and acquisitions, 229
  postwar years, 184
  textbooks (1980s), 281
  trade publishing, 230
Programming Business Computers (McCracken, Weiss, and Lee), 249
promotion. *See also* advertising
  author, 254
  direct mail, 179, 256
  group, 256
  specialized for each title, 256
Psychology and the Challenges of Life (Nevid and Rathus), 362
Psychology in Action (Huffman, Vernoy, and Williams), 312, 349, 423
Public Law 480, 209
public libraries. *See also* libraries
  beginning of, 67
  Civil War and, 67–68
  New York Public Library, 208, 428, 443–444
  number of (1990), 273

Public Library of Science (PLoS), 442
published titles
  changes (1929–1940), 160
  Charles Wiley (1807–1826), 31
  U.S. (1929–1949), 160
publishers
  bookseller relationship (postwar years), 193
  British, American title acquisition (1841–1846), 91
  competitive terrain (1980s), 271
  distribution systems (1960s), 257
  in helping authors craft books, 194–195
  market knowledge, 195
  newspaper/magazine cooperation (1820s), 41–42
  as "Philistines" and "rogues," 31
  pirating British books, 22
  portfolio selection, 458
  profitability of leading U.S. publishers (1974), 247
  proliferation (1970s and 1980s), 273
  risk, in era of rapid technological change, 441
  risk, in journals, 442
  STM, 217, 254, 319–320
  understanding of supply and demand (1920s), 159–160
  Wiley rank (1948–1959), 175
Publishers Association, 246
Publishers' Weekly, 221
publishing
  in antebellum America, 65–73
  as business, 12, 188
  business approaches (1950s and 1960s), 202–203
  computer revolution and, 9
  culinary, 396
  as durable business, 459
  early copyright laws and, 26
  educational (1980s), 279–286
  as entrepreneurial venture, 257
  financing, 217
  functions, 5
  important topics, 6
  journals, 289–292
  medical, 292–293
  modern, transition to, 101–141
  New York as center, 26–27
  printing and bookselling combination (early 1800s), 32
  professional, 287–288
  program development, 11
  as pure entrepreneurship, 458
  road to, 20–24
  slowdown (1825–1826), 58
  society, 380–381
publishing companies. *See also specific companies*
  family control, 12
  growth, 4
  ownership (postwar years), 192
  today, 4
Publishing Group, 316

publishing industry
  government regulation (World War II), 173–175
  growth (1800–1865), 70–73
  growth (1830–1860), 66
  railroad impact, 69–70
  revenue (1820 to 1856), 69
"Publishing Without Boundaries," 459
PubMed Central, 442
The Puzzle of the Tacoma Narrows Bridge Collapse (Fuller, Zollman, and Campbell), 309
PWS-Kent, 273

Q

QED Information Sciences, 390
Qualitative Organic Analysis (Kamm), 150, 151
Quick Calculus, 227
Quinn & Boden, 164

R

R&D. *See* research and development
R. D. Irwin
  profitability (1976), 247
  as Wiley competition, 281
R. R. Bowker, 271
Radio Telegraphy and Telephony (Duncan and Drew), 151
railroads
  in 1840s, 69–70
  in 1850, 70
  first transcontinental line, 108
  in Second Industrial Revolution, 102
Random House
  beginning of, 144
  CRM purchase, 271
  editors, 254
  going public, 217
  as top-tier publisher (1958), 216
  as Wiley competition (1980s), 281
  Wiley territory invasion (mid-1980s), 310
Rational Geometry (Halsted), 134
The Raven and Other Poems and Tales (Poe), 13, 86
readers
  in 1920s, 156
  benefit from international copyright law, 92
  number of (1840–1860), 67
reading
  1950s through 1970s, 211
  between the wars, 155–159
Reasons for the Inexpediency of Chartering a National Bank, 73
Recipes for Two (Glass), 182
Recollections of Curran, 36
Red Pottage (Cholmondeley), 121
Red Sage Project, 368

REDEL acquisition, 373
RedShift, 356
Reed, 273
reference-linking service, 372
Reformation of Medical Science (Channing), 77
Relationship Marketing (Gordon), 412
Religion of the Indian Tribes, 36
religious titles
  Charles Wiley & Co., 36
  Van Winkle & Wiley, 34
  Wiley & Putnam, 79
Remarks on the Currency of the United States, 73
Remarks on the Slavery Question in a Letter to Jonathan Phillips (Channing), 79
The Remedy, in a National Bank of the People, 73
renewal planning, 338–343
  challenge, 339
  distribution system, 340
  electronic technology products, 339
  fiscal 1993 as turning point, 339–340
  focus and, 336–338
  GBN help, 340–341
  process introduction, 336
  reporting groups reorganization, 338–339
  scenario planning, 340–342
  strategic plans (1991–1995), 339
  workplace improvements, 340
Renouf Publishing, 134
Rensselaer Polytechnic Institute catalog, 111
reorganization
  in 1985, 310
  in 1990, 338–339
  College Division, 224
  direct reports (1966), 224
  editorial program (1964), 222–223
  Interscience Division, 223–224
  Interscience merger and, 222
  New Media Department (1968), 225
  occupational division, 228
  Pesce, 346
  Professional and Reference Book Division (1965), 223
  schools division, 223
  vice presidents, 223
  Wiley-Interscience Division, 225
Reports of Cases Argued . . . in the Supreme Court (Cranch), 30
Repository of Useful Knowledge, 78
reprinting, copyrighted material, 138
Research and Development Committee, 277
research and development funding. *See also* GDP
  sources, 367
  trends, 366
  U.S. federal as percentage of GDP (1976–2008), 366
  U.S. by source (1953–2004), 367
research libraries (1960s and 1970s), 208–209
Resistance of Materials (Seely), 151

retail trade. *See* booksellers
returns
    first acceptance (1922), 131
    logistical/financial problems, 257
    policies (1960s), 257
    teachers (1920s), 131
    Wiley (1957), 257
    Wiley (1960s), 258
    Wiley (1970s), 258
revenue. *See also* earnings
    Blackwell Publishing (2006), 432
    Interscience (1960), 217
    Wiley (1922), 459
    Wiley (1941), 459
    Wiley (1957), 211
    Wiley (1957–1962), 216
    Wiley (1957–1969), 212
    Wiley (1962), 217
    Wiley (1971–1979), 265
    Wiley (1971), 263
    Wiley (1979–1983), 268
    Wiley (1980–1990), 311
    Wiley (1980), 459
    Wiley (1989–2007), 346
    Wiley (1991–1998), 342
    Wiley (1992–2002), 429
    Wiley (1997–2007), 455
    Wiley (1999), 459
    Wiley (2006), 459
    Wiley (2007), 455
    Wiley Asia (1993–1998), 414
    Wiley Business, Law, and General Books Division, 385
    Wiley Canada (1989), 297
    Wiley Canada (2002), 412
    Wiley guidelines (1988–1997), 315
    Wiley Higher Education Group (1998–2003), 363
    Wiley Japan (1984–1989), 299
    Wiley Professional/Trade Group (1997), 391
    Wiley Professional/Trade Group (1998–2001), 393
    Wiley Professional/Trade Group (2002), 397
    Wiley STM (2002), 398
    Wilson Learning (1982), 306
reviews
    as blessing and danger, 255
    New York Times, 255
    textbook, 127–128
revolving credit, 203
Richard Carvel (Churchill), 113, 121
Richard D. Irwin, 217
Rienzi (Bulwer), 43
risk
    assessing and managing, 457
    Internet, 441
    investment (1980s), 278
    journal publishing, 289, 442
    trade publishing, 229–230

robber barons, 101, 103
Robinson Crusoe (Defoe), 25
Rocks and Rock Minerals (Pirsson), 150
Roman Antiquities, 36
Romania delegation, 244–245
Ronald Press, 232
royalties, 137
Rugby For Dummies (Guthrie), 404

S

Sailor's Floating Library, 25
St. Clair Press, 229, 284
sales
    forecasting, 251
    growth (1820–1870), 78
    online, 421
    textbooks (1982–1985), 275–276
    used textbooks (late 1980s), 280
    Wiley (1945–1959), 203
    Wiley (1950s), 194
    Wiley (1962), 222, 249
    Wiley (1978), 274
    Wiley (2007), 12
    Wiley, by business sector (1954–1959), 213
    Wiley Canada (1985), 297
    Wiley decline (mid-1980s), 309–310
    Wiley international (1982), 294
    Wiley Ltd. (1989), 296
    Wilson Learning (1983), 308
sales representatives. *See also* travelers
    Higher Education, 362
    PC use, 321
    wireless tablet PC use, 321
sales volume, 12
Salmagundi (Irving), 39
Sampling Inspection Tables (1944, 1945, 1959, 1970, 1998), 6
Samuel Bagster & Sons Bibles, 133
Saunders, as Wiley competitor (1980s), 281
The Scarlet Letter (Hawthorne), 83
scenario planning
    Higher Education, 341
    Professional/Trade Group, 341
    in renewal, 341–342
    STM, 340–341
    in technology step-up, 429
school library volumes (1934), 168
School Telemachus, 36
schools division (1966), 223
science
    excitement (1950s through 1970s), 210–211
    in making universities, 109
    in Second Industrial Revolution, 109
Science Editions, 230
Science of Physiognomy, 35

science titles
  Charles Wiley & Co., 36
  list downturn (1980s), 281
  prices (early 1900s), 130
  production costs, 253
  Wiley & Putnam, 75
  Wiley (1980s), 285
The Sciences: An Integrated Approach (Trefil and Hazen), 350
scientific, technical, and medical (STM) publishers. *See also* STM,
     Wiley
  Alan R. Liss as, 319–320
  Interscience as, 217
  market (1990s), 366
  promotion, 254
  R&D funding and, 366, 367
Scientific, Technical, and Medical business, 10
Scientific American, 231, 289
Scientific Press, 123
The Scientific Observer (Matheson), 231
Scott Foresman
  profitability (1976), 247
  Time acquisition, 271
  as Wiley competitor (1980s), 281
Scoville Memorial Library, 24
Scripta Technica, 292
Second Bank of the United States, 74
Second Industrial Revolution
  defined, 101–102
  inventions, 108–109
  John Wiley & Sons orientation, 108–110
  knowledge of technology, 102
  railroad climax, 102
  robber barons, 101, 103
  science expansion, 109
Second Treatise [of Civil Government] (Locke), 6
self-teaching guides (Wiley series), 227, 330
series books
  agricultural science, 134–139
  Biochemical Preparations Series, 177–179
  development (1958), 216
  manifestation of, 134
  math series, 134
  new editions, 137
  nonprinted manuscripts, 138–139
  nuclear science, 177
  postwar period, 177–179
  prepublication promotion, 138
  proposals, 137
  royalties, 137
  social science, 179
  Structure of Matter Series, 177
series editors
  Davidson as, 139
  manuscript review, 139
  new editions, 137
  reviewers and, 128
  Wiley letterhead, 134

ServSafe titles, 396
Seven Lamps of Architecture (Ruskin), 106, 107
SGML (Standard Generalized Markup Language), 423
Shanghai office, 450
Shanghai Scientific and Technical Publishing Company (SSTP),
     302–303
Sherman Antitrust Act, 246
shipping
  department in Starrett Lehigh Building, 257
  overseas markets, 191
  Wiley (mid-1960s), 257
Silent Spring (Carson), 6
Silver Burdett, 271
Simon & Schuster, 144, 216
Simplified Drafting Practice (1953), 6
Singapore operation, 412, 450
A Sketch of Bolivar in His Camp (Paulding), 62
Sketch of the Civil Engineering of North America (Stevenson), 99
The Sketch-book of Geoffrey Crayon (Irving), 13, 33, 38, 39, 46
Slavery in the United States (Sampson), 79
SmartBooks, 353
social libraries, 24–25, 67
social science series, 179
society publishing
  editorial work, 382
  expansion (19th century), 380
  initiative, 380–381
  relationships (2001), 382
software
  industry (mid-1980s), 308
  purchasing decisions, 285
  simulations, 353
Software Division, 285
Software Practice and Experience, 239
Solar Heating (Beckman, Klein, and Duffie), 287
Some Presses You Will be Glad to Know About, 168
Somerset distribution center, 274, 275, 316–317
Sons of Liberty, 20
Soros on Soros: Staying Ahead of the Curve (Soros), 387, 418
The Soul of a New Cuisine (Samuelsson), 396
South Africa, Wiley in, 419
South-Western Publishing, 271
Soviet Union
  Brad Wiley trip to, 243–244
  bureaucracy, 244
  cooperation with, 245
  courtship of, 243–245
  delegations to, 243
  in Universal Copyright Convention (UCC), 243
  Wiley revenues (early 1980s), 299
space race, 211
specialized books, direct mail promotion, 132
Springer-Verlag, 273
Sputnik, 196, 198, 207, 217
The Spy (Cooper), 13, 33, 41, 45, 47, 48, 49, 50
stagflation, 271
Stainless Iron and Steel (Monypenny), 151

Stamp Act riots, 20
Standard Generalized Markup Language (SGML), 423
Statics (Meriam), 186
Statistical Annals of the United States (Seybert), 44
Steam Power (Hirshfeld and Ulbricht), 138
steam technology, 72
steel production (post-Civil War), 108
stereotyping
    defined, 71
    plates, 71–72
    technology, 29
    United States introduction, 72
Sterling & Company, 325
STM, Wiley, 339, 366–372. *See also* scientific, technical, and
        medical (STM) publishers
    in 1989, 332
    acquisitions, 373–380
    Amazon.com and, 384
    book market strategy, 384
    books, 383–385
    British, 402
    business-level plan, 341
    Cochrane Collaboration, 380
    competitor analysis, 368
    CrossRef, 372
    EBM initiatives, 381
    electronic delivery platform, 370
    as global operation, 385
    Global team, 399
    Journal of Image Guided Surgery, 368–370
    journal prices, 367
    lead in global publishing, 399
    leadership, 366, 367
    Library and Advisory Boards, 370
    online journals, 368–370
    opportunities/challenges (1990s), 367–368
    publishing centers, 367, 380
    Red Sage Project, 368
    revenue (2002), 398
    scenario planning, 340–341
    society publishing, 380–382
    society relationships, 382
    "spirit of Ealing," 370
    Wiley InterScience launch, 371
stock
    Black Monday market collapse, 335
    certificates, 454
    creation of two classes of stock, increasing family control, 325
    fluctuations (1980s), 325
    on New York Stock Exchange (1995), 452
    ownership, 454
    prices (1982–1990), 326
    prices (1989–2007), 343
    prices (1997–2007), 454
    recapitalization (1982), 325
The Stones of Venice (Ruskin), 106
Strasbourg office, 403

Strategic Customer Care (Brown), 412
Strictures on a Pastoral Letter, 34
Structure of Matter Series, 177
The Structure of Matter (Rice and Teller), 177
The Structure of Matter (Teller), 230
student focus groups, 353
subscriptions
    book clubs (post-Civil War), 130
    books sales by (Charles Wiley), 33
    prepublication, 5
    product emphasis, (1991–1995), 339
    renewal rates, 289
Sudoku For Dummies (Heron and James), 404
Suggestions on the Banks, 73
Summary of the Law of Nations (Bradford), 33
supplementary materials for textbooks, 184
swifts in typesetting, 159
SWOT analysis, 203, 234
Synergy, 441
Synthesis Coalition, 351
System of Mineralogy (Dana), 13, 80, 329
Systematic Identification of Organic Compounds (Shriner), 150

T

Tax Saving Strategies, 377
Take My Family ... Please (Lautens), 297
takeover speculation about Wiley, 325, 426
Tales for Fifteen (Cooper), 51
Tamerlane (Poe), 86
The Task and Other Poems (Cowper), 34
Teamsters Union, 274
Technical Insights acquisition, 373
technical titles
    Charles Wiley & Co., 36
    Van Winkle & Wiley, 34
    Wiley & Putnam, 75
technology
    audio market, 309
    customer/content interaction, 444
    interactive videodisc, 309
    nineteenth-century advanced, 71–72
    product market growth, 342
    in Second Industrial Revolution, 102, 109
    software market, 308–309
    stereographic, 29, 71–72
    as threat and opportunity, 277
Technology Press (MIT), 178–179
Technology Steering Committee (TSC), 400
Tehran Book Fair, 451
Tehran office, 419
telecommuters, first, 324
telegraph, 108
telephone, 108
Television: The Electronics of Image Transmission, 6
Television (Morton), 151

TES (Training and Educational Services), 354, 357
Textbook of Geology (Ives), 129
Textbook of Organic Chemistry (Holleman), 14, 141
textbooks
    authors (early 1900s), 126–127
    cloth versus paper, 214
    degree of difficulty, 135
    design/illustrations, 184
    development, 216
    as digital product, 447
    evolution (1950s), 183
    evolution as learning tool, 186
    geography (1980s), 285
    introductory, 214
    low-priced reprints (1950s), 239
    online content search, 4
    physics (1980s), 285
    postwar years, 182–185
    pricing (mid 1980s), 280
    publishing economics, 446
    reviewers, 127–128
    revolution (1950s and 1960s), 214
    sales (1980s), 269
    sales (war and postwar years), 172
    seasonality, 203
    solicitations (1920), 126
    supplementary materials, 184
    trends in majors and, 214
    used-book market, 280, 446
    Visualizing series, 448
    Wiley (post-Civil War), 126–128
    writing challenge, 127
    writing style (1950s), 182
themes, 8–12
Theories of Personality (Hall and Lindzey), 208, 226, 249
The Theory and Practice of Landscape Gardening (Downing), 75–77
Theory of Quantized Fields (Bogoliubov and Shirkov), 299
Theory of Transverse Strains (Hatfield), 127
Thera*Scribe*, 389
Thermodynamic Properties of Steam (Keenan and Keyes), 166
Third Avenue offices, 222
third century
    navigation through, 457
    strategic plan, 456
    Wiley Vision, 459
Tiananmen Square, 334, 335
Ticknor & Fields, 83, 99
timeline, Wiley family, 13–15
Tokyo office, 415
Tontine Coffeehouse, 18
Toppan Printing Company, 239, 241
trade embargo (1807), 22
trade publishing
    as anti-cyclical, 229
    opportunity exploration, 229–232
    profits, 230

risk, 229–230
    Wiley and Basic Books joint venture, 230
    Wiley publicity, 230
    Wiley titles, 230–231
    Wiley view as revenue stream, 230
trademarks, Wiley, 445
Traditional Market Agreement (TMA), 246
Training and Educational Services (TES), 357
translations
    in 1965, 242
    Arabic-language, 242
    Chinese For Dummies program, 417
    first, 134
    For Dummies, 395–396
    requests (1953), 192
    rights, 242
    Spanish, postwar years, 191
transportation revolution, 27
Tratec, 305
travel publications
    Charles Wiley & Co., 36
    Frommers, 393, 404, 449–450
    John Wiley publication, 62
    in print and electronic delivery, 449–450
    Van Winkle & Wiley, 34
travelers. *See also* textbooks
    characteristics of, 170
    as college sales representatives, 170
    former, 185
    Midwest, 185
    New England, 185
Travels in Greece, Palestine, Egypt, and Barbary During the Years 1806 and 1807 (Chateaubriand), 34
Travels in North America (Lyell), 88
Travels in Various Countries in Europe, Asia, and Africa (Clarke), 34
A Treatise on Agriculture, 36
A Treatise on the Resistance of Materials (Wood), 127
The Triangle: A Series of Numbers upon Three Theological Points (Whelpley), 31, 32, 33, 60
The Truth About Publishing (Unwin), 159
turnaround of Wiley business
    attempted, 316–317
    Business, Law, and General Books (BLG) growth, 320
    Ellis and, 319–320
    employees during, 318, 327
    expectations, 318
    family decision, 327
    Harper & Row's list acquisition, 317
    Higher Education (1990s), 348–349
    internal "venture fund," 318
    layoffs, 316
    Liss acquisition, 319–320, 332
    lists sales to Macmillan, 316
    McMullin and, 314–319
    sours, 317–321
    stockholders and, 319

we versus they atmosphere, 319
write-offs, 316
"twigging phenomenon," 212
200 Gooey, Slippery, Slimy, Weird & Fun Experiments
(VanCleave), 389
"Two Thousand and Seven," 268
Two Years Before the Mast (Dana), 47
two-thirds men (as hired printing press workers), 40
type stamping, 259
Typee (Melville), 13, 59, 83–85
typesetting
in cousins' era, 159
in digital production, 422
photocomposition machines, 259–262
Photon, 259–262
speed increase (1841–1854), 72

U

Ullman's Encyclopedia of Industrial Chemistry, 384
Uncle Tom's Cabin (Stowe), 6
United Kingdom, 402–405. *See also* Chichester offices, and John
Wiley & Sons Ltd.
United Publishing and Promotion Company, 303
U.S. Customs and Border Protection Agency, 445
U.S. information centers, 191
The United States and England (Paulding), 34
United States International Book Association, 191
United States Military Academy, 64
Universal Copyright Convention (UCC), 243, 305
The Universal Receipt [Recipe] Book, 33
University of Chicago monographs, 168
University of Phoenix, 347
University of War, 172
university presses (post-World War II), 168
Urban Systems, 231
Uruguay, exports to, 189

V

The Valley of Shenandoah (Tucker), 51
Value Reporting Revolution (Eccles), 404
Van Nostrand Co.
book pricing (1965), 253
as one-man show, 264
publishing volume, 121
as Wiley competitor, 112
Van Nostrand Reinhold
lists, 391
Wiley acquisition, 391
as Wiley competitor (1980s), 281
Van Winkle & Wiley
addresses, discourses, orations, 34
cookbooks, 33

defined, 31
dissolution, 35
history titles, 34
juvenile titles, 34
legal titles, 34
literature, 34
medical titles, 33, 34
political economy titles, 35
religious titles, 34
technical titles, 34
travelogue titles, 34
Vanguard Press, 144
VCH Publishing
in 1960s through 1980s), 375
acquisition, 336, 373–380
acquisition cost, 373, 376
background, 374–375
East Germany library integration, 375
integration, 376
Wiley-VCH name, 376–380
Velasco: A Tragedy in Five Acts (Sargent), 77
Venezuela, exports to, 189
The Versatile Organization, 313
Vietnam War aftershock, 268
A View of the Lead Mines of Missouri, 36
Viking Press, 144
A Visit to Texas, 62
Visualizing Geology (Murck, Skinner, and Mackenzie), 448
Visualizing textbook series, 448
vocational market, 228
Von Holtzbrinck Group, 271, 273
Voyage Round the World, 35

W

W. C. Brown, as Wiley competitor (1980s), 281
W. F. Etherington & Co., 164
Wadsworth, as Wiley competitor (1980s), 281
WAIS (Wide Area Information Servers), 368
Wal-Mart, 387
War and Peace (Tolstoy), 75
War of 1812, 31, 34
warehouse clubs, 387
warehouses. *See also* distribution centers; distribution systems
British, 296
changes (1990s), 340
establishment, 257
regional, 257
Warren, Gorham & Lamont, 273
The Warren Buffet Way (Hagstrom), 387
Waverley (Scott), 34
The Wealth of Nations (Smith), 25
Web logs (blogs), 442
Web Publishing Technology (WPT), 357

Web-offset printing, 158
Weeds of Witches (Bailey), 96
A Week on the Concord and Merrimack Rivers (Thoreau), 87
Weight Training For Dummies (Baker, Neporent, and Schlosberg), 409
Weight Watchers New Complete Cookbook, 396
Western Distribution Center (Utah). *See also* distribution centers
    closing, 316
    worker strike and, 275
Whig Knickerbockers, 81
White, Weld & Company, 217
The Whitefooted Deer and Other Poems (Bryant), 81
wholesale trade
    book auction, 41
    early 1800s, 33
Wide Area Information Servers (WAIS), 368
wikis, 442
Wiley & Halsted
    dissolution, 41
    formation, 38
    political economy titles, 44
    publications, 38–40
    scientific publishing, 44
Wiley & Putnam
    American Book Circular, 80
    authors, 82–88
    beginning of, 65, 73
    book reviews, 77
    at Broadway bookstore, 65
    careers launched by, 87–88
    as critical success, 88
    dissolution, 95
    early years, 73–79
    economic policy titles, 73–74
    education titles, 73
    as enterprising publishers, 77
    fiction, 75
    as library distributor, 78
    The Library of American Books, 82–83
    The Library of Choice Reading, 81–82
    London office, 77, 95
    magazines, 78
    mathematics titles, 74
    medical titles, 74–75
    military titles, 75
    as most connected publisher, 88
    nonfiction titles, 74–75
    philosophy titles, 75
    in recession, 73
    religious titles, 79
    scientific titles, 75
    technical titles, 75
    wholesale department, 96
Wiley, Charles
    book business and, 41–44
    in book trade, 26–28
    business phases, 29–31
    Charles Wiley & Co., 35–38
    Cooper relationship, 47–50
    death, 51, 52
    early author relationship, 50
    Irving relationship, 38–39
    marriage, 21
    New England manuscripts, 27
    print shop beginnings, 29–31
    start in publishing, 22–24
    Van Winkle partnership, 31–35
    Wiley & Halsted, 38–40
Wiley, Charles (1835–1916)
    formation of John Wiley & Son. 104–106
    as vice president and treasurer, 124
Wiley, John
    American Monthly publication, 61–62
    in antebellum America, 65–73
    apprenticeship, 53
    as book agent, 60
    book fair, 97–98
    as church deacon, 59
    craft instincts, 138
    engineering titles, 65
    at father's death, 58
    George W. Long partnership, 63–65
    gift books, 68
    glory years, 80–89
    Halsted partnership, 99
    as international book merchant (1850s), 97–99
    James Fenimore Cooper and, 63
    marriage, 60
    Nassau Street bookstore, 60
    orientation to Second Industrial Revolution, 108–110
    post-Putnam, 96–99
    sons partnership beginning, 104–106
    Wiley & Putnam, 73–89
    World War II, 171, 172–175
Wiley, William Bradford
    as assistant manager, 169
    authors and, 213
    background, 169
    "books of caliber," 171
    as CEO, 200
    as chairman of the board, 271
    Chapman & Hall relationship, 191–192
    in company transition, 200
    computers and, 199
    as Curtis G. Benjamin Award recipient, 201
    death of, 264, 344
    European strategy, 191–192
    as heir apparent, 195
    mergers, 216–222
    Navy enlistment, 171
    as president, 197, 200
    profile, 201

protégé, 200
scientific excitement and, 210–211
senior managers, 200
Soviet Union trip, 243–244
as "stubborn patriarch," 326, 327
success, 200
as vice president and treasurer, 194
Vietnam War and, 201
at Wiley 150th year celebration, 198
Wiley, William Bradford II
1980s period, 330
as chairman, 421–426
Wiley, William Halsted
background, 103, 104–106
Brooklyn Bridge opening, 105
death of, 120, 141
Edison connection, 103
editorial contracts, 124
joining company, 103
leaving company, 141
as Major Wiley, 106
as mechanical engineer, 119
Osgood episode, 103
profile, 120
screening books/authors, 124
Wiley output under, 121
wintertime Southern excursions, 124
Wiley, William O.
in adding company titles, 126
as company owner, 148
as company president, 146
increase of book titles, 141
profile, 146
retirement, 171
Wiley Arabooks, 242, 293
Wiley Australia. *See also* Jacaranda Wiley
For Dummies titles, 409
history, 405
revenue growth (2002), 408
sales model, 408
trade program, 408–409
The Wiley Bulletin, 176, 253, 256
Educational Edition, 257
end of, 257
Science and Industry Edition, 256
Wiley Canada
in 1980s, 296–297
distributor for Charles Scribner's Sons, 297
publications, 297
publishing program expansion, 410–411
revenue (1989), 297
revenue (2002), 412
sales (1985), 297
sports titles, 412
turnaround, 297
U.S. title support, 409–410
Wiley Custom Publishing System, 355

Wiley Eastern Ltd.
in 1980s, 298
concessional existence, 298
debt, 298
management, 415
reprints of U.S. titles, 241
Wiley Encyclopedia of Electrical and Electronics Engineering, 384
Wiley Europe, 403
Wiley Faculty Network (WFN), 358–359, 447
Wiley Foundation, 440
Wiley France, 387
Wiley India
Dreamtech and, 416, 451
management, 415
Precise Custom Textbook Series, 447, 451
Wiley International Editions (WIEs)
in 1981, 294
launch, 239
printing of, 239–240
simultaneous publication, 240
Wiley InterScience
ArticleSelect, 373, 444
customer base (1999), 371
customer base (2002), 373
customer feedback, 371
daily user sessions, 373
enhanced features, 373
journal availability via, 372
launch, 371, 401
MobileEdition, 373
Pay-Per-View, 373, 444
as service provider, 373
Synergy merge, 441
as way of life, 371–372
Wiley Japan
in early 1980s, 299
journals, 418
revenue (1984–1989), 299
Wiley Law, 390
Wiley Learning Technologies (WLT)
Alpha-Omega as, 306
markets question, 312
pilot tests, 306–307
Wiley Pathways, 448
The Wiley Prize in Biomedical Sciences, 440
Wiley Singapore, 11
Wiley Sound Business Cassettes, 309
Wiley Southeast Asia, 298–299
Wiley Systems, 228
Wiley trademarks, 445
Wiley Vision, 459
Wiley Web Tests, 356–357
Wiley-Blackwell. *See also* Blackwell Publishing
common publishing ethic, 441
due diligence, 438
formation, 438
global enterprise, 438

Wiley-Blackwell *(continued)*
  increased capabilities, 439
  integration, 432
  journals, 439
  leadership, 438–439
  online products, 439
  open market competition, 443
  revenue growth potential, 439
Wiley-Chapman partnership, 133–134
Wiley-IEEE Press book series, 384
Wiley-Interscience division, 225
Wiley-Interscience merger
  analysis, 221
  distribution network, 220
  improved governance, 220
  Interscience scientific journals, 220
  Interscience technical encyclopedias, 219–220
  Interscience titles, 219
  outside directors, 220
  as part of larger trend, 217
  personality/cultural conflicts and, 221
  post-merger conflict, 221
  Publishers' Weekly creation, 221
  reorganization and, 222–225
Wiley-Nauka Scientific Publishers, 299
WileyPLUS
  activity monitoring, 421
  development, 355
  as *eGrade Plus* evolution, 355, 359
  flexibility, 447
  functions, 421, 447
  homework with, 447
  relaunch, 358, 401
  student use, 4
  Wiley-Blackwell, 439
Wiley-VCH. *See also* VCH Publishing
  Akademie Verlag sale, 376
  emergence, 376
  in-house editorial operation, 376
  leadership, 376
  pan-European journals, 377–380
  staff, 10
William Morrow, 144
Wilson Learning Company
  failure, 311–312
  as growth source, 307
  management training competition, 311
  operating autonomy, 311
  performance (1984–1990), 310
  promise of, 305–308
  revenue for purchase, 306
  sales (1983), 308
  Wiley acquisition, 278, 306
  Wiley sale of, 338
  Wilson Alliance for Research and Development, 308
Windows XP For Dummies (Rathbone), 15, 377

Win-Win Negotiating (Jandt and Gillette), 309
wireless tablet PCs, 321
"Wizard of Menlo Park," 102
Woman in the Nineteenth Century (Fuller), 85
women
  emergence at Wiley, 233–235
  role of, 234–235
  Stoll as first leader, 235
word processing, faculty training, 286
word-of-mouth advertising, 256
worker strike (EDC 1979), 275
worklife
  computers and, 420–421
  Wiley (1980s), 321–325
  Wiley (1990s), 340
  Wiley (post-Civil War), 124–126
workshops, 349
The World of Wiley, 257
World War II. *See also* postwar years
  book market expansion, 172
  Hamilton as president, 172
  market share during, 173
  occupational market, 174
  Wiley margins, 175
  Wiley revenue during, 172
World Wide Web
  Berners-Lee browser, 334
  CERN announcement, 334
  defined, 335
  distribution impact, 423
  journal availability, 370
  launch, 339
  publishing changes coming from, 341
Wrightbooks acquisition, 393

X

Xerox
  copy machines, 259
  Steve Jobs daylight raid, 273
XML (Extensible Markup Language), 423

Y

Year Book Medical Publishers, 293
You and Your Job (Davis and Wright), 161
You Can't Take It With You: The Common Sense Guide to Estate Planning for Canadians (Foster), 411
Young Americans, 81, 82, 88
Your Carriage, Madam! (Lane), 182

Z

Zeitschrift für anorganische und allgemeine Chemie, 380
Zuno Digital Publishers, 370